BLACKLISTED

ALSO BY PAUL BUHLE

Marxism in the United States

C. L. R. James: The Artist as Revolutionary

Popular Culture in America

History and the New Left: Madison, Wisconsin, 1950–1970

Encyclopedia of the American Left
(co-edited with Mari Jo Buhle and Dan Georgakas)

The Immigrant Left in the United States (co-edited with Dan Georgakas)

The Tragedy of Empire: William Appleman Williams
(with Edward Rice-Maximin)

C. L. R. James's Caribbean (co-edited with Paget Henry)

Tender Comrades: A Backstory of the Hollywood Blacklist
(with Patrick McGilligan)

Images of American Radicalism (with Edmund Sullivan)

*Taking Care of Business: Samuel Gompers, George Meany, Lane Kirkland
and the Tragedy of American Labor*

Insurgent Images: The Agitprop Art of Mike Alewitz

The New Left Revisited (co-edited with John McMillian)

ALSO BY PAUL BUHLE AND DAVE WAGNER

A Very Dangerous Citizen: Abraham Polonsky and the Hollywood Left

Radical Hollywood

*Hide in Plain Sight: The Hollywood Blacklistees in Film and Television
(1950-2002)*

BLACKLISTED

The Film Lover's Guide
to the Hollywood Blacklist

Paul Buhle
and Dave Wagner

palgrave

First published by PALGRAVE MACMILLAN™ in 2003
175 Fifth Avenue, New York, N.Y. 10010 and
Houndmills, Basingstoke, Hampshire, England RG21 6XS.
Companies and representatives throughout the world.

PALGRAVE MACMILLAN IS THE GLOBAL ACADEMIC IMPRINT OF
THE PALGRAVE MACMILLAN division of St. Martin's Press, LLC
and of Palgrave Macmillan Ltd. Macmillan® is a registered trademark
in the United States, United Kingdom and other countries. Palgrave
is a registered trademark in the European Union and other countries.

Library of Congress Cataloging-in-Publication Data
Buhle, Paul, 1944-
    Blacklisted : the film lover's guide to the Hollywood blacklist /
Paul Buhle and Dave Wagner.
      p. cm.
    ISBN 1-4039-6145-X (pbk.)
    1. Motion picture industry—United States. 2. Blacklisting of
entertainers—United States. 3. Blacklisting of authors—United
States. 4. Motion pictures—United States—Catalogs. I. Wagner,
Dave. II. Title.

PN1993.5.U6B84 2003
384'.8'0973-dc21
                                                    2003046025

A catalogue record for this book is available from the British Library.

First Palgrave Macmillan edition: September, 2003
10 9 8 7 6 5 4 3 2 1

Book design by Planettheo.com

Printed in the United States of America.

CONTENTS

INTRODUCTION

This volume is a directory of films written, directed or produced, all or in part, by victims of the Hollywood blacklist—or by those who escaped blacklisting by providing "friendly" testimony to congressional committees in search of victims. The designations are simple and straightforward: each victim's name is marked with a bullet (•) and the name of each future friendly witness with a dagger (†). Some few artists—those who took their punishment for years and then capitulated—are marked with both. We have also included some work by those who were "graylisted"—artists who were not named before a congressional committee but were effectively excluded from filmmaking for a period of years (their names are not marked). And we have included a number of films that may not have had blacklistees among their credits but that concern themselves directly with the story of the blacklist.

For the most part, we have not included films by any given artist made after that artist gave "friendly" testimony, because the renunciation of old commitments by the writer or director nearly always meant that the political themes of their older work disappeared, whether because the artist changed his or her political views or submitted to de facto censorship. We have, however, included a selection of post-testimony features from certain key figures, such as Clifford Odets and Robert Rossen, whose later films represent a redirected social criticism rather than a self-imposed silence or censorship.

The reader is asked to take special note of the fact that the bullets and daggers in the list of films have been applied exclusively to those artists who were members of the Hollywood branches of the Communist Party-USA. Conservative actors and directors, Cold War liberals and others who appeared as "friendly witnesses" against the Left before Congress are not designated with these diacritical marks. Also excluded from this designation are the many artists who were sympathetic or close to the CP-USA but not members; to include the films of all of the latter would be a task well beyond the scope of this volume and would represent a lexicon of the films of the Popular Front—an undertaking of encyclopedic dimensions, because a large minority of films made in the late 1930s through the mid- to late-1940s would of necessity fall into this broader category.

Even party membership did not mean necessarily that an artist designated with a • or a † was a dedicated political activist. Far from it. It is true that the Hollywood Left led the way in organizing film industry unions, especially the Screen Writers Guild; included in its number nearly all of the film capital's leading antifascists (with an interruption during the eighteen months of the Hitler-Stalin Pact of 1939-1941); drew upon much of the best theatrical talent from Broadway; and established a lively social scene filled with cocktail parties, poker games, literary and musical salons and political discussions that were a source of great appeal to Hollywood's newcomers (and no doubt one of the reasons why so many unlikely figures, including Ronald Reagan, wanted to join). Jewish Hollywoodites, particularly those who were "progressive" (or left-liberal) and trying to carve out personal lives and careers in a society in which anti-Semitism was still tolerated and widespread, found the communist milieu of artists and intellectuals stimulating and comfortable—notwithstanding the Pact period—and, particularly during the war, a source of good career contacts. For all but a handful, their political identity remained, in their way of thinking, secondary to their lives and careers.

Then the moment came when they had no choice but to make a choice. At that point, the artists' political identity no longer seemed so secondary. Those artists who formally or informally attached themselves to the Left, for as little as a few months or for as long as decades, all paid the price when they were required, if they wanted to continue working in films, to renounce their (by this time mostly past) beliefs and to "name" their co-workers, friends, lovers, cousins, wives and husbands. In most cases, they could not bear to become informers. And so the overwhelming majority accepted some form of career-ending exile.

The lucky ones found television work, returned to theater or became expatriates rather than capitulate to what they viewed as public humiliation and undisguised anti-Semitism at the hands of politicians whose continued political careers often depended on the pursuit of race-based politics at home (the exclusion of black voters). Sometimes sneeringly referred to as "swimming-pool communists," most of the artists held firm, giving up their swimming pools rather than submit to what they viewed as ethical blackmail. It should be no surprise, then, that, looking back on their careers, these artists would regard their work as often more political than they had realized themselves. It is this commonality of political and aesthetic views as expressed *in the films themselves* that we have sought to discover in this book.

We have analyzed about 900 films in this volume, in most cases providing at least a sketch of the plot line and characters (the elements of filmmaking most influenced by the blacklist victims, who were overwhelmingly screenwriters). We have also noted where appropriate the role of cooperative or like-thinking progressive actors (or producers, directors, and, in a few cases, cinematographers and composers). Finally, we have remarked on the popular appeal and the artistic merit of particular films and their role in film history. About 400 of the films regarded as the least important (usually, deep B-productions) or those with minimal involvement by blacklistees are summarized quite briefly, without full credits.

The range and quality of films is, naturally, enormous. And that's part of the point. If one's only knowledge of the political content of the films made in Hollywood from the beginning of sound to 1980 derived solely from the ancient claims of conservative witnesses at congressional committees, Cold War liberals in the popular magazines, conscience liberals in books and journals, and the blacklistees themselves in books and interviews (when they were at last permitted to utter an opinion), one would come away with the impression that, while some efforts were made to introduce "subversive" ideas into the film medium, very little "got through." At most there may have been the inappropriate depiction of a happy Russian peasant or a worrisome line delivered by Ginger Rogers in TENDER COMRADE; otherwise, it was argued by nearly everyone, the executives in a studio's "front office" managed to keep a lid on the ideas if not on the talent of the Hollywood Left. That most people in Hollywood agreed on this master narrative was largely a matter of convenience on one side and dashed hopes on the other. The studios were eager to encourage the notion that their vigilance had resulted in politically pure entertainment, and the left-wing writers and directors were all too aware that they had never made the kinds of radical and uncompromising films they had really wanted to make (although some finally did, after they went into exile).

Nevertheless, as this book demonstrates, the collective contribution of these artists to popular filmmaking was astonishing. It reached across every narrative, from the silly to the serious, and every kind of genre, from the humblest comedy to the most illuminating dramas; it included spurious material meant to provide no more than a moment's distraction, and substantial reflections on the most important matters of the day. While the number of films included here is small compared to the Hollywood output of thousands of films (particularly in the 1930s and 1940s), it contains a surprising number (though of course far from all) of the best films Hollywood ever made—including some films that have been undeservedly forgotten and that we hope will be retrieved. Assembled for the first time in a common context, these films add up to a treasury of the artistic efforts and social attitudes of Progressive Hollywood in the era of the Popular Front and its trailing penumbra of political activism that reaches down to the present day.

Because the study of film in this historical category has emerged only in recent years, the significance of the connections established necessarily remains controversial and open to rebuttal. The actual influence of radical artists over the products of large studios varied a great deal from film to film, but one key historical point is not in dispute: the history of Hollywood can be seen as a struggle for artistic freedom—first for control over dialogue and characterization comparable to that enjoyed by playwrights in New York; then, in the new cinema after CITIZEN KANE, in which the writer-director team emerged, for control over most of the rest of the narrative (excluding the ending, over which the studios retained an unyielding control); and finally after World War II, for total artistic freedom, when artists of all specialties (emphatically including the stars) attempted to break from the studios by setting up their own independent production companies

The history of that struggle can be read in the films themselves. Left-wingers who felt like little more than white-collar slaves forced to produce kitsch in an industry that could be thoroughly unglamorous when seen from the inside nevertheless sometimes had been able in the first decade of talkies to transform mundane story assignments into something very like art objects that contained personal meanings for vast audiences. Later, when studios urgently sought "message" films (World War II marked a high point), they were invited to build on themes of social solidarity, antifascism, sometimes criticism of the fey or feckless rich, and, increasingly after 1945, criticism of anti-Semitism and racism. More important, they were invited to create or recreate on film certain character types beloved of the film audience: the idealistic hero or moody outsider, the hard-pressed but courageous heroine, the spunky kid and loving elders, not to mention certain improbably intelligent animals, from dogs to horses and even an occasional seal. Then, as the war years faded into the "Age of Anxiety," the foreground of the Hollywood film was increasingly occupied by the psychologically troubled, victims of betrayal and ever-more complex characters rarely if ever seen on the screen before, including brooding teenagers, victims of discrimination and others whose rage at society gave meaning to their otherwise inexplicable deviant behavior.

Of course, this is too simple a description of "Golden Age" American films either as art or as commerce. The ups and downs of the movie business as well as the political logic of American society at large pose paradox upon paradox for any large overview of the history of film content. No generalization can be absolute, and not even the ebb and flow of censorship can provide an unshakeable foundation. Conservative political influence remained so strong that themes had to be disguised deep in the cinematic subtext. But disguise was a skill learned early on in the history of the industry. The emergence of sound films at the very end of the 1920s ensured the employment of hundreds of screenwriters, who occupied a status so low (at dinner parties, as the joke went, they were seated "below the salt and the hairdressers") that they had to struggle for a decade just to gain some degree of control over their on-screen credits. Moreover, the autocratic behavior of movie moguls and their compliant bureaucracy, and the tight artistic censorship (embedded in studio practices as early as 1930) left them precious little creative freedom in areas of their key interest. Films favoring unionization and films opposed to European fascism were as unlikely as films favoring free love. Nevertheless, in the margins of the films, and sometimes squarely within the mainstream of Hollywood narrative, progressive and radical artists managed to create unforgettable cinema with extraordinary messages.

Wartime, it should be remembered, was very nearly the peak of theater attendance that climaxed in 1946, just before a sudden and precipitous decline. Writers who had been quietly banned for their union activities and for suspiciously "red" sympathies suddenly got as much work as they wanted during the war, if rarely the kind of work they wanted. Movies in the widest range of genres showed a radical or at least humanistic tinge. Afterward, the independent studios that began to spring up were responses not only to the desire for freedom in filmmaking but also to the descent of the Iron Curtain—American-style—over Hollywood. In this period, both within the old studios and the new independent companies, film noir emerged in its full glory, bearing the particular genius of American artistry in the crafts of directing, screenwriting, acting, cinematography and music. Radicals were among the most talented and prolific of the *noiristes*, at long last beginning to reach their full artistic potential even as they realized that the end was drawing near.

Still, the blacklist was never really "The End." For the lucky ones, it was only a dreadful interregnum. Just as their credits continued to appear on older films on late-night television while the writers and directors themselves were banished, the social themes stayed alive, more or less, in a much-reduced Hollywood. Under pseudonyms and fronts, blacklist victims continued to write some of the most admired films of the day. Meanwhile, many of the best blacklisted artists sought their fortunes abroad, and after years of delay and disappointment, a few (especially the directors) made brilliant second careers, accomplishing artistically what would never have been possible in Hollywood.

The blacklistees' return to Hollywood began, one artist at a time, during the early 1960s. The Vietnam War and popular opposition to it, within Hollywood as in the larger society, soon prompted a final wave of creative energy by once again turning dissent into good business. Time was running out on the life energies of these aging artists, but the sympathies of the younger generation were running with them. Unfortunately, the mixture of social themes, big budgets and stars famous for their rebelliousness often did not succeed artistically or commercially. Hollywood had been bypassed by the creative phase of world cinema during the 1950s and 1960s, and its products continued to pay the price. But here and there, the kinds of films dreamed of by radicals during the distant 1930s and 1940s actually took shape, artistically and politically, even in genres like westerns. It was a last and at times glorious flowering. By the end of the sixties, with the help of educated audiences exposed to European and Japanese films and newly organized into film societies—and demanding to see a more sophisticated craftsmanship from Hollywood—the formerly blacklisted artists began to turn out some of the masterpieces of the era, such as Waldo Salt's screenplay for MIDNIGHT COWBOY (1969), to take just one example.

Today, long after the collapse of communism as an international movement, the old battles seem like ancient history. By 1997, the Screen Actors Guild and what had become the Writers Guild hosted a series of ceremonies, symposia and public exhibitions that offered apologies and exoneration to the victims of the blacklist. It was admitted by the common consent of the creative community (if not all conservative or Cold War liberal critics), that the filmmakers had never been guilty of subverting American society—or even wanting to. They were not a revolutionary party; they were liberals leaning leftward, naïve about the Soviet Union but fervent in their commitment to antifascism and to multiracial, multicultural democracy on the home front. Most of all, they were members of the film community, and it was in this very specific identity as artists that the survivors of the blacklist were welcomed home at last. *Blacklisted: The Film Lovers' Guide to the Hollywood Blacklist* is in effect another marker of homecoming and of their audiences' rediscovery of the blacklistees' work.

Before you, film lover, lies a highly selective version of Halliwell's or Maltin's film guides, the famous movie joining the obscure, the deserving cheek-to-cheek with the undeserving, the spectacle with the low-budget, the art film with the imitations of films that deserve no imitation. Use this tool and bear in mind that nothing can replace the joy (and the occasional pain) of watching the films themselves.

A NOTE ON SOURCES AND METHODS

Every effort has been made to track down long-buried information about the specifically uncredited contributions that were made to particular films and what films were written during the height of the blacklist under assumed names.

Creative conflicts that had significant repercussions have also been noted. Often, such details have never been made public before, or only in our earlier work or in the definitive reference volumes.

Doubtless, the identification of some important script contributions, especially during the 1950s, has been lost because of secrecy and the death of the participants. We have provided whatever useful details we could glean from our own interviews with some of the figures whose work is discussed. The wealth of the material is so great that some readers may wish to pursue their own research to gather further elusive details. We can only hope so, and welcome any corrections or new discoveries for future editions.

This book is published in the middle of a great transition between two information technologies, from printed books to the Internet and from video-cassette to DVD. Because of the technical requirements of this book, the fruits of both technologies had to be consulted: the definitive *AFI Catalog of Feature Films,* 1893-1950 and 1961-1970, as well as the vastly more accessible but less reliable Internet Movie Database (www.imdb.com). Whenever possible, we resolved the differences in favor of AFI, but of necessity for technical reasons (including the lack of a digital access to the AFI database), we sometimes had to draw selectively on both regardless of conflicts in the data. And along with the inevitable and regrettable errors in a work of such an accumulation of details, ambiguities of fact will have crept in that readers of a certain inclination will long to regard as blunders or worse but that may represent nothing more than differences in editorial preferences in the best sources. To give just one example, AFI and other sources tend to date films from their domestic release, while IMDB often seems to prefer to date foreign films from the year they were released in the United States. Similarly, some sources give the date on which production was completed (preferring to emphasize the historical context of the film's creation), while other sources prefer to date a film to the day it was released (to emphasize its historical context for the audience). Many other variations of this kind show up in the reference works. If for no other reason, the reader should bear in mind that this book is not intended to resolve these kinds of questions of fact. It is a convenient form of a handbook for the filmgoer and TV-watcher. It is also, not incidentally, a rather extensive if informal set of footnotes to our several volumes on the history of the blacklist.

The same slow and awkward transition from the aging VHS technology to the adolescent (for movie collectors) DVD technology makes it difficult to provide the reader with timely or reliable sources for the films mentioned in this volume. Only a minority of the films are easily available on video (or DVD) for sale or rental, but a surprising number can be found on Ebay and a considerable majority can be seen on cable and satellite TV channels, several of which are devoted almost exclusively to films of the Golden Age. Another portion exists in film archives, such as those at the Library of Congress and the University of California at Los Angeles. Some of the remainder may be found in the catalogs of specialized dealers in videos who supply the collectors' market. For the most contemporary leads on the dealers in these markets, we refer the reader to the appropriate section of the annual *Movie and Video Guide* edited by Leonard Maltin and to the monthly publication *Big Reel* (700 East State Street, Iola, WI 54990), which primarily serves the 35 mm collector but also contains advertising from some of the most specialized VHS and DVD dealers, often students of film in their own right.

In some cases, the films, like the filmmakers themselves, may be gone forever; they may be lost or been purposely destroyed or simply turned to powder from neglect. Some films, we may hope, are awaiting rediscovery in some remote film vaults in Europe, where so many blacklisted writers and directors worked during the darkest years, or in aging film libraries of old UHF TV stations.

For those who may wish to pursue this subject in more detail, we refer the reader to the authors' earlier work:

Patrick McGilligan and Paul Buhle, *Tender Comrades: A Backstory of the Hollywood Blacklist*. Interviews with many of the survivors of the blacklist.
Paul Buhle and Dave Wagner, *A Very Dangerous Citizen: Abraham Lincoln Polonsky and the Hollywood Left*. A study of the Hollywood Left's most admired intellectual and writer-director.
Paul Buhle and Dave Wagner, *Radical Hollywood*. An overview, with many details, of the Left story up to 1950.
Paul Buhle and Dave Wagner, *Hide in Plain Sight*. The story after 1950, including television and the impact of the acting style called Method.

KEY TO THE TEXT

Prod:	Producer
Dir:	Director
Scr:	Screenwriter
Story basis:	Writer and title of narrative on which the screenplay is based

•	Blacklisted
†	"Friendly Witness"
•†	Blacklisted and later gave "friendly" testimony

Internal title in SMALL CAPITALS means the film is described elsewhere
   in this volume.

n.d. — no date established

STUDIOS

Col	Columbia
E-L	Eagle-Lion
MGM	Metro-Goldwyn-Mayer
Para	Paramount
PPC	Producers Pictures Corp
PRC	Producers Releasing Corporation
Rep	Republic Pictures
RKO	RKO Films
20th	Twentieth Century-Fox
UA	United Artists
U-I	Universal-International
WB	Warner Brothers

GLOSSARY

B-FILMS—Low-budget productions, sometimes from "poverty row" (the smallest) studios like Monogram and Producers Releasing Corporation (PRC) and the low-budget "units" of lesser studios like Republic. B-film standards include hasty shooting schedules, few sets and fewer recognized stars, appearing most often in established genres like westerns, crime stories and slapstick comedy. By the late 1940s, low-budget productions also contributed films noir that were occasionally regarded later as aesthetic achievements.

BLACKLIST—The systematic exclusion from employment of workers considered troublemakers. The term can be traced back to the practices of landowners in the Irish countryside of the nineteenth century who compiled a "black list" against those known for Irish Republican sympathies. From the later nineteenth century in the United States, "blacklist" has been used to describe the similar proscription by agreement of employers in associated industries or localities to ban employment of those known to be strikers, strike sympathizers or—above all—strike organizers. It was most notoriously associated with the use of company spies in industries such as the railroads, in which corporations employed outside agencies (notably the Pinkerton Agency) or created their own elaborate system of spying on secret and public meetings. The "blacklist" was used informally against individual employees known for union sympathies as early as the teens (against some professional baseball players, for example) and in the film industry during the 1930s. But after 1947 the practice became systematic (often denied by studio executives). The Screen Actors Guild and the Screen Writers Guild inserted "blacklist" provisions in their own constitutions in 1951, barring anyone who would not swear a loyalty (i.e., anticommunist) oath. These clauses were stricken in the 1960s.

BREEN OFFICE—Catholic conservative Joseph Breen's assumption of power at the Production Code Administration (see THE CODE) prompted this informal designation. The Office grew stronger through the 1930s, but with the approach of war and growing challenges from studios, the Breen Office was put increasingly on the defensive from 1939 onward. In 1941, Breen resigned. He was replaced by his former assistant, Geoffrey Shurlock. Hollywood's patriotic contributions to the war effort, not least by left-wingers, diminished public (and political) criticism of the industry. The eagerness of wartime audiences for franker treatment of moral issues—especially but not only GIs on leave—prompted further challenges. By the later 1940s, and notwithstanding the growing "red scare" against supposed communist influence on a handful of films, the influence of the Code eroded. Postwar European imports, and to a lesser degree American independent films willing to defy the Code, broke down its influence. The "rating system" that eventually followed never worked well and lost much of its authority with the release and grand commercial success of MIDNIGHT COWBOY, the first acclaimed film to be rated "X."

THE CODE—Popular shorthand for the production code, itself a euphemism for censorship, that was formally adopted by the film industry in the early 1930s. Responding to well-publicized complaints about "immorality" and its effect on the public, the Motion Picture Producers and Distributors of America (MPPDA) in 1922 hired Will Hays as "czar" and referred to his authority as the "Hays Office." No formal rules were put into effect until more pressure was exerted in 1931, near the dawn of the sound film, that expressed particular displeasure with sex and violence but also any hint of radicalism or sentiment opposed to racism or in support of labor. Under the Production Code Administration, or PCA, films were systematically screened, often sent back to studios for excision and sometimes re-writing, but these efforts proved so inadequate in guarding the public that critics (most potently authorities in the Catholic and Episcopal churches) demanded further restrictions. The creation of a Production Code Administration (PCA) in 1934 gave Joseph Breen an unprecedented authority as a censor, his role affirmed with a certificate stamped on every accepted film print. Any film made earlier may be considered "pre-Code."

FRIENDLY WITNESSES—Those Communists who, after being "named" as party members (or sometimes merely as "sympathizers") by other witnesses to House Committee on Un-American Activites (HUAC) hearings, exonerated themselves by admitting guilt, declaring their patriotism and providing the committee with the names of others. Some of the most famous included directors Elia Kazan and Robert Rossen and actors Lloyd Bridges and Sterling Hayden.

FRONT—A real person who allowed his or her name to be used by a blacklisted writer on a screenplay, a practice adopted by the later 1940s in Hollywood and used more infrequently in television (where pseudonyms were often employed instead). The basis for a front was often nothing more than friendship, but just as often in some measure pecuniary. The "front" collected a certain percentage of the fee for writing and turned over the balance to the blacklistee. The humorous as well as the more painful results of this deception were dramatized in THE FRONT, directed by blacklistee Martin Ritt, written by blacklistee Walter Bernstein, and starring Woody Allen.

GRAYLIST—A term used to describe those writers, actors, directors, technicians and others who were never actually "named" in congressional testimony but who were nevertheless refused employment in films and often in television as well. The "graylist," conducted so informally that its victims could never be altogether sure that it existed apart from the fact of its persistence—often attributed to an unwillingness to write a patriotic statement directed against blacklistees—started in 1950 and faded away by the mid-1960s. Many on the graylist, having lost their place in the industry, never worked in it again.

HAYS OFFICE—See THE CODE

HOLLYWOOD BLACKLIST—A term generally used to described those several hundred members of the film industry who were "named" at hearings between 1947 and 1951 and were prevented from working unless or until they provided "friendly" testimony to investigators.

HOLLYWOOD NINETEEN—The 19 members of the film industry called in 1947 for the first round of congressional testimony. They were producer-director-writer Adrian Scott; directors Herbert Biberman, Edward Dmytryk, Lewis Milestone, Robert Rossen and Irving Pichel; actor Larry Parks; and writers Alvah Bessie, Bertolt Brecht, Lester Cole, Richard Collins, Gordon Kahn, Howard Koch, Ring Lardner, Jr., John Howard Lawson, Albert Maltz, Samuel Ornitz, Waldo Salt and Dalton Trumbo. The choice of these 19 was highly arbitrary; several had never been Communists, and other Hollywood Communists had been far more active politically. Significantly, no veterans of World War II were on the list. After the first ten witnesses had refused to cooperate at the September 1947 hearings, the hearings were temporarily suspended.

HOLLYWOOD TEN—The ten witnesses called first at the HUAC hearings of 1947, namely Adrian Scott, Herbert Biberman, Edward Dmytryk, Alvah Bessie, Lester Cole, Ring Lardner, Jr., John Howard Lawson, Albert Maltz, Samuel Ornitz and Dalton Trumbo. All of these had been known Communists in Hollywood. Each served the maximum sentence, a year in jail, for contempt of Congress; the U.S. Supreme Court, with only Justices Hugo Black and William O. Douglas dissenting, refused to hear an appeal in April 1950.

HOUSE COMMITTEE ON UN-AMERICAN ACTIVITIES—Known popularly as the House Un-American Activities Committee with the acronym HUAC, the Committee was formed in May 1938. Although nominally concerned with the potential disloyalty of fascist as well as communist sympathizers as world war approached, like the Federal Bureau of Investigation it concerned itself almost exclusively with Communists. Also like the FBI, it was generally led by men deeply imbued with racist values, suspicions of Jews as disloyal to the white race as well as to the United States, and indeed, suspicions of all liberals as "soft" on national and race values. The first Hollywood hearings of HUAC, during 1940-1941, foregrounded anti-Semitic suspicions of supposed Jewish desires to drag the nation into a European war. These hearings also brought forward "patriotic" conservatives, such as Adolph Menjou, known to sympathize with fascist causes and eager to purge Hollywood of its Communists and liberals. The hearings ended with Pearl Harbor. Hearings returned in 1947 with new vigor and publicity for the Committee, suspended with the court challenge of the Hollywood Ten, and returned from 1951 to 1953 following a Supreme Court victory in 1950. The name of HUAC was changed to the Internal Security Committee in 1969 and abolished in 1975.

INDEPENDENT PRODUCTION—Any film produced outside the realm of the half-dozen major and handful of minor studios. During the 1930s, small-scale productions were launched, often on the basis of an individual star (such as juvenile singer Bobby Breen) and with rented equipment, for a series of films or even one film. During World War II, shortages of film stock nearly eradicated the independents, but they arose again shortly afterward with new vigor, most prominently as vehicles for certain stars such as Dick Powell, to make films with more creative freedom. The Red Scare hit the field of creative talent hard, as did the rise of television. Independent production, never absent, took hold again as a serious factor from the later 1950s with international productions and star vehicles, growing still more important in the last decades of the century.

LEFT—A term borrowed from the assembly of the French Revolution, in which the most revolutionary element happened to group on the leftward side. Thereafter, socialists and anarchists in Europe were designated "Left," followed naturally by the communists, in Europe and elsewhere. Not often used before the Depression in the United States, it was common thereafter, supplemented by such derogatory terms as "Red" (from a favorite color of socialists), "Commie," "comsymp" (communist sympathizer), "CPL" (follower of the Communist Party "line," or official views on any given subject), and so on. "Far Left" was also sometimes used to indicate communist (or "Trotskyist," i.e., a follower of Leon Trotsky) rather than socialist or liberal.

NOIR—A designation adopted from the French critics and only commonly used by U.S. scholars and critics from the 1950s onward. Film noir conveys the meaning of a "dark" film characterized by single-source lighting, moody characters, pointed and often cryptic dialogue, and decidedly downbeat moral lessons (if any).

POPULAR FRONT—A shortened version of the "Popular Front Against War and Fascism" declared at Communist International meetings in 1935, it served as symbol and substance of a new approach toward noncommunists. Expectations of early revolution vanished in this dramatic change of tactics, and alliances with socialists (in the United States, mostly with liberals) were urged, mainly but not only to combat the increasing danger of global fascism. The Popular Front allowed a relatively small Communist Party-USA to enter the Democratic Party, the labor movement mainstream and the Roosevelt New Deal administration at many levels, resulting in great short-term influence but also charges of "subversion" (because Communists, fearful of attack, often did not announce their status). The Popular Front expired with the Hitler-Stalin Pact in 1939, and was formally succeeded by the "United Front" during wartime, but the latter term never gained great popularity in the United States, while the Popular Front came to stand for an all-around aggressive liberalism-cum-radicalism with vigorous support of industrial unions and the causes of nonwhites, along with support for the Soviet Union.

PROGRESSIVES—A term often used, especially from the middle 1940s, to describe those who were sympathetic toward many of the causes of the Communist Party and Popular Front, likely signing petitions or appearing at fund-raising events but never joining the party. During the 1930s, "liberals" had been an encompassing term, but anticommunist liberals went on the offensive shortly after the close of the World War II, leaving organizations such as the Progressive Citizens of America and its affiliate, the Hollywood Independent Citizens on Art, Sciences and the Professions (popularly known as HICCASP). Throwing their energy into support of Henry Wallace on the Progressive Party ticket in 1948, prominent "progressives" such as Katharine Hepburn, Humphrey Bogart, Danny Kaye and many more found themselves badly isolated and threatened with blacklisting. Most simply went silent or (like Lucille Ball and Judy Holliday) exculpated themselves by "playing dumb."

UNFRIENDLY WITNESS—Those who refused to testify before HUAC, often invoking the Fifth Amendment right against self-incrimination, or otherwise refused to name their associates while admitting to their own political beliefs; this nearly always resulted in blacklisting.

BLACKLISTED

A

Abbott and Costello Meet Captain Kidd (1952)

WB. Prod: Alex Gottlieb. Dir: Charles Lamont. Scr: Howard Dimsdale,• John Grant. Cast: Bud Abbott, Lou Costello, Charles Laughton, Fran Warren, Hillary Brooke, Bill Shirley, Leif Erikson

By this time, Abbott and Costello were winding down, bereft of the talents of Robert Lees• and Fred Rinaldo,• who wrote the comics' best scripts. In their place, Howard Dimsdale got the opportunity for his last credit (along with slapstick veteran John Grant), before Hollywood's Iron Curtain fell. According to a family biography of Costello, the strictly nonpolitical Grant refused the rotund comedian's demand that he sign a loyalty oath and was barred from the last five years of the partners' film work.

Still, this badly edited and eccentrically tinted Cinecolor feature with Charles Laughton (and Frances Farmer's ex-husband, Leif Erikson) offers an amusing romp modeled on ABBOTT AND COSTELLO MEET THE INVISIBLE MAN. The boys once again get plugged into a fading film genre with endless gags, jolly songs, a little gender-role reversal (old hat to Lou, but especially popular at the time in Jane Russell/Bob Hope pairings) by buccaneer Warren. Look out, she has the sword!

Heading back into some Hollywood version of the real-life Captain Kidd's history, Abbott and Costello find themselves on a pirate island (in the Caribbean? They call it Tortuga). Entrusted with a love letter from Warren, they confuse this document with a treasure map. Laughton, by this time long since a prince of hams, floats serenely above the meager plot. 70 min., color.

Abbott and Costello Meet Dr. Jeckyl and Mr. Hyde (1953)

Howard Dimsdale• made an uncredited script contribution to this odd plot bringing together British suffragettes with Boris Karloff as the good doctor and stuntman Eddie Parker in an ape suit as his alter ego. Mostly chase scenes and animal jokes.

Abbott and Costello Meet Frankenstein (1948)

U-I. Prod: Robert Arthur. Dir: Charles T. Barton. Scr: Robert Lees,• Frederic I. Rinaldo,• John Grant. Cast: Bud Abbott, Lou Costello, Lon Chaney, Jr., Bela Lugosi, Lénore Aubert, Jane Randolph, Glenn Strange, Frank Ferguson

Arguably the best Abbott and Costello, or at least up there with HOLD THAT GHOST, THE WISTFUL WIDOW OF WAGON GAP and LITTLE GIANT. Certainly it remains the most popular: it is played regularly on cable networks at Halloween and said to be the all-time cult favorite of The Grateful Dead's (late) Jerry Garcia. Screenwriter Lees considered this one the closest to the original script, the terseness of the gags explained by Costello's refraining from ad-libs. The casting helps, because Chaney and Lugosi (who after this had little but Ed Wood features to look forward to) brilliantly play it straight even in the ludicrous circumstance of Frankenstein and Dracula and the Wolfman popping up in a single feature. Occasional songs don't hurt, but Lou's timing is the draw in scene after scene.

The boys are flunkies as usual, as Lugosi plans to install Lou's brain in a Frankenstein monster. The Werewolf, played with all the sincerity that Chaney will later give to the ex-con character in THE DEFIANT ONES, tries to warn them of the danger while shifting in and out of his hairy secret identity. Meantime, various romances and pseudo-romances blossom, including Aubert's pretense at falling in love with hapless Lou to get a warm body ready for a transplant. Even Vincent Price makes an appearance (his voice, anyway). Among the scenes Lees liked best is one that has the boys working in the museum stock room opening packages. Dracula steps out of a box and Lou alone sees him and gasps, while Bud as always refuses to believe a word that the pudgy actor says. Delightful action follows. 83 min.

Abbott and Costello Meet the Invisible Man (1951)

UI. Prod: Howard Christie. Dir: Charles Lamont. Scr: Robert Lees,• Frederic Rinaldo.• Cast: Bud Abbott, Lou Costello, Nancy Guild, Arthur Franz, Adele Jergens, Sheldon Leonard, William Frawley, Gavin Muir

Another of the final Abbott and Costello films before the blacklist and one of the best efforts by Lees and Rinaldo. The boys' graduation from detective school in the first moments of the film is a classic (its satire of academic formalities is a B-version of the Marx Brothers' *Monkey Business*) and is followed in later films by similar riffs on detective and horror pics. Notwithstanding the usual premise of finding the guilty and vindicating the innocent, the crime narrative has never looked sillier.

A boxer (Franz) accused of murdering his manager must elude the cops while proving his innocence, so he appropriates the serum of the late Invisible Man. Endless invisibility gags (long since mined by left-wing writers in works from THE INVISIBLE WOMAN to television's *Topper*) take up the slack of a thin plot. What we take to be reality is merely an illusion within this political and comedic tradition. The high point comes when Lou agrees to step into the boxing ring. The renowned timing of the duo seems a bit off as they show their age or perhaps the stress of repetition. This film also lacks the flagrant sexual ambivalence that served Lou so well on other occasions. Nifty special effects, however, stand the test of time and of future computer animation. Actor Sheldon Leonard, seen here in one of his last screen appearances as a mobster before he became a real-life television mogul (producer of shows starring Danny Thomas and Dick Van Dyke), hired his old blacklisted Hollywood friends on the sly. 82 min.

Accent on Love (1941)
20th. Assoc. Prod: Walter Morosco, Ralph Dietrich. Dir: Ray McCarey. Scr: John Larkin. Story basis: Dalton Trumbo,• "Man With a Shovel" (n.d.). Cast: George Montgomery, Osa Massen, J. Carrol Naish, Minerva Urecal, Thurston Hall, Irving Bacon, Leonard Carey, Oscar O'Shea

Occasionally interesting thirties social drama about realty exec Montgomery, fired for refusing to advertise premium rents for slum apartments. Despised by wife Urecal (daughter of the boss, Hall) and alienated from his middle-class life, he turns ditch digger, surrounded by kindly working-class folks and pretty blue-collar girl Massen. Assuming the mantle of the people's champion, he becomes the tenants' spokesman. Ridiculous ending has Hall repenting, urging his snooty daughter to let Montgomery divorce her and turning the realty company over to his soon to be ex-son-in-law! Trumbo's original story never had a chance. Strictly in the sentimental vein, with Naish nice as the working-class papa. 61 min.

Accident (1967)
Cinema V. Distributing/London Independent Producers. Prod: Joseph Losey,• Norman Priggen. Dir: Joseph Losey.• Scr: Harold Pinter. Novel basis: Nicholas Mosley, *Accident* (1966). Cast: Dirk Bogarde, Stanley Baker, Jacqueline Sassard, Michael York, Vivien Merchant, Delphine Seyrig, Alexander Knox, Harold Pinter

Often described as Losey's best film. Pinter rewrote a script from a novel about two Oxford dons and the Austrian princess (and student) they are both in love with but who is engaged to another student-aristocrat. As in the novel, there is a car crash in which the male aristocrat (York) is killed, and one of the dons (Bogarde) carefully covers up the princess' role as driver. Pinter and Losey turned Bogarde, the mildly irritable bourgeois, into a monster who derives courage from his own self-disgust and the vulnerability of those close to him. The sexual conquest of the princess is a perverse victory over Baker, the charismatic colleague who gets both the media attention and the girls whom Bogarde has secretly craved.

The politics of the film are clear enough: "Aristocrats were made to be killed," as Bogarde says. But the real politics are textual (or subtextual) and visual, with sweeps of peaceful, beautiful British countryside and an Oxford-looking historic campus (actually St. John's) undercut by psychic and physical violence. Bogarde's wife (Merchant), eight months pregnant, is characteristically excluded from intellectual conversation; meanwhile, Bogarde and Baker battle out their virility on the tennis court. Pinter plays a former student of Bogarde's who humiliates him. The senior don consoles himself by engaging in a mini-affair with the provost's daughter (Seyrig). A return to the accident of the title frames the horrifying conclusion. Brilliantly directed, with wonderful casting—especially Bogarde, a homosexual actor who understood Losey's outsider status and worked with him frequently. No major American distributor would touch it, spelling disaster at the box office. It nevertheless remains a classic of British film. 105 min., color.

The Accusing Finger (1936)
Para. Prod: A. M. Botsford. Dir: James P. Hogan. Scr: Madeleine Ruthven, Brian Marlow, John Bright,• Robert Tasker. Cast: Paul Kelly, Marsha Hunt,• Kent Taylor, Robert Cummings, Harry Carey, Bernadene Hayes, Joseph Sawyer, DeWitt Jennings, Russell Hicks, Jonathan Hale.

This exceptional anti–capital punishment drama, and early Hollywood Communist Party member Ruthven's only worthwhile credit, probably owed more to real life ex-con Tasker's own experiences and reflections. A deputy district attorney (Kelly) nicknamed "Hotseat" is determined to send another young man to the chair—until he is framed on a murder charge and faces the chair himself. Young Bob Cummings is charming as a hillbilly lad destined for electrocution. In courtroom oratory, he offers the moral to a senator (Carey), who is putting in a congressional bill to end execution and gives the best reasons to the jury. 62 min.

An Act of Murder (1948)

U-I. Prod: Jerry Bresler. Dir: Michael Gordon.•† Scr: Michael Blankfort,† Robert Theoren. Story basis: Ernst Lothar, *The Mills of God* (1935). Cast: Fredric March, Edmond O'Brien, Florence Eldridge, Geraldine Brooks, Stanley Ridges, John McIntire, Frederic Tozere, Will Wright, Clarence Muse

This early euthanasia courtroom drama has upright Pennsylvania judge March realizing that Eldridge, his wife of 20 years, has a fatal and horribly painful illness. Refusing to clue her in but taking her on a second honeymoon, he seeks to end her agony (expressed in the noir style in a house of mirrors) by overdosing her on potentially toxic medication. Unable to take the pressure, he purposefully drives into an embankment, leaving her dead. Once scornful of bleeding-heart liberal lawyers (like potential son-in-law O'Brien) who spoke of the heart and not the letter of the law, he finds himself in the docket. An interesting small moment has a colleague recall March's idealistic youth, apparently on the Left in the early New Deal days. His erstwhile nemesis O'Brien then defends him and finally gets at the truth. Meanwhile, there is lots of rumination on legal ethics. It looks like a run-up to television's *The Defenders* (1961-1965)— written substantially by blacklistees under pseudonyms—except this time it's an elite figure who is morally innocent even if legally guilty. According to FBI documents subsequently released, it was shown that March had been a supporter of the 1930s Hollywood Left, and Eldridge was close to the party if not an actual member. 91 min.

Act of Violence (1948)

MGM. Prod: William H. Wright. Dir: Fred Zinnemann. Scr: Robert L. Richards.• Story: Collier Young. Cast: Van Heflin, Robert Ryan, Janet Leigh, Mary Astor, Phyllis Thaxter, Taylor Holmes, Berry Kroeger, Connie Gilchrist

A gripping treatment of World War II memories haunting its survivors in a society that cannot grasp what the veterans have been through—and worse, does not want to be bothered—the film opens with Ryan on a Manhattan street, dragging himself into his apartment for a gun and leaving town on a bus. He shows up in L.A. exurb Santa Lisa during a Memorial Day parade where Heflin, a successful contractor, is busy dedicating a housing development. (The stiff-legged Ryan dragging

himself through the path of a marching band at right angles, to punctuate his alienation from postwar society, is a special Zinnemann touch.) Heflin has a wife (Leigh), family and a seemingly secure future. But he had betrayed Ryan and others under his command in a Nazi prison camp, revealing their plan to escape. Van Heflin is keenly aware of his own guilt ("I was an informer. It doesn't make any difference why I did it. . . . They even gave me food, and I ate it. . . . To save one man, me. . . . Ten men dead and I couldn't even stop eating.")

At a Los Angeles builders' convention full of drunks waving flags and chasing skirts, Ryan begins a chase that winds through the dark streets of L.A. while Heflin winds up in a bar with a washed-out prostitute (the best of Astor's later roles), who hires him a hit man to get rid of his nemesis, and reminds him, "You're the same man you were in Germany." Astor, Leigh and Ryan's girl Thaxter reveal that violence is a man's game and that they are powerless to stop it. Fine urban cinematography and script make this one of the most important and overlooked noirs. Carl Foreman• wrote an important B film on similar themes in THE CLAY PIGEON. Director Zinnemann, already auteur of the unique (and Oscar-winning) postwar location film THE SEARCH (1948), went on to direct several more notable left-written films, including THE MEN, scripted by Foreman. ACT OF VIOLENCE began to receive its due only with fuller appreciation of Zinnemann decades later. 82 min

Action in Arabia (1944)

RKO. Prod: Maurice Geraghty. Dir: Leonide Moguy. Scr: Phillip MacDonald, Herbert J. Biberman.• Cast: George Sanders, Virginia Bruce, Lénore Aubert, Gene Lockhart, Robert Armstrong, H. B. Warner, Michael Ansara

Looking suspiciously like another entry for Sanders' Falcon character, this one has the intuitive detective as an antifascist newspaperman. It also has the pasted-together quality of its production history: Ernest B. Schoedsack and Meriam Cooper had shot desert footage back in 1937 for a proposed picture on Lawrence of Arabia, then put the project on the shelf, from which it was recovered for this project (and augmented by more location footage shot in California by Robert Wise). Still, the film is surprisingly charming at many points. Repeatedly on the verge of exposing Nazi plots, Sanders is blocked in his efforts by U.S. embassy officials around the world seeking to keep the lid on any behavior that disrupts business relations. In Damascus, Orientalized as both the "oldest city in the world" and the most treacherous, he learns that the Nazis plan to unite Arab tribespeople against the Allies and take over the Suez Canal.

The suave Sanders is at his best feigning the gambler and playboy. Romance combines with intrigue, with Virginia Bruce as double agent actually working for the Free French. Sometimes described as the classic B exotic war film or a much-reduced CASABLANCA, *Action in Arabia* resembles more a "Terry and the Pirates in the Desert" (minus the comic strip heroes' right-wing politics). Even the double agents can be charmingly two-faced, as the nastiness of the Nazis is driven home. 75 min.

Action in the North Atlantic (1943)
WB. Prod: Jerry Wald. Dir: Lloyd Bacon. Scr: John Howard Lawson.• Story basis: Guy Gilpatric. Cast: Humphrey Bogart, Raymond Massey, Alan Hale, Julie Bishop, Ruth Gordon, Sam Levene, Dane Clark

One of the best of the propagandistic World War II films showing the élan of the antifascist fighters. Lawson's script locates the ever-romantic Bogey first on a ship doomed by German torpedos, then ashore where he finds Bishop, his true love and new wife—before he is swept back to sea with Captain Massey and a new determination to halt the Nazis on the high seas. Cinematography and direction apparently followed Lawson's carefully scripted realism closely, making this film (along with Lawson's SAHARA and COUNTER-ATTACK) one of the three Hollywood movies closest in spirit to *Battleship Potemkin*.

The sailors fight boredom, bad food and intramural differences while real trouble awaits. Sam Levene plays the autodidact Jewish intellectual and left-winger who must be allowed to combine his ethnic heritage with those of others (no African Americans exist here and, unlike most combat films, no other ethnic identifications are important). In the crucial political scene at what is clearly a National Maritime Union hall (i.e., a Popular Front hotbed) in New York, Levene explains to mates just what the struggle against the fascists is all about: the precondition for a different and better world.

For a time it turns into a commander's film as we follow Massey on shore to visit his wife (the wonderfully tender, middle-aged Gordon), then back on ship where more torpedoing brings in Bogey as his replacement. By that time air-to-ship bombardment, anti-aircraft fire and assorted mayhem take over. The boys have got to get to Murmansk to resupply the Russian allies, and in such an upbeat progressive flag-waver, they're bound to make it somehow. Critics loved it as stirring and authentic. 126 min.

Adam Had Four Sons (1941)
A sentimental Ingrid Bergman vehicle about a French governess watching over a family after the wife's death. Michael Blankfort† co-adapted a contemporary novel about a stockbroker's household after World War I, the fighter pilot son and the would-be seductress (played memorably by Susan Hayward).

Adventure in Manhattan (1936)
The remake of a silent film about a crime reporter's adventures, co-scripted by Sidney Buchman• and adapted by an uncredited John Howard Lawson.• A chestnut plot used to this day, it has crooks putting on a stage performance with plenty of noise (here a play about WWI trench warfare with plenty of gunfire) to cover their real play: tunneling into a bank to make off with the loot.

Adventures of Captain Marvel (1941)
Rep. serial. Prod: Hiram S. Brown Jr. Dir: William Witney, John English. Scr: Ronald Davidson, Arch B. Heath, Joseph F. Poland, Sol Shor,† Norman S. Hall. Story basis: Captain Marvel, *Whiz Comics* (assorted writers). Cast: Tom Tyler, Frank Coughlan, Jr., Louise Currie, Robert Strange, Harry Worth, Bryant Washburn, John Davison, George Pembroke, Peter George Lynn, Reed Hadley, Jack Mulhall, Tetsu Komai

This 12-episode serial (first part 31 minutes, the others 19) is the "origin story" of the comic book hero, less spectacular (and less interesting) than the printed version, but with the same "SHAZAM!" transformation and cloud of smoke. Coughlin's Marvel is a foot bigger (not just more muscular, a la Superman/Clark Kent) than his diminutive if occasionally courageous alternative identity, Billy Batson, played by Tyler. The plot drags, and without the background scenery of the Flash Gordon serials' Ming Palace and fanciful creatures, becomes repetitive and downright dull. But aficionados will enjoy the Republic Pictures' special effects team working to make Marvel's takeoff and flying look "real" (not leaping like Superman but lifting off in a more birdlike manner, obviously a magical power and not just the effect of being from another planet).

The story turns on an evil capitalist who has subverted an archaeological journey to vaguely Afghani region to study relics of a lost world. Disguising himself as a local legend, "The Scorpion," this villain seeks to keep for himself the ancient device discovered by the archeologists that would enable him to dominate the world—a series of lenses capable of destroying anything within their focus ("the power of the sun"). To prevent this, a necromancer-wizard gives Billy the verbal formula that transforms him into "The World's Mightiest Mortal."

In the end, Marvel provides a small Popular Frontish message: "a world of freedom, justice and hope for all men" would find a good use for this untapped power, but the present world would place it in the wrong hands. He throws the weapon into molten lava to "burn the memory from the minds" of the current generation. The ultimate weapon is too much of a burden for any individual or nation to bear (presidents Roosevelt and Truman weren't listening). Friendly witness Shor, a decade later, brushed aside congressional queries about the contents of his old films by dismissing them as juvenile adventures. 240 min.

Adventures of Casanova (1948)
E-L. Prod: Leonard S. Picker. Dir: Roberto Galvadón. Scr: Crane Wilbur, Walter Bullock, Karen DeWolf.• Story basis: Crane Wilbur. Cast: Arturo de Córdova, Lucille Bremer, Turhan Bey, John Sutton, George Tobias, Noreen Nash, Lloyd Corrigan, Fritz Leiber

An exotic military romance drama with left-wing undertones. In 1793, Austrian armies are ruthlessly crushing Sicilian rebels, and only the great lover Casanova (Córdova) can save the day. In this wholly imaginary history, he is the son of a disinherited nobleman and leaps into action, directing a guerilla war, kidnapping the chief of police and bartering captives for bread for the masses. Meanwhile, his Lady (Bremer) refuses betrothal to another and escapes dressed as a page boy. Córdova is almost trapped by another lady (Dalva) but, swept away by his lovemaking, she lets him escape. Sidestepping an execution and after much further confusion, he barely prevents baddie Sutton from bedding Bremer in a forced marriage. The production was shot entirely in Mexico, and, according to studio publicity, marked the first time that a foreign director (the accomplished Gavaldón) had been hired to direct a U.S. company abroad. 83 min.

The Adventures of Huckleberry Finn (1939)
MGM. Prod: Joseph L. Mankiewicz. Dir: Richard Thorpe. Scr: Hugo Butler• (uncredited contribution by Waldo Salt•). Novel Basis: Mark Twain, The Adventures of Huckleberry Finn (1885). Cast: Mickey Rooney, Walter Connolly, William Frawley, Rex Ingram, Lynne Carver, Jo Ann Sayers, Minor Watson, Elisabeth Risdon

A natural for left-wing writers, this film was Butler's breakthrough as a writer of children's scripts, his métier until the blacklist. According to his widow, Jean Rouverol Butler, the film reduced the plot to slapstick far more than Hugo Butler had intended and Twain's own narrative would have made possible. Still, the film earnestly seeks to follow the lad from one escape to another with a fleeing slave. Rooney as Huck is an engagingly rebellious Missouri lad who believes Abolitionists are the lowest possible creatures but also that his friend "Nigger Jim" has a right to freedom. He also enjoys the adventure of emancipating him by rafting toward the free state of Illinois. The performance of Rex Ingram as Jim seems antique to modern eyes but by 1930s film standards avoided the usual minstrelsy-style stereotypes; he is portrayed as a man eager to escape slavery but not so urgently as to betray his comrade Huck.

Butler introduced a steamboat captain with Abolitionist sentiments, roughly in keeping with Twain's own racial and political sensibilities. By this means, Huck races upriver to rescue Jim from a lynch mob. More than a small element of "white savior" mentality is at work here, but with a sort of antifascist flair and a repeated show of dignity for Ingram. William Frawley and Walter Connolly, as hucksters, are thrown in for laughs and to set up Huck to play Juliet in drag. 89 min.

The Adventures of Martin Eden (1942)
Col. Prod: B. P. Schulberg. Dir: Sidney Salkow. Scr: W. L. River.• Cast: Glenn Ford, Claire Trevor, Evelyn Keyes, Stuart Erwin, Dickie Moore, Ian MacDonald, Frank Conroy, Rafaela Ottiano, Regina Wallace

Along with a much better film, THE SEA WOLF (1941), this is the only left adaptation of a novel by Jack London, the revolutionary American writer with the biggest international audience (thanks in no small part to translations and enthusiasm for his work in the old Eastern Bloc). Like the movie Jack London (1943), done with a slightly bigger cast, it nevertheless suffers from an inability to capture the protagonist's boisterous and melancholy prose.

Ford is presented realistically as a sailor aboard a veritable hellship who keeps a diary of the captain's brutality and the eventual mutiny it inspires. But he has difficulty getting it published to expose conditions and to free his comrade, Erwin, imprisoned for the mutiny. At first embittered at his lack of success, Ford suddenly enjoys renown with a novel but falls into a romance with rich girl Keyes, whose patronage leaves him still more bitter. This novel, one of London's best, leaves the protagonist plunging into the ocean in a suicide. The Hollywood ending is considerably more chipper. 87 min.

The Adventures of Robinson Crusoe (1954)

UA. Prod: Óscar Dancigers, Henry F. Ehrlich. Dir: Luis Buñuel.• Scr: Hugo Butler,• Luis Buñuel. Novel basis: Daniel Defoe, *Robinson Crusoe* (1720). Cast: Dan O'Herlihy, Felipe de Alba, Jaime Fernandez, Chel López, Jóse Chávez, Emilio Garibay

Despite the fact that O'Herlihy as Crusoe was nominated as best actor at the 1954 Academy Awards, and in the face of the continuing popularity of the theme (see Tom Hanks in *Castaway*), this film remains virtually impossible to find. Some critics think it's among Buñuel's best, not least for the dream sequence in which Crusoe's father rebukes him for his wayward adventurousness and a scene in which, hungry for the sound of another human voice, he climbs into the Valley of the Echo and shouts out a Psalm. Key to the story is the parable of colonialism in Crusoe's slave, Friday, whose unconditional freedom Crusoe must acknowledge before he can count himself free. 90 min.

Affairs of Geraldine (1946)

A Jane Withers B-vehicle co-scripted by Arthur Strawn• and Lee Loeb (a frequent writing partner with Harold Buchman•). A small-town girl leaves good guy at the altar, heads for the big city and big trouble but finally comes back to home and virtue.

Affairs of Jimmy Valentine (1942)

Robert Tasker, a left-winger mysteriously murdered in Mexico before the blacklist, co-scripted this adaptation from an old-time plot (Broadway circa 1910) that was in turn taken from an O. Henry short story and used three times previously for films about the loveable, retired safecracker called back into action.

Affairs of Martha (1942)

MGM. Prod: Irving Starr. Dir: Jules Dassin.• Scr: Lee Gold,• Isobel Lennart.† Cast: Marsha Hunt,• Richard Carlson, Virginia Weidler, Spring Byington, Allyn Joslyn, Frances Drake, Majorie Main, Melville Cooper, Inez Cooper

A delightful (and utterly obscure) social class comedy and Dassin's first directorial effort, this film finds the gentility of a WASPy Long Island village and its domestic servants almost up in arms against each other. Someone's maid, according to the New York papers, has written an exposé of "her" rich local family. Skeletons threaten to fall out of the closet: swindlers' copper deals, adulterous affairs and other embarrassing private foibles of the powerful. Hunt and Main are the primary attractions here. Hunt the serving girl married the young man of the house (in a stupor; he sobered up and left town before consummating the marriage) and now determines to tell all. Main is the spirited cook who leads the local servants in an all-out strike threat, offering a running commentary on the hazards of romance for women and on the silliness of the employing class. Along with *Barnacle Bill* and *The Wistful Widow of Wagon Gap*, this is one of the noted lesbian comic actress' best films. Director Dassin later wrote off his earliest Hollywood efforts, but this one has plenty of life. 69 min.

Afraid to Talk (1932)

A major Broadway social drama by George Sklar• becomes a minor and botched film despite script contributions by Sklar and Albert Maltz.• A bellboy observes a mob rub-out and a morally tainted DA decides to indict him, and a system just as corrupt nearly sends him to the hotseat. In the play he is martyred, a symbol of Depression fatalism. Here he survives in a Hollywood ending that removes the sting.

Air Cadet (1951)

Robert L. Richards• penned this minor adventure in which combat-jockeys learn how to use airborne flamethrowers. Lots of aerial acrobatics.

Air Hostess (1949)

One of the last films of philosopher Rousseau's collateral descendant, Louise Rousseau,• who tackled romance and adventures of the proliferating stewardess field (not to be confused with an earlier film of the same name, 1933). A contemporary women's film treating the lives and loves of three stewardesses, *sans* the eros, or ersatz eros, of later treatments.

Air Raid Wardens (1943)

Howard Dimsdale• made an uncredited script contribution to this Laurel and Hardy antifascist effort (their only one), with some charming moments as hapless owners of a small-town bike and radio shop who fail at enlistment but catch the Nazi spies, notably disguised as loud-mouthed patriots.

Aladdin and His Lamp (1952)

Howard Dimsdale• teamed up with Left ally Millard Kaufman in Walter Wanger's debut as a Monogram producer—a giant step downward and not the last for Wanger, who was about to renounce the Left and move to productions abroad. This Aladdin loves the princess, has the lamp and enjoys triumphs that kids will like best. Not to be confused with several animated features (the most recent by Disney) of the same character. Nedrick Young• appears as a supporting actor.

Algiers (1938)

UA. Prod: Walter Wanger. Dir: John Cromwell. Scr: John Howard Lawson,• James M. Cain, (script contribution: Harold Buchman•). Film basis: *Pépé Le Moko* (1937). Cast: Charles Boyer, Sigrid Gurie, Hedy Lamarr, Joseph Calleia, Alan Hale, Gene Lockhart

One of the classic Hollywood films that, between *The Sheik* and the many World War II dramas, constructed North Africa as a semi-European, semi-exotic zone where anything goes. Charles Boyer is the charming criminal who feels he must escape the Casbah to experience Paris (he sees the Arc de Triomphe in his imagination). But he will surely be captured by the police—in the person of his friendly inspector-adversary, Calleia—if he leaves his protected home turf. His love interest in middle-class European Lamarr brings him down from early cockiness, but he is certain to be undone by his hot-blooded Algerian girlfriend (Gurie), who would rather betray him than lose him to a rival. According to recent research, James Cain was hired to write the first 20 minutes, easing the otherwise exaggerated dramatics of Lawson, who had months before he delivered the final version of BLOCKADE to Wanger.

The real interest in this film, however, lies in its treatment of the near Middle East, featuring romantic and amiably crooked half-European male characters and a Europeanized police force that must attend to the law but can't help being fond of its criminal counterparts. European men are escaping from something unspecified in advanced civilization, while European women are drawn into this maelstrom on the wings of boredom with their usual roles and out of a passion for half-Oriental lovers.

Algiers, Lamarr's first U.S. hit, might well be compared with director Irving Pichel's evocation of Egypt in TEMPTATION and with two other key blacklistee-written films, CASABLANCA and John Berry's• forgotten 1949 CASBAH, a musical version of *Algiers*. 96 min.

Alibi Ike (1935)

Edward Chodorov• produced and added a script contribution to this adaptation of the elder Ring Lardner's short story about a hick baseball pitching sensation who has an excuse for everything. Cavern-mouthed Joe E. Brown is the whole show here, along with some great sight gags.

Alice Adams (1935)

RKO. Prod: Pandro S. Berman. Dir: George Stevens. Scr: Dorothy Yost, Mortimer Offner,• Jane Murfin. Novel basis: Booth Tarkington, *Alice Adams* (1921). Cast: Katharine Hepburn, Fred MacMurray, Fred Stone, Evelyn Venable, Frank Albertson, Hedda Hopper, Hattie McDaniel

One of the films that established Katharine Hepburn as the game gamin who can return from deep depression to her full moral stature—giving in, when necessary, to resolve romantic crises. Here, she plays the pretty adolescent daughter of invalid clerk Stone in a small Indiana town. She is enchanted when a son of the gentry, MacMurray, asks her to dance, but is unable to handle the situation. He walks her home and she is embarrassed at the modesty of her house. Meanwhile, Venable as Mother Adams henpecks kindly but helpless dad (Stone), blaming his personal failure for Hepburn's inability to catch a hot prospect. With confusion around the theft of a chemical formula invented by her former beau, she is certain that she has lost McMurray forever. Not to worry: things straighten out in small town America and even businessmen can reconcile their differences. The film is better than it sounds, thanks mainly to Hepburn. Social themes suffer, however, by comparison to almost any other Hepburn pic of this era. 135 min.

Alice in Wonderland (1950)

Lou Bunin Productions. Prod: Lou Bunin. Dir: Dallas Bower. Scr: Albert Lewin, Henry Myers• (uncredited: Edward Eliscu•). Novel basis: Lewis Carroll, *Alice in Wonderland* (1865). Cast: Carol Marsh, Stephen Murray, Pamela Brown, Ernest Milton, Felix Aylmer, Joyce Grenfell, David Reed

A commercially doomed French-based production with a mixture of live action and Lou Bunin puppets, released disastrously within days of a Disney full-animation version. The Bunin production, drawing upon the talents of various former employees of Disney, was less sugary, zanier and truer to the literary original, with many wonderful scenes of queenly tyranny, surrealistic singing and dialogue. British actress Carol Marsh was chosen at the last moment when British authorities, presumably acting on State Department command, barred the travel of a younger actress; Marsh was too old for the part and her singing was stilted at best. Yet many quirky pleasures remain for viewers of this film, until recently very difficult to obtain. 83 min.

All Night Long (1961)

This jazz performance film co-scripted by Paul Jarrico• (as "Peter Achilles") with Nel King, is a dubious adaptation of *Othello*. Dave Brubeck, Tubby Hayes and Charles Mingus are the real stars, although the marriage of a black band leader to a modern-day Desdemona would be more interesting if Patrick McGoohan (playing the romantic rival) had better lines. Producer Robert Roberts, who worked with lefties at Enterprise Studios, stumbled badly here as well.

All Over Town (1937)

Rep. Prod: Leonard Fields. Dir: James W. Horne. Scr: Jack Townley, Jerome Chodorov.• Story basis: Richard English. Cast: Ole Olsen, Chic Johnson, Mary Howard, Harry Stockwell, Franklin Pangborn, James Finlayson, Eddie Kane

The first Olsen and Johnson film, this was a distinctly low-budget effort but their first connection with the screenwriting Left, a collaboration that reached a peak with Robert Lees' and Fred Rinaldo's script for CRAZY HOUSE. Olsen and Johnson naturally play themselves, this time as a vaudeville team trying to land a job with their singing seal. Finding a closed theater, they pose as oil millionaires, and after a shooting, think Sally the seal has swallowed the contract. They take her on a roller coaster ride to make her throw it up (but she loves the ride, while the men get ill). After being kidnapped (and saved by Sally, who hits a kidnapper with a bowling ball), they run down the real killer—or rather, Johnson runs him down as Olsen provides a play-by-play imitation of radio sportscasters, a gambit they improve upon in *Crazy House*. Bad editing and camera work mar this film, but the "rehearsal" scene offers the team a chance to do their regular theatrical stuff—if not with the psychedelic excellence of the later film, a favorite of doped-out campus regulars of the seventies for very good reasons. 61 min.

All of Me (1934)

This play-based pre-Code film was co-adapted by Sidney Buchman.• Student Miriam Hopkins turns down professor Fredric March, insisting that marriage ruins true love. A tragic sequence of pregnancy and false charges follow. Co-star George Raft's real-life bodyguard had a supporting role.

All Quiet on the Western Front (1930)

An uncredited, minor script contribution by Gordon Kahn,• about a German teacher courageously delivering an antiwar lecture to students about to become soldiers, made this Kahn's first produced Hollywood effort. Lewis Milestone directed and produced the most expensive film in U.S. history to date, as well as one of the most awarded and undoubtedly the strongest pacifist film made in Hollywood. Lew Ayers (himself a noted pacifist) starred as a German adolescent taught war-lust who lives through the horrors and returns from war disillusioned with it all.

All the King's Men (1949)

Col. Prod, Dir, Scr: Robert Rossen.† Novel basis: Robert Penn Warren, *All the King's Men* (1946). Cast: Broderick Crawford, John Derek, Joanne Dru, John Ireland, Mercedes McCambridge, Shepperd Strudwick, Katherine Warren, Ralph Dumke, Will Wright, Grandon Rhodes, H. C. Miller, Richard Hale, Helene Stanley, Paul Ford, John "Skins" Miller•

One of the half-dozen most awarded films of any left-wing director or writer and Rossen's own commercial and personal triumph shortly before his days as a friendly witness (and his ultimate return to prestige filmmaking with THE HUSTLER). The film compares poorly to a number of earlier Rossen films (BODY AND SOUL) in poetic use of camera and script, but it forcefully relates the colorful tale of late Louisiana governor Huey Long (described by Franklin Roosevelt as the "most dangerous man in America") as American liberals chose to remember it.

The novel focused on the journalist. In this version, the center is the charismatic small town politician who in his success finally destroys his family and himself. McCambridge, as his right-hand woman, plays the crucial role, coaxing idealistic newspaperman Derek to stay with the team until the moral disaster is complete. Crawford as the Kingfish is brilliant but lacking the particular qualities that made Huey Long unique in the South. In real life, Long was the son of a prominent Louisiana socialist, successfully united black and white citizens as no state leader north or south since Reconstruction and was assassinated while in the process of elaborating a challenge to the New Deal with the aid of constituencies both to Roosevelt's left and right.

Academy Awards went to Crawford, Rossen (for best picture); nominations to John Ireland, McCambridge (in her film debut), and to Rossen again (best script). Voted best film of the year by New York film critics eager to make a safely liberal political choice. 109 min.

The Amazing Doctor Clitterhouse (1938)

Anatole Litvack Productions (WB), First National Pictures. Prod: Anatole Litvak. Dir: Anatole Litvak. Scr: John Wexley,• John Huston. Play basis: Barré Lyndon, *The Amazing Dr Clitterhouse* (1937). Cast: Edward G. Robinson, Claire Trevor, Humphrey Bogart, Allen Jenkins, Donald Crisp, Gale Page

A fine crime feature with Robinson as the Park Avenue physician who decides to analyze criminal behavior by becoming the mastermind of a criminal gang. He hadn't counted on the boss being a tough-talking dame (Trevor) who, in a typical Wexley aside, explains that the real criminals are the bankers and tenement-house owners. Nor had he counted on an especially mean mug (Bogart) enraged by Trevor's romantic feelings for his new rival.

Some of the best of the film returns to the familiar Runyonesque territory of run-of-the-mill thieves with low educational levels (and probably low IQs) but many loveable qualities. Among them, Robinson quickly becomes a cultural hero. The plot grows less convincing as the film unspools, but Robinson and Trevor remain interesting. Bogart is too one-dimensional here to be up to par. This is Huston's first screenwriting credit, thanks (according to his longtime friend Wexley) to the older writer's sponsorship. Huston's memoirs failed to acknowledge the debt. 87 min.

The Amazing Mr. X (aka The Spiritualist, 1948)

Bernard Vorhaus• directed and Ian McLellan Hunter• co-scripted this deep B-weirdo film, with a fake spiritualist, a blackbird "familiar," and many of the pleasantly odd moments later associated with the Creature Feature television anthologies, including a scoundrel far more enticing than the good guy.

The Amazing Mrs. Holliday (1943)

Co-scripted by Leo Townsend† from a story by Sonya

Levien and a so-so vehicle for Deanna Durbin, this film was attacked at the time by critics as exploiting war themes for the sake of a successful musical. Director Jean Renoir himself was rumored to have stalked off the set in a disagreement ignited by Durbin's ego. What remains is a story of a young American schoolteacher in China who smuggles nine orphans into her homeward-bound ship. The best (or worst) moment is Durban singing "Rock-a-Bye Baby" in Chinese.

Ambush (1949)

A typical Sam Wood western of cowboys versus Indians, which was, however, also a real-life battle between right-wing Wood and left-wing writer Marguerite Roberts.• He won, she later recalled (last scene: flag snapping in the breeze replaces a kiss), but suffered a fatal heart attack a year later while leading the charge against the Hollywood Left.

Among the Living (1941)

Para. Prod: Sol C. Siegel. Dir: Stuart Heisler. Scr: Lester Cole,• Brian Marlow. Story basis: Lester Cole,• Garrett Fort. Cast: Albert Dekker, Susan Hayward, Frances Farmer, Harry Carey, Gordon Jones, Dorothy Sebastian, Clarence Muse

The film begins with its strongest moment, at a cemetery, where the late southern mill baron is lauded by town notables and sneered at by mill workers standing outside the gates. It was pronounced by the *New York Times* the "dreariest film of the year." House Committee on Un-American Activities (HUAC) hearings later inadvertently revealed that far more radical dialogue about class and race had been cut from the script. What remains is an extremely odd performance by Dekker (known in real life for modest participation in wartime Popular Front activities) in a dual role as twins: the maddened son, kept in a locked room for decades, and the son who was sent away to school and told that his brother had died. The two come into contact again when the death of the baron prompts the insane one to steal their father's body from their mother's side in the family plot.

This is an early film treatment of domestic violence, which causes the son who shares his mother's agony to go berserk under the patriarchal thumb. Violence begets violence: when a reward is wrongly offered for him as the killer of a mill girl, a typically bloodthirsty and money-hungry mob erupts. One fine scene has sane brother Dekker and his wife (played by Farmer—her last film before herself being sent to a real-life insane asylum) wrestling with the tale's moral implications. Even so, *New Masses* reviewers regarded it as one of Hollywood's best contemporary features. It is also memorable for the cinematography of Theodor Sparkuhl, who had been active in 1920s German classics and later worked for Jean Renoir. 78 min.

Anchors Aweigh (1945)

MGM. Prod: Joe Pasternak. Dir: George Sidney. Scr: Isobel Lennart.† Story basis: Natalie Marcin. Cast: Gene Kelly, Kathryn Grayson, Frank Sinatra, José Iturbi, Dean Stockwell, Pamela Britton, Billy Gilbert

A Gene Kelly wartime musical with a lot of classy hoofing and warbling (Sinatra is Kelly's singing voice) over a mighty thin plot. Kelly and Sinatra (in the flesh) are gobs on leave in Hollywood (!), with Gene the Don Juan and Frankie the hopeless drip. Kelly falls hard for Grayson, an extra with a boy to care for. Believing through most of the film that his pal is in love with her (he actually has eyes for chubby, funny Britton), Kelly smiles while Grayson dances and sings. He has his own singing and spectacular dancing to do, and not all that much dialogue survives or, apparently, is necessary.

Most memorable (which is to say steadily recycled in film history retrospectives), Kelly offers a dance duet with the animated character Tom, of Tom and Jerry. That's the high point of the film, although critics rightly praised the film as another of Pasternak's fluid productions. It earned an Academy Award for best score (with songs by Jules Styne and Sammy Cahn), and nominations for best actor, best color cinematography, best picture, and best song. 139 min., color.

And Now Tomorrow (1944)

Para. Prod: Fred Kohlmer. Dir: Irving Pichel.• Scr: Frank Partos, Raymond Chandler. Cast: Alan Ladd, Loretta Young, Susan Hayward, Barry Sullivan, Beulah Bondi, Cecil Kellaway

One of those forties soapers in which social uplift and genuine moral vision are combined in the romantic intrigues and medical moments that figure in so many women's films. Young, a debutante from the richest family in a New England industrial town, is deaf from meningitis despite the efforts of the best doctors in the world. She postpones marriage to beau Sullivan (an upright scion himself) while she seeks further help. Ladd, a working-class boy whose immigrant father was fired (just before Christmas!) from the factory that Young's family ran, has gone through medical school with the help of the town doc (kindly Kellaway) and now practices in a blue-collar clinic in Pittsburgh. A scientific investigator in his off hours, he comes up with a serum that, the doc thinks, might work on Young. But he still resents her class privilege, about which she is more than deaf. She watches him operate on a poor child, daughter of a working-class woman who remembers Young with hatred and then forgives her. The ending is never in doubt, but after 1950 no one would believe it. 85 min.

Angel on My Shoulder (1946)

The thematic sequel to HERE COMES MR. JORDAN, but less successful by far as co-written by Roland Kibbee.† There is also a rare comic performance by progressive former Yiddish theater actor Paul Muni in a difficult role as a murdered convict who wakes up in Hell, where the devil (Claude Rains) offers him a chance to get even—as a respected judge. Onslow Stevens is best as a psychoanalyst utterly confused by Muni's wildly vacillating behavior. Remade in 1980 as a film for television, directed by John Berry.•

Angels with Broken Wings (1941)

A cheapie musical directed by Bernard Vorhaus,• it was denied release in Latin America because of the involvement of a villain, played by Gilbert Roland, in a scheme of quickie Mexican divorces.

Angels with Dirty Faces (1938)

W.B. Prod: Sam Bischoff. Dir: Michael Curtiz. Scr: John Wexley,• Warren Duff. Story basis: Rowland Brown. Cast: James Cagney, Pat O'Brien, Humphrey Bogart, Ann Sheridan, George Bancroft, Billy Halop, Bobby Jordan, Leo Gorcey, Gabriel Dell, Huntz Hall, Bernard Punsley, Joe Downing, Edward Pawley

A superior crime drama and an all-time Cagney favorite, tainted but not ruined by its bow to the moral authority of church and state. Cagney and O'Brien are boyhood pals in the slums, pursued by the cops for trying to steal from a railroad car. O'Brien is caught, does his time, and returns to the old neighborhood as a priest, while Cagney escapes into a life of crime. When finally arrested, he agrees to take the fall in return for $100,000 when he is released.

Cagney and O'Brien thereafter do a dance of loyalties and separations. The career criminal seeks to impress the slum kids with his money and his toughness and shares

O'Brien's hatred for the crookedness of urban politics. He kills O'Brien's enemies outright when he learns that they plan to assassinate the priest, then he finds himself on death row, with his priest pal begging him to turn "yellow" so that the kids won't want to be like him. In the famed gripping (if also maudlin) climax, he willfully gives up the pose of toughness that has been his greatest pride. Along with the critically admired DEAD END, *Angels with Dirty Faces* launched Jordan, Gorcy, Hall and others as the Dead End Kids and BOWERY BOYS through dozens of B-pics, many of them written by the Hollywood Left. Box office was boffo; Oscar nominations went to Cagney, to Roland Brown for best original story, and to Curtiz for best direction. 105 min.

Another Language (1933)

A pre-Code theatrical adaptation produced by Walter Wanger, co-scripted by Donald Ogden Stewart• with an adaptation by Gertrude Purcell,† this film has newlyweds contemptuous of stodgy middle-class values in contrast to the younger generation's boredom, bohemianism and inclination toward adultery.

Another Part of the Forest (1948)

Universal Prod: Jerry Bresler. Dir: Michael Gordon.•† Scr: Vladimir Pozner.• Play basis: Lillian Hellman,• *Another Part of the Forest* (1946). Cast: Fredric March, Dan Duryea, Edmond O'Brien, Ann Blyth, Florence Eldridge, John Dall, Dona Drake, Betsy Blair, Fritz Leiber, Whit Bissell, Don Beddoe, Wilton Graff, Virginia Farmer,† Libby Taylor, Smoki Whitfield

This prequel to THE LITTLE FOXES (1941) is best remembered cinematically for progressive cameraman James Wong Howe's innovative use of middle range shots, allowing a theatrical intimacy in conversational situations. It is less remembered for screenwriter Pozner, who fled the blacklist to Paris and was later disfigured in a bomb attack by right-wing terrorists.

Here we learn how the wicked Hubbard family of *The Little Foxes* came by their greed and conniving nature. It all goes back to "the wah" (i.e., between the states) and the way the fortune was gathered: by raising the price on necessities during the worst of the conflict. March, as the old storekeeper and family patriarch who wishes he could put the guilt to rest, is beset with a hopelessly troubled wife (Eldridge) and daughter (Blyth) who want nothing more than to get out, preferably to Chicago; and by a no-good son, Duryea, who wants to spend his share and a great deal more on good times and women. His brother O'Brien, no

success as a salesman, is also out of luck in his hopes for a large loan to start a business. Blair, an utterly batty relative, and Dall, a neighbor who wishes he could woo Blyth, help fill out the list of the hopeless. 107 min.

Another Thin Man (1939)

Third in the Thin Man series and the fifth film made on the story basis of famed detective novelist and left-winger, Dashiell Hammett.• Lacks Hammett qualities other than a certain heavy-drinking sophistication that the Popular Frontish *New Yorker* crowd would have recognized.

Are Husbands Necessary? (1942)

A Tess Slesinger and Frank Davis† adaptation of a popular novel by the same name, this film has Ray Milland and Betty Field as a feuding couple wanting to have a baby but unable to pull family expenses together because of her scatterbrained spending. Though mostly sitcomic, it has some clever dialogue and high moments with the Three Stooges singing and Milland clumsily breaking up a fancy ball thrown for financial aristocrats.

The Argyle Secrets (1948)

Cyril Endfield• scripted and directed this adaptation of his own radio play about a reporter getting the goods on Nazi spies. The new Eronel production company did not survive, but the film shows hints of a major talent in chrysalis.

Arkansas Judge (1941)

A hillbilly gab-fest with unusually distinguished writers and equally unusual social drama. Ring Lardner, Jr.,• Ian McLellan Hunter• and Gertrude Purcell† all worked on this adaptation of an Irving Stone novel. Slander suits, courtroom and mob scenes, false accusations and (finally) a good arrest mark the cornpone plot. Roy Rogers, in one of his few non-westerns, plays a young attorney.

Arkansas Traveler (1938)

An old-fashioned newspaper drama co-scripted by Viola Brothers Shore,• with George Sessions Perry and co-starring Irvin S. Cobb. The local political boss plans to build a dam at taxpayer expense; the press exposes the hidden agenda in the bond issue, although advertisers pull out. Threatened with bankruptcy and loss of press freedom, the reformers use an unexpired radio license and build a makeshift transmitter in one night, tipping the election.

Army Girl (1938)

Samuel Ornitz• co-scripted this Republic gendered B-effort about a somewhat rebellious Army commander's daughter.

The Asphalt Jungle (1950)

MGM. Prod: Arthur Hornblow, Jr. Dir: John Huston. Scr: Ben Maddow,•† John Huston. Story basis: W.R. Burnett. Cast: Sterling Hayden,† Louis Calhern, Jean Hagen, Sam Jaffe,• John McIntire, Marc Lawrence,† Teresa Celli, Marilyn Monroe

Often described as one of the best crime films of all time and a nominee for many Academy Awards, it elaborates a jewel robbery planned by mastermind con Sam Jaffe and backed by corrupt lawyer Louis Calhern. A carefully assembled group of criminals falls because each criminal mistrusts all the others. Their personal circumstances, moreover, reveal the clash between the lure of the caper and the reality of domestic life (troubled wives, sickly kids and a deep sense of alienation and despair always close at hand). Hayden, whose relationship with Hagen fails even as he nears arrest, finds himself unable to return to anything like normal life—not so far from the real-life Hayden, a remorseful friendly witness. Marilyn Monroe as semi-moll is notable.

The last of Huston's noir features, it strongly reflects the contributions of Maddow (one of his last films before he was blacklisted) in an effective adaptation of Burnett's story. The dialogue is sharp and Jaffe is brilliant as the gang boss; he was nominated as best supporting actor on his way to a destroyed career. The film was remade as CAIRO (1963), written by Joan Scott, herself blacklisted as former executive secretary of the left-led (and quickly busted) Television Writers of America, the young Norman Lear's labor affiliation. *Asphalt Jungle* was admired for its cinematic finesse but attacked by Bosley Crowther among others for its amoral acceptance of criminals as worthy subjects. 112 min.

The Assassination of Trotsky (1972)

Cinnette-CIAC-Dino De Laurentiis. Prod: Norman Priggen. Dir: Joseph Losey.• Scr: Nicholas Mosley, Massolino D'Amico. Cast: Richard Burton, Alain Delon, Romy Schneider, Valentina Cortese, Giorgio Albertazzi

This film is regarded by several generations of Leon Trotsky's followers as definitive proof of Losey's Stalinist impulses, not altogether incorrectly. We see here the last days, in 1940, of the exiled revolutionary in Mexico, with Burton the aging and somewhat cranky if still loveable intellectual who innocently adopts assassin Delon (lover to Schneider, an unbalanced aide to Trotsky), leading to the left-wing political crime of the century. The larger political context of the Moscow Trials, a crushed Spanish Civil War and impending world war is sloughed off for symbolic dread. Lots of Mexican footage in place of the character development by Burton/Trotsky shows Losey at his weakest. Reviewers gave Cortese high marks as Trotsky's loyal wife but gave little credit to the film otherwise. Shot in English, it was destined for failure outside the enraged (and culturally influential) Trotskyist following in Britain. 103 min., color.

Atoll K (1950)

The last outing for Laurel and Hardy, scripted by an uncredited Howard Dimsdale• and directed by John Berry• in his first project in European exile after the blacklist. A bottom-of-the-bucket French-Italian production had the boys inheriting a Pacific island that was almost worthless after taxes and customs. A storm lands them instead on a deserted atoll. Stuck with a French cook and an Italian stowaway, they set out like Robinson Crusoe to make some kind of life. But the island's supply of uranium for making bombs brings in the superpowers. Rich possibilities for political satire go mostly if not entirely unrealized.

Autumn Leaves (1956)

Para. Prod: Robert Aldrich. Dir: Robert Aldrich. Scr: Jack Jevne, Lewis Meltzer, Robert Blees. (Principal writers: Jean Rouverol Butler• and Hugo Butler,• both uncredited). Story basis: Jean Rouverol Butler. Cast: Joan Crawford, Cliff Robertson, Vera Miles, Lorne Greene, Ruth Donnelly, Maxine Cooper

The tale of an aging, unmarried woman (Crawford at the late edge of her classic form) who falls in love with a young man but whose good sense is overcome by his ardor. Beautifully cinematic scenes later became stock film sexuality, including Crawford first afraid to show herself in a bathing suit at the beach, then being pulled joyfully into the waves by Robertson, both surrounded by symbolic explosions of surf.

At the very moment we are ready to take pleasure in the triumph of love over age, however, the bottom falls out. The story has a sub-basement of despair, madness and in-law incest (Robertson's mind has been unhinged by learning that his father is sleeping with his, Robertson's, first wife) that qualify it as a precursor to Hitchcock's *Psycho*, but with a feminist underpinning. This last of Crawford's half-dozen films written by blacklistees, was (through director Aldrich) also notably the bridge to her later horror period; at 51, she is matched up with Robertson in the first of his roles as an unbalanced innocent. At one point, the psychiatrist— continually invoked as the higher authority—jeers at Crawford, who fears losing Robertson by assisting his cure, "You're not the patient. Or are you?" Of course, by this point in the fifties, everyone was a patient. 108 min.

Avalanche Express (1979)

The film that convinced screenwriter Abraham Polonsky• to retire once and for all. Producer-director Mark Robson died in the final stages of the shooting, and lead Robert Shaw succumbed before the film reached audiences.

Football star Joe Namath is inexplicably cast as a CIA man in a cowboy outfit in a Cold War drama that makes no sense for Polonsky's politics or aesthetics.

Avenging Rider (1943)

RKO. Prod: Bert Gilroy. Dir: Sam Nelson. Scr: Harry O. Hoyt, Morton Grant.• Cast: Tim Holt, Cliff Edwards, Ann Summers, Davison Clarke, Norman Willis, Karl Hackett, Earl Hodgins

A memorable banker-and-swindler drama, with Holt inadvertently on the wrong side of the law until he can straighten things out. The rancher and his sidekick "Ukelele Ike" visit an old pal and find him shot dead. Pursuing the crooks, they draw the fire of the sheriff and have to go underground. Happily, the doctor's daughter (Summer) is around to help. At last they piece the crime together (literally, a playing card cut into five pieces) and get Clarke, the wicked banker who has almost made away with a wagonload of gold bullion. Ike's contribution, beyond humor, is that forgotten cowboy adaptation of a Harlem hit, "Minnie the Mountain Moocher." 55 min.

B

Babes on Swing Street (1944)
Howard Dimsdale• screenplay; lightweight musical comedy with Ann Blyth, Peggy Ryan, Andy Devine and Leon Errol, in stage night at a settlement house where teachers raise money and attention to attract music school candidates for scholarships.

Bachelor Apartment (1931)
This skirt-chasing comedy hurt screenwriter John Howard Lawson,• tempted back to Hollywood, because it was dramatically vapid and a commercial failure. Lowell Sherman, at once director and star, could hardly have created a worse vehicle for himself.

Bachelor Daddy (1941)
One of Robert Lees• and Frederic I. Rinaldo's• lesser efforts, despite Edward Everett Horton in lead of this film in the "Baby Sandy" series, with the child deposited in an exclusive Bachelor's Club. A favorite Hollywood plot, highlighted by an in-joke subplot about a nonexistent film serial called *The Phantom of the Mesa*.

Back Door to Heaven (1939)
Odesso Pictures. Prod. William K. Howard. Dir: William K. Howard. Story: William K. Howard. Scr: John Bright,• (Robert Tasker, uncredited). Cast: Jimmy Lydon, Wallace Ford, Aline MacMahon, Anita Magee, Jane Seymour, William Harrigan, Stuart Erwin, Patricia Ellis, Kent Smith, Van Heflin, William K. Howard

Perhaps the best single example of the class theme in a thirties film. Damaged by low production values and uneven editing but with many vivid moments, it attracted much critical attention at the time. Said to be the life story of producer-director Howard's childhood pal, the film is a Christian socialist fable about poor boy Lydon (with a mean drunk for a father) caught stealing a harmonica to play for high school graduation. He is sent to an abusive work farm and from there to prison. The finest moment in the film has

the cast of high school chums in later life, articulating, one by one, how capitalism, encapsulated in the effects of the Depression, stole their dreams.

Ford accidentally meets his childhood sweetheart just before he tries to stop a robbery and is then wrongly apprehended and sentenced to death. In a courtroom scene foreshadowing *Knock on Any Door*, he is defended by another high school classmate. Doomed nevertheless, Ford escapes and returns to his hometown, where his class is holding a reunion. MacMahon exploits wonderfully sentimental moments to the hilt as the now-retired teacher who has always understood the forces of fate. In a memorable soliloquy against class hatred, Ford pleads with the victims of society to change the world but to hold no grudges. This was the last major film of screenwriter Bright, who gave Cagney his best early hits. A militant trade unionist, Bright was already exiled from first-class features, a full decade before the blacklist. Tasker, his collaborator (also a former San Quentin inmate) and fellow party member, died mysteriously in Mexico City in 1945. 85 min.

Back Pay (1930)
The weepy Francis Edward Faragoh• adaptation of a Fannie Hurst novel about a girl in an oppressive small town who runs away to the big city and lives with a war profiteer, then returns to the blinded serviceman who is her true love.

Back Roads (1981)
CBS Theatrical Films (WB). Prod: Ronald Shedlo. Dir: Martin Ritt.• Scr: Gary Devore. Cast: Sally Field, Tommy Lee Jones, David Keith, Miriam Colon, Michael V. Gazzo, Dan Shor, M. Emmet Walsh, Barbara Babcock

A poorly conceived Ritt project shot shortly after Field won an Oscar for Ritt's NORMA RAE. Here she plays a loser, a $20 Southern hustler who knows she can't win but refuses to admit it. "Whores," she quips, are "high school girls doing it for nothing." After a well-intended Tommy Lee Jones (a car wash attendant who made a light living as a boxer taking dives) throws a punch at a cop harassing her, they hit the road together. Janet Maslin in the *New York Times* praised Field as one of the nouveau heroines drawn from daily life, in effect a liberated woman, if always bound somehow by middle-class moral aspirations. Most critics didn't like it much, and the gate was disappointing. 94 min.

Back to Bataan (1945)
RKO. Exec. Prod: Robert Fellows. Asso. Prod: Theron

Warth. Dir: Edward Dmytryk.•† Scr: Ben Barzman,•
Richard H. Landau. Story basis: Aeneas MacKenzie,
William Gordon. Cast: John Wayne, Anthony Quinn,
Beulah Bondi, "Ducky" Louie, Fely Franquelli, Richard
Loo, Philip Ahn, Lawrence Tierney

The first film about heroic Filipinos that seeks to
deal with the complex issues of Filipino nationalism,
including the earlier U.S. conquest of the island and the
apparent tardiness of the American response to Japanese
conquest early in the war. Wayne is not altogether
predictable as the American colonel sent to prepare
locals for the landing at Leyte Gulf and the massive
reconquest to follow. In tense pep-talks, he even praises
Filipino resistance in the Spanish-American War while
laying accusations of oppression most heavily upon the
Spanish.

Wayne's key maneuver is to bring in Quinn, who as
the grandson of a martyr in the anti-Spanish struggle
offers a unifying national symbol. Back in action against
the Japanese, and ever the generic Third World male,
Quinn is slow to arouse but fiery when lit. Beulah Bondi
as an American schoolteacher puts on a fine Anna Louise
Strong–like performance as the Christian converted to
anti-imperialism. Ducky Louie is the plucky Filipino kid
and heroic figure of the resistance. The courage of the
locals is demonstrated as well as praised, and the Japanese behavior as military conquerors none too overdrawn. The film lacks the candid assessment of racism
that marred each phase of U.S. actions in the Philippines,
but it was a big box office success. 95 min

Badman's Territory (1946)
With a story basis by Bess Taffel• and Clarence Upson
Young for Randolph Scott and George "Gabby" Hayes, this
western has a crusading newspaperwoman determined to
attack crime and corruption in a frontier community. It's
mostly action in this mangled recounting of the Oklahoma
Land Rush (and a big commercial success).

Bad Men of Tombstone (1949)
A tedious gold-mine western scripted by Arthur Strawn•
and Philip Yordan (best known for grabbing credits
without lifting a pen). Progressive Barry Sullivan plays
the often sympathetic outlaw destined to bite the dust.

The Bad News Bears Go to Japan (1978)
John Berry• was embarrassed at this commercial job,
starring Tony Curtis and the kids; at least it ended the

series. His one other children's film, Maya, shows what
he could do with the genre.

Bagdad (1949)
An over-the-top costume drama based on a story by
Tamara Hovey• about a Bedouin princess educated in
Britain, who returns home to find her father murdered
and her tribe endangered. Even worse, she encounters the
evil British colonial ruler of Bagdad, delightfully hammy
Vincent Price. Mild anticolonialism; mostly music and
intrigue. More painfully memorable in retrospect, after
repeated U.S. invasions of Iraq.

The Bandit of Sherwood Forest (1946)
Col. Prod: Leonard S. Picker, Clifford Sanforth. Dir:
George Sherman, Henry Levin. Scr: Wilfred H. Petitt,
Melvin Levy.† Story Basis: Paul A. Castleton, The Son of
Robin Hood (1940). Cast: Cornel Wilde, Anita Louise, Jill
Esmond, Edgar Buchanan, Henry Daniell, George
Macready, Russell Hicks

The only Robin Hood film written by a lefty anticipates the historic 1950s television series written by so many
of them. Forbidden by lawsuit to use "Robin Hood" in the
title, this one is really a "son of," custom-made for the
physical antics of Wilde. Returning from the Crusades,
Wilde finds that the efforts of his father to keep tyranny at
the gates (at least inside the gates of Nottingham) have
been swept away by the Normans with the help of all-too-
willing collaborators (shades of World War II, among many
in the film). This Robin Hood is actually an aristocrat, as
was his father, and his domain over the forest is a sort of
noblesse oblige. But his struggle against the new regime is
noble in more than one way; he comes close to leading a
revolutionary uprising until the usual comradely cooperation (more than a little like partisan warfare behind German
lines) saves the day. 86 min., Technicolor.

The Bang-Bang Kid (1968)
Spanish-Italian spaghetti anti-western comedy directed by
Stanley Prager,• with a robot gunfighter. Lefties made a
number of Euro-westerns worth watching, but this isn't
on the list.

Barnacle Bill (1941)
MGM. Prod: Milton Bren. Dir: Richard Thorpe. Scr: Jack
Jevne, Hugo Butler.• Story basis: Jack Jevne. Cast:
Wallace Beery, Marjorie Main, Leo Carrillo, Virginia

Weidler, Donald Meek, Barton MacLane, Connie Gilchrist

Many charming moments enliven this sentimental blue-collar story of an old sailor and the middle-aged but romance-minded woman he dangles on a string. An all-too-familiar plot, but not far removed from life: boat-owner Beery, constantly in debt, wants Main's financial backing (she runs her father's cafe for working stiffs), but does not want to be tied down. When his cute daughter (Weidler) shows up, Main is easily enticed into a dream of having a husband and family, with the child as her own. A strong supporting cast includes the ever-pleasant Carrillo as the protean proletarian of the docks.

Realistic commercial fishing scenes and a harborside church service capture the life of the community, while a trained pelican harassing our heroes for their fish is the revenge nature takes on those who compete for her riches. The inevitable sea disaster brings Beery to his senses—out of his fantasies of an exotic trip with male-bonded Carrillo and into grudging married bliss. Not considered as tasty as *Tugboat Annie* (with the same top stars), but comparable in its use of Beery and more realistic in camerawork. 90 min.

The Barefoot Mailman (1951)

An uncredited Alfred Lewis Levitt• co-scripted this adaptation of a novel about a nineteenth-century mail carrier to distant and untamed sections of Florida. Schemer Robert Cummings reforms, and Will Geer• played his last supporting part before the blacklist (and his triumphant return in television's *The Waltons*).

The Barretts of Wimpole Street (1934)

MGM. Prod: Irving Thalberg. Dir: Sidney Franklin. Scr: Ernest Vajda, Claudine West, Donald Ogden Stewart.• Play basis: Rudolf Besier, *The Barretts of Wimpole Street* (1930). Cast: Norma Shearer, Fredric March, Charles Laughton, Maureen O'Sullivan, Katherine Alexander, Una O'Connor, Ian Wolfe

A film that astonishes by evolving, toward the end, from a romantic women's melodrama into a smashing gendered polemic. The apparently neurasthenic Shearer (as Elizabeth Barrett) comes alive at the prospect of mating with March (Robert Browning) and finally confronts patriarchal tyranny in the wonderfully hateable person of her father (Laughton), the domestic tyrant who has apparently killed his kindly wife with his demands (hidden in Christian sanctimony) and now presides over the adolescents, with special concern for O'Sullivan and

Shearer. As he learns that he can no longer dominate Shearer by keeping her in bondage to her supposed sickly nature, he comes close to revealing that he has a near-incestuous desire to keep her apart from the world and close to him forever. The others he merely bullies. Shearer, overacting as usual, often comes close to tears but summons up the courage to sneak away (with her dog, so Laughton does not have the consolation of having the mutt murdered). Not many lines of poetry are actually uttered, but the audience would not likely have enjoyed the Brownings' verse anyway. Stewart bragged in his memoirs of having rewritten it in record time of two weeks. 110 min.

Bar 20 (1943)

This lesser but enjoyable Hopalong Cassidy feature co-scripted by Michael Wilson,• Morton Grant• and Norman Houston has jewels and cash, including Hoppy's savings, stolen from a stagecoach. George Reeves, future television Superman, co-stars.

The Beast with Five Fingers (1946)

WB. Prod: William Jacobs. Dir: Robert Florey. Scr: Curt Siodmak (uncredited script contribution by Harold Goldman•). Story basis: William Fryer Harvey. Cast: Robert Alda, Andrea King, Peter Lorre, Victor Francen, J. Carrol Naish

Described by *Variety* as "among the most scary [films] ever made" and scored delightfully by Max Steiner, this film offers a thin plot with fine special effects and a sometimes astounding performance by Lorre, who has most of the best moments in Warner's only horror film of the 1940s.

In an Italian village at the turn of the century, a wealthy man who loved to play piano is slowly dying while a mad but seemingly harmless quack (Lorre) tries to discover the mysteries of fate through astrology. Meanwhile, a pleasant local con artist (Alda) and former musical composer is urging the old man's nurse (King) to flee and begin her life afresh. After the old man dies in an accident, his hand seems to be on the loose, playing the piano and killing or attempting to kill various people by strangling them—just as a ruthless American would-be heir (and his son) announce their determination to contest the will that gives everything to King. Slowly, suspicion turns toward the psychotic Lorre. The subdued political angle reveals acquisitive Americans, whose manners and aspirations clash with the artistic and bohemian impulses of the Italians. 88 min.

Beasts of Berlin aka *Hitler—Beast of Berlin,* aka *Goose Step* (1939)
PPC. Prod: Ben Judell. Dir: Sherman Scott. Scr: Shep Traube.• Cast: Roland Drew, Steffi Duna, Greta Granstedt, Alan Ladd, Lucien Prival, Vernon Dent, John Ellis, George Rosener, Bodil Rosing, Hans Heinrich von Twardowski

First screen credit for Ladd was this left-wing ardent bit of antifascism. An underfunded film with an international cast (including a handful of German refugees), it was released three times amid the sweep of political and military events. An oral history of screenwriter Traube recalls it as almost an underground event because it bucked so hard against the trend (one slow to reverse) of avoiding offense to German distributors. It was re-released twice, in 1941 and 1943, never gaining an audience.

The film traces the efforts of German antifascists to overthrow Nazism. They meet in a tavern, printing leaflets urging resistance to the Gestapo. The greatest emotional crisis comes when Drew's wife, Duna, announces that she is pregnant and wants to leave for the United States. Drew is caught and tortured when the owner of the tavern is forced to admit he is a leader of the group. Von Twardowski, who had been infiltrating the Nazis, gets drunk and tells the names of the members—causing all to be sent to the same concentration camp. Although tortured at the order of the camp commandant, Drew manages to escape (with the help of a "good German" camp guard) and is brought to Switzerland, where he reunites with Duna and his child. 87 min.

Beauty for the Asking (1939)
RKO. Prod: B. P. Fineman. Dir: Glenn Tryon. Scr: Paul Jarrico,• Doris Anderson. Story basis: Edmund L. Hartmann. Original story idea: Grace Norton, Adele Buffington. Cast: Lucille Ball, Patric Knowles, Donald Woods, Frieda Inescort, Frances Mercer, Leona Maricle, Whitney Bourne

A story straight out of Jewish business life (headstrong woman makes a fortune on beauty aids) is joined to the stock love-lost-and-regained plot of many women's films. Things being what they were in Hollywood, entrepreneurialism offered a narrative test for character. Memorable mostly for the star Ball (a former Communist elector and future witness, denying everything but unwilling to name anyone), in one of her early leading roles.

A working stiff, Lucy loses her man just as she begins to market her product, a "revolutionary" face cream that saves its user time and effort. Later she is bankrolled by the very heiress that rat Knowles left her for, and still later must decide whether or not to take him back. Happily, she has one of those nice guys conveniently at hand—an assistant conspicuously unembarrassed to work for a woman boss. Lucy is properly full of dignity through all this. But bereft of either physical comedy (she does that much better in a few contemporary Three Stooges shorts) or the proper material for a proper weepy, even she can't drag the story very far. Future blacklistee Jarrico, who earned his first real screen credit here, was on his way to better things. 68 min.

Becky Sharp (1935)
Pioneer Pictures. Prod: A. Rouben Mamoulian. Dir: A. Rouben Mamoulian. Scr: Francis Edwards Faragoh.• Play basis: Langdon Mitchell, *Becky Sharp* (1899), adapted from the William Makepeace Thackeray novel *Vanity Fair* (1848). Cast: Miriam Hopkins, Frances Dee, Cedric Hardwicke, Billie Burke, Nigel Bruce, Pat Nixon

A talky film that, like so many literary adaptations, inevitably passes over many interesting parts of the famed novel. But it nevertheless possesses real and sometimes surprising strengths. Hopkins richly deserved her Oscar nomination for her characterization of the poor girl raised in rich company, scheming to live above her station by playing continually and cynically upon male vanity. Raised as an orphan, she comes of age in pursuit of a rich husband but draws only dullards and rakes and one extraordinary decadent (Hardwick) who understands her only too well. "Men are dying for their country and I'm dying for breakfast," she says as the Napoleonic Wars climax at Waterloo.

More fascinating than Becky in her glory is Becky in her downfall. Blowsy and desperate, reduced to being a cabaret singer but nevertheless drawn to one selfless deed, she still has some delightful wickedness in her, directed mostly at her detestably hypocritical Christian in-laws. A great climax offers one of the most morally daring moments in 1930s films. From a technical standpoint, it's not the first film but the first feature film to be shot with the three-strip Technicolor technique. It cost $950,000 to make and poor receipts slowed further use of the technological breakthrough. 83 min.

Bedtime for Bonzo (1951)
Universal. Prod: Michael Kraike. Dir: Frederick de Cordova. Scr: Val Burton,• Lou Breslow. Story: Raphael David Blau, Tod Berkman. Cast: Ronald Reagan, Diana Lynn, Walter Slezak, Lucille Barkley, Jesse White, Herbert Heyes, Herbert Vigran

A triple irony: future blacklistee Burton writes for Reagan (in one of his last screen appearances before turning to television and General Electric, his corporate-political backer); by this time, Reagan is already a big winner in the Hollywood blacklist but due to become much bigger (he negotiated the Screen Actors Guild [SAG] out of most television residuals, and decades later, wore an SAG union button as he busted the air traffic controllers, setting off the era of widescale labor defeat). Here, playing way, way over his head, he is a psychology professor. Happily, the chimp is a Method actor.

Reagan brings Bonzo into his home to prove that heredity wins over environment. Lynn, the ex-farmgirl housekeeper, babysits the chimp but gets in the way of his engagement to Barkley. Like J. Fred Muggs on contemporary television, Bonzo acts "human" (or child-like), mugging at the camera and acting up, thus reorganizing the humans' lives. Inevitably, Reagan and Lynn will get together as sweethearts and lovers—but not until the honeymoon, and not without Bonzo! A very liberal interpretation would suggest that the plot makes monkeys out of typical Cold War–era college intellectuals. 83 min.

Before Dawn (1933)

Director Irving Pichel's• warm-up for films with social themes—and a fair bit of hack work—of the later 1930s and 1940s. A mixup of psychoanalysis, crime and romance.

The Beguiled (1971)

Off-center Civil War drama with escaped Southern soldier Clint Eastwood hidden in a boarding school of horny girls and a hornier administrator. Director Don Siegel, usually dynamic to a fault, can hardly sustain the narrative here. Script by Albert Maltz• as "John B. Sherry."

Behave Yourself! (1951)

RKO. Prod: Jerry Wald, Norman Krasna. Dir: George Beck.† Scr: George Beck and Frank Tarloff.• Cast: Farley Granger, Shelley Winters, Margalo Gillmore, William Demarest, Francis L. Sullivan, Hans Conried, Sheldon Leonard, Marvin Kaplan, Elisha Cook, Jr., Glenn Anders, Lon Chaney, Jr.

A winning satire of gangster films by veteran radio scriptwriter (and future TV writer of note) Tarloff, along with future friendly witness Beck. Granger, a quietly progressive (and more quietly gay) actor joins Winters, an often noisily progressive one (like Granger, careful enough to avoid the blacklist) in an emotional triangle with the inevitable mother-in-law, played by Gillmore. He wants to wear the pants and to get into wife Winters' pants more often than he does, but living under her mother's roof, appears permanently outnumbered—until a pooch belonging to a mobster accidentally enters the household. A mob hit and lots of confusion follow, with Conried and Leonard as screwball criminals tracked by equally screwy detectives. The modest Tarloff claimed that he joined the project because Beck was exhausted, and the studios fled to television. His next movie was made almost a decade later in Britain, the uncredited but memorable *School for Scandal*. 81 min.

Behind City Lights (1945)

A women's drama scripted by Richard Weil.• Lynne Roberts' character leaves a small town for big city life where she becomes entangled with crime before returning to her old boyfriend and the country.

Behind the Eight Ball (1942)

A musical with story and co-screenplay by Stanley Roberts,† at its best when the Ritz Brothers hog the camera.

Beloved Bachelor (1931)

Para. Producer unknown. Dir: Lloyd Corrigan. Scr: Sidney Buchman.• Cast: Paul Lukas, Dorothy Jordan, Charles Ruggles, Vivienne Osborne, Leni Stengel, John Breeden, Harold Minjir, Marjorie Gateson, Alma Chester

A pleasant little sentimental outing with Lukas laying it on thick as the kindly sculptor who adopts little Jordan after her mother's death. Growing up in his studio, with Lukas' old friends Ruggles and Breeden, she comes of age as he grays at the temples. At the time, winter-spring relationships were no less common but still controversial, and so her love for Lukas is the hinge for complications. She is convinced that he is in love with Osborne, an old flame, and he can't believe that she wants a father-figure as lover. The audience has guessed the outcome long beforehand. Ruggles, then beloved as a comic figure (here, as often before the Code, playing hilarious drunken scenes), comes off best as the delightfully silly uncle type. 74 min.

Best Man Wins (1948)

Col. Prod: Ted Richmond. Dir: John Sturges. Scr: Edward Huebsch.• Story basis: Mark Twain, "The Celebrated

Jumping Frog of Calaveras County" (1865). Cast: Edgar Buchanan, Anna Lee, Robert Shayne, Gary Gray, Hobert Cavanaugh, Stanley Andrews, George Lynn, Bill Sheffield, Marietta Canty, Paul E. Burns

A rare and rarely seen but excellent translation of Twain to the screen, thankfully lacking most of the Hollywood sugaring apparent in even the sturdy first sound version of THE ADVENTURES OF HUCKLEBERRY FINN. This one, shot on a B budget but with good casting and excellent direction, puts across the story of the wandering gambler who returns to his home town to learn that his wife has divorced him and intends to remarry. The famous jumping frog owned by the peripatetic Buchanan, and the training of a dog for a race, keeps moppet Gray on his dad's side as mom is eventually won back over. The best film of the unlucky Huebsch (he once said he suffered heart attacks after producers gutted his most earnest political screenplays) until he began working with Robert Aldrich in a late comeback. 73 min.

The Betsy (1978)
Harold Robbins' novel was adapted by Walter Bernstein,• and presents a corporate auto giant and his frisky family. A strictly commercial project for everyone involved, but Laurence Olivier always delivers; here he draws from the same well he used to play Nazis, but winks at the material. Could anyone blame him?

Beware of Ladies (1937)
Irving Pichel• directed this comedy about a reporter (Betty White) separated from her husband and covering a politician with whom she falls in love. Borderline hanky-panky.

Beyond the Last Frontier (1943)
Morton Grant• co-scripted this Texas Rangers tale (with Smiley Burnette for laughs and Bob Mitchum as a heavy) about a gang running contraband through Ranger territory. Variety reported that the film audience snickered through unconvincing plot complications.

The Big Break (1953)
A gambler's story and failed Broadway show by Arnold Manoff• (co-starring his wife, the blacklisted future Oscar winner, Lee Grant). The drama was interestingly adapted by Lee Gold,• but the promising film died thanks to the political atmosphere.

The Big Cat (1949)
E-L/William Moss Pictures. Prod: William Moss. Dir: Phil Karlson. Scr: Morton Grant,• Dorothy Yost. Cast: Lon McCallister, Preston Foster, Peggy Ann Garner, Forrest Tucker

A strange Depression drama about a rural southwestern ranching area suffering decades of drought. Youngster McAllister, son of a woman who fled the valley after a violent quarrel by two men over her, shows up to find his uncle, the woodsman Foster. Nearly jumped by a cougar rampaging the countryside, he discovers that his supposed refuge from the poverty of city life is full of old clan-like hatreds. But his uncle dreams of restarting a bark extraction business and the lonely but spirited local teenager Garner immediately McAllister as a likely fiancé.

While the preacher urges reconciliation, promising the possibility that God will forgive and bring the valley rain, the boy ponders. Unable to shoot a buck, he hears his kindly uncle explain that killing is proper only for subsistence and that "everything is Man's fault anyway." The big cat (with a $150 reward on its head) offers the action that moves the plot, but proves less threatening than the emotions of the inhabitants. It is, nevertheless, the symbolic issue that must be resolved as the boy reaches for manhood and a life in the valley. Director Karlson, known for his human interest themes, frequently worked with the Left both before and after the blacklist. 75 min., color.

Big City (1937)
MGM. Prod: Norman Krasna. Dir: Frank Borzage. Scr: Dore Schary, Hugo Butler.• Story: Norman Krasna. Cast: Luise Rainer, Spencer Tracy, Charles Grapewin, Janet Beecher, Eddie Quillan, Victor Varconi, Oscar O'Shea, Helen Troy, William Demarest, John Arledge, Irving Bacon, Regis Toomey, Guinn "Big Boy" Williams, Jack Dempsey, James J. Jeffries, "Slapsie Maxie" Rosenbloom, Jim Thorpe, Man Mountain Dean, Ruth Hussey.

Romantic comedy with plenty of proletarian solidarity of a perversely individualistic quality. Rainer is a Russian refugee married to cabbie Tracy. Taxi bosses try to trap cabbies into criminal activities by using "labor agitator" Beecher to stir up trouble, ultimately accusing Rainer of transporting a bomb. Threatened with deportation, she goes underground and enjoys the support of cabbies wised up to the real issues, until she realizes that all will suffer until she gives herself up. She is saved from deportation on the night she gives birth. Meanwhile, the taxi bosses try to give the independents a lesson, but get one in return. Watch for boxers and wrestlers Dempsey, Jeffries, Rosenbloom, Thorpe, and Dean as themselves, the loveable pugs. This is the debut film of Ruth Hussey, often cast as the unmarried, strong career girl. 80 min.

The Big Clock (1948)

Para. Prod: Richard Maibaum. Dir: John Farrow. Scr: Jonathan Latimer, Harold Goldman.• Novel basis: Kenneth Fearing, *The Big Clock* (1946). Cast: Ray Milland, Charles Laughton, Maureen O'Sullivan, George Macready, Rita Johnson, Harry Morgan, Elsa Lanchester

Based on a novel by left-winger Fearing and said to be modeled after the publishing business tyranny of the Hearst empire, this is a fast-paced thriller with Milland at his noir best. A talented newsman, he has left his young wife in emotional exile since signing on with *Crime Story* magazine seven years earlier. Just as he struggles to extricate himself, even at the cost of his job, boss Laughton (brilliant as a predatory capitalist) murders the former model who had been pursuing Milland. This resets the plot clock, for Milland has only 72 hours to find the real murderer. Hired by Laughton supposedly to crack the case for a magazine exclusive, he learns, step by step, that the clues point more and more toward himself. With the police closing in, he is trapped in the nightmare world of Laughton's imperial tower (an ostentatious office building shot from ominous angles). He must take on all the odds and every authority. Brilliantly tense, the film nevertheless contains some delightfully odd moments, including Lanchester as dotty bird-lover. Remade as *No Way Out* (1987) with far less impact and no politically adequate villain. 95 min.

The Big Guy (1939)

Universal. Assoc. Prod: Burt Kelly. Dir: Arthur Lubin. Scr: Lester Cole.• Story Basis: Wallace Sullivan, Richard K. Polimer, "No Power on Earth" (N.d.). Cast: Victor McLaglen, Jackie Cooper, Ona Munson, Peggy Moran, Edward Brophy, Jonathan Hale, Russell Hicks, Wallis Clark

Another in a series of prison dramas, this one barely more than a standard B-adventure for Cooper, the innocent youngster trapped in a web of crime and conspiracy. While showing off his car to friends, he is compelled to drive a getaway for escapees. Temporary warden McLaughlen, who has been kidnapped by the escapees after being treated badly by his own superiors, discovers that Cooper (sentenced to hang) is not guilty after all. But Cooper stages a breakout and McLaughlen is shot, dying before he can testify but leaving a portentous affidavit.

Film has an excess of melodrama, and is far less successful than a better film made seven years later from the same source, *Behind the High Wall*, with Sylvia Sidney. 78 min.

The Big Knife (1955)

Associates and Aldrich. Prod-Dir: Robert Aldrich. Scr: James Poe. Play basis: Clifford Odets,† *The Big Knife* (1949). Cast: Jack Palance, Rod Steiger, Ida Lupino, Shelley Winters, Wendell Corey, Jean Hagen, Ilka Chase, Everett Sloane, Paul Langton

A delayed 1940s film or premature 1960s film with a handful of actors close to the blacklistees, *The Big Knife* offers a glimpse of 1950s social drama at its best. It's a lesser Hollywood counterpart of the contemporary television play, where the Left writers hid themselves while making a living and waiting for an opening. Poe adapted Odets' pre-blacklist play with as much success as possible under these conditions, including a budget of less than a half-million dollars and a 15-day shooting schedule.

Palance is the Odetsian writer who comes to Hollywood after taking part in important social (read: left-wing) theater, as in Odets' *Waiting for Lefty*, and is soon corrupted by money. Seeking to desert the palace of lies, he is held fast by studio executive Steiger (said to be miming Columbia's Harry Cohn) through his possession of a terrible secret. To survive, Palance must betray his integrity, his faithful assistant and everything else meaningful to him. Well-played by Steiger, Lupino, Corey and Hagen, among others—quite as if they yearned for the more solid material available before the red scare. Winters is a bit off for the avant-garde treatment, a bit too obvious as usual, but she makes a solid effort. The melodrama was done better on stage and in a later theatrical television production. Panned on release by Odets-hating Pauline Kael, among others, as a vendetta against Hollywood. 111 min.

The Big Night (1951)

Waxman Productions. Prod: Philip A. Waxman. Dir: Joseph Losey.• Scr: Stanley Ellin, Joseph Losey• (script contribution: Hugo Butler•). Novel Basis: Stanley Ellin, *Dreadful Summit* (1948). Cast: John Barrymore, Jr., Preston Foster, Joan Lorring, Howard St. John, Dorothy Comingore,• Philip Bourneuf, Howland Chamberlain

A remarkable film noir, Losey's swan song before his flight to Europe. Son of modest tavern-owner Foster, Barrymore is the shy and sensitive type who is razzed and roughed up by his proletarian peers for his innocence. When sports writer St. John comes into his father's bar after hours and canes and humiliates him, Foster refuses to tell his son what it's all about, and Barrymore sets out for revenge with his father's pistol. The mystery of why a man would silently take a beating from a sadistic newspaper columnist in front of his adolescent son drives the story, which takes the form of the boy's discovery of the meaning of "manhood" told against a hallucinatory tour of the sins of the Big City at night.

Key to the film are two plot points that the Production Code forbade, but were contained in the novel; a mother's infidelity and the Catholic Church's strictures against divorce. It's enough to summarize the central plot point this way: the mother, not the father, committed the story's original sin.

Little wonder, with so little explained or even explainable under contemporary rules, that the film is in so many places incomprehensible. But it is an extraordinary failure. In a single shot, Losey reveals the genius to come; as a guilty and desperate boy who by now has taken his vengeance wanders the streets, he comes upon a church with a pair of imposing Romanesque towers. As he turns away and slouches down a side street, the camera pulls back to a wide shot to reveal, in a devastating equation, a pair of industrial cooling towers and the church spires (of the same height) across the street. Comingore, ditched (and her child taken away) by husband and friendly witness screenwriter Richard Collins,† was herself dramatized in GUILTY BY SUSPICION, in which her character commits suicide rather than endure a long mental collapse, as happened in real life. 75 min.

The Big Show-Off (1945)

With a co-screenplay by Richard Weil,• this film stars Arthur Lake (of the Blondie series) as a nightclub singer who pretends to be a professional wrestler, and Lionel Stander• as the club owner.

A Bill of Divorcement (1940)

A remake of the Katharine Hepburn 1932 hit, with Dalton Trumbo's• rewrite doomed from the outset despite good writing, fine reviews and good performances from leads Maureen O'Hara, Adolph Menjou, Fay Bainter and Herbert Marshall. A daughter's shock at realizing her father is congenitally mad with "bad blood" (a quasi-racial concept already outdated by 1940) could only be overplayed.

The Bishop's Wife (1947)

Goldwyn. Prod: Samuel Goldwyn. Dir: Henry Koster. Scr: Robert E. Sherwood, Leonardo Bercovici.• Novella basis: Robert Nathan, "The Bishop's Wife." Cast: Cary Grant, Loretta Young, David Niven, Monty Woolley, James Gleason, Sara Haden, Gladys Cooper, Elsa Lanchester, Karolyn Grimes, Tito Vuolo, Regis Toomey, Sara Edwards

One of Goldwyn's biggest hits of the season. According to Bercovici's account, he invented romantic qualities for the angel, Grant, who visits minister's wife Young to cheer up her life with the dull and duty-bound Niven. In fact, he is so romantic that only the pure-as-driven-snow morality of Young can overcome the devilish temptation and assist hubby Niven to become more attentive, more interesting and more of a chum to daughter Grimes. Nominated for best picture, best director, best film editing and best music, and praised as a "delightful and appropriate" Christmas film from its first moments of release. Remade in 1996 as *The Preacher's Wife*, directed by Penny Marshall and starring Denzel Washington. 109 min.

The Black Cat (1941)

Universal. Prod: Burt Kelly. Dir: Albert S. Rogell. Scr: Robert Lees,• Fred Rinaldo,• Eric Taylor, Robert Neville. Story basis: Edgar Allan Poe, "The Black Cat" (1843). Cast: Basil Rathbone, Hugh Herbert, Broderick Crawford, Bela Lugosi, Gale Sondergaard,• Anne Gwynne, Gladys Cooper, Cecilia Loftus, Claire Dodd, John Eldredge, Alan Ladd

Earliest of the left-written comedy satires of horror classics (written, in substantial part, by left-wingers just a few years earlier), although not nearly as good as *Abbott and Costello Meet Frankenstein* or similar features. Not to be confused with the 1935 Edgar Ulmer feature of the same name, which was no less loosely based on Poe but a wonderfully rendered antiwar allegory. The 1941 version is only a detective story, but with too few thrills for a thriller or gags for a comedy.

Loftus is the eccentric who owns an old mansion, keeps dozens of cats and even has a crematorium for them. She is found murdered after she disappoints her heirs by recovering from an apparently fatal illness. Sondergaard, her housekeeper, is distinctly mysterious and terribly afraid of a black cat, which she regards as an omen of death. (Indeed, a statue of a black cat stands over the crematorium). Lugosi, by this time in real life a major figure in the leftish and antifascist Hungarian Democratic Federation, plays the caretaker who seems to be scheming but is only simple-minded. Her relatives Rathbone (an adulterous cad) and Cooper are only the two most prominent relatives waiting for her to die, while Crawford (not yet billed as

"Broderick") is trying to buy the house for a client. Pudgy Herbert, brought by Crawford to assess the house's valuables, plays it strictly for gags—a sort of Costello without Abbott. Ladd has few lines and no action.

One inhabitant after another dies mysteriously in standard thriller fashion. Meanwhile, Gwynne, the good relative, is en route to fall in love with Crawford. A slow climax with many twists, mostly slowing down the action, produces an unlikely, semi-sympathetic killer. In real life, Sondergaard was married to producer-director Herbert J. Biberman• and with him was destined for the blacklist. Ladd, Lees and Rinaldo were shortly due for much better material and bigger pics during the wartime wave of Left cinema. 70 min.

Black Eagle, the Story of a Horse (1948)
Edward Huebsch• adapted an O. Henry short story about a drifter who gets himself involved in horse skullduggery and clears out again to rejoin hoboes.

The Black Hand (1950)
A well-received Italian American drama with story basis by Leo Townsend,† starring Gene Kelly, J. Carrol Naish, Teresa Celli and Marc Lawrence.† In some ways a precursor to the *Godfather* films. The misery of turn-of-the-century Manhattan Italians turns them toward acceptance of the mafiosi. Their victory (this a bit of forties optimism) over crime control comes by fully realizing their Americanism.

Black Like Me (1964)
Walter Reade-Sterling Inc. Prod: Julius Tannenbaum.• Dir: Carl Lerner.• Scr: Gerda Lerner, Carl Lerner. Book basis: John Howard Griffin, *Black Like Me* (1961). Cast: James Whitmore, Roscoe Lee Browne, Will Geer,• Walter Mason, John Marriott, Clifton James, Dan Priest

The only film directed by blacklisted film editor Carl Lerner, and the only one co-scripted by future famed women's history scholar Gerda Lerner. This alone would make the film of interest, but it is also arguably the most tough-minded of the civil rights features in its references to interracial sexuality and its conspicuously unmelodramatic treatment of the daily life of blacks in the small town South. Taken from the best-selling account by Griffin of his travels disguised as a black man, it has Whitmore as the native Texan and military veteran dying his skin to pass as black while the civil rights battle heats up the social atmosphere.

Critics complained of the erratic story line, and indeed the film is only a series of episodes with an occasional flashback. But critics also admitted its occasional power. Whitmore hitchhikes from town to town, experiencing prejudice, sometimes danger, occasional sexual temptation, regular doses of kindness from black folks and, here and there, enough white liberality to maintain his hope for peaceful change.

The left-wing quality of this treatment is driven home by the cross-class version of racial egalitarianism (in contrast to the standard liberal blanket judgment against the lower-class redneck) and by the daring of the sexual discourse. Will Geer,• in another of his bad-guy roles, is the epitome of racist sexuality: picking up Whitmore, he describes his own adventures with black women and repeatedly demands to know whether Whitmore's wife has had liaisons with white men. Whitmore recalls wondering whether his wife might think differently about him as a (temporary) black man. And he must ponder whether to enter into his own liaison with a pleasantly ordinary (and realistically portrayed) black woman. In short, there is lots to watch here; an early signpost to the return of the Hollywood Left and the contemporary limits of cinematic politics. 105 min.

Blackmailer (1936)
Harold Buchman• was one of three screenwriters of mystery melodrama who morphed toward comedy in midstream, in part (according to *Variety*) due to censorship of the themes involved in the successful blackmailing of a presumably respectable (but still young) wife for romantic sins of her pre-married days.

Black Orchid (1958)
A soapy Martin Ritt• project for stars Sophia Loren and Anthony Quinn as improbable middle-agers, the entrepreneur and criminal's widow who spend most of their time trying to persuade their assorted children that they can make it work.

The Black Room (1935)
Col. Prod: Robert North. Dir: Roy William Neill. Scr: Arthur Strawn,• Henry Myers.• Story basis: Arthur Strawn. Cast: Boris Karloff, Marian Marsh, Robert Allen, Thurston Hall, Katherine DeMille, John Buckler, Henry Kolker, Colin Tapley, Torben Meyer

A superior horror melodrama set somewhere in the Middle Ages, the film depicts the grim hand of tradition that free-minded youth seek to escape. Legend predicts that when twin sons are born to a baronial family that lives in a Tyrolean castle, one day the younger will kill the older. Twins are born, the younger is sent away to prevent tragedy, and 20 years pass. Then the evil older brother requests the return of his brother. Meanwhile, as in so many of these films, rumors make the villagers restless, terrified and likely to lash out. In this case, the older brother murders a woman who threatens to expose their affair, and in turn murders his younger brother, then assumes his identity. Only the mastiff knows who is who, as the surviving brother lays a plot to win the hand of the woman he craves, accusing his rival for her hand of his own murders. The ending is classic Gothic, containing the perennial consolation of the horror genre—revenge against the evil ones in high places. 70 min.

The Black Widow (1947)

A Republic serial co-scripted by Sol Short† and an unintentionally hilarious postwar conspiracy featuring a spy manipulator with a generic Asian (or Indian) quality; the guru-poppa who appears magically in a puff of smoke; and honest Americans who finally, after many reels, break the racket. No apparent anticommunism, unless the Chinese, with a real-life revolution in their homeland, are once again the Yellow Peril.

Blind Alley (1939)

An interesting jailbreak drama by Michael Blankfort,† considered one of the first films to treat psychological issues in a mature fashion. The criminal takes refuge in the home of a psychology professor (Ralph Bellamy), who cures him by probing his damaged childhood but cannot prevent his fate. The Breen office first sought to block production, relenting to a censored version. The story was remade as more noirish THE DARK PAST a decade later.

Blind Date See Chance Meeting

Blockade (1938)

Walter Wanger Productions. Prod: Walter Wanger. Dir: William Dieterle. Scr: John Howard Lawson.• Cast: Madeleine Carroll, Henry Fonda, Leo Carrillo, John Halliday, Reginald Denny, Vladimir Sokoloff, Robert Warwick, Fred Kohler, Carlos De Valdez, Peter Godfrey, Nick Thompson, Rosina Galli, William B. Davidson, Lupita Tovar, Katherine DeMille

The 1930s film most often regarded as a political triumph of the Hollywood Left, and from that point of view Lawson's most successful outing by far. When Spanish farmer Fonda finds himself towing the wrecked auto of the wealthy and educated Madeleine Carroll, the two are fascinated with each other, although romance is impossible. When the civil war begins with Francisco Franco's attack, Fonda urges resistance and becomes a leader in the peasants' army. Involved in antifascist intrigue, he shoots and kills Caroll's father, a Franco spy. Disbelieving her father's guilt, and desperate to get away from the situation, she plays a part in the blockade of Fonda's home territory.

In a bid for realism, we see through an English observer's eyes a starving city besieged by fascists and watch a supply ship torpedoed. Although another ship awaits, the population grows steadily more desperate for outside assistance. Fonda delivers the first propaganda blow for the future Second Front, appealing to the world not to stand idly by as the fascist curtain falls across Europe. 84 min.

Blond Cheat (1938)

Joan Fontaine plays a sneaky, sexy crook in this low-budget drama co-scripted by Viola Brothers Shore.•

Blonde Alibi (1946)

A proletarian intrigue with a cabbie, the mob, a missing Bible and an occasional comic turn. Story by Gordon Kahn.•

Blonde Crazy (1931)

WB. Prod: Unknown. Dir: Roy del Ruth. Scr: Kubec Glasmon, John Bright.• Cast: James Cagney, Joan Blondell, Louis Calhern, Noel Francis, Raymond Milland, Guy Kibbee, Polly Walters, Charles Levinson, William Burress, Peter Erkelenz, Maude Eburne, Walter Percival, Nat Pendleton

One of the underrated "escapist fare" gems of the early 1930s that helped establish Cagney's persona not only as a tough guy sweet on women but as someone who is tortured by his own inner conflicts and doomed by the contradictions of class. In this film, Cagney is a talented grifter who falls quickly in love with a working-class girl (Blondell). She slaps him delightfully, intending to put him in his place, but soon he draws her into his scams as she understands how easy it can be to escape the hard work, near-poverty and fatalism of working-class life.

Soon they're living in a big city hostel, where they meet Calhern, passing counterfeit bills and intending to fleece Cagney of his accumulated stake. Eventually, after a jewelry caper, Cagney avenges himself on Calhern but is caught by the law. Blondell, who has married a broker, finds her new bourgeois life unbearably dull. Cagney repents too late and faces years in prison (the last line has Cagney singing, "If I had the wings of an angel, over these prison walls I would fly. . . ."). Blondell wants him to go straight, but he can't see any other way out of the Depression life and, inasmuch as he intends to rob the rich, can't quite see what he is doing as morally wrong. Brilliant in its understatement. 79 min.

The Blonde from Singapore (1941)

Edward Dmytryk•† directed this low B-feature about a pilot and a mechanic who poach pearls to buy a plane and join the Far East Royal Air Force in the war effort. Florence Rice is the showgirl blonde.

Blondie

Between 1938 and 1950, Columbia made 28 features on the Chic Young comic strip then so popular that it remained the lead comic in Sunday color sections in newspapers across the country for decades. The most political "Blondies" were made during World War II and written by Constance Lee• and Karen DeWolf,• both of whom were later blacklisted. Penny Singleton, who played the lead through virtually the entire series, had a political life as well. After her film career, as vice president and executive secretary of the American Guild of Variety Artists, Singleton defied show business moguls and mob leaders alike by leading the Radio City Rockettes on strike in 1966.

The comic strip was a satire on Depression social fantasies that begins where the "happy ending" left off. Blondie was originally a 1920s flapper, a ditzy free spirit, née Blondie Boopadoop (this before the advent of Betty Boop), who in 1933 marries a millionaire (hence Dagwood Bumstead's comically "aristocratic" name). But Dagwood's parents disapprove of Blondie and disinherit their son, who now becomes a working stiff at an architectural firm with the irascible Mr. Dithers as his boss. He is now the familiar figure of the classic American boob, a good-hearted soul amiably incompetent at middle-class family life until he is scolded into line by his wife.

If much of this backstory is forgotten in the suburban tales to follow, some always lingers. The first entry in the political cycle, this time by DeWolf alone, was *Blondie in Society* (1941), in which the title really means dog society—the world of the pedigreed pooch to which the Bumsteads are now strictly outsiders. A grade school pal borrows $50 from Dagwood (Arthur Lake), pays him off with a Great Dane, and Blondie enters it in the big dog show. A Dane-fancier (William Frawley, later of *Lucy* fame) is also a major client of Dagwood's architectural firm, and confusion ensues when, thanks to Blondie singing "Trees" with a boys choir, the Dane takes first prize. Many of the pretensions of middle-class society are punctured in strange, small moments.

Lee and DeWolf teamed up for *Blondie for Victory* (1942). Easily the most didactic of the series, this episode highlights striking and often contradictory images of women's roles during the war. Blondie and other local housewives have enlisted so vigorously in the war effort that husbands face total chaos at home, with Dagwood worse off than most others because of his characteristic bumbling and with two young children in the house. Blondie organizes a uniformed housewives' mobilization, asserting that no obstacle (certainly not husbands) can be allowed to stand in the way of their patriotic war work. Jonathan Hale as Mr. Dithers meanwhile seeks to bully Dagwood into silencing Blondie as the madcap complications unfold and an unwitting celebrity "lonely soldier" pleads his case to be left alone by women so he can fight the war. The counterattack against women's mobilization succeeds—or does it backfire? The plot grows dim in a stunning newsreel-style parade of women's uniforms on the battlefront and home front.

The two radical screenwriters teamed up again for another turn at Popular Front wartime humor in *Blondie's Blessed Event* (1942). Blondie's approaching childbirth throws Dagwood into new fits of failure at his job. Sent off to Chicago to speak to a business convention, he runs into unemployed artiste and schnorrer Hans Conried, whose script for Dagwood's talk leaves the architects in stunned silence. The message: husbands can dispense with architects and be their own home-builders with the scrap materials available. The charlatan-freeloader returns to California with Dagwood and moves in until Blondie puts her foot down. The only surprise is the appearance of Win-the-War bureaucratic agencies eager to enlist what they mistakenly think is Dagwood's expertise.

A 1943 film, *It's a Great Life*, is so obscure that it has eluded the omniscient Maltin's list of titles. This one also has many animal jokes. A Dagwood confused by domestic noise thinks he hears Dithers order him to buy a *horse* rather than the *house* the boss really wanted. Forced to live with his error, Dagwood explains to Blondie that he has taken in a refugee, and Blondie's heart melts before she learns that he has actually bought a nag. Then the family falls in love with the animal, which spends much of his time in the house, when not taking Dagwood to work. Dizzy times at the office are followed by a foxhunt (Daisy makes friends with the fox, and allows Dagwood to reign victorious). At the film's close, Daisy and the horse converse, perhaps the inspiration for similar TV interlocutions to come.

In 1945, Connie Lee wrote the first of the two films she did without DeWolf for the series. In *Life with Blondie*, Marc Lawrence† makes an unlikely appearance. Heavy on the animal humor, this Blondie has Daisy displacing Dagwood as head wage-earner of the household, with all the jibes inherent in the turnabout. Considered a menace to the neighborhood and nearly caught by the dog catcher, Daisy inadvertently becomes Pin-up Pup of the GIs, a cover dog of the press and advertising model for Daisy Soap. Bringing in more income than Dagwood, the dog sits in his office chair as Dagwood endures ridicule from family and officemates, a level of contempt for the patriarchal ego softened only a little by Blondie. Unable to complete an overdue architectural plan that Mr. Dithers needs to borrow a half-million dollars, Dagwood stumbles from disaster to humiliation to disaster again. To keep the plot moving, a couple of hoods (Lawrence and Douglas Fowley) threaten a kidnapping, but nothing spoils the delightful mood of the ridicule of gender roles. 64 min.

Finally, in 1946, Lee wrote *Blondie's Lucky Day*. This time boss Dithers is off on an apparent two-week business trip, leaving Dagwood in charge of the office. Raising Blondie's hopes that he might prove a success in life after all, Dagwood is invited to the mayor's office, where the assorted big shots are hiring discharged veterans. Intently puffing a cigar (it makes his voice squeak), Dagwood is morally coerced into hiring Anita Louise, a Women's Army Corps (WAC) officer. Gender conflict at the office raises specters of *Nine to Five*. Dithers unexpectedly returns after losing a major account and is intent upon firing the extra help. Postwar recession, redundancy and the employee fantasy of an independent operation complicate the usual family nonsense as Dagwood sets up a business in competition with Dithers.

Blood on the Sun (1945)

UA. Prod: James Cagney (William Cagney, uncredited). Dir: Frank Lloyd. Scr: Lester Cole.• Story basis: Garrett Fort. Cast: James Cagney, Sylvia Sidney, Robert Armstrong, Wallace Ford

A taut and not overly orientalized (or at least racialized) drama of an antifascist newspaperman in 1940 Japan who must play detective to get to the bottom of a murder of two friends. This is a suddenly older James Cagney, just a few years after playing pug proletarians, now an executive who is still spiritually and sometimes physically the fighter.

In a typical Left script gambit, Cagney finds himself more politically aggressive than the U.S. Embassy, which tries to keep a lid on controversy. Editor of an English-language daily in Tokyo, he breaks the story of Japanese strategic plans to assault U.S. bases in the Pacific. Soon thereafter, he goes onboard ship to see off a husband and wife leaving for the States and finds them dead in their cabin. Surrounded by Japanese government security figures (strangely, or not so strangely, acting like FBI men), he is contemptuous rather than polite. Some American businessmen and journalists would prefer not even to discuss what the Japanese are doing to China; Cagney's character correctly sees it as a model for their plans elsewhere. In an odd subplot, the emperor is a sympathetic old guy now surrounded by evil militarists—perhaps a spin on the real-life postwar U.S. decision to let the figurehead continue rather than putting him on trial for collaboration with war crimes. The production effort by brothers Cagney foreshadowed the brief burst of quality independent films just ahead. 98 min.

Blossoms in the Dust (1941)

MGM. Prod: Irving Asher. Dir: Mervyn LeRoy. Scr: Anita Loos (uncredited script contribution: Hugo Butler•). Story basis: Ralph Wheelwright. Cast: Greer Garson, Walter Pidgeon, Felix Bressart, Marsha Hunt, Fay Holden, Samuel S. Hinds, Kathleen Howard

A classic Greer Garson-as-noble-woman melodrama, this one is very affecting and based on a real life story and is a valuable case of Left writers delivering on social themes around the "strong" woman. Edna Gladney, daughter of a comfortable family, sees her adopted sibling humiliated by documents revealing "illegitimacy," and when she loses her own child to a fatal accident, turns her sympathies toward foundlings. Soon she has established a day nursery especially suited to the needs of the working mothers who toil at her husband's Texas mill. When he dies, leaving her financially set for life, she launches the Texas Home and Aid Society in Fort Worth, mainly to assist adoption. As she comes to appreciate the pariah status of "illegitimate" children, their background noted on birth certificates and even on passports, she lobbies fearlessly in the state legislature for the overturn of existing laws.

A tour-de-force performance even for this tested trouper won Garson an Oscar nomination (*Blossoms* won an Academy Award for best interior decoration, for those Texas-like parlors) and left millions of hankies dripping. By playing upon the innocence of children and the mother-surrogate kindness of the female social reformer, the film managed to make an unusual statement about the irrelevance of documented bloodlines for the future citizen and the strength of one woman to confront the political system for the good of the community. An early and not altogether successful experiment in color film, *Blossoms* also won an Oscar nomination for best color cinematography. 99 min., Technicolor.

The Blue Max (1966)

The big-ticket British production of a Ben Barzman• adaptation, starring George Peppard, James Mason and Ursula Andress, in a German World War I pilot's tragic story; arguably a critique of German militarism, hardly a daring target. Peppard fades quickly and so does the film.

Blues in the Night (1941)

WB. Prod: Henry Blanke. Dir: Anatole Litvak. Scr: Robert Rossen.•† Play basis: Edwin Gilbert, "Hot Nocturne" (unproduced). Cast: Priscilla Lane, Richard Whorf, Betty Field, Lloyd Nolan, Jack Carson, Elia Kazan,† Wallace Ford, Billy Halop, Peter Whitney, Howard Da Silva•

A deeply moody piece about Jewish yearning to play black music, this was one of later friendly witness Rossen's stronger scripts. The film opens in a club where law school kid and clarinet player Kazan tries to get his pals together to start a band ("You see, I'm a student of jazz," he says later, offering details to impress). Thrown into jail for fighting, they listen as an African American "sings the blues" in the next cell and eventually set out on a road tour that covers the old South (with footage of blacks picking cotton as a sort of gloss). As critics have observed, the free spirit of the boxcar-riding group (Priscilla Lane) becomes no one's "girl," a remarkable feature of the film.

The attempt to find the "real America" drifts into a predictable romance with, however, some oddly surrealistic moments of montage, all apparently staged by rising cameraman and later cult director Don Siegel. The typical cinematic mixture of jazz and modern classical music has prize barrel-house musician Jigger (Whorf) seduced by torchy Field into leaving the band, leading to a "neuropsychiatric episode" that prevents him from playing the piano, from which he finally recovers to play his own composition, à la Gershwin! The film is notable also for a delightful cameo by future blacklistee Howard Da Silva as a bartender. Most songs were written by composer Harold Arlen, a Buffalo cantor's son, Broadway songwriter and frequent collaborator with Yip Harburg. 88 min.

Body and Soul (1947)

Enterprise Productions/UA. Prod: Bob Roberts. Dir: Robert Rossen.† Scr: Abraham Polonsky.• Cast: John Garfield, Lilli Palmer, Hazel Brooks, Anne Revere,• William Conrad, Joseph Pevney, Canada Lee, Lloyd Gough•

One of Polonsky's two master works of this period (along with FORCE OF EVIL) and among the half-dozen finest boxing films ever made—and certainly the one with the strongest feminist underpinning. Garfield, determined to make his way up from the tenements after his father is killed in a random street shooting outside the family's candy store, looks to fight promoter Gough. His mother, played brilliantly by Revere (in a scene reminiscent of *National Velvet*, in which she gives much the same antimaterialist speech to little Elizabeth Taylor), makes one last, hopeless effort to make him see reason, to know "what he is fighting for." Garfield knows all too well, but plunges ahead like a man doomed.

As success looms, Garfield deserts girlfriend Palmer (who comes to live with Revere, the two bonding against him) and takes up with Brooks, a gang moll. Before the big fight—which he is programmed to lose, making a fortune by betting against himself—he accepts the final humiliation. His trainer and friend (Lee), a former champ with a brain disorder caused by too many punches, refuses to counsel Garfield to take a dive, rebels against Gough and dies on the spot. A big commercial hit for little Enterprise, making *Force of Evil* possible. 104 min.

Boom (1968)

John Heyman Production/Universal Pictures. Prod: John Heyman, Norman Priggan. Dir: Joseph Losey.• Scr: Tennessee Williams. Play basis: Tennessee Williams, *The Milk Train Doesn't Stop Here Anymore* (1964). Cast: Elizabeth Taylor, Richard Burton, Noël Coward, Joanna Shimkus, Michael Dunn, Romolo Valli

Described uncharitably by *Variety* as "an actors' exercise," this picture was a typically unsuccessful effort to make theater (a Williams set piece about the bored and decadent rich) into film. Shot in Sardinia and in the Dino De Laurentiis Studio in Rome, it revolves mainly around Taylor, an aging, rich and repeatedly married harridan who spends a great deal of her time berating those around her. Burton, as a poet, comes in for much of the abuse; so does

27

BORN TO BE WILD (1938)

Coward, a gay blade from Capri; but she has plenty left for her doctor (Dunn) and servants. Her nouveau-riche clothes and manners struck reviewers as somewhat off. But the film presents playwright Williams at the social edge of his mostly symbolic dramaturgy. Burton has the best of it with his Burtonesque, spoiled bohemian mannerisms and the direction of Losey to set the scene with some much-needed drama. 112 min., color.

Boomerang! (1947)

A documentary-style crime drama directed by Elia Kazan† with a cast that included non-cooperator Jane Wyatt (a non-Communist who nevertheless paid the price and won, leaving Hollywood for television's *Father Knows Best*), Lee J. Cobb,† and solid progressive Ed Begley Sr. A priest is murdered in Bridgeport, Connecticut, and detectives work methodically to find the real killer after the wrong man is nearly convicted.

Border Patrol (1943)

UA/Para. Prod: Harry Sherman. Dir: Lesley Selander. Scr: Michael Wilson.• Characters created by Clarence E. Mulford. Cast: William Boyd, Andy Clyde, Jay Kirby, Russell Simpson, Robert Mitchum, George Reeves, Claudia Drake, Duncan Renaldo

One of Wilson's four Hopalong Cassidy films and politically the sharpest, dealing with the complex issues in the tortured history of colonization. Happily for him and the plot, wickedness is concentrated in a single mine-owning operation not so different from the one he tackled in the infinitely better-known SALT OF THE EARTH, also scripted by Wilson, over a decade later.

Even though he has promised to respect Mexican autonomy by staying on the Texas side of the U.S. border (despite his two sidekicks' longing for the food and companionship across the Rio Grande), Hoppy runs into trouble as he helplessly watches a rider shot dead on the Mexican side. A señorita (Drake) arrives with a posse and forces the three *gabachos* into Mexican custody. There they hear about frequent disappearances among the locals: Mexicans who come north to work in a silver mine—where, it was said, the conquistadors had worked enslaved Indians to death centuries earlier—are never seen again. Traveling to the mine, Hoppy and friends encounter Mitchum, the gun-toting guard (his film debut), as the first symptom of a little totalitarian state. The owner has indeed kidnapped the Mexican workers and will not let them leave. Escaping from a rigged trial and riding to the mine, Hoppy rouses the workers, frees them and tells

the owner that he will face charges for practicing peonage (made illegal under the New Deal, though rarely enforced) and forced labor. This is superior Popular Front filmmaking, intended for juvenile audiences but a rouser for anyone with a heart. 63 min.

Born Free (1966)

Carl Foreman• Productions. Prod: Sam Jaffe, Paul Radin. Dir: James Hill. Scr: Gerald L. C. Copley (pseudonym for Lester Cole•). Book basis: Joy Adamson, *Bonfire, A Lioness of Two Worlds* (1960). Cast: Virginia McKenna, Bill Travers, Geoffrey Keen; Peter Lukoye, Omar Chambati, Bill Godden, Robert Cheetham, Robert S. Young, Geoffrey Best, Surya Patel.

This ground-breaking animal liberation feature is shot through with blacklistees and their pals, like Hollywood old-timer Sam Jaffe (not to be confused with the blacklisted actor of the same name). It closely follows the bestseller by Adamson of how the gamekeeper's wife in Kenya raised Elsa the lion cub and set her free after reeducating her in the arts of living on her own in the wild, and it made for a superior family film. Lush African color scenes, rapport of husband Travers and wife McKenna, problems and prospects of life for whites in Africa all emerge with grace and compelling interest. The last shot finds Elsa with her own cubs (and mate)—perhaps overdone as the idealization of domesticity. Assaulted by Pauline Kael (who as so often smelled a red), it was adored by the *New York Times* and most critics, apparently ignorant of Copley's real identity. The sequel, *Living Free*, was not as successful critically or at the box office. 95 min., color.

Born to Be Wild (1938)

Rep. Asst. Prod: Harold Shumate. Dir: Joseph Kane. Scr: Nathaneal West (uncredited: Samuel Ornitz•). Cast: Ralph Byrd, Doris Weston, Ward Bond

Film is a B- (or perhaps C-) production about two California working stiffs hired to drive a mysterious shipment (it turns out to be dynamite) to a town over the mountains. Despite the premise, this is no *Wages of Fear*. The plot, complicated by a cute woman with a cute dog, wavers wildly between road action and fistfights, and Byrd occasionally breaks out in song. Nonetheless, the film is memorable for its contemporary variations on the "registered plot" of the westerner foiled in his attempts to make a fortune by cornering the water or real estate markets, and for the odd script collaboration of talented left-wing novelists West (*Miss Lonelyhearts*) and Ornitz (*Haunch, Paunch and Jowl*). Here and there, their whimsical radicalism appears, as when the truckers are temporarily halted by a lunatic who is determined to develop empty desert space and tries to persuade them to buy worthless land. It was a cynical but altogether accurate prediction of the region's future. The film is also fascinating as one of several leftish movies to feature Ward Bond, who later became one of the most right-wing actors and activists in real-life McCarthy-era Hollywood. 66 min.

Born to Sing (1942)

An otherwise unmemorable juvenile let's-put-on-a-show musical, scripted by an uncredited Richard Weil,• made memorable by the addition of the Earl Robinson–John Latouche "Ballad for Americans," staged so elaborately by Busby Berkeley that it sticks out like a happy sore thumb. Leo Gorcey, Sheldon Leonard and Margaret Dumont are wasted in the effort.

Boston Blackie Goes Hollywood (1942)

Interesting mainly as an early directorial effort of Michael Gordon,•† although mercifully his only one among the 14 Blackie films made over nine years (the first director of the series was Edward Dmytryk•†). The incompetence and stupidity of the police as much as star Chester Morris' suave qualities made the series a success.

Bowery Boys

One of the curiosities of Martin Scorsese's 2002 film *Gangs of New York* was his depiction of the Bowery Boys as a real-life nineteenth-century proletarian Irish gang striding through Manhattan streets in striped shirts and two-foot stovepipe hats. It was a long way from "Sach" and "Slip," the two street mugs in the long-running Monogram series played by Leo Gorcey and Huntz Hall. The gang first appeared under a different name in *Dead End*, Sidney Kingsley's play about the hopes and realities of slum life, which was brought to the screen by Lillian Hellman; the young street-kid actors were propelled into an unanticipated stardom. Through all the permutations of gang names and studios, about 85 films involved the boys, some 48 of which were made under the Bowery Boys monicker. Billy Halop, Bobby Jordan, Gabriel Dell, Bernard Punsley and, above all, Hall and Gorcey (sometimes joined by Gorcey's brothers) became successively cast members of ANGELS WITH DIRTY FACES and several other films at Warners, then Universal, with at least four distinct major series (not counting serials), most of which were bound up inextricably with the Left. Playwright/screen-writer John Wexley• wrote for them as the Dead End Kids, Edward Eliscu• and Lew Amster• for the Little Tough Guys, and Carl Foreman• for the East Side Kids. Foreman also wrote and directed for the Bowery Boys (two of their best), and was joined in the writing by Cyril Endfield• and famed proletarian novelist Albert Bein.• One of the East Side Kids, Hally Chester, went on to become Hal E. Chester, producer of left-wing B-films during the 1940s, and finally more strictly commercial products in Britain of the 1950s-1960s.

It would be easy to sentimentalize the appeal of a group of comic sidekicks whose urban adventures involved the same opponents as the Three Stooges—Nazis, crooks and snobs—but an enjoyable comic mayhem, albeit in the context of an ethnic or class solidarity, was generally the most the Boys could summon. In *Bowery Blitzkrieg* (1941), as *Variety* noted, they grew up from their Dead End days with a script, owing at least slightly to a contribution from Carl Foreman, deft enough to overcome the trite plot. (Its producer, Sam Katzman, also did horror cheapies with blacklisted writers during the 1950s-1960s.) To the tune of "The Sidewalks of New York," the film opens in a gym in which boxing is clearly the way out of a life of poverty and petty crime. Gorcey, the most appealing of the boys, formerly drawn to stickups, has made up his mind to become a champ. As expected, neighborhood gangs try to pull him back down, and he actually gives blood to help a pal when he should be strengthening himself for the big fight. Hull, the tough cop with a heart of gold, and Henry, his girl, are bowery grownups as practical reformers, reaching out one kid at a time.

Spooks Run Wild (1941) was the unlikely start for the man who wrote HIGH NOON, Foreman's third directorial outing en route to the art film and the second Bowery Boys film. Bela Lugosi is in top form, given the material, as an innocent if somewhat weird magician who is wrongly mistaken for a serial killer by the nervous boys, who find themselves sharing a house overnight with him. The match-up of humor and horror marked the transition of Lugosi and Karloff to self-parody (notably with Abbott and Costello in a series of hit films written by Robert Lees and Fred Rinaldo) and perhaps the disintegration of the 1930s horror motif in general amid the greater horrors of the real world. In *Junior Army* (1942), Bein provided the story basis (much the same cast here but not using the name Bowery Boys). Child star Freddie Bartholomew is on hand when the boys learn that Nazis have infiltrated the old neighborhood gang and aristocratic Freddie helps his new Bowery pals—poor but fiercely patriotic—help the Allied cause. In *Mr. Hex* (1946), written by Endfield, the boys' favorite singer has to quit to take care of a sick mother, so they scratch around for money. Mobsters hire an "evil eye" character to offset the hypnotized Hall's somnambulant strength of ten. Endfield's *Hard Boiled Mahoney* (1947), another fisticuff slapstick affair, was the future director's final effort in the series, offering up another case of mistaken identity before adopting what amounted to a new identity of his own in Britain.

Bowery to Broadway (1944)

A show biz musical, scripted by Bart Lytton,† of beer garden life in turn-of-the-century New York, with a weak plot but strong cast, including Maria Montez, Jack Oakie, Turhan Bey, Leo Carrillo and Andy Devine.

Boy Slaves (1939)

RKO. Prod and Dir: P. J. Wolfson. Scr: Albert Bein● and B. Harrison Orkow. Story basis: Albert Bein. Cast: Anne Shirley, Roger Daniel, James McCallion, Walter Ward, Charles Powers, Johnny Fitzgerald, Frank Malo, Paul White, Walter Tetley, Charles Lane, Alan Baxter, Arthur Hohl, Norman Willis, Roy Gordon

The last of the imprisoned juvenile cycle that began with *Mayor of Hell*. Here, homeless and wandering boys in the South are given over by a judge to supposed gainful employment in a turpentine camp (a very real-life experience for Southern prisoners). Forced into debt by prices at the company store, brutalized with hunger and overwork, they attempt a revolt. Crushed, they plot a letter to the President's wife (without saying so, obviously the humane Eleanor Roosevelt) explaining their plight. When this too fails, they flee. Anne Shirley, as a sort of house slave (by implication, also a sexual victim), persuades them to give themselves up and seek justice in the legal system. There are some powerful scenes and a realistic setting amid the melodrama by Bein, a fine if forgotten proletarian novelist (*Youth in Hell*, 1930). 72 min.

The Boy with Green Hair (1948)

RKO. Prod: Stephen Ames (also Adrian Scott●). Dir: Joseph Losey.● Scr: Alfred Lewis Levitt,● Ben Barzman.● Story basis: Betson Beaton. Cast: Dean Stockwell, Pat O'Brien, Robert Ryan, Barbara Hale

An early mark of director Losey's skill was also studio executive Dore Schary's lavish bow (in Technicolor) to the theme of peace. Schary made himself known as a friend of the Left, en route to offering them bigger and better things before he defected to the side of the blacklisters. In a nutshell, this is a big-budget

political art film that under better circumstances might have launched a genre. Critics spotted the weaknesses but attributed them to a didactic script rather than meddlesome censorship by Howard Hughes, who had just bought the studio.

It is also a touching family film, and in that sense resembles a number of the Left's shots across the bow of the mainstream cinema such as *Lassie Come Home* and *So Well Remembered*. Child actor Stockwell plays a boy raised by a single father, the loving Irish working-class character beautifully enacted by O'Brien. Stockwell's hair inexplicably turns green when he hears talk of another world war, and the two must cope together with the consequences. If the metaphor is odd, it is also oddly effective, with the boy meeting in dream-like circumstance the child refugees of the most recent war. With touches of science fiction at points, the film delivers a political punch but also benefits from the talent of Levitt, a former Terrytoons animation screenwriter, in dealing with children's consciousness. Stockwell's growth in self-understanding, with the assistance of kindly Ryan and Hale, makes the film memorable. Scott bowed out as producer to mollify Hughes, but the kindly Ames continued the essential thrust of the film. 82 min., color.

The Brave Bulls (1951)

Col. Prod and Dir: Robert Rossen.† Scr: John Bright.● Novel basis: Tom Lea, *The Brave Bulls* (1949). Cast: Mel Ferrer, Anthony Quinn, Miroslava Stern, Eugene Iglesias, José Torres, Charlita, Alfredo Aguilar

An exceptionally well-received film that foreshadowed the 1950s work of the Left exiles in Mexico. On the heels of Rossen's triumph in ALL THE KING'S MEN, this drama of a bullfighter struggling against his fear is used as a semi-realistic look at the world of blood sport and its crowds. The matador as both a symbolic hero and a manipulated icon is played brilliantly by Ferrer in his best screen performance. His manager, played by Quinn, and his mistress, the unknown Stern (never destined to make it in U.S. films), helpfully complicate emotions, while the location shooting and mostly Mexican cast prompt a sense of realism rare in treatment of south-of-the-border themes. 108 min.

The Brave One (1956)

King Brothers. Prod: Irving Rapper. Dir: Irving Rapper. Scr: Robert Rich (pseudonym for Dalton Trumbo●). Cast: Michael Ray, Rudolfo Hoyos, Jr., Joi Lansing, Elsa Cardenas, Fermín Rivera, Carlos Navarro

Winner of a best screenplay Oscar for "Robert Rich" (who failed to show up at the awards ceremony, much to the academy's embarrassment), this family film combines the love of animals and subtle politics of several other Left creations (most notably of screenwriter Hugo Butler• in his collie tales) with the Mexican themes that the Hollywood progressives had been moving toward in the postwar era. (*Viva, Zapata!* was the best-known, even if it was plucked from the hands of left-wing artists; others, such as FIESTA, were little more than well-meaning kitsch.)

At the peak of his American screen career, a child (Ray) adopts a bull that was born to a dying cow and raises it as his own. His father, a poor farmworker, has been deprived of almost everything, and soon the bull will be taken away by the *patrón* as well. Meanwhile, history lessons at the boy's grade school conspicuously stress Mexico's national resistance against the European colonizers and the pride of Indian identity. That connection is never made explicitly with the bullfight (that would be asking too much in 1956), but the boy and the bull grow up together facing danger and what is certain to be a tragic ending. Or will they? The film is memorable for the bullfighting scene, whose outcome, however improbable, is possible, according to aficianados. Beautifully shot, nominated for an Oscar for editing, *The Brave One* is a tribute to the blacklistees in exile and their skill in adapting creatively to their situation and their surroundings. 100 min., color.

Breakfast for Two (1937)
A romantic comedy co-scripted by Viola Brothers Shore• and directed by Lillian Hellman's• ex-husband Alfred Santell, with Barbara Stanwyck as the woman so determined to reform wastrel Herbert Marshall that she takes over the family shipping empire.

A Breath of Scandal (1960)
An uncredited Sidney Buchman• collaborated with his old friend Sidney Howard on this lightweight Sophia Loren vehicle about a Viennese princess who rebels against her father (Maurice Chevalier) when she meets a handsome American in Italy. Angela Landsbury is a scheming aristocrat.

The Bribe (1949)
First-rate Marguerite Roberts• dialogue is wasted on wooden lead roles, with Robert Taylor as an ex-GI uncovering smugglers and Ava Gardner on a Caribbean island. Villains Vincent Price and John Hodiak are the best thing in the film, which was panned by reviewers as thin and obvious. This was the last big-budget (MGM) film noir made in Hollywood and too self-conscious by half. Roberts' work deserved better.

The Bride Wore Boots (1946)
One of Irving Pichel's• lesser directorial efforts, despite casting of Barbara Stanwyck and Robert Cummings as mismatched marrieds amid horse races.

The Bride Wore Crutches (1940)
This Shepard Traube• directorial outing is an abysmal comedy adventure of a would-be cub reporter and hoods Edgar Kennedy and Lionel Stander,• who manage to provide at least a few laughs.

The Bridge on the River Kwai (1957)
Col. Prod: Sam Spiegel. Dir: David Lean. Scr: Pierre Boulle (uncredited: Michael Wilson,• Carl Foreman•). Novel source: Pierre Boulle, *Le pont de la rivière Kwai* (1954). Cast: Alec Guinness, William Holden, Sessue Hayakawa, James Donald, Geoffrey Horne, André Morell, Ann Sears

One of the most celebrated films of the period, even if audiences and critics were apparently unaware that the credited screenwriter spoke and wrote no English. Wilson received the script credit decades later, posthumously.

The story turns on a battle of personalities between two strong commandants, Japanese POW commander Hayakawa and his prisoner, British colonel Guinness. The Japanese are desperate to connect by rail their control of resource-rich Burma with Southeast Asia to reach the ports of the Pacific theater. To make the link, they exploit the labor of British and allied troops captured early in the war. Key to the project is a railroad bridge. Guiness throws himself into its construction as a way of clinging to his class privilege and the imperial habits of command, but along the way he loses sight entirely of the war goals. William Holden suffers no such illusion and quietly hatches a scheme to blow up what Guiness is building. Holden's plan punctures the Guinness character and exposes him as the ultimate militarist, committed to the project and to the authority of the state—any state—even if it means helping the Japanese win the war.

Lean's work was highly praised by American left-wingers and did his best work on this film. More than a little credit for that went to the sharpness of Wilson's writing. As in the later *Planet of the Apes*, also based on a Boulle novel, Wilson managed to drain some of the worst colonial attitudes form the original; it had not eluded literary critics of the novel that the Japanese played much the same role as captors in the original narrative that the gorillas played in *Planet*. By the time Wilson was done with the screenplay, all traces of this sort of thing had been removed.

The famous climax cost Lean $250,000 to shoot, but viewers appreciated every minute, because it contained some of the most effective cross-cutting in the service of suspense ever put on the screen. Oscars and nominations were measured by the pound: best actor, best adapted screenplay (Wilson's and Foreman's lost Oscar), best color cinematography, best director, best picture, and more. 161 min., color.

Broadway (1942)
A creaky nostalgic adaptation by John Bright• and Felix Jackson (a German refugee best remembered for working on DESTRY RIDES AGAIN) of the old days, with speakeasies, colorful mobsters and leggy chorines.

Broadway Bill (1934)
A slight horse racing drama, uncredited for writer Sidney Buchman• or director Frank Capra. However, it brought the two into a working team with magnum success a few years later in MR. SMITH GOES TO WASHINGTON.

Broken Arrow (1950)
20th. Prod: Julian Blaustein. Dir: Delmer Daves. Scr: Michael Blankfort† (front for Albert Maltz•). Novel basis: Elliott Arnold, *Blood Brother* (1947). Cast: James Stewart, Jeff Chandler, Will Geer,• Debra Paget, Basil Ruysdael, Arthur Hunnicutt, Jay Silverheels

Proclaimed with only slight exaggeration to be the first Hollywood film to take the side of the Indians (actually, a handful of features since *Laughing Boy* in 1935 had portrayed individual Indians sympathetically, as martyrs to the settlement of the West), *Broken Arrow* has been castigated in recent years for its historical inaccuracy, for putting Paget in red makeup and for other offenses. Nevertheless, it is a powerful film, with the unmistakable narrative intelligence of Maltz in every scene—as in his only other western, TWO MULES FOR SISTER SARA. In its popularity (it was later made into a TV series) and its impact on public sympathies, *Broken Arrow* is comparable to *Dances with Wolves* in the 1990s. It was the ninth-largest-grossing picture in 1950.

Michael Blankfort's name appears on the film as the screenwriter because at the time he was close to Maltz (who broke off the friendship after Blankfort told HUAC that his cousin, Henry Blankfort• and ex-wife, Laurie Blankfort,• were members of the Communist Party). Stewart plays a former cavalry scout in an Arizona frontier town of the 1870s who wants to open lines of communication with Cochise in his domain in the Chiracahua Mountains. Taking his life in his hands, Stewart enters Cochise's land as a lone diplomat for peace, arguing that the chief show his willingness to deal by preserving the U.S. Mail from attack. In the meantime, Stewart wins the confidence of the Apaches by saving the life of an Indian boy and learning the language and customs of the tribe, even wooing shy maiden Paget. He also seeks to calm the racist white townsfolk, led by an enraged Geer, who want to string him up. Later, the peace is broken when the townspeople fall on Stewart and the Apaches in a stream bed.

The film works largely because of Stewart's aw-shucks, democratic and humane affect, and because Chandler's Cochise falls squarely within the "noble savage" of local-color tradition. As for its historical accuracy, the casual reader in Arizona history will recognize the massacre of 18 Apache men, women and children at Aravaipa Creek in 1871 by gunmen from Tucson, angered in part at the loss of their federal subsidies that followed a negotiated truce with the Indians. Chandler won an Oscar for best supporting actor. 93 min.

The Broken Melody (1934)
Best remembered of Bernard Vorhaus'• 1930s British *oeuvre* because of the star power of John Garrick and Merle Oberon; a composer is exiled to Devils Island, and returns to make his saga into an opera.

The Brotherhood (1968)
A mediocre crime film directed by Martin Ritt,• largely the result of Kirk Douglas's craving to star in just such a film. Supporting cast of Alex Cord, Irene Papas, Luther Adler• and Susan Strasberg cannot save a transatlantic tale of a quarreling crime family torn between Old World customs and new social realities.

Brute Force (1947)
U-I. Prod: Mark Hellinger. Dir: Jules Dassin.• Scr: Richard Brooks. Story: Robert Patterson. Cast: Burt Lancaster, Hume Cronyn, Ella Raines, Yvonne De Carlo,

Howard Duff, Ann Blyth, John Hoyt, Anita Colby, Roman Bohnen, Sam Levene, Jeff Corey,• Jay C. Flippen

A terse prison drama scripted by a leftist fellow-traveler and the screenwriter of HOME OF THE BRAVE has director Dassin near the peak of his pre-blacklist skills. The warden's lieutenant played by Cronyn is a sadistic brute whose calculated dehumanization of prisoners incites an inmate rebellion. The warden himself (Bohnen), who seems unaware of the whole scene, is strongly reminiscent of an FDR type whose saintly demeanor hides his brutality. Prisoners, meanwhile, organize into something close to a band of revolutionaries.

The prisoners have respite only in memories of the outside (especially their wives or lovers, seen through a heavily romantic tint) and in their determination to pull down Cronyn, whatever the cost. The film thus asserts its central allegory: the world is the prison and the prison is the world. No escape is possible. Violence is the ruling principle, and violence is the only possible response—even if it is a hopeless one. It has many powerful moments, due less to the story line than to the directorial energy of Dassin. 95 min.

Buck Privates (1941)
This film launched former Robert Benchley shorts writers Robert Lees• and Federic I. Rinaldo• into spectacular success as Abbott and Costello's best script team, but here only as uncredited script contributors. It's really a variety show featuring the singing Andrews Sisters, although subtextual politics appear when a wealthy draftee reveals himself as a typical chiseler, seeking to pull family strings to get out of the service. Shemp Howard of the progressive-minded Three Stooges has a rare supporting role.

Buck Privates Come Home (1947)
U-I. Prod: Robert Arthur. Dir: Charles Barton. Scr: Robert Lees,• Frederic Rinaldo,• John Grant. Story basis: Bradford Ropes, Richard Macaulay. Cast: Bud Abbott, Lou Costello, Tom Brown, Joan Shawlee, Nat Pendleton, Beverly Simmons, Don Porter

A curious mixture of postwar GI experience and sheer slapstick, this film is marked by moments of candid resentment against military authority unacknowledged during the war. But it also shows the receding of Abbott and Costello into images of their celebrity selves, literally including the movie posters for themselves that the actors innocently come across in the film.

Bound for home on a troop ship, the boys (Lou in particular) articulate the collective rage at the military brass, condensed into sergeant Brown, formerly a Manhattan beat cop whose attempted arrest of the two street peddlers drove them to the Army recruiters in the first place. They have another reason to resist authority: a little refugee French girl who has adopted the always sexually ambivalent Lou as (in Lou's words) her mother. Sneaking her in against Army regulations, they join a midget racer team with a former GI buddy, and Lou inadvertently begins one of the longest and wildest slapstick automobile scenes on film (his car has wings and flies!). Most remarkable is the wartime footage of the first minutes that gives the film a documentary montage of GIs returning home—not quite losing their resentment, but eager to make a new life for themselves in a changed America. 77 min.

Burma Convoy (1941)
Co-screenplay by Stanley Rubin† for a film described by the *Times* as a masterpiece of the unintended cliché, with missing jewels, Maharaja, sea voyage and all.

Bury Me Dead (1947)
Bernard Vorhaus• directed this Karen DeWolf• co-script of a wife, thought dead, who shows up at her own funeral and accuses her philandering hubby of attempting to murder her. Exceptionally weak B-film, despite interesting premise and one of June Lockhart's best efforts.

Buy Me That Town (1941)
Para. Prod: Sol C. Siegel. Dir: Eugene Forde. Scr: Gordon Kahn.• Story: Martin Rackin, Murray Boltinoff, Harry A. Gourfair. Cast: Lloyd Nolan, Constance Moore, Albert Dekker, Sheldon Leonard, Barbara Jo Allen, Edward Brophy, Warren Hymer, Horace MacMahon

This is the only full-scale comedy with solo script by Kahn, a Marxist bohemian who did his most lucrative work on Roy Rogers oaters before the blacklist struck. Despite its B-production values, this film has all the charm of the then-popular Damon Runyon–style gangster pic of rascals with good hearts. *Variety* called it "one of the most entertaining B entries of the season."

Planning the takeover of a Depression-ridden town for gambling purposes, the mobsters find out that the burg is dead broke and facing extinction. They cleverly turn a profit by transforming the jail into a sort of country club, in which mobsters seeking immunity from more serious charges can hang out comfortably. Soon, the hoosegow costs $1,000 per week. Meanwhile the boys become public spirited (ex-arsonist Hymer is memorable as the fire chief). While the state cops breathe down their necks and comedienne Allen reveals her love for the big lug Brophy, the film races toward a comic climax that is not altogether comic: war spending offers commercial salvation. Never for a moment serious about itself, *Buy Me That Town* offers a sustained joke about crime and the law in tough times. 70 min.

C

Ça Va Barder (1954)

Societe nouvelle dispas. Prod: Unknown. Dir: John Berry.•
Scr: John Berry, Henri-François Rey. Cast: Eddie Constantine, May Britt, Jean Carmet, Henry Cogan, Jean Danet

Exile Berry created this low-budget but exceedingly popular French detective tale by transforming a mediocre British detective novel into an over-the-top romp, with abundant satire of American cinematic gestures. In the process, he helped create a most improbable French film idol, Eddie Constantine, a real-life former Broadway dancer, Hollywood bit-player and Paris crooner. Both character and actor were made internationally famous a few years later by director Jean-Luc Godard in *Alphaville*. The original hardly made it to American shores.

In *Ça va Barder*, the Constantine figure, a hard-drinking, womanizing American in Paris, punches and shoots his way though a fleet of tropical freighters to win back an old girlfriend (Britt) who is now hooked up with her smuggler-boss. The French audience could enjoy it without ever taking it seriously. 82 min.

Cabin in the Sky (1943)

MGM Prod: Arthur Freed. Dir: Vincente Minnelli. Scr: Joseph Schrank. Play Basis: Lynn Root, John LaTouche, Vernon Duke. Cast: Ethel Waters, Eddie ("Rochester") Anderson, Lena Horne, Louis Armstrong, Rex Ingram

A famed black musical punctuated (or arguably, shaped) by the lyrics of Yip Harburg• and the tunes of Harold Arlen, Vernon Duke and Duke Ellington, the film was adapted from the smash Broadway hit that reputedly integrated musical theater with its road company. In the film version, however, whites are altogether absent, making the somewhat later STORMY WEATHER (where whites are scarce) the first integrated musical film in which blacks do not play subservient roles. Nonetheless, *Cabin in the Sky* was a Hollywood breakthrough, if a financial failure.

The folk-musical quality of the film is built around Ethel Waters as the long-suffering religious wife and Eddie Anderson as the wayward, gambling husband. Satan's crew (hustlers sporting attractive horns and lots of ghetto humor) set out to take his soul, while the heavenly hierarchy is impelled to judge him mercifully, thanks to the incessant prayers of Waters to "The Boss." Over at the side of the action, "bad woman" Horne also wants Anderson. Frustrated at his near-reform from sin, the devils arrange for him to win the Irish Sweepstakes—or was it just a dream, as Anderson lay near death, Waters praying by his side? In the stage version, temptress Georgia Brown was primarily a dancer, played by Katherine Dunham; in the film, Horne was mostly a singer, but this was enough of an acting part to be a debut. In Hollywood-style recycling, tornado footage from *The Wizard of Oz* was used.

The plot matters less than the songs and the dance numbers, at least one of which (furious dancing in a black club) puts later Spike Lee recreations to shame. Songs "Cabin in the Sky" (with Waters looking on high, and Anderson eager for life down here) and "Honey from the Honeycomb" (sung successively by Horne and Waters) are especially engaging—arguably some of the best moments ever in film musicals. For the film, the team of Arlen and Harburg added three new pieces: "Li'l Black Sheep," "Happiness is a Thing Called Joe," and "Life's Full of Consequence." Inquisitors of HUAC later asked Harburg if "Joe" was actually a cryptic invocation of Joseph Stalin! 98 min.

Caged (1950)

WB. Prod: Jerry Wald. Dir: John Cromwell. Scr: Virginia Kellogg, Bernard C. Schoenfeld.† Cast: Eleanor Parker, Agnes Moorehead, Ellen Corby, Hope Emerson, Betty Garde, Jan Sterling, Lee Patrick, Olive Deering, Jane Darwell, Gertrude Michael

The best and most realistic of the jailed-women dramas, usually exploited for sadism and implied lesbianism. These elements are not absent but are handled with rare intelligence. Parker is a young woman imprisoned as an accessory to a robbery in which her boyfriend died. She's revealed to be pregnant, is watched over in kindly fashion by assorted cons and persecuted by the sadistic matron. Warden Moorehead is aware of mistreatment but unable to end the system of favoritism and payoffs or even find the budget for a psychologist. The prison system is a horror, and these women are mere victims, in trouble thanks to their bad choice in men. Un-Hollywood pessimism has the warden predicting, "You'll be back!" Co-screenwriter and erstwhile investigative journalist Kellogg claimed she'd spent four weeks in some of the worst women's jails to get realistic material. The script got an Oscar nomination, as did Parker and Emerson. 96 min.

Caged Fury (1948)

Pine-Thomas. Prod: William H. Pine, William C. Thomas. Dir: William A. Berke. Scr: David Lang.† Cast: Richard Denning, Sheila Ryan, Mary Beth Hughes, Buster Crabbe, Frank Wilcox

This archetypal circus or carnival tale features bold women put to the test by the lust and/or love of good and/or bad men. Brave and confident lion tamer Hughes (she shows no fear behind the whip) is murdered when the bad-guy clown (Crabbe in an unusual villain role) strings a secret wire to make her escape from the cage impossible. Ryan, expected to take the place of Hughes and to fall willingly into his arms, instead takes up with Denning, who saves her and the circus when Crabbe starts a fire. Before these developments, however, she has to establish her determination not to give up her career for a family: becoming a star is all she has ever dreamed of. Short on plot and even more so on production values arranged by the two "Dollar Bills," Left-collaborators Pine and Thomas, the independently produced *Fury* is long on self-conscious female characterization. Perhaps only an unusual woman would place herself in a cage with a ferocious (nonhuman) beast, but those who do earn our respect for their fearlessness. At a final moment, however, the pregnant Ryan hints she will leave the circus after all—to have kids. 60 min.

Cairo (1963)

A remake of THE ASPHALT JUNGLE with Adrian Scott's• wife Joan Scott• writing (as "Joanne Court"), her single career advance beyond Disney scenarist and television writer. It is also one of suave George Sanders's last interesting films.

Calamity Jane and Sam Bass (1949)

U-I. Prod. Leonard Goldstein. Dir: George Sherman. Scr: Melvyn Levy,† Maurice Geraghty. Story basis: George Sherman. Cast: Howard Duff, Yvonne De Carlo, Dorothy Hart, Lloyd Bridges,† Milburn Stone, John Rodney, Charles Cane, Marc Lawrence,† Walter Baldwin, Nedrick Young•

An overly complex but interestingly gendered yarn of law and order versus justice in the Old West, with Technicolor providing the evidence of higher-than-usual studio aspirations. Duff is the never-shot-a-gun stranger in an East Texas town, looking for honest work and hoping someday to own a ranch. De Carlo is the sheriff's

sister who falls for him, despite her brother Stone's (ill-founded) suspicions. Duff—soon to be graylisted in real life for his success starring in a Dashiell Hammet–based show—is magic with horses because of his creature-feelings for them; he meanwhile attracts the ardent attention of tomboyish Hart, who as Calamity Jane gets the best part in the film.

Adventures follow as Duff finds himself on the wrong side of the law, thanks to the swindlers who run Abilene and poison the horse he bought to win the big race. He and his friends become outlaws to win back the money that ranchers had bet on him. Though Hart throws aside her own reputable career to follow him into out-lawry (and repeatedly throws herself at him), he never loses his craving for an ordinary life with family. The result is a few good scenes, lots of shoot-'em-up action, and a sinking sense that, somehow, this just can't be the real story of the historical characters. 85 min., color.

Call of the Canyon (1942)

A contemporary war profiteer saga has Oklahoma ranchers cheated by a purchasing agent with no patriotism whatever, Gene Autry as the singing cowboy (forced, at gun point, to yodel on the radio) and Smiley Burnett as his comic sidekick. Marc Lawrence,† in a rare western appearance, is once again the ideal gangster. Maurice Rapf• co-wrote the story basis.

Campus Rhythm (1943)

A musical cheapie co-scripted by Frank Tarloff,• who privately pleaded with scholars to drop the credit from recorded memory. Professional singer Gale Storm enrolls in school to get away from her career, but acquires a boyfriend, puts on a show and so on.

Can't Help Singing (1944)

A Deanna Durbin vehicle co-scripted by Leo Townsend,† this film earned an Oscar nomination for Jerome Kern and Hans J. Salter as music directors and another for their song, "More and More." Yip Harburg• contributed lyrics for "Any Moment Now" to Kern's music, as the Technicolor musical traces Durbin's travels across country in the mid–nineteenth century to join and marry an old boyfriend. On the way she realizes she has fallen in love with another.

The Canterville Ghost (1944)

MGM/Loew's. Prod: Arthur Field. Dir: Jules Dassin.• Scr:

Edwin Blum. Story basis: Oscar Wilde, "The Canterville Ghost" (1887). Cast: Charles Laughton, Robert Young, Margaret O'Brien, William Gargan, Reginald Owen, Rags Ragland, Peter Lawford

This wartime piece (and director Dassin's third feature film) combines a major opportunity for Laughton to play the ham, little Margaret O'Brien the cute kid, Robert Young the soldier who fears his own cowardice, and the English people at large to be charmingly eccentric hosts for their well-meaning occupiers. Of all these, however, it is Laughton who faces center stage as the castle ghost. He has successfully frightened generations of dwellers and guests but is himself descended from a long line of yellow-streaked lords. Prancing and shuddering, he recalls Bert Lahr as the Cowardly Lion, while O'Brien plays a British Shirley Temple who happens to be mistress of the castle in which the Yanks are being housed. Young and Laughton fall into much clever repartee, broken off when Young is sent to France where, predictably, he freezes up in combat. Returning disgraced, he is presented with another opportunity to prove himself. Didactic moral: the British, America's cousins, deserve saving. 96 min.

Captain Scarlett (1953)

A prototype for the *Adventures of Robin Hood* television series, with a similar bold lad (played by the same actor, Richard Greene). It co-starred one of Hollywood's up-and-coming left-wing screenwriters, Nedrick Young,• in his last major acting role (Young would go on to co-script THE DEFIANT ONES but never achieve his promise as the Errol Flynn–type of dashing swash-buckler of the screen). It was also screenwriter Howard Dimsdale's• biggest-budget project, just before his descent into the blacklist and much uncredited work in children's television shows. Scarlet is the dispossessed noble who returns to his beloved France to find rotten snob Royalists squeezing the peasants during the post-Napoleonic Restoration.

Captain Sindbad (1963)

Delightfully cheesy King Brothers production co-scripted by Harry Rellis (pseudonym for Guy Endore•) and Samuel B. West (pseudonym for Ian McLellan Hunter•) in this third filmed Sindbad feature. Guy Williams of television's *Wild Bill Hickock* fame is the hero who saves a princess while enduring endless challenges, natural and supernatural, set before him by a literally heartless villain. It was regarded as great fun at the time, and has remained a holidays keep-the-kids-busy television perennial since.

A Captive in the Land (1990)

Ask Soviet-American Films, Gloria Productions, Gorky Film Studios. Prod: John Berry.• Dir: John Berry. Scr: John Berry, Lee Gold.• Novel basis: James Aldridge, *A Captive in the Land* (1962). Cast: Sam Waterson, Alecksander Potapov, T. Hol, Victor Ignatyev, Aleksei Ivashchenko

Rare script collaboration for Lee Gold, who worked largely in French television from the 1950s onward, and filmed in the former Soviet Union, this is a détente tour de force completed out of time—contemplated for decades but only produced as the East Bloc fell. Waterson and Potapov, playing a U.S. microbiologist and Soviet flyer, respectively, are stranded together in the Arctic winter and must work out their social relations to survive until they are rescued by one side or the other, and in the process finding the humanity in each other. The "cold" in Cold War is an enemy to both. Deserves to be much better known. 89 min.

Captive Wild Woman (1943)

A bizarre old-style exploitation feature, directed by Edward Dmytryk.† An unbalanced surgeon, played by John Carradine, turns an ape (played by the exotic starlet Acquanetta) into a female of obvious sexual desirability but ambiguous humanity. Everything goes fine until she becomes jealous of Evelyn Ankers—then look out! As Dmytryk used stock footage for HITLER'S CHILDREN, he uses old 1933 footage (from *The Big Cage*) to fill holes in the narrative. He notably did not direct *Jungle Woman* (1945), the sequel.

Captured! (1933)

A war drama with an antiwar flavor, scripted by Edward Chodorov• and starring Leslie Howard with Douglas Fairbanks, Jr. and Paul Lukas. POWs in Germany riot against their captors and scheme against each other over old love affairs and assorted encounters (including the rape and murder of a German woman). These were themes banned from Hollywood films just a few years later.

The Cardinal (1963)

With an uncredited script contribution by Ring Lardner, Jr.,• this highly awarded film was just critical (and also supportive) enough of the clergy, and just liberal enough politically, to capture the public reputation of the church in modern times. Protagonist Tom Tryon wanders through the Papal bureaucracy and eventually finds a real cause in the U.S. South, where black Catholics are terribly persecuted, and where he is attacked and symbolically crucified. Lardner could not recall, later, whether the strongest racial scenes were written by himself or by his friend and fellow progressive, Gore Vidal.

Career (1939)
Dalton Trumbo• scripted this story of the rise of an Iowa boy torn between a medical career and marrying the local banker's daughter. Some of the themes were later more fully developed by assorted (and mostly uncredited) lefties in IT'S A WONDERFUL LIFE. Anne Shirley played the daughter—and married Adrian Scott• a few years later, still later divorcing the lone producer of the Hollywood Ten while giving friendly testimony against him.

Career (1959)
A theme reworked, once more by Dalton Trumbo• (now working under a pseudonym), of a young man's struggle to rise, this time as a would-be Broadway actor, played by Anthony Franciosa in one of his best films.

The Careless Years (1957)
A true oddity and very rare, this film can best be seen as a dress rehearsal for some themes of Kazan's Splendor in the Grass—but without the glamor. Co-written under fronts by Mitch Lindemann• and John Howard Lawson,• the story is about class and the adult sexual hypocrisy exposed when two very young people, a poor boy and a girl from a wealthy family, fall in love, play by the rules but are prevented from marrying. Unusual for its frank sympathy for the teens against the adult world and for its Lawsonian class-based realism, Careless Years moves toward the cinematic revolutions of the 1960s-1970s.

Carnival Story (1954)
Dalton Trumbo• scripted this film anonymously for the exploitation-minded King Brothers, director Kurt Neumann, and stars Anne Baxter and Steve Cochran. Like CAGED FURY, it's a study of female strength of character in circus surroundings: a sexually exploited, pretty war survivor who joins a road troupe just to stay alive. She reluctantly agrees to marry the high-diver, a cad whose accidental death prompts her to take ever-greater chances to maintain the fascination of the bloodthirsty crowd. Baxter is finally saved by the circus strong man and dimwit Gropo (played by Ady Berber), a cult figure of sorts destined to reappear in the later satirical television series

developed by Mel Brooks, Get Smart. At its best, the moody film approaches European neo-realism in a repudiation of contemporary Hollywood styles.

Carolina Moon (1940)
This Connie Lee• story basis is a remake of Tumbling Tumbleweeds (1935), this time set in the South. Gene Autry and Smiley Burnette save elderly Carolina plantation owners from the depredations of a swindler.

Casablanca (1942)
WB. Prod: Hal Wallis. Dir: Michael Curtiz. Scr: Howard Koch,• Julius J. Epstein, Philip G. Epstein. Play basis: Murray Burnett, Joan Alison, "Everybody Comes to Rick's" (unpublished). Cast: Humphrey Bogart, Ingrid Bergman, Paul Henreid, Claude Rains, Peter Lorre, Sydney Greenstreet, Conrad Veidt

An all-time Popular Front favorite, Casablanca received several Academy Awards (best picture and best screenplay), in addition to many nominations, but was no box office smash, nor even a particularly well-remembered classic—until its revival by the antiwar generation of the 1960s-1970s (including a considerable boost from Woody Allen's Play it Again, Sam). Now considered one of the best films ever made, it combines the antifascist schmaltz perfected by so many screenwriters who were later blacklisted with the element other films too rarely possessed: an absolutely overpowering love story.

Bogart, personally sympathetic to Hollywood's communists, plays the ultimate disillusioned politico but undisillusioned romantic, in this case (for viewers who listen closely) a former gunrunner in the 1935 Ethiopian campaign and a fighter for the Spanish Loyalists—very likely with the communists, who were most of the foreign volunteers. Just a few years later he finds himself, as the troubled Rick, running the Café Americain in Morocco under German occupation. Reviving an earlier romance with the luminous Bergman, now the wife of antifascist leader Henreid trying to escape, he must choose between the nobility of love and the nobility of the cause, each of which had eluded him once but both of which now seem tantalizingly within reach. The political story is deepened by Rick's mysterious friendship with the head of the Vichy police (Rains), whose apparent cynicism is more than a match for Rick's own. Throw in Lorre, Greenstreet and Veidt, and the result is a film that never fails to surprise even upon repeated viewing.

According to Koch, a principled Popular Front liberal who refused to name names and was blacklisted for his trouble, many of the most famous lines were written by the more experienced Epstein twins ("What is your nationality?" "I'm a drunkard"), who abandoned the project when it fell behind schedule and disaster loomed (they had great dialogue, no story). Facing a deadline of two weeks with only a quarter of the screenplay done, Koch wrote feverishly, erecting the narrative scaffolding at times with the help of Bogart over a bottle of the star's whiskey. By the time shooting started, the screenplay was only half-finished, and soon Koch was engaged in a test of wills with the director on the question of whether the love story would be subordinated to the political story (it was Curtiz who insisted on the flashback to the train station in Paris). In the end, the two stories meshed flawlessly. A tense collaboration in the most collaborative art at the height of the Popular Front had produced an almost accidental masterpiece. 102 min.

Casbah (1948)
A musical remake of *Algiers* with songs by Yip Harburg's• collaborator Harold Arlen, among others. It may be most memorable as director John Berry's• only musical and co-writer Arnold Manoff's• only film success before the blacklist and later uncredited triumph as scriptwriter (with Abraham Polonsky and Walter Bernstein) of television's *You Are There*. The plot is never taken seriously, as career criminal Tony Martin gets into trouble by breaking away from dark lover Yvonne De Carlo as he seeks to return to France. The Katherine Dunham Dancers add a large note of exoticism, and the song "For Every Man There's a Woman" (nominated for an Oscar) was a winner with audiences.

The Case Against Brooklyn (1958)
"Raymond T. Marcus" (Bernard Gordon•) and the uncredited Julian Zimet• scripted a fact-based drama of bookmakers taking over an inside section of the police force. It was a fact-based close reading of a bookie operation, if rather far-fetched in the legal clean-up.

The Case of the Lucky Legs (1935)
An unmemorable Perry Mason outing based on Erle Stanley Gardner novels; this one, adapted by Jerry Chodorov,• was second in a series of seven.

Case of the Missing Man (1935)
This hackish crime drama claimed the documentary "this is New York" angle familiar to contemporary Left aesthetics. The protagonist, a down-on-his-luck photographer, snaps random New Yorkers and inadvertently captures the image of a dangerous criminal. Scripted by Harold Buchman• and his frequent partner Lee Loeb.

Casey's Shadow (1978)
One of Martin Ritt's• lesser efforts should have been an adequate vehicle for the blacklistees' pal Walter Matthau, but it was an all-too-sentimental story of a washed-up trainer, his horse, his son and the inevitable big race. Ritt, a handicapper of great skill, reputedly fooled himself. "Ethnic" scenes in bars with Matthau in a mustache, talking Cajun, are the best thing in the overly long film, which cost $3.5 million to produce. Lacking sex or romance, it never had a chance, and failed at the box office.

Cass Timberlane (1947)
MGM. Prod: Arthur Hornblow, Jr. Dir: George Sidney. Scr: Donald Ogden Stewart,• Sonya Levien. Novel basis: Sinclair Lewis, *Cass Timberlane* (1945). Cast: Spencer Tracy, Lana Turner, Tom Drake, Mary Astor, Albert Dekker

An interesting adaptation and update of famed Lewis novel has Tracy as the crusty judge and widower who has buried his ideals beneath boredom (not entirely: a wealthy dowager says that he subscribes to magazines that nobody has ever heard of "except the FBI") with his routine existence on the bench and the social life of the ruling class in a middle-sized Minnesota town. By accident, he meets a young working-class woman who has caricatured him in a court room sketch and is not at all impressed with his status. Tracy soon descends literally and metaphorically from the heights to the flats, umpiring a softball game in her neighborhood. As he begins to woo her, she sees her kindly father in him and has aspirations for knowledge and culture that he can supply.

His social set is scandalized not so much by the age as the class difference. The film bogs down in the supposed dilemmas of the couple and her temptations, offering only hints that many middle-class women are restless with the spiritual narrowness in every prairie town that novelist Lewis described. Still, two match-ups are at times memorable; Tracy with Turner and scriptwriter Stewart with Levien (whose credits stretch from *The Hunchback of Notre Dame* to *Oklahoma!*, and whose daughter was Tamara Hovey•). 119 min.

Cat Ballou (1965)

Col. Prod: Harold Hecht,† Mitch Lindemann.• Dir: Elliot Silverstein. Scr: Walter Newman, Frank Pierson. Novel basis: Roy Chanslor, *The Ballad of Cat Ballou* (1956). Cast: Jane Fonda, Lee Marvin, Michael Callan, Dwayne Hickman, Nat "King" Cole, Stubby Kaye, Reginald Denny, Bruce Cabot

Oscar-winning Lee Marvin, playing the drunkest gunslinger in the West, thanked the horse at the Academy Awards ceremony, as well he might have. It sits on its rump and even walks sideways. The plot, such as it is, is taken from a novel of the same man who wrote JOHNNY GUITAR, so perhaps it is no surprise that *Cat* is in many ways a send-up of the earlier film, with Fonda sending for "Kid Shelleen" to help fight the local railroad baron's men, who are killers of her father. This picture was also the highlight of Lindemann's foreshortened career. 96 min.

Caught (1949)

Enterprise. Prod: Wolfgang Reinhardt. Dir: Max Ophüls (uncredited: John Berry•). Scr: Arthur Laurents. Cast: Barbara Bel Geddes, James Mason, Robert Ryan, Art Smith, Curt Bois, Natalie Shafer

The Hollywood debut of James Mason and a casting-against-type romantic curiosity better remembered for its directors and actors than for its contents. It was also the last completed project of Enterprise, the strongly Left-influenced independent company that made a series of remarkable films (including FORCE OF EVIL) and collapsed shortly before its most-talented figures were blacklisted. In mid-film, as an effort to boost the studio's reputation, Berry was replaced by Ophüls and later dropped from the credits.

Seen another way, this is a woman's film of distinction with a certain antimaterialist outlook common to blacklistee efforts. Its real star, Barbara Bel Geddes, struggles to make her own way in the world decently and meaningfully, if only because her marriage is so dissatisfying. New to New York and enrolled in finishing school, she talks casually about finding a rich man and successfully lands him in Ryan. There is no doubt whatever that the tortured millionaire was shaped from Howard Hughes' legend; reputedly, Hughes insisted that if he were to be portrayed, Ryan was the only one to do it properly.

Ryan marries just to vex his psychoanalyst(!) and immediately returns to his real interests: making money and manipulating people. Bel Geddes goes off to find a job in Manhattan's Lower East Side at the office of a pediatrician and obstetrician. Her boss is a sane and humanitarian Mason (considerably less powerful than in his mentally troubled roles), who has thrown away the good life of practicing on uptown neurotics to make a difference among the poor. Mason's speeches to her on the emptiness of materialist values and the necessity to instruct patients in the healthy life are vintage thirties themes realized in forties films, and the closest that Popular Front sympathizer Laurents—graylisted for his political sympathies and his homosexuality—got before *The Way We Were*. Secretly pregnant after a brief and unsuccessful reunion with the Ryan character, Bel Geddes sets the stage for a final clash with his world—nothing surprising, but strangely warming. 88 min.

The Cavern, aka Sette contro la morte (1964)

Dalton Trumbo• remains uncredited for this extremely obscure film, directed by Pado Cianchini and Edgar Ulmer, making it the third Ulmer title to use a blacklisted writer (the others were Gordon Kahn• and Julian Zimet•) in a career never far from the Left. As usual for Ulmer, *Cavern* is very low-budget, a German-Italian production about Americans, Brits, French and Russians trapped in an underground cavern awaiting rescue, with tempers flaring over the same issues that separate the nations above ground. If an overly obvious allegory, it is also interesting and bold for its time.

The Ceremony (1963)

Ben Barzman• scripted, and Laurence Harvey and Sarah Miles starred in this indifferent adventure story with a prison escape, a sexual triangle and a struggle over loyalties. It was shot in Spain.

Champagne Waltz (1937)

A shmaltzy-waltzy feature about Viennese musical culture, featuring Strauss standards and modern tunes with "book" by Billy Wilder and Hy S. Kraft.• Semi-memorable fantasy scene when lovers imagine the way the waltz palace looked in its best days and when "The Blue Danube Waltz" was played for Emperor Franz Josef.

Champion (1949)

UA. Prod: Stanley Kramer. Dir: Mark Robson. Scr: Carl Foreman.• Cast: Kirk Douglas, Marilyn Maxwell, Arthur Kennedy, Ruth Roman, Lola Albright

This Foreman treatment of a Ring Lardner, Sr., story won six Academy nominations (including best supporting actor for Kennedy and best film score) and one actual

Oscar (best film editing). It was regarded by Foreman as the first film to use the "jump cut," an editing device intended to skip the most obvious exposition (and thus demanding more from audiences). Often regarded as one of the finest cinematic boxing dramas because of its detailed accuracy, *Champion* is actually a moral drama of class mobility at the price of the loss of social or family solidarity. Foreman later told Columbia University interviewers than he had never been very politically acute; but his ability to portray integrity (or the lack of it) was highly refined. Kramer, who fancied making leftist films, notoriously fired him amid the production of HIGH NOON, when Foreman refused to become a friendly witness. *Champion* is also memorable as an early vehicle for Douglas to express his mixture of muscular virility and modern neurosis. This time it is the egotism of the strong rather than (as in THE STRANGE LOVES OF MARTHA IVERS) the loss of nerve of the morally weak.

A slum boy with a crippled brother, riding the boxcars, is beaten and in desperation becomes a brutally skilled pugilist. Intent on heading west for a share in a restaurant, he learns on arrival that the place has been sold. He woos the proprietor's daughter but agrees to marry only under compulsion, and deserts her at the first opportunity. Mauling his opponents in the ring, he grows more cynical as he becomes more famous. He especially enjoys stealing wives or girlfriends, then dumping them. Conclusion poses whether the ever-loyal brother can bring himself to cover up for the celebrity black sheep one last time. 99 min.

Chance Meeting aka *Blind Date* (1959)

Sydney Box Associates/Independent Artists. Prod: Luggi Waldleitner and David Deutsch. Dir: Joseph Losey.• Scr: Ben Barzman,• Millard Lampell.• Dir: Joseph Losey. Cast: Hardy Kruger, Stanley Baker, Micheline Presle, Robert Flemyng, Gordon Jackson

The Losey film that built on his artistic successes with budget film noir in England (*The Sleeping Tiger*, TIME WITHOUT PITY) and sets the pace for his best-known work to follow shortly. For much of his subsequent career preoccupied with portraying the use of sexual energy by the upper-middle class to secure property relations, Losey here offers a prelude. A young Dutch artist (Kruger) succumbs to the seductions of a much older woman (Presle), only to discover that she is the wife of a powerful politician who has used Kruger as bait in an elaborate scheme to preserve her threatened class privileges. While the relation between prey and predator always has a sexual dimension, no matter how elaborate the game, Losey insists, the prey is invariably a form of property. British film

favorite Baker, with the rock-hard jaw of the Scotland Yard detective, sees through the plot, but there is no kindness extended to the Dutch son of the working class (the painter's mural, a paean to his coal-mining ancestors, dominates a number of scenes). The same themes would become familiar elements in later Losey films, notably in THE SERVANT and ACCIDENT, where they would be developed with much more sophistication and without the obligatory trappings of the mystery thriller. Released in England as *Blind Date*, the film would be one of the few Losey films ever to attract favorable notice in the U.S. press. Even so, distribution was stopped in its tracks by the lingering red scare. The Catholic War Veterans and Cardinal Spellman threatened to picket the theaters if it were given a major release (instead, it appeared almost invisibly on a double bill with *It Happened in Naples*). Lampell claimed he had inserted the sensibility of Vincent Van Gogh's letters to his brother Theo in painting studio scenes. 93 min.

Charlie Chan's Greatest Case (1933)

Fox. Prod: Sol M. Wurtzel. Dir: Hamilton MacFadden. Scr: Lester Cole,• Marion Orth. Novel basis: Earl Derr Biggers, *The House Without a Key* (1925). Cast: Warner Oland, Heather Angel, Roger Imhof, John Warburton, Walter Byron, Ivan Simpson, Virginia Cherrill, Francis Ford, Robert Warwick, Clara Blandick

This was the third of the Charlie Chan feature films, but based on the first of the Chan novels and follows the Pathé (silent) serial of 1926. Like others of the series, it has the curious affect of "otherizing" Chan in a sympathetic way, as the Confucian detective (and no doubt a Chinese counterpoint to the increasing demonization of the Japanese as the rising "Yellow Peril"). For the 1930s, the South Seas (in this case Hawaii) was an exotic location, even in urban Honolulu.

Chan, as a Hawaiian police detective, is faced with a huge and feuding American family (with some of its members going native, partying with locals), marriage proposals, mysterious telegrams and packages, rampant blackmailing and a shipboard smallpox quarantine—not to mention a corpse. No one but Chan could sort it out—certainly not the moviegoers. But the series was one of the 1930s "B" standards for Fox and a slight source of embarrassment in later decades because Asian actors were nowhere to be seen. 70 min.

Charlie McCarthy, Detective (1939)

Frank Tuttle† directed and Edward Eliscu• co-wrote (including lyrics for the musical number "I'm Charlie

McCarthy, Detective") this slight comedy using famed ventriloquist (and ardent antifascist) Edgar Bergin's two famous dummies, Charlie and Mortimer Snerd. Best moment has Charlie commenting sarcastically on a surrealist painting; the worst is a bit of Stepin Fetchit–style African American humor.

The Chase (1966)

Horizon/Lone Star/Col. Prod: Sam Spiegel. Dir: Arthur Penn. Scr: Lillian Hellman.• Novel basis: *The Chase* (1956), adapted from the play by Horton Foote of the same name (1952). Cast: Marlon Brando, Jane Fonda, Robert Redford, E. G. Marshall, Angie Dickinson, Janice Rule, Miriam Hopkins, Martha Hyer, Robert Duvall

One of those late Lillian Hellman snafus (like TOYS IN THE ATTIC) that suggest Dashiell Hammett may actually have written sections of Hellman's earlier film scripts, while she reached her own mark with legitimate theater during the 1930s-1950s. In this case, her work faced repeated rewrites and reshooting from an overly ambitious producer, and got a very rough reception from critics. An overly mannered Brando is cast as sheriff of a small Southern town assigned to catch fugitive Redford on his way back home to see wife Fonda. The town is loaded with racists, alcoholics, Christian nuts and secular sluts, all of them impeding the sheriff's progress through one long—very long—night. Penn's direction was destroyed by his removal from the set. Spiegel took over, looking as though he were still groping for a way to guide an audience through the emerging social chaos of the time. Penn found it shortly (in *Bonnie and Clyde*) while this was the last of Spiegel's great misadventures, following triumphs with ON THE WATERFRONT, THE BRIDGE ON THE RIVER KWAI, and LAWRENCE OF ARABIA. 133 min., color.

Chasing Danger (1939)

One of those French Foreign Legion adventures with rebellious Arabs. Leonardo Bercovici• provided the story basis.

Chasing Yesterday (1935)

An exceedingly odd drama adapted, from an Anatole France novel, by Francis Faragoh• about a bookseller in *fin de siècle* France who tries to sell his book collection to save an orphan.

Che! (1969)

Michael Wilson• once described this film as his greatest professional disappointment. A sympathetic screenplay was eviscerated by producer Sy Barlett in a cold-blooded act of cinemacide. If it had been shot as Wilson wrote it, the film would have shown Che's development unsentimentally, with a clear-eyed hardness; instead, Che is a nutty romantic with a gangster's ruthless streak, eager to risk all-out nuclear war (in the Cuban missile crisis) rather than suffer a blow to his ego. A great screenwriter's last film, now difficult to find, richly deserving its obscurity. (Happily, the original screenplay has survived.) With Omar Sharif as Che; Jack Palance is still more improbable as Fidel Castro.

Chicago Confidential (1957)

The plot concerns an attempted takeover of a union by mobsters—an effort by "Raymond T. Marcus" (scriptwriter Bernard Gordon•) to bring labor issues into late noir. Noir cult actor Elisha Cook, Jr., among others, sets the scene.

Chicken Wagon Family (1939)

A hillbilly comedy about Cajuns and their movements across the South to Manhattan. Viola Brothers Shore's• adaptation of a John Barry Benefield novel is funny in parts, thanks to Jane Withers, Leo Carrillo, Marjorie Weaver and Spring Byington.

A Child is Born (1939)

WB. Exec. Prod: Hal Wallis (Assoc. Prod: Samuel Bischoff). Dir: Lloyd Bacon. Scr: Robert Rossen.† Play basis: Mary McDougal Axelson, *Life Begins* (1932) Cast: Geraldine Fitzgerald, Jeffrey Lynn, Gladys George, Gale Page, Spring Byington, Eve Arden

This is a surprisingly good second filming of Alexson's play (in 1932, it starred Loretta Young) and an unlikely project for Rossen, whose slum proletarians, mobsters and molls seem out of place among all the kindly nurses and dedicated surgeons. But there is a connection: Fitzgerald has been condemned to 20 years in prison for a killing (never explained) that she claims was self-defense but the jury has ruled a murder. Her faithful husband (Lynn) has obviously built his life around her and is frustrated when the police guard at the hospital keeps him away from her. In the crucial scenes at the maternity ward, we find the usual cast of types—Byington, a mother of five who is expecting number six; George, a show biz wife whose husband never wanted the child and is about to replace her in the vaudeville act and perhaps in his life; and so on. At the crucial moment, the doctors warn that they must try to save either the life of Fitzgerald or her child, and she must choose. 79 min.

Child of Manhattan (1933)

A pre-Code gender melodrama built around a respectable family inheriting a dance hall named "Loveland," in which they must confront the realities of lower-class life. A scion sent to investigate meets the taxi dancer who supports her impoverished family, and makes her his mistress, followed by pregnancy, a still-birth, and an improbable Hollywood ending. This is an interesting early example of the work of Preston Sturges (who wrote the play basis) and of Gertrude Purcell,† a screenwriter often chosen in the thirties for credible characterizations of women.

The Children's Hour (1961)

UA/Mirisch-World Wide Productions, a William Wyler Production. Prod-Dir: William Wyler. Scr: Lillian Hellman.• Play basis: The Children's Hour (1934). Cast: Shirley MacLaine, Audrey Hepburn, James Garner, Miriam Hopkins, Veronica Cartwright, Fay Bainter

Nearing the end of a long Hollywood career often connected with the Old Left, Wyler remade his own first cinematic version of Hellman's play, originally retitled These Three (1934) for the film. In that version, Hellman's first important screen credit, the lesbian themes of the stage play were carefully scrubbed out and replaced with the implication of an emotional ménage à trois between two women and a man—by the end of the century a touchier theme than lesbianism.

In the remake, the lesbian themes of the Broadway play are restored, although the word is never mentioned and, according to a later interview with Hepburn, never even discussed among the cast. Once again, the theme illuminates the tension of two teachers who are maliciously and falsely attacked by student gossip but who discover in the act of denying the physical truth of the allegation a belated realization of its emotional validity. In this version, the talkiness of the original screenplay has been reduced and a certain realism added, largely through the cinematography of Franz Planer. But if the issues had in a sense moved on (if not terribly far), the original film version contained more dramatic tension, the pseudo-revelations seemed more potentially destructive and the resolution, however obliquely stated, somewhat more surprising. Still, for a theme so little explored, this is an important effort, the more so in Hollywood history for being treated twice

without the decadence or sickness that had long been attributed to homosexuality. MacLaine is not at her best here, but in her credible effort she reveals how much she lost by coming so late to Left-written features. It also marks, like The Americanization of Emily, the unique role of Garner as too-young-to-be-left (and also too cynical), but engagingly iconoclastic in his choices and not afraid to be daring. Predictably savaged by Hellman's political enemies in the world of prestigious reviewers, it survives as a fascinating memento. 107 min., color.

China's Little Devils (1945)

A neglected Chinese resistance film with story and script by Sam Ornitz• in a B-production with refugee children (played mostly by Asian actors) assisting downed U.S. flyers, finally sacrificing their own lives for the Allied cause.

Chip Off the Old Block (1944)

A light-hearted Donald O'Connor service musical co-scripted by Leo Townsend† around the show put on by a naval academy and the romance of cadet O'Connor with a descendent of old-time musical theater actresses.

A Christmas Carol (1938)

MGM. Prod: Joseph L. Mankiewicz. Dir: Edward L. Marin. Scr: Hugo Butler.• Novel basis: Charles Dickens, A Christmas Carol (1843). Cast: Reginald Owen, Gene Lockhart, Terence Kilburn, Leo G. Carroll, Lynne Carver, Ann Rutherford, D'Arcy Corrigan, Ronald Sinclair, Lionel Barnham, Barry MacKay

This first U.S. sound version of Dickens' classic is closest both to the author's class-conscious sentimentalization of the poor and to his psychological insight into the mentality of heartless employers. Dispensing with much of the sappiness of other renditions, it goes straight to Dickens' point about social class and sticks to it. Canadian-born Butler, with the help of splendid casting, created an icily supernatural succession of ghosts full of historical lessons. The Ghost of Christmas Past, this time a fairy-like maiden, beautifully evokes the cramped childhood that led to Scrooge's stingy nature. The Father Christmas–looking Ghost of Christmas Present shows the working class enjoying itself. The spectral Ghost of Christmas Future does not speak but only gestures toward the lonely tomb Scrooge will inhabit. The political effect is diminished by Scrooge's conversion, but never entirely. The sins of the age are laid at the feet of the rich. 69 min.

El Cid (1961)
Samuel Bronston Productions. Prod: Samuel Bronston. Dir: Anthony Mann. Scr: Philip Yordan, Fredric M. Frank, Ben Barzman• (uncredited script contribution: Bernard Gordon•). Cast: Sophia Loren, Charlton Heston, Raf Vallone, Geneviève Page, John Fraser

An epic that some might regard as possessing a renewed contemporary significance in the "battle of civilizations," *El Cid* is another product of the Bronston/Yordan production mill in Spain. It comes at the tail end of the era of spectacles, increasingly done on tight budgets. What the duo did have was one of the best directors then working, two huge stars, Miklós Rósza as a composer and blacklisted writers who needed work. Without Loren, though, nothing would have happened, and when she took a look at the first draft she turned down the project. Loren, who had seen GIVE US THIS DAY and admired it, agreed to go ahead only if Barzman rewrote the screenplay, which he hurriedly did, following the stage version by Pierre Corneille as closely as he could. The rush shows in the resulting story about how the Christian knight Rodrigo Diaz and his army pushed the Moors out of Spain in the eleventh century, but there are fine touches, notably the cinematic trick of tying a dead warrior to his horse and sending him into battle to scare the hell out of the enemy. 182 min., color.

Cigarette Girl (1947)
A musical comedy with slight story by Edward Huebsch• about the bar girl who becomes a singing star.

The Cincinnati Kid (1965)
The script by Ring Lardner, Jr.• was ruined, according to Lardner himself, by Terry Southern's rewrites and the bad direction of Norman Jewison. Steve McQueen is the kid of the title, a poker player determined to make his mark by defeating the grand old champ, played by Edward G. Robinson. The fine supporting cast of Ann-Margret, Karl Malden, Tuesday Weld, Joan Blondell and Rip Torn (even a cameo by Cab Calloway) shows moments of brilliance, but is wasted on the romantic plot.

Cinderella (1950)
Walt Disney's animation smash followed many filmings of the story from silent days onward, in the United States and Europe. Maurice Rapf,• one of the uncredited scripters, insists that he contributed the rebellious quality that sets off this Cinderella from predecessors. This

was also notable as the first animated film since *Bambi* that had a single story line. An instant and spectacular success, it was the sixth-largest-grossing film of 1950. It also proved to be the swan song at Disney for left-wing writers, save those few who deceived the boss by working under pseudonyms a bit later—a bitterly ironic consequence because they admired his artistic seriousness despite his politics.

Circle of Two (1980)
Milton Byrman/Film Consortium of Canada. Prod: Henk Van der Kolk. Dir: Jules Dassin.• Scr: Thomas Hedley, Jr. Novel basis: Marie-Therese Baird, *A Lesson in Love* (1973). Cast: Tatum O'Neal, Richard Burton, Kate Reid, Patricia Collins, Robin Gammell, Nuala Fitzgerald

A small, odd and stagey film with unlikely pairing of O'Neal and Burton. She's an artistic-minded teenager alienated from her New England environment, notwithstanding a couple of loving and would-be-understanding parents in Gammell and Collins. He's a used-up bohemian, aged 60, a modernist painter whose time has gone, taking his artistic resolve along with it. They meet when she goes to a pornographic film and pursues him into his studio, where she learns about the trials of the artistic life and gains some confidence in herself. About the time she begins insisting upon physical contact, her parents find out. Things are headed for disaster until psychiatrist Reid, who has most of the answers, steps in. A bittersweet tone clings to the proceedings, whose lumbering predictability and sentimentality is softened by O'Neal's effort. Dassin was properly abashed at having undertaken the project. 106 min., color.

Circus World (1964)
Co-scripted by Julian Halevy (a pseudonym for Julian Zimet•). This Cinerama clunker shot in Spain has John Wayne, Claudia Cardinale and Rita Hayworth as a dysfunctional, extended circus family.

Citizen Kane (1941)
Mercury Productions, RKO. Prod: Orson Welles. Dir: Orson Welles. Scr: John Houseman (uncredited: Herman J. Mankiewicz, Orson Welles). Cast: Orson Welles, Joseph Cotten, Dorothy Comingore,• Agnes Moorehead, Ruth Warrick, Ray Collins, Erskine Sanford, Paul Stewart, William Alland†

Although the only person connected with *Kane* to be blacklisted directly was actress Comingore (who refused to testify and eventually committed suicide), film historians like Joseph McBride and others believe that Welles, a Wisconsin native and a self-described socialist, was an early victim of the blacklist because he was cut down by a studio system that viewed him as a threat. It was true that *Citizen Kane* lost money, and while that was unforgivable in Hollywood then as now, the movie also changed filmmaking forever, not least in terms of what would be considered permissible social and political content. Welles was in one sense the American Jean Renoir, a director who was able to deploy the sentiments of the Popular Front not merely in antifascist propaganda but in examinations of the class structure and the ideology of daily life. THE MAGNIFICENT AMBERSONS, taking as a text Welles' beloved Booth Tarkington, was to have been his adventure into "poetic realism" in looking at the U.S. middle class, just as his *It's All True* was to be a heightened and more intense use of the same techniques in a radical exploration of the life of the dispossessed in Brazil. If those two films were "French," *Citizen Kane* was "German" in the sense that it deliberately used the devices of the epic stage that Welles had already mastered as a director of theater and radio, incorporating visual documents of every variety to astonish the audience (rather than to entertain them). Welles' artistic and critical success was a challenge to the studio system itself, holding out the promise of emancipating film art from rigid industrial organization. *Kane* hit the Hollywood film community like a thunderbolt, and there would be no going back. His genius producer from radio days, John Houseman, escaped the blacklist but was solidly left-wing; at the end of a long career as acting teacher, Houseman served as mentor of a young Robin Williams.

This film is the familiar Horatio Alger story turned on its head, showing how, through hard work and dedication, a man could transform a merely large inherited fortune into an empire and still end up a complete failure as a human being. Along the way it showed the social effects of the concentration of the power of the news media in the hands of a few tycoons like William Randolph Hearst, the subject of the film, lessons of particular value in postmodern America. 119 min.

City for Conquest (1940)

First National Pictures/WB. Prod: Anatole Litvak. Dir: Jean Negulesco, Anatole Litvak. Screenplay: John Wexley.• Novel basis: Aben Kandel, *City for Conquest* (1940). Cast: James Cagney, Ann Sheridan, Frank Craven, Donald Crisp, Arthur Kennedy, Anthony Quinn, Elia Kazan,

George Tobias, Blanche Yurka, Lee Patrick, Thurston Hall

One of the great boxing tales in the pug-with-a-conscience tradition, and easily one of Cagney's best. A blue-collar fighter who doesn't want to fight has a brother (and roommate) who is a would-be composer of a symphony based upon the sensibility and aural atmosphere of metropolitan life. After a poverty-driven change of heart, Cagney nearly becomes the world champ. Then a foe's dirty fighting leaves him sightless but philosophical ("I can see things now that I never saw before"), a pathetic newsie, still in love with the girl who had shunned him for a moneyed boyfriend. She eventually understands how wrong she has been, and in a display of masochism, the humbled Cagney celebrates her return to him in a news kiosk just as his brother's symphony, played by a concert orchestra, is heard over the radio. Through his pain and his vicarious attachment to his brother's success in creating music of and for the masses, he has achieved a moral triumph.

Wexley, the best of Cagney's writers (uncredited for earlier contributions to another of the star's best, THE ROARING TWENTIES), had no rival in writing the working-class intellectual of the leftish 1930s-1940s archetype that was at the heart of the Cagney character. Tending toward the maudlin, especially in the boxer's own completely forgiving and self-abnegating nature, it was at its strongest an affirmation of proletarian virtues against the temptations of capitalist corruption. Left to his own devices, the screenwriter would have preferred never to leave Broadway. The production was a landmark in another way: William Cagney served as assistant producer, a first small step toward the Cagneys' independent production company of BLOOD ON THE SUN. 101 min.

City Without Men (1943)

Puritan-B. P. Schulberg/Col. Prod: B. P. Schulberg. Dir: Sidney Salkow. Scr: W. L. River,• George Sklar,• Donald Davis. Story basis: Budd Schulberg,† Martin Berkeley.† Cast: Linda Darnell, Michael Duane, Sara Allgood, Edgar Buchanan, Leslie Brooks, Glenda Farrell, Margaret Hamilton, Sheldon Leonard

The unusual result of a failed effort by aging mogul B. P. Schulberg to establish a regular production company, this low-budget film can be seen thematically as the prison-drama version of TENDER COMRADE. Unlike that film, however, the boarding house is not a collective, the women are unhappy and no babies are born. But the women still suffer together and make a life for themselves. Darnell does little acting, but the cast around her—both the drunken and disgraced lawyer played by Edgar

Buchanan and the circle of women—make up in character acting what the plot loses along the way.

The premise is shaky. Enlisted sailor Duane is about to ship out after marrying fiancée Darnell. But when he sees suspicious activity in the harbor, he gives chase and is accused by the Japanese spies of being their employee. Sent to prison for five years, he meets the usual run of Runyonesque gangsters (especially the warm and fuzzy mobster, Sheldon Leonard), while Darnell settles into the adjoining small industrial town, where she is refused a teaching position and goes to work in a laundry with the rest of the household of women that she has made her own. After an attempted prison break and during a bang-up patriotic conclusion, Buchanan gives a fine Popular Front speech about the character of American justice. 75 min.

Clash By Night (1952)

A Fritz Lang project from play basis by Clifford Odets†, made months before his friendly testimony. It was heavily adapted by Alfred Hayes, the unblacklisted former Communist (a lyricist for "I Dreamed I Saw Joe Hill Last Night," sung most famously by Paul Robeson) and the uncredited American collaborator on Rossellini's *Paisan*. Class struggle has changed to gender struggle as the catch is down in Monterey fisheries, and Barbara Stanwyck is the returnee who sought to escape working-class life (as mistress of a prominent California politician) but failed. Robert Ryan, whose stripper wife has abandoned him, becomes her depressed and violent paramour until her dumb-but-faithful boat captain husband, played by Paul Douglas, reels her back in. The film may be most notable for its opening, which has fishing boats returning to shore, and for supporting actress Marilyn Monroe as a factory worker waking and going off to join others in a realistically depicted fish cannery assembly line. *Clash* was bitterly attacked by Catholic authorities as immoral.

Claudine (1974)

20th./Third World Cinema. Prod: Hannah Weinstein. Dir: John Berry.• Scr: Lester Pine, Tina Pine. Cast: James Earl Jones, Diahann Carroll, Eric Jones, Lawrence Hilton-Jacobs, David Kruger, Adam Wade, Yvette Curtis, Socorro Stephens

This was the last film produced by Weinstein, former theatrical attorney and aide to 1948 Progressive Party candidate Henry Wallace, and later a British TV powerhouse who brought Ring Lardner Jr,• Adrian Scott,• Ian McLellan Hunter,• Robert Lees• and others into the famed British *Adventures of Robin Hood* television series and

assorted clones of the middle-to-late 1950s. *Claudine* was also the first American film for Berry since his blacklisting and the relaunch of his film career in France. Intended to be an African American romantic/realist comedy, it succeeded in doing something new, the realistic depiction of ghetto life. But like all of the 1970s "black theme" films written and directed by ex-blacklistees (with the notable exception of SOUNDER, directed by Martin Ritt and made as a sentimental pastoral), it failed to spark a popular response. Probably white audiences weren't buying anything else. *Claudine* is also choppy and evidently under-budgeted, weighted down by a desire to do too many things at a time when even the best efforts by whites were suspect for black audiences.

And yet, the story of the Harlem garbage man and the single mother of six, meeting at her maid's job in the suburbs, has all the charm that the late Popular Front aesthetic could muster. James Earl Jones and Carroll have real dignity and even some all-too-human flaws. Conflicts and contradictions of poverty, off-the-books jobs and welfare also register. Hilton-Jacobs, as the Black Power teen of the family, is just political and surly enough. The political ending, an amiable confrontation with the cops during the wedding of the adults, seems tacked on but is the final mark of the film's commitment. Jones, who struggled through THE GREAT WHITE HOPE and had some bad experiences with left-wingers' disapproval at his stage portrayal of Paul Robeson, is at his best in this politically understated setting. 92 min., color.

The Clay Pigeon (1949)

RKO. Prod: Herman Schlom. Dir: Richard Fleischer. Scr: Carl Foreman.• Cast: Bill Williams, Barbara Hale, Richard Quine, Richard Loo, Frank Fenton, Frank Wilcox, Marya Marco, Robert Bray, Martha Hyer, Ann Doran

Foreman, in his first (if modestly) acclaimed dramatic effort after writing for the Bowery Boys, reportedly based the story on a real incident in which a former serviceman recognized his Japanese prison guard on the streets of Los Angeles. Williams, as always the innocent (as in DEADLINE AT DAWN), plays a sailor who awakens from a coma to find that he is accused of turning informer during World War II in a Pacific POW camp. The ensuing chase to prove his innocence yields few surprises but has a taut pace and strong punctuations by the talented Fleischer, with Foreman's political message delivering the final wallop. Patriotic war vets discover that some of their old comrades had collaborated with the Japanese enemy to the point of going into business with them after the war, framing or killing anyone who got in the way. The film raised the uneasy question about the relation between fascism and postwar business-as-usual. 63 min.

Cleopatra (1963)

Sidney Buchman• co-scripted (his first legit post-blacklist screen credit) this laborious Nile spectacular, which was not as bad as it was treated by critics (who could hardly sit through the $40 million, 243-minute theatrical version, later heavily cut for television). Reportedly, a crowd of 10,000 gathered in Manhattan hoping to see the premiere, thanks largely to the romantic rumors connecting the two stars, Elizabeth Taylor and Richard Burton. Taylor's Cleo is a book lover (she blocks the destruction of the world's biggest library) who forbids persecution of the Jews. She also fools around a lot, especially with Burton. The film won several Oscars, but strictly for the technicians.

Close-Up (1948)

John Bright•, his friend Max Wilk (a pioneer of television drama) and an uncredited Richard Collins•† co-scripted this film, based on a James Poe story, billed as the first to be shot entirely in Manhattan in a decade. But a mediocre plot and talky gags dominate this fantasy of a top Nazi hiding out in Gotham after the Third Reich collapses.

Cocktail Hour (1933)

A continental drama with the "white telephone" flavor of so many early Depression films, giving a risqué look at the behavior of the upper class—and a taste of gender dynamics. Scripted by Gertrude Purcell.†

Code of the Rangers (1938)

A Tim McCoy western written by Stanley Roberts† (and with music by Connie Lee•) in which the hero realizes that his brother is the real outlaw. The unusual ending has a prospective marriage.

College Scandal (1935)

A campus murder mystery by Marguerite Roberts,• with too many twists and turns around questions of fraternity-sorority misdeeds. A student is about to print rumors of a romance between the daughter of a chemistry professor and an instructor; the murders are eventually traced back to a fatal heart-attack during a fraternity hazing. Compares unfavorably to SORORITY HOUSE, treating social class

in the Greek system, but interesting as part of a sustained effort to treat the conservative wing of campus life.

Colonel Effingham's Raid (1945)

20th. Prod: Lamar Trotti. Dir: Irving Pichel.• Scr: Kathryn Scola. Novel basis: Berry Fleming, Colonel Effingham's Raid (1943). Cast: Charles Coburn, Joan Bennett, William Eythe, Donald Meek, Allyn Joslyn, Elizabeth Patterson

Pichel's World War II–era foray into progressive patriotism, adapted from a popular novel by a noted Southern writer about the sanctity of American traditions and the rush to bury the past. In this case, Southern tradition is embodied in a retired army colonel, played with great gusto by Coburn, whose extravagant acting and girth fill the screen.

The colonel has returned to the small Southern town where his distant cousin, Eythe, is a youngish journalist in an office of jaded press veterans (and one fresh idealist, perky Joan Bennett). Coburn organizes everything around himself in military fashion and launches a crusade to save Monument Square (dedicated to the lost cause of the Confederacy) from being renamed for a late, crooked politician. To halt the destruction and desecration of a historic town hall, he swings comically (but with more than a hint of constitutional heroism) back into action against the smarmy latecomers of the newest New South. "Genial is the word for this film," wrote a Times critic, and genial it is. 72 min.

Colorado Sunset (1939)

Stanley Roberts† co-scripted this early Gene Autry film for Republic, with lots of music from the Texas Troubadours, about a dairy war featuring a conspiratorial group of law officers hijacking farmers' trucks, and ownership of the radio station by a sister of the head conspirator. The use of the radio to transmit secret messages reflects the anxieties of 1939, perhaps most of all the very real prejudice of media against American intervention in the coming world war.

Colt Comrades (1943)

UA/Harry Sherman Productions. Prod: Harry Sherman. Dir: Lesley Selander. Scr: Michael Wilson.• Novel basis: Bliss Lomax, Colt Comrades (1939). Cast: William Boyd, Andy Clyde, Jay Kirby, George Reeves, Victor Jory, Robert Mitchum

This is a male, western match for TENDER COMRADE, with analogous left-wing input and consequences: the fascists at home (water thieves and swindlers) versus the antifascists (Hopalong Cassidy and the community of small ranchers). The film is notable as Wilson's first Hoppy feature and Robert Mitchum's western debut (the first ten minutes, before he's shot down), and is equally notable for Boyd's articulation of the left-wing western code, essentially "No Justice, No Peace." (When the "law" is lynch law, Hoppy pulls his two six-shooters.) In a happy ending, his laughable sidekick Clyde strikes water while drilling for oil, making it possible to break the monopoly of the bankers on cattle-raising while saving the good-spirited ranchmistress in the process. Despite such success, Hoppy and his two pals cannot themselves be reconciled to settling down to ranch life, as they had sworn to do. The weak and oppressed await them further down the trail. 67 min.

Come Closer, Folks (1936)
An oddly appealing Harold Buchman• tale (co-scripted with Lee Loeb, from a story by Aben Kandel) of a small-town hustler who turns honest and wins the girl.

Comin' Round the Mountain (1951)
The last of the Robert Lees• and Frederic I. Renaldo• Abbott and Costello films, and the least in every sense from laughs to social content. It has a Broadway singer searching for gold in hillbilly land but discovering family feuds, romance and Kentucky voodoo. The best material has Margaret Hamilton (the Wicked Witch from THE WIZARD OF OZ) in a cameo appearance as the local pin-pusher, setting in motion a sequence of love-potion comical mismatches—but it's mostly long, greasy beards, funny hats and familiar urban jokes about rural idiocy.

Coming Home (1978)
Jayne Prod/Jerome Hellman Prod. Dir: Hal Ashby. Scr: Waldo Salt,• Robert C. Jones. Cast: Jane Fonda, Jon Voight, Bruce Dern, Penelope Milford, Robert Carradine, Robert Ginty

The kind of highly awarded antiwar drama the Left liked before 1941 and after 1946, with a sensitivity toward injured vets' sexuality not seen since THE MEN. "Make Love, Not War" applied to the rehabilitation center in which paralyzed Vietnam vet Voight suffers while trying to regain self-confidence and Vietnam protester Fonda helps him, mostly as friend but also as lover. Her husband, the macho Dern, an emotionally paraplegic officer still clinging to the fantasy of victory in far-off jungles, is a

more pathetic creature in his own way than the guys in the wheelchairs.

In workshops intended to help develop the plot with the right notes, Salt interviewed hundreds of Vietnam veterans and discovered that many of their own images of their experiences had been shaped by earlier Vietnam films. Criticized for oversimplifying themes but successful in conveying the complex emotions of the time, the film was an unqualified success. The sixties music soundtrack made the same point in a different way. The film won Oscars for best actor and actress and best screenplay, and garnered nominations galore in other categories, in the United States and abroad. Unfortunately, a planned documentary slated to use the interview footage with returned veterans fell through, and with it a major opportunity for Fonda to add a major producer credit to her artistic antiwar work. 126 min., color.

Confessions of a Nazi Spy (1939)
First National Pictures/WB. Exec. Prod: Hal Wallis, Jack Warner. Assoc. Prod: Robert Lord. Dir: Anatole Litvak. Scr: John Wexley.• Cast: Edward G. Robinson, Frances Lederer, George Sanders, Paul Lukas, Henry O'Neill, Dorothy Tree,• Lya Lys, Grace Stafford, James Stephenson, Hedwiga Reicher, Sig Ruman, Lionel Royce

One of those antifascist films destined to give future blacklisted screenwriters qualms that they had once boosted the FBI and pointed toward internal subversion as a pressing problem for American society. Of course, they saw things differently in the late 1930s, when Confessions, along with Juarez, marked what was considered by the Hollywood Left a step forward toward relevance. But this tale of treachery used too broad a brush. Dealing fast and loose with isolationist sentiment, Confessions seemed by implication to link all popular resistance to war with sympathy for the German-American Bund. It also helped to inspire an early congressional inquiry into Hollywood in 1939, when Southerners who actually were sympathetic to the German cause hauled up Warner execs for questioning about making pro-war propaganda. (The Warners fought back—this time.) Nazi sympathizers in Milwaukee actually burned down a theater that played the film, and two Polish exhibitors were murdered in their own theaters. The New York premier opened with security guards. But it was only a foretaste of much more sophisticated patriotic wartime cinema to come from the Hollywood Left.

Former Hungarian matinee idol Lukas plays the dentist who runs an espionage network with the help of Nazi officials in Washington, including (with suspiciously shaven head) Sanders. O'Neill is the German Army deserter who wants to make a homeland reputation and a living for himself but stumbles into the hands of U.S. officials and gives them the opportunity to shut down the network. FBI man Robinson is both deft and alert in pursuit. The most powerful moments in the film purport to show Bund meetings whipping up hatred for democratic values, while the most pathetic suggest that America is virtually unarmed against foreign subversion. The question of the fate of Jews in Germany is largely suppressed or sublimated in the process, although references of Nazi sympathizers to "those people" are unmistakable. 104 min.

Conrack (1974)

Martin Ritt• directed this overly long and disappointing adaptation of a Pat Conroy novel about a rebellious Southerner's attempt in the 1960s to bring education to black kids in South Carolina. Following THE GREAT WHITE HOPE and *Sounder*, it was the director's last effort to confront the issues of racism, through the experience of a teacher embracing the lives of virtually illiterate black children on Daufuskie Island, off the South Carolina coast, in 1969. Irving Ravetch† and Harriet Frank, Jr., who wrote and co-produced the film with Ritt, fell back upon the "education" formula in *The Blackboard Jungle* (1955) and others, by now badly outdated.

Conspiracy (1939)

RKO. Prod: Cliff Reid. Dir: Lew Landers. Scr: Jerome Chodorov.• Story: John P. McCarthy, Faith Thomas. Cast: Allan Lane, Linda Hayes, Robert Barrat, Charley Foy, Lionel Royce, J. Farrell MacDonald, Lester Matthews, Henry Brandon

A Central American exotic film with antifascist and anti-imperialist overtones, it has seaman Lane discovering contraband cargo en route to a military dictator. Remarkably, he eludes state security forces and makes his way to Hayes, the beautiful leader of the people's revolutionaries. Her comrades order him killed, but he slips away. Lots of adventures include gun battles, a run for the border, and a lover's choice (hers) between romance and guiding her people in their revolt against oppression. 58 min.

Conspiracy of Hearts (1960)

This British-made World War II drama with nuns protecting Jewish children in Italy was written by Adrian Scott• in a failed and strictly forgettable attempt to reestablish his film credentials.

Copacabana (1947)

Beacon Prod. Prod: Sam Coslow. Dir: Alfred E. Green. Scr: László Vadnay, Howard Harris, Allen Boretz.• Story basis: László Vadnay. Cast: Groucho Marx, Carmen Miranda, Steve Cochran, Gloria Jean, Andy Russell, Earl Wilson

Groucho without the other Marx Brothers is like a beer without the head (and not up to the Groucho of fifties television). His match-up with Carmen Miranda is nonetheless suitably bizarre. She plays the talented half of an unsuccessful show biz act as well as a long-standing, increasingly frustrated fiancée. At the end of their financial rope, Groucho sees his real future as her agent. He doubles the fun and confusion by booking her twice, once as a Latin American firecracker and simultaneously as "Fifi" (in a veil). Somehow, no one notices the similarity. Meanwhile, Groucho plots steadily, usually with catastrophic results. The plot is just thick enough to hold together the succession of production numbers, some of them Miranda-style campiness, one or two with some actual *echt* Groucho. 92 min.

Cornered (1945)

RKO. Prod: Adrian Scott.• Dir: Edward Dmytryk.•† Scr: John Paxton, Ben Hecht (uncredited). Story and Adaptation: John Wexley.• Cast: Dick Powell, Walter Slezak, Micheline Cheirel, Nana Vale, Morris Carnovsky,• Edgar Barrier, Luther Adler,• Nestor Paiva

This film is historically important to the history of HUAC hearings and the deeper lore of McCarthyism because this was the second RKO feature for the production team of Scott, Dmytryk and Paxton after the wildly successful MURDER, MY SWEET. Dmytryk later claimed that, on behalf of the Communist Party, Wexley had exaggerated Nazi influence in wartime Argentina (the film's setting). There seems little doubt that Wexley transformed a nonpolitical Hecht screenplay treatment (an American tracks his brother's murderer to the West Indies) into what Wexley intended to be a tense antifascist melodrama along the lines of CASABLANCA. What Dmytryk failed to mention, however, was the extraordinary pressure the team came under from representatives of Nelson Rockefeller, the U.S. government and RKO brass well before shooting started; they wanted to scrap any but the most elusive references to Argentina's antifascist resistance and to the fact that its Nazi problem ran a good deal deeper than a group of sympathizers in elite social circles. In spring 1945, rather late in the game as far as the war was concerned, Argentina broke off diplomatic relations with an all-but-defeated Germany, and the U.S. government wanted to save its new ally from embarrassment.

RKO was so concerned about Dmytryk getting the message that they packed him off to Argentina for a personal tour. It was all a measure of how quickly the left-wing cinematic heroes of 1943 and 1944 had become the goats of 1945 as World War II wound down and their views once again became inconvenient. Most of the internal correspondence on these matters was kept by producer Scott, but only recently discovered among his papers. Dmytryk waited until Scott was dead to give his highly questionable account of the making of this film.

The effect of the outside pressure on the film was perhaps predictable. Although reviews were generally good, judging it to have just the right exotic suspense, even the most appreciative critics thought the movie long and convoluted. Powell, a Canadian war hero fresh from a German POW camp seeking the conspirators behind his French wife's murder, knows only that a Vichy official betrayed her. He follows the official's trail to Switzerland and then to Buenos Aires. There he discovers a nest of Nazi sympathizers among the social set. He fails to recognize in this set an improbable and still more secret antifascist ring dedicated to locating war criminals and collaborators—the organization Wexley had originally cast as an "underground" (i.e., communist) organization, and definitely not in the upper crust. Powell is captured and beaten and lapses into one of the "blackouts" he suffered as a POW (recalling for most fans a famed scene in MURDER, MY SWEET), and hardly knows whether he has at last found his revenge. Lots of noir action and tough talk present Powell at his Bogartian best, the action heightened by the lack of a love interest, now replaced by a compelling desire to straighten out the past. 102 min.

Cotton Queen (1937)

Directed by Bernard Vorhaus• in his British period, it is notable not for its romantic plot but for its sequences of Midland cotton workers at the factory and at play. Rare documentary footage was incorporated to cut costs and give a flavor of blue-collar life in the Depression years.

Counsel for Crime (1937)

Dull legal drama with occasional hints of flaws, or worse, in the legal system. A senator's adopted son and assistant D.A. prosecutes his own (biological) father in a crooked legal firm. Co-scripted by Harold Buchman.• Favorite tough guy Marc Lawrence† has a supporting role.

Counter-Attack (1945)

Col. Prod: Unknown. Dir: Zoltan Korda. Scr: John Howard Lawson.• Play basis: Janet• and Philip Stevenson,• *Counter-Attack* (1943), based on Russian play *Pobyeda* (n.d.), by Ilya Vershinin and Mikhail Ruderman. Cast: Paul Muni, Marguerite Chapman, Larry Parks,† Harro Meller, Roman Bohnen,• George Macready, Erik Rolf, Ludwig Donath,• Rudolph Anders, Philip Van Zandt

An extraordinary experiment in film drama, apparently lost to audiences after World War II but now recovered if still largely unavailable. Along with BLOCK-ADE, ACTION IN THE NORTH ATLANTIC and SAHARA, it forms part of expressionist playwright Lawson's cycle of social realism on film. Based indirectly on a contemporary Russian drama (and an unsuccessful theatrical production in the United States), it traces the Red Army struggle against German occupation in 1942, as engineers secretly build an underwater bridge facing German lines for Russian tanks to counterattack. Of the small forward group that seeks to spy on enemy positions, only Russians Muni and Chapman survive. They find themselves guarding seven German soldiers, including an officer, with only one gun. Desperately awaiting the arrival of their troops, the two fight sleep and carry on conversations with the prisoners, who reveal themselves as various German types—one instinctively antifascist (logically played by Donath and happy to defect), others who share their commanders' racist views toward non-Aryans. Worst of all, predictably, is the murderous officer who cockily insists that Germany will triumph. Muni's loyal German shepherd plays a key role. One of Muni's best. 90 min.

The Courageous Dr. Christian (1940)

A less notable Jean Hersholt feature in the "Dr. Christian" series, this one directed by Bernard Vorhaus• and written by the team of Ring Lardner, Jr.• and Ian McClellan Hunter.• Appalled by the misery of the homeless, the doc demands that the city council build decent public housing, but to no avail. An epidemic of spinal meningitis finally compels a quarantine of "Squatterstown" and the town's conscience is awakened.

Cowboy (1958)

Adaptation of a Frank Harris novel starring Glenn Ford and Jack Lemon, written by Dalton Trumbo• under a front. Lemon learns the lesson that to grow up to be a real American cowboy you have to move to the left and be tough enough to stand up to the bosses. Obvious if not unpleasant melodrama leavened with a few comic moments.

Cowboy and the Señorita (1944)

First film that paired "King of the Cowboys" Roy Rogers with real-life characterful divorcée and teenage single mother Dale Evans, it was written by Gordon Kahn,• a Rogers filmscripting regular. Plot is the usual western stuff with Rogers falsely accused of a crime, Evans engaged to a conniving businessman before the truth is known, Fuzzy Knight thrown in for laughs and the Sons of the Pioneers yodeling.

Crack in the World (1965)

A mediocre sci-fi eco-warning adventure co-scripted by Julian Zimet• about the explosion of a bomb that cracks the layer surrounding the magma at the earth's center. Made on the cheap in Spain, with special effects the real star of the subfeature.

Crack-Up (1946)

RKO. Prod: Jack T. Gross.• Asst. Prod: Sam P. Engel. Dir: Irving Reis. Scr: John Paxton, Ben Bengal,• Ray Spencer.• Story basis: Fredric Brown, "Madman's Holiday" (Detective Story, July 1943). Cast: Pat O'Brien, Claire Trevor, Herbert Marshall, Wallace Ford, Erskine Sanford, Mary Ware

A strange and often wonderful film with many odd connections to the blacklist, Crack-Up is a sophisticated attack on the pretensions of high modernism by expert practitioners of low modernism, in this case writers of a noir thriller. The film determinedly exposes snob values in art, abstract expressionism and phony surrealism while reflecting on themes of the unconscious (in true surrealist spirit).

The writing talent was key. The most prominent was Paxton, a friend and frequent collaborator of Edward Dmytryk•† and Adrian Scott,• who for reasons never determined was not blacklisted. Party members Bengal and Spencer, on the other hand, were thrown out of Hollywood before they could get established. Bengal was a celebrated radical playwright with the New Theatre League in New York before heading for the west and oblivion, while Spencer joined the circle of exiled blacklistees in Mexico City, where he is mostly remembered for eventually marrying the widow of novelist B. Traven. The screenplay is based on an obscure story by Brown, an eccentric Milwaukee newspaper proofreader who emerged during the 1940s as a major crime and science-fiction pulp novelist.

The film opens on an apparently crazed man crashing through the doors of the "Manhattan Museum" with a wild tale about surviving a train wreck. A flashback begins with a lecture in the museum by this same man, a populist art critic (O'Brien) who likes to bait aesthetes like his wealthy bosses, the museum patrons. During the lecture, O'Brien defends popular tastes in art and then ridicules a painting that is clearly a satire on the work of Salvador Dali, who was always in bad odor on the Left for the commercial quality of his painting and later for informing on fellow Spaniard and surrealist filmmaker Luis Buñuel. (The incident cost Buñel a museum job and threw him into penury, according to his memoirs.) In the same scene, a painter starts raving that O'Brien is hostile to "abstract emotional values," and the critic concedes as much. This also anticipates later actual events: during the Cold War, U.S. intelligence agencies funded exhibitions and galleries devoted to abstract expressionism.

Once this pointed material is out of the way, the story settles into a proper whodunit, with cops and art critics on the trail of a wealthy art collector and thief who uses forgeries to cover his crimes. Part of the joke is that the elitist thief, who justifies his mania for acquisition by saying, "museums cater to dolts," has such lower-middle-class tastes (Gainsborough and Dürer). Red herrings are everywhere as the body count rises and O'Brien comes to doubt his own sanity, then discovers that he has been manipulated by the wartime discovery of sodium pentathol, here called "narco-synthesis," which "puts honesty on a scientific basis." In the wrong hands, it also puts corruption on a scientific basis, the film warns, in a characteristic note of anxiety about the peacetime uses of technological breakthroughs made for war. A rare and inspired movie. 93 min.

Craig's Wife (1936)

Col. Assoc Prod: Edward Chodorov.• Dir: Dorothy Arzner. Scr: Mary C. McCall, Jr. (script contribution by Edward Chodorov, uncredited). Play basis: George Kelly, Craig's Wife (1928). Cast: Rosalind Russell, John Boles, Billie Burke, Jane Darwell, Dorothy Wilson, Alma Druger, Thomas Mitchell

An important film, rare for its period: written, directed by and starring women, albeit in the vein of perverse strength of character. Based on a prize-winning 1920s play, it was first a silent feature, and finally remade in 1950 as HARRIET CRAIG (with Anne Froelick• co-scripting). Of the three equally soapy versions, this is emphatically the best, in no small part because of Russell's presence (the part ensured her rise as a major unglamorous woman star, with a character too overpowering to be considered feminine), but also because of the slant given to the plot.

A woman uncomfortable in a man's world has determined to make herself comfortable on her own terms, in her own home. To that end, she easily sacrifices sociality (she virtually refuses entry to any nonrelative and worries about any water stain or dirt from the presence of her in-laws), brushes aside sisterhood (regarding almost all women as potential rivals) and is repelled by the idea of having children. Her husband, the blindly adoring John Boles (a turnabout from his classic role as the cad in *Back Streets*), awakens only slowly and only after her actions turn murderous. And yet, while Russell is constantly fussy and self-involved, she exhibits an almost inadvertent pathos, the desperate response of a woman who cannot satisfy herself with the usual wifely consolations. The left-wing magazine *New Masses* accurately complained that in the stage version she was poor and had every reason to obsess about her home; the middle-class movie version made her just an obsessive. 73 min.

Crazy House (1943)

Universal. Assoc. Prod: Eric C. Kenton. Dir: Edward F. Cline. Scr: Robert Lees,• Frederic I. Rinaldo.• Cast: Ole Olsen, Chic Johnson, Cass Daley, Patric Knowles, Martha O'Driscoll, Thomas Gomez, Percy Kilbride, Richard Lane, Andrew Tombes, Hans Conried, Billy Gilbert

One of Lees and Rinaldo's best scripts and certainly the finest of the three Olsen and Johnson filmed farces because of the effectivness of the in-house satire aimed at the film industry. The antic pair arrive in Hollywood and stage a madcap parade to call the studio's attention to their return to filmmaking, then quickly learn that the studio is all too aware and that they have been barred from the lot as a menace. They have themselves shot from a cannon over the studio walls, and a secretary greets them calmly—until she finds out who they really are, then jumps into her desk, which swallows her whole! And so it goes as the two make a film about their own filmmaking adventures.

Dance numbers and cameos fill up much time, and the theft of the film print (while an audience is at a decisive preview) compels the pair to put on one of their usual "Hellzapoppin" shows with lots of surrealistic imagery. One of the memorable gags is the name of the studio: Miracle Pictures. The sign says it all: "If it's a good picture, it's a Miracle." 80 min.

Crime by Night (1944)

Jane Wyman, playing the Girl Friday to a private dick,

headed a lesser cast of sorry figures in a spy-and-murder story co-scripted by Richard Weil.•

Crime Wave (1954)

Late and inexpensively produced noir written under a pseudonym by Bernard Gordon• is the screenwriter's moodiest and perhaps his best film. It has Sterling Hayden† (the bitterly regretful friendly witness) and future tough guy Charles Bronson in a mob story of gang remnants going under. Realistic street scenes and interiors of working-class L.A., juke box jazz, hash house regulars—everything but the absence of non-whites gives superior flavor and pointed action.

The Criminal (The Concrete Jungle, 1960)

Anglo-Amalgamated Productions/Fanfare. Prod: Jack Greenwood. Dir. Joseph Losey.• Scr: Alun Owen. Story basis: Jimmy Sangster. Cast: Stanley Baker, Sam Wanamaker,• Grégoire Aslan, Margit Saad, Jill Bennett, Rupert Davies, Patrick Magee

Losey closed out the 1950s with the last of his English films that were destined to remain obscure. Like Losey's EVE, *The Criminal* starred a riveting performance by Baker and was mutilated in the editing room when the distributors insisted that 35 minutes be cut from the original 130 (and then on cutting another 11 minutes for its U.S. release). As with *Eve*, film buffs can only wonder at what great moments were lost along with the minor scenes whose excision has led to confusion on a few important plot points. What is left, however, is a story that shows a highly original director trying to wriggle out of the commercial corset that had confined him for a decade (the aptly named Anglo-Amalgamated Productions never aimed higher than the *Carry On, Nurse* series).

Baker plays a tough but honorable and independent criminal in the manner of Burt Lancaster in I WALK ALONE. After his release from a stretch in prison he finds his old network of thieves taken over by a new class of corporate gangsters, experts at the deal, the set-up and the double-cross. Wanamaker, by then probably the most prominent blacklisted American actor in England, plays the type with particular relish, protesting that it's all just "business." When Baker organizes the theft of £40,000 from a racetrack and then stashes it to let it cool off, he is betrayed and sent back to prison, where he becomes the object of an elaborate conspiracy to force him to reveal where he hid the loot. But the focus is never on the caper. This is Losey's FORCE OF EVIL, where the long arm of business reaches out from the boardroom into social relations of every kind, turning friendship, loyalty and love into small change. 97 min.

The Crimson Canary (1945)

One of Henry Blankfort's• better efforts, starring Noah Beery, Jr. (later of *The Rockford Files*) with then-left folksinger Josh White (later a friendly witness) and Coleman Hawkins and Oscar Pettiford making a rare appearance as musicians on their way from an obscure nightclub in San Francisco to bigger venues.

Cross Creek (1983)

EMI. Prod: Robert Radnitz. Dir: Martin Ritt.• Scr: Darlene Young. Novel basis: Marjorie Kinnan Rawlings, *Cross Creek* (1942). Cast: Mary Steenburgen, Peter Coyote, Alfre Woodard, Rip Torn, Dana Hill

Gender classic of Martin Ritt, and one of Steenburgen's most enduring performances, based on the life of local-color novelist Rawlings, as she resettles in the Florida Everglades and there comes across the oddball characters (eventually including real-life Hollywood progressives Coyote and Torn) who reset her agenda and provide her the material to become a literary success. Treated badly by some critics for its nondramatic plot of a woman relearning (after a successful career as a journalist) to write the fiction that she seeks to create, it drags at points, but the lush photography and Ritt's sympathetic direction, showing Rawlings/Steenburgen's growing into the surroundings, makes the film memorable and at some points extraordinarily touching. 122 min., color.

The Cross of Lorraine (1943)

MGM. Prod: Edwin H. Knopf. Dir: Tay Garnett. Scr: Michael Kanin, Ring Lardner, Jr.• (Ian McLellan Hunter,• uncredited script contribution), Alexander Esway, Robert Hardy Andrews. Novel basis: Hans Habe, *A Thousand Shall Fall* (1921). Cast: Jean-Pierre Aumont, Gene Kelly, Cedric Hardwicke, Richard Whorf, Peter Lorre, Hume Cronyn, Joseph Calleia

One of the most politically articulate war films made by Americans about non-Americans. The repeated use of "The Marseilles," rousing the internationalist as well as nationalist subtextual messages of the French Revolution, suggests that something more than victory over Nazism is at stake. As the title reveals, even religious imagery will be put to good purpose.

The film opens on French boys of various types running off to fight the German invaders, including a Chilean antifascist (read: communist), a secret collaborationist and the usual run of rural and urban, middle- and working-class folks. Prepared to die in the struggle, they are betrayed by their Vichy government.

They find themselves in a German prison camp, and the story revolves in some ways around the traitor among them, brilliantly played by Lorre. Great cruelty ensues (the Nazis "amputate the enthusiasm" of one resister by mutilating him), and the possibility of escape opens with inside information that the Germans themselves regularly fake a mission across the border to France to acquire contraband goods. The escapees learn from a neighborhood boy that the Americans have entered Africa, and now the resistance will begin in earnest. Villagers willfully set themselves upon destruction of their collective hearth: "It takes courage to burn our homes . . . let us scorch the earth, they will find nothing but ashes when they get here." As townsfolk march into the mountains we hear the Marseilles, and sunshine gathers behind them: an unforgettable ending. The National Board of Review gave Hardwicke and Garnett special awards based on several films including *The Cross of Lorraine. The New York Times* called it "heartening." 90 min.

Crossfire (1947)

RKO. Prod: Adrian Scott.• Dir: Edward Dmytryk.•† Scr: John Paxton. Novel basis: Richard Brooks, *The Brick Foxhole* (1945). Cast: Robert Young, Robert Mitchum, Robert Ryan, Gloria Grahame, Sam Levene, Jacqueline White, Steve Brodie, Lex Barker

The third collaboration between producer Scott, Dmytryk and Paxton (after MURDER, MY SWEET and CORNERED) and the last before the blacklist, this proved a favorite film for the Congressional investigating committees to attack. The story occupies a narrative landscape somewhere between film noir and a "message" film. Unlike its predecessors, which had smaller budgets but were politically much sharper, this one was expensive and high-profile but highly successful, because it cashed in on the mini-wave of films about anti-Semitism. It also showed Ryan at the peak of his considerable acting skills as a twisted creature who is obsessed with finding Jews to attack.

One of four army buddies on leave, Ryan beats a sympathetic and philosophical Jewish civilian (Levene) to death out of pure malice. Most of the film follows the investigation, including false leads and another murder by Ryan. The plot foregrounds Young as the police detective who makes democratic pronouncements, while the fair-minded GI Mitchum eventually sees the necessity of bringing a psychotic to justice.

This may be the weakest of the various collaborations of the progressive production group because the film lacks Dick Powell as the noir lead and because avuncular Young smoking a pipe seems two-thirds of the way to *Father Knows Best*. Mostly, though, the film requires a harder edge to escape being maudlin. Grahame, Young, Dmytryk, Scott and Paxton all received Academy Award nominations. 86 min.

The Crowd Roars (1932)
Lesser John Bright● collaboration with Jimmy Cagney, shot and written at the Indianapolis 500 (supporting actor William Arnold was actually winner of the 1930 race), according to Bright from true stories about drivers and their romances, but badly cut at director Howard Hawks's insistence.

Cry of Battle (1963)
Blacklist-return action-epic with some of the Left's favorite actors. Directed by Irving Lerner● and scripted by Bernard Gordon● from the war novel *Fortress in the Rice,* with a cast that featured Van Heflin and Rita Moreno (including a memorable nude bathing scene), it depicted heroic Filipinos leading the guerilla resistance movement against the Japanese and preparing the way for the final Allied victory.

Cry, the Beloved Country (1951)
London Film Prod. Prod: Zoltan Korda, Alan Paton. Dir: Zoltan Korda. Scr: Alan Paton (fronting for John Howard Lawson●). Novel basis: Alan Paton, *Cry, the Beloved Country* (1948). Cast: Canada Lee, Charles Carson, Sidney Poitier, Geoffrey Keen, Reginald Ngeabo, Joyce Carey

Extraordinary film banned for more than 40 years in South Africa while forgotten in the United Kingdom and the United States, then remade lavishly in 1995 for James Earl Jones. This was Lawson's last major dramatic film and also the last for Canada Lee, under severe pressure from HUAC and soon to be dead of a stroke. Shot stunningly on location in African shanty towns and closely following Apartheid-opponent (and political moderate) Paton's novel, it traces the story of a country minister who comes to Johannesburg in search of his son. Once there, he encounters in swift succession a daughter who has become a prostitute, a brother with no moral

responsibility for family and the trail of a son who has been sent to prison for a petty offense and while on parole has murdered a noted white reformer. The racial and economic system shows the victims trapped into something worse than submission: a cowed silence and self-victimization. The plot hangs on Lee's encounter with the farmer and typical Boer racist who is the father of the murder victim. Too liberal and Christian for many tastes, with great sympathy not only for the ministers who assist Lee (Poitier, in his first important film role, is strong) but also for police official Keen and other well-meaning officials within the system. Touching and at points almost overwhelming. 103 min.

Curse of the Werewolf (1961)
Better-than-average Hammer Films exploitation feature was only nominally based on Guy Endore's● masterpiece, *The Werewolf of Paris* (1931). In the original, the action was set in the context of the Paris Commune of 1870-1871 and the siege of the city. What remains is Endore's notion of lycanthropy as a hereditary disorder precipitated by social conditions, brought on here by aristocratic cruelty. The genius of the novel lay in diminishing the mere horror of lycanthropic murder when surrounded by the larger horrors of war.

Curtain Call (1940)
A Dalton Trumbo● backstage satire about producers who buy a bad play from an innocent in order to break a contract. Barely diverting but, amazingly, boffo at the box office; its plot inspired *Footlight Fever* and, perhaps, Mel Brooks' *The Producers* as well.

Custer of the West (1967)
Revisionist western made in Cinerama and written by Bernard Gordon● and Julian Zimet,● it somewhat ironically traces the life of the general through 140 adventure-packed minutes. Filmed in Spain with Spaniards as Indians. This may be the first film to ridicule Custer's inflated view of himself.

Cynthia (1947)
Vehicle for teen star Elizabeth Taylor, co-scripted by Harold Buchman,● was described by Bosley Crowther as "gooey candy," a tale of the emergence of a dewey-eyed teenager into adolescence and puppy love with Jimmy Lydon, veteran of the Henry Aldrich films. Future senator

George Murphy plays the fearful father who does *not* know best.

Cyrano de Bergerac (1950)

UA/Stanley Kramer Productions. Prod: Stanley Kramer. Dir: Michael Gordon.•† Scr: Carl Foreman.• Play basis: Edmond Rostand, *Cyrano de Bergerac* (1897). Cast: José Ferrer,† Mala Powers, William Prince, Morris Carnovsky,• Ralph Clanton, Lloyd Corrigan, Virginia Farmer,† Edgar Barrier, Elena Verdugo

A much-hailed drama inspired by the life of the seventeenth-century author, already filmed in several low-budget French and Italian versions. Alexander Korda had intended a British production with Orson Welles, but when that fell apart, Kramer bought the rights (including a script by Ben Hecht), then ordered a new start by Foreman.

The familiar story has the richly beschnozzled poet, secretly in love with his cousin, use a handsome friend as a front. The background that is often forgotten is the French-Spanish military conflict, which ups the ante. Later, with the pal dead for 14 years, Cyrano visits Roxanne in her convent and she realizes his true identity only after he has been mortally wounded in revenge for his satirical literary jabs. The script is more than serviceable for the extra-long and often melodramatic plot, and the direction may be Gordon's best dramatic work. Ferrer, who renounced the Left in friendly testimony, won an Oscar in this, his best film role. Steve Martin did a bloodless comic version in 1987, and Kramer planned but never actually made an all-black version. Ferrer starred once more in a 1963 British remake. 112 min.

D

Dakota (1945)
Carl Foreman• wrote the story basis for this western set piece suited to John Wayne. As son-in-law of a Chicago capitalist, he battles Ward Bond, the land swindler of the unsettled territory, and defends the wheat farmers for the economic boom ahead against the incoming railroad lines. The wheat field arson scene is most memorable. Above-average oater based on a novel by Edna Ferber.

The Daltons Ride Again (1945)
Henry Blankfort• provided some dialogue for this pictur-esque and well-cast borderline B-western with the famil-iar plot of the brothers on the loose, resembling (as in many other films) the legendary Jesse James gang. Land is grabbed by the railroad barons and blamed on the brothers until they prove their innocence.

Dancing Feet (1936)
The old plot of the millionaire's daughter (here, a grand-daughter) and the ambitious proletarian who loves her. She's mistaken by the bellboy for a dance-hall hostess and turns a musical show into a big hit. Scripted by Jerome Chodorov.•

Dancing on a Dime (1940)
Para. Prod: A. M. Botsford. Dir: Joseph Santley. Scr: Maurice Rapf,• Allen Rivkin. Story: Max Rolpé, Jan Lustig. Cast: Grace McDonald, Robert Paige, Peter Lind Hayes, Eddie Quillan, Frank Jenks, Virginia Dale, William Frawley, Carol Adams, Lillian Cornell

Peppy backstage musical treats a Works Progress Administration/Federal Theater troupe about to go under due to cuts in Congress (caused, in real life, by a conservative backlash against New Deal programs, accompanied by considerable red-baiting and the earliest Hollywood "investigations"). A group of boys formerly rehearsing for an abandoned WPA show move into a theater and there discover a roll of counterfeit cash that enables them to pay bills until opening night. Only a great deal of fast footwork (both literally and figuratively) allows them to save the show and save themselves from jail. Kindly New Deal administrator Frawley makes pro-duction possible. 74 min.

The Dancing Pirate (1936)
Pioneer Pictures. Prod: John Speaks. Dir: Lloyd Corrigan. Scr: Ray Harris, Francis Edward Faragoh.• Story basis: Emma-Lindsay Squier, "The Dancing Pirate," *Colliers* (1927). Adaptation: Jack Warner, Brois Ingster. Cast: Charles Collins, Frank Morgan, Steffi Duna, Luis Alberni, Victor Varconi, Jack La Rue, Alma Real, William V. Mong, Mitchell Lewis, Julian Rivero, John Eberts

Touted as the first color "dancing musical," with an original script by Robert Benchley displaced in the pro-cess, just two original songs by Rogers and Hart remain. A fascinating if often confused comedy-fantasy, it finds Collins first teaching waltz lessons to young women (helping them become "modern"—willing for a male embrace in public) in 1820 Boston. Kidnapped by pirates(!) in Boston to work on their ship, he escapes to the coast of then-Spanish California, where he is treated as a spy and scheduled for execution—until the daughter of the *alcalde* hears that he is a dance teacher. In one of the first of the film's delightful scenes, the women of the village save him from the hangman at the last moment; a bit later, as the daughter (his sweetheart) faces marriage with a villain, our hero assists a successful rebellion of oppressed but basically friendly Indians, who in happy triumph dance most amazingly à la Busby Berkeley. The subtext is rich in oddities but the film flopped and set back color production for years. 85 min., color.

Dangerous Corner (1934)
One of co-scripter and early Hollywood Communist Party member Madeleine Ruthven's• few credits, a play-based caper film with a trick double ending that re-introduces the romance of the story and produces a different out-come—a subtlety more or less ruined when the studio cut the running time.

The Daring Young Man (1942)
Col. Prod: Robert Sparks. Dir: Frank R. Strayer. Scr: Karen DeWolf,• Connie Lee.• Cast: Joe E. Brown, Marguerite Chapman, William Wright, Roger Clark, Lloyd Bridges†

Forgotten gem from the writer-director team of the *Blondie* series, starring the famed Big Mouth actor of the era in a dual role of sharpie grandmother (with lines like, "You'll never know the pleasure of putting a slug into a pay phone") and her naive grandson. Young Brown, a shy repair shop owner, has his building blown up around him by Nazi saboteurs, including a young Bridges. Encouraged by radio reporters who want to make him into a personal example of red-blooded patriotic response, he tries to enlist in every armed service and is turned down by each as physically unfit. An extremely silly plot follows with Brown as instant bowling sensation whose ball is guided by radio controls (guided by Nazis agents, now using him as their inadvertent agent). Best scenes: grandma taking over the old folks home with loaded dice, and a politically awakened Brown in a Douglas Fairbanks parody, swinging from chandeliers. Worst scene: Brown in blackface. But DeWolf and Lee dialogue is lively and Brown possesses real charm as the little man. His granny impersonation perfectly foreshadows Jonathan Winters in all the quirky gendered nuance. 73 min.

The Dark Angel (1935)

Hackish Lillian Hellman,• co-scripted with Mordaunt Shairp; a stiff-upper-lip drama of two World War I flyers and the girls they both love. 105 min.

Dark City (1950)

A script contribution by Leonardo Bercovici• helped lift this noir into a minor classic—a property originally purchased by Hal Wallis for Burt Lancaster, who would have been perfect for the picture. Hopelessness, weirdness, nightmare presences abound, as Charleton Heston plays the role of a hopeless gambler wandering through life. 98 min.

The Dark Corner (1946)

20th. Prod: Fred Kohlmar. Dir: Henry Hathaway. Scr: Jay Dratler, Bernard C. Schoenfeld.† Story basis: Leo Rosten (*Good Housekeeping*, July-Aug. 1945). Cast: Lucille Ball, Mark Stevens, Clifton Webb, William Bendix, Kurt Kreuger, Cathy Downs, Reed Hadley, Constance Collier

Well-regarded melodrama about a private eye (Stevens) who falls victim to a murder frame. Not long from jail, he tries to resume a normal life as a private dick, with Ball as his lively, sharp-tongued secretary (and daughter of a big-league umpire). But he finds himself unable (as society at large seemed unable) to escape the past, in the person of a former partner (Krueger), up to old swindling tricks. Intermittently depressed at the hand

of fate, Stevens offers up the film's most famous line to Ball, "I feel all dead inside. I'm backed up in a dark corner and I don't know who's hitting me." Clever cinematography has his office dark, Bendix glittering horribly in his identity of "White Suit," a sadistic hit man named for his outfit, and considered by some later critics a stand-in for the repressed gay type. Some wonderful city shots (including a carni-style entertainment gallery at night) and lots of existential action. 99 min.

The Dark Past (1948)

Another Freudian spinoff with dream sequences written by Michael Blankfort† and based on the 1939 film hit *Blind Alley*, in turn based on a play by James Warwick. An escaped prisoner holds family hostage but the shrink he kidnaps (Lee J. Cobb†) convinces him that his unhappy childhood holds the secret. 75 min.

Day of Triumph (1954)

This extraordinarily obscure, low-budget final film of Irving Pichel• narrates the story of the Zadokites, a communistic Christian sect that arises after the death of the Savior, proclaims the revolution, and is repressed violently by the Romans. Lee J. Cobb† played Zadok, the prophet-leader, Joanne Dru played Mary Magdalene, and Robert Wilson played Jesus, with the young Mike Conners as a disciple.

Dead End (1937)

Goldwyn. Prod: Samuel Goldwyn. Dir. William Wyler. Scr: Lillian Hellman.• Play basis: Sidney Kingsley, *Dead End* (1936). Cast: Humphrey Bogart, Joel McCrea, Sylvia Sidney, Wendy Barrie, Claire Trevor, Marjorie Main, Leo Gorcey.

Adaptation of Kingsley's socially conscious Broadway hit is set near the East River, where the rich have moved into luxury apartments towering over the slums. The upstairs/downstairs setting finds the wealthy gangster (and former neighborhood kid) Bogart wanted by the law, but comes back to find his mother and his childhood sweetheart. Menially employed architect is McCrea torn between a neighborhood girl and a once-wealthy lass from the heights of pre-Depression affluence. Several of the future BOWERY BOYS, led by Leo Gorcey, are seen for the first time here, as neighborhood ruffians with drunk or absent fathers and no prospects of escaping their environment. The adults have hardly more options, and it is here that Hellman (or Kingsley) makes crypto-political hay. We learn that McCrea's girl Wendy Barrie is on strike, and

Bogart's girl is dying of syphilis (in contrast to the play, the film suggests unconvincingly, with a cough, that it is tuberculosis) while his destroyed mother disowns him. The kids and McCrea grope for a second chance. 93 min.

Deadline at Dawn (1946)

RKO. Prod: Adrian Scott.• Dir: Harold Clurman. Scr: Clifford Odets.† Story basis: William Irish (Cornell Woolrich). Cast: Susan Hayward, Paul Lukacs, Bill Williams, Joseph Calleia, Osa Massen

Boyish sailor Williams, out on a 24-hour leave, is caught up in a murder case after he accidentally takes money from a woman he picked up while drunk. In a few hours, he will be due back on ship; the night unfolds in what is taken to be a typical blue-collar Manhattan, Bronx or Brooklyn neighborhood. A series of workaday characters, most of them benevolent proletarians, respond with interesting reflections about their lives. At dawn, the morose but articulate cabbie Lukacs ("At best, I am not a happy man"), who drives Williams and a laconic Hayward wherever they wish, untangles the mystery and philosophizes to Hayward, "The terror and horror you feel are from being alive." Deserted by his wife years earlier for another man, he committed the murder himself to protect his daughter from a vicious blackmailer.

The only Odets-written film to achieve stature as a film noir (and the only film collaboration with the famous Group Theatre figure Clurman), it offers heavily stylized dialogue of an intelligent, thoughtful working class; the film is doomed, as artwork, by its conceptual driftiness, which diminishes the best use of otherwise convincing noir atmosphere and camera work. 83 min.

Deadly Trap, aka La maison sous les abres (1971)

Written by Sidney Buchman,• produced obscurely in France but directed by René Clement in one of several collaborations with blacklistees. This muddled thriller cuts against the Cold War grain in the saga of an ex-CIA agent who works as an ad agency writer (and is pursued by his former bosses) rather than return home to suffer with his disturbed wife, the real star of the film, Faye Dunaway.

Death Kiss (1932)

Gordon Kahn's• first full credit is a stage-set whodunit with Bela Lugosi in a non-horror role, disappointing because he has so little opportunity for his signature monster-melancholy.

Death of a Salesman (1951)

Col. Kramer Productions. Prod: Stanley Kramer. Dir: László Benedek. Scr: Stanley Roberts.† Play basis: Arthur Miller, Death of a Salesman (1949). Cast: Frederic March, Mildred Dunnock, Kevin McCarthy, Cameron Mitchell, Howard Smith, Royal Beal, Don Keefer, Jesse White, Claire Carleton, David Alpert, Elizabeth Fraser, Patricia Walker

Only the red scare and the contempt that Cold War liberals as well as conservatives had for the unbending Miller can explain why this Kramer production failed to reach a wide audience or get friendly notices. Viewed as an intolerably prestigious left-winger by his critics, Miller captured American society's lower-middle-class sales ethos brilliantly. Columbia executives even mulled producing a documentary praising American salesmen to be shown in tandem with the film, but instead simply pulled Salesman from the theaters after limited screenings.

The film version was based pretty much exactly on Miller's Pulitzer Prize–winning (and hit Broadway) drama, with all the main stars except March repeating their performances. The aging salesman of the title tries to figure out what's gone wrong with his life and his family acts out their related anxieties. This version is remembered as Kevin McCarthy's film debut. The tele-film starring Dustin Hoffman and John Malkovich (1985) is much superior, but this early version deserves a second look. 115 min.

Decoy (1946)

Bernard-Brandt. Prod: Jack Bernhard, Bernard Brandt. Dir: Jack Bernhard. Scr: Nedrick Young.• Story basis: Stanley Rubin.† Cast: Jean Gillie, Edward Norris, Robert Armstrong, Herbert Rudley, Sheldon Leonard, Marjorie Woodworth, Philip Van Zandt, Carole Donne, John Shay

A neat little noir by Young, whose career was shortly ruined, and by Rubin, who went on after friendly testimony to decades of hack work in television as a writer-producer, sometimes arranging jobs for blacklistees. Decoy features an all-time femme fatale played by British actress Jean Gillie, whose character kills and humiliates men and is utterly incapable of guilt. The melodrama opens with Gillie as head of a small mob, dying and apparently eager to tell all to "honest cop" Sheldon Leonard (in a change from his usual mobster roles). As she tells the story, she arranged to have an executed prisoner's body absconded, with the idea that he can be revived and tell where he has hidden $400,000 in a bank job. On the road with a map and looking for the loot, she fakes a flat tire, double-crosses her partner, and runs over his body again and again—with pleasure.

Close to GUN CRAZY but without the implied compromise of romance. In her last gasp, she laughs at the sympathy of her interviewer. 76 min.

The Defiant Ones (1958)
UA. Prod: Stanley Kramer Dir: Stanley Kramer. Scr: Nathan E. Douglas (pseudonym for Nedrick Young•), Harold Jacob Smith. Story basis: Harold Jacob Smith. Cast: Tony Curtis, Sidney Poitier, Theodore Bikel, Lon Chaney, Jr., Charles McGraw, Cara Williams

Producer-director Kramer's bravest social film has convicts Poitier and Curtis chained to each other when a prison van overturns. They make their escape in the deep South. Real-life folksinger and civil rights activist Bikel is brilliant playing the former lawyer who has become a painstaking sheriff, a humane man chained to his job. A surprisingly vigorous Chaney, in his last serious film role (and his first in many years), is the turpentine-camp leader who stops a lynching when Poitier and Curtis are captured, revealing himself as a former chain-gang member. If the framing of quarrels between Poitier and Curtis seem dated, the literal mutual bondage and the existential hopelessness of their mutual condition carry the film along convincingly—although Lenny Bruce's comedy routine about Hollywood producers inviting a black character up to polish their cars in Beverly Hills offered a chilling reminder of liberal film's limitations. The film won Oscars for best screenplay (Young avoided an appearance at the ceremony) and for best black and white cinematography as well as many nominations. 97 min.

De Sade (1969)
Cyril Endfield• directed an unsatisfying and unsuccessful version of the story of the dissolute old reprobate (played by Keir Dullea). Lost for years, it has been reissued on DVD, but has few high points within a narrative mess. The best moment is doubtless a scene in which the notorious count, on a tear, virtually destroys a noble house, an evident metaphor for feudalism. The fascination of the Left (including the surrealists and novelist Guy Endore•) for De Sade has been better served elsewhere.

Desert Fury (1947)
Big-budget Technicolor bore with script by the usually interesting Robert Rossen,† and the talented noiriste A. I. Bezzerides, based on a novel by Ramona Stewart. John Hodiak, Burt Lancaster and most especially Mary Astor are wasted on melodrama, as gamblers love and quarrel among themselves.

Desire Me (1947)
This production, based on a screenplay by Marguerite Roberts• and Zoe Akins, came out so badly that director George Cukor successfully had his name removed. An apparent widow lives alone on the French coast until a stranger comes along and seeks to take her husband's place (literally). Nice touches, like an old village festival, not much more.

Destination Tokyo (1943)
WB. Prod: Jerry Wald. Dir: Delmer Daves. Scr: Delmer Daves and Albert Maltz.• Story basis: Steve Fisher. Cast: Cary Grant, John Garfield, Alan Hale, John Ridgely, Dane Clark, Warner Anderson, William Prince, Tom Tully, Peter Whitney, Faye Emerson, John Forsythe

A rare match-up of Grant and Garfield (a skirt-chasing proletarian seaman with a smallish role) contrasts the suave and fatherly captain of a submarine with the rough and courageous crew. Most of the film is devoted to action as the sub slips behind a Japanese destroyer into Tokyo Bay, gains information for bombing raids and fights its way out again. The distinctly leftish heart of Tokyo lies in the treatment of the "ordinary Americans" from many walks of life (although none are minorities): some are devoted family men, others roustabouts, still others shy virgin teens. Garfield is superb as his superficial toughness poorly disguises a good heart. The rest of the cast similarly shows the atmosphere of sacrifice and courage that helps explain why the "good war" could be remembered so well and so affectionately. Named best film of the year by the New York Times, with an Academy Award nomination for best story. 135 min.

Destry Rides Again (1939)
Universal. Prod: Joe Pasternak. Dir: George Marshall. Scr: Felix Jackson, Gertrude Purcell,† Henry Myers.• Story: Felix Jackson. Novel basis: Max Brand, Destry Rides Again (1930). Cast: Marlene Dietrich, James Stewart, Mischa Auer, Charles Winniger, Brian Donlevy, Allen Jenkins, Warren Hymer, Irene Hervey, Una Merkel, Billy Gilbert, Dickie Jones

One of the funniest westerns ever made, Destry was conceived by antifascist German refugees from Berlin film circles (Pasternak, Jackson and Dietrich) as a satire on the conventions of the U.S. genre they regarded with as much amusement as affection. As Hollywood partners, they chose experienced screenwriters and radicals Myers and Purcell, and together the unlikely crew told the story of a sheriff who is a kind of *sthetl filosof*-cum-Marxist intellectual who orders milk at the bar and prefers parables to pistols for solving social problems (even though he is a crack shot). The story celebrates the virtues of pacifism but finally urges intervention to defeat fascism. When sheriff Stewart reluctantly straps on his guns for the final shootout, the womenfolk mock his individualism by picking up their rolling pins and storming the saloon en masse. Many splendid scenes separate the presumed virtues of American life from its all-too-obvious vices. The film helped restore a sagging Dietrich career and made her version of "See What the Boys in the Back Room Will Have" into a future camp favorite. 94 min.

The Devil Commands (1941)

Interesting horror film with touches of noir and a large step up for director Edward Dmytryk•† has widower-scientist Boris Karloff trying to reach his dead wife through a contraption. Anne Revere• is great as former spiritualist faker who begins to believe in her powers.

The Devil-Doll (1936)

Universal. Prod: Ted Browning. Dir: Ted Browning. Scr: Guy Endore,• Garrett Fort, Erich von Stroheim. Story: Ted Browning. Novel basis: Abraham Merritt, *Burn Witch Burn* (1933). Cast: Lionel Barrymore, Maureen O'Sullivan, Frank Lawton, Robert Greig, Lucy Beaumont

A nearly forgotten horror classic, based on a story by director Browning (best remembered for *Freaks*), with many of the familiar elements of revenge and justice for the underdog. Here the centerpiece is a bank swindle that finds Barrymore on Devil's Island for a crime he did not commit. He escapes to a jungle hovel where bizarre post-Malthusian experiments are conducted in the miniaturization of animals and human beings, in order to reduce the necessities for feeding and clothing the world by five-sixths(!). Back in Paris with the secret formula, Barrymore disguises himself as an old woman (he never takes off his earrings till the final scene) and pretends to run a doll shop, while actually coaching the human miniatures into a vengeful crime spree against the swindlers. *Devil-Doll* takes a sentimental proletarian turn when Barrymore seeks to clear his name for the sake of his daughter, to assist her prospective husband, a taxicab driver. But the images that remain are the special effects—wonderful for contemporary film technology:

dolls that come alive, upset the private lives of the rich, and even engage in Apache dancing with each other. The thumbprint of thirties radical novelist Endore is unmistakable. 79 min.

The Devil is Driving (1937)

Story basis by Harold Buchman• and frequent partner Lee Loeb for cheapie social drama about a cook arrested on a drunken-driving rap and the ethical dilemma of an honest District Attorney torn between duty and sentiment.

The Devil's Playground (1937)

This forgettable remake of 1928 silent film *Submarine*, produced by Edward Chodorov,• co-scripted by Jerome Chodorov• and Dalton Trumbo• has two Navy diver pals in love with the same gal.

Diamond Head (1963)

One of Marguerite Roberts'• last films and one of the first big-budget melodramas aimed at racism in paradise (Hawaii). Charlton Heston plays a patriarchal plantation owner romantically linked to a native girl, while his daughter (Yvette Mimieux) determines to marry a mixed-race physician. The racist-capitalist, personified in the film community's real-life right-wing leader, won't cross the line; but the next generation is determined to do so—in the name of love, naturally.

Dinner at Eight (1933)

Top-drawer George Cukor comedy-drama of manners from Broadway's Kaufman-Ferber production, with Donald Ogden Stewart's• additional dialogue, has the very rich maneuvering against each other in the midst of Depression despair. The most famous throwaway line is apparently Stewart's: when the slinky but vacuous blonde (Jean Harlow) frets that machinery is taking away all the good occupations, sublime old battle-ax Marie Dressler quips, "Oh, my dear, that's something you never need worry about."

Diplomaniacs (1933)

RKO. Prod: Sam Jaffe. Dir: Wiliam A. Seiter. Scr: Joseph L. Mankiewicz and Henry Myers.• Story basis: Joseph L. Mankiewicz. Cast: Bert Wheeler, Robert Woolsey, Marjorie White, Louis Calhern, Phyllis Barry, Hugh Herbert, Richard Carle

Splendid farce with Wheeler and Woolsey at the top of their game in the most political of the anarchic comedies and the gifted Myer's (MILLION DOLLAR LEGS) last crack at slapstick genre. The boys set up a barber shop in the Oklahoma Territory, where a local Indian tribe presses them into service as diplomats to a Geneva peace conference. After a series of crazed digressions, they arrive in Switzerland only to discover that the stuffed shirts talking about peace are in fact representatives of arms merchants whose real interest is war. The high point comes near the end, during a speech about "harmony among the nations," when a right-wing provocateur throws a bomb into the chamber. When the smoke clears, all of the delegates are in blackface, singing a gospel song about peace (for what is probably the only time in film history, the blackface is oddly respectful). The boys go home thinking they have achieved their goal, but when they show up they are drafted and now face the consequences of war themselves. No wonder the working title was *In the Red*. An enduring film. 61 min.

Dishonored Lady (1947)

This has an uncredited script contribution by David Lang† to a play adaptation starring Hedy Lamarr as the woman in question—a sexually active, successful magazine executive who is mysteriously unhappy with her life. She needs a shrink to tell her that she is another of the lost women of modern times, badly in need of a husband and family. Within a few years, Hollywood's real-life Communist-connected lay therapist was similarly convincing his patients that their loyalties were mistaken, and that they should give friendly testimony. Lang didn't need to be convinced.

Divorce in the Family (1932)

MGM. Prod: Harry Rapf. Dir: Charles Reisner. Scr: Delmer Daves. Story basis: Delmer Daves, Maurice Rapf.• Cast: Jackie Cooper, Conrad Nagel, Lewis Stone, Lois Wilson, Jean Parker, Louise Beavers

The first real credit for studio scion Maurice Rapf (still a freshman at Stanford, and overseen by his father, never a radical) is a sadly overlooked film about a Depression family. It centers on Cooper's difficulties in adjusting to his parents' separation and his mother's remarriage to a kindly doctor. The father, a hard-working anthropologist always away on digs, is one of those men "who should never have married," as he admits, and his mother is a kindly if a bit too fashionable middle-class Sacramento woman seeking the usual sources of domestic

bliss. With his brother off at military school, Cooper gets himself into assorted kinds of trouble and finally runs away from home, triggering a crisis. Very Cooperesque (i.e., cute), but avoids easy answers and clichés (except for the ending). 78 min.

Dixie Dugan (1943)

Commercially unsuccessful adaptation of popular, folksy comic strip by screenwriting team Lee Loeb and Harold Buchman.• The perky girl of the title finds herself in hectic and deeply bureaucratic wartime Washington, D.C. She gets a secretarial job with a boss who wants to get rid of her by assigning her a public survey; the results are sensational, and the government has to learn from its lower servants, with family problems and laughs on the side. The intended series flopped.

A Doctor's Diary (1937)

The screenplay by Samuel Ornitz• and Joseph Anthony of medical melodrama, in the framework of the Group Theatre drama *Men in White*, which in its film version revolutionized popular dramatic treatment of hospitals and helped create clichés spun out in endless films (some written by reds) and television series with continuing left-liberal connections. In *Doctor's Diary*, an earnest young physician is engaged to the daughter of the hospital's president but neglects her to find a cure for polio. All ends happily—except in New Zealand, then suffering a real-life epidemic, where showings of the film were banned.

Doll Face (1945)

An adaptation credited to Harold Buchman,• for a play by famed stripper Gypsy Rose Lee has a badly exploited singer-dancer forced into the lowest entertainment bracket. Young Perry Como sings "Hubba Hubba," and his acting career ends here.

A Doll's House (1973)

Tomorrow Entertainment. Prod: Richard F. Dalton, Joseph Losey•. Dir: Joseph Losey. Scr: David Mercer. Play basis: Henrik Ibsen, *A Doll's House* (1879). Cast: Jane Fonda, David Warner, Trevor Howard, Delphine Seyrig, Edward Fox

Fonda in her peak artistic (and most activist) years is a bit over her head in an art film and suffers in comparison with the Claire Bloom/Anthony Hopkins version (1989), but this is nevertheless an achingly sincere performance. Losey's usual mordant tone is largely absent here in the story of the turn-of-the-century struggle for women's emancipation (a stage favorite for generations of the Left). Losey's recruitment of Fonda—then notorious for her visit to North Vietnam—prompted a war over Mercer's script, which had diluted Ibsen's feminist message in assorted ways. Seyrig, an acclaimed European actress and also a determined feminist, was quoted at the time as saying, "I wish I weren't in this movie." But many parts of the film, including Seyrig's own supporting role, nevertheless stand up well, as do the changes Fonda insisted on in the script. A particularly beguiling scene has Fonda as an almost childlike doctor's wife showing her ankles while dancing an Italian tarantella for bourgeois dinner guests at a winter party. Losey is superb in sketching the surrounding scene of the Scandinavian middle class and its patriarchal center. The film almost disappeared due to political controversy, but finally made it past the art theaters and into the mainstream—thanks to ABC's *Sunday Night at the Movies*. 106 min., color.

Don Giovanni (1979)

Opera Film Poduzione/Gaumont/Camera One/ Antennae2/Janua Films. Prod: Ralf Liebermann. Dir: Joseph Losey.• Adaptation: Joseph Losey. Opera basis: Lorenzo da Ponte, Wolfgang Amadeus Mozart, *Don Giovanni* (1787). Cast: Ruggero Raimondi, John Macurdy, Edda Moser, Kiri Te Kanawa, Kenneth Riegel, José van Dam, Teresa Berganza, Malcolm King

A five-million dollar, multinational co-production set on the lovely Venetian islands. Losey rendered the seemingly apolitical Giovanni, a sexual gourmand, into a figure more contemporary to the French Revolution than to Mozart's own period; he unaccountably opens with an epigram from Antonio Gramsci about the Europe of the 1930s ("The crisis consists precisely in the fact that the old is dying and the new cannot be born; in this interregnum a great variety of morbid symptoms appears.") Nonetheless, this *Don* is one of the half-dozen finest opera films ever made, helped enormously by the great Te Kanawa and Raimondi's well-realized subversive egoist Giovanni. Losey overcomes the necessarily static quality of the form with brilliant camera strokes that surround their subjects. The film was celebrated in England and France, while viciously attacked by critics in the United States, notably Vincent Canby of the *Times* (for using close-ups!). It was the final evidence that Losey would never be forgiven in his home country during his lifetime. 98 min.

Don Juan Quilligan (1945)

Comedy directed by Frank Tuttle,† with Anne Revere• supporting a cast that included William Bendix, Phil Silvers and Joan Blondell. But the talent was wasted on the miserably scripted tale of an accidental bigamist.

Don't Gamble with Love (1936)

A forgettable feature scripted by Lee Loeb and Harold Buchman,• with a cast that included Ann Sothern and Irving Pichel• (the director's last Hollywood acting part of note). One good feature: casino owner Bruce Cabot, convinced to go legit, quickly learns that all business operates on the same moral standard.

Double Alibi (1940)

B-crime drama written by Harold Buchman• with a nifty ending. Wayne Morris's character, on the run after his estranged wife is murdered, poses as a crime reporter until exposed by a health columnist. He convinces her of his innocence; together they set out to find the real criminal.

The Double Man (1967)

Frank Tarloff• was called in at the last minute to concoct a script around ski action footage shot for a doomed production. Yul Brynner, an old friend of the Left, did duty as a CIA agent and his East German double.

Dragon Seed (1944)

MGM. Prod: Pandro S. Berman. Dir: Jack Conway. Scr: Marguerite Roberts,• Jane Murfin. Novel basis: Pearl S. Buck (1943). Cast: Katharine Hepburn, Walter Huston, Agnes Moorehead, Turhan Bey, Akim Tamiroff, Hurd Hatfield, Aline MacMahon, Henry Travers

A remarkable evocation of anti-Japanese resistance in traumatic and changing times for China, unquestionably dated by its use of non-Asian actors but well-scripted and full of strong performances. Although extremely long, it is narratively tight and fast-paced. The script was adapted from the best-selling novel of Pearl S. Buck that dated from her own crypto-Maoist days (1943), effectively utilizing her theme of the strong and somewhat westernized young woman as a fine vehicle for a Popular Frontish Hepburn.

With Huston and MacMahon as the loving older parents, Bey as their somewhat bohemian son and Hepburn as the independent-minded daughter-in-law, the opening scenes feel like Asia in the Old West (as seen by Hollywood). Even with epicanthic folds applied by the makeup department, Hepburn cannot shake the Yankee look until her acting ability kicks in, as when she stands up to speak at a meeting called by students to promote anti-Japanese resistance (she's called home by her more traditional husband.) By loving her, by giving her a book (something unknown for women unless they were educated concubines), he wins her heart—just in time for the volunteers' trek south to rebuild Chinese industry. After their village is bombed and the cadre return, the cruelty of the Japanese and the treachery of collaborators takes center stage, once again giving Hepburn the chance to play the heroine. Through it all, the puzzled Huston and MacMahon stand by as commentators on changing times, mediating between the old, destroyed insularity and the different, better world to come. 145 min.

Dream Wife (1953)

Odd film co-scripted by Alfred Lewis Levitt• with Herbert Baker and Sidney Sheldon (also the director) for a big-budget production. Business traveler Cary Grant is entranced by a princess in an oil-rich Middle Eastern kingdom raised, like all women in the culture, to make her future husband happy. Back home he's the unhappy fiancé of Deborah Kerr, a State Department exec already married—to her job. He offers marriage to the princess but only Kerr herself can speak the language! Resulting confused ménage, as the princess becomes an American-type female consumer, together with bedroom farce (no sex, of course), typify Hollywood's wrestling with the transition from 1940s to 1950s film.

Duffy's Tavern (1945)

Based on the popular radio show, this film was critically panned but also one of the top 35 grossing films of 1945-1946. Its artificial plot has famed radio figure Archie the barkeep drive owner Duffy into debt by serving meals to veterans thrown out of work when a photographic company closes due to wartime shortages. Several left-wing connections: associate producer Danny Dare,† actor Howard Da Silva,• and most of all writer/pianist Abe Burrows,† then a popular guest at Hollywood Left social gatherings, soon to abandon his friends in disgraceful fashion, but helpful in getting distant cousin Woody Allen a leg up in show biz.

Dulcy (1940)

Written by the Broadway comedy team of Jerome Chodorov• and Joseph Fields (with Albert Mannheimer). The movie is all Ann Sothern as charming naïf, here joined to Asian American child character actor Donald Huie as a Chinese war orphan proving a crucial piece of the plot in a typical gesture to the times.

Dust Be My Destiny (1939)

WB. Dir: Lewis Seiler. Scr: Robert Rossen.† Cast: John Garfield, Priscilla Lane, Alan Hale, Frank McHugh, John Litel, Billy Hallop, Henry Armetta, Stanley Ridges, Bobby Jordan

Classic Rossen realism of the period. The incarcerated victim of a justice system that wrongly convicted him, Garfield serves his sentence and attempts to ride the rails to a job, but is picked up for trespassing and jailed again, at a prison farm where a sadistic foreman (Hale) drives him ever further into despair. Luckily and unluckily, Hale's daughter (Lane) falls for him, and as they plan a getaway, Garfield is compelled to defend himself against his prospective father-in-law. On the run again but this time with a loving companion, he finds decency in small town folk, takes honest work until exposed, and faces the hard decision to go back. A subproletarian (but better production value) version of Edgar Ulmer's later noir Detour (1945), Garfield is the classic version of the ordinary guy wronged by the system. 88 min.

Dynamite (1929)

MGM. Prod: Cecil B. DeMille. Dir: Cecil B. DeMille. Scr: John Howard Lawson,• Gladys Unger, Jeanie Macpherson. Play basis: John Howard Lawson, Processional (1925). Cast: Conrad Nagel, Kay Johnson, Charles Bickford, Julia Faye, Joel McCrea

A very early romance talkie about class struggle and the first written by a blacklistee. Overplotted for film (based on a Lawson stage play), it's the tale of rich girl Johnson, who will lose her inheritance if she doesn't marry. She marries coal miner Bickford, who has been sentenced to die for a murder he did not commit (and spends his time in jail worrying about his daughter, pathetic little Faye). To everyone's surprise, he gets off when the real murderer is revealed. After some confusion, Johnson goes to the coal patch town in Pennsylvania where Bickford has returned to work and tries (without, of course, actually consummating the marriage) to work something out—and then decides spontaneously to become a good wife and mother. Old boyfriend Nagel comes to find her, with still more confusion to follow, including a coal mine disaster, lots of sentimentalism and some real class tensions. Remarkable and predictive of the way class will be treated in the compromises that leftist screenwriters found they had to make, *Dynamite* is remarkable as well for the rare mise en scène of a blue-collar village. 129 min.

E

Eagle in a Cage (1971)

Group W Films. Prod: Millard Lampell,• Fielder Cook. Dir: Fielder Cook. Scr: Millard Lampell. Cast: Kenneth Haigh, John Gielgud, Ralph Richardson, Billie Whitelaw, Moses Gunn, Ferdy Mayne, Georgina Hale, Michael Williams

Historical piece on Napoleon in exile on St. Helena. Originally a television *Hallmark Hall of Fame* drama and Emmy winner for Lampell, it was reshot as a film with Lampell co-producing in Yugoslavia, adding a black general (although none served with Napoleon, some had been in his army elsewhere), played memorably by Gunn. The film never loses its theatrical quality, but with Richardson and Gielgud, staginess is a virtue.

The solidly left-wing lines are delivered entirely by Richardson, cast as the British physician assigned to care for a Napoleon who cannot rebut charges of war crimes but who insists that statesmen are not bound by moral law. Meanwhile, he philosophizes broadly, recalling his young and romantic days with Whitelaw, Napoleon's old girlfriend and currently Gunn's wife, and he frolics improbably with Hale (in the real history, the character was age 14), an island girl who dreams of fame and glory. The film never strays too far from the *Hallmark* style of uplift, but Gielgud saves the drama at weaker moments as an emissary from London with plans to unleash the general once again upon the French ruling class. Receiving the Emmy, Lampell told the audience, "I think I should mention that I was blacklisted." It earned a headline in the *New York Times* back pages, and helped to finish off the blacklist. 98 min., color.

Earl of Puddlestone (1940)

Rep. Prod: Gus Meins. Dir: Gus Meins. Scr: Val Burton,• Ewart Adamson. Cast: James Gleason, Lucile Gleason, Russell Gleason, Harry Davenport, Lois Ranson, Tommy Ryan, Eric Blore, Betty Blythe

One of the Higgins Family series initiated by writer Eddie Eliscu several years earlier, and the most ill-starred. Producer-director Meins, arrested on real-life morals charges, committed suicide, and the studio initially removed his name from the credits. Otherwise, and as so often with this series (in a theme later exploited by *The Beverly Hillbillies*), country rubes prove wiser than city folks. In this case, Ransom is excluded from a community charity show by a snooty matron, and the family sets about improving its social position. Grandad Davenport learns that a search is on for the American heir of a British lordship and hires a con man to proclaim son James Gleason the real Earl of the title. The family's status soars: Ransom returns to a show, a butler is hired to teach the family manners and while the businessman-son is out of town, the Higgins family moves to a mansion. When the con man threatens to tell all, the Higginses kidnap him and call him an insane member of the family. At a grand ball for the social set, all the cards are turned up. 67 min.

Earth vs. The Flying Saucers (1956)

Col. Prod: Charles H. Schneer. Dir: Fred F. Sears. Scr: Curt Siodmak, Bernard Gordon• (credited as "Raymond T. Marcus"). Cast: Hugh Marlowe, Joan Taylor, Donald Curtis, Morris Ankrum, John Zaremba, Thomas Browne Henry, Grandon Rhodes, Larry J. Blake

One of the more remarkable of the low-budget Cold War saucer films by virtue of its anti–Cold War themes (Americans unite with Russians against the common enemy). This is not the tradition of friendly aliens bearing gifts of peace, however (as in IT CAME FROM OUTER SPACE). In fact, these invaders turn out to be flying fascists. Technologically advanced, they are soldiers from a "disintegrated star system" sent on a mission to subjugate earthlings. Most memorable are the images of alien spacecraft slicing through the Washington Monument or crashing into the Supreme Court or, in the film's climax, into the capitol dome of Congress (for many viewers, Ray Harryhausen's stop-motion animation must surely have been the film's high point). But it is impossible not to regard such images as an act of revenge by a writer (Gordon) publicly humiliated by subpoenas summoning him to a public interrogation of his political beliefs and the frightening of his children by hovering FBI agents. Still, Gordon insisted that he also had something else in mind. In the film, the external threat is so terrible that the Soviet Union and the United States, at each others' throats since 1945, now declare worldwide peace and return to their alliance, as in the good old days of the antifascist crusade against the common enemy. Securing planetary safety for what may be presumed to be a more cooperative future through the guidance of a functioning United Nations, they spare humanity twice over. No congressman would dare make such a proposal. (Nor was the suggestion of oral sex between newlyweds in a moving car ever noted by critics or audience, Gordon once noted with a sense of wonder.) 83 min.

Earthbound (1940)

20th. Prod: Sol M. Wurtzel. Dir: Irving Pichel.• Scr: John Howard Lawson,• Samuel G. Engel. Story basis: Basil King, "The Ghost's Story" (n.d.). Cast: Warner Baxter, Andrea Leeds, Lynn Bari, Charley Grapewin, Henry Wilcoxon, Elizabeth Patterson, Russell Hicks, Christian Rub, Ian Wolfe, Lester Scharff, Reginald Sheffield, Pedro de Cordoba

One of those "weird" fantasy pictures, so popular in times of mass slaughter, situating characters between life and death with assorted angels or other supernatural beings mediating and compelling self-reflection. Director Pichel had shortly before directed a low-budget Biblical epic, THE GREAT COMMANDMENT (1939, actually released in 1942) and had a feeling for the territory. In *Earthbound*, an American (Baxter) traveling in France meets an old man who warns him that his time on Earth is almost up. Arriving in Paris after leaving his wife on a mountain-climbing trip, he meets his lover, equally adulterous and the wife of the man he admires most. Shaken, he tells her he wants to break it off. She kills him and, from beyond the grave, he attempts to bring about reconciliations. It ends on a strangely beautiful note—a true Pichelean moment, with a hand holding the ghost of a dead bird. 67 min.

East Side, West Side (1949)

MGM. Prod: Voldemar Vetluguin. Dir: Mervyn LeRoy. Scr: Isobel Lennart.† Cast: Barbara Stanwyck, James Mason, Van Heflin, Ava Gardner, Cyd Charisse, Nancy Davis, Gale Sondergaard•

Successful soaper from a popular romance novel, with a sometimes strong women's message. English-accented smoothie Mason (in his third U.S. film) is a skirt-chasing husband vowing to be (more) faithful to heiress Stanwyck, but ex-girlfriend Gardner is back in town, and this is one explosive sexpot, twirling men around her claws like necklaces. Heflin plays the former slum kid who has come back between European adventures, perhaps for the CIA. Falling in love with the betrayed wife, he gets all the good-guy lines. The plot is better than it sounds because of the intelligent banter among women about men and the bitter expressions of class resentment by Gardner. A bonus: Cyd Charisse sings. By coincidence or not, the hardest-hitting television drama series of the following decades, written

largely by blacklistees and starring several of the most left-wing actors of the day including blacklistees, took over the title (*East Side/West Side*, 1965-1966). Arnold Perl• was executive producer. 108 min.

Edge of Darkness (1943)

WB. Exec Prod: Jack Warner. Dir: Lewis Milestone. Scr: Robert Rossen.• Novel basis: William Woods, *Edge of Darkness* (1942). Cast: Errol Flynn, Ann Sheridan, Walter Huston, Nancy Coleman, Tom Fadden, Judith Anderson, Helmut Dantine, Ruth Gordon, Roman Bohnen, Dorothy Tree,• Morris Carnovsky•

That the notoriously right-wing (and during the 1930s, reputedly profascist) Errol Flynn was chosen to lead a fictive people's war against the Nazi occupation of Norway is one of those little ironies of Hollywood casting. Still, Milestone and Rossen could not have chosen a more dashing figure for this rather shallow but heart-lifting drama. Actually shot in Carmel-by-the-Sea (another one of those ironies: moving the camera angle just a hair, they could have caught the plush digs of Hollywood's leftish bohemian set), it depicts the tiny fishing village of Trollness, discovered to be flying the national flag in occupied Denmark. Nazi troops find, to their astonishment, Danish partisans and Nazi dead piled up in the streets.

In a film-long flashback, we learn about the making of the resistance through a dawning awareness of the full cruelty of the occupiers and the shamelessness of the collaborators (most of all the owner of the canning factory, determined to hang onto his property). With most of the young men gone, women and old-timers fill the ranks of the hastily assembled underground, which must strike hard to aid the national movement. Flynn successfully pulls together the irregular troops, but it is the subterranean strategy meeting of the townsfolk and the sight of them marching through the streets armed with everything available that provides the lasting and stirring images. Critics complained about a mixture of Ibsen, Chekov and standard RKO and about a Norwegian anthem sung in English, among other incongruous details. Ordinary folks no doubt found it moving. 120 min.

Edge of the City (1957)

MGM. Prod: David Susskind. Dir: Martin Ritt.• Scr: Robert Alan Aurthur. Cast: John Cassavetes, Sidney Poitier, Ruby Dee, Jack Warden, Kathleen Maguire

This is producer David Susskind's initial move from television to film, with his left-wing connections (he had earlier produced several shows with graylisted writers) and outspoken social values intact. It's also Ritt's debut as film director, with one of the most talented liberal television writers delivering a strong script. Made as a drama for TV (in which black actors had begun to get a few parts as developed as those of their white counterparts), it was reshot for film, where no such black roles had yet been risked in McCarthy era Hollywood. It's particularly interesting as the first lead for Sidney Poitier, an outspoken liberal, and for Ruby Dee, a notable left-winger too young (or recent in her fame) to be on the blacklist.

Cassavetes is a young man AWOL from the army. Taking a job on New York's loading docks, he runs into mean foreman Jack Warden (whose role closely resembles the sergeant he played in World War II films, without the benevolent side) and helpful fellow worker Poitier. Shown the ropes and made into a friend by the black proletarian, he takes a place to live "uptown" in a largely nonwhite neighborhood evidently bordering Harlem. He is introduced to a progressive social worker (Kathleen Maguire), who is fast friends with former social worker and Poitier's wife (Dee). The two women have it all over the men in both culture and education, but the four enjoy social evenings together, sometimes even discussing racism.

Heroic Poitier protects Cassavetes, and a racially tinged confrontation with Dee changes him, in the key ideological moment of the drama. Bosley Crowther, in the *Times*, praised the film's seriousness and compared it to CASABLANCA. 85 min.

Edison, The Man (1940)

Sequel to YOUNG TOM EDISON but not as good politically or in any other way. Hugo Butler• had co-scripted the tale of the frustrated youngster, more energetic and insightful than society seemed to allow, as a rebel of sorts; but the man was far more businessman than inventor in real life, and that could hardly be the depiction that the studio would demand (or that Butler as solo screenwriter apparently chose, for that matter). Instead, the "Wizard of Menlo Park," played by Spencer Tracy, is conveyed through sentimentalism and a great deal of MGM fantasy.

Edward, My Son (1949)

MGM. Prod: Edwin H. Knopf. Dir: George Cukor. Scr: Donald Ogden Stewart.• Play basis: Robert Morley, Noel Langley, *Edward, My Son* (1949). Cast: Spencer Tracy, Deborah Kerr, Ian Hunter, James Donald, Mervyn Johns, Felix Aylmer, Leueen MacGrath

A rather stagy production made in Britain as the blacklist was closing in, about a Canadian capitalist who owns a big business in the United Kingdom and has resided there for some years. A melancholy figure, he speaks to the camera as if to a stage audience about the loss of his 23-year-old son (never seen), adding, "I want your opinion." The film flashes back to the lower-middle-class life of younger Kerr and Tracy, poor but eagerly expecting a baby and thinking about buying what they need on the installment plan. Soon, their newborn son has to be put into a plaster cast because of the weakness of his nerves, and Kerr learns that she can't have another child. Tracy proposes hiking the insurance on his failing business and setting a fire to bring him the money to pay for his son's operation—and more. Many complications follow, with Tracy complaining that after the war, everything in England has gone sour. A dark and enigmatic film, not without virtues. 112 min.

Ellery Queen and the Murder Ring (1941)

Second of the Ellery Queen mystery films, this one was co-scripted by Gertrude Purcell† and starred Ralph Bellamy, who was meant for better things than a hospital murder.

Emergency Squad (1940)

Another example of Edward Dmytryk's•† climb from the Bs to the As, working every genre available to him. Youthful reporter heads for the police station looking for a story and uncovers a financial swindler's scheme to bilk stockholders by blowing up sections of a tunnel under construction, bringing shares down to rock bottom.

Escapade (1955)

Pinnacle. Prod: Daniel M. Angel, Hannah Weinstein.• Dir: Philip Leacock. Scr: Gilbert Holland (pseudonym for Donald Ogden Stewart•). Play basis: Roger MacDougall, *Escapade* (1953). Cast: John Mills, Yvonne Mitchell, Alastair Sim, Jeremy Spenser, Andrew Ray, Marie Lohr, Peter Asher

Under a title that suggests a caper-romance, this is in fact an important film about post–World War II pacifism (more cryptically, the early "Ban the Bomb" movement in England). It is also the great Donald Ogden Stewart's last, magnificent effort at political drama. Adaptation was his highest skill, and in this outing the idealism of youth is pitted ironically against both the Cold War nationalism and the male authoritarianism of the elder generation, even of the quasi-Left. Mills is a doctrinaire pacifist who is busy writing and speaking for disarmament—so busy that he ignores his family, sending his three boys off to what the British call public school and sending wife Mitchell into a barely suppressed rage. Just as she struggles to explain why she is going to leave Mills, the boys of the school organize a quiet conspiracy. After eldest son Ray (acting on the boys' plan) steals a small plane to dramatize a petition from various schools declaring their unwillingness to fight in future wars, and then appears to have been lost in the Alps en route to Vienna, everyone rallies to the boys' side. At the close of the film, grandmother Lohr delivers the peace sentiments as a generational statement of the promise to come, while the boys prepare to light a bonfire (like boys in other British schools) signaling that Ray has indeed landed and the message has been carried forth. This film illuminates an otherwise bleak period of film history and is not to be missed. Weinstein was the original émigré producer who hired many blacklisted writers for fifties British TV. 87 min.

Escape (1940)

MGM. Prod: Lawrence Weingarten. Dir: Merwyn LeRoy (additional scenes, George Cukor). Scr: Arch Oboler, Marguerite Roberts.• Novel basis: Ethel Vance, *Escape* (1939). Cast: Norma Shearer, Robert Taylor, Conrad Veidt, Alla Nazimova, Felix Bressart, Albert Bassermann, Philip Dorn, Bonita Granville, Blanche Yurka

One of the first anti-Nazi films (along with CONFESSIONS OF A NAZI SPY) and one of the best dealing with German civilian life. German-born American actress Nazimova is awaiting death in a concentration camp while her American-born son (Taylor) searches for her. He takes up with a countess (Shearer), herself compromised with a Nazi lover, and meanwhile Nazimova has taken a coma-inducing drug that she had secretly carried. Shearer sacrifices herself to a stricken Nazi (played by the superb German antifascist Conrad Veidt) to allow an escape. Melodramatic but, in the circumstances, still effective. At this late date, it was among the first militantly Hollywood anti-Nazi films set in contemporary Europe, with a cast including prominent exiles. 98 min.

Escape from East Berlin (1962)

Independent, low-cost production, directed by Robert Siodmak, with Millard Lampell• the last of four writers. A fact-based melodrama about the Berlin Wall, interesting because a blacklistee takes on Communist government oppression.

Escape to Paradise (1939)

Stock project for co-scriptwriter Ian MacLellan Hunter• and Bobby Breen Productions, the last in the series for Breen, the kid with the golden voice. In an unspecified Latin American locale, the lower-class lad helps a female tourist find love with a kindly maté-tea grower, who believes in the musical traditions of the masses.

Eve (1962)

Interopa/Paris Films Productions. Prod: Raymond Hakim, Robert Hakim. Dir: Joseph Losey.• Scr: Hugo Butler,• Evan Jones. Novel basis: James Hadley Chase, *Eve* (1945). Cast: Jeanne Moreau, Stanley Baker, Virna Lisi, James Villiers, Ricardo Garrone, Lisa Gastoni

This film marks director Losey's break with melodrama and his first opportunity, after a swooning essay about him appeared in an influential French film magazine in 1960, to show what he could do with a good script. It also marks, lamentably, the last good script of Hugo Butler, increasingly trapped in exile, with deteriorating health. The politically sympathetic Welsh actor Stanley Baker, who had earlier appeared in Losey's BLIND DATE and THE CRIMINAL, joined him again in this stylish and intense film, which, before the notorious Hakim brothers ripped it apart in the editing room, was considered by British critic Kenneth Tynan an equal to the director's masterpiece, THE SERVANT.

Some while before the action of *Eve* begins, a Welsh miner has died after finishing a novel, which his brother (Baker) appropriates as his own. After the book is a hit, Baker acquires his own Italian island and the beautiful Lisi as a fiancée. Then he meets the title figure, a high-class prostitute played with feline slyness by Moreau; she is even more cynical and corrupt than he, and so the one other person who can forgive him for stealing his dead brother's work. Dark obsession pervades the rest of the film, the first appearance of the director's own great theme that bourgeois sexuality is an acting out of property relations. 115 min.

Ever Since Venus (1944)

Writer Connie Lee• of BLONDIE fame contributed to this comic tale of a fuss over a new lipstick mischievously called "Rosebud" (after the famous sled in CITIZEN KANE). Ina Ray Hutton and Her Orchestra keep the jams moving. The real significance of the film is its Hollywood lore: Ms. Hutton's orchestra was the model for the "all-girl band" in *Some Like It Hot*.

Every Saturday Night (1936)

Remembered by Edward Eliscu• as the project that brought him back to Hollywood following severe disillusionment and made him a successful screenwriter after serving as lyricist for a handful of films (including *Whoopee, Great Day, Rockabye*, and DIPLOMANIACS). He went to see the stage production and "found it a most enchanting American story about a family, without the fake clichés of romance or a chase." It was later known as the Higgins Family, in several more low-budget features. The film structurally resembles the contemporary family radio shows, with fun-filled teenagers emerging as a comic class after the rise of the modern high school early in the Depression (see HENRY ALDRICH).

Ex-Champ (1939)

Gordon Kahn• wrote the story basis for this boxing melodrama about a champ who lives in the past, working as a doorman to support his family.

Executive Action (1973)

National General Pictures. Prod: Edward Lewis, Dan Bessie. Dir: David Miller. Scr: Dalton Trumbo. Story basis: Donald Freed and Mark Lane. Cast: Burt Lancaster, Robert Ryan, Will Geer,• Gilbert Green, John Anderson, Ed Lauter, Sidney Clute, Lloyd Gough,• Dick Miller

Trumbo's last screenplay was cast with any number of old friends and allies and seemed doomed (or conspired against) for that reason from its inception. Herbert Magidson, an L.A. businessman active in the antiwar movement, was said to have put up most of the money, buying the property from Donald Sutherland. Rumors of CIA "interest" in the project and threats against it were voiced at the time of production.

The film was shot in 1960s staccato fashion, making the narrative sometimes difficult to follow, but the main line of speculation is one pursued by investigator Mark Lane into the JFK assassination. Freed had written about the trial of Julius and Ethel Rosenberg and a book about the Black Panther conspiracy trial in New Haven. The books suggested that wealthy right-wingers ordered the hit because Kennedy was, according to them (rather improbably), not only about to sign the test-ban treaty but to pull out of Vietnam and (entirely improbably) to "lead the black revolution." Lancaster and Ryan played the right-wingers credibly, but Ryan's death a few weeks after the film was completed more than hinted that it was doomed. By the time it was released, NBC had decided to ban advertising of the film "on the basis of not meeting NBC standards." ABC and CBS also turned down advertising for it. Against all this pressure, an already weak project was doomed. 91 min.

Exodus (1960)

UA. Prod: Otto Preminger. Dir: Otto Preminger. Scr: Dalton Trumbo.• Novel basis: Leon Uris, *Exodus* (1958). Cast: Paul Newman, Eva Marie Saint, Ralph Richardson, Peter Lawford, Sal Mineo, Lee J. Cobb,† John Derek,† Hugh Griffith, Jill Haworth, David Opatoshu, George Maharis

The follow-up to Trumbo's blacklist-breaking (for him) SPARTACUS offers a foreshadowing of other dreadful big-star films he would soon undertake, in the vein of THE SANDPIPER and *Hawaii*—in this case made worse by the historical distortions in the literary source itself. Looking like a preparation for the conspiratorial view of Islam (and Arabs in general) after the Cold War, it offers some touching glimpses of Jewish refugees escaping Cyprus and evading the British blockade but is mostly stuck in stereotypes. Paul Newman is a leader of the emerging Israeli military operation, Eva Marie Saint is his loving nurse, and life-long progressive David Opatoshu plays a sympathetic militant of the murderous Irgun. The film won an Oscar for the score, the best thing in it, but even this element is badly overblown. 210 min., color.

Eyes of the Underworld (1943)

Crime drama co-scripted by Arthur Stawn† about the rise in auto thefts after the start of World War II because of shortages created by rationing.

F

the authorities of still being a jewel thief, if not worse) drawn into a murder case in a resort somewhere outside Manhattan. Newswoman Harriet Hilliard fancies him and spends a lot of time trying not to act jealous of other women around him; she has, however, plenty of sarcastic one-liners about men in general and the Falcon in particular. Not surprisingly for wartime, the case turns into a criminal conspiracy to steal war bonds and change their serial numbers.

The Face Behind the Mask (1941)
A mystery tinged with horror is interesting largely thanks to Peter Lorre in the starring role as a recent Hungarian immigrant whose face is hideously scarred in a hotel fire. Unable to get work, considering himself lost, he falls into criminal activity, hoping to raise the money for plastic surgery. Co-script by Paul Jarrico.•

Face in the Rain (1963)
Filmways-Calvic Production. Prod: John Calley. Dir. Irvin Kershner. Scr: Hugo Butler,• Jean Rouverol,• based on a screenplay by Guy Elmes. Cast: Rory Calhoun, Marina Berti, Niall MacGinnis, Massimo Giuliani

One of the late antifascist features of the blacklistees, this one a vehicle for Calhoun, executive co-producer of the Italian production. Berti is the real star as the wife of an imprisoned Italian antifascist who accepts German officer MacGinnis as her lover in order (she believes) to protect her husband. Calhoun, an American who is sent to aid the partisans but has made up his mind to survive, takes up residence in her attic, aided by her son (child actor Giuliani). Her motivations are probed, along with the effects of war on women's condition and choices. A well executed if slightly dated but still above-average Hollywood treatment of war themes. Also notable for camerawork by Haskell Wexler, a most important Left continuator in Hollywood. 98 min.

Fail-Safe (1964)
Splendid anti-nuke vehicle for Henry Fonda (playing the president during a global crisis) adapted by Walter Bernstein• from contemporary best-seller. Made for television in 2000, produced by George Clooney.

The Falcon Strikes Back (1943)
One of 16 Falcon films made during the 1940s and one of the two directed by Edward Dmytryk•† has the suave detective and former master criminal (always suspected by

The Fall of the Roman Empire (1964)
Para. Prod: Samuel Bronston. Dir: Anthony Mann. Scr: Ben Barzman,• Basilio Franchina, Philip Yordan (uncredited contribution: Bernard Gordon•). Cast: Sophia Loren, Stephen Boyd, Alec Guinness, James Mason, Christopher Plummer, Anthony Quayle, John Ireland, Mel Ferrer, Omar Sharif

A spectacle made on the cheap in Spain in the typical Bronston and Yordon pinch-penny fashion but with some important moments, notably a speech by the Greek soldier-philosopher Timonides (Mason) delivered to the Roman Senate, a warning against the hubris of empire and the needless creation of enemies by military adventurism. Neither Barzman's writing (Yordan spent his time on arranging the mis en scène in the money shots for the trailers), nor Mann's masterful hand nor the presence of Plummer and Guiness could compensate for the rigid execution of an aging genre or for Boyd's wooden acting. Still, when the truly big-budget *Gladiator* appeared 35 years later, *Empire* suddenly seemed to have aged rather well by contrast. For the film, Gordon consented to be hauled in to write a love scene for Loren, who is basically ornamental. All of later Roman history is condensed into the final year, with Guinness as Marcus Aurelius about to descend from emperorhood, Plummer his would-be royal successor. 188 min.

The Family Next Door (1939)
One of a projected new series of family comedies by Mortimer Offner,• Edward Eliscu's• (and director George Cukor's) intimate friend from high school days in New York. Unlike the Jones Family series (see EVERY SATURDAY NIGHT), also scripted by Eliscu, this one lacked the sitcomic flavor that kept audiences coming back. At any rate, no more were made.

Fargo Kid (1940)
Reviewers complained that star Tim Holt spoiled the usual shoot 'em up by hiding a bankroll in his gun during the

first reel—from then on he had to use his fists! The second of the obscure Fargo Kid series has Holt hired to be an outlaw. After outwitting a gunman and borrowing his identity (along with the bankroll of $5,000), he searches for and locates a sympathetic old-timer prospecting near a gold vein. Another oater written by Morton Grant.• The real star is the scenery itself: Utah's Escalante Mountains.

Father Goose (1964)

Universal Prod: Robert Arthur. Dir: Ralph Nelson. Scr: Peter Stone, Frank Tarloff.• Story basis: S. H. Barnett. Cast: Cary Grant, Leslie Caron, Trevor Howard, Jack Good, Sharyl Locke, Pip Sparke, Verina Greenlaw, Stephanie Barrington, Jennifer Berrington, Laurelle Felsette, Nicole Felsette

This Oscar-winning wartime feature owes its origin to British-exiled blacklistee Tarloff transforming a remake of African Queen in the Pacific to a tale of an American beachcomber drafted into being a coastwatcher on a South Pacific island. Supposedly guarding against the threat of the Japanese, he mainly tends to a group of female orphans watched over by schoolmistress Leslie Caron. Stone essentially polished the dialogue after Tarloff. In the outcome, Grant's harmless blustering amid the opposite sex and Caron's schoolmarmish coquettery is comically set off by Howard's role as the acute Australian commander. Considered lightweight by critics, Goose became the favorite of many World War II veterans: so harmless, so lovable. 118 min., color.

Fellow Traveller (1989)

BBC/HBO. Prod: Michael Wearing. Dir: Phillip Saville. Scr: Michael Eaton. Cast: Ron Silver, Hart Bochner, Imogen Stubbs, Daniel J. Travanti, Katherine Borowitz, Jonathan Hyde, Alexander Hanson

One of the best of the efforts to treat the Hollywood blacklist and easily the best to approach the loaded issues of Jewishness as well as the oddball role of a prominent psychoanalyst in the coaxing of friendly testimony, Fellow Traveller deserves a wider viewing.

Silver, Bochner and Travanti are inspired as, respectively, the screenwriter, his Brooklyn boyhood friend (and rising film star) and the apparently benevolent shrink. In one particularly effective scene, studio writers, directors, and producers gather around a Beverly Hills swimming pool in the middle 1940s to collect money for the war effort, certain in their own minds that history has vindicated their left-wing politics. Then comes the dreaded repression, resisted not only for political reasons but for reasons of Jewish cultural solidarity as well (the anti-Semitism behind the blacklist was evident from the start). Silver is shown leaving his wife (Borowitz) to write for the television show Adventures of Robin Hood in England; it's the only reference on film to the most successful television work (along with You Are There) done by the Left in the 1950s. Jewish pretty boy Bochner, who wears a Star of David around his sculpted neck, has a breakdown that ends with him spilling the beans—and committing suicide, the broken conscience of a generation.

Silver wants to feel at home in the British Left, then organized (by the real-life E. P. Thompson) under the aegis of the Ban the Bomb movement. But he can't, and the film yearns for a strong conclusion. It comes with Travanti, who has become a social democratic anti-Communist insisting that the blacklist is a good thing—thus revealing himself as an extraordinary rat of the Arthur Koestler/Congress for Cultural Freedom variety. A brave film, filled with accurately observed details. 97 min.

Fiddler on the Roof (1971)

UA. Prod: Norman Jewison. Dir: Norman Jewison. Scr: Joseph Stein (Joseph Fields, uncredited). Multiple bases: Broadway musical by Joseph Stein, Jerry Bock and Sheldon Harnick, from Sholom Aleichem stories; play The World of Sholom Aleichem by Arnold Perl• (1956), uncredited. Cast: Chaim Topol, Norma Crane, Leonard Frey, Molly Picon, Paul Mann, Rosalind Harris, Michele Marsh, Neva Small, Candy Bonstein

Back in the dark days of the 1950s, blacklistee television writer and occasional screenwriter (with a posthumous co-credit for MALCOLM X) Perl had devised a traveling show, "The World of Sholem Aleichem," drawing on the famed Yiddish writer's short stories for a small cast (with fellow blacklistee Jack Gilford often in the leading role) playing mostly local Jewish institutions. A road success, it germinated indirectly into a long-running Broadway musical starring Zero Mostel,• about the dairyman Tevye and his marriageable daughters in a Ukrainian shtetl. Eventually it could claim 35 million viewers in more than 30 nations and adaptations in a dozen languages. Its music could be (and was) enjoyed by those who had little interest and no sympathy for the short story writer's humanitarian outlook. Uncredited playwright Joseph Fields was a long-time collaborator with Edward Chodorov,• raising the prospect of yet more quiet blacklist work on the final film script.

The film, directed by a gentile (whose other credits were to include Jesus Christ, Superstar) and starring the Israeli Topol in place of Mostel, lost something in the process. The musical score by Jerry Block took great liberties with the original author's notions, and the choreography by Jerome Robbins† steals the show even while effectively enhancing the images of anti-Semitic pogroms. The Jewish world created is, in all, a little Disneyfied. And yet Tevye manages to speak, as Aleichem did, for the downtrodden of the world; his daughters emerge as if etched from real types; and even the radical student who becomes a son-in-law, wounding Tevye by renouncing religion, is treated with the seriousness of his cause. The village looks at least a little like a *shtetl* (filming took place near Zagreb, Yugoslavia), and the color palette was reportedly adapted from Chagall's paintings.

As a narrative of life before dispersal from centuries-old locations, *Fiddler* is also most curiously and cryptically a vindication of the somewhat chastened (and re-Judaized) blacklistees. Yet so much has its performance become a definition of Jewishness—like *Schindler's List* in another generation—that assimilated Jews and avowed nationalists can view it as an explanation of diasporic history while enjoying it as pure entertainment. Also like *Schindler's List*, it raked in the Oscars: best actor, best art direction/set design, best director, best picture, best supporting actor. Golden Globes: best actor and best film–musical comedy. 181 min., color.

Fiesta (1947)
Exotic musical co-scripted by Lester Cole•, with music in part by Aaron Copland,• highlighting the lives of an aristocratic Mexican family, with Esther Williams as the good-natured spitfire educated in the United States, determined to marry an American. Best scene is her cross-dressing as her artistic brother, to fight a bull. Ricardo Montalban's first U.S. film.

55 Days at Peking (1963)
Dreadful pseudo-history directed by Nicholas Ray, in which big stars play Anglo-Americans and other Euros facing the horror of the Boxer Rebellion. Some slight effort is made to explain the suffering of ordinary Chinese, but mostly the film remains politically clueless, while it drags on and on. A Philip Yordan project, it was one of Bernard Gordon's• first proper credits coming off the blacklist.

Fighting Bill Carson (1945)
Louise Rousseau• wrote this Buster Crabbe western with an analytical flair. When Crabbe disrupts a stage holdup and in the process rescues a lobbyist at the Texas state legislature who had used his influence to get a charter for the local bank, citizens want to make the lobbyist head of the new bank. He declines because it turns out he was the mastermind behind the stage robbery. Justice, needless to say, triumphs.

Fighting Devil Dogs (1943)
A forgotten bit of Americana that is actually a re-edited compilation of a Republic serial shot in 1938 about a couple of lieutenants in the Marine Corps in China and Manchuria. Co-written by Sol Shor,† it featured so much mayhem and bloodshed that the first run was actually cancelled by Fox theaters on the West Coast because children ran out of the theater or hid behind the curtains. Five years later, deep in World War II, the gore no longer seemed so shocking.

Figures in a Landscape (1970)
A strictly minor Joseph Losey• movie written, oddly enough, by star Robert Shaw from a novel by Barrie England. Shaw and co-star Malcolm McDowell have escaped from an unidentified prison in an unidentified country for nameless reasons, hike their way across hundreds of miles of barren landscape, stealing from nameless peasants along the way as they dodge the real star, a helicopter with an extraordinarily skilled pilot who can do stunts six feet off the ground. It all adds up to very little, though a few scenes are memorable. If the lines Shaw wrote for himself are often banal, he put his heart into delivering them. Losey, who agreed to direct the film under duress from Shaw, was disheartened at the result.

Finger of Guilt (aka The Intimate Stranger, 1956)
E-L. Prod: Alec Snowden. Dir: Joseph Walton (Joseph Losey•). Scr: Peter Howard (Howard Koch•). Cast: Richard Basehart, Mary Murphy, Constance Cummings, Roger Livesey, Mervyn Johns, Faith Brook

A film less interesting for Losey's skilled direction or the Koch script than its insider look at contemporary British film studio life. Basehart is the former promising young Hollywood director who dallied with an actress who was also the producer's wife. He thereby lost his career and finally landed in London, where he also landed the daughter of one of the big B-filmmakers (modeled perhaps on Eagle-Lion, which produced any number of B-films written by left-wing and assorted other Americans). The studio is out of date and Basehart wants to make a flashy new hit, for which he has brought over his ex-sweetheart (Brook) to star under false pretenses of potentially renewed romance. Then a series of mysterious letters arrives, demanding that he respond to an old lover (whom he insists he never met) in the United Kingdom. His career and his life come apart until the conspiracy is ferreted out. There are some psychological twists, but not enough of them; unlike other British features by Losey or Koch, this has no evident social or political theme, unless it may be the ruinous effects of false accusation against a filmmaker. Livesey is most interesting as the aging studio chief, and the black-and-white cinematography of Cummings, Losey's inamorata of the moment, is luminous. 95 min.

First Comes Courage (1943)

Col. Prod: Harry Joe Brown. Dir: Dorothy Arzner. Scr: Melvin Levy,† George Sklar.• Story basis: Elliott Arnold. Cast: Merle Oberon, Brian Aherne, Carl Esmond, Fritz Leiber, Erville Anderson, Erik Rolf, Reinhold Schunzel, Isobel Elsom

A most unusual antifascist pic directed by lesbian Arzner who was, after the birth of the talkies and until the 1970s, practically the only top-flight woman director (notwithstanding interesting Ida Lupino low-budget films with left-wing writers). Here, Oberon is a Norwegian girl seemingly friendly to a Nazi major but actually involved in passing information to the Allies through Leiber, the town doctor. She marries Nazi Esmond, who is then assassinated by Leiber. The plot thickens as British commando Aherne, who met her before the war, is sent on a secret mission and, after some furtive courting, begs her to return with him. She bravely resists love's call and personal safety until commandos land. Stiff acting reduces ideological oomph, but the female lead offers a strongly gendered antifascist message. This was successful Broadway playwright Sklar's only artistic film success among many disappointments. 88 min.

First Love (1939)

Universal. Prod: Joe Pasternak. Dir: Henry Koster. Scr: Bruce Manning, Lionel Houser (uncredited story basis: Gertrude Purcell,† Henry Myers•), based on a fairy tale recorded by Charles Perrault, "Cendrillon, ou la petite pantoufle de verre" (1697).Cast: Deanna Durbin, Robert Stack, Eugene Pallette, Helen Parrish, Lewis Howard, Leatrice Joy, June Storey, Frank Jenks, Kathleen Howard, Thurston Hall, Marcia Mae Jones

A vehicle for child actress Durbin and the first sound version of Cinderella (the pre-release alternative title), following a silent film starring Mary Pickford (and preced-

ing the Disney film and assorted musicals). Here, the fairy tale is done in contemporary style. Orphan Durbin regrets graduating from Miss Wiggins' school for girls because her wealthy relatives have no interest in her. She settles in with the servants, who love her for her singing and her good heart. After some social embarrassment, she is invited to a gala ball but has only her unfashionable graduation dress to wear. The servants secretly buy her an outfit with their savings and arrange to have a friendly cop stop the family limo and hold it at the ball until midnight. Durbin enchants everyone with her voice, but slips away after kissing Stack. Her envious cousin fires all the servants and she leaves the house for Miss Wiggins, singing Puccini's "One Fine Day" as Stack arrives to sweep her away. The Disney animated version, scripted in part by Maurice Rapf,• has a stronger Cinderella, willing to fight for herself—and also funny mice. 84 min.

Fisherman's Wharf (1939)

Principal Productions (Bobby Breen Productions). Prod: Sol Lesser. Dir: Bernard Vorhaus.• Scr: Bernard Schubert,† Ian McLellan Hunter,• Herbert Clyde Lewis. Cast: Bobby Breen, Henry Armetta, Leo Carillo, Lee Patrick, Rosina Galli, Leon Belasco

A vehicle for the boy singing sensation Breen (star of a half-dozen films, the first two directed or written by reds), this is on one level a child's story of realizing he is adopted, that he wants to run away from home and that he can return to what has always been a loving adopted family. On another and more important level, however, it contains an unforgettable evocation of Italian American working-class life in the late 1930s (not to mention some unforgettable pet seal tricks).

As the film opens, the fleet returns from fishing (as in CLASH BY NIGHT more than a decade later, in a somewhat more stylized fashion but still using real footage). Breen is singing and the concertina sees heavy use. We see a loving relationship between a boy and (apparently) his father, beautifully played by Armetta; a blue-collar home; and the slow recognition that a sister-in-law from Seattle (taken in because of her misfortune) is from a distinctly higher social class. As she schemes to shame Armetta into abandoning the share-and-share-alike method of dividing the profits from fishing for a standard capitalist approach (his friends successfully go on strike, forcing him to abandon his temporary folly), her effete and bratty son lets slip the truth about Breen's paternity. A veritable idyllic childhood is seemingly ruined, but no tragic ending is possible in a film like this. Melodrama aside, the camera work of life near the docks, the dialect-heavy dialogue and the general ambience convey something that the A-films of ethnic life entirely miss. Breen never again got quite so good a setting for his talent—and then his voice changed. 72 min.

5 Branded Women (1960)

Prod: Dino De Laurentiis. Dir: Martin Ritt.• Scr: (uncredited: Michael Wilson,• Paul Jarrico•), Ivo Perilli. Novel basis: Ugo Pirro, *Jovanka e le altre* (1959). Cast: Silvana Mangano, Jeanne Moreau, Barbara Bel Geddes, Vera Miles, Carla Gravina, Van Heflin, Richard Basehart

A film central to the backstory of the blacklist, whose true authorship (Wilson and Jarrico) was undisclosed for years. For reasons that remain unclear, Ritt hated the film, perhaps because of the difficult shooting conditions (in Yugoslavia), but it is invaluable as a record of the sensibility of disillusioned Hollywood CP-ers who clearly saw an opportunity to comment on their own situation after revelations about Stalin, the revolt in Hungary in 1956 and its repression by the Soviet Union. *Women* explores with great passion the question of how a dissenting minority within a larger political movement can assert its legitimate interests without compromising the success of the common struggle. The dissenters are women who know their concerns have been overlooked but manage to force them into the foreground and, in some sense, prevail. Many blacklistees were in a similar position, clinging to the ideals of the Popular Front even during the Cold War, a loyal but dissenting minority.

A group of Slovenian women in World War II discover they have all been seduced by the same German soldier. After he is castrated by partisans—who then turn around and disgrace the women as well by shaving their heads—the "branded" women take to the hills and become scavengers for food and weapons. Soon they evolve into a partisan guerrilla squad; this unlikely band of disciplined killers eventually links back up with the very partisans who had shaved their heads, and together they form a united front against their common fascist enemies. Between firefights, the women learn military discipline (partisans are executed for dereliction) even as they insist on the right to express their love physically to whomever they please.

After the finely crafted opening scenes, the film slows down a bit, but patient viewing is rewarded. In one memorable scene (not in the book), the writers have a partisan disguise himself in an enemy uniform and, during a showing of Nazi propaganda newsreels from the front, deliver a film canister to the unsuspecting army projectionists. When the reviewing stand blows up, taking along

with it a dozen or more German officers, the scene becomes a kind of aesthetic statement: movies should be social explosions. Still difficult to find, this film is a prime candidate for restoration. 115 min.

Five Came Back (1939)

RKO. Prod: Robert Sisk. Dir: John Farrow. Scr: Jerry Cady, Dalton Trumbo,• Nathanael West. Story basis: Richard Carroll. Cast: Chester Morris, Lucille Ball, John Carradine, Wendy Barrie, Kent Taylor, Joseph Calleia, C. Aubrey Smith, Patric Knowles

Strange low-budget and choppy film that displaces class and social anxieties to the Central American jungle, where a planeful of Americans has crash-landed. Calleia, an existential anarchist under escort as a prisoner to a South American republic, is the key figure in several ways, because he accepts the consequences of the crash: cooperative living. Elderly Smith, an anthropology professor, and his wife, Knowles, return to the love they felt for each other and the simple pleasures they lost with the death of a child decades earlier. Ball expresses a disgust with the American society she lives in, and a willingness to stay behind when the repaired plane can only carry five passengers. Calleia seizes the gun and proclaims that because return means death for him, he alone has the right to decide who goes and who stays.

The rest of the film, from the excitement around child Wendy Barrie to the approach of drumming (and head-shrinking) Indians, to the leadership of captain Morris, is stock window-dressing for the cryptic social criticism. The plot was remade as *Back from Eternity* in 1956 by John Farrow, with Robert Ryan and Rod Steiger, but with a distinct dilution of social theme. 75 min.

5 Card Stud (1968)

Para. Prod: Hal B. Wallis. Dir: Henry Hathaway. Scr: Marguerite Roberts.• Novel basis: Ray Gaulden, *5 Card Stud* (1968). Cast: Dean Martin, Robert Mitchum, Inger Stevens, Roddy McDowall, Katherine Justice, Yaphet Kotto

Notable mainly for Martin's performance as a western antihero and for writer Roberts's return from the blacklist decades after writing many B-westerns, leading to her final success, the Oscar-winning TRUE GRIT. A deepening of the psychological themes in film noir since the 1940s had meanwhile resulted in the "dark western," making her own efforts in that direction possible.

Roberts's rendering of the novel is clumsy at times but has a definite charm to make the best of Martin's talent—which is strictly for playing Dino. Like so many westerns but without the pretension to any seriousness, Martin is the good-bad cardsharp who has the love of several women (bodily, the bathhouse owner Stevens; and spiritually, the oppressive and cranky rancher's daughter, Justice), but must contend with the usual bad guys involved in the murder of the members of a perennial poker game, notably the psychotic McDowall, tortured by Oedipal conflicts. A memorable if smaller role is played by Kotto (later the head of the detective division in television's *Homicide*) as a barkeep and Martin's pal. 103 min., color.

5 Fingers (1952)

20th. Prod: Otto Lang. Dir: Joseph L. Mankiewicz. Scr: Joseph L. Mankiewicz (and Michael Wilson,• uncredited). Novel basis: L. C. Moyzisch, *Operation Cicero* (1950). Cast: James Mason, Danielle Darrieux, Michael Rennie, Walter Hampden, Oscar Karlweis, Herbert Berghof, Ben Astar, John Wengraf

This brilliant, revisionist account of spy activity during World War II has the mousy valet of British diplomatic aristocracy and bureaucracy (more or less the same thing) in Turkey successfully stealing secrets, for the Germans, under their noses because they regard the commoner as a nonperson incapable of such action. Based on a true story (the secrets happily went unused), it shows Mason at the apex of his acting brilliance. Adapted as a television series with no bite. 108 min.

The Fixer (1968)

MGM. Prod: Edward Lewis. Dir: John Frankenheimer. Scr: Dalton Trumbo.• Novel basis: Bernard Malamud, *The Fixer* (1966). Cast: Alan Bates, Dirk Bogarde, Georgia Brown, Hugh Griffith, Elizabeth Hartman, David Opatoshu, Carol White

This adaptation of Malamud's Pulitzer Prize–winning novel dramatized a real historical incident: the Russian trial in 1911 of a Jewish handyman whose plight and its international impact helped publicize the pervasive anti-Semitism in that pre-revolutionary society. Notable as one of the first major Hollywood dramas with themes of Jewish victimization. Ironically but most effectively, Bogarde, the government investigator and a favorite actor of exile director Joseph Losey, gets the best lines.

Bates is a *shtetl* lad who abandons home for Kiev, arriving just in time for a "minor" pogrom, echo of the 1905 incidents that drove so many to seek refuge in the United States. In a fascinating sexual scene, he is lured into bed by a *shiksa* daughter of a leading anti-Semite but

at the last moment detects that she is having her period, and he rejects her as "unclean." This leads indirectly to his downfall: he takes risky work, in which he can be arrested under false charges of killing a gentile boy in a ritual murder. He is pursued by a Czarist system evidently seeking to channel social discontent into populist anti-Semitic sentiment. State's attorney Bogarde discovers the truth, while the tortured and humiliated Bates endures the adversity without confessing, and learns as well as gives lessons in morality. The final scenes possess a rare cinematic power. Cold War critics ruthlessly mowed it down and buried it. 132 min., Metrocolor.

The Flame and the Arrow (1950)

Norma F. R. Productions. Prod: Frank Ross, Harold Hecht.† Dir: Jacques Tourneur. Scr: Waldo Salt.• Cast: Burt Lancaster, Virginia Mayo, Aline McMahon, Nick Cravat, Robert Douglas

Waldo Salt's last credit before the blacklist features a leftish guerilla facing off against a tyrant determined to conquer turf and extract taxes. The genial freebooter eventually learns that he can no longer avoid the national (or regional) struggle by going it alone. Meanwhile, he woos the lady fair, who is nominally pledged to some rascally royal. In this version of the generic struggle against wrongdoers, Lancaster is the wilderness prince of the mountains around Lombardy surrounded by veritable acrobats who love to outjump as well as outwit and outfight the imperial conquerors. He also expresses some pleasantly ecological themes, a love for birds (choosing the section of the forest where the emperor's hawks do not rule) and for the nonmaterialistic simple life of wooden bowls and no servants. His son has been captured by the newly appointed representative of the crown, and he must recapture the boy while overthrowing the urban regime. His men enter town the night of the carnival, and get to show their stuff. McMahon is especially good as a village woman's leader who explains politics to Lancaster and to Mayo. 88 min., color.

Flame of Calcutta (1953)

Mysterious maiden appears in eighteenth-century India to assist the brave British officer in going after a villainous prince. Based on a story by Sol Shor.†

Flaxy Martin (1949)

Virginia Mayo in the title role as a femme fatale, mistress at once of a mobster and a mob lawyer, concealing each relationship with the other and promising each that they will "go away together." A working-class girl (played by Dorothy Malone) offers love and redemption. David Lang† provided the story basis and wrote the script.

Flight to Mars (1952)
Monogram. Prod: Walter Mirisch. Dir: Lesley Selander. Scr: Arthur Strawn.• Cast: Cameron Mitchell, Marguerite Chapman, Arthur Franz

As director Selander turned from westerns to sci-fi, he continued to deploy left-wing writers. This film saw the first use of color in the genre. Perhaps the main benefit is the resonance of the tints in the exotic outfits—sharp shoulder pads and miniskirts for the women, but pre-aerobics clothes-of-the-future businesswear for the men. The plot rehearses the usual crash and welcome by the natives (living in tunnels), who unfortunately want to save their own civilization by invading Earth. Interplanetary romances inevitably complicate things (politics elsewhere in the galaxy is just as full of would-be manipulators), and the protagonists run (or fly) for their lives. An allegory rather than mere hack work, it is a study of a society that has met its doom with the worst possible strategies—giving power over to demagogues rather than democrats. 72 min., color.

Florida Special (1936)
Para. Prod: Albert Lewis. Dir: Ralph Murphy. Scr: David Boehm, Marguerite Roberts,• Laura Perelman, S. J. Perelman. Story basis: Clarence Budington Kelland. Cast: Jack Oakie, Sally Eilers, Kent Taylor, Frances Drake, Claude Gillingwater, J. Farrell MacDonald, Sidney Blackmer, Matthew Betz, Sam Hearn, Dwight Frye, Garry Owen, Clyde Dilson, Mack Gray

A Hollywood extravagance of expensive sets and threadbare story lines is more interesting for what might have been—with the leftwing sympathizer S. J. Perelman collaborating on the script—than for what resulted. The studio built a version of Pennsylvania Station and hired top writers to handle this mundane mystery comedy. Oakie mugs through his act as a newspaper reporter who unintentionally boards a train for Florida with rich pal Taylor, who has just broken off an engagement with Drake. She happens to be on the same train and soon has her jewels nabbed. By the time the train reaches Virginia, multiple kidnappings and rescues have taken place and cops are on hand to sort things out. Oakie learns that he is fired but he has the story of a lifetime, while Taylor makes off with the hostess (and former girlfriend of a

mobster) whom he has met and saved along the way. As Roberts later commented, she was only hired as "an inexpensive writer to develop ideas" and a script "now and then," but had the consolation of knowing that such hack work "didn't take much out of me." 70 min.

The Flying Irishman (1939)
RKO. Prod: Pandro S. Berman. Dir: Leigh Jason. Scr: Ernest Pagano, Dalton Trumbo.• Cast: Douglas (né Clyde) "Wrong Way" Corrigan (as himself), Paul Kelly, Robert Armstrong, Gene Reynolds, Donald MacBride, Eddie Quillan, J. M. Kerrigan

Remarkable if factually dubious production about an American underdog, played by the historical character himself. Real-life Corrigan supposedly intended to fly from New York to Los Angeles but landed instead in Ireland, less likely by mistake than as a publicity stunt. The film recounts the story of a boy who wanted urgently to fly, despite all the odds (mostly class-based) against him. As the family's finances wither after his father dies, and after putting a brother through college, he saves enough money to buy an airplane, but his pilot's license is denied repeatedly: he has a weak heart, and can't get into the trade without the flying hours that ex-military pilots (and upper-class men trained professionally) easily acquire. Loaded down with far more gasoline than the plane should hold, he makes the wrong-way flight and eventually gets a hero's welcome on his return to New York. Corrigan's acting was stiff, but he exuded a certain sincerity. Gene Reynolds, who played the boy version of Corrigan, grew up close to the Left and went on to produce M*A*S*H for television. 71 min.

Footsteps in the Dark (1941)
WB. Exec Prod: Hal B. Wallis. Prod: Robert Lord. Dir: Lloyd Bacon. Scr: John Wexley,• Lester Cole.• Play basis: Ladislas Fodor, Bernard Merivale, Jeffrey Dell, Blondie White (n.d.). Cast: Errol Flynn, Brenda Marshall, Ralph Marshall, Ralph Bellamy, Alan Hale, Lee Patrick, Allen Jenkins, Grant Mitchell, Lucile Watson, William Frawley, Roscoe Karns, Turhan Bey, Jack La Rue

A lighthanded comedy for Flynn, the swashbuckler about to become a war hero, about an investment councilor who secretly writes mystery novels and happens upon a murder that he believes he can solve. The sly comedy plays out as he pursues stripper Patrick as a likely suspect, then turns toward Marshall, a romantic possibility. Not enough good moments, except for Flynn fans. 96 min.

Forbidden Street aka *Britannia Mews*, aka *Affairs of Adelaide* (1949)

20th. Dir: Jean Negulesco. Scr: Ring Lardner, Jr.• Novel basis: Margery Sharp, *Britannia Mews* (1946). Cast: Maureen O'Hara, Dana Andrews, Sybil Thorndike, Diana Hart, Anne Butchart

Lardner later expressed bitter regrets about this melodrama's re-editing, which, in his view, just about robbed it of any value. Produced in London, it is a nineteenth-century class drama about a squalid slum and an artist who marries a beautiful young woman of the upper class (O'Hara), who learns the hard lessons of survival when she is disowned for her foolishness. The film is worth watching for the evolution of O'Hara's character, with the help of Lardner's shrewd dialogue and for her occasionally splendid acting. Many images are memorable, but Lardner was right about the editing: the class line melts into melodrama. 90 min.

Force of Evil (1948)

Enterprise Productions. Prod: Bob Roberts. Dir: Abraham Polonsky.• Scr: Abraham Polonsky, Ira Wolfert. Novel basis: Ira Wolfert, *Tuckers' People* (1943). Cast: John Garfield, Beatrice Pearson, Thomas Gomez, Roy Roberts, Marie Windsor, Howland Chamberlain, Paul McVey, Barbara Woodell, Stanley Prager,• Beau Bridges

One of the deservedly most famous films of the Hollywood Left, and along with Polonsky's two scripted pre-blacklist films, BODY AND SOUL and I CAN GET IT FOR YOU WHOLESALE, part of the classic trilogy of noir's Marxist master. It turns a stock portrayal of mobsters into an effective moral tale of family struggle among Jews, reflecting the moral dilemmas in the world outside.

Garfield, this time not a pug but a corrupt lawyer, is moving up fast in the policy ("numbers") racket, so named because the poor put their insurance policy money into a weekly gamble instead. To complete the centralization of the mob's control, Garfield must recruit the operation of his brother, Gomez, an honest crook with a bad heart who sacrificed to send Garfield to law school. The film pivots on Garfield's corruption of Gomez's trusted secretary, Pearson, who wants an honest life but is lured by Garfield because (as he tells her) she really wants to be corrupted or is, at least, unable to resist.

Step by step they go down, Gomez with them, showing that crime is capitalism and capitalism, crime. Scenes of confrontation between the resistant Gomez and Garfield are perhaps the most memorable. The terse script comes as close to theatrical Odets as any film, including

Odets' own. "We have a real new talent in the medium, as well as a sizzling piece of work," the *New York Times* reviewer reflected. Too bad Polonsky had so little time to practice it. (Robert Aldrich, studying at the knee of the master, was assistant director). 78 min.

Forever Amber (1947)

20th. Prod: William Perlberg. Dir: Otto Preminger. Scr: Ring Lardner Jr.,• Philip Dunne. Novel basis: Kathleen Winsor, *Forever Amber* (1944). Cast: Linda Darnell, Cornel Wilde, George Sanders, Glenn Langan, Glenn Langan, Richard Haydn, Jessica Tandy, Anne Revere,• Leo G. Carroll, Robert Coote, John Russell

Some fun at the beginning and end, according to Lardner, but precious little in between. Actually, this is one of the films that seemingly threatened the Production Code, thanks to the frank amorality of the lead, who beds her way from poverty to fortune. Set in England at the time of the Great Revolution (1644), it sheds a lot of light upon class privilege but not much on the politics. Sent to prison on false charges, Darnell turns crooked, is discovered by the aristocracy, lives through the Black Plague, repeatedly loses the man she really loves and hopes the best for her son. An Academy Award nomination went to David Raksin† for best music. 138 min.

Forever and a Day (1943)

RKO. Prod. and Dir: René Clair, Emund Goulding, Cedric Hardwicke, Frank Lloyd, Victor Saville, Robert Stevenson, Herbert Wilcox. Scr: Charles Bennett, Michael Hogan, Christopher Isherwood, Gene Lockhart, Donald Ogden Stewart.• Cast: Brian Aherne, Robert Cummings, Ida Lupino, Charles Laughton, Herbert Marshall, Ray Milland, Claude Rains, Buster Keaton, Elsa Lanchester

A magnum RKO production rallying sympathy to British cause by marshalling big names from all sides of the camera (almost, but not entirely, the "All English Cast" claimed by publicity), with a transhistorical and trans-class claim on English traditions through the story of one house's inhabitants from 1804 to almost 1944. High points among the dozen or so vignettes include the plucky wives who figured out their husbands' business for them, the lordly figures who nevertheless acted in the common English good and the servants (Laughton and Lanchester) who ham it up with their favorite characterizations. The house, now occupied by an Englishwoman and a distantly related American (whose side of the extended family has always been part of the story: the literal Anglo cousins of Americans), is bombed out, but will be rebuilt, like

England itself. If only partly created by the Left, *Forever* nevertheless has the essential stamp of the pro-Allied Left film, albeit with fewer references to the good common people. Described accurately as having "once-in-a-life-time cast and directing." 104 min.

Forgotten Faces (1936)

Para. Prod: A. M. Bostford. Dir: Ewald André Dupont. Scr: Marguerite Roberts,• Robert Yost, Brian Marlow. Story basis: Richard Washburn Child, "A Whiff of Heliotrope." Cast: Herbert Marshall, Gertrude Michael, James Burke, Robert Cummings, Jane Rhodes

Previously made under the same title by Paramount in 1928, the film retains some of the pre-Code spice (without much else). Marshall is a gambling-house entre-preneur, distrusted and disliked by his adulterous wife, Michael. Finding her in the arms of another man, he shoots the lout and turns himself in, leaving his baby with police sergeant Burke. Seventeen years later, as mom is working in a burlesque house, she conspires to blackmail her former in-laws. Will her nearly grown daughter (Rhodes) ever be able to marry without a shadow of her "bad mother"? 71 min.

Forty Thieves (1944)

One of the cycle of four Hopalong Cassidy features written by Michael Wilson• of later fame who took these assign-ments just as seriously as he did LAWRENCE OF ARABIA. Hoppy has cleaned up the county from a previous adventure, is appointed sheriff and commences running for his first election. The saloon owners, angry because he is bad for business, rig the election. He gracefully concedes defeat but soon reasserts himself with his shootin' irons when he discovers evidence of vote fraud. Armed, domestic version of antifascism wins the day.

Four Sons (1940)

20th. Prod: Darryl F. Zanuck, Harry Joe Brown. Dir: Archie Mayo. Scr: John Howard Lawson.• Story basis: I. A. R. Wylie, "Grandmother Bernie Learns Her Letter," *Saturday Evening Post* (1926). Cast: Don Ameche, Eugenie Leontovich, Mary Beth Hughes, Alan Curtis, George Ernest, Robert Lowery, Lionel Royce

Even at this late date, Hollywood was still backing away from the anti-Nazi film, with very few featuring members of the heavily left-wing German refugee com-munity. A version of this story was made in 1928 by John Ford, but of course without the anti-Nazi update,

which owed everything (except the disillusionment) to Lawson.

The film hails back to pre-invasion Czechoslovakia in 1936, where widowed Leontovich cares lovingly for her sons. Dad was killed in the last big war, and she is happy to see one of her sons (Lowery) leaving for America. Another (Curtis) supports the Nazis, while a third, our protagonist (Ameche) is a patriotic Czech. They try to make peace at Curtis's wedding, but the bridegroom is called to duty to kill a captured spy before he talks. Time passes, and the family reconciles until the eve of the Nazi invasion. Ameche learns from his brother that a list has been compiled of locals to be murdered and rushes out to warn them, accidentally shooting his brother. Hughes, Curtis's widow, denounces him, and he is killed in turn. The last son is drafted by the Germans and falls in battle. Presented with a medal, the mother wryly observes that the first time she was so awarded, her husband had died for the Germans. Finally, Hughes realizes that the war is wrong, and with her son and Leontovich, they head for America. At times overwrought, but understandably so for the time and place. 89 min.

The Fox (1968)

Motion Pictures International. Prod: Steve Brody, *The Fox* (1923). Dir: Mark Rydell. Scr: Lewis John Carlino, Howard Koch.• Story basis: D. H. Lawrence. Cast: Sandy Dennis, Anne Heywood, Keir Dullea, Glyn Morris

A heavily symbolic feminist and lesbian drama that marks the characteristically difficult return of the black-listed artist into the maelstrom of sixties avant-garde film. Too many arty shots and poses along with the repressed histrionics of a typical Sandy Dennis outing mar the drama of two former schoolgirl pals trying to live as men-free adults on an isolated farm in winter, troubled only by hard work and the intrusion of a fox raiding the hen house. Into this icy, would-be Amazonia where Dennis had settled in as the domestic and Heywood the outdoorswoman comes the remarkably vulpine Dullea, grandson of the farm's previous owner. Making himself the handyman and phallic figure of the household, he precipitates emotional crises. The attrac-tion of both women to him divides them, and his romantic approaches to Heywood (enacting a sex scene Koch could not have written in earlier decades) threaten to overwhelm her. His exit triggers the third act. At times overdrawn, the film nevertheless gives Heywood her best and most credible part as a woman caught between two kinds of life—making this a film badly in need of recovery. 110 min., color.

Framed (1947)

Col. Prod: Jules Schermer. Dir: Richard Wallace. Scr: Ben Maddow.•† Story basis: John Patrick. Cast: Glenn Ford, Janis Carter, Barry Sullivan, Edgar Buchanan, Karen Morley,• Jim Bannon, Barbara Woodell, Paul E. Burns

An above average noir women's pic with Carter as the dame who consorts with Sullivan to find a pigeon and rope him in. Ford, reduced from mining engineer to out-of-town truckdriver, is seduced by Carter, who plans to embezzle a quarter-million with the help of Sullivan, a local bank vice president. She needs a fall guy who looks like Sullivan, but as the robbery unfolds, she falls for Ford. The bulk of dramatic tension involves Ford trying to figure out her motives, and take the guilt off his would-be mining partner, played lovingly by Buchanan. 82 min.

Frankenstein (1931)

Universal. Prod: Carl Laemmle, Jr. Dir: James Whale. Scr: Garrett Fort, Francis Edward Faragoh.• Story basis: Mary Wollstonecraft Shelley, Frankenstein (1818). Cast: Colin Clive, Mae Clark, John Boles, Boris Karloff, Edward Van Sloan, Frederick Kerr, Dwight Frye, Lionel Belmore, Marilyn Harris

In his first important credit (in some ways, his most important), Faragoh took over the script late, gave the power of speech to the scientist's "dummy" assistant, added a bit of humor and most important, gave the "monster" the humane touches that actor Karloff later insisted endeared him to children as the true victim of the tale. Wollstonecraft, who had subtitled her novel "the Modern Prometheus," had something similar in mind—perhaps even the emerging industrial worker who was created by patriarchal industrialism and then abandoned to his fate and tortured nearly to madness. Deservedly, this is considered the best of the screen adaptations, which began in 1910, reemerged as satire in the 1940s, and continued into the 1980s-1990s in a variety of forms. It was one of the ten best-selling films of the year and one of the most expensive to produce, at nearly $300,000. In another irony, this was the film that helped touch off a unionization drive in Hollywood: actor Karloff, tortured by the acid used to take off his makeup at night and insulted by the studio publicity warning pregnant women to flee at the sight of him in costume, set his mind on the Screen Actors Guild, of which he was a pioneer (he was also, like Bela Lugosi, a frequent ally of the Left).

The story line is simple. As the film opens, the Count (played by Clive) and his assistant are seen digging up a corpse, which they mean to reanimate. They need, however, a new brain, and having dropped the one he was assigned to take, assistant Frye substitutes the brain of a criminal. Van Sloane, as the Count's former professor, makes his way to the castle where the two use electricity to bring the "monster" to life. The mentally tortured creature escapes and accidentally drowns a child before he is hunted down by villagers bearing torches. 71 min.

Friendly Persuasion (1956)

Allied Artists. Prod: William Wyler, Robert Wyler. Dir: William Wyler. Scr: Michael Wilson• (originally uncredited). Story basis: Jessamyn West, "Friendly Persuasion," 1945. Cast: Gary Cooper, Dorothy McGuire, Anthony Perkins, Richard Eyer, Robert Middleton, Phyllis Love

Wilson's genius in this originally uncredited screenplay is felt from the first moments of the story about a Quaker family living in a border state during the Civil War. It combines two of the family themes used by left-wingers of the period with uncommon skill: the relations between children and animals and the domestic situation of women who discover their strength in unexpected ways.

Wilson was particularly interested in and adept at women's themes, and many of his most successful films before the blockbusters that closed out his career were devoted to them. In fact, he began working on a screenplay for Friendly Persuasion soon after a volume of Jessamyn West's short stories appeared in 1945. As in SALT OF THE EARTH and 5 BRANDED WOMEN, Wilson took up the theme of women in an internal struggle within a minority group, in this case the Quakers in a border state during the Civil War. West's heroine shows the backsliders in the local fellowship and in her own family how to practice their pacifist beliefs while refusing to fight against invading Confederate troops.

In the film that was eventually made (and for which Wilson, by this time on the blacklist, was denied credit), the standard of the faith is planted squarely by McGuire, who prevents bloodshed by sharing her food with Southern soldiers and winning their respect. Every other member of the family has temporized in some way—yielding to the temptations of martial glory, arguing the essential evil of the enemy. Even when McGuire successfully makes the philosophical point, those around her find ways to elude it. In the end there is little doubt that the film—again, as made—was an apology for the Cold War and necessary for all Americans, including devout pacifists, to abandon their principles and rally to arms. Even so, Wilson managed to preserve the essential message in a running joke about a boy and a nasty goose that loves to ambush him, a parable of violence and Quaker resistance that was apparently too subtle (and too funny) for the front office to tamper with.

Friendly Persuasion is in places a beautiful film, but Wyler's compromises in the handling of the story's political concerns were made mostly at the Quakers' expense and now may be regarded as a measure of the moral loss of Quaker influence in public affairs. (West was herself Richard Nixon's second cousin). The film nevertheless charmed the French, whose film industry insiders must have known the true authorship; it took a *Palme d'Or* at Cannes in 1957. 131 min.

From Hell to Heaven (1933)

Sidney Buchman• wrote the screenplay for a Lawrence Hazard stage piece (*Good Company*), a horse-race melodrama with assorted inhabitants of a hotel counting on the big race to change their lives. Bookie Sidney Blackmer takes a bet for Carole Lombard, who left him years earlier for a rich man; meanwhile, David Manners desperately needs to win $500 he embezzled to keep wife Adrienne Ames in comfortable style. And so on. Murder confounds a drifty plot.

From This Day Forward (1946)

RKO. Prod: William L. Pereira. Dir: John Berry.• Scr: Hugo Butler• (uncredited script contribution: Clifford Odets†). Story basis: Garson Kanin, adaptation, from Thomas Bell novel, *All Brides Are Beautiful* (1936). Cast: Joan Fontaine, Mark Stevens, Rosemary DeCamp, Harry Morgan, Arlene Judge, Bobby Driscoll

The most expressively optimistic film of the postwar Left, this is literally working-class cinema. Based on a 1941 novel by lefty Bell (which begins with the happy thought that on a Jewish holiday, the Bronx looks like a city in the midst of a general strike) and updated as well as de-ethnicized, it traces the saga of a blue-collar couple, played touchingly by Fontaine and Stevens. Camera angles around the High Bridge in the Bronx, shots of the factory floor and in their apartment work wonderfully to extend the moods of urban hope and industrial realism.

He is a machinist, bombardier and would-be artist; she works at a bookstore and dreams of having a family. They married shortly before his induction, a past we see only in flashbacks. The continuing class reality is defined by her extended family and their economic hard times. Her sister DeCamp, married to cheerfully unemployed blue-collar oaf Morgan (the actor destined to co-star in both the most right-wing and most left-wing TV shows in

broadcasting history, *Dragnet* and *M*A*S*H*), warns Fontaine dourly about the unhappiness of marriage and kids. Their mother is a miser counting funds for old age. Meanwhile, demobilization brings only a return to blue-collar normalcy, including factories handing out layoff slips. In a twist that would seem anomalous during later decades, Stevens innocently contributes his drawings to an art volume suppressed as pornography and must take a guilty plea or go to jail.

Somehow, despite all their problems, the couple has the confidence in themselves, their future family and their society that would soon slip away—at least for the vision of a more cooperative, egalitarian America and not just a richer one. A studio hit. 95 min.

The Front (1976)

Col. Prod: Martin Ritt,• Charles H. Joffe. Dir: Martin Ritt. Scr: Walter Bernstein.• Cast: Woody Allen, Zero Mostel,• Herschel Bernardi, Michael Murphy, Danny Aiello, Andrea Marcovicci, Julie Garfield

One of Allen's best films but, contrary to popular misunderstanding, not one of his own creation. Former blacklistees Ritt and Bernstein had floated a project about the blacklist unsuccessfully until the screenwriter's friend Allen was presented as a possible lead. He is indeed perfect for the part of a delicatessen clerk who, thanks to high school pal Murphy, altogether innocently finds himself acting as a "front" (the bylined writer but not the actual author) for blacklistees writing for television. Like a number of real-life fronts, he begins with great success and then runs into trouble when he is put on the spot to come up with scripts that he obviously can't write alone. Finally, the witch-hunters close in. His girlfriend pleads with him to take a stand and not become a friendly witness, but he only fumbles his way toward morality. Like all the principals in the film, he is emblematically Jewish.

Mostel, playing the overweight and overwrought victim he truly was as a blacklisted actor (unable to work even on his beloved Broadway for much of the 1950s), takes a famous filmic leap out the window—standing symbolically for the suicides, early heart attacks and strokes suffered in real life by blacklistees (and in particular for the suicide of Phillip Loeb, long-time co-star of *The Goldbergs*). Cold Warriors like the *New York Times'* Walter Goodman, ever eager to return to the attack on the Hollywood reds, savaged the film. Better disposed critics (including some of the blacklistees themselves) suggested that the mixture of comedy and drama did not quite come off, that the displacement of the blacklist narrative from movies to television muddied the issue, or more simply that Mostel's over-the-top performance was not in keeping with the seriousness of the issues. Most of these views have faded with time and the film has held up under decades of repeated viewing. Virtually unmarketed when it was released, *The Front* has deserved its long life. 94 min., color.

Fugitive from a Prison Camp (1940)

In this Stanley Roberts† story, working stiff Phillip Terry hopes to win Marian Marsh by joining a gang of outlaws and convincing her brother, George Offerman, Jr., to go straight. Arrested instead as an accomplice, he dreams of creating a work camp in which young offenders can be segregated from hard cons.

The Fuller Brush Man (1948)

An unlikely comedy based on a novel by accomplished noir and western screenwriter (and later TV producer) Roy Huggins† has Red Skelton as the brush man, stumbling across a murder and solving it with the help of girlfriend Janet Blair.

F.T.A. (1972)

A concert film of the antiwar vaudeville troupe of Jane Fonda and Donald Sutherland among others, reaching U.S. military bases around the world with a peacenik message (the title is an abbreviation for "Fuck the Army") for soldiers at the height of the despair over Vietnam. It gives lots of its footage to the servicemen themselves. Scripted in part by Dalton Trumbo,• with Sutherland delivering recitations. Attacked by the loyalist press, the film died and disappeared. Some fugitive copies are rumored to be available via the Internet.

Fuzzy Settles Down (1944)

Companion to Louise Rousseau's• FIGHTING BILL CARSON (which she also wrote for Buster Crabbe), this time about control of a Western town's community newspaper instead of the bank.

G

Galileo (1975)

Cinévision Ltée. Prod: Ely A. Landau. Dir: Joseph Losey.• Scr: Barbara Bray, Joseph Losey. Play basis: Berthold Brecht,• *Das Leben Galilei* (1938). Cast: Topol, Tom Conti, Edward Fox, John Gielgud, Ian Hoare, Margaret Leighton, Michael Lonsdale

Frustrating because it could have been so much better, but the central problem was that casting Israeli actor Topol, forever identified as the milkman Tevye, was an invitation to excess. The invitation was accepted. In addition, Brecht's style and purposes so consistently undercut the expectations of cinema, and so a first viewing of this story of the suppression of a Great Idea can be somewhat tedious. However, more patient viewing opens on the vistas of Brecht's own copious landscapes, in which ideas are taken seriously and drive the action without the benefit of easy stage emotions.

Losey had wanted to make this film for years, ever since directing a famous stage production in Hollywood and New York, starring Charles Laughton, that was widely misunderstood. It accounts for the persistent misinterpretation of Losey as a Brechtian. 145 min.

The Gay Señorita (1945)

Anglo businessman (Jim Bannon) sets his sights on converting a Latino neighborhood in California into a factory zone but changes his mind while falling in love with a gay (really only cheerful) señorita, played by Jinx Falkenburg. The film is interesting for its celebration of Hispanic California (L.A.'s Sandoval Lane), but mainly because of its being the Columbia debut for film composer-lyricist Jay Gorney• (in a script co-written with Edward Eliscu,• actually credited as producer), and for its cast of Latino actors.

The General Died At Dawn (1936)

Para. Prod: William LeBaron. Dir: Lewis Milestone. Scr: Clifford Odets.† Story basis: Charles G. Booth. Cast: Gary Cooper, Madeleine Carroll, Akim Tamiroff, Dudley Digges, Porter Hall, William Frawley

Odets' maiden voyage into Hollywood scriptwriting, fast from his Broadway left-wing triumphs, was for one of the most distinguished "social problem" directors (ALL QUIET ON THE WESTERN FRONT, etc.). The result was widely considered the writer's sell-out, an impression that Odets himself likely encouraged with his revulsion at piling up the dollars he also urgently wanted. The film has suffered further from the embarrassment of later viewers at non-Asians playing so many Asian parts, often with pidgin English. Nor does it have the virtue of, for instance, DRAGON SEED, with Katharine Hepburn making all the political points.

And yet *The General* is far from a bad film, for its time. Within 90 seconds of the opening, Coop has punched out an American businessman who expresses pleasure in the way a warlord and business partner have been squeezing the Chinese masses. (Cooper later claimed to know nothing about communism, and, who knows?, maybe he was not alert enough to figure out that he was plumping for alternatives to Chiang Kai Chek's crookedness). The film develops into an almost average exotic spy drama, with Carroll sneaking weapons funds away from courier Cooper, and Coop seeking to recover the cash while Caroll falls in love with him.

The General is rescued from the usual clichés by Coop's references to the struggling masses, by the supporting performances of Tamiroff (as a brutal but cultured warlord), Digges (a bug-eyed American conspirator) and Frawley (a boozed-up American corporate type). Even Odets himself has a cameo. Still, the film drags, and Carroll is like a femme fatale out of silent film with too much mascara; Coop needed a stronger matchup. 98 min.

Gentleman's Agreement (1947)

20th. Prod: Darryl F. Zanuck. Dir: Elia Kazan.† Scr: Moss Hart. Novel basis: Laura Z. Hobson, *Gentleman's Agreement* (1947). Cast: Gregory Peck, Dorothy McGuire, John Garfield, Celeste Holm, Anne Revere,• June Havoc, Albert Dekker, Jane Wyatt, Dean Stockwell, Nicholas Joy

One of the premier anti–anti-Semitism films of all time, this box office hit was viewed sarcastically in the film colony as a stern warning not to mistreat a Jew—he could turn out to be a gentile. Peck is a successful magazine journalist determined to get at the heart of the continuing discrimination against Jews, from high society to the hoi polloi. So he does the almost unthinkable, letting it be known that he is Jewish.

The drama that follows is predictable, but with some deeply affecting moments. Peck experiences social slights and casual insults stoically, but realizes with some anguish that he has exposed his family (especially his son, Stockwell) to the plight of "those people." Garfield and Revere make the movie's points, however. As the working-class guy and former GI, Garfield insists he doesn't want sympathy for "the poor little Jews" like himself but justice for everyone ("Don't force me to make a speech"). The gentile mother Revere, who carries her high ideals into practice, insists that for her part she will overcome illness to live on to see something finer than an American Century, a Russian Century or an Atomic Century.

The best scene, apart from Garfield and Revere, has the loving but fearful wife McGuire explaining to their son that he is safe and secure because, thank God, they aren't *really* Jewish, and rationalizing to Peck that she has no reason to feel guilty about not being Jewish, poor or anything else disabling. (When the son cries out, "They called me a dirty Jew and a stinking kike," McGuire answers, "You're no more Jewish than I am, it's just a horrible mistake," and to Peck, "I'm glad. There I said it. I'm glad I'm not [Jewish]. Like you're glad you're good-looking instead of ugly, rich instead of poor . . . you can never understand that.")

Peck's moral reserve suits him well, as does the director's. If it had been made a few years later, Kazan would have somehow turned the film into a paean to American virtues. The film earned many Academy Awards and nominations, including awards for Peck for best actor, Kazan for best director, Zanuck for best picture; nominations included Dorothy McGuire for best actress, Revere for best supporting actress, Moss Hart for best screenplay, and Harman Jones for best editor. 118 min.

Ghost Valley Raiders (1946)

Average Don Barry oater, his first series western, with a few interesting moments thanks to a Connie Lee• story basis. Outlaws are diverting the stagecoach, stealing gold and murdering the passengers. They get away with such atrocious behavior because (as usual in such films) the town banker is in league with them. Falsely accused of the robbery-killings, Berry's character lets it be believed that he is the "Tolusa Kid" who recently shot his way out of prison.

G.I. Honeymoon (1945)

GI couple Gale Storm and Peter Cookson have just wedded, but every effort to consummate the marriage is interrupted by army emergencies. A Richard Weil• screenplay provides evidence that amid global events and record-high theater attendance, censorship was loosening its grip.

The Giant Behemoth (1959), aka The Behemoth

Artists Alliance. Prod: David Diamond, Ted Lloyd. Dir: Eugene Lourie, Douglas Hickox. Scr: Eugene Lourie, Daniel James.• Story basis: Robert Abel, Alan J. Adler. Cast: Gene Evans, André Morell, John Turner, Leigh Madison, Jack MacGowran

A highly enjoyable low-budget anti-nuke feature opens with scientist Evans, a marine biologist veteran of Bikini, lecturing on the dangers of nuclear testing and the silliness of referring to "safe" levels of radiation. The voice-over warns of the sea we know so little about striking back some day. The warning is realized in the appearance of a sea monster apparently hidden all this time and now dying of radiation poisoning. It invades London, ravaging neighborhoods until it is destroyed. The film pointedly includes news reports of massive fish kills in North America, and dead fish with radioactive poisoning crowding the shores. The best part of the film, however, is the view of London streets during the late 1950s. 72 min.

Gigolette (1935)

Gordon Kahn• wrote this low-budget speakeasy women's drama about taxi dancers, youth rebellion and the struggle for romance. The protagonist's father commits suicide and she can make a living only by hiring on at a notorious sucker joint in Manhattan. She strikes up a romance with a bruised patron, whose parents at first reject her.

The Girl Friend (1935)

Col. Prod: Sam J. Briskin. Dir: Edward Buzzell. Scr: Gertrude Purcell,† Benny Rubin. Story: Gene Towne, C. Graham Baker. Cast: Ann Sothern, Jack Haley, Roger Pryor, Thurston Hall, Victor Kilian, Ray Walker, Inez Courtney, Margaret Seddon

The prolific Purcell wrote this early Ann Sothern comedy in which Pryor and pals hoped to spend the summer mooching on a farm after intercepting the script of an aspiring playwright-farmhand and posing as big-city theatrical producers. When they try to avoid actually producing the play, they are outsmarted at every turn by Sothern until they are forced to put on the show (now with their own script) in a rented barn with local talent.

A rainstorm blows in on opening night and confusion reigns when all of the displaced animals come back to the barn for cover. Many other antics kick up along the long comic highway to a happy ending. The spirit of the film was captured in plans for a publicity campaign in which a studio representative was to visit all 48 states and recruit an actual "buxom milkmaid" from each state for a high-kicking musical number. Genius of the system, indeed. 67 min.

The Girl from Jones Beach (1949)

Star Ronald Reagan was going over from Left to Right in the leadership of the Screen Actors Guild, en route to cheerleading for the blacklist and negotiating a contract that deprived actors of nearly all potential TV residuals. Allen Boretz• wrote this forgettable comedy about the search for a perfect young woman for a product promotion. Warners suspended Lauren Bacall for refusing to accept the role.

The Girl Most Likely (1957)

This mediocre remake of TOM, DICK AND HARRY (the screenplay co-written by Paul Jarrico• and nominated for an Oscar) stripped out the pleasures of the original. This version, which moves the class content into the foreground and is basically a musical (Jane Powell's last), did not credit Jarrico, but he claimed to have taken part.

Girl Rush (1944)

When screenwriter and friendly witness Mac Benofft appeared before the House Committee on Un-American Activities to rationalize and apologize for his past connections, he found himself apologizing just as heartily for *Girl Rush*, on which he made a mere script contribution. A tale about Barbary Coast vaudevillians at the end of their rope, it is notable for mildly risque songs ("Annabella's Bustle") and for the plot of bankers who want to keep the West free from settlement, and women (aka showgirls) who take charge of even the roughest galoot.

Give Us This Day aka Salt for the Wise (1949)

J. Arthur Rank/Eagle-Lion Films. Prod: Rod E Geiger, Nat A. Bronsten, Edward Dmytryk.•† Dir: Edward Dmytryk. Scr: Ben Barzman.• Novel basis: Pietro Di Donato, *Christ in Concrete* (1939). Cast: Sam Wanamaker,• Lea Padovani, Kathleen Ryan, Charles Goldner, Bonar Colleano, Bill Sylvester, Nino Pastellides, Philo

Hauser, Sid James, Karel Stepanek, Ina De La Haye, Rosalie Crutchley, Ronan O'Casey, Robert Rietty, Charles Moffat

Heartfelt screen version of the great Italian American "proletarian novel" and perhaps Wanamaker's finest film performance, here at the very start of his exile to the United Kingdom, where he devoted himself to stage acting and to the physical recreation of Shakespeare's Globe Theater (completed not long after Wanamaker's 1993 death). This film was made possible because Dmytryk had already been blacklisted in 1947 and convinced Barzman as a political duty to follow him to London to make movies in an effort to break the blacklist. An orgy of cost-cutting nearly led to the production's collapse, and some people, like writer Barzman, never got paid.

Nevertheless, the film captures to a considerable degree the life of New York Italian immigrant bricklayers during the Depression and their neighborhood on the Lower East Side, around Mulberry Street. Some wonderful scenes (a wedding feast in particular) and the acting of wife Padovani, bricklayers Colleano and Goldner, along with protagonist Wanamaker, aptly evoke Donato's world. The heavy Catholicism of the novel was too much for the Left writer and director, and the cinematic temptation to render religious and deeply symbolic themes into family narratives (in this case, a hard-luck story of the couple and their children) simplified the novel's sometimes elusive message.

The film is notable for its intense naturalism, heightened by Dmytryk's experience in film noir, which led to the occasionally unpredictable (and effective) camera angle. Like SALT OF THE EARTH, *This Day* pointed technically and thematically to the kind of narratives left-wing filmmakers in the United States would surely have developed if they had been allowed to. This very important film was never given adequate marketing in America and had all but disappeared except among collectors until it was re-released in 2003. 90 min.

Glamour for Sale (1940)

Hollywood path-breaking screenwriter John Bright• penned this crime picture about an escort racket (i.e., prostitution), the innocent who is trapped in it and the good cop who cracks the case and saves her.

The Glass Key (1935)

A mediocre version of Daniell Hammett's• novel, starring George Raft, this film was a crime story without the psychological twists of the novelist's work. Heavily censored by the Breen Office for violence and hints of sexual sadism, it was enjoyed enough by audiences to make it one of the big hits of the 1936-1937 season.

The Glass Key (1942)
Para. Prod: Fred Kohlmar. Dir: Stuart Heisler. Scr: Jonathan Latimer. Novel basis: Dashiell Hammett,• *The Glass Key* (1931). Cast: Brian Donlevy, Veronica Lake, Alan Ladd, Bonita Granville, Joseph Calleia, Richard Denning, William Bendix, Margaret Hayes

Hammett's novel is considered one of his most enigmatic and confusing, but the film became one of the best Hammett adaptations after THE MALTESE FALCON. It is also, not by accident, Ladd at his noir best (as in THIS GUN FOR HIRE): blunt and nervy.

The plot is almost impossible to summarize, and in some ways a mere frame for the American-style moral debauchery. In brief, it revolves around a reform candidate for the Senate pledging a cleanup of vice. Donlevy is the political boss now supporting Denning; Ladd is the aide who was lifted from the gutter by Donlevy but discovers that reform is only a ploy for a power-grab. Indeed, the senator's son has been having an affair with Donlevy's sister and so on, into the night, until the end comes rather suddenly and without any great satisfaction to anyone, including the audience. But like *The Maltese Falcon*, the point is the mood of betrayal and not the series of false romances, purloined documents, murders and coverups. In this and in the various gestures of pathology (some hinting of homosexual ties), it is a thirties gangster film updated to foreshadow the best of noir. 85 min.

God's Little Acre (1958)
Security Pictures. Prod: Sidney Harmon. Dir: Anthony Mann. Scr: Philip Yordan (as Ben Maddow•†). Novel basis: Erskine Caldwell, *God's Little Acre* (1933). Cast: Robert Ryan, Aldo Ray, Tina Louise, Buddy Hackett, Jack Lord, Fay Spain, Vic Morrow, Rex Ingram, Michael Landon

Entrepreneur Yordan snatched the credits from his writing stable of blacklistees in one of his premier successes before turning to cheap foreign productions with still other blacklisted talents. From a later perspective, the treatment of white Southerners seems caricatured, but the sympathy of Maddow, Mann and brilliant star Robert Ryan for these deeply ignorant and sincere rednecks is sincere. Ryan, the patriarchal poor white farmer, is convinced, even more than his no-good sons, that his granddaddy's gold mine is somewhere on the property. Meanwhile his daughter, played by Louise, grows up voluptuous and is courted by buffoon Hackett. Novelist Caldwell's sympathies with the 1930s left-wing perspective, at the root of the sympathetic-and-critical treatment of Southern whites, come through strongly here, as in Martin Ritt's several contemporary Southern art-film features. 118 min.

The Go-Between (1971)
Col. (MGM-EMI World Film Services Prod). Prod: John Heyman, Norman Priggen, Dennis Johnson. Dir: Joseph Losey.• Scr: Harold Pinter. Novel basis: L. P. Hartley, *The Go-Between* (1953). Cast: Julie Christie, Alan Bates, Dominic Guard, Margaret Leighton, Michael Redgrave, Michael Gough, Edward Fox

Unusual for the Losey canon because of its dramatic subtlety. Thanks to Pinter's skillful adaptation of the Hartley novel, this film is among Losey's best, with all of his familiar themes of the relation between class and sexuality expressed with great restraint and refinement— and perhaps for that reason one of his biggest successes in the United Kingdom. Proleptic flash-forwards of the sort used toward the end of MIDNIGHT COWBOY were cut at the insistence of the producers, a loss to film history (and awaiting restoration).

The turn-of-the-century story finds child actor Guard as a boy clearly from another class visiting for a month with a schoolmate's family. He falls into the summer routine of the leisure classes, while a farm on the estate provides the allure of hardworking, boisterous and colorful Bates. A superb Julie Christie uses Guard to deliver secret messages between herself and Bates, with whom she is gamboling even while engaged to an affable, colorless viscount (Fox), a diversion she takes as her due in exchange for fulfilling her duty to class, family and England by marrying (but not unhappily) for money. Mistress of the household Leighton watches over the scene anxiously, unable to change the details but certain of the class-weighted outcome. The film won an Oscar nomination for Leighton (best supporting actress), and British Academy Awards for her and for Fox. 118 min., color.

Going Hollywood (1933)
MGM. Prod: Walter Wanger. Dir: Raoul Walsh. Scr: Donald Ogden Stewart.• Story basis: Frances Marion. Cast: Bing Crosby, Marion Davies, Stuart Erwin, Fifi D'Orsay, Ned Sparks, Patsy Kelly

The first Stewart script and the first by any future blacklistee for a big-budget musical. It's full of silliness, but a distinctly campy quality in the satire is a celebration of studio days.

Stuck among prudish old maid types (the obviously "bad" women's culture) as a schoolteacher back East, Davies hears a broadcast of crooner Crosby and resolves to find romance and self-realization in Hollywood. Most conveniently, Crosby is himself about ready to go to make movies, and they meet repeatedly en route, with obstacles to romance provided by Bing's oh-so-French girlfriend and co-star D'Orsay.

The best parts of the film are Davies' dream fantasies, in which lavish production numbers offer a lush surrounding of heterosexual heaven (from a women's standpoint, naturally). The determinedly overplayed backstage story of directors' misplaced martial bellowing, stars throwing tantrums and their last-minute replacement by fresh nubility (D'Orsay by Davies) anticipates the roasting of Hollywood in Olson and Johnson's CRAZY HOUSE but is treated here with crisp Stewart verbal cleverness rather than Lees-and-Rinaldo-style sight gags. Charming moments are weighed down somewhat with mediocre musical interludes. 80 min.

Gold for the Caesars (1964)

One of Arnold Perl's• rare film credits (along with MALCOLM X, though he was much better known for TV work like *East Side/West Side*). Millard Lampell• contributed to the script but earned no credit for this low-budget Italian sandal epic about an architect-slave ordered to search for gold while repelling attacks from warring Celts. Jeffrey Hunter starred.

Golden Boy (1939)

Col. Prod: William Perlberg, Rouben Mamoulian. Dir: Rouben Mamoulian. Scr: Lewis Meltzer, Daniel Taradash, Sarah Y. Mason, Victor Heerman. Play basis: Clifford Odets,† *Golden Boy* (1937). Cast: William Holden, Barbara Stanwyck, Adolphe Menjou, Lee J. Cobb,† Joseph Calleia, Sam Levene, Don Beddoe, Charles Halton

Performed by the Group Theatre, working from Clifford Odets' play, this film suffered somewhat in the adaptation. Gone are the Odetsian phrases, with only a handful of exceptions, and the theatrical climax has been Hollywoodized. John Garfield would have been a better choice than Holden, and so forth. But the acting in general is so good and the cinematography so stunning that the rather tired fight-game story line sags only occasionally.

In the classic Hollywood ethnic displacement from Jewry, the lower-class boy with the loving, cultured Old World father is Italian. Cobb (in the most warm-hearted performance of this later friendly witness's career) plays Dad to the hilt, a grocer about to give son Holden—in his first starring film role—an expensive violin for his twenty-first birthday. Sam Levene is on hand as the wisecracking son-in-law who wants nothing but the money for a cab of his own. Temptation enters by way of boxing, which Holden has taught himself as a means to get the recognition that a decade of fiddling hasn't given him. Stanwyck is fight promoter Menjou's girl, a former down-at-the-heels near-streetwalker whom he has pulled up and plans to marry. Beddoe is the Old Jew (rather, Old Italian) of the family circle on hand for quips ("Beating a wife, it's the first step to fascism").

Partly to win Stanwyck's love and partly to spite her, Holden wins bout after bout—until the big challenge in The Garden, where he kills the Chocolate Drop Kid with a blow (the visual images of the black section of the audience and the twisted faces among the whites are all stunning). He must gain absolution from the Drop's Christian father and try to carry his burden, which is surely easier to take when you also get the dame. Gangster Calleia, with a flicker of Italian American pride amid his corruption, is the last obstacle ("You used me like a gun," Holden charges), as in BODY AND SOUL—which could be easily called the improved version of *Golden Boy*. 99 min.

Golden Earrings (1947)

Abraham Polonsky• wrote his first screenplay for Marlene Dietrich in her role as a gypsy queen on the lam from the Nazis and poured his heart into dramatizing the political peril of the gypsies, but scarcely a word of his dialogue survived. Dietrich's first role in three years (she was in Europe entertaining the troops) was ridiculed for her stringy hairdo and her darkened skin, and her colorful tribe for being as much against women's choice in marriage as against the Nazis.

Go Man, Go! (See THE HARLEM GLOBETROTTERS)

The Good Humor Man (1950)

Frank Tashlin adapted the Roy Huggins† novel *Appointment with Fear* for this Jack Carson vehicle, in which an innocent ice cream man untangles his involvement in a robbery with the help of his customers.

The Great Commandment (1939)

Cathedral Productions. Prod: John T. Coyle. Dir: Irving Pichel.• Scr: Dana Burnett. Cast: John Beal, Albert Dekker, Maurice Moscovitch, Marjorie Cooley

One of those notably low-production-value Biblical dramas in which the parents (really the fathers, because the mothers stay mostly out of sight) are classically Jewish, the daughters dark-skinned and the sons often look suspiciously like Gentiles. Here, a Zealot who is also a Rabbi's son in a village near Jerusalem has been raised to be a scholar but sees the only hope for his oppressed people in a concerted uprising against Rome.

Beal leaves behind his career and his betrothed for the sake of the armed struggle. But Jesus (in one of those film tricks, we only hear the voice and his point of view) is a pacifist! Our hero is imprisoned, it turns out, during the crucifixion, and the Roman soldier whose life he saves had actually thrust a sword into the side of the suffering Savior. The Zealots, evident victims of imperialism, suffer for the worldwide moral (but not political or economic) transformation. All this is odd to contemplate because *Great Commandment* could be taken as an antiwar statement of Party member Pichel—or perhaps a final hoped-for peace to follow the impending world calamity. It was not released until 1942, and then mainly through church showings, perhaps changing its reception dramatically

Pichel, the best known of the Hollywood Nineteen to elude both prosecution and friendly testimony, worked abroad in his last two pictures, both of them religious dramas. His DAY OF TRIUMPH takes another, more existential shot at approximately the same subject. The much better known MARTIN LUTHER, on *Times* critic Bosley Crowther's top-ten list for that year, is also an abundantly metaphorical treatment of McCarthyism, again in the religious frame. 85 min.

The Great Flamarion (1945)

Rep. Prod: William Wilder, W. Lee Wilder. Dir: Anthony Mann. Scr: Anne Wigton, Heinz Herald, Richard Weil.• Story basis: Anne Wigton, based on Vicki Baum, "Big Shot," *Colliers* (1936). Cast: Dan Duryea, Erich von Stroheim, Mary Beth Hughes

A "bad woman," minor noir film interesting mainly as a vehicle for the aged von Stroheim to reprise his cinematic history and portray the "ugly" but strong-charactered figure first humiliating himself and then seeking personal justice.

A vaudeville trick shooter's act rests upon a masochistic (for the time, typically psychoanalytic)

scenario: he portrays the angered husband who surprises and then confronts a wife or lover by shooting several items held out from her body, and then with more shots barely misses her paramour as the latter stands before a mirror. This foreshadows the plot-line: Hughes wishes to get away from Duryea, her alcoholic husband, and through false promises of love, convinces the otherwise solitary and single-minded von Stroheim to kill him "accidentally" during the act. He awaits her later at a lavish hotel, then realizes she is not coming; he loses everything but the will to track her down. In Mexico City, a ragged and broken von Stroheim seeks to avenge the betrayal. 78 min.

The Great Jasper (1933)

Prod: David O. Selznick. Dir: J. Walter Ruben. Scr: H. W. Hanemann, Richard Weil,• (uncredited: Robert Tasker, John Bright•). Novel basis: Fulton Oursler, *The Great Jasper* (1930). Cast: Richard Dix, Edna May Oliver, Florence Eldridge, Wera Engels, Walter Walker, David Durand, Bruce Cabot, Betty Furness, James Bush

Enough immorality and class tension to make this a good pre-Code example of Hollywood luridness, scripted in part by writers who knew well the dark side of American life. Working stiff Dix is the only man in a small 1890s industrial town able and willing to operate the new electric trolley. In return, capitalist Walker invites Dix and his puritanical wife Eldridge to spend the weekend at his place. There, Dix seduces Walker's wife, and the results show up in nine months. Ten years later, Walker invites Dix back into his house, makes the postponed accusation and fires him. Dix takes sustenance from an alcoholic astrologer, and when she dies, he becomes The Great Jasper of a carnival act. More years pass, and Dix's illegitimate son becomes a playboy band leader who seduces his half-brother's fiancée, played by a young Betty Furness. 85 min.

The Great Man's Lady (1942)

Para. Prod: William A. Wellman. Dir: William A. Wellman. Scr: W. L. River.• Story: Seena Owen, Adele Rogers St. Johns. Story basis: Vina Delmar, "The Human Side" (1939). Cast: Barbara Stanwyck, Joel McCrea, Brian Donlevy, Thurston Hall, K. T. Stevens, Lucien Littlefield

An early example of winning-the-west revisionism. Stanwyck, according to studio lore, was fitted with a special apparatus to keep her bent over sufficiently to play a woman of more than 100 years, a trick that nearly works. In the kind of role she would play repeatedly (on television just as memorably as films), she is, through flashbacks, the frontier wife as tough as her man or tougher. In fact, McCrea plays a simp and a drunkard who has to be directed and compelled to greatness as a champion of the little people.

The film opens with a statue unveiled of the late senator, founder of the Manhattan-looking Hoytsville. There, in a mansion huddled between skyscrapers, is his reputed ex-wife. The reporters push in for the real story, which Stanwyck reveals to a young female would-be biographer. The Great Man was an adventurer who eloped with the society girl to the Great Plains, where he planned a town without capital, based on his landholding. There he lost his stake to a fast-talking gambler, Donlevy, who is so smitten with Stanwyck that he allows her to win it all back. Hubby heads out for his fortune, while Donlevy keeps her company. Years and several locations later, she discovers that McCrea has gone on to a second wife, believing Stanwyck dead, and is now in league with the corrupt railroad barons. Her selfless task is to straighten him out and to articulate the real values of people's progress: development of the West along democratic principles of hard work and a piece of the pie for everyone (at least for white folks, but maybe even Mexicans and Chinese as well). 90 min.

The Great Sioux Uprising (1953)

U-I. Prod: Albert J. Cohen, Leonard Goldstein. Dir: Lloyd Bacon. Scr: Melvin Levy,† J. Robert Bren. Story basis: Gladys Atwater. Cast: Jeff Chandler, Faith Domergue, Lyle Bettger, Glenn Strange

A better and more complex film than the average contemporary western, but (viewed less sympathetically) also an exceedingly odd mixture of political clichés and rewritten historical events. Domergue and potential fiancée Strange are horse dealers in Oklahoma during the Civil War, faced with the possibility of a sudden windfall: the Union Army is willing to pay almost any price for replacement mounts. The only extra herds, however, belong to the Indians. The stealthy Strange, already known for cheating horse ranchers in the prices he negotiates between them and the army, uses his crew of no-goodniks to steal hundreds of Sioux ponies, claiming he bought the horses "up north."

Meanwhile, former Union Army surgeon Chandler comes to town, sick of trying and failing to heal the dying soldiers. Enlisting himself as a vet, he figures out the real deal while falling in love with Domergue. Wise to Indian ways, he has already saved a chief's horse and has the credibility to talk peace when Strange seeks to provoke

war. A remarkable moment: a Confederate delegation promises full support to an intertribal council, but an ethnic Cherokee general actually beats a slave, exposing the hypocrisy of the Confederates—allowing Chandler to explain that the war is really for the abolition of slavery. 80 min.

The Great White Hope (1970)

20th. Prod: Lawrence Turman. Dir: Martin Ritt.• Scr: Howard Sackler. Play basis: Howard Sackler. Cast: James Earl Jones, Jane Alexander, Lou Gilber, Joel Fluellen, Chester Morris, Robert Webber, R. G. Armstrong, Hal Holbrook, Beah Richards, Moses Gunn

A problematic adaptation of the Broadway hit on the life and times of boxing champ Jack Johnson (also played by Jones on the stage), the first black heavyweight title-holder. His achievement provokes the white establishment at the turn of the century when he takes up with white divorcee Alexander, and he is arrested for violating the Mann Act. He flees to Canada and across Europe, determined to keep boxing but finding few challengers. Ritt was reportedly reluctant to film a stage play after several unhappy experiences, but was persuaded by Turman, then riding high from producing The Graduate, to take the job. The film version, weighted down by the narrative problems of the play (just as Ritt had feared) and no success at the box office, nonetheless collected a slew of awards, including a nomination for best actor and actress for Jones and Alexander, and a nomination for best adaptation for Sackler from the Writers Guild. 103 min., color.

The Greatest (1977)

Col. Prod: John Marshall. Dir: Tom Gries. Scr: Ring Lardner, Jr.• Book basis: Muhammad Ali, Herbert Muhammad, Richard Durham, The Greatest—My Own Story (1975). Cast: Muhammad Ali, Ernest Borgnine, Lloyd Haynes, John Marley, Robert Duvall, David Huddleston, Ben Johnson, James Earl Jones, Dina Merrill, Paul Winfield, Annazette Chase, Mira Waters

A surprisingly good film that bombed with most of the reviewers and disappeared from the theaters—no doubt thanks to the unpopularity of Ali's political positions—but it stands up to scrutiny as a biopic, even next to the vastly more lavish Ali.

It is doubtful whether Ali did much of the writing of his autobiography, and the absence of a single negative moment (except, perhaps, his near-assignation with a white prostitute when he happens to hear about

Malcolm X speaking nearby) make the historical qualities of the film unreliable. But the racial pathos of the
South, where Cassius Clay grew up, his disillusionment
with his Olympic status (he symbolically tosses his
medal off a bridge), his defiance of promoters and the
army as he embraces his Muslim faith, are all undeni-
able. Lardner's script gives Ali more opportunity to
speak his mind than all the talks he delivered for the
Nation of Islam at antiwar rallies and black-connected
events. He does so volubly (in the years before repeated
big-money fights damaged his brain). Borgnine, as
Angelo Dundee, has a pretty small role but performs it
creditably, and James Earl Jones as Malcolm X is briefly
brilliant. Lardner, Jr., rightly complained of the low
budget, accelerated shooting schedule and dreadful
editing. The surviving film has all the difficulties of, say,
Will Rogers, Jr., starring in *The Will Rogers Story*, but
more of the virtues, particularly for the diehard Ali fan.
102 min., color.

Green Grass of Wyoming (1948)
Followup to *Thunderhead—Son of Flicka* and inheritor of
the mantle of the original *My Friend Flicka*, scripted by
Francis Faragoh.• It received an Academy Award nomination for cinematographer Charles G. Clarke. This story has
a young girl's favorite horse become a champion trotter,
as written by friendly witness and B-film specialist Martin
Berkeley.†

Guide for the Married Man (1967)
Considered risqué at the time of distribution, decades later
it seems considerably less daring than the most ordinary
television comedy. It was dreamed up by Frank Tarloff•
during his British sojourn, based on the experiences of a
fellow exile evading his wife's suspicion until, in the end,
he realizes inevitably that their marital love is true. Tarloff
persuaded his friend Walter Matthau to play the lead and
the studio to let Gene Kelly direct his first nonmusical.
Robert Morse and Inger Stevens are enjoyable, and a
dozen cameos (Lucille Ball, Carl Reiner, Phil Silvers and
Sam Jaffe• among the progressives) round out the cast.
89 min., color.

Guilty by Suspicion (1991)
WB. Prod: Arnon Milchan, Alan D. Blomquist. Dir: Irwin
Winkler. Scr: Irwin Winkler (uncredited: Abraham Polon-
sky•). Cast: Robert DeNiro, Annette Bening, George
Wendt, Patricia Wetting, Sam Wanamaker,• Chris Cooper,
Ben Piazza, Martin Scorsese, Barry Primus, Gailard Sar-
tain, Stuart Margolin, Joan Scott•

This is a movie that should have been great—great
cast, big subject, strong production values. But Irwin
Winkler in his directing debut mangled the original script
by Abraham Polonsky so badly that Polonsky took his
name off the film. The original was about a Communist,
but Winkler turned him into a liberal (DeNiro) who
refused, for confused and personal reasons, to testify before
the House Committee on Un-American Activities and was
blacklisted for his silence. In fact, only a handful of liberals
who had never been part of the Popular Front were ever
blacklisted, so the story gets off on the wrong foot from the
opening scene. Indeed, DeNiro has no political views to
speak of throughout the film, and it becomes difficult to
sympathize with a man who appears to be the essentially
willing victim of a huge misunderstanding.

Some scraps of Polonsky's script, based on his 1956
novel *Season of Fear* (also the original title of the screenplay) are still telling: the anxiety of old friends over casual
conversations, the strain on marriages, the suicidal
impulses, the sudden disappearances of longtime associates and the suffocating social atmosphere created by the
ubiquity of two-bit informers. The character who burns
his personal library of Marxist classics in the garden while
a party swings on in his living room is based on real-life
friendly witness and screenwriter Richard Collins† and his
wife, Dorothy Commingore (divorced by Collins and
destroyed by the blacklist), as Polonsky has told interviewers.

Annette Bening and George Wendt are memorable
(she for her first real appearance as a star and he for slicing
the ham so assiduously), but one can only wonder what
the film might have been if something close to the original
story had been shot. Cameos of several surviving blacklistees, especially Sam Wanamaker and Joan Scott, are
interesting historically. 105 min., color.

Gun Crazy aka Deadly Is the Female (1949)
King Bros Production/UA. Prod: Frank King, Maurice
King. Dir: Joseph H. Lewis. Scr: MacKinley Kantor,
Millard Kauffman (front for Dalton Trumbo•). Cast:
Peggy Cummins, John Dall, Berry Kroeger, Morris Car-
novsky, Anabel Shaw, Harry Lewis, Nedrick Young,•
Rusty Tamblyn

Trumbo and Lewis at their wooliest in one of the
most carefully studied and admired of B-films. It opens on
strong thirties notes but quickly develops themes of youth
rebellion and Cold War *anomie* that anticipate dozens or
perhaps hundreds of later, lesser films.

Cummins plays a carnival sharpshooter who meets her match in Dall, a young man with a fascination for handguns who grew up in a poor family as a crack shot but with a contrary hatred for killing (not unlike Johnny Guitar). He is happy in his job with a small arms manufacturer when he meets Cummins. She lures him into a life of crime and adventure on the road. It never becomes clear what motivates Cummins beyond a generalized boredom with what she sees as the confining working-class life; but it's a type that would become familiar enough in the films of the seventies.

The picture is deservedly famous for Lewis' three-and-a-half minute sequence of a bank robbery, shot from the back seat of the getaway car in one take from the moment the car enters the small town until it clears the cops. "By refusing to cut to another angle," film historian Dan Wakeman wrote, "Lewis makes the spectator an accomplice to the robbery, forced to play out the scene in real time and from the viewpoint of the protagonists." GUN CRAZY was rediscovered upon its release on video in the early 1990s, and in 1996 was enshrined in the list of 100 top American movies of all time by the fan magazine *Movieline*. 86 min.

The Guns of Navarone (1961)

Col. Prod: Carl Foreman.• Dir: J. Lee Thompson. Scr: Carl Foreman. Novel basis: Alistair MacLean, *The Guns of Navarone* (1957). Cast: Gregory Peck, David Niven, Anthony Quinn, Stanley Baker, Anthony Quayle, James Darren, Irene Papas, Richard Harris, Gia Scala

This World War II actioner heroizes an attempt by Allied commandos and partisans to blow up the heavy German guns that control passages between Greek islands and block the escape of trapped British forces. The film was presumably intended to continue the enormous success Foreman (with fellow uncredited blacklistee Michael Wilson) had enjoyed just a few years earlier in adapting Pierre Boulle's novel for David Lean in THE BRIDGE ON THE RIVER KWAI—but Thompson was no Lean. The production suffered from lumbering exposition and an explosion fetish, matched by a cast mostly going through the motions. The major exception is real-life socialist Baker, who plays a Bogart-like disillusioned veteran of the Spanish Civil War restored in spirit for one more struggle. The film got a handful of Oscar nominations from an Academy eager to recall the "Good War," but, more understandably, won only for best special effects. 157 min., color.

H

Half a Sinner (1940)

Low-budget comedy-drama with a story basis by Dalton Trumbo• and the occasional good gendered moment with actress Heather Ange, playing a schoolteacher in a peck of trouble with cops and gangsters.

Hangman's Knot (1952)

Col. Scott-Brown Productions. Prod: Harry Joe Brown. Dir: Roy Huggins.† Scr: Roy Huggins. Cast: Randolph Scott, Donna Reed, Lee Marvin, Claude Jarman, Jr., Frank Faylin

The film opens on the startling image of a group of what appears to be U.S. civilians ambushing a company of U.S. cavalry in the desert. Actually, the attackers are a troop of Confederate soldiers in disguise and far from home ambushing a shipment of army payroll gold. Scott plays a Confederate officer who learns only after the successful ambush that the war is over, meaning the spoils are now private booty. After the Southerners decide to divide the loot and go home, outlaws besiege them in a stage way station. As a British critic noted, the gold repeatedly changes its character, becoming by turns an unexpected personal reward for sacrifice in war, a desperate shortcut to happiness and finally a moral encumbrance whose weight threatens to drag everyone down around it. One of Scott's best oaters anticipates the cycle of six B-westerns he made with director Budd Boetticher over the next few years, among the best ever made. Huggins—who insisted that the film's opening was a kind of reverse-optic Marxism, the right of states to leave the Union—was soon to abandon film for television, a gain for the new medium, a loss for film. 81 min.

Hangmen Also Die (1943)

T. W. Baumfield. Prod: Arnold Pressburger, Fritz Lang. Dir: Fritz Lang. Scr: John Wexley• (with a contribution by Bertolt Brecht•). Cast: Brian Donlevy, Walter Brennan, Anna Lee, Gene Lockhart, Dennis O'Keefe

Czechoslovakia is under occupation when a dreaded Gestapo chief is assassinated. The protagonist must escape arrest to preserve the underground resistance, but the Gestapo orders mass killings until he is caught. After many tangles, the resisters manage to implicate the chief local collaborator with the Nazis, a brewery owner, as the assassin. The occupation authorities are ordered to close the case, finally, even though Berlin intelligence knows the collaborator is innocent. In short: they have been beaten, foreshadowing ultimate victory.

Many fine scenes communicate a sense of dread with the genius of the true dramatist's sense of detail, as when a Gestapo agent splits a sausage with his fingers, spritzing grease in all directions. The German-speaking playwright and radical Wexley had been hired as a buffer between Lang and Brecht, according to Lang's best biographer. And according to Brecht's journals, Wexley appropriated the screen credit by marking as his own ideas on the pages he and Brecht collaborated on. Sure enough, Wexley took the credit to Screen Writers Guild arbitration and won, giving Brecht an additional reason to leave the United States (he was called before HUAC and grilled without its members having the remotest idea of his stature). The somewhat overlong drama lacks complex characterization, and some of the politically strongest scenes are also the most aesthetically rigid, but the antifascist politics are among the best ever enunciated in popular film. 140 min.

Happy Anniversary (1959)

Fields Productions/UA. Prod: Ralph Fields. Dir: David Miller. Scr: Jerome Chodorov,• Joseph Fields. Play basis: Jerome Chodorov, Joseph Fields, Anniversary Waltz (1954). Cast: David Niven, Mitzi Gaynor, Carl Reiner, Loring Smith, Monique van Vooren, Patty Duke, Elizabeth Wilson

The swan song of a team that had a half-dozen Broadway musicals and as many film collaborations in the decades before the blacklist. This time it's a fifties-style family piece, with the usual zany dialogue, single friends, annoying parents, troublesome but loveable kids, and one more twist: the recollection of premarital assignations in a hot-sheets hotel. Niven is tortured by memories of more romantic-erotic (if also completely faithful) days of youth. 83 min.

Happy Go Lucky (1943)

The Michael Uris• story basis provided a framework for lots of singing and a few comedy mixups in this generally humdrum picture. On some generic island stop-off of a Caribbean cruise, working girl and would-be gold digger Mary Martin furiously pursues millionaire Rudy Vallee. Thanks to independent-minded expatriate Dick Powell, who wants to start up an oyster business but lacks the capital, the film has some complications and another lead vocalist. Voodoo love potions, tropical rainstorms, side-kick Eddie Bracken's pratfalls and similar nonsense round out the exotic-location romance.

Hard Traveling (1985)

New World Pictures. Prod: Helen Garvey. Dir: Dan Bessie. Scr: Dan Bessie. Novel basis: Alvah Bessie,• *Bread and a Stone* (1941). Cast: J. E. Freeman, Ellen Geer, Barry Corbin, James Gammon, Jim Haynie

An homage by the younger Bessie and his companion Garvey to the elder Bessie, who died the year this film was made. In 1940, with the Depression lingering, drifter Freeman takes a job as a handyman in small town California. There he meets pretty widow Geer (daughter of blacklisted actor Will Geer•) and after failing at every attempt to make a living for the family, including her two sons, he turns to crime. Shooting a shopkeeper opens the pit to perdition. His one happy year is contrasted with his bitter childhood (poverty made worse by the beatings first of a stepfather, then reformatory guards). Reviewers labeled it a "period weepie," with murder victim Corbin overdrawn as unworthy of sympathy and lover Geer as the thoughtful schoolteacher who loves poetry. Oversimplified, but empathetic. 99 min.

The Harlem Globetrotters (1951)

Sidney Buchman• Enterprises. Prod: Buddy Adler. Associate Prod: Alfred Palca.• Dir: Phil Brown. Scr: Alfred Palca. Cast: Thomas Gomez, Dorothy Dandridge, Bill Walker, Angela Clarke, Reese "Goose" Tatum

A unique film in many ways, not least for the confusion created by two versions of the same story made within three years. This original version in 1951 was one of producer Sidney Buchman's last films, with a first-credit screenplay by Palca, who immediately went on the blacklist. In 1954 it was remade under the jazzier title *Go Man, Go!* and this version became widely confused in the minds of viewers—able to see one on the black entertainment cable channels, the other on Turner Classic Movies—with its predecessor. The remake had Ruby Dee in the place of Dandridge and Dane Clark rather than Gomez in the role of Coach Abe Saperstein, but Palca's screenplay was recycled more or less intact (with Arnold Becker as a front for Palca). The original is also unique for its use of the promising Dandridge, whose acting career was blocked at every turn by the sparseness of roles for African American women and whose life ended tragically in 1965. Both movies feature a dozen of the Harlem Globetrotters themselves, most prominently the towering center, Goose Tatum.

The narrative is a straightforward black self-improvement story with the once formidable character actor Gomez (FORCE OF EVIL) as the white coach who condescends in giving advice to a promising but highly individualistic player with the higher purpose of inspiring the team to cooperation and winning ball games. 78 min.

Harriet Craig (1950)

Col. Prod: William Dozier. Dir: Vincent Sherman. Scr: Anne Froelick,• James Gunn. Play basis: George Edward Kelly, *Craig's Wife* (1926). Cast: Joan Crawford, Wendell Corey, Lucile Watson, Allyn Joslyn, Ellen Corby

Third (and last) version of a popular stage feature of the 1920s, probably best captured cinematically by Dorothy Arzner's 1936 CRAIG'S WIFE. This version is pretty strictly a Crawford vehicle, one of the earliest indications that the former Charleston dancer and sex symbol was going to become an aging crazy lady, often quite unsympathetic, for most of the rest of her screen career. This time the element of repressed sexuality that enlivened Rosalind Russell in *Craig's Wife* has just about vanished and with it some of the badly needed social explanation for the protagonist's actions. Married to the kindly suburban professional Corey, Crawford has come to look upon her house as her only possession and safety in a world strictly ruled by the battle of the sexes. Her father left her mother, a memory that seems more prominent in the earlier version, in which Russell told all rather more sympathetically—as a warning—to a younger woman. What remains is a sort of Hedda Gabler thirst for revenge, with Crawford manipulating Corey ruthlessly: lying, demanding his attention with feigned illness and otherwise acting out. In the end, Corey has the good sense to walk away, and the viewer feels more victorious over the destructive Crawford than sympathetic to her plight. Screenwriter Froelick (this was her last film) claimed the Crawford character was more three-dimensional before the rewrites, and that may well be, as Hollywood was moving swiftly toward the era of the selfish wife and bad mom. Sherman, in an autobiography, claimed that he also was (although never named in testimony) effectively blacklisted because of his engagement with lefties from Federal Theater onward. 94 min.

Harrigan's Kid (1943)

One more racetrack story, this one with a screenplay co-credit by Martin Berkeley,† and an uncredited contribution by Henry Blankfort,• about a would-be jockey whose handlers sell his contract to gruff but kindly capitalist, landing the cynical kid on a vast horse farm in bluegrass country. Film is better than the standard plot, thanks to a strong performance by supporting actors as a gang around the stables.

Hatful of Rain (1957)

Michael V. Gazzo's play about youthful heroin addiction gained screen time with Fred Zinnemann's direction and a script written by Gazzo, Alfred Hayes and Carl Foreman.• Working-class family life is given the once-over in a film that was courageous at the time for not preaching, offering the portrayal of a sympathetic druggie played by Don Murray, a former GI who got hooked in Korea.

The Hawk (1935)

Affiliated Pictures. Prod: Herman Wohl, J. D. Kendis, John Conrad. Dir: Edward Dmytryk.•† Scr: Griffin Jay. Story basis: James Oliver Curwood, "The Coyote" (n.d.). Cast: Yancy Lane, Betty Jordan, Dickie Jones, Lafe McKee, Don Orlando, Marty Joyce

Dmytryk's first film, after years of work at Paramount as an editor, made by a small independent company for a reputed $5,000 (although Dmytryk's autobiography is doubtful in a raft of assertions), and shot at Monogram from the script of an unknown and probably unpaid screenwriter. The result was a western melodrama not very different from hundreds of others of its kind but a foreshadowing of Dmytryk's skill in using limited resources to produce pulpy attractions.

As his mother is dying, young man Lane is told that his real name is Jack King and is given a locket. Over at the Triple X ranch, his father (McKee) is still hoping to find the misplaced son. By a remarkable coincidence (except in novels and films), Lane/King soon finds himself at work on his father's ranch. The ranchhouse crew, ranging from little Dickie Jones to cowgirl–foster daughter Jordan, to Zandar, a wonder dog, help unravel a rustlers' tangle and guide Lane and Jordan to the obligatory romantic conclusion. 55 min.

He Ran All the Way (1951)

UA. Prod: Bob Roberts, John Garfield (uncredited). Dir: John Berry.• Scr: Guy Endore• (front for Hugo Butler• and Dalton Trumbo•). Story basis: Sam Ross (uncredited adaptation: Dalton Trumbo).• Cast: John Garfield, Shelley Winters, Wallace Ford, Selena Royle, Bobby Hyatt, Gladys George, Norman Lloyd

Most memorable as John Garfield's last moment on camera, it is also memorable for introducing Winters as a Left "type" (less-than-beautiful, warm if chubby, given to melancholy), a role she was destined to play for the best part of her career. Garfield plays the neurotic criminal on the run, a small-time thief who has panicked in a bank job and wounded a guard. Heading for a place to hide the loot, he meets Winters and goes home with her to meet her family. When they return from a film, he pulls his gun, certain they know he is on the lam. His mixture of fear and paranoia is matched by theirs in a scary world in which cops often come in shooting at anything that moves.

Deep noir, made not long before Garfield's sudden death (and one of the most moving funerals in Manhattan history). His face in the final frame expresses the unforgettable image of what the blacklist was doing to some of America's best popular artists. Desperate and ill in real life, he was drinking heavily with a heart problem, under terrible pressure as his world fell apart. The entire production, with the collaboration of many of Hollywood's most talented leftists, has the sense of a terribly sad swan song. 76 min.

Heaven With a Barbed Wire Fence (1939)

20th. Exec Prod: Sol Wurtzel. Dir: Ricardo Cortez. Scr: Dalton Trumbo.• Story basis: Dalton Trumbo, Leonard Hoffman, Ben Graumantzohn. Cast: Jean Rogers, Raymond Walburn, Majorie Rambeau, Glenn Ford, Nicholas Conte, Eddie Collins, Ward Bond, Irving Bacon, Kay Linaker

A borderline "A" Depression drama that introduced Glenn Ford (soon to be a favorite sentimental-but-tough Popular Front actor). Ford heads West from Manhattan to realize his dream in a ranch property. Hitching cross country, he hops in the back of a truck but is discovered along with Rogers, disguised as a boy. She follows him and a new pal as they hop a freight. Driven from the train, they land in a hobo camp. After more troubles, the three travel on together, and Roberts tells them how her parents were killed by fascists in the Spanish Civil War. Eventually, she is arrested as an illegal alien and Ford agrees to marry her. Finally landing in Arizona, Ford finds the ranch is a mess—but Roberts comes along to convince him that with enough work it can be built into a "barbed wire heaven." Some of the best of the film can be found in character actors like Walburn as the hobo "professor" and his girlfriend, barkeep Rambeau—all of them "types" in an economic slump that brings together people of all kinds. 65 min.

Heldorado (1946)

Rep. Prod: Edward J. White. Dir: William Witney. Scr: Gerald Geraghty, Julian Zimet.• Cast: Roy Rogers, Dale Evans, George "Gabby" Hayes, Paul Harvey

One of the less memorable Rogers/Evans pairings but occasionally interesting for its modern-day setting (Las Vegas, celebrating its annual rodeo, styled "Heldorado" after the gruff qualities of earlier pioneer life) and for Evans as the ever-perky upper-class girl brought down a notch but not diminished by cowboy-singer and detective Roy. The film is also interesting for the Sons of the Pioneers' self-mocking evocation of western braggadocio. The villains are, as usual, a mixture of rough characters and the deceitful upper-middle-class, in this case including one of the administrators of the rodeo. An early example of Zimet, who went on to write a western of a higher order, THE NAKED DAWN. 70 min.

Hellcats of the Navy (1957)

Morningside Production. Prod: Charles H. Schneer. Dir: Nathan Juran. Scr: David Lang.† Raymond T. Marcus (i.e., Bernard Gordon•). Novel basis: Charles A. Lockwood, Hans Christian, *Hellcats of the Sea* (1955). Cast: Ronald Reagan, Nancy Davis, Arthur Franz, Robert Arthur, William Leslie

A time capsule of the Cold War, containing many frozen ironies of the era that were much less visible at the time, not least in the allegory of leadership provided by Ron and Nancy in their first and only starring roles together; in the often rather dreadful dialogue by Lang, who had testified against his friends to keep his job and elude the blacklist that Reagan had benefited from and encouraged (as FBI informant T-10); and in the fact that, laboring away anonymously below decks was an unrepentant Communist screenwriter, Gordon, trying to save a sinking action melodrama.

The story poses the not unfamiliar question: Should a captain put his entire command at risk to save one man, who also happens to be a romantic rival? Along the way, Reagan is asked what he intends to do after the war. The response: "I'm going into the surplus business." 82 min.

Hell Drivers (1957)

Acqua and Rank Film Org. Prod: Benjamin Fisz. Dir: Cyril Endfield.• Scr: Cyril Endfield. Story: Joe Kruse. Cast: Stanley Baker, Herbert Lom, Peggy Cummins, Patrick McGoohan, Jill Ireland, Gordon Jackson, David McCallum, Sean Connery

This film marked Endfield's exit from anonymous low-budget work. Shot in VistaVision, it is a tough story of ex-con Baker hauling cargo over rough roads and conspiring to cross crooked boss Lom. Watch for McGoohan and Connery, on their way up to transatlantic star status. This is the old Endfield of TRY AND GET ME, good left-wing noir (removed, for political reasons, to Britain); not easy to find but worth the effort. 108 min., color.

Heller in Pink Tights (1960)

Para. Prod: Marcello Girosi, Carlo Ponti. Dir: George Cukor. Scr: Walter Bernstein,• Dudley Nichols. Story basis: Louis L'amour. Cast: Sophia Loren, Anthony Quinn, Margaret O'Brien, Steve Forrest, Edmund Lowe

Bernstein's exit from the blacklist, thanks to Cukor, an old ally of various personalities in the Hollywood Left. This lighthearted western traveling show has Loren in the lead and Quinn as the entrepreneur who promotes the show, swindles the backers whenever possible, and really loves Sophia (who wouldn't?). The theme of dealing with the theatrical business under financial duress and political pressure (on the frontier) proved irresistible to its creators, perhaps too much for them to take it seriously. Reviewers, no doubt sick of humorless westerns by this time, liked the atmosphere of theater in the rough. 100 min., color.

Hemingway's Adventures of a Young Man (1962)

20th. Prod: Jerry Wald. Dir: Martin Ritt.• Scr: A. E. Hotchner. Story basis: Ernest Hemingway short fiction. Cast: Richard Beymer, Diane Baker, Corinne Calvet, Arthur Kennedy, Jessica Tandy, Susan Strasberg, Eli Wallach, Ricardo Montalban, Dan Dailey, Fred Clark, Paul Newman, Juano Hernandez

A lot of fine acting (and directing) talent is frittered away here in Ritt's final collaboration with Wald, a prominent producer who mourned the blacklist's effect on films but is better remembered for putting his name on scripts largely written by others. This film is almost an anthology of tales about young Beymer's experiences in the First World War era. The lad helps deliver a baby, rides the rails, becomes an ambulance driver for the Italians, takes a bullet, falls in love with a nurse and, finally, comes home to find things worse than ever. Such traumas might drive anyone to artistic expression, and they make a writer out of a thinly disguised Hemingway. Strasberg is the nurse and Newman and Hernandez are punchy fighters.145 min., color.

Henry Aldrich

Para. Prod: Sol C. Siegel. Dir: Hugh Bennett. Scr: Val Burton.• Play basis: Clifford Goldsmith, *What a Life!* (1938). Cast: Jimmy Lydon, Charles Smith, John Litel, Olive Bakeney, Vaughan Glaser

From 1939 to 1944, Paramount released a series of 11 features about a decent but bumbling high school student who continually gets into trouble because his grasp of social reality is shaky—smarter kids find it easy to blame their misfired schemes on him. Like Dagwood Bumstead in the BLONDIE series, Henry was raised in a well-to-do family (his father is a stuffy Princeton alum) and this accounts for much of his lack of practicality, as well as his desirability to the girls, who alternatively mother him and bail him out of trouble.

The character was created by Clifford Goldsmith, whose play *What a Life!* had a Broadway run of 538 performances in 1938-1939. In the lead role of the touring version of the show was Eddie Bracken, who collected anecdotes from teachers during his travels and used them to create the radio (later TV) series *Our Miss Brooks*, a crypto-feminist vehicle for smart-aleck high school teacher Eve Arden in conflict with an authoritarian principal. Both the Aldrich and Brooks series were early responses to the new universal American experience of the high school (in 1920, only a third of U.S. children got as far as high school, but during the Depression, the states began to require attendance as a way of reserving available jobs for adults).

The Henry Aldrich series is usually perceived as a less pretentious and less expensive version of MGM's Andy Hardy, but if MGM won a Special Oscar for its "achievement in representing the American way of life" for the sentimental and domestic Hardy series, the more satirical, school-oriented Aldrich series views the upper-middle class more skeptically. Some of that difference was no doubt the work of blacklistee Val Burton, who wrote seven of the nine screenplays.

The first adaptation of Goldsmith's play was written by the unlikely duo of Charles Brackett and Billy Wilder. That film and the first sequel starred Jackie Cooper (in *What a Life* and *Life with Henry*), after which the Aldrich saga continued in 1941 with Burton as screenwriter in *Henry Aldrich for President* and James Lydon replacing Cooper. The series was Burton's one big success in films, very much akin to that of Connie Lee• in the BLONDIE series and to the collection of left-wingers working on the BOWERY BOYS and JOE PALOOKA films.

In Burton's *Henry Aldrich for President* (1941), Henry is nominated for class president as a gag by a snooty rich boy, but Henry becomes a serious candidate when one of his opponents, a cute girl, develops a crush on him and leaves the race in his favor. Lots of complications follow when Henry is accused of stealing a rival's speech and stuffing ballot boxes. A strained action climax finds Henry and his perennial pal Dizzy in a wild airplane ride. *Variety* complained that the one serious and tragic scene with the father (Litel) might make bobby-soxer audiences uncomfortable.

If Burton's first script had some dark notes, they were few compared to the real intensity of *Henry Aldrich, Editor* (1942), Burton's second entry. This time Lydon learns where an arsonist will strike next and, by printing the information, positions himself as the main suspect. In a way that Andy Hardy never imagined, *Editor* raised serious questions about press freedom and the risks real journalists must sometimes take. *Henry and Dizzy* (1942), also written by Burton, was one of the best in the series, thanks to sidekick Charles Smith, cameos by some aging child actors (the famed "Alfalfa" of Our Gang, Carl Switzer) and a bang-up lakeside plot.

Henry Aldrich Swings It (1943) was the next and most musical entry, part of the teen-swing craze of wartime, with Henry forming a band. He is also in love with his music teacher, prompting confusion when dad grows dubious and mom draws the worst conclusions (64 min.). In *Henry Aldrich Haunts a House* (1943), Henry becomes an improbable super-teen after swallowing a mysterious chemical formula and enjoys the usual haunted-house gags in the style of Abbott and Costello. *Henry Aldrich Plays Cupid* (1944) has Henry playing matchmaker for the kindly if blustery principal, Vaughan Glaser. The last of the series, *Henry Aldrich's Little Secret* (1944) is, laugh-for-laugh, the weakest. Henry loses his charm as a baby sitter for a troubled infant.

Her First Romance (1940)

Monogram. Prod: I. E. Chadwick. Dir: Edward Dmytryk.•† Scr: Adele Comandini. Novel basis: Gene Stratton-Porter, *Her Father's Daughter* (1921). Cast: Edith Fellows, Wilbur Evans, Jacqueline Wells, Alan Ladd, Roger Daniel, Judith Linden, Marian Kerby, Marlo Dwyer, Otila Nesmith

A campus romance with a gender-conscious twist but not half so keen as the Trumbo-scripted SORORITY HOUSE. Fellows finds herself beset from all sides. Bookish but wanting love and attention, she is invited to a formal dance as a cruel sorority trick. Her half-sister and guardian refuses even to buy her a dress, but her proletarian pal Kerby, the family cook, finds her an outfit and conspires to get her to the dance. As in so many such stories, without glasses and in snappy clothes she is attractive, but learns of the prank and refuses to go into the dance until visiting opera star Evans happens by to escort her. Nasty guardian Wells also happens to be on hand with her own beau (Ladd in an early, non-action and non-existential, part), whom she has stolen away from Linden. A smash at the event, Fellows even performs a duet with Evans, and after some complications, happiness reaches even more unimaginable heights. 77 min.

Her Sister's Secret (1946)

PRC. Prod: Henry Brash. Dir: Edgar Ulmer. Scr: Anne Green.• Novel basis: Gina Kaus, *Dark Angel* (1934). Cast: Nancy Coleman, Margaret Lindsay, Philip Reed, Felix Bressart, Regis Toomey, Henry Stephenson, Fritz Feld, Winston Severn , George Meeker, Helene Heigh, Frances E. Williams

One of several films directed by the erratic, prolific, and left-leaning independent refugee producer Ulmer (whose big credits include the original *Black Cat*, the cult DETOUR, and the Yiddish classic *Green Fields*) with a handful of collaborators destined for the blacklist. In this outing, Ulmer and Green tried to bring some light to the then-taboo issues of illegitimacy. Coleman gives her baby to Lindsay to raise, creating a host of emotional and legal complications. Low production values as on other PRC features, but the film's subject and sincerity makes it a gender-conscious cinematic document, like the contemporary NOT WANTED. 86 min.

Here Comes Mister Jordan (1941)

Col. Prod: Everett Riskin. Dir: Alexander Hall. Scr: Sidney Buchman,• Seton I. Miller. Play basis: Henry Segall, *Heaven Can Wait* (n.d.). Cast: Robert Montgomery, Claude Rains, James Gleason, Evelyn Keyes, Edward Everett Horton, Rita Johnson, John Emery

Every bloody military conflict brings a flurry of films from Hollywood invoking the hope of life-after-death (as did the depressed mood of the 1980s), nearly all of them intended to be cheerful and uplifting. In this fantasy, one of the best of the subgenre, death is debonair in the form of Claude Rains. His assistant is the bungling new angel in the heavenly bureaucracy, Edward Everett Horton.

Robert Montgomery, a principled Hollywood conservative (and father to one of Hollywood's later progres-

sives, Elizabeth Montgomery of *Bewitched* and socially minded television films), is in top form as the prizefighter on the verge of a title bout who crashes his own plane and is mistakenly ripped from his mortal coil by the blundering Horton (left alone, he would have pulled through somehow). To make amends, Rains must find him a suitable new body, and the first choice is a millionaire about to be bumped off by wife Johnson and executive assistant Emery. In the new drag of the millionaire's bones, the boxer falls for Keyes, hires former trainer Gleason (the classic Irish boxing type), and it all looks good until further complications set in.

This film was a great hit at the time, thanks perhaps to its sense of consolation. A big box office hit, it won Academy Awards for best screenplay (Miller and Buchman) and Segal (best original story), Hall (best director), and Montgomery (best actor) 94 min.

Here Comes Trouble (1936)

20th. Assoc. Prod: John Stone. Dir: Lewis Seiler. Scr: Robert Ellis, Helen Logan, Barry Trivers. Story basis: John Bright,• Robert Tasker. Cast: Paul Kelly, Arline Judge, Mona Barrie, Gregory Ratoff, Sammy Cohen, Edward Brophy, Halliwell Hobbes, Andrew Tombes, Ernie Alexander Mischa Auer, Richard Powell

One of those curious proletarian crime comedy-intrigues of the Depression years, penned by two close collaborators and early Hollywood Communists, Bright and ex-con Tasker. The story centers on a purloined ruby, but the thin plot is almost incidental to the ambience and action.

Two stooge-like jewel thieves, Brophy and Tombes, plan to lift the Mahal Ruby on a tour boat sailing into Havana. They are put off by a ruse and, once on land, soon thrown in jail for bar fighting and watch the ship leave port without them. On ship, meanwhile, an ill and badly exploited stoker hits an abusive officer with a shovel, also bursting a steam pipe, forcing shipmates Kelly and Cohen (a diamond-in-the-rough named "Grimy") to prevent a boiler explosion. More intrigue follows, and after the ship docks in New York, Barrie almost gets away with the jewel—when Cohen's pet monkey stumbles across something quite magnificent. Not to be confused with a Spencer Tracy melodrama of the same name. 62 min.

Heroes of the Hills (1938)

Rep. Prod: William A. Berke. Dir: George Sherman. Scr: Betty Burbridge, Stanley Roberts.† Story basis: Stanley

Roberts, Jack Natteford. Cast: Robert Livingston, Ray Corrigan, Max Terhune, Priscilla Lawson, LeRoy Mason, James Eagles, Roy Barcroft, Barry Hays, Carleton Young

One of the abundant Three Mesquiteers series, sometimes featuring John Wayne and less often a left-wing writer or two, with the kind of social uplift theme articulated here. This time around, the Mesquiteers (Livingston, Corrigan and Terhune) capture inmates Mason and Eagles, who explain that the former has bad lungs and needed fresh air to survive. Sounding like New Dealers, the Mesquiteers also suggest to the authorities that the prison relieve its overcrowding by creating trustee positions for work on nearby ranches. But like modern entrepreneurs, builders of a forthcoming prison addition need to nip the experiment in the bud. They shoot at the trustees, making it look as if the convicts mean to "escape," and get a shock when the victims reassemble rather than disperse. The lesson is plain but effective: Some prisoners, at least, are more honest than the men who want to make fortunes from the prison system. 56 min.

Hey, Rookie (1944)

Col. Prod: Irving Briskin. Dir: Charles Barton. Scr: Henry Myers,• Jay Gorney,• Edward Eliscu.• Story basis: E. B. Colvan, Doris Colvan. Cast: Ann Miller, Larry Parks,† Joe Besser, Joe Sawyer, Jimmy Little, Selmer Jackson, Jack Gilford,• Charles C. Wilson, Bob Evans, Doodles Weaver

Originally an army camp musical developed with the guidance of three left-wing screenwriters, then picked up by Hollywood after it held the stage of L.A.'s Belasco Theater for 36 weeks early in the war. The thin plot deals with a musical-comedy producer who is drafted and assigned to put on a show to entertain fellow soldiers. The "Khaki Go Wacky" look of the gags and songs helped make lead Larry Parks a star, briefly elevated to public notice the eventual Three Stooges fill-in Besser (then best known for the Broadway vaudeville "Sons 'o Fun"), and offered a screen debut for Gilford, a left-wing nightclub comic best remembered for later TV sitcoms and films like *Hold That Tiger*. Despite the generous sprinkling of talented Hollywood leftists, the film had no class line to speak of except the real class identities of most of the characters—but more than a pinch of patriotic antifascism. This film remains practically unavailable. 77 min.

The Hidden Room (1949) See *Obsession*

High Noon (1952)

Stanley Kramer Productions. Prod: Stanley Kramer (uncredited Assoc. Prod: Carl Foreman•). Dir: Fred Zinneman. Scr: Carl Foreman. Story basis: John W. Cunningham, "The Tin Star" *(Collier's)* (1947). Cast: Gary Cooper, Thomas Mitchell, Lloyd Bridges, Katy Jurado, Grace Kelly, Otto Kruger, Lon Chaney, Jr., Harry Morgan, Ian MacDonald, Lee Van Cleef, Sheb Wooley, Jack Elam

Perhaps the pivotal movie of the blacklist, *High Noon* established the western as the genre in which the Cold War would be debated and, because it was an uncompromised (if often misunderstood) masterpiece whose author was literally run off the set for political reasons, the clearest evidence that the crackdown against Hollywood was a conscious act of political censorship. What might have happened if Foreman had been subpoenaed before shooting began rather than close to the end? The near-certainty that the movie would not have survived in the present form suggests how many films were literally censored out of existence because the most gifted generations of filmmakers never got to make them.

The tale turns on several effective gimmicks, notably the use of real time to tell the story (punctuated by the frequent cutting away to a clock face) and a Tex Ritter narration in song revealing the innermost fears of the marshal. But the film relies on much more than gimmicks. All of the social forces of contemporary America are depicted in their relative responses to the threat of a common enemy, namely McCarthyism as a junior form of revived fascism (brought back from its defeat in World War II in the figure of convicted murderer Frank Miller, now inexplicably pardoned in much the way that certain Nazi war criminals were protected in the United States with the help of McCarthy and Richard Nixon). As each institution fails to support the law officer—the judiciary from the start, then the church and municipal government—the rout of the old Popular Front is shown to be absolute. The mayor (Mitchell) sums up the lack of interest in resisting the common threat this way: "People up North are thinking hard about this town . . . thinking about sending down money, money to put up stores and to build factories. . . . But if they're going to be reading about shooting and killing in the streets—everything we worked for will be wiped out in one day." In short, finance capital trumps social justice.

Foreman left little doubt, in interviews later in life, that the allegory was about Hollywood and his own lonely struggle to remain on the set and working, but it works just as well for the nation as a whole at the time. Critics in what was then the budding neoconservative movement hated the film for all the wrong reasons, a sacrifice of critical acumen that became conservatism's historical point of separation from any effective role in the debate over film content. 85 min.

High Tension (1936)

A comedy co-scripted by Edward Eliscu• with an abundance of absurdist elements. A pulp-magazine adventure writer has based her stories about a deep-sea diver on the life of her boyfriend, who repairs cables at the sea bottom. Adventures and melodrama are less fun than the characterizations.

High Wall (1947)

MGM. Prod: Robert Lord. Dir: Curtis Bernhardt. Scr: Lester Cole.• Play basis: Alan R. Clark and Bradbury Foote. Cast: Robert Taylor, Audrey Totter, Herbert Marshall, Dorothy Patrick, H. B. Warner, Warner Anderson

An important psychoanalytic drama about a former air force pilot who received head injuries, later diagnosed as haematoma. Found in an overturned car with his wife strangled, he chooses at first to suffer alone as he is moved from jail to psychiatric clinic en route to probable trial and execution. The district attorney, sure that he is faking, is especially eager to see him burn, but he meets sympathetic psychiatrist Totter, who helps him recover his memory and demonstrate his innocence. Not the most compelling example of the psychological genre, but it has a nice Southern setting for the clinic, somewhat believable fellow patients, and showcases Taylor's intense (some would say overdramatic) acting style. One more interesting case of the war-tortured veteran, and one of the rare successes of Cole's at effective melodrama. 99 min.

His Exciting Night (1938)

Universal. Prod: Ken Goldsmith. Dir: Gus Meins. Scr: Pat C. Flick, Edward Eliscu,• Morton Grant.• Play basis: Katharine Kavanaugh, Adam's Evening (1934). Cast: Charles Ruggles, Richard Lane, "Slapsie Maxie" Rosenbloom, Marion Martin, Stepin Fetchit, Ona Munson, Frances Robinson, Georgia Caine, Regis Toomey, Stanley Hughes, Benny Baker

Screwball comedy with a dose of gender politics. Amid his wedding reception, Ruggles is duped by his boss (Lane) into traveling to the apartment of glamour girl Martin. "Caught" by her real husband (played by Slapsie Maxie), he and Martin escape in a cab—only to be driven by a cabbie, an aspiring singer, into a lake

when he can't hit a certain high note! Everyone thinks Ruggles and Martin are dead, except Rosenbloom, who wants to kill Ruggles. Much more confusion follows until at last the sneaky boss (who feared that Ruggles was going to steal one of his most valuable accounts) is exposed and the usually timid Ruggles is emboldened by Martin to stand up for himself. A funny surprise ending rounds it all off. Eliscu quipped about the film 50-some years later, "It wasn't *my* exciting night." 61 min.

His Greatest Gamble (1934)

A father-and-daughter film co-scripted by Sidney Buchman• has a gambler steal his young daughter from his estranged wife. Sent to prison for a murder that he did not commit, he learns over the years that his ex-wife has caused the child to grow up neurasthenic and desperately unhappy. He escapes from prison, poses as her uncle, and assists her in making a life with her true love. Solid soap.

His Kind of Woman (1951)

Howard Hughes. Prod: Robert Sparks. Dir: John Farrow, Richard Fleischer (uncredited). Scr: Frank Fenton, Jack Leonard, Earl Fenton (script contribution by Roy Huggins,† uncredited). Story basis: Gerald Drayson Adams, *Star Sapphire* (n.d.). Cast: Robert Mitchum, Jane Russell, Vincent Price, Tim Holt, Charles McGraw, Raymond Burr, Jim Backus, Philip Van Zandt, Dan White, Carleton Young, John Mylong

This stylized tropical noir is a near-perfect vehicle for a Mitchum and Russell romance, with some scene-stealing by Price. Huggins contributed edgy but not great lines like this: Mitchum: "I'm a professional gambler." Russell: "Aren't we all."

The classic loner, Mitchum is offered a sum to show up at a Mexican resort and cool his heels. He eventually learns that a big-time crook deported from the United States, played by the hefty Burr, is going to return with a new identity, and Mitchum may be the fall guy. While waiting, Mitchum falls into a romance with lounge singer Russell, meets her old boyfriend Price (a swashbuckling film star who yearns for *real* adventure) and a cast of ugly Americans, including the lecherous Backus (later the voice of Mr. Magoo).

Full-figured Russell's strapless gowns offer gratifying distractions from her acting inability. Mitchum does better just by playing Mitchum, the blue-collar existentialist. 120 min.

Hit the Hay (1945)

Typical Judy Canova populist comedy, written by Richard Weil,• with the hillbilly girl improbably making a splash in the world of opera.

Hit the Ice (1943)

Universal. Prod: Alex Gottlieb. Dir: Charles Lamont. Scr: John Grant, Robert Lees,• Fredric I. Rinaldo.• Story basis: True Boardman. Cast: Bud Abbott, Lou Costello, Patric Knowles, Elyse Knox, Sheldon Leonard, Four Teens, Johnny Long and His Orchestra

A musical full of production numbers, including skating extravaganzas, that has too little of the always inventive Lees/Rinaldo dialogue but many pleasing moments. Sheldon Leonard, the crypto-Jewish gangster surrounded by dummies, is especially charming as set against those lower-middle-class failures, Abbott and Costello.

The duo of photographers from a Manhattan working-class neighborhood are the least successful of the old gang: Everyone else is moving up in the world, from New York to Los Angeles. Seeking to better themselves as sidewalk cameramen, they are inadvertently caught up in a scheme to rob a bank. The boys photograph the robbers and are mistakenly taken to be the thieves. To clear themselves, they pursue the gang to a winter resort village, where misadventures turn into antics in the woods and on the ski slope. Lots of opportunities for songs. There are few wartime antifascist references, and some critics even carped that precious film stock was being wasted; escape-seeking war workers loved it, however. 82 min.

Hitch Hike Lady (1935)

Rep. Prod: Nat Levine. Dir: Aubrey Scotto. Scr: Gordon Rigby, Lester Cole.• Story basis: Wallace MacDonald. Cast: Alison Skipworth, Mae Clarke, Arthur Treacher, James Ellison, Warren Hymer, Beryl Mercer, J. Farrell MacDonald, Christian Rub, Harold Waldridge, Ward Bond

A sentimental road comedy-drama with ample evidence that the dispossessed and marginally criminal road types of the thirties have some qualities unappreciated in the larger society. Skipworth is a near-broke British matron traveling to America to rejoin her son. Unbeknownst to her, his letters about owning an orange farm, "Rancho San Quentin," refer to a less pleasant location. Determined to get to California on her last $40 and sharing a ride west with Mae Clarke, she is robbed and reduced, for a short time, to hitchhiking (the only connection in this misnamed B-feature). Meanwhile, Clarke and trailer salesman Ellison keep the secret about her son from her, hoping all will turn out for the best as they drive a trailer to California. Luckily they have already gathered up two more loose souls, Treacher and Hymer; Treacher borrows $500 from gangster pals against the reward out on Hymer's head. After assorted other adventures (including an orange-judging contest), they arrive in California together, Treacher buys an orange ranch, Skipworth's son gets out on parole, and all ends happily. 76 min.

Hitler's Children (1943)

RKO. Prod: Edward A. Golden. Dir: Edward Dmytryk.† Scr: Emmet Lavery. Book basis: Gregor Ziemer, *Education for Death: The Making of a Nazi* (1941). Cast: Tim Holt, Bonita Granville, Kent Smith, Otto Kruger, H. B. Warner, Hans Conried.

The low-budget box-office smash (it had the biggest grosses in RKO history to that time) that gave Dmytryk a leg up for better assignments during the war. Mixing documentary footage of Nazi rallies with patriotic appeals to Americans and a dash of Goethe and Beethoven, it has also been called "exploitation" for its use of political and sexual issues, but is hardly excessive for a wartime feature. The film is also notable for B- cowboy star Holt in a serious dramatic feature, a sign that little was expected from the production.

Granville is a German-born girl sent back to Germany by her New York parents to live with her grandparents so she will not lose touch with her cultural roots. Next door to her new school is the "Horst Wessel School" for members of the Hitler Youth preparing for careers in fascism, Holt among them. The two begin to fall for each other. She resists at first; he doesn't, and that sets the thin plot into motion. The narrator, American-school pedagogue Kruger, watches them fall in love, quotes passages from *Faust* celebrating freedom, and then tries to rescue her from what is discreetly called a labor camp. Granville's eventual escape from the camp into the sanctuary of a church brings onstage a German Catholic bishop who denounces Hitler at every opportunity.

The camp is actually one of the infamous *Lebensborn* SS maternity centers for unwed German mothers, which were supposed to become a breeding ground for Himmler's officer corps but that by war's end had collapsed into "adoption" centers for childless SS couples (for whom blond Polish children were kidnapped). The idea of a state-run sex camp was a shocking theme for Hollywood, but whatever titillation there may have been in the film was more than balanced by the equally shocking depiction of the forced sterilization of politically dissident German women. For all of its quirkiness as a documentary melodrama, the film has a sincerity that rescues it from mere historical oddness. 82 min.

Hitler's Madman (1943)

PRC. Prod: Seymour Nebenzal Dir: Douglas Sirk. Scr: Peretz Hirschbein, Melvin Levy,† Doris Malloy. Story basis: Bart Lytton,† "Hangman's Village" (apparently unpublished). Adaptation: Albrecht Joseph, Emil Ludwig, Edgar G. Ulmer (uncredited). Cast: Patricia Morison, John Carradine, Alan Curtis, Ralph Moran, Howard Freeman, Ludwig Stossel, Edgar Kennedy, Al Shean, Jimmy Conlin, Ava Gardner (uncredited).

A film based on a real-life incident in Lidice, Czechoslovakia, where a famous Nazi officer was assassinated and the town wiped out in revenge (HANGMEN ALSO DIE dealt with the same material). Interesting as the U.S. film debut for refugee German director Sirk (a socialist veteran of the Bavarian revolution of 1918) and for Hirschbein, a famed Yiddish short story writer who had also written several of the best-known Yiddish films for director Edgar Ulmer. The elusive Nebenzal, a German American with close ties to the German Left, produced films by G.M. Pabst and both versions of M (by Fritz Lang and Joseph Losey). Unfortunately, typical PRC "poverty row" production values robbed this effort of much of its potential. 84 min.

Hitting a New High (1937)

RKO. Prod: Jesse L. Lasky. Dir: Raoul Walsh. Scr: Gertrude Purcell,† John Twist. Story basis: Robert Harari, Maxwell Shane. Cast: Lily Pons, Jack Oakie, John Howard, Eric Blore, Edward Everett Horton, Eduardo Ciannelli, Luis Alberni, Jack Arnold, Leonard Carey

A definite curiosity as a Purcell-style women's film and a farce that didn't make it: the studio lost big bucks and singer Pons never appeared in a nonconcert feature again. The plot was too wild for anyone outside the slapstick zone to pull off. Oakie, press agent for millionaire aesthete and would-be big game hunter Horton, hears Pons singing in a jazz club and plants her in the jungle as "the Bird Girl" opera singer for Horton to "discover." Dressed only in feathers, she charms him, but back in the United States she is found out by her jazz-band leader boyfriend, Howard. So she sings jazz at night and opera during the day. The situation is too fragile to last long, so which musical form (and which man) will she choose? 85 min.

Hold That Ghost (1941)

Universal. Prod: Alex Gottlieb (uncredited). Assoc Prod: Burt Kelly, Glen Tryon. Dir: Arthur Lubin. Scr: Robert Lees,• Fred Rinaldo,• John Grant. Cast: Bud Abbott, Lou Costello, Richard Carlson, Joan Davis, Mischa Auer, also Ted Lewis and the Andrews Sisters

One of the most literate of the Abbott and Costello scripts and easily one of the funniest, in no small part thanks to Joan Davis's comedic talents. (According to writer Lees, Costello nearly ruined the film with his jealousy over Davis, fearing her humor would draw attention away from him.) The boys are gas station attendants who accidentally inherit a road house formerly owned by a mobster. Davis, an out of work radio actress, shares a ride in a jitney with scientist Richard Carlson and is caught up in the ensuing excitement.

A series of apparently supernatural events keeps the unwilling guests (dumped by the jitney driver) fluttering in the road house, where the mobster's money is hidden and where fellow mobsters soon make trouble. As Davis falls in love with Lou and the group entertain themselves with antic dancing, things get steadily more confusing. Respectability is in short supply among the proletarian protagonists. Critics complained of too many familiar props, such as secret panels, clutching hands, and similar contraptions, and of the predictable response from Lou (who can't convince Bud of anything, naturally). But when they work, they work: when Costello tries to hang up his pants, a bedroom wall in front of him turns 180 degrees, changing the room into a gambling den, which disappears again in another moment. 86 min.

Holiday (1938)

Col. Prod: Everett Riskin. Dir: George Cukor. Scr: Donald Ogden Stewart,• Sidney Buchman.• Play basis: Philip Barry. Cast: Katharine Hepburn, Cary Grant, Doris Nolan, Lew Ayres, Edward Everett Horton, Henry Kolker, Binnie Barnes, Jean Dixon, Henry Daniell

One of the best screwball comedies of all time, thanks to the superb writing team of Stewart and Buchman, and one of Hepburn's most charming pre–Spencer Tracy films—certainly her most antibourgeois. Stewart is considered to have returned Hepburn from "box office poison" status with this and THE PHILADELPHIA STORY, which like Holiday was adapted from a grandly successful Broadway play by Barry.

Grant, an executive of lower-class origins, is betrothed to rich girl Doris Nolan. Once he enters the fat cat household, however, he meets the rebellious sister,

Hepburn, and the alcoholic brother, Ayers. Unlike Nolan, who thrives in the midst of luxury and the prospect of a big career for her future husband, the siblings have been crushed by the burden of wealth. Ayers wanted to be a musician, Hepburn wanted a meaningful career—both are stuck and happy only when recalling childhood.

And that is in a way the solution, when Hepburn brings Grant's liberal-bohemian older friends (Horton and Donnelly) up to her former playroom during a dreadfully stuffy party downstairs. By revealing to her the bohemian side of "Johnny," they allow her to take him from her sister without suffering guilt. Special political moments appear when Hepburn offers sarcastic remarks at a typical businessman and former childhood chum who says he loves doing business in "some other countries" (Italy, Germany?) where unions aren't a problem any more. 95 min.

Holiday Affair (1949)

RKO. Prod: Don Hartman. Dir: Don Hartman. Scr: Isobel Lennart.† Story basis: John D. Weaver, "The Man Who Played Santa Claus," *McCall's* (1948). A Christmas Gift." Cast: Robert Mitchum, Janet Leigh, Griff Barnett, Wendell Corey, Esther Dale, Harry Morgan

In this romantic family drama with a strong underlying class theme, Leigh is a war widow who can't put aside the past. Her young son is the "man of the house," while she is engaged to the kindly but passionless lawyer Barnett. Along comes the ex-GI Mitchum, hardly more than a blue collar-drifter who works at a department store at Christmas, but who has the inclination to give away most of what he owns. Achieving a natural rapport with her son, he woos Leigh, who must choose between instant respectability and the possibility of real love. Interesting in part because Mitchum offers sage advice about healing the wounds of war, without however seeking to return Leigh to a wholly domestic world. A major box office failure for Mitchum, an actor far better suited for noir. 87 min.

Holiday in Havana (1949)

Col. Prod: Ted Richmond. Dir: Jean Yarbrough. Scr: Robert Lees,• Frederic I. Rinaldo,• Karen DeWolf.• Story basis: Morton Grant.• Cast: Desi Arnaz, Mary Hatcher, Ann Doran, Steven Geray

A rare story with credits for no fewer than four screenwriters who were later blacklisted. Arnaz's first feature has a Cuban carnival as the backdrop for music, comic adventure and romance. Desi is a lowly hotel

bellboy who yearns to become a professional bandleader in the kind of semi-urban folk culture typical of the 1940s-1960s Caribbean, in which popular music was both a representation of mass sentiment and a way out of the slums.

Because of a hotel mixup, Arnaz is sure that Hatcher—visiting her homeland after an education in the United States—has scorned his invitation to write music for her. When he sets off for Havana in a beat-up bus with a ragged but talented group of musicians, she accidentally joins him to sing in the carnival. En route, they duck the police, encounter his family (who believes the two have married) and fall in love. Nothing spectacular but never dull and full of high spirits, with Desi at his very best as the vital musician. 73 min.

Holiday in Mexico (1946)

MGM. Prod: Joe Pasternak. Dir: George Sidney. Scr: Isobel Lennart.† Story basis: William Kozlenko. Cast: Ilona Massey, Walter Pidgeon, Jane Powell, Roddy McDowall, Xavier Cugat, José Iturbi

Foolish romantic mixups in Mexico City's diplomatic circles serve as an excuse for some good musical numbers showcasing the pianist-conductor Iturbi at the "higher" end of musical culture and Cugat at the more vigorous "lower," with thrush Powell in her MGM debut. Notwithstanding the talented Lennart, so little thought was given to characterization that the Hays Office complained about the stereotyping of Mexicans, after which a few roles were upgraded. Lennart went on to better things, and the Hollywood Left to better movies about Mexico. 128 min., color.

Hollywood Boulevard (1936)

Para. Prod: A. M. Botsford. Dir: Robert Florey. Scr: Marguerite Roberts.• Story basis: Faith Thorns. Cast: John Halliday, Marsha Hunt,• Robert Cummings, C. Henry Gordon, Esther Ralston, Esther Dale, Frieda Inescort, Francis X. Bushman, Gary Cooper

Another insider's look at the biz, full of almost credible details and ample up-and-coming extras as well as colony old-timers; interesting but flawed by over-complicated backstage plotting. This film may be most notable as an early opportunity for character actress Marsha Hunt—no Communist but a liberal who refused to testify against her friends and fellow union activists—in a co-starring role.

Broke ex-star Halliday agrees to have his ghost-written memoirs sold to a gossip mag for $25,000, but the publisher's wife was one of the star's past lovers. Meanwhile, daughter Hunt, who hates Hollywood, falls for studio junior writer Cummings. At a Hollywood night spot, Cummings accidentally slugs Halliday, the first of psychological and physical blows (including a gunshot from his former lover) that bring the old egoist to his senses. The real film director, Florey, much later claimed in an interview that the plot was lifted from his 1927 experimental short, *Life and Death of 9413—a Hollywood Extra*. 75 min.

Hombre (1967)

20th. Prod: Irving Ravetch,† Martin Ritt.• Dir: Martin Ritt. Scr: Irving Ravetch, Harriet Frank, Jr. Novel basis: Elmore Leonard, *Hombre* (1961). Cast: Paul Newman, Frederic March, Richard Boone, Cameron Mitchell, Barbara Rush, Martin Balsam

A classic reversal of western themes by Ritt, Newman and the writing team, with remarkable casting all around and a strong antiracist story line. Raised by Apaches, white man Newman is assisting a stagecoach full of settlers in the 1880s across treacherous territory while he battles an Indian agent and other whites who have stolen the Indians' land or hold deeply racist views. The last 20 minutes are spellbinding, with the Anglo-Christian half of Newman's heritage prevailing over what might have been the wiser, more stoic and Apache half. Even Anglo viewers will be more ambivalent about that now than when the film was released. Critics rightly compared this to the ending of BROKEN ARROW. One of the last major U.S. westerns before the genre was transformed by the Euro-western. 111 min.

Home of the Brave (1949)

Screen Plays Corp. Prod: Stanley Kramer. Dir: Mark Robson. Scr: Carl Foreman.• Play basis: Arthur Laurents, *Home of the Brave* (1946). Cast: Lloyd Bridges,† James Edwards, Frank Lovejoy, Jeff Corey•

Foreman's first political film of note, the most hard-hitting of the antiracist (rather than anti-anti-Semitic) topical films in the later 1940s, and also one of Lloyd Bridges' last opportunities in a left-wing film. It is a fascinating psychological drama to boot (with Corey substituting for the usual German-accented psychoanalyst—the war situation made that too unlikely). Based on a novel about a gay soldier, the plot was almost but by no means entirely transformed: some sexual tension remains, another lingering source of fascination for this film.

The story is seen in flashbacks, through the memories of a black soldier who has lost the use of his legs after surviving a difficult test in combat. During a secret mission in the Pacific War, a small group of volunteers found itself divided over racial questions when the last of the volunteers is the black Edwards. Bridges, the lead volunteer, is sympathetic but sees the overwhelming necessity of getting the job done (mapping the territory for later invasion). The seemingly Southern-raised, vividly racist white (Lovejoy) sets the plot in motion with his constant barbs; when he is killed, Edwards wonders if he wasn't happy about it, a twist on the battlefield angst of the typical war film. Corey must help him work it out.

Seen at the time as daringly liberal, it stands up well against PINKY and the other liberal dramas of the day. It also demonstrates Foreman's talent for action drama that would serve him well in HIGH NOON (which, oddly, was the working title for this war film). 88 min.

Honeymoon (1947)

Another simple-minded South-of-the-Border exotic feature, with an uncredited contribution by Isobel Lennart† to a Michael Kanin script; for a grown-up Shirley Temple. A soldier on a three-day pass in Mexico, desperately missing his girl, is rewarded by Temple, determined to bend all the rules in crossing the border to marry him. Franchot Tone is the kindly Mexican police official who finally makes it possible.

Honeymoon Ahead (1945)

Val Burton• wrote this lost musical comedy about a prison choir that simultaneously lands a radio contract and loses one of its best voices. What to do? Frame him back into prison.

Honky Tonk (1941)

MGM. Prod: Pandro S. Berman. Dir: Jack Conway. Scr: Marguerite Roberts,• John Sandford.• Cast: Clark Gable, Lana Turner, Frank Morgan, Marjorie Main, Claire Trevor, Albert Dekker, Chill Wills, Henry O'Neill, Veda Ann Borg

This was MGM's biggest money-maker in 1941, no doubt because of the enduring appeal of the always unlikely pairing of Gable and Turner (she was just 20 years old here, Gable twice that). But it never got the critical attention it deserved, perhaps because it was the original dark western—not film noir, certainly, but a deeper look at the corruption of the west than had ever been dared before. This was the sole Hollywood credit for the Marxist novelist Sandford and a rare collaboration with wife Roberts (and her strongest film until she returned from the blacklist decades later to write, among other screenplays, TRUE GRIT).

Gable plays a con man sick and tired of being tarred and feathered and thrown out of villages in the Midwest. He hops a train for Nevada, where he intends to take over a town of his own. To his delight, officials in his new digs are as corrupt as he (the sheriff owns the saloon and the judge skims from the fines). Social progress has been held back by these officials' unwillingness to share the loot with the citizens, so Gable runs a "reform" slate to take over town government and wins, giving the citizens their end of the booty in the form of schools and churches. Along the way, Gable must deal with the love of a good woman (Turner, the judge's daughter, representing the higher corruption) while contemplating the opportunities provided by a bad woman (Trevor). Gable's power is challenged by the older order, and the way he meets the challenge while dealing with the parallel conflicts in his personal life fills out the rest of this very watchable and intelligent parable. A measure of its power is the epilogue that appears on the screen at the end: "And when I die don't bury me deep / Leave one hand free to fleece the sheep." 105 min.

Hotel Berlin (1945)

WB. Prod: Louis F. Edelman. Dir: Peter Godfrey. Scr: Alvah Bessie,• Jo Pagano. Novel basis: Vicki Baum, *Hotel Berlin* (1944). Cast: Helmut Dantine, Andrea King, Raymond Massey, Faye Emerson, Peter Lorre, Alan Hale

An adaptation of the Baum novel in the *Grand Hotel* tradition but now about the last months of Nazism as seen in the comings and goings of guests in a respectable hotel. The aristocratic and decadent Prussian officers stand in contrast to ordinary Germans who are terrified but prepared to join (or at least sympathize with) the resistance as it shows its capacity to challenge those in power. For Bessie and others, the film was intended to provide an antidote to the theory of "collective guilt" while showing the historically based class privilege at the center of Nazi authority. German military official March, knowing something is terribly wrong and plotting Hitler's assassination even on the way to his own suicide, can still say to a friend, "Prepare better for the next war. We must never lose again." Dantine, the partisan agent, is meanwhile hidden in the hotel; Lorre plays the apparently maddened Nazi intellectual who actually writes pro-Allied propaganda. Emerson, an officer's mistress, is really a courier, and other ordinary people begin to challenge Nazi authority as the old order breaks up. The film ends with a joint message of Churchill, Roosevelt and Stalin coming over the illegal radio.

This film has been criticized for finding good Germans too easily, but in fact recalls (albeit too far in advance for precise accuracy) a little-known rising of "antifas" shortly after the fall of the Nazis and before being repressed by Russians, British and Americans on all sides of the new dividing lines. Excellent performances and a notable appearance by real-life ardent antifascist Lorre make the scenario more gripping and perhaps more credible. 98 min.

The House I Live In (1945)

RKO. Prod: Mervyn LeRoy, Frank Ross. Dir: Mervyn LeRoy. Scr: Albert Maltz.• Cast: Frank Sinatra and a bunch of kids

Winner of an Academy statuette, this film short, centered on Sinatra's singing, was evidently the fruit of an exchange of letters between Sinatra and Maltz after the release of the screenwriter's PRIDE OF THE MARINES earlier in 1945. The "House" is the United States, and, through Sinatra's defense of a boy being chased by young ruffians—then gathering around while he sings about the meaning of it all—is a call for tolerance of ethnic differences. Lyricist Abel Meeropol, who also wrote "Strange Fruit," was to be the father who adopted the sons of Julius and Ethel Rosenberg. Seen as a major statement of the Popular Front sentiment, it stresses the multiculturalism at the heart of the American way and the source of the victory over fascism. The blandness of the message—no minorities are present, not even Jews, and the boy picked on could be either Catholic or Protestant—needs to be seen in the context of the times. 11 min.

The House of the Seven Gables (1940)

Universal. Assoc. Prod: Burt Kelly. Dir: Joe May. Scr: Lester Cole• (also dialogue director). Novel basis: Nathaniel Hawthorne, *The House of the Seven Gables* (1851). Adaptation: Harold Greene. Cast: George Sanders, Margaret Lindsay, Vincent Price, Alan Napier, Nan Grey, Dick Foran, Cecil Kellaway

Cole's adaptation of the Hawthorne classic captures many of the strengths of the novel, including the troubling sense of historical guilt in a society whose wealth grows from its greed to exploit the virgin continent—and the associated recklessness of a patriarchal society. But Cole unsubtly shifted its political point (and expressed surprise in his memoirs that critics did not notice) by identifying the Pyncheons as slave traders, with Sanders as the summa of wickedness and Price remarkably cast as the abolitionist antidote.

Unconsciously acting out a seventeenth-century curse by Matthew Maule, whose land was stolen by the Pyncheons, patriarch Emery summons the two Pyncheon sons home to announce that the house will be sold. This enrages the evil son, played brilliantly by Sanders, who believes a treasure is hidden somewhere on the property. (In one of the best scenes, good son Price, a left-liberal in real life, notes that the portraits on the wall depict thieves, swindlers and counter-revolutionary traitors.) After Emery changes his mind, he suddenly drops dead. Sanders seizes the opportunity to accuse the innocent Price of murder, conspiring to send him to prison for life and gain control of the property. The house, however, was deeded to daughter Lindsay, who devotes herself to freeing Price.

Time passes and Price meets a fellow convict, who has been sentenced to the same prison for abolitionist activities. By an all-too-remarkable coincidence, the convict happens to be Maule's descendant and namesake. Decades later, young cousin Grey comes to live in the mansion, and thereby hangs the rest of the tale. Condemning everyone to emotional wretchedness, the predatory and pseudo-aristocratic Sanders often steals the picture as he seeks to control everyone around him. In both political and aesthetic terms—and despite its lack of reputation—this is one of the most interesting adaptations of a historic American novel ever, and certainly the best of the studio days. 89 min.

The House on Carroll Street (1988)

Orion. Prod: Robert F. Colesberry, Peter Yates. Dir: Peter Yates. Scr: Walter Bernstein.• Cast: Kelly McGillis, Jeff Daniels, Mandy Patinkin, Jessica Tandy

A small film set in 1951 and hence in the heart of the McCarthy period, and in that sense a followup to Bernstein's script for THE FRONT. Yates relied overmuch on melodrama, and so the film has been largely ignored, but from at least one angle it can bee viewed as a revival of Jewish progressivism at a time when the Popular Front character of much anti-Nazi sentiment was being forgotten.

A young woman played by McGillis is already under suspicion by the FBI and fired for her ties with the Left. She inadvertently overhears a plot to smuggle former Nazis (including SS officers) into the United States, a reference to the real-life projects Overcast and Paperclip. McGillis tries to get the news to the FBI, while on the run to elude a virtual death sentence. FBI agent Daniels, perhaps the least believable character, is hard to sell on the idea, even though a phone call to the Pentagon's contemporary Joint Intelligence Objectives Agency (which secretly, on Truman's orders, ran 765 Nazi scien-

tists and engineers into the country in 1945-1955), would have confirmed that McGillis was telling the truth—and promptly shut down the narrative. Daniels eventually joins the crusade, but the romance, in a small bow to realism, is doomed. Still, its very possibility illuminates the decency of some ordinary nonpolitical people in the 1950s (unfortunately, few in the FBI were inclined to protect civil liberties by resisting J. Edgar Hoover's commands, and fewer still did so), as well as the hopeful image of gentile and Jew reaching out to each other across formidable barriers. Final scenes in Grand Central Station also evoke Hitchcock. 101 min., color.

The Howards of Virginia (1940)

Col. Prod: Frank Lloyd. Dir: Frank Lloyd. Scr: Sidney Buchman.• Novel basis: Elizabeth Page, The Tree of Liberty (1939). Cast: Cary Grant, Martha Scott, Cedric Hardwicke, Alan Marshal, Richard Carlson, Paul Kelly, Irving Bacon, Tom Drake, Anne Revere, Ralph Byrd, Alan Ladd

This film may properly be regarded as Buchman's historical prequel to his screenplay for MR. SMITH GOES TO WASHINGTON: it explains the revolutionary and patriotic foundation of national liberty, which may have been betrayed but still gives reason to fight. Sometimes titled Tree of Liberty, it is a typical Hollywood production of the day, combining New Deal and patriotic themes.

Grant is the son of a poor Virginia tidewater farmer who went off to fight the Indians (with the promise of 1,000 acres of land for every fighter) in the 1760s and was killed. The oldest son of a shattered family, the lad grows up friends with Thomas Jefferson, an instinctive rebel at school and a would-be frontiersman. Marrying into the Virginia aristocracy, Grant takes Martha Scott to his backwoods settlement, where (to his delight and her horror) they mix democratically with the common folk, drink corn liquor, square dance and help raise a neighbor's barn. Grant is dragged into state politics (he wants internal improvements) and wrangles with his brother-in-law Hardwicke, a haughty Tory, before joining Patrick Henry in the House of Burgesses. A creator of the new patriotism, he naturally becomes an officer in the Revolutionary Army.

By the end (after being reconciled with his long-separated wife), Grant envisions a nation free of hatred (including class hatred) and free of an aristocracy. Although slavery evidently continues (Grant's own help seem to be well-treated, with as little made of it as possible), the march against Nazism appears almost to have begun already. Many corny and even repellent moments are offset if not overcome by New Deal kitsch and the occasional jab at the rich as lacking true patriotism—and *their* use of slaves as a mark of their real nature. Richard Carlson's Thomas Jefferson is no more inaccurate than future Hollywood accounts, in itself a tribute to screenwriter Buchman. Academy Award nominations went to Richard Hageman (best music) and Jack Whitney (best sound recording). 117 min.

The Hucksters (1947)

MGM. Prod: Arthur Hornblow, Jr. Dir: Jack Conway. Scr: Luther Davis (unattributed script contribution: Edward Chodorov•). Novel basis: Frederic Wakeman, *The Hucksters* (1946). Adaptation: George Wells. Cast: Clark Gable, Deborah Kerr, Sydney Greenstreet, Adolphe Menjou, Ava Gardner, Keenan Wynn, Eddie Arnold

Chodorov was brought in to sharpen this already well-plotted and intelligent film about the "ad game" and its business morals. It features some especially stirring revelations about the tyranny of the big client (radio advertisers who, in real life, hired writers and often made up the radio blacklist) and the slavish eagerness of ad agencies to comply.

Gable is the evidently middle-class ex-GI who wants a career in advertising and believes he is worth a good salary; Kerr the military widow of social standing who becomes his first catch for a soap testimonial. But ad exec Menjou drunkenly admits that he has betrayed an ex-partner to get where he is. Greenstreet is great as the soap baron who knows soap is all the same except for the ads and who insists upon his own style for them (here as silly as ads in real life), which modern singers (the romantic competition, Gardner) abhor. Love will out, but on the way Gable avenges himself against Greenstreet. Strong finish to a must-see film. 115 min.

Hud (1963)

Para. Prod: Irving Ravetch,† Martin Ritt.• Dir: Martin Ritt. Scr: Irving Ravetch, Harriet Frank, Jr. Novel basis: Larry McMurtry, *Horseman Pass By* (1961). Cast: Paul Newman, Melvyn Douglas, Patricia Neal, Brandon De Wilde, John Ashley

Modern cowboy Newman, a wildly successful womanizer and bar brawler in a smallish town near the Texas family ranch, is an emotional mess. He suffers from some hidden hurts that emerge quickly enough—overly stern father Douglas and guilt for driving the car that crashed and

killed his brother, the favorite of the family, a decade earlier. But his real problem is his determination to treat other people like objects. His nephew De Wilde, son of his late brother, is emerging into puberty and drawn to Newman but simultaneously repelled, demonstrating something that first seems a virginal shyness but becomes more clearly a sense of right and wrong, a connectedness to community and its history.

But what are the rights and wrongs of the modern west? Here the film, perhaps constrained by the novel, ignores the history of racism and ecological damage, and celebrates the work ethic that keeps the ranch together. Patriarch Douglas's resistance to "punching holes in the earth" (unwillingness to lease out oil options) thereby seems heroic in a nostalgic sense. Conservatives and Pauline Kael nevertheless despised the film as unbalanced and unfair to American virtue.

Notwithstanding the strong acting of Newman and Douglas, *Hud* would have remained little more than an interfamily quarrel if it were not for the issues raised by the characters of Neal and De Wilde. The housekeeper, a divorcee, becomes a mother substitute for the lad while inspiring offhand sexual ardor in Newman. A rape-attempt scene, daring for 1963, occasions a final disillusionment in Newman after hoof-and-mouth disease has compelled the eradication of all the ranch's stock and the economic ruination of the Old Way. The filmmakers were shocked when it turned out that young men in the audience actually identified with the morally repugnant Hud. It was, nevertheless, one of Ritt's biggest films and one of Newman's best, winning Academy Awards for Neal (best actress), and best black and white photography. 112 min.

Hudson's Bay (1940)

So-so historical drama about the men and women involved in the founding of the Hudson's Bay Company in the late seventeenth century to exploit the fur trade in northern Canada. Lifted by a great cast, including Paul Muni, Gene Tierney and Laird Cregar. The prolific Irving Pichel• directed, and an uncredited David Lang† contributed to the script.

Hullabaloo (1940)

A very funny movie about the radio biz, an aged "road show casanova" and the struggle for a novelty show and a sponsor, written by Left friend Nat Perrin (briefly but never officially on the blacklist), with an uncredited assist by Val Burton.•

Humoresque (1946)

WB. Prod: Jerry Wald. Dir: Jean Negulesco. Scr: Clifford Odets,• Zachard Gold. Story basis: Fannie Hurst, "Humoresque" (1919). Cast: John Garfield, Joan Crawford, Oscar Levant, J. Carrol Naish, Joan Chandler, Tom D'Andrea, Peggy Knudsen, Robert Blake

The only matchup of Garfield and Crawford is also a matchup of the weepie women's film with the Odets-style class drama (with an apparently ethnic, cryptically Jewish family). A lavish production with extended musical sequences that sometimes disguise, sometimes reinforce the tension. Practically everyone in this world, from the rich and bored to the lower-middle class, looks up to the classical violinist in ways that would baffle future generations. Crawford, as an adulterous society patron, derives a mixture of orgasmic pleasure and romantic pain from the music.

Garfield, as usual, is the lower-class kid whose family (excepting his mother) has no patience for a boy who fiddles through the Depression. Oscar Levant, in his finest and fullest film appearance, offers a constant stream of mordant comments—many of them very funny reflections on the philistinism of American culture—as he acts as best pal and temporary companion for cast-aside Chandler. The violinist experiences stage success but personal torment in the dilemma that pits his whole social background (articulated by his mother) against Crawford's world of privilege. Even or especially in moments of pain, Garfield's determination "to live" is a fine example of the Popular Front mentality. 125 min.

Hurry Sundown (1967)

Written by blacklisted blue-collar worker Bert Gilden• (with his wife, Katya Gilden, a mildly successful novelist, and Horton Foote), starring Jane Fonda, Michael Caine and Robert Hooks in a revisionist drama about the twentieth-century south, with plenty of adultery, racism and greed. Condemned by the Catholic Board of Review and for that reason alone, fun to see.

The Hustler (1961)

20th. Prod: Robert Rossen.† Dir: Robert Rossen. Scr: Robert Rossen, Sidney Carroll. Novel basis: Walter Tevis, *The Hustler* (1959). Cast: Paul Newman, Jackie Gleason, Piper Laurie, George C. Scott, Myron McCormick, Murray Hamilton, Michael Constantine, Jake LaMotta, Vincent Gardenia

The last of Rossen's many fine proletarian dramas and probably the best as well as one of the most successful Hollywood features by a former red, thanks to Rossen's tight direction, and good editing and casting. It is a superb evocation of life above the slate table and a penetrating performance by the "Great One," Jackie Gleason as Minnesota Fats. The film was also characteristic of the Left social drama adapting to changing times: here the outsiders evidently have lower-class origins, but they *choose* the outsider status of the pool room life, whether for existential reasons, for sport or for art. Newman is the proven best (after beating Gleason at the start of the picture) and, like Kirk Douglas in CHAMPION and Garfield in BODY AND SOUL, turns ruthless, dumping his long-time manager for the driven but insulting impresario-hipster Scott (in a chiseled performance updating Lloyd Gough in the Garfield picture). He also picks up Laurie, a boozy, depressed broad who craves love and has real insight into those around her but is always on the edge of falling back into self-destructive behavior.

Heading into Louisville for the big money (Myron McCormick is the apparently gay aristocrat willing to pay for superior action), Newman also heads toward disaster; the cynical individualism around him leads to betrayal and to moral and spiritual collapse. Newman becomes an outsider even among the outsiders, giving him the opportunity to make the kind of existential statement at the core of the left-wing art film. *The Hustler* chimes with Walter Bernstein's memory from the late 1940s that Rossen had planned a film like this for a long time. The speeches had arguably been better ten or fifteen years earlier, and the black-and-white cinematography was by now self-conscious. But this is a remarkable movie in every sense, and, as Rossen's last important film, stands as his epitaph. It won Oscars for best art/set design and best black-and-white cinematography, along with nominations for best picture, best screenplay, best actor, best actress, best supporting actor, and more. 134 min.

I

I Can Get it for You Wholesale (1951)
20th. Prod: Sol C. Siegel. Dir: Michael Gordon.•† Scr: Abraham Polonsky,• Vera Caspary.• Novel basis: Jerome Weidman, *I Can Get it for You Wholesale* (1962). Cast: Susan Hayward, Dan Dailey, George Sanders, Sam Jaffe,• Harry Von Zell

Made on the cusp of the blacklist and based on an unsavory novel, this film had a lot against it right from the start, and the central problem was almost insurmountable: how could one make Hayward the most cynical imaginable career woman, willing to sleep her way through her business plan, and yet reconcile her to the Hollywood notion of domestic bliss? Answer: you couldn't really, but you could take a lot of swipes at the double standard and invoke Sam Jaffe as an Eastern European *zeyde* (grandfather) to sort out the moral issues, concluding with the immortal line, "When it comes to choosing between people and money, we'll go bankrupt every time."

Wholesale answers the question about how radical artists could get their messages through in products whose every detail was controlled by the budgets and the front office and reviewed carefully before release. It was through the application of the higher narrative skills of adaptation, metaphor and characterization to a popular medium where no one expected to find them. And so Polonsky was able to transform what was essentially an anti-Semitic novel into a fable containing the important moral lesson of secular Yiddishkayt: the legacy of centuries' old anti-Semitic oppression leading its victims to a humanist universalism. 91 min.

I Love Trouble (1948).
In a novel adapted by Roy Huggins† from his own novel, Franchot Tone stars as a detective investigating the mysterious past of the wife of a wealthy client. A snappy mystery with a nicely humanistic ending.

I Stand Accused (1939)
This B-crime drama written by Gordon Kahn• has some interesting touches of lower-class life. When two law partners go different ways as their practice fails, questions of right and wrong are posed in the courtroom and outside.

I Stole a Million (1939)
Universal. Prod: Burt Kelly. Dir: Frank Tuttle.† Scr: Nathanael West. Story basis: Lester Cole.• Cast: George Raft, Claire Trevor, Dick Foran, Henry Armetta, Victor Jory, Joseph Sawyer, Robert Elliott, Tom Fadden, John Hamilton

This drama of class resentment written by oddball Marxist fantasist West runs out of gas but has some great early moments. Raft is a taxi driver who realizes he has been cheated by the company when he thinks he has bought his own cab after making many credit payments. Reclaiming his money, he faces arrest for supposed "robbery." When he escapes from the police with the cuffs still on his wrists, his real life of crime begins. He can get them off with the help of a con only if he agrees to take part in a bank robbery. Between hired "jobs," he enters a flower shop with intentions of a holdup, but instantly falls in love with clerk Trevor. Determined to go straight, Raft cleans up in a crap game and buys a little garage. But the police find his trail again, and once more he is forced into robbery. The plot bogs down into a quasi-gangster tale of the "million dollar bandit." One more example of how West never was allowed to do his best work in Hollywood. 80 min.

I Walk Alone (1948)
Para. Prod: Hal B. Wallis. Dir: Byron Haskin. Scr: Charles Schnee. Adaptation by Robert Smith, John Bright.• Play basis: Theodore Reeves, *Beggars are Coming to Town* (1945). Cast: Burt Lancaster, Lizabeth Scott, Kirk Douglas, Wendell Corey, Kristine Miller, Georges Rigaud, Marc Lawrence,† Mike Mazurki, Mickey Knox,• Roger Neury

Strong performances by Lancaster, Douglas and Scott lift this above-average crime-revenge pic. Lancaster is just emerging from 14 years in the can for masterminding a bootleg operation. His ex-partner Douglas, meanwhile, has used the profits to build up a fashionable casino, with heiress Miller as his part-time squeeze (and torch singer Scott as his girl). He thinks he can bring the enraged, almost maddened Lancaster back in as a subordinate, but times have changed, crooks use double-entry accounting on both sets of books, and thugs like Burt have lost their cost-effectiveness. 97 min

Identity Unknown (1945)

Rep. Assoc. prod: Walter Colmes, Howard Bretherton. Dir: Walter Colmes. Scr: Richard Weil.• Story basis: Robert Newman, "Johnny March" (n.d.). Cast: Richard Arlen, Cheryl Walker, Roger Pryor, Bobby Driscoll. Lola Lane, Ian Keith, John Forrest, Sarah Padden

A strange little sui generic, low-budget Popular Front allegory in which a soldier comes out of a VA hospital unaware of his identity. He might be one of three soldiers whose dog tags were found in a bombed German house. Taking the name of Johnny March (as in the song, "When Johnny Comes Marching Home"), he seeks to return to each of three homes he may have had. Each one has its own personal tragedy, mirroring the general situation of bereaved home-fronters: a missing son, missing husband or missing father. After the odyssey, an Army psychiatrist discovers that he is none of these, and by popping a classroom question, gets him to remember that, oh yeah, he's actually a history professor! 71 min.

If Winter Comes (1947)

MGM. Prod: Pandro S. Berman. Dir: Victor Saville. Scr: Marguerite Roberts,• Arthur Wimperis. Novel basis: A. S. Menteth-Hutchinson, If Winter Comes (1921). Cast: Walter Pidgeon, Deborah Kerr, Angela Lansbury, Binnie Barnes, Janet Leigh, Dame May Whitty, Reginald Owen

Made previously in 1923 for another war, this stiff-upper-lip drama puts Kerr and Pidgeon in a British town on the verge of war. Seemingly destined for one another, they break apart after a series of misunderstandings, as Pidgeon marries the suspicious and jealous Lansbury. Kerr, a patrician but a true defender of the people's war against fascism, finds herself defending the honor of Pidgeon and of his maid, Leigh, who was impregnated by a fiancé killed in the war. Back from assisting at the front, she saves her good name, but they can't marry without harming others (and perhaps the cause of national unity), and so they take their consolation in their own moral code. Kerr is perfect for the long-suffering role, but the plot is unequal to her or writer Roberts' best efforts. 97 min.

If You Could Only Cook (1935)

Col. Assoc. prod: Everett Riskin. Dir: William A. Seiter. Scr: Howard J. Green, Gertrude Purcell.• Story basis: F. Hugh Herbert. Cast: Herbert Marshall, Jean Arthur, Leo Carrillo, Lionel Stander,• Alan Edwards, Frieda Inescort, Gene Morgan, Ralf Harolde, Matt McHugh, Richard Powell

A typical thirties we're-not-really-having-sex comedy buoyed by a fine cast, billed misleadingly by Columbia as a "Frank Capra production" until Capra sued the company (and got them to offer him rights to You Can't Take it With You). Business exec Marshall goes on vacation, disillusioned with his old life after his plan for a new car design is turned down by the board of directors. As he wanders in a park, he meets the unemployed Arthur, a college professor's daughter who assumes he is out of a job like her. Intrigued by her, Marshall agrees to apply with her as a husband-and-wife cook-and-butler team for former bootlegger Carrillo. Poor Marshall has to sleep on the porch when they only get one bed in the servant's quarters. When the bootlegger learns of this arrangement and begins romancing Arthur, Marshall is driven to sneaking into his own office to "steal" his own design drawings so he can use them to impress Arthur. The still-innocent Arthur tries to sell them to another manufacturer, and the whole crazy scheme starts to collapse until the redoubtable Lionel Stander steps in. 75 min.

I'll Love You Always (1935)

Col. Prod: Everett Riskin. Dir: Leo Bulgakov. Scr: Vera Caspary,• Sidney Buchman.• Story basis: Lawrence Hazard. Cast: Nancy Carroll, George Murphy, Raymond Walburn, Arthur Hohl, Jean Dixon, Robert Allen, Harry Beresford, Paul Harvey, Howard C. Hickman, Adrian Morris, Claudia Coleman, Irving Bacon, Mary Foy, Elaine Baker

A B-romance with a typical Depression theme and oddball details. Engineering student Murphy and his new wife Carroll (a Shakesperian actress in the making) head for Manhattan. The proletarianizing experience is nearly overwhelming: he becomes a moving man who takes his frustrations out on the loving wife. She, in a one-sided self-sacrifice, refuses a lucrative job offer in Chicago—and unbeknownst to him, becomes a taxi dancer in a Chinese restaurant(!) to keep up family finances. When he learns the truth, he demands a divorce and decides to take an engineering job in Russia(!!). But he fights with his would-be employer, gets into still deeper trouble, and heads toward the Hollywood ending. This kind of eclectic, odd-angled plotting (from two old hands) would soon be displaced by more fixed genres. 75 min.

The Impossible Years (1968)

MGM. Prod: Lawrence Weingarten. Dir: Michael Gordon.•† Scr: Bob Fisher, Arthur Marx, George Wells. Play basis: Bob Fisher, Arthur Marx. Cast: David Niven, Lola Albright, Chad Everett, Ozzie Nelson, Christina Ferrare

An often-mocked exploitation flick with a few more interesting angles than its reputation allows. A Hollywood farce playing off the sexual revolution, middle-class parental anxiety in particular (and to a lesser degree, stirrings of campus revolt), has prof and shrink Niven en route to the top of his department at some University of California campus that sounds a lot like Berkeley—or is it UCLA? He has a fast-pitch assistant, Everett, who comes up with snazzy titles for his books, and is even willing to ghost-write them. His sexy daughter (Ferrare) has him in trouble, though, by carrying around a placard on campus with a single expletive on it (à la Berkeley's "Filthy Speech Movement," following the Free Speech Movement). Just as worrisome even for indulgent academic parents is her steady dating, her absence from classes she hates, her insistence on going unchaperoned on a students' weekend in Catalina and the agitation of her boyfriend's father and fellow psychologist, ol' Ozzie N., who acts like he could more easily be worrying about David or Ricky. Lots of leering near-sexuality here, including a beatnik painter and his nude painting of Ferrare. But (what is this, the thirties?) no sex. 92 min., color.

In a Lonely Place (1950)

Col. Prod: Robert Lord. Dir: Nicholas Ray. Scr: Andrew Solt. Cast: Humphrey Bogart, Gloria Grahame, Frank Lovejoy, Carl Benton Reid, Art Smith, Jeff Donnell

Often viewed as a metaphorical—or censored—treatment of the blacklist experience, the adaptation of a novel about a tortured screenwriter (Bogey, once a big success, now almost forgotten) is considered a noir classic. It may also be seen as the gesture of left-leaning director Ray, saved from the blacklist only by Howard Hughes' personal intervention, to his fallen friends. Like real-life Bogart, who lost courage as the investigation of Hollywood continued and covered himself with patriotic declarations, his character is defeated and perpetually drunk. Even Ray, who was never forced to make such a declaration, went a similar direction during the decades after his making of the classic teen noir *Rebel Without a Cause* (with Clifford Odets† on the set dispensing guidance).

After asking a hat-check girl over to his apartment to help outline an adaptation of a novel, Bogart later learns that the girl was killed after she left his apartment. He meanwhile falls into a passionate relationship with Grahame, his neighbor and a defeated starlet (and a potential witness). Innocent or guilty (and we do not learn until late in the film), the writer is not a nice guy:

a World War II officer (one of his men is now a cop, played by noir favorite Lovejoy) who remains enigmatic but does his job well, Bogey has become a brawler who comes close to murdering a driver for pushing his car off the road. Grahame's quest for love exists under a shadow whose true nature we never learn. Evocative but enigmatic, the film was definitely unequal to the weight placed upon it. 94 min.

In Caliente (1935)

First National, WB. Prod: Edward Chodorov.• Dir: Lloyd Bacon. Scr: Edward Chodorov, Julius J. Epstein, Jerry Wald. Story and adaptation: Warren Duff, Ralph Block. Cast: Dolores del Rio, Pat O'Brien, Edward Everett Horton, Leo Carrillo, Glenda Farrell

Latino exotica with a dash of low-budget Busby Berkeley, this film looks forward to those 1940s big-production conga-line films. O'Brien is a magazine editor and Horton, still looking the butler type but here actually his financier publisher who is intent on getting him out of Manhattan long enough to keep him from marrying a golddigger who threatens to drain the magazine's funds. Picking a spot at random on a globe, he chooses Agua Caliente in northwest Mexico. Here, music is in the air, and the Latinas are lovely (especially professional dancer del Rio) but distrustful of men (in this case her manager Carrillo, who is prone to gambling away their earnings). Through a series of blunders and misunderstandings, del Rio is "hired" to divert O'Brien and does so in grand style, including some splendid dance numbers more spectacular than Berkeley's (Judy Canova's novelty chorus cameo comes and goes too quickly). A big jump for Chodorov into the mainstream after making tough social-issue films like MAYOR OF HELL just a few years earlier. 84 min.

In Old California (1942).

Co-scripted by Gertrude Percell,† this stock western traces a Boston pharmacist's journey in the Gold Rush of 1849, where he finds local corruption and roots it out.

In Our Time (1944)

WB. Prod: Jerry Wald. Dir: Vincent Sherman. Scr: Ellis St. Joseph, Howard Koch.• Cast: Ida Lupino, Paul Henreid, Alla Nazimova, Nancy Coleman, Mary Boland, Victor Francen, Michael Chekhov

A long, long antifascist romance that gets tangled up in details, unlike screenwriter Koch's usual narrative clarity. Lupino is a lowly aide to a fussy British antique buyer shopping Warsaw in 1938 in search of bargains. She meets and falls in love with kindly Polish aristocrat Henreid, then finds herself swept up in his family and the impending international crisis. High government official (and uncle of her husband) Francen is practically a Nazi collaborator, as well as a haughty traditionalist—with a suspiciously Dracula-like lilt to his accent. Against the weight of tradition and in the face of crisis, Lupino sets out to bring the peasantry of Henreid's estate into modern times with tractors and profit-sharing. At first, they ignorantly resist the new technology in what could almost be taken as a series of Polish jokes. Then comes the German invasion, prompting the aristocracy at large (including Francen) to flee, while the peasants prepare to struggle heroically. In contrast to the decadent classes, they (and Henreid and Lupino with them), will almost certainly die in the name of Poland. Actually a British actress from an Italian stage family, Lupino was just making a transition to Hollywood and is here the perky American antifascist girl right down to the bone. 110 min.

In This Our Life (1942)
WB. Prod: Hal B. Wallis, David Lewis. Dir: John Huston. Scr: Howard Koch.• Novel basis: Ellen Glasgow, In This Our Life (1941). Cast: Bette Davis, Olivia deHavilland, Billie Burke, Hattie McDaniel, Lee Patrick, Walter Huston

A historical drama very much in the mood of Lillian Hellmans' hit THE LITTLE FOXES, with much the same mixture of corruption and eccentricity. Seen against the background of World War II and with Popular Front liberal Huston choreographing Koch's adaptation, the political metaphors come through loud and clear.

Bette Davis swiftly makes this her movie as the unbalanced woman who craves what she has missed in her life (and perhaps what many Southern women missed). The daughter of a failed businessman and niece of a manipulative and successful one, she tires of her own husband and goes after her sister's, ruining both their lives. She runs over a pedestrian and seeks to place the blame on an exemplary young black man who dreams (with the vision of his mother, maid Hattie McDaniel) of attending medical school. Her blatantly vicious racism—in a popular plot drawn from real Southern life and frequently repeated in race-oriented films of the next decade or so—exposes the larger system of beliefs. Delightfully perverse moments with tobacco magnate uncle, who patronizes her in ways bordering upon incestuous desire that she freely indulges, wheedling him with her charms. 97 min.

Inherit the Wind (1960)
Lomitas Productions/MGM/UA. Prod: Stanley Kramer. Dir: Stanley Kramer. Scr: Nathan E. Douglas (Nedrick Young•) and Harold Jacob Smith. Play basis: Robert E. Lee, Jerome Lawrence, Inherit the Wind (1955). Cast: Spencer Tracy, Fredric March, Gene Kelly, Dick York, Donna Anderson, Harry Morgan, Claude Akins, Elliott Reid, Philip Coolidge

The same pair who wrote THE DEFIANT ONES deliver here for producer Kramer once again in an old-fashioned Popular Front drama (anticipated in the Rossen screenplay for They Won't Forget) about the 1920s-1930s South, with a stock cast of characters. This time it's the "Scopes Monkey Trial," with outsider Gene Kelly miscast as E. K. Hornbeck, a transparent stand-in for H. L. Mencken, Morgan as the Dixie judge, Claude Akins as minister, March as the character of defense attorney Clarence Darrow (March's real-life wife Florence Eldridge played his loyal mate) and Spencer Tracy as the William Jennings Bryan character. This revisiting of claims to Biblical infallibility among a barely literate population and its opportunist leading officials obviously drew upon the sentiments of the civil rights era, even without any reference to race. The writers and director/producer had scored hugely in The Defiant Ones only three years earlier, and took on a project floating around Hollywood for years, nabbing big stars for a major courtroom drama. Devotees of William Jennings Bryan found the portrayal of him condescending at best and the degree of freedom-taking with historical events too typically Hollywood. The result was windy, but perhaps the best that liberalism had to offer on the brink of Camelot, and the last good credit earned (albeit pseudonymously) by Ned Young en route to further disappointment and an early grave. 127 min.

Intruder in the Dust (1949)
MGM. Prod: Clarence Brown. Dir: Clarence Brown. Scr: Ben Maddow.• Novel basis: William Faulkner, Intruder in the Dust (1948). Cast: David Brian, Claude Jarman, Jr., Juano Hernandez, Porter Hall, Elizabeth Patterson

A remarkable film for the time, this Faulkner adaptation was almost certainly a model for To Kill a Mockingbird (good white lawyer defends endangered black resident against racists) but was attacked bitterly by Communist Party theorist V. J. Jerome for not properly "class-angling" the drama. The critic had his point: racism here is never seen as a part of the class matrix of Southern society but as a cohesive part of a monstrous naturalism in which whites can lynch and then send condolences to the family, feeling no sense of contradiction. Maddow would have answered the charge as Paul Jarrico did similar complaints about race in the late 1940s film: the Left did the best that it could within an extremely restrictive set of rules.

Juano Hernandez plays a stubborn old black man arrested for supposedly killing a white man and is immediately threatened with a lynch mob. Brian, the boy through whose eyes the drama is seen, has himself been stung by Hernandez's pride but persuades his father to take up the case. We learn about the joys of racism as a perverse psychological compensation—and we see convincing mob action. But the moral is a universal one (the need to do right), rather than a historical one (the need to come to terms with some dreadful element in contemporary American society). 87 min.

The Invisible Man Returns (1940)

Universal. Assoc. Prod: Ken Goldsmith. Dir: Joe May. Scr: Kurt Siodmak, Lester Cole.• Story: Joe May and Kurt Siodmak Nvel basis: H. G. Wells, *The Invisible Man* (1897). Cast: Vincent Price, Cedric Hardwicke, Nan Grey, John Sutton, Cecil Kellaway, Alan Napier, Forrester Harvey

Inferior entry in the fantasy series on invisibility, neither as distinguished as *The Invisible Man* with Claude Rains nor as campy as two comedy films by Lees and Rinaldo, THE INVISIBLE WOMAN and ABBOTT AND COSTELLO MEET THE INVISIBLE MAN. In a hesitant stab at serious drama, Price is charged with the murder of his brother, and becomes invisible with the help of scientist Sutton. Price is going insane from the serum and needs the antidote. After confusion and a struggle in a mine, the real murderer is discovered. Not long after this feature, Price's persona acquired a much-needed hamminess that made up for the generally miserable plots of his films. 81 min.

The Invisible Woman (1940)

Universal. Prod: Burt Kelly. Dir: Edward Sutherland. Scr: Robert Lees,• Fred Rinaldo,• Gertrude Purcell.† Story basis: Kurt Siodmak, Joe Mayo. Cast: John Barrymore, Virginia Bruce, John Howard, Charlie Ruggles, Oscar Homolka, Margaret Hamilton, Shemp Howard

Comedy peaks early when store model Bruce becomes a guinea pig for scientist Howard's experiment in invisibility. A working girl, she takes a much-deserved revenge on her mean-spirited department store boss, compelling him to simultaneously raise wages and reduce hours at work.

The social element all but disappears as the show goes on the road in Charlie Ruggles' snowbound cabin and is replaced by a Topper-like humor of mysteriously moving objects, unexpectedly reappearing faces and bodies. Department store heir Barrymore and Bruce move toward a romantic (and cross-class) romance. Barrymore the uncapitalistic rentier reprises his benevolent, class-crossing role in THE PRESIDENT'S MYSTERY. 72 min.

Isle of the Dead (1945)

RKO. Prod: Val Lewton. Dir: Mark Robson. Scr: Josef Mischel,• Ardel Wray. Cast: Boris Karloff, Ellen Drew, Marc Cramer, Katherine Emery, Helen Thimig, Alan Napier

A superior Lewton production, unique for returning Karloff from the horror genre to historical drama. Here, the veteran actor is used to his best advantage as the tough-as-nails Greek general. At the turn of the century, Karloff faces the prospect of a plague wiping out his army, which is about to face an enemy perhaps not so dreadful as what nature has to offer—or perhaps he only faces nature's revenge for the hubris of conquest. Trapped on a small island, he becomes more and more ruthless in his effort to keep the disease from spreading, in the end condemning all the inhabitants to an inescapable death. Rumors of active vampires, never more than a spectre, add another ominous dimension. But the real enemies are the damaged social relations that armed conflict merely reinforces. Death stalks the inhabitants and their commander alike as the prospects for endless armament and endless war loomed on the real-world horizon. 72 min

It Ain't Hay (1943)

One of the most thinly plotted Abbott and Costello features. In spots still fun, it was co-written by Allen Boretz• (author of the immortal stage play *Room Service*, adapted for a Marx Brothers film). Here the madcappery is inspired by horses, racing and gambling, losing when you thought you won and vice versa.

It Came from Outer Space (1953)

U-I. Prod: William Alland.† Dir: Jack Arnold. Story basis: Ray Bradbury. Scr: Harry Essex. Cast: Richard Carlson, Barbara Rush, Charles Drake, Russell Johnson, Kathleen Hughes, Joe Sawyer

Adapted from a story by Ray Bradbury at his radical apex—a Hollywood liberal usually if not always willing to stand up for the blacklistees—and set up by former Communist and future friendly witness Alland, this is the original of the liberal-minded "invasion from space" films. Scientist Carlson and his wife Rush are newcomers in a desert town but eager to be good citizens. Imagine, then, when they observe the descent of a spaceship (looking very much like a comet). On investigation, they learn that aliens have crash-landed to repair their ship; Carlson pleads with sheriff Drake to restrain himself, while pressure builds for a lynch mob to "clean out" the aliens, holed up in a worked-out mine. Although they look like giant eyeballs, and put fear into townsfolk by assuming the shape of familiar human beings, they mean no harm. In fact, there is a suggestion that they possess advanced knowledge of social organization, as the film unambiguously defends what it describes as the aliens' "better ideas"—which the Americans in the film are too "frightened" to accept. Director Arnold, a vivid anticommunist and perhaps (as a former filmmaker for the International Ladies Garment Workers Union) the most authentic New York–style social democrat in Hollywood, would go on to direct more Alland films, cross the ocean to guide antinuke classic *The Mouse That Roared*, and end his career on another commercial fantasy setting: *Gilligan's Island*. 80 min.

It Can't Last Forever (1937)
Harold Buchman• and partner Lee Loeb penned this story of theatrical agent Ralph Bellamy and journalist Betty Furness and a radio act, finding themselves embroiled in mob activity and helping police solve a big jewel robbery. Good title, minor effort.

It Could Happen to You (1937)
Nathanael West and Samuel Ornitz• scripted this story about the struggle between a good brother and a bad brother in a language school whose headmaster manipulates and blackmails his students. The so-so drama is elevated by a few remarkable scenes, like the opening one at a picnic, with a Popular Front vision of melting-pot Americanism tempered by a sense of cultural retention of ethnic "types" (including German Americans), and a shared vision of a roughly egalitarian society.

It Happened in Brooklyn (1947)
MGM. Prod: Jack Cummings. Dir: Richard Whorf. Scr: Isobel Lennart.† Story basis: J. P. McGowan. Cast: Kathryn Grayson, Peter Lawford, Frank Sinatra, Jimmy Durante,

Gloria Grahame, Marcy McGuire, Aubrey Mather, Bobby Long, Billy Roy, William Haade, Tamara Shayne

A box office smash with a thin but adequate script and Sinatra at his half-serious acting best. He's a soldier coming back from Europe with a secret photo not of a girl but of the Brooklyn Bridge. A nurse, also from Brooklyn, challenges his credentials because he does not seem as open and friendly (i.e., too shy, the Sinatra pose for a series of films around this time) as a Brooklynite should naturally be.

When he lands in Brooklyn, amid the bustling crowds and *heymishe* characters, Sinatra by chance lands a ride with Grayson, who hates her home city and teaches music at a local high school because she can't make it in opera. The coincidences multiply, of course, and Sinatra sees her again when he goes to visit old pal and mentor Durante, janitor at the self-same school. Complications arise when Lawford, a British lord who wants to learn swing, shows up for tutelage and falls in love with Grayson, who reciprocates as she moves toward success in the big time. Will Sinatra give her up? The film may persuade viewers that there really was magic in Brooklyn before the Dodgers eloped to L.A. André Previn makes his screen debut at the tender age of 17. 105 min.

It's a Wonderful Life (1946)
Liberty Films. Prod: Frank Capra. Dir: Frank Capra. Scr: Frances Goodrich, Albert Hackett, Frank Capra, Jo Swerling (additional scenes), Michael Wilson.• (Uncredited: Dalton Trumbo,• Clifford Odets,† Dorothy Parker,• Myles Connelly). Story basis: Philip Van Doren Stern, "The Greatest Gift" (1945). Cast: James Stewart, Donna Reed, Lionel Barrymore, Thomas Mitchell, Henry Travers, Beulah Bondi, Frank Faylen, Ward Bond, Gloria Grahame, H. B. Warner

The real story behind this film remained unknown for years, until film scholar Joseph McBride dug it out for his Capra biography. The film itself languished until the 1970s, when its unusual combination of film-noir pessimism about American life and contrasting comic optimism about the power of community was more recognizable. McBride discovered that some of the most talented Hollywood left-wingers had worked on the screenplay without credit, although some mystery remains about the exact role of each. But apparently, Trumbo adapted the Stern short story for the screen; Odets and Connolly (the only conservative in the project) rewrote the adaptation; Parker reworked the dialogue; and Wilson gave it all a "polish." The principal writers,

Goodrich and Hackett, were themselves highly accomplished writers and noted liberal activists (and falsely accused of being Communists by the American Legion in 1952 for their role in the 1943 Hollywood Writers Mobilization). Famed *New Yorker* writer Dorothy Parker's role remains undetermined.

In any case, the meaning of the film is inescapable: Stewart, as the custodian of the only institution in town that stands between working people and the predations of Barrymore's omnivorous bank, is too valuable to his community and has too great a social conscience to act out the individualist daydreams of the ordinary American schmo, a situation he bitterly resents until he discovers how dark the alternatives are and just how blessed is the community he has helped create. The political message is contained in a remark the incompetent but lovable Uncle Billie (Mitchell) makes to the banker: "After all, Potter, some people like George had to stay at home. Not every heel was in Germany and Japan." 130 min.

Ivanhoe (1952)

MGM. Prod: Pandro S. Berman. Dir: Richard Thorpe. Scr: Noel Langley, Marguerite Roberts• (originally uncredited). Adaptation: Aeneas MacKenzie. Novel basis: Sir Walter Scott, *Ivanhoe: A Romance* (1820). Cast: Robert Taylor, Elizabeth Taylor, Joan Fontaine, George Sanders, Emlyn Williams, Finlay Currie, Felix Aylmer

A remarkable post-Holocaust treatment of the King Richard theme so popular in a handful of contemporary films and the blacklistee-written television series, *The Adventures of Robin Hood*. In this case, Robert Taylor is a handsome if humorless Ivanhoe determined to ransom good King Richard, restore the Saxons to power and overthrow the wicked Normans, led by a deliciously evil Sanders. All this would be rather familiar except that Ivanhoe saves the life of a Jewish merchant (Aylmer) and, after returning the wounded man to York, is espied by his beautiful daughter, Elizabeth Taylor. Complications abound, in part because our hero is already betrothed to the virtuous noblewoman played by Fontaine, creating a familiar triangle between the "dark" and "light" woman, except that here the dark one is the more heroic.

The film is endowed with lots of action, as virtuous Saxon woodsmen pour what seem like millions of arrows into the Normans. The nobles escape with Elizabeth Taylor in tow, and after a witch trial (shades of the blacklist!) of her as a nature-healer, they threaten a vast pogrom against all the Jews of England, including herself unless she converts to Christianity. She would rather die, and after more complications she finally must, in one sense or another (Sanders, evil but sentimental, swears while dying that she belongs to him still) obviously to prevent intermarriage or at any rate breeding with the English nobility. Lots of wonderful great side glances at the details of tyranny, such as iron collars for serfs. Freeborn Englishmen strive to restore their freedom—with a return to their own monarchy! Staggeringly inaccurate as history, the film is often real fun with occasional punch. Arguably the young, uncorrupted Elizabeth Taylor's best film after NATIONAL VELVET and the last time she plays, with any credibility, a role other than a glorified harlot (or harridan). 106 min., color.

J

Jailhouse Rock (1957)

Avon Productions. Prod: Pandro S. Berman. Dir: Richard Thorpe. Scr: Guy Trosper. Story: Ned (i.e., Nedrick) Young.• Cast: Elvis Presley, Judy Tyler, Mickey Shaughnessy, Vaughn Taylor, Jennifer Holden, Dean Jones, Anne Neyland

One of Elvis Presley's better films has a virtually unknown backstory connected to the blacklist. In the face of studio objections, writer Young successfully claimed screen credit for the original story behind the drastically altered screenplay—written in turn by an old friend of the Hollywood Left—a prison drama in the familiar Left mode from the thirties that morphed into a music vehicle for the rock star. Along with *Wild In the Country* (the last script that Clifford Odets delivered) and *Flaming Star* (where he plays a half-breed suffering discrimination), *Jailhouse* captures the rock great empathetically as a Southern prole struggling to realize himself. How much of *Jailhouse Rock* one can attribute to Young's work is difficult to say, but look for one key scene in which Elvis goes to a cocktail party of upper-middle-class professionals with jazz on the "hi-fi." From the context, they are undoubtedly bohemians and probably left-wingers. 96 min.

Jennie (1940)

20th. Prod: Sol M. Wurtzel. Dir: David Burton. Scr: Harold Buchman,• Maurice Rapf.• Story basis: Jane Eberle, "Heil, Jennie," *Story* magazine, 1939. Cast: Virginia Gilmore, William Henry, George Montgomery, Ludwig Stössel, Dorris Bowdon, Rand Brooks, Joan Valerie Ritz Quigley, Hermine Sterler, Irving Bacon, Harlan Briggs, Almira Sessions

A remarkably strong crypto-feminist or anti-patriarchal drama, rightly celebrated (though rarely available). The patriarch of a German American Midwest family (Stössel) refuses to permit his would-be violinist son to accept a scholarship in Chicago to study music. Son Brooks is to stay at home in the shoe business. Stössel permits his other son to marry but only if he brings bride Gilmore back home to live with them. Afterward, dad becomes enraged when Gilmore encourages third son Montgomery to grow flowers. As more of the past comes to light, the poisonous fruit of the authoritarian European tradition grows clearer. When daughter Bowdon sneaks off to see a boyfriend, dad orders her out of the house; when she returns later, ill and abandoned, Gilmore insists on helping her, even when dad orders her and her husband to leave, too. Living modestly, she works to divide the family against the tyrant. The original working title, "Heil, Jennie," suggested an anti-Nazi angle mostly lost (or disguised) in the transformation of the plot into an immigrant-style American family drama of the old ways versus the new. 78 min.

Joe Palooka

Monogram Series. Prod: Hal E. Chester. Series Dirs: Cyril Endfield,• Reginald Le Borg, Jean Yarbrough. Series Scr: Cyril Endfield, Stanley Prager,• Nedrick Young,• Henry Blankfort,• Stanley Rubin,† Mande Collins, Albert DePina. Story basis: Ham Fisher, *Joe Palooka* (comic strip). Cast: Leon Errol, Joe Kirkwood, Jr., Elyse Knox, Lina Romay, David Bruce, George O'Hanlon, Lyle Talbot, Virginia Welles, Sheldon Leonard, Stanley Prager,• Morris Carnovksy,• Marc Lawrence,† Joe Louis, Elisha Cook, Jr.

A veritable film school of budding left-wing directors and writers, this low-budget Monogram series started in 1946 and wrapped up in 1951 (a 1934 film with Jimmy Durante, PALOOKA, is discussed separately). The series was based very loosely on a Depression comic strip whose name derived from the slang word for an incompetent boxer that had entered the language around 1924 (origin unknown). Joe is a wide-eyed innocent blond pugilist of uncertain ethnic background who needs an irascible Irish manager and an obese rival to keep him punching properly. The films are difficult to find but good examples of the kind of sub-basement cultural entry points that left-wingers carved out for themselves when they lacked better connections in Hollywood.

Joe Palooka, Champ (1946), the first entry in series, set out guidelines for what followed, including most of the gags and stars (Elyse Knox was later replaced, Robert Coogan was chubby rival Humphrey for two features, and some comic support is added by future Stooge Joe Besser). Leon Errol, one of the enduring figures of comic film shorts, had his longest run here. Some notably talented figures like Morris Carnovsky appear in one film or another, apparently by virtue of personal and political connections to the production team. In line with the creators' intent, even legendary champ Joe Louis has a cameo, and several other real-life boxers, including Henry Armstrong and Manuel Ángeles Ortiz, make brief appearances.

In the first outing, gangsters steal the manager's champion fighter, so Knobby Walsh (Errol) sets out to find a replacement. He discovers Kirkwood, Jr., working in a gas station and in the usual genre fashion (but with a few more laughs) trains him to become champ. *Joe Palooka in the Knockout* (1947) was, by contrast, the least comic of the series. A boxer dies in the ring, apparently at the hands of our hero, prompting him to retire. On a tip from his fiancée Marshall, Knobby and Joe investigate the possibility that he died of a drug administered by gamblers. *Joe Palooka in Winner Take All* (1948) has lots of ring footage.

Variety offered up kudos for maximum action with minimum budget. This time comedy vet William Frawley is Knobby, funny in a sort of sitcom way (just as Errol had that 1930s film affect). Gamblers attempt to bring down the odds on Palooka's championship bout, then resort to various tricks to get him to throw the fight. Sheldon Leonard, once again, is the gambler. *Joe Palooka in the Big Fight* (1949) is fast-paced, overplotted but marked with comic moments (mostly Errol's) and surprisingly crisp dialogue—Prager's biggest writing success until he returned from the blacklist. A gang frames Kirkwood with a drunk rap just before a big fight so they can put their own candidate in the ring. As the conspiracy fails, they set to frame him for murder. Sought by the cops, Kirkwood undertakes his own manhunt, with a bang-up conclusion. *Joe Palooka in the Counterpunch* (1949) has Kirkwood on a trip to South America, where he aids a professor in delivering an Inca statue to a museum. Along the way he gets involved with counterfeiters until friends bail him out of trouble. In *Joe Palooka Meets Humphrey* (1950), the next-to-last entry, Joe and his new bride are en route to a honeymoon when they meet Humphrey, who informs them that he has been scheduled for a rematch with Joe. The fat man is an embarrassment, and Errol pretends to be an English lord (and fight manager) to get the fight cancelled. *Joe Palooka In Humphrey Takes a Chance* (1950) the last left-wing entry, has Knobby take Joe, his wife and Humphrey to a village where the chubby one can run for mayor, providing a nice satire on contemporary political styles and the typical Court House ring.

John Meade's Woman (1937)
Para. Prod: B. P. Schulberg. Dir: Richard Wallace. Scr: Herman J. Mankiewicz, Vincent Lawrence. Story basis:

John Bright,• Robert Tasker. Cast: Edward Arnold, Francine Larrimore, Gail Patrick, George Bancroft, John Trent, Aileen Pringle, Sidney Blackmer, Willard Robertson, Johathan Hale

One of a small number of films during the 1930s-1940s (a rather more famous one was Paul Jarrico's• MEN OF THE TIMBERLAND) that dealt with deforestation and reforestation, a popular issue during the Works Progress Administration days of the New Deal. This one chronicles the life of a lumber king, played by Arnold, who ignores the pleas of employee Bancroft to reforest rather than convert the forest land to wheat fields. Ruthless and indifferent to the coming Dust Bowl, he continues to repossess farms lost to debt in the Depression. The heroic Larrimore, a farm girl who has come to Chicago and met capitalist Meade there, turns to organize the farmers against him. When he demands that a militia be turned against the riotous farmers, a local sheriff tells him that nature has its own militia—the dust storms, to wipe away the men who wiped away the forest that protected the soil. The last moments of the film are dramatized by a dust storm. Larrimore was a member of the well-known left-wing Adler acting family (Luther, Stella and Celia) and made her screen debut here. 80 min.

Johnny Allegro (1949)
Karen DeWolf• and Guy Endore• wrote the screenplay for this tale of an ex-gangster played by George Raft hired by the Treasury Department to stop a counterfeiter in a standard undercover investigation plot. Raft drags down the proceedings with his usual flat affect and acting inability, but the cast is brightened by the presence of Will Geer.• A waste of brilliant novelist Endore's time, not to mention everyone else's.

Johnny Got His Gun (1971)
World Entertainment. Prod: Bruce Campbell. Dir: Dalton Trumbo.• Scr: Dalton Trumbo. Cast: Timothy Bottoms, Diane Varsi, Jason Robards, Jr., Donald Sutherland, Kathy Fields

With son Christopher Trumbo as associate producer and with an uncredited assist from John Bright,• this is a family (and Hollywood left-wing) effort to make father Trumbo's famed 1939 pacifist novel into an avant-garde film. Unfortunately, the central theme of Bottoms' psychic horror as war casualty and object of medical experiments (he lacks arms, legs and face) also reduces the rest of the story into fragments. This is too bad, because many moments of the film are truly charming or truly weird. Erotic romance with sexually emancipated working-class girl Varsi (her father is an ex-Wobbly who gives the couple the bedroom of his shotgun shack) has great power, despite its brevity, in the pair's mutual shyness and (this is 1971) her unglamorous nudity; so do some moments of Robards as the father of the childhood Johnny, and a definitely over-the-top Sutherland as a recurrent and befuddled Jesus, sending the boys off to suffering and death. The pacifist theme, always intentionally central, fatally slips away. 111 min., color.

Johnny Guitar (1954)

Rep. Exec. Prod: Herbert J. Yates. Dir: Nicholas Ray. Scr: Philip Yordan. Novel basis: Roy Chanslor, *Johnny Guitar* (1954). Cast: Joan Crawford, Sterling Hayden, Mercedes McCambridge, Scott Brady, Ward Bond, Ben Cooper, Ernest Borgnine, John Carradine, Royal Dano, Dennis Hopper (uncredited)

Yordan apparently served as the front for a screenplay whose early drafts were written by Ben Maddow,•† but Maddow later told an interviewer that he had no memory of writing any of the screenplay. In fact, the key artistic decisions may have been made, apparently for the only time in her career, by then-fading star Joan Crawford, working for a budget studio for the first time and perhaps solicitous about it. According to Yordan, it was Crawford who decreed that the final shootout take place between herself and McCambridge. In any case, the Chanslor novel had already called for a final gunfight between Emma and another female character, and it was this showdown of the Amazons that became the center of interest for auteur cultists (along with a number of elliptical classical allusions). Since Chanslor had already worked out the essential characters and their relations, the question of screenplay authorship has in any case receded from film scholars' concerns.

Director Nicholas Ray, a radical rescued from the blacklist by patron Howard Hughes, still had the commercial triumph of *Rebel Without a Cause* ahead of him as he undertook this film, in which a guitar-playing stranger rides into a town polarized between forces led by the local cattle baron (Bond) and a former saloon worker (Crawford) who, based on inside information, has managed to build a bar and casino on the site of a coming railroad line. Her sexual history, association with outlaws and assertiveness in business have turned the local equivalent of the White Citizens' Council

against her, and she sends for help in the form of Johnny (Hayden), a highly skilled gunman of uncertain value after he turns up a guitar-toting pacifist. (Ray's luminous photography of the guitar as Johnny rides into town in the opening scenes is one of the best things about the film.) Some critics thought they saw symbolism in the figure of Ward Bond—in real life one of the biggest enforcers of the blacklist in Hollywood—as the leader of a band of Puritans on horseback who, clad in avenging black, were bent on running the European-style bohemians out of town. The allegorical interpretation alas, sustains interest longer than the film. 110 min.

Johnny O'Clock (1947)

Col. / J. E. R. Productions. Prod: Edward G. Nealis. Dir: Robert Rossen.† Scr: Robert Rossen. Story: Milton Holmes. Cast: Dick Powell, Evelyn Keyes, Thomas Gomez, Lee J. Cobb,† Ellen Drew, Nina Foch, Jeff Chandler (uncredited)

One of Rossen's minor efforts was a vehicle for Powell, then at his peak as the light-drama actor who briefly became (with Alan Ladd) a favorite among left-wing writers and directors to play noir leads, sometimes in his own production companies. A staunch Hollywood Republican, Powell was nonetheless a civil liberties–style defender of the Left, considering the red-baiting campaign both ungentlemanly and unbusinesslike.

Here Powell makes himself an indecent man drawn to decency—quite a trick and almost successful, but hobbled by the lack of an actual plot. Professional gambling impresario Powell has a deal with casino boss Gomez that is about to go sour because Ellen Drew is murdered and because another gambler (Chandler, in one of his early supporting roles) wants to take over the territory. Powell falls in love with her sister, Keyes, while trying to crack the case and keep himself out of trouble with the mob or the law.

Lots of throwaway "tough" lines are swapped, especially between hard-boiled Powell ("Trouble and worry and count the letters. That's my life.") and showgirl Keyes. Cobb, another of those friendly witnesses who later despised himself for naming his friends, works well as the police detective who plays a waiting game. The best scene is the climax, as Gomez learns that his squeeze (Drew) is physically repelled by him and in love with Powell. As in FORCE OF EVIL, which remains Gomez's single great performance, he manages to sum up all the self-hatred that was possible inside the circle of personal and social corruption depicted by

Rossen and fellow Left writers and directors in such passionate detail. 98 min.

Jolson Sings Again (1949)

Col. Prod: Sidney Buchman.• Dir: Henry Levin. Scr: Sidney Buchman. Cast: Larry Parks, Ludwig Donath,• William Demarest, Barbara Hale, Bill Goodwin

One of the first films that Sidney Buchman produced in his promising career at Columbia, and one that is painful to watch today for multiple reasons. Buchman, who had long since broken with the Communist Party on principle, nevertheless refused to talk to HUAC on principle and lost his career. Parks, who had been the Communists' foremost personality within the Screen Actor's Guild, begged not to be forced into the gutter—but went anyway, naming names, which was practically the end of *his* career, too.

As bad as the backstory might have been, the movie, even though it continued the Mammy-singing entertainer's career where *The Al Jolson Story* left off (the film that made Parks a star in 1947), mercifully spares the audience the blackface routines, toning things down to the point that Jolson becomes a displaced balladeer wandering through the era of Sinatra. Even so, he rolls his eyes and spreads his fingers in unmistakably minstrel gestures. Those who actually saw Jolson perform for the soldiers in World War II recall what the film leaves out, namely the dirty jokes that, along with the Mammy routines, were Jolson's real bread and butter.

Compared to the gestures and the music (the soundtrack is Jolson's voice), the plot is inoffensively mild. When *The Al Jolson Story* ended, his wife left him for wanting to go back on stage. Parks goes wild, singing a little but not enjoying it, then living a playboy's life. The key to this film is that the Jewishness is entirely in his parents, especially Donath, the bearded ancient who offers sage advice, among many other Yiddish gestures. Mama, who acts in mama's expected ways of wanting Al to eat kosher and find a nice Jewish girl, drops dead, and Papa's songs bring Jolson back to something of his old self (in a scene that softens considerably the catharsis provided by the original *Jazz Singer* for a secular age). To pay his emotional debts, Parks helps lead American entertainers in committing themselves to play for the troops across the world (many odd moments here, including a version of "Chinatown" sung in Italy!).

After a physical collapse, Jolson meets Southern-accented nurse Hale, and the predictable romance begins. Strangely, or not so strangely, this offers one more brick of evidence in the successful assimilation of a great

American hack. Norman Brooks played Jolson in a last fictional screen appearance in *The Best Things in Life are Free* (1956), a slogan Jolson himself would never have abided. 96 min., color.

The Jolson Story (1946)

Sidney Buchman• was mercifully uncredited for this giant hit, starring SAG Communist Larry Parks and Evelyn Keyes. Closely modeled on *The Jazz Singer* (1927) rather than Jolson's own roustabout, strictly careerist, womanizing life. The Jewish boy reprimanded for singing secular songs runs away to become an entertainer. Where *The Jazz Singer* had a religious ending, *The Jolson Story* points toward assimilation.

Juke Box Jenny (1942)

Universal. Assoc. Prod: Joseph G. Sanford (Joseph Gershenson). Dir: Harold Young. Scr: Robert Lees,• Frederic I. Rinaldo,• Arthur V. Jones, Dorcas Cochran. Cast: Harriet Hilliard, Ken Murray, Donald Douglas, Iris Adrian, Charles Halton, Sig Arno, Reed Hadley, William Ruhl, Don Dillaway, Claire Du Brey, James Flavin

Not the finest moment for Lees and Rinaldo, with scant dialogue, but in what *Variety* described as a vehicle for "offbeat tunes" there can be found an underlying women's teen (and female) theme with some charm. A recording company executive wants to record "jive" music (forties jump swing) but is forced by chief shareholder and prospective mother-in-law to keep it strictly classical until a mix-up involving a drunken marriage throws everything into confusion and, ultimately, jive and commerce triumph. "Swing It Mother Goose," a generational statement of sorts, compares with jive numbers (and the story line) in Edgar Ulmer's *Jive Junction* (1943). 61 min.

Jumping Jacks (1952)

Para. Prod: Hal B. Wallis. Dir: Norman Taurog. Scr: Robert Lees,• Frederic I. Rinaldo,• Herbert Baker. (Additional dialogue: James B. Allerdice, Richard Weil.•) Story basis: Brian Marlow. Cast: Dean Martin, Jerry Lewis, Mona Freeman, Don DeFore, Robert Strauss, Richard Erdman

Robert Lees wrote the script for this film in 1944 for Abbott and Costello, too late for a World War II pic. It was revived for the Korean conflict and offered to a new team on the verge of becoming a box office hit. There are some charming satires of military life, but Jerry

Lewis's comedy was even broader and certainly more aggressive than Lou Costello's vaudeville prole. Who could imagine even the quasi-feminine Lou in an Army barracks, tossing his clothes one-by-one over a screen in striptease style, as Lewis does? The studio took out ads in the industry papers to state its regrets for having to credit blacklistees Rinaldo and Lees on this film (they could have added, but did not, fellow blacklistee Richard Weil). 96 min.

Jungle Flight (1947)

An action film based mainly on aerial shots of cargo planes in action, with a minor dose of Latin American romantic exoticism. Produced by the "two dollar bills" (William H. Pine and William C. Thomas) who dabbled in Left filmmaking. The story basis was by David Lang.†

The Jury's Secret (1938)

Universal. Assoc. Prod: Edmund Grainger. Dir: Edward Sloman. Scr: Lester Cole,• Newman Levy. Story basis: Lester Cole. Cast: Kent Taylor, Fay Wray, Jane Darwell, Nan Grey, Larry J. Blake, Fritz Leiber, Leonard Mudie, Samuel S. Hinds, Granville Bates, Halliwell Hobbes, Edward Broadley, William B. Davidson

Hollywood Ten writer Cole wrote no fewer than four "wrong man" plots, a studio favorite, for Universal in the late thirties, and this was one of the sharpest in social criticism. It keys on the turmoil following a flood that kills 400 people in "Midland City," ruled by a ruthless tycoon, phony philanthropist and inspirational newspaper columnist, Brandon Williams (Hinds). He writes a series encouraging the townsfolk to rebuild even as he makes preparations to leave town to escape the mess, but left-wing critic Walter Russell (Taylor) steps forward to insist that Williams remain in town until he uses his influence to build a flood-control project. Instead, the tycoon plots to cover his flood losses by shorting stock in the largest local public company and causing its collapse, enriching himself at the expense of most of the other citizens. When a failed novelist in his employ discovers the plot, he murders Williams, but the killing is blamed on someone else. Social criticism morphs into a courtroom suspense melodrama of the familiar kind.

The Breen Office objected to what it called "the kidding and ridiculing of the administration of justice" throughout the film, and in particular to a line about "a powerful lobby in the United States Senate." The studio toned things down a bit, but Cole's points were inescapable. 65 min.

Just Off Broadway (1942)

A detective Mike Shayne (Lloyd Nolen) movie, this one written by Arnaud d'Usseau,• with a few bright notes—mainly Phil Silvers as a commercial photographer showing up at inappropriate moments.

K

Keeper of the Flame (1942)

MGM. Prod: Victor Saville. Dir: George Cukor. Scr: Donald Ogden Stewart.• Novel basis: I. A. R. Wylie, *Keeper of the Flame* (1942). Cast: Spencer Tracy, Katherine Hepburn, Richard Whorf, Margaret Wycherly, Forrest Tucker, Frank Craven, Horace McNally (i.e., Stephen McNally), Percy Kilbride, Howard da Silva•

The last of Stewart's important screenplays in feature films (he later claimed that Hollywood could not make stories this radical), *Keeper* also arguably marks the didactic political highpoint of the Tracy/Hepburn matchup, and of Cukor's work as well. Brilliantly written and subtly acted, it is seen by film historians as a thinly disguised attack on isolationism and especially on Charles Lindbergh, who featured prominently in the "America First" movement. But the narrative outstrips the formalities of the plot and, in any case, under Cukor's direction the sparks that fly between Tracy and Hepburn occupy the foreground.

Tracy is a reporter called back from Europe to cover the death of a famous American patriot. Hepburn, the hero's widow, is kept from public attention and seems anxious to protect her dead husband's memory—and, we come more and more to suspect, to cover up his real-life activity. A young da Silva, playing the chauffeur and groundskeeper who was saved by the hero during the First World War but was humiliated in the decades after, offers the key to the truth. Toward the end of the film, we begin to discover that a fascist plot to rouse hatred against unions, blacks and Jews was short-circuited by the hero's death. Hepburn's vivid reticence and Tracy's shy mixture of growing passion and respect for her feelings makes it the most unusual, least gruff and most politically evocative of their films. 100 min.

Keeping Company (1940)

Minor fare written by Adrian Scott• with Harry Ruskin and James Hill, about a small town businessman-father overwhelmed by his wife (whom he invariably calls "Chief") and his three daughters. It suggests the later power of LIFE WITH FATHER but is much weaker, and a box office flop.

The Kid from Cleveland (1949)

Herbert Kline Prod. Republic. Prod: Walter Colmes. Dir: Herbert Kline. Scr: John Bright.• Story basis: Herbert Kline. Cast: George Brent, Lynn Bari, Rusty Tamblyn, Tommy Cook, Ann Doran, John Beradino, Louis Jean Heydt, K. Elmo Lowe, Bill Veeck and the Cleveland Indians baseball team

A remarkably touching low-budget drama about a troubled boy from a single-parent home (his father was killed in the antifascist conflict) and the sportswriter who saves him from falling into juvenile delinquency. Good baseball footage includes portions of Indians games, locker room talk, and especially Larry Doby (the American League's first African American player). Director Kline—former editor of the brilliant, influential 30s radical magazine, *New Theater and Film*—managed to avoid the blacklist. 89 min.

Kind Lady (1935)

MGM. Prod: Lucien Hubbard. Dir: George B. Seitz. Scr: Bernard Schubert. Play basis: Edward Chodorov.• Story basis: Hugh Walpole, "The Silver Casket." Cast: Aline MacMahon, Basil Rathbone, Mary Carlisle, Frank Albertson, Dudley Digges

Adapted for film from a Broadway stage favorite written by Chodorov, who had adapted it from Walpole's story. Kindly but filthy rich old maid living alone with her servants is surrounded by a fabulous collection of paintings and many expensive trinkets. She opens her home first to the visiting (and obviously impoverished) painter who admires her collection; and then to the painter's wife, who stages a fainting spell to gain extended privileges for herself and her husband in the house. As in Losey's• THE SERVANT but in the spirit of material rather than spiritual corruption, they soon take over, holding her hostage until the resolution. It was remade in 1951 in a less available version under the same title and with improved casting, including Ethyl Barrymore as the grand dame and Angela Lansbury as one of the plotters. 76 min.

King and Country (1964)

BHE Films, Landau/Unger. Prod: Joseph Losey,• Norman Priggen. Dir: Joseph Losey. Scr: Evan Jones, John Wilson. Story basis: James Landsdale Hodsen. Cast: Dirk Bogarde,

Tom Courtenay, Leo McKern, Barry Foster, James Villiers, Peter Copley, Derek Partridge

Among the many antiwar films made by the black-listees and their immediate circle of sympathizers, this is the least compromising. It preserves the power and immediacy of theater on film and is the fulfillment of the old promise and dream of the Depression of a film medium that would reach beyond the middle class to the working people it took as its subject. Ironically, Losey reached this artistic opportunity at about the same moment he gave up on the prospects for the modern working class to change society. Although the film was equally a demonstration of Losey's disgust for the English ruling class's willingness to subordinate every shred of decency to the close-order drill of established class relations, it is also Losey's farewell to the working class that, in the pitiful figure of Hamp (Courtenay), apologizes for any inconvenience it may have caused on its way to oblivion.

Bogarde plays an officer-lawyer in World War I who argues for the defense at Hamp's court martial for desertion, with death the possible penalty. He explains that the soldier deserved forgiveness because he was disoriented by the exhaustion of too many years at war and bad news from home. The court martial decides that Hamp must be made an example of; the officers are organizing another attack, after all, and the boys must be "encouraged" to keep up discipline. A painful, rage-inspiring, unique film. 86 min.

King of the Newsboys (1938)

Rep. Assoc. Prod and Dir: Bernard Vorhaus.• Scr: Louis Weitzenkorn, Peggy Thompson. Story basis: Samuel Ornitz,• Horace McCoy, Jack Natteford. Cast: Lew Ayres, Helen Mack, Alison Skipworth, Victor Varconi, Sheila Bromley, Alice White, Horace MacMahon, Ray Cooke, Jack Pennick, Mary Kornman, Gloria Rich, Oscar O'Shea, Marjorie Main (uncredited)

An extremely obscure but highly interesting film in the Vorhaus style, a thirties feature akin to his British films, with lots of atmosphere if not much plot. An impoverished young man who enjoys being a slum personality connected slightly with organized crime proposes marriage to his childhood sweetheart, who is shown at home in a tenement with her drunken father, hopeless mother and many siblings. Ayres promises big things, but the Helen Mack character prefers a local mobster. Ayres then makes himself the "king" of the film's title by building a distribution network that becomes a track tipsheet. As he grows rich, Mack realizes how wrong she

was in abandoning him, but Ayres now regards her as damaged goods and sees the mobster's face whenever she approaches. In this thematic, the working class must strive to escape poverty individually, but glimpses of more cooperative possibilities are ever-present (from their new view of the docks, where they dreamed of sailing off to Europe, they realize that their ship of dreams was actually a garbage scow). 65 min.

A Kiss for Corliss (1949)

Strand Productions. Prod: Colin Miller. Dir: Richard Wallace (asst. dir: Robert Aldrich, uncredited). Scr: Howard Dimsdale.• Story basis: Howard Dimsdale. Characters: F. Hugh Herbert. Cast: Shirley Temple, David Niven, Tom Tully, Virginia Welles, Darryl Hickman

Shirley Temple's final film before a graceful retirement, which is remarkable enough without even considering the higher irony that the kindly hand extended to help her step down from the pumpkin carriage of her career was Communist Dimsdale's. The film was the sequel to Kiss and Tell (1945), a domestic comedy that pretended to be shocked by the notion that any teenage girl selling kisses would actually possess some erotic ulterior motives. Temple was the pubescent Corliss Archer in both films, a role producers originally had hoped would be played by Rita Hayworth, an actress of an entirely different wattage. An artifact of interest to navigators of film history. 88 min.

Kiss the Blood Off My Hands (1948)

Harold Hecht-Norma Productions. Prod: Richard Vernon. Dir: Norman Foster. Scr: Leonardo Bercovici.• Novel basis: Gerald Butler, Kiss the Blood Off My Hands (1940). Adaptation: Ben Maddow,•† Walter Bernstein.• Cast: Joan Fontaine, Burt Lancaster, Robert Newton, Lewis L. Russell, Aminta Dyme, Jay Novello

A minor but extremely important film noir written by the elusive Bercovici and adapted by Maddow and Bernstein. Its unique sensibility was contained in the unlikely title, which was approved after the producers complained to the Production Code that it was Butler's own for his novel, originally published in the United Kingdom. This Lancaster vehicle has Burt as an embittered GI in postwar London who has inadvertently killed someone in a bar brawl and finds himself falling in love with nurse Fontaine and blackmailed by the brilliantly insidious cockney, Newton. Lancaster's masochism has never been lovelier, and the streets of London are alive with stylized proletarian realism. 79 min.

The Kissing Bandit (1948)

Isobel Lennart† co-scripted (with John Briard Harding) and Joe Pasternak produced Frank Sinatra's second-most-embarrassing film (after *Johnny Concho*) and one of the bigger Technicolor-musical flops of the day, in a fantasy that has Kathryn Grayson as fantasy lover.

Kitty Foyle (1940)

RKO. Executive Prod: Harry E. Edington, David Hempstead. Dir: Sam Wood. Scr: Dalton Trumbo• (additional dialogue, Donald Ogden Stewart•). Novel basis: Christopher Morley, *Kitty Foyle* (1939). Cast: Ginger Rogers, Dennis Morgan, James Craig, Gladys Cooper, Ernest Cossart, Eduardo Ciannelli

An Academy Award–winning performance from Rogers as the Philadelphia Irish working-class girl with big class and gender problems. Was her grandfather actually on the Main Line, i.e., the prestigious settlements that followed the rail tracks out from the city center? (Not exactly. He worked on the crew that built it). In adolescence, she daydreams about a prince coming to sweep her away. As the Depression hits, she gets work at a magazine edited by Mainliner Dennis Morgan and they fall in love. The Cinderella scenario crashes when the magazine fails and she goes to work selling perfume in New York. The young and idealistic physician Craig pursues her. (Rogers' role is a kind of working-class socialist of the type she would come to regret in her years as enemy of the Left; director Wood was another iron-clad reactionary.)

The reappearance of Morgan intensifies the conflict between her desire for the shopgirl's version of the American Dream and her sense of dignity combined with propriety (he asks her to go away with him, but he cannot or will not divorce his wife). The *mise en scène* is beautifully expressive of Kitty's inner turmoil, making it one of the most accomplished women's films of the period. In addition to the Academy Award to Rogers, there were nominations for best director, best picture, and best script. 108 min.

Knickerbocker Holiday (1944)

PCA. Prod: Harry Joe Brown. Dir: Harry Joe Brown. Scr: David Boehm, Harold Goldman,• David Cook, Rowland Leigh. Adaptation: Thomas Lennon. Play basis: Maxwell Anderson, *Knickerbocker Holiday* (1938). Cast: Nelson Eddy, Charles Coburn, Constance Dowling, Shelly Winters, Percy Kilbride, Chester Conklin (uncredited)

This adaptation of Anderson's popular play, with music by Kurt Weill• (and four songs added for the film), is the perfect wartime Popular Front production of a historical musical comedy. In old New Amsterdam, the jolly Dutch burghers who make a fat living with all sorts of illegal trade face two new problems. Coburn, a pompous king's emissary, is coming to take charge; and much worse, Eddy as Peter Stuyvesant is inventing freedom of the press for the common folk (who are also jolly, but oppressed and much more svelt).

This involved plot barely offers relief from music (a self-conscious character looks at Eddy and then the camera and asks, "Is he going to sing again?"), but follows Eddy to meet with representatives of other colonists, then back home to stop Dowling from marrying the increasingly dictatorial Coburn. The fantastic windup includes Eddy rousing the masses musically to an insurrectional frenzy. "September Song," sung in only a couple verses by Coburn, slips by almost without notice. And yet it is all a perfect period piece. In the end, democracy will be exhorted and even the Indians quietly approve. Wonderfully caricatured, the unfree colonial America is about to be overcome by the forces that will eventually produce the New Deal. Academy Award nomination for music (including Kurt Weill). 85 min.

Krakatoa, East of Java (1969)

This film vies with *Zombies of Mora Tau* for the title of worst blacklistee-written film of all time—a disaster pic co-scripted by Bernard Gordon• with a nineteenth-century Dutch East Indies ship sailing near the famous volcano explosion. No wonder they were in trouble: the real island of Krakatoa is *west* of Java.

L

Lady Be Careful (1936)
Dorothy Parker• and Alan Campbell (with Harry Ruskin) wrote this slight drama about a sailor betting his buddy that he could kiss a cabaret girl first. The deathly dry Parker suggested having the two sailors kiss instead.

Lady from Nowhere (1936)
A so-so crime drama written by Arthur Strawn• from a story by Ben Grauman Kahn. The story is helped by Mary Astor's role as a tough Manhattan hotel manicurist who witnesses a murder and goes on the lam to Connecticut where she works as a waitress.

The Lady Gambles (1949)
U-I. Prod: Michael Kraike. Dir: Michael Gordon.•† Scr: Roy Huggins.† Story: Lewis Meltzer, Oscar Saul. Adaptation: Halsted Welles. Cast: Barbara Stanwyck, Robert Preston, Stephen McNally, Edith Barrett, John Hoyt, Leif Erickson

This is the first feature made about Las Vegas, whose big mob joints like The Flamingo had opened just two years earlier. The classic "problem film" poses Stanwyck as the "table crawler" who suddenly and unexpectedly becomes a compulsive gambler when faced with the temptation of the glitter and fast money.

Intense acting by Stanwyck is underlined by characteristic psychological themes. Her sister (Barrett) has spurned offers of marriage in order to care for a helpless sibling, and is now a frustrated spinster who lives with Stanwyck and Preston, tearing them apart. Stanwyck is obviously vulnerable—even ready to snap—when they go on a working vacation in Vegas. There, they face new romantic problems: gambling house exec McNally makes a romantic play while inveigling her into betting—until she loses her head. Psychology wears thin and the film droops heavily toward the end, but a determined Stanwyck holds the screen. 99 min.

Lady in Distress (1942)
British spin on a familiar plot (with uncredited contribution by Gordon Kahn•) and starring Michael Redgrave with Paul Lukas, about a mentally unbalanced illusionist.

Lady Scarface (1941)
RKO. Prod: Cliff Reid. Dir: Frank Woodruff. Scr: Arnaud d'Usseau,• Richard Collins.† Cast: Dennis O'Keefe, Judith Anderson, Frances E. Neal, Mildred Coles, Eric Blore, Marc Lawrence,† Marion Martin

Cheapie mystery-romance-drama misses its chance to make gun-totin' gang boss Anderson into a female George Raft, evidently because detective cop O'Keefe and snooping reporter Neal are too busy stumbling over each other and falling in love in the process. Anderson as boss Slade might have been intensely interesting but instead is only intermittently so. Too pretty for the Ma Barker type, she brooks no disagreement from her "boys" and carries out the job herself when necessary. For her part, reporter Neal is an avid career-woman, bucking police attempts to keep her off the case. But all the forces of right are with the cops, and as they do their duty, the film grinds on toward its inevitable conclusions, dramatic and romantic. 66 min.

A Lady Without Passport (1950)
MGM. Prod: Samuel Marx. Dir: Joseph H. Lewis. Scr: Howard Dimsdale.• Story basis: Lawrence Taylor. Adaptation: Cyril Hume. Cast: Hedy Lamarr, John Hodiak, James Craig, George Macready, Steven Geray, Bruce Cowling, Nedrick Young, Steven Hill, Robert Osterloh, Trevor Bardette, Charles Wagenheim, Renzo Cesana, Esther Zeitlin

Romantic melodrama about a very real contemporary dilemma: the ease of getting passports for certain kinds of immigrants (those fleeing communist countries, including many with Nazi or fascist pasts, who were hidden and protected by authorities) and the extreme difficulties for others (refugees without relatives or resources). Lamarr has been dawdling around the U.S. embassy in Havana waiting for a passport and becomes the perfect tool for immigration officer Hodiak to entice smugglers of aliens. As reviewers commented, for an ex-resident of a German concentration camp (and probably, if not identifiably, Jewish), Lamarr's character sure looks undamaged and wears nice clothes. Leader of the smugglers Macready is more romantic than sinister—considerably more romantic than Hodiak, who finally gets the girl as well as the crooks. Location shots in Miami and Havana are interesting. 72 min.

Land of Fighting Men (1938)

An independent B-picture with an interesting story basis by Stanley Roberts† and tunes and lyrics by Connie Lee• has a land monopolist manipulating a range war for his own buying spree.

Land of the Open Range (1941)

RKO. Prod: Bert Gilroy. Dir: Edward Killy. Scr: Morton Grant.• Story: Lee Bond. Cast: Tim Holt, Ray Whitley, Lee "Lasses" White, Janet Waldo

A fascinating replay of the notorious 1891 Oklahoma Land Rush, in which former Indian Territory was put up for grabs and the folks with guns got the best and the most. In this case, a notorious banker and land salesman has died after serving time in jail for swindling, and he leaves his huge ranch to all those who have served at least two years in prison—but they have to rush for parcels of it.

Holt is the deputy sheriff who finds himself defending elderly reformed convict Whitley, whose perky daughter (Waldo) stands up for decency and peace. Against Holt's usually good judgment, she insists that good can be found in (almost) anyone and successfully promotes a reconciliation. Inevitably, some of the bad guys are really bad, and plot to seize land by the river and dam up the water to control the town. After some gunplay, and Holt himself racing a horse on a bet, things begin to clear up. Dams and water companies are good if only they work hand-in-hand with the ranchers. As usual in Holt films, Lee "Lasses" White is on hand as "Whopper," the laughably colloquial and superstitious sidekick who might be said to combine most of the traits (eye rolling, superstition and musicality) given to African American male actors in this era. 60 min.

The Las Vegas Story (1952)

Howard Hughes Production/RKO. Prod: Samuel Bischoff, Robert Sparks. Dir: Robert Stevenson Scr: Earl Felton, Harry Essex (uncredited: Paul Jarrico•). Story basis: Jay Dratler. Cast: Victor Mature, Jane Russell, Vincent Price, Hoagy Carmichael, Brad Dexter, Gordon Oliver, Jay C. Flippen, Will Wright, Ray Montgomery, Colleen Miller, Bill Welsh

A small film about the neon town in the early 1950s and a romantic triangle that makes this film little more than a vehicle for Mature and Russell, with precious few political themes or noir edges. (Or perhaps it's just a knockoff of CASABLANCA for the rubes.)

Nightclub singer Russell and GI Mature had a thing during the forties (with unmarried sex hinted at more broadly than was possible a few years earlier), but they had split. Piano player Carmichael tells the story, as he did repeatedly in other films in those years. She returns years later with Price, a business executive past bankruptcy seeking to recoup his fortunes at the crap tables. Mature, by now a cop, tries to do the right thing with kids running away to get married (hints at pregnancy here, again pressing the edges of the allowable). He finds himself back in love (and realized lust) with Russell while a diamond necklace of hers is stolen and Price is arrested. Only Jane Russell fans could get something out of this one.

The political upshot was bigger than the film itself, as Jarrico sued to get his credits and Hughes' attorneys successfully defended the firm by pointing to the "morality" clause in the Screen Writers Guild contract: Jarrico had proven his moral turpitude by refusing to be a friendly witness to HUAC! 88 min.

Lassie Come Home (1943)

MGM. Prod: Samuel Marx, Dore Schary. Dir: Fred M. Wilcox. Scr: Hugo Butler.• Novel basis: Eric Knight, Lassie Come Home (1940). Cast: Roddy McDowall, Donald Crisp, Dame May Whitty, Elizabeth Taylor, Edmund Gwenn, Elsa Lanchester

The first and easily the best of the Lassie films, this tear-jerking children's story (brilliantly handled by Butler) is about the sentimental qualities of Lancashire working-class society, the British love and admiration for pet dogs and the extraordinary (if somewhat unbelievable) ability of a collie to travel hundreds of miles, swim rivers, fight evildoers and make her way back to the boy who loves her. It is also a wartime theme of class reconciliation, as a Scots lord and his daughter (Taylor, en route to National Velvet and permanent stardom) see the goodness of the boy's family and adopt them, in effect, with the collie that they have purchased and who has three times run away. Some of the tenderest moments show the wanderer Gwenn, and along Lassie's trail an aged, lonely couple who adopt Lassie temporarily, as if in solace for a son lost in the war. Probably most memorable for child viewers, however, are the action shots of Lassie ("playing herself," according to the credits) swimming, running and otherwise celebrating the role. 88 min., color.

The Last Crooked Mile (1946)

A play by Robert L. Richards• provided the story basis for this adapted radio drama about a private eye seeking an elusive valuable missing coin and tangling with the inevitable torch singer, until a bank official is disclosed as the real rascal.

The Last Man (1932)

Francis Faragoh• supplied the dialogue for this spooky drama of a detective finding an abandoned ship with only two sailors still alive. Notable for early color sequences.

The Last Mile (1932)

K.B.S. Films. Prod: Samuel Bischoff. Dir: Samuel Bishoff. Scr: Seton I. Miller. Play basis: John Wexley,• The Last Mile (1930). Cast: Howard Phillips, Preston Foster, George E. Stone, Noel Madison, Alan Roscoe, Paul Fix, Al Hill, Daniel L. Hayes, Alec B. Francis, Louise Carter, Edward Van Sloan

An important Broadway drama terribly distorted by Hollywood production. Among the jailhouse-and-jailbreak films of the time, this version was unquestionably sympathetic in its portrayal of the prisoners and their desperation, as well as the violence of the uprising that follows. Yet it bitterly disappointed playwright Wexley by toning down the violence and killing off his real protagonist for a more sympathetic one who was actually innocent of the crime for which he was convicted. 78 min.

The Last Mile (1959)

Vanguard Production/United Artists. Prod: Max Rosenberg. Dir: Howard W. Koch. Scr: Milton Suborsky, Seton Miller. Play basis: John Wexley,• The Last Mile (1930). Cast: Mickey Rooney, Clifford David, Dan "Red" Barry, Alan Bunce, Frank Conroy, Michael Constantine, Clifton James, Leon Janney, George Marcey

A death-row drama redux of Wexley's play with the suspiciously lefty production company, it marked a small-scale blacklistee return feature made outside the major studios on a small budget entirely in New York, with a fine, largely theatrical cast. A disclaimer before the credits noting that such conditions belonged to the past gives the film a retro feel for the thirties theatrical ambience. While apparently undercutting parallels to current capital punishment controversies (the same year, killer Caryl Chessman went to the chair in California despite widespread protests that foreshadowed 1960s uprisings), the disclaimer could not prevent analogies. The Last Mile may be the last old-fashioned statement of the blacklistees.

As a fine study of group tension, it also speaks to the psychological "otherization" of late 1950s and early 1960s films: everyone is waiting, and each execution is a reminder of the common fate. A new arrival, Rooney, sets the tone: he is welcomed into a community of the lost, who have nevertheless retained some degree of humanity and caring. As their inhumane treatment by prison officials continues, they revolt, anticipating the hopelessness of any escape. Moral questions fade as Rooney takes charge, answering society's cruelty in acts of cruelty against its representatives. At last he chooses death rather than submission, an anticipation of the "revolutionary suicide" theme that will become so popular later. 81 min.

The Last Outpost (1951)

David Lang† provided the story for the first starring western role for future president Ronald Reagan, at the time FBI informant T-10 and president of the Screen Actors Guild. Reagan is the courageous Confederate spy sent West to pick up a gold shipment. Posing as a Union officer visiting the Western town, he woos Rhonda Fleming (who earlier felt deserted by him) and learns that the Apaches intend to attack the town. The village is saved by Reagan and his fellow Confederates who, now attired in the proper uniforms, join with the arriving Union soldiers to smash the Apaches. The future reconciliation of whites (especially white men) against common enemies can readily be foreseen. In an interesting sidelight that (like Reagan's battle films) might have formed the future president's pseudo-historical pseudo-memory, all nonmilitary federal agencies are seen as corrupt and overbearing.

The Last Posse (1953)

Seymour Bennett's• last (credited) film, written with his wife Connie Lee• (Bennett, of BLONDIE fame) and Kenneth Gamet, and with the Bennetts also supplying the story basis. A moralistic and medium-budget western about a sheriff's son who realizes that his father and the town's leading citizens did wrong by appropriating stolen money.

Laughter (1930)

Para. Prod: Unknown. Dir: Harry d'Abbadie d'Arrast. Scr: Herman J. Mankiewicz, Donald Ogden Stewart.• Story basis: H. D. Harry d'Abbdie d'Arrast, Douglas Z. Doty. Cast: Nancy Carroll, Fredric March, Frank Morgan, Leonard Carey, Diane Ellis

An early Stewart talkie with his characteristic dry-witted comic treatment of the ruling class. Here Morgan is "C. Morton Gibson," a stock speculator who makes almost ten million bucks on a good day. Wife Carroll, a former showgirl, considers him a very dull fellow, and while he piles up the dough she hangs out with young composer March. She has earlier convinced Carey, a would-be paramour, not to blow his brains out, but a little later she must persuade the wild Ellis (the financier's daughter by an earlier marriage) not to elope with the scorned fellow. Time and again, Morgan's money and prestige save his family from embarrassment if not disgrace. But what does it leave him with in the end? 85 min.

Laura (1944)

20th. Prod: Otto Preminger. Dir: Otto Preminger, Rouben Mamoulian. Scr: Jay Dratler, Samuel Hoffenstein, Elizabeth Reinhardt (uncredited: Ring Lardner, Jr.•). Novel basis: Vera Caspary,• Laura (1943). Cast: Gene Tierney, Dana Andrews, Clifton Webb, Lane Chandler, Vincent Price, Judith Anderson, Grant Mitchell, Dorothy Adams

This famous noir film has Andrews the snooping detective looking for the murderer of Tierney while gazing at her portrait and interrogating her two boyfriends, the prissy Webb and the conniving Price. In the process, we learn that Tierney was not only beautiful but a quick study who, on meeting noted literary celebrity and newspaper columnist Webb (the actor's film debut), used him to develop a list of advertising clients and a big reputation. But there's at least something odd here: middle-aged Webb has no sexual attractiveness—indeed, has the effeminacy of the contemporary Hollywood gay image—while Tierney is swathed in it. Unfortunately, the film builds up irresistibly to Tierney choosing the "real man," our detective-protagonist. Along the way, there are some fine performances. The film won an Oscar for black-and-white cinematography, and nominations for best director, interior decoration, screenplay and supporting actor (Webb). Interestingly, the lingering memory of the film is its eerie theme, written by friendly witness David Raksin.† 85 min.

The Law vs. Billy the Kid (1954)

A Sam Katzman cheapie written by "John T. Williams" (i.e., Bernard Gordon•), who rehearses the old they-made-me-a-criminal outlaw narrative. Lots of western local Technicolor work raises the film above normal Katzman par (Variety proposed it as "standard fare for the outdoor program market," meaning drive-ins), but

Gordon—who also scripted THE LAWLESS BREED, also about a populist outlaw-hero—delivers on the wronged-man theme.

The Lawless (1950)

Pine and Thomas Productions/Paramount. Prod: William H. Pine, William C. Thomas. Dir: Joseph Losey.• Scr: Geoffrey Homes (pseudonym for Daniel Mainwaring). Cast: Macdonald Carey, Gail Russell, John Sands, Lee Patrick, John Hoyt, Lalo Rios, Maurice Jara, Walter Reed, Herbert Anderson, Argentina Brunetti, William Edmunds, Gloria Winters, John Davis, Martha Hyer, Frank Fenton, Paul Harvey, Felipe Turich, Tab Hunter

Breaking loose from RKO and setting himself up with two B-film co-producers known as the "Dollar Bills," Losey planned a gripping drama about racial intolerance and class values in Latino California. John Hubley,• an animator fired by Disney and en route to a career as a distinguished independent (with wife Faith), served as uncredited production designer, planning the main sequences in rural districts around Sacramento in dozens of locations (all on a $400,000 budget). It was, in retrospect for Losey, "the closest to the kind of film that I'd have chosen to make" in those days: a socialist shocker with a raging mob of racists.

Real-life Marysville becomes Santa Marta ("the friendly city") shortly after the war, where Latinos are jeered by local rednecks (Jara, an Army veteran, says, "I forgot what I was coming back to.") As the "fruit tramps" struggle to make a decent life, both sides of the racial line (emblemized in the world-weary liberal reporter Carey and the idealistic Latina, Russell) are in turmoil over worsening racism and the better lives that postwar prosperity offers only to whites. A massive brawl breaks out at a Hispanic neighborhood dance when a carload of Anglo punks descends on it, looking for trouble. Rios hits a cop by accident and, panicking, steals a car to escape. Soon, local reporter Russell (who covered the dance and riot for her Spanish-language weekly) pleads on behalf of the captured young men while their lawyer advises them to plead guilty. An emotional confrontation between Carey and Russell suggests that he used to be an idealistic (read: Popular Front) journalist who has sold out for a comfortable spot in a small town. Meanwhile, the scandal sheet in Stockton, conspiring with right-wing plants in the wire services, stirs the pot with phony headlines until TV reporters get involved, and by this time events reach the boiling point. After Carey realizes his error and editorializes against the popular racial sentiment, crowds riot again, this time smashing the newspaper office and everything in it. Afterward, a moralist among them pleads with Carey not to leave town: "We need someone to yell at us when we forget our decency and look the other way." Perhaps the first film, certainly the first left-wing film, that shows television reporting as part of the mainstream's self-vindication. Early Losey at his best.

The premiere was held in San Antonio, Texas, under the sponsorship of the League of United Latin American Citizens (LULAC). 83 min.

The Lawless Breed (1953)
Biopic of John Wesley Hardin, the outlaw destined to be romanticized by Bob Dylan. Director Raoul Walsh sought to create an action drama, and screenwriter Bernard Gordon (by this time working under pseudonyms, here "John T. Castle") complied. The result was unfortunately dulled by the performance of Rock Hudson (although he was not as lifeless in this film debut as in later films).

Lawrence of Arabia (1962)
Horizon Pictures/Col. Prod: Sam Spiegel. Dir: David Lean. Scr: Robert Bolt (uncredited: Michael Wilson,• credit restored 1996). Book basis: T. E. Lawrence, *Seven Pillars of Wisdom* (1922). Cast: Peter O'Toole, Alec Guinness, Anthony Quinn, Jack Hawkins, José Ferrer, Anthony Quayle, Claude Rains, Arthur Kennedy, Donald Wolfit, Omar Sharif

One of the great spectaculars in the original sense and Wilson's return to the big time (although his credits on this film were not granted until after his death), the film was also a triumph for producer Spiegel, with Bolt doing the adaptation from Lawrence's oddball orientalist literary classic. Spiegel, fresh from THE BRIDGE ON THE RIVER KWAI (with the uncredited Wilson doing the hard script writing there, too), looked upon location shooting as a big-ticket adventure and proof that the independents could handle this mega-genre as well as the majors. Indeed, with seemingly endless desert vistas filled with inspired cinematography and a huge score, 200-plus minutes was barely long enough to contain everything. A little like Warren Beatty in the second half of *Reds*, star O'Toole grows gradually smaller in the vast cinematic landscape, with Lawrence's real motives in organizing a sort of pan-Arabic guerilla force against the Turks during World War I foggy at best. The screenplay hints that Lawrence was an avatar of the earliest English explorers who combined a love of exotica with a bit of honest self-

disgust at the pleasure they took in conquering the world—a suggestion made in a scene that indicates Lawrence rather enjoyed a good caning at the hands of the "wogs" (the scene was cut for the initial release and restored decades later). To Wilson, Lawrence was apparently an inexplicable ideologue (*Seven Pillars* offered evidence of more mystical motivations), but the screenwriter and the star strode over all of these ambiguities magnificently. 227 min. (restored version), color.

The League of Frightened Men (1937)
One of a handful of Nero Wolfe detective dramas, this was the only one scripted (actually co-scripted) from the Left, by Guy Endore.• The murder of three Harvard alumni is brilliantly solved by Wolfe (played by Walter Connolly) and his assistant (Lionel Stander•).

Legend of Lylah Clare (1968)
The Associates and Aldrich Co-Production/MGM. Prod: Robert Aldrich. Dir: Robert Aldrich. Scr: Hugo Butler,• Jean Rouverol (Butler).• Teleplay basis: Robert Thom, Edward DeBlasio, "Legend of Lylah Claire" (1963). Cast: Kim Novak, Peter Finch, Ernest Borgnine, Milton Selzer, Rossella Falk, Gabriele Tinti, Coral Browne, Valentina Cortese, Jean Carroll, Michael Murphy

Originally a 1963 *Dupont Show of the Week* television drama starring Tuesday Weld, this remake is fuller, more avant-garde, and far more over-the-top in its campiness. Behind the façade and additional layers of supernatural melodrama, the blacklisted Butlers helped Aldrich fashion a memorable (if sometimes incoherent) critique of Hollywood and of commercial filmmaking. Noted by reviewers as a return by Aldrich to the themes of THE BIG KNIFE 13 years earlier, it is interesting as another of Aldrich's collaborations with the Left, this one intended as a building block in establishing Aldrich's production company.

Hollywood agent Selzer sets the film in motion by "discovering" an ingenue who resembles the late film star Lylah Claire. Dying of cancer, he wants to do one artistically worthy film project as producer, and he wants to evoke the memory of the one fascinating actress he discovered. He proposes the project to Claire's former director and husband, Finch, who is doubtful about reviving a ghost but agrees when he meets wistful siren Novak.

The film begins to dip seriously as the biopic proceeds and Novak plays a double role, supernaturally recovering the memories of Claire. Still, some fascinating moments occur in the struggle to control the production.

A melodramatic ending doesn't spoil the oddity of this film, which was written mainly by Hugo Butler as he was dying of brain cancer and was completed by his wife, Jean Butler. Aldrich believed that Novak was not up to the part but also confessed that trying to make the audience believe in the dual Lylah Claire had been too much to expect. The film's length makes problems worse; and yet there is a certain verve to Novak's final revelation of lesbianism—a contemptuous gesture, twisting the knife in her tormentors, and that helps explain at least some of the psychological action. 130 min.

The Letter (1940)

WB. Prod: Robert Lord, Hal B. Wallis, Jack L. Warner. Dir: William Wyler. Scr: Howard Koch• (uncredited script contribution: Anne Froelick•). Cast: Bette Davis, Herbert Marshall, James Stephenson, Frieda Inescort, Gale Sondergaard,• Bruce Lester, Elizabeth Earl, Sen Yung, Willie Fung

This dramatic adaptation by Howard Koch of a Somerset Maugham short story was an exotic vehicle for Bette Davis (Koch soon became famous for CASABLANCA). A bored wife of a planter in the Maylasian tropics, Davis jealously shoots her lover to death and then concocts a lie to justify self-defense. Her lawyer (Marshall), a friend of Davis's husband, learns about a damning letter to the murdered man and gets the go-ahead from her deceived husband to buy it. As the case proceeds and he comes to understand her better, Marshall is psychologically seduced by her charismatic ruthlessness. Through hypocritical appeals to justice, he manages to get her off.

But this is only the setting for the melodramatic last act. The Maugham story has her facing prison, but the Koch adaptation gives something more dramatic and haunting—true to the noir mood (scarcely developed by 1940) and to Davis's talents for self-destruction. According to Froelick's own account, as Koch's assistant (and uncredited script contributor to his earlier radio triumph, "War of the Worlds"), she provided dialogue for Davis' scenes and accepted noncredit status. In return, Koch put her in place for her own screenwriting career, which became more and more promising until she was blacklisted. 95 min.

A Letter for Evie (1945)

MGM. Prod: William H. Wright. Dir: Jules Dassin.• Scr: Alan Friedman, DeVallon Scott. Story: Blanche Brace. Cast: Marsha Hunt,• John Carroll, Hume Cronyn, Spring Byington, Pamela Britton, Norman Lloyd, Donald Curtis, Therese Lyon

One of those early films that made Dassin cringe later but proved quite serviceable at the time on the bottom of double bills (in this case, often with the lefty BANDIT OF SHERWOOD FOREST). A sentimental war drama about Cronyn and Hunt as pen pals—an innocent soldier and an equally innocent young thing who have never met. The shy Cronyn substitutes handsome and wolfish Carroll for himself, resulting in the expected complications, with Cronyn as comic star. 89 min.

Letter from an Unknown Woman (1948)

Rampart. Prod: John Houseman. Dir: Max Ophüls. Scr: Howard Koch.• Novel basis: Stefan Zweig, *Brief einer Unbekannten* (1923). Cast: Joan Fontaine, Louis Jourdan, Mady Christians, Marcel Journet, Art Smith, Carol Yorke, Howard Freeman, John Good, Leo B. Pessin, Erskin Sanford

A left-wing collaboration with Ophüls (like CAUGHT, in which he replaced John Berry), for another small production company, this film was organized by Joan Fontaine and William Dozier and most likely doomed by the blacklist's shutdown of available talent. A young Viennese woman falls in love with a handsome concert pianist. They have one night together, and after he promises to return but doesn't, she marries another man to give the pianist's child a name. Years later they meet again, but by this time he has forgotten her entirely. He reads a letter from her, written after that meeting but just before the climactic events of the film. A simple story, but Koch and Houseman, Fontaine and Jourdan handled the details in a delightfully moody look back at a lost (and by contrast to what followed, extraordinarily innocent) era of pre–World War I central Europe. 94 min.

Life Begins at Eight-Thirty (1942)

20th. Prod: Nunnally Johnson. Dir: Irving Pichel.• Scr: Nunnally Johnson (uncredited: F. Scott Fitzgerald). Play basis: Emlyn Williams, *Yesterday's Magic* (1942). Cast: Monty Woolley, Ida Lupino, Cornel Wilde, Sara Allgood, Melville Cooper, J. Edward Bromberg,• William Demarest, Hal K. Dawson, William Halligan, Milton Parsons, Inez Palange, Charles La Torre

A high-budget and cleverly cast behind-the-footlights comedy drama about the alcoholic sentimental ex-headliner (Woolley) and his self-sacrificing crippled daughter (Lupino) given a second chance when she gets a suitor (Wilde) and the boozer gets a chance to return to the stage in a starring role.

The film is one of many assignments given to Johnson, one of Fox's favorite (and best) producers, with the hard-working Pichel. This is a strictly sentimental piece. Father and daughter lived together in a crumbling Manhattan boarding house, where dad gets a chance to make a comeback as King Lear in a stylish production and swears off the sauce, only to learn his daughter is about to leave him for a suddenly acquired suitor. Woolley's delightfully wrought hamming fills the screen: from the quiet, dignified sober character to the brilliantly acid and wildly hilarious drunk and then back, best of all as a lush Santa Claus. Compare this to Pichel's other sentimental pictures, like *The Great Rupert* (in which Jimmy Durante has the Woolley role and Lupino's is recast as, yes, a pet squirrel). 85 min.

A Life of Her Own (1950)

MGM. Prod: Voldemar Vetluguin. Dir: George Cukor. Scr: Isobel Lennart.† Cast: Lana Turner, Ray Milland, Tom Ewell, Louis Calhern, Ann Dvorak, Barry Sullivan, Margaret Phillips, Jean Hagen, Phyllis Kirk, Sara Haden, Hermes Pan

A sappy vehicle for Turner with only a bit of the gender consciousness hinted in the title and little of the verve of the usual Cukor film. She's a Kansas girl who has come to New York to make a career as a model. Quickly sizing up the social relations for models and the men who can own them, she becomes the penthouse-dwelling mistress of sympathetic Montana mine owner Milland. Key to the story is her hand-wringing over whether she ought to walk out on him when she learns that his wife is an invalid who needs him more than she does. Reviewers considered it a throwback to the "white telephone" films of the middle 1930s, and in many ways it was. But now and then Turner turns it on as a career woman who hits the glass ceiling early and finally has to figure out her own alternatives. The best scenes, however, belong to Dvorak, an embittered fellow model who has seen it all. 108 min.

Life With Father (1947)

WB. Prod: Robert Buckner. Dir: Michael Curtiz. Scr: Donald Ogden Stewart.• Play basis: Howard Lindsay, Russell Crouse, *Life With Father* (1939) based on a memoir by Clarence Day, *God and My Father* (1932). Cast: William Powell, Irene Dunne, Elizabeth Taylor, Edmund Gwenn, Zasu Pitts, Jimmy Lyndon, Martin Milner

One of Stewart's wittiest scripts (arguably the sharpest after HOLIDAY, if not his most socially compelling), offering an especially keen version of the theme familiar to French drama: the subtle subversion of the patriarch by wife, children and the servant class.

Clarence Day's popular reminiscences, first published in the *New Yorker* and later frequently collected in books, provided glimpses of family life in Gaslight Manhattan that were loving but definitely unheroic. Powell is perfect as the successful businessman who simply cannot understand the purely formal nature of his authority. Dunne, in one of the best of her famous maternal roles, carries on the charade by bowing to his authority and insisting that their four sons do as well—while twisting him around their (but especially, her) little fingers. Pitts provides a bit more laughter as the annoying cousin who drops by to stay.

The children's antics are sitcomic, a mild version of Lucy; at their worst, they sell neighbors patent medicine that kills a pet dog. Mostly, their behavior involves spending more money than Powell would imagine reasonable for something like a carriage ride or a new suit of clothes. These incidents mainly provide structure for the dialogue. Stewart's genius, faithfully reflected in Curtiz's direction and the casting choices, was to remain always suspended between the propriety of the bourgeois pater familias, upset at small indignities, and the love within the family that heals all wounds. The film earned Oscar nominations for best actor (Powell), best art direction/set direction, and best color cinematography. 118 min., color.

Lights of Old Santa Fe (1944)

The second pairing of Roy Rogers and Dale Evans, co-written by Gordon Kahn,• is a modern tale of a rodeo company in financial trouble. Roy helps Dale, a spunky entrepreneur who has just about run out of luck thanks to a sneaky business partner who wants to compel her to sell the abandoned ranch she owns because the government is about to pay top dollar for the land. Gabby Hayes supplies the physical comedy, this time more the doddering old man than the mental "idjit." The syncretic high point is the "Cowboy Polka."

A Likely Story (1947)

RKO. Prod: Richard H. Berger. Dir: H. C. Potter. Scr: Bess Taffel.• Script contribution, Waldo Salt.• Story basis: Alexander G. Kenedi. Cast: Bill Williams, Barbara Hale, Sam Levene, Lanny Rees, Dan Tobin

Strictly light but often funny fare, engaging on several levels for the student of film. The plot combines the then-popular theme of a misunderstood medical diagnosis throwing the protagonist into the expectation of an early demise, the Damon Runyon crooks-with-a-heart-of-gold engaged in good deeds and the girl-in-the-city plot.

The film opens with Williams just mustered out of the army after spending time in a hospital for his penchant for day-dreaming his way into a faint (imitating the symptoms of a bad heart). He meets aspiring artist Hale, her kid brother Rees and minor mobster (just out of Sing Sing) Levene on a train to Manhattan. The plot quickly thickens. Falling in love with Hale, Williams determines to help her buy back the family house in Menominee Falls, Wisconsin, by borrowing on his life insurance. Lovable mobster Levene (whose former casino boss has gone so legit that he works nights in a defense factory) puts up $5,000 to collect the half-million when Williams dies.

Much of the interest is directed to child actor Rees, who plays the expected kid role of bringing his sister and Williams together. The unconquerably stubborn woman sacrifices her art when she meets her love match in tenement surroundings of steadfast working-class ethnics who speak broken English. So much for art and feminism. 88 min.

Lilith (1964)

Col. Prod: Robert Rossen.† Dir: Robert Rossen. Scr: Robert Rossen. (Uncredited: Robert Alan Aurthur). Novel basis: J. R. Salamanca, *Lilith* (1961). Cast: Warren Beatty, Jean Seberg, Kim Hunter,•† Gene Hackman, Peter Fonda

Rossen's last film evokes the early 1960s and the concerns of his late work, such as issues of social disorientation (see *David and Lisa*, with blacklistee Howard da Silva, among others) that were nicely concentrated in the novels of the day by the influential Salamanca. Protagonist Beatty is a psychological drifter, back from the army (presumably Korea) in his home town, unable to stick with work or find a life. Offering to work at a mental sanitarium for the wealthy, he is warned by Hunter that it will be a degrading, low-paying job. But he persists and meets the first crew of what will evolve in later sixties films into the usual run of harmless if severely disturbed inmates (including young Hackman). Among them is the deeply manipulative Seberg, spurning the love of the hopelessly insecure Fonda. Who has the tighter grip on reality?, Beatty wonders, as he begins to slide into his own breakdown.

Hunter's character remains hooded but vaguely fascinating, her benevolence too good and a bit too seductive to believe. In real life, she was blacklisted, moved to television and finally succumbed to the pressure and became a friendly witness. Jean Seberg was ferociously persecuted and hounded to suicide by the FBI for her support of radical causes, especially the Black Panthers. Rossen never ceased surrounding himself with talented people on the edge. 114 min.

The Limping Man (1953)

Banner Pictures. Prod: Donald Ginsberg. Dir: Charles De laTour. Scr: Ian Stuart Black, Reginald Long (uncredited script contribution: Cyril Endfield.•). Story basis: Anthony Verney. Cast: Lloyd Bridges,† Moira Lister, Leslie Phillips, Hélène Cordet, Alan Wheatley, Rachel Roberts, Jean Marsh

First British job for Endfield, who actually rose above his standard B-Hollywood work as he gravitated toward directing low-budget but also more artful pictures. This one, interestingly, stars Bridges, who never quite gave up his sentimental picture of himself as progressive, despite having given friendly testimony to HUAC. Good pace, good acting (all Brits except Bridges), but the melodrama runs out of plot (with a familiar twist).

Bridges is an American GI returning to London after six years to take up again with Lister, a rather thrill-crazy actress. The day he arrives, a man whom he was talking to is assassinated by a sniper. British cops Wheatley and Phillips become more and more suspicious of Bridges, who determines to crack the case himself. 76 min.

Little Caesar (1931)

First National. Prod: Hal B. Wallis, Darryl F. Zanuck. Dir: Mervyn LeRoy. Scr: Francis Faragoh,• Robert N. Lee, Robert Lord (uncredited: Darryl F. Zanuck). Novel basis: W. R. Burnett, *Little Caesar* (1929). Cast: Edward G. Robinson, Douglas Fairbanks Jr., Glenda Farrell, William Collier, Jr., Sidney Blackmer, Ralph Ince, Thomas E. Jackson, Stanley Fields, Maurice Black, George E. Stone, Armand Kaliz, Nicholas Bela

Deservedly renowned classic of the genre and the first of the in-effect adaptations (including another crime classic twenty years later, THE ASPHALT JUNGLE) of the nonprogressive but brilliant Burnett by left-wing screenwriters. Like his friend and comrade John Wexley, Faragoh had just the touch for making criminality a revenge for the hatred of official society felt by the early

1930s film audience; but he lacked the good fortune of Wexley to keep working with a genuine star (Cagney, for several more years).

The unforgettable Rico, played by Robinson (himself a definite film progressive until the blacklist approached), is more than a mug. Like "the public enemy" in the movie of the same name, he is a social type, a man who relishes his stature as a criminal and his power over the refined types whom he despises (and over women as well). Starting his notorious career knocking over gas stations, he joins a mob run by a mysterious king of the underworld. He also runs the life of his moll (Farrell). Eventually, Rico stages a raid on a cabaret owned by his rivals, in the process murders a police commissioner and then challenges one after another of competing figures until only the "king" stands in his way. His downfall lies in the decency of his pal, played by Fairbanks, and his own vanity, which clever detective Collier plays on to trap him in a shootout. "Is this the end of Rico?" Yup, but only the beginning for the genre. 80 min.

The Little Foxes (1941)

RKO. Prod: Samuel Goldwyn. Dir: William Wyler. Scr: Lillian Hellman● (additional dialogue: Arthur Kober, Dorothy Parker,● Alan Campbell.●) Play basis: Lillian Hellman, The Little Foxes (1939). Cast: Bette Davis, Herbert Marshall, Teresa Wright, Richard Carlson, Dan Duryea, Patricia Collinge, Charles Dingle

Hellman's cinematic high point (along with WATCH ON THE RHINE), with the notable assistance of Wyler, Parker and husband Campbell in bringing the stage production to the mass audience. Bosley Crowther, normally a master of understatement, called it "one of the most cruelly realistic character studies yet shown on the screen," a judgment that 50-some more years of movies has not changed.

The story of second-generation carpetbaggers in the American South circa 1900, all eager for the family estate, sets up greed in all Hellman's favorite ways (race is hardly a factor here—that theme was never her forté). The wickedest of them is Davis, who replaced Tallulah Bankhead from the theatrical version. (Much of the cast carried over, including Duryea.) Davis conspires regularly against brothers Duryea and Dingle for the old man's money while neglecting husband Marshall, the most decent member of the clan, finally letting him die of a heart attack by denying him the needed medicine. Her daughter, Wright, is the lucky one, eloping with Carlson so as to escape the deadening atmosphere. Greg

Tolland's camerawork foreshadows the breakthroughs of James Wong Howe in the film's prequel, ANOTHER PART OF THE FOREST. There is nothing like Foxes in revealing the power of the cash nexus to reduce human beings to worms. Prestigious Hellman-haters, like literary critic Diana Trilling, viewed capitalism as the liberating alternative to its rivals, and therefore harped determinedly on the assorted personal and political sins of Hellman and Hammett; but Hellman-haters never really discuss the power of her talent. 116 min.

Little Giant (1946)

Universal. Prod: Joseph Gershenson. Dir: William A. Seiter. Scr: Walter DeLeon. Story basis: Paul Jarrico,● Richard Collins.† Cast: Bud Abbott, Lou Costello, Brenda Joyce, Jacqueline de Wit, George Cleveland, Elena Verdugo, Mary Gordon, Pierre Watkin

The most politically effective of the Abbott and Costello comedies, perhaps because the prime source of humor is not another popular cultural icon (such as Frankenstein or the Wolf Man) but the folklore of capitalism itself. Also unique because the duo do not appear as partners but as antagonists.

A farm boy in Cucomunga, Lou takes a recorded correspondence course in salesmanship. Brimming with confidence in the power of the sales talk to get people to buy what they do not need, he leaves his old mother and loving girlfriend to make it big in Los Angeles, where his uncle works for a door-to-door vacuum cleaner sales company. There he runs into Abbott, playing the crooked boss, and immediately blunders into getting fired. Exiled to Stockton, he accidentally sets a one-day sales record and is brought back to L.A., where after many misadventures he exposes the essentially predatory nature of salesmanship itself. 92 min.

The Little Minister (1934)

RKO. Prod: Pandro S. Berman. Dir: Richard Wallace. Scr: Jane Murfin, Sarah Y. Mason, Victor Heerman (script contributions: Mortimer Offner,● Jack Wagner). Play basis: Sir James M. Barrie, The Little Minister (1897). Cast: Katharine Hepburn, John Beal, Alan Hale, Donald Crisp, Lumsden Hare, Andy Clyde, Beryl Mercer, Billy Watson, Dorothy Stickney, Mary Gordon, Frank Conroy, Eily Malyon, Reginald Denny

This popular fin de siècle British play was made twice as silent films in the United States. This sound version was budgeted at $650,000 and was a loss for the studio. It should have been perfect for Hepburn, but contributed to her reputation as an uppity woman who would have to be redeemed later through softening, glamorizing and finally pairing with gruff Spencer Tracy. The sentimental class and regional ambience of Scottish industrial village culture, which meant so much to earlier audiences (the play was produced for American radio as well), did not play well with U.S. movie viewers.

Nevertheless, it's quite an odd piece of Scottish (actually, pseudo-Scottish) historical drama. It concerns diminutive preacher Beal, who has devoted himself to becoming the parson his widowed mother wants him to be. His diminutive stature reflects his timorous character, which makes him "just the right size" in every sense for Hepburn. She dresses like a gypsy (and was apparently left behind by them as a baby), but is actually the fiancée of the local lord and somehow totally unknown to the townsfolk. They first hear her singing on the Sabbath (quite a sin), and then in a series of forest encounters she befriends Beal, who later joins the town government only to find himself in the middle of a protest against the lowering of wages by manufacturers of the weaving district. Hepburn, instinctively radical, fools him into sounding the horn for the working people to gather as the soldiers approach. He speaks against violence, but she convinces the crowd to gather up stones and pelt the invaders (and even puts a clod in Beal's hand so that he inadvertently hits the commander).

As Beal becomes increasingly intoxicated with her in a series of delightful exchanges ("Can a man love a woman against his will?") they become the object of rumor, and he is considered unreliable by puritanical Presbyterian elders. In desperation to save him, Hepburn vows to "go away" and convinces the lord to take her to Europe for a honeymoon after a hasty marriage. Hepburn was never a more charming vixen, wooing and wheedling her man into idealism while deeply desiring his love. 110 min.

Little Miss Nobody (1936)
One of a series of vehicles for Jane Withers co-written by Edward Eliscu• and his friends to play on the spunky image of the child actor (a rival to Shirley Temple). She's a foundling who conspires to prevent the adoption of an orphan home playmate (Betty Jean Hainey) without herself by faking a fire drill and turning the hose on the son of the would-be adopter.

The Living Ghost (1942)
An inauspicious beginning for Howard Dimsdale's• curious and often fascinating career in various zones of B-features.

Plump, kidding detective James Dunn finds a house full of suspects for the apparent murder of its patriarch (who isn't really dead after all, just missing). Too many twists and turns and too many bad jests. A big snore.

The Locket (1946)
Although she never received the writing credit she deserved, Norma Barzman• wrote the essential scenes in this tale of a man who discovers that his wife has some neurotic compulsions, including kleptomania, left over from conflicts in her childhood. The premise cleverly allowed Barzman to exploit two hot film trends simultaneously: psychoanalysis and the technique of advancing a story backwards, i.e. through flashbacks, the latter used here as a peeling away of memories, some false and some true. The result is a complex and memorable little RKO noir.

The Long, Hot Summer (1958)
Jerry Wald Prod./20th. Prod: Jerry Wald. Dir: Martin Ritt.• Scr: Irving Ravetch,† Harriett Frank, Jr. Story basis: William Faulkner short stories. Cast: Paul Newman, Joanne Woodward, Anthony Franciosa, Orson Welles, Lee Remick, Angela Lansbury, Richard Anderson, Sarah Marshall, Mabel Albertson

The first Newman/Woodward pairing and the first of Ritt's Southern dramas—a region he favored from college days in the South before he became a New York actor and blacklistee. A fine Faulkner adaptation with Welles as the small-town tycoon who gets his own way until he hires casual laborer Newman, on the move from trouble he caused in a nearby county. Pretty soon he stirs romantic feelings in Welles' unmarried but independent-minded daughter (Woodward), and intense resentment from failed son Franciosa. Such is Welles' psychological makeup or sneaking fondness for the schemer of the LITTLE FOXES variety that he encourages the resulting conflict. Remick, as the lame-brain wife of Franciosa, and Lansbury as a spirited (even lusty) middle-aged Southern belle stir the pot further, but the characters often seem to provide stagey dialogue for the real picture of the rural South at its hottest, delivered convincingly in lush color and CinemaScope. The overlong story finally bogs down, but the film would nevertheless last—unlike Peyton Place, Wald's Calvinist film about small town scandal, which was a bigger hit with a less convincing backdrop and script. The pasted-on happy ending is troublesome, but the film was a big step up for Newman and Woodward, now moving toward the blacklistee-style realism that would quickly become their specialty. 118 min.

The Long Night (1947)

RKO. Prod: Raymond Hakim, Robert Hakim, Anatole Litvak. Dir: Anatole Litvak. Scr: John Wexley.• Screenplay basis: Jacques Viot, *Le jour se lève* (1939). Cast: Henry Fonda, Barbara Bel Geddes, Vincent Price, Ann Dvorak, Howard Freeman, Moroni Olsen, Elisha Cook, Jr., Queenie Smith

A remake of the last great film of the French Popular Front before the German invasion of World War II, Marcel Carné's *Le jour se lève* (*Daybreak*)—a simple story but also a complex allegory about the dispossession of the wartime working class, here successfully translated to the U.S. screen by the experienced Warner Brothers team of Wexley and Litvak.

In the original, Jean Gabin played a French worker who locks himself up in his room after killing a vaudevillian who trains both his dogs and his women with torture, including a young woman Gabin had fallen in love with. The grim mood of the film perfectly captured the pessimism of a France on the eve of World War II as sectors of the country's upper-middle class prepared to welcome the Germans.

The U.S. version casts Fonda as a veteran of the Battle of the Bulge disillusioned by the failing hope that life would be better after the war. As the film opens, a blind man (Cook) is climbing the stairs of a rooming house when he hears gunshots, which turn out to be fatal for a middle-aged man who comes crashing down the stairs. When the cops are summoned, more bullets tear through the door at the top of the stairs. It's Joe (Fonda), who is now a desperate criminal, surrounded by cops who would like nothing more than to get rid of the problem by pumping him full of holes. In a long flashback, we learn that Joe is morose over two failed love affairs, one with the assistant (Bel Geddes) of the vaudevillian (Price) and the other with the more-or-less innocent young woman (Dvorak) whom both he and Price have been wooing. This four-way tug of hearts is the frame for exploring class relationships and eventual murder and retribution. The social allegory does not translate effortlessly from prewar France to postwar United States, and the ending is changed to meet front-office demands, but it is nonetheless an artful attempt to capture the sense of an important French film that very few Americans could have had the opportunity to see.

This is one of the more important postwar noir films, made on the cusp of the repression in Hollywood. Soon work of this kind would disappear, and indeed the film was lost for decades until video sleuths at Kino International rediscovered and re-released it in 2000. Among other things, it is a reminder of the directing skills of the Russian-born Litvak, who survived blacklisting in Berlin and Paris before coming to the United States in the 1930s,

and left again as soon as the Hollywood blacklist began (though he was never named). 101 min.

Lord Jeff (1938)

MGM. Prod: Frank Davis, Sam Wood. Dir: Sam Wood. Scr: James Kevin McGuinness (uncredited: Frank Davis, Sam Wood, Walter Ferris). Story basis: Bradford Ropes, Val Burton,• Endre Boehm. Cast: Freddie Bartholomew, Mickey Rooney, Charles Coburn, Herbert Mundin, Terry Kilburn, Gale Sondergaard,• Peter Lawford, Walter Tetley, Emma Dunn, Monty Woolley, Peter Ellis, George Zucco, Matthew Boulton

Dedicated to the founder of orphanage homes in England and best remembered as the American debut of British-born Peter Lawford, this film, like BLOSSOMS IN THE DUST, is an evocation of the good-heartedness of those who care for orphaned children. Also notable as one of the first cases involving screenwriters' credits: Ropes took out a full-page *Variety* ad asserting that he had written two-thirds of the dialogue.

In London, youthful scalawag Bartholomew works with Sondergaard to bilk jewelry stores. Bartholomew is caught and sent to Dr. Barnardo's Home for Orphaned Boys. The kindly director Coburn and his wife Dunn try to steer Bartholomew right, but he remains a tough case. Rooney, one of the fellow inmates, refuses to inform on an escape plan and so is barred from a student cruise on the *Queen Mary*. Bartholomew's former gang pals try to get him to rejoin them, and when he refuses, frame him with some jewels. 85 min.

Loss of Innocence (1961)

Howard Koch• adapted Rumer Godden's novel, *The Greengage Summer* (1958), for this visually romantic but uninspired continental drama about a girl, adeptly played by Susannah York, who is forced to grow up through a love affair. More interesting is the depiction of the wine country, with a visit to historic Reims.

Lost Angel (1944)

MGM. Prod: Robert Sisk. Dir: Roy Rowland. Scr: Isobel Lennart.† Story basis: Angna Enters. Cast: Margaret O'Brien, James Craig, Marsha Hunt,• Philip Merivale, Henry O'Neill, Donald Meek, Keenan Wynn, Alan Napier, Sara Haden, Kathleen Lockhart, Walter Fenner, Howard Freeman, Elisabeth Risdon, Robert Blake

A vehicle for little O'Brien, a wartime Shirley Temple (but a more capable actor), showing an iconoclastic view of scientific child-rearing. Poor Margaret is being raised to become a genius by specialists (like Professors O'Neill and Meek) in an insular clinic. She is a young know-it-all but never has any fun, and at the first opportunity makes her escape with the help of reporter Craig. Through him, she gets to be a "real" little girl—and then some. Runyonesque gangster Wynn is so charmed by her that he goes straight, and Craig falls into the arms of Hunt, who as a nightclub dancer first makes O'Brien jealous, then shows her what a glamorous mom looks like. 91 min.

Lost Horizon (1937)
Col. Prod: Frank Capra. Dir: Frank Capra. Scr: Robert Riskin (script contribution: Sidney Buchman•). Novel basis: James Hilton, Lost Horizon (1933). Cast: Ronald Colman, Jane Wyatt, John Howard, Edward Everett Horton, Thomas Mitchell, Margo, Isabel Jewell, H. B. Warner, Sam Jaffe,• Richard Loo

Columbia's most expensive film to that time is arguably an antiwar drama about a utopia where the woes of the world remain unknown—with a bit of H. Rider Haggard's She-like fantasy thrown in. Ironically, the Brits who are the main protagonists have been rescued (actually, kidnapped) from the Chinese revolution by Ronald Colman, diplomat and author. Their plane crash in Asian mountains leaves the handful stranded in a mysterious valley paradise. Their lama-guide H. B. Warner (in yellow face) explains that the society of Shangri-La was created centuries before by a Belgian priest, Father Perrault—a high lama who still runs the place! And what's more, he is none other than Marxist Sam Jaffee! Inspired by the high lama's message of freedom and peace, Colman goes into the Valley of the Blue Moon and comes across the lovely Wyatt, who confesses that it was her idea that Colman be kidnapped because his books had expressed an idealism compatible with Shangri-La's. Everything subsides into peace, harmony and crypto-socialism until fellow Britisher John Howard, Colman's brother, grows restless and vows to escape from paradise regardless of the risk. Finally persuading Colman to go along, he precipitates disaster for them all. The mood of the film is what has endured. 133 min.

Louisa (1950)
U-I. Prod: Robert Arthur. Dir: Alexander Hall. Scr: Stanley Roberts.† Cast: Ronald Reagan, Charles Coburn, Ruth Hussey, Edmund Gwenn, Spring Byington, Piper Laurie, Scotty Beckett, Jimmy Hunt, Connie Gilchrist, Willard Waterman, Marjorie Crossland, Martin Milner, Terry Frost, Dave Willock

One of nearly a half-dozen red-written films (and as apolitical textually or subtextually as the rest) to feature the future right-wing president, but a tale improved by the comedy of old age romance with the great sentimental actor Gwenn and future sitcom star Byington as his would-be amour. Three-generation romantic complications are cross-fertilized in a suburban setting that looks ahead to television, with the thirties-style recognition of economic woes now forgotten, and with social embarrassment substituting for social angst. 89 min.

Louisiana Purchase (1941)
Para. Exec. Prod: Buddy G. DeSylva. Dir: Irving Cummings. Scr: Jerome Chodorov,• Joseph Fields. Stage musical basis: Irving Berlin, Morrie Ryskind, Louisiana Purchase (1940), based on a story by Buddy G. DeSylva. Cast: Bob Hope, Vera Zorina, Victor Moore, Dona Drake, Irene Bordoni, Raymond Walburn, Max "Slapsie Marxie" Rosenblum, Frank Albertson, Phyllis Ruth

Based on the hit Broadway musical by mainstream comedy scripter Ryskind (a Hollywood right-winger who eagerly gave testimony against the future blacklistees), this Hope vehicle offers all the evidence anyone needs that social values were either missing or dreadful in at least some of the work blacklistees did. Light comedy fare with many Hope wisecracks and lots of mediocre music offers a modest send-up of a Fred Allen–style "Senator Foghorn" South, full of oddball but actually rather sympathetic white American Dixiecrats.

Hope is implicated in a crooked merchandising company and can get off the hook only by blackmailing a senator, a scheme that coincides with Mardi Gras time in New Orleans. He enlists Zorina, an Austrian refugee from the Nazis, and simultaneously falls in love with her. She lures the dumb and middle-aged Moore into a compromising situation, then has moral qualms—and complications flourish. Remarkably, New Orleans bordello owner Bordoni also gets into the act, and Rosenblum is on hand as an enforcer. More remarkably, the Mardi Gras parade turns up not a single non-white face in the crowd! In the climactic scene, Hope filibusters the Senate by reading Gone with the Wind. 95 min., color.

Love Affair (1939)
RKO. Prod: Leo McCarey. Dir: Leo McCarey. Scr: Delmer Daves, Donald Ogden Stewart.• Story: Leo McCarey, Mildred Cram. Cast: Irene Dunne, Charles Boyer, Maria Ouspenskaya, Lee Bowman, Astrid Allwyn, Maurice Moscovitch

The original and best version of a film McCarey remade in 1957 as *An Affair to Remember* with Cary Grant and Deborah Kerr (the film was remade a second time, miserably, in 1994 with Warren Beatty) is a combination witty romance-drama and tearjerker, exceptionally strong on the gender line.

Fellow cruise voyagers Boyer (the famous playboy en route to marry an heiress) and Dunne (of modest background, with a business career and no marriage in sight) fall in love. The perky Dunne, intent at first on resisting Boyer's advances (telling him that the continental style of lovemaking will never, at least in the United States, "replace baseball"), caves in after they visit his aged grandmother in enchanted Majorca. But he has no occupation, and he wants to prove himself. They agree to meet in six months at the top of the Empire State Building. She is prevented from meeting him by a tragic coincidence, and so the longed-for embrace is postponed through a series of sad misunderstandings until the end of the tale, by which time the audience has exhausted its folded linen.

Along with Katharine Hepburn elsewhere, Dunne provides Stewart (and his collaborators) the best opportunity he will have to compare hard-working ordinary folks (here the honest middle class) with the idle rich and to push the battle of the sexes into a wider social drama. 87 min.

Love Begins at Twenty (1936)

First National Pictures/WB. Prod: Brian Foy (uncredited). Dir: Frank McDonald. Scr: Dalton Trumbo,• Tom Reed. Play basis: Martin Flavin, *Broken Dishes* (1929). Cast: Hugh Herbert, Warren Hull, Patricia Ellis, Hobart Cavanaugh, Mary Treen, Dorothy Vaughan, Clarence Wilson, Robert Glecker, Anne Negel

One of Trumbo's domestic comedies, unpleasantly memorable for its henpecked husband theme but lightened by O. Henryesque humor. Herbert's wife Ellis and his boss Cavanaugh both pick on him constantly. Robbed of bonds he has been sent to deposit, he is told that he has to make up the difference himself. A failure in his wife's eyes, he is repeatedly compared to the man she could have married. When left behind to wash dishes while his wife goes to the movies, he drinks too much, winds up at a lodge meeting and gets the missing bonds slipped back into his coat pocket. 57 min.

Love Happy (1950)

Artists Alliance/UA. Prod: Lester Cowan, Mary Pickford. Dir: David Miller, Leo McCarey (uncredited). Scr: Mac Benoff,† Frank Tashlin, Ben Hecht (uncredited). Story

basis: Harpo Marx. Cast: Groucho Marx, Chico Marx, Harpo Marx, Vera-Ellen, Ilona Massey, Marion Hutton, Raymond Burr

A very late Marx Brothers (just the favorite three) lumped uneasily into the "Let's Put On a Musical" format for famed silent screen star Pickford's own production company. Many moments of fun, with some of the pleasure in seeing Chico and Harpo near retirement, their faces lined and their physical stunts cut back but their zest almost undiminished. At last, Harpo got one of his own stories made, but probably a decade too late: this is a fondly faded version of the 1930s, very much minus Margaret Dumont. It's not so much that they lack the energy as that the thematic moment has passed.

A diamond smuggling (and murder) ring of pretty silly criminals, headed by an overaged femme fatale (who can still put the "whammy" on men, a kind of science-fiction power that predictably backfires with Harpo), plants their jewels in a tin of sardines and then loses the can to omnivorous light-fingered Harpo. Meanwhile, a musical run by and for young actors is threatened with being closed before it even opens, and a romance between the leading figures is even more predictably endangered. Groucho is the detective trying to find out the phone numbers of the chorus girls. Fast-talking Chico is meanwhile Harpo's intermediary (best gag moment has him once more interpreting Harpo's pantomimes, first in person and then over the phone!), as well as the hustler who keeps the show going when it teeters toward financial collapse. 85 min.

Love Has Many Faces (1965)

One of the comeback films for Marguerite Roberts• that she could not take seriously. Lana Turner is an aging former beauty who wants desperately to hold onto her beachboy husband (Cliff Robertson) when he starts running around with cutie Stefanie Powers.

Love Is On the Air (1937)

One of Morton Grant's• few non-westerns, an early seminoir and Ronald Reagan's screen debut. A president of the local Better Business Bureau disappears after announcing that he can prove a club owner is part of organized crime. Reagan, a radio announcer here as in real life, is almost fired for defending the missing man, then demoted to the children's hour, which he takes on location, broadcasting kids in their daily activities. There he gets the clues to pursue the disappearance and finds fresh cement under a garage, evidently concealing a body. Vindicated, he returns to his job triumphant. A curiosity.

Love Me Forever (1935)
A musical with crime plot co-written by Sidney Buchman.• When loveable mobster Leo Carillo falls hard for opera singer Grace Moore, he builds his life around her, including a night club—but she falls for someone else.

Lucky Boy (1929)
Viola Brothers Shore• wrote the story for this Georgie Jessel ripoff of the popular Al Jolson Jazz Singer theme, with a touch of George M. Cohan thrown in. Son of a Bronx jeweler, Jessel (playing himself) wants to hit the big time in show biz, while dad (William H. Strauss) thinks he should stay put, mending watches and inspecting diamonds.

Lucky Legs (1942)
B-comedy star Jinx Falkenburg inherits a million dollars, plunging her into an assortment of predicaments. Written by Stanley Rubin.†

Luxury Girls (1952)
The only fully realized screenplay of Norma Barzman.* Shot in Italy under the direction of Bernard Vorhaus,* it tells the story of an exclusive boarding school where one of the girls gets pregnant and, in choosing an abortion, draws the sympathy of her classmates. (After she attempts suicide, her parents agree to the procedure.) Both screenwriter and director flew under the radar, borrowing names for the credits. Distributed in Europe under the title of *Fanciulle di lusso,* it surfaced in the U.S. only in 2003.

M

M (1951)

Col. Prod: Seymour Nebenzal. Dir: Joseph Losey.• Scr: Norman Reilly Raine, Leo Katcher, Waldo Salt.• Screenplay basis: Thea von Harbou, Fritz Lang, Paul Falkenberg, Adolf Jansen, Karl Vash (based on an article by Egon Jackson). Cast: David Wayne, Howard da Silva, Luther Adler, Martin Gabel, Steve Brodie, Raymond Burr, Glenn Anders, Karen Morley,• Norman Lloyd, John Miljan, Walter Burke, Roy Engel, Jim Backus

Remake of Fritz Lang's 1931 German classic about a serial murderer of children. In this update, the killer (Wayne) terrorizes Los Angeles and leaves only one clue: he takes the victims' shoes. Da Silva is the police inspector who must follow a crooked trail. Threatened by the generalized police crackdown, the local mob sends out the word that it will find the killer and bump him off. A pool hustler eventually places the letter "M" in chalk on the killer' s back. As a little girl points to the letter, Wayne rabbits and the gangsters give chase. Brought to a cab company garage and subjected to a kangaroo court, Wayne pleads to be punished. Only the arrival of the cops keeps the crowd from ripping him apart. Best scene: as per Lang's original, Wayne is alone in his apartment, playing a flute and fondling a victim's shoes, turning a lump of clay into a child-like figure and crushing it suddenly. Although closely following the original, Losey and the new scriptwriters managed to increase the emphasis on the need to understand the abnormal psychology of extreme criminal behavior (in place of public panic and the lynching impulse). Interestingly, Nebenzal produced both the Lang and Losey versions. 87 min.

Ma and Pa Kettle at Waikiki (1955)

U-I. Prod: Leonard Goldstein. Dir: Lee Sholem. Scr: Jack Henley, Harry Clork, Elwood Ullman. Story basis: Connie Lee• [Bennett], from characters created by Betty MacDonald, *The Egg and I* (1945). Cast: Marjorie Main, Percy Kilbride, Lori Nelson, Byron Palmer, Loring Smith, Lowell Gilmore, Mabel Albertson, Esther Dale, Ida Moore

The actual footage of this film was shot years earlier and held back while other Kettle sagas were released. Eventually, some nine films pretty much exhausted the material. This is the last film released with Pa (Kilbride), leaving most of the cast to stumble on through two more. Sholem was a veteran with long ties to Hollywood progressives, including several script collaborations with Harold Buchman and a marvelously radical *Superman and the Mole Men*, which he directed. Lee's story was accepted before the curtain fell and remained on the print even after she was blacklisted.

Pa Kilbride, normally the hesitant type, is time and again thrown into action by Ma, played to the hilt by the large and vigorous Main. In this case, a cousin in Waikiki is not well and begs Kilbride to take over his pineapple-canning factory while he recuperates. Main and eldest daughter Nelson head for Hawaii, where pop has managed to blow up the plant and get himself snarled in a conspiracy involving a competitor trying to corner the canned fruit business. Pa Kettle as any kind of tycoon can only be farcical, and maybe that was the point. 79 min.

Macao (1952)

RKO. Prod: Alex Gottlieb. Dir: Josef von Sternberg (uncredited: Nicholas Ray). Scr: Stanley Rubin,† Bernard C. Schonfeld† (uncredited: Edward Chodorov•), Norman Katkov, Frank L. Moss. Cast: Robert Mitchum, Jane Russell, William Bendix, Gloria Grahame, Thomas Gomez, Philip Ahn

Exotic Mitchum actioner with "she of the full-figured girdle" and Thomas Gomez in what would be yellow face if the film weren't black and white. The island off China is one of those notorious dens of sin and sex, whose émigré Americans are misfits of various sorts. Mitchum shot a man in a fight, Bendix apparently did some financial juggling and Russell (who has some good tough-talking lines in the first half hour), a small-time con artist, seems a lot like a call girl looking for a fresh start or at least a new location. Casino owner Ahn, a bigger crook, is bored with chippie Grahame and wants to get his hands on Russell; police chief Gomez is trying to figure out who's working with the American cops. Before that's all straightened out, Mitchum and Russell go through a romantic interlude and tumble. The film is more style than substance, with loud echoes from Sternberg's two Shanghai films. The heavy use of left-wingers (including Ray, brought in at the end to finish the project) suggests not a conscious effort to make a red movie but a desperate attempt to give some clarity of motives to a sinking plot. 81 min.

Mackenna's Gold (1969)
Col./Highroad Production. Prod: Carl Foreman,• Dimitri Tiomkin. Dir J. Lee Thompson. Scr: Carl Foreman. Novel basis: Heck Allen (as "Will Henry"), *Mackenna's Gold* (1963). Cast: Gregory Peck, Camilla Sparv, Omar Sharif, Julie Newmar, Keenan Wynn, Telly Savalas, Dick Peabody, Ted Cassidy, Eduardo Ciannelli, Lee J. Cobb,† Burgess Meredith, Edward G. Robinson, Eli Wallach, Raymond Massey, John Garfield, Jr. (i.e., David Garfield), Victory Jory (narrator)

This movie raised high hopes because it was Carl Foreman's return to the American screen in the genre he transformed with HIGH NOON. In fact, Foreman refashioned the Allen novel into a kind of sequel to the Hadleyville saga. In the original, men refused to back up the U.S. marshall in a showdown because they feared the notoriety would spoil the chances of investment from interested parties "up North." Here the impulse that favored capital investment over social justice leads the same men to join the sheriff on a wild goose chase for buried gold based on little more than a sketchy Indian map. It all winds up, predictably, in a laissez-faire free-for-all full of gunfire and treachery. The result is an overlong, confusing actioner with occasional glimpses of a magnificent opportunity lost. 128 min., color.

The Macomber Affair (1947)
UA. Prod: Benedict Bogeaus, Casey Robinson. Dir: Zoltan Korda. Scr: Casey Robinson, Seymour Bennett.• Adaptation: Seymour Bennett, Frank Arnold. Story basis: Ernest Hemingway, "The Short Happy Life of Francis Macomber" (1944). Cast: Gregory Peck, Joan Bennett, Robert Preston, Reginald Denny, Carl Harbord, Jean Gillie, Earl Smith, Frederic Worlock

This was to be Seymour Bennett's opening to the big time, but it came too late (his wife Connie Lee of the BLONDIEseries was also slated for the blacklist); it may be one of the two best films made (along with *For Whom the Bell Tolls*) from Hemingway fiction.

Treacherous wife Joan Bennett despises her big-game hunter husband Preston, and he deserves it. When he backs down from a confrontation with a lion, she gives him the raspberry, cuckolds him with guide Peck, and finally gives him a bullet in the back of his head. He survives, though (unlike the original story), and meanwhile she gets hers from Peck, who recognizes her for the creature that she is. Lots of atmospheric outdoor scenes and hunting shots underline the rugged charm of the film for at least some viewers. Hollywood ending (and beginning) is unconvincing but does not ruin a tight drama. 89 min.

Madame DuBarry (1934)
WB. Exec. Prod: Jack L. Warner, Hal B. Wallis. Dir: William Dieterle. Scr: Edward Chodorov• (also story basis). Cast: Dolores del Rio, Reginald Owen, Victor Jory, Osgood Perkins, Verree Teasdale, Ferdinand Gottschalk, Anita Louise, Maynard Holmes, Henry O'Neill, Hobart Cavanaugh, Dorothy Tree,• Virginia Sale, Camille Rovelle

Costume drama about DuBarry, introduced to the court of Louis XV by Duc de Richelieu; she soon reorders the entire scene to fit her own infamous demands, like the summer night she orders up a sleigh ride and all Paris' sugar is used for the purpose. In a gesture of defiance, she shows up at court in a nightgown after the Duc de Choiseul (O'Neill) has her gown stolen to prevent her appearance.

The third remake of the story is the most lavish WB production to that date and a major career step for Chodorov, who shows how imperial decadence is the collective delusion of a class sensing its own demise. Even the lower orders of the aristocracy share this awareness. (Louis: "What are you trying to do to France?" DuBarry: "Only what it is doing to me.") The mood is set throughout by long quotes from Mozart's *Marriage of Figaro*, whose political purpose (with librettist Da Ponte) was not far from Chodorov's. Interestingly, the Catholic Church put the film on its "condemned" list, probably in gratitude to DuBarry's memory, because of her role in a real-life plot to bring down Choiseul after he tried to expel the Jesuits from France. 79 min.

The Mad Martindales (1942)
Francis Edward Faragoh• was called in to do the film version of a Wesley Towner adaptation of an unproduced German play, which may explain why Twentieth Century-Fox asked German director Alfred L. Werker to direct. The story turns on an eccentric *fin de siècle* San Francisco family up to its ears in antiques and debt, and the efforts by the daughters to marry well.

Mademoiselle Fifi (1944)
RKO. Prod: Val Lewton. Dir: Robert Wise. Scr: Josef Mischel,• Peter Ruric. Story basis: Guy de Maupassant, "Madamoiselle Fifi" (1882) and "Boule de Suif" (1880). Cast: Simone Simone, John Emery, Kurt Kreuger, Alan Napier, Jason Robards, Sr., Helen Freeman, Norma Varden, Romaine Callender, Fay Helm

An extraordinary historical allegory about social class and collaboration with an occupying army, at times cheesy and at times full of subtle insights. Simone, as the patriotic laundress from a country village, finds herself caught up in the Prussian invasion of France in 1870 (an all-too-evident metaphor for the Nazi invasion of France). Trapped in a horse-drawn carriage with a group of would-be upper-class expatriates, she learns that they are eager to collaborate with the enemy for the sake of their own security, comfort and pocketbooks. Only one is different, an intellectual agitator who fled the armed resistance after making strong speeches.

When she finally submits to having dinner with a Prussian officer for the sake of the others, she is treated by them as a tart. Leaving the journey to become an urban laundress, she experiences the same collaboration among her working-class sisters. But the revolutionary follows her, and the idealistic young town priest takes up the struggle as well. Like the later resistance, it is a lone, almost existential decision to confront the conquerors. Interesting to compare carriage scenes with those in Ford's *Stagecoach*, also based on de Maupassant. 69 min.

Madigan (1968)

Universal. Prod: Frank P. Rosenberg. Dir: Don Siegel. Scr: Abraham Polonsky,• Howard Rodman (under pseudonym Henri Simoun). Novel basis: Richard Dougherty, *The Commissioner* (1962). Cast: Richard Widmark, Henry Fonda, Inger Stevens, Harry Guardino, James Whitmore, Susan Clark, Don Stroud, Michael Dunn, Steven Ihnat, Raymond St. Jacques, Lloyd Gough,• Sheree North

The *policier* that returned the long-blacklisted Abraham Polonsky to the big screen under his own name after 17 years. It was already a bit of an anachronism when it was filmed because Dougherty's novel dealt with the social tensions of the Kennedy years. By the end of the decade, with inner cities everywhere on fire and the National Guard in the streets, the precinct station was no longer the right stage for the exploration of moral ambiguities.

The spare plot involves a pair of detectives who head for Brooklyn to interview a suspect in illegal gun trafficking they had sent to jail years earlier. The suspect manages to distract and disarm them and steal their weapons, the equivalent of stealing their honor as cops, and the rest of the film is the story of how they risk their lives to get their guns back. Along the way the rigid and moralistic inspector (Fonda, in top form) is revealed to be the source of problems in morale because he can't distinguish between institutional corruption and the petty give-and-take between cops and criminals that are a prerequisite for any productive interaction at all. The film is saved by the

intelligence of Polonsky's screenplay and Don Siegel's always fluent direction. 101 min.

Madigan's Millions (1968)

A late Stanley Prager• screenplay about an unlikely U.S. Treasury agent, played by Dustin Hoffman, tracking down money owed the government by an Italian American gangster who has returned to Europe. Painful even for the most ardent Hoffman fans.

The Magic Face (1951)

Col. Prod: Mort Briskin, Robert Smith. Dir: Frank Tuttle.† Scr: Mort Briskin, Robert Smith. Cast: Luther Adler,• Patricia Knight, William L. Shirer, Ilka Windish, Heinz Moog, Jaspar Von Oertzen, Charles Koenig, Anton Mitterwurzer, Annie Maier, Hermann Ehrhardt

Curious and heartfelt production by the director of THIS GUN FOR HIRE, one of the last of the otherwise modestly talented Tuttle's three dozen films (most made before 1935) and the very last before his friendly testimony. Adler, one of the premier theatrical figures of the Group Theatre, made relatively few film appearances, yet in the same year he also appeared in Joseph Losey's• remake of M.

A master German actor and impersonator (Adler) insinuates himself into Hitler's inner circle, becomes his valet, kills the boss, takes his place and leads Germany to defeat. A bizarre fantasy with surprisingly little political content but worth seeing just for the fact that it could be made. 88 min.

The Magnificent Ambersons (1942)

RKO. Mercury Productions. Prod: Orson Welles. Dir: Orson Welles. Scr: Orson Welles. Novel basis: Booth Tarkington, *The Magnificent Ambersons* (1918). Cast: Orson Welles (narrator), Joseph Cotten, Dolores Costello, Anne Baxter, Tim Holt, Agnes Moorehead, Ray Collins, Erskine Sanford, Richard Bennett

This coulda-been-a-masterpiece was butchered down to 88 minutes from 132, with a rewritten ending and the sacrifice of a full five minutes from the rich ballroom scene that was to establish the characters, their interrelations and the social space they inhabit. Perhaps in part because Welles' CITIZEN KANE had lost money, RKO chief George Schaefer panicked when he saw the first cut, citing "somber music" and uneasy audience reaction at the preview (although recovered comment cards showed many were also highly favorable). The film, about the rise and decline of a Midwestern family, had been cut to Welles' specifications, but by this time he was off in Brazil shooting a good-neighbor film at the request of Nelson Rockefeller, who hoped to use U.S. Popular Front culture to help keep sympathy for fascism at bay there. Some accounts say Welles neglected the task of the final editing, but modern research shows he sent long and detailed instructions back to Hollywood for the revision, nearly all of which were ignored by Schaefer—now with a rival (Charles Koerner, soon to be new RKO chief) and a Welles-hater, breathing down his neck. The Hollywood Left had by now reached its high-water mark of political influence, but the spatchcocking of *Ambersons* on the editing table is properly regarded as the beginning of the end of the Left's artistic influence (perhaps culminating in the gutting, strictly for political reasons, of RKO's CORNERED). In 2002, the A&E television channel remade the film at 150 minutes using the Welles shooting script and later instructions, and successfully laid to rest any doubt that Welles knew best. A skeleton at 88 min.

The Majestic (2001)

Castle Rock Entertainment. Prod: Frank Darabont. Dir: Frank Darabont. Scr: Michael Sloane. Cast: Jim Carrey, Martin Landau, Laurie Holden, Bob Balaban, Brent Briscoe, Amanda Detmer, Allen Garfield, Hal Holbrook, Ron Rifkin, Donald Ogden Stiers. James Whitmore

A Jim Carrey vehicle that is also the latest and among the best explorations of the blacklist to be treated in a feature film. In true Capraesque style, the political saga is squeezed down to fit a small town and its loyalties. But this town, in 1951, somewhere north of L.A., curiously named "Lawson" (the connection with blacklisted writer John Howard Lawson would be impossible to miss), is fated to defend a writer accused—wrongly, as so often—of holding dangerous radical ideas or at the least of dangerous past associations.

The plot not improbably situates Carrey as a hack writer on his way up when he is hit by a subpoena, based on nothing more than a meeting he'd attended years earlier in the company of a girlfriend. (She has since become a television writer, and happily ratted him out to save herself.) After his current girlfriend abandons him, Carrey drunkenly drives north, plunges his car off a bridge—and is found, now an amnesiac, by the kindly doctor played by Whitmore. Again, for insiders, this is particularly delicious: lifelong progressive Whitmore played every role that Left (and other) writers gave him with a broad humanist approach, and in this role he would minister to the victims he'd known well in real life.

Through an accident of mistaken identity (and the power of unfulfilled longing), Carrey becomes the returned war hero who was believed dead. He acquires a pseudo-father in Landau, the owner of a closed and apparently abandoned movie theater and a girlfriend (Holden) who is about to become a civil liberties lawyer and reads him the Bill of Rights. Eventually Carrey recalls his true identity, and about the same time he is "discovered" by the FBI and arrested for flight. In the penultimate scene, he appears in front of HUAC in what is a reprise of the film's opening moments, when footage of the real hearings run under the credits, with John Howard Lawson among those seen resisting questions. Carry must decide whether to desert his career prospects in Hollywood to confront the evil-doers or abandon his hopes as a writer.

Critics complained that the film was maudlin, too obvious in its metaphors and a bad use of Carrey's comic genius to boot. These charges, even when not entirely wrong, were often ungenerous or openly cynical and in some cases purposeful exaggerations. 152 min.

Make Believe Ballroom (1949)

Col. Prod: Ted Richmond. Dir: Joseph Santley. Scr: Albert Duffy, Karen DeWolf.• Story basis: Albert Duffy. Cast: Jerome Courtland, Ruth Warrick, Ron Randell, Virginia Welles, Al Jarvis, Frankie Lane, King Cole Trio, Kay Starr, Jimmy Dorsey, Gene Krupa

An extraordinarily sweet and optimistic movie about two teenagers, carhops at an L.A. drive-in restaurant, whose encyclopedic knowledge of contemporary popular music brings then into conflict over which of them will win a large prize in a radio publicity contest. This slender plot covers a frankly commercial purpose, namely to publicize the then-popular radio show of the same title whose gimmick was to have deejay Jarvis introduce the latest recorded hits with fictional patter describing elegant but imaginary ballroom scenes in which the bands were supposedly playing.

The unlikely result of this weak foundation was the blacklisted DeWolf's finest screenplay, one in which she managed to elevate an early effort at multilevel marketing into a touching depiction of the hopes and aspirations of the postwar Los Angeles working class. Not surprisingly, the dream is not of stronger unions and higher pay but of joining the lower-middle class by owning a drive-in restaurant at which gorgeous carhops in miniskirts and roller skates swoop among the cars like swallows along the eaves; where neon shines with a Technicolor brilliance and the staff summons the highest octaves for the utopian anthem, "Hamburger Heaven." The film is, alas, rarely shown on TV and must be seen to be believed, but it is an example of what a sympathetic (and inspired) writer could achieve even with material hauled up from the bottom drawer of commercial culture. 78 min.

Make Way for a Lady (1936)

Gertrude Purcell• wrote the screenplay for this story of a 15-year-old (Anne Shirley) determined to find a new wife for her widowed father (Herbert Marshall). She causes confusion all around when she mistakenly concludes that a new neighbor, pulp novelist Margot Graham, is the woman of dad's dreams. Actually, he is dreaming of someone else.

Make Your Own Bed (1944)

WB. Prod: Alex Gottlieb. Dir: Peter Godfrey. Scr: Francis Swann, Edmund Joseph. Adaptation: Richard Weil.• Play basis: Harvey J. O'Higgins, Harriet Ford, *On the Hiring Line* (1919). Cast: Jack Carson, Jane Wyman, Alan Hale, Irene Manning, George Tobias

Wartime romp straight out of the Three Stooges style of anarchic populism, with German spies, a mixed-up detective and extremely silly rich people. A rich couple (an unhappy wife and former actress who is compelled by munitions-maker Hale to move with him to the suburbs) have a big servant problem. A very funny scene puts Hale at a Manhattan employment agency full of other rich people desperate for butlers and maids.

Carson, who has a bad record of attempting to arrest the wrong people, becomes convinced (after overhearing radio actors rehearsing their lines) that the place is being overtaken by Nazis who plan to blow up Hale's factory. Meanwhile, romantic mixups galore confuse Wyman and Carson, Hale and Manning with Bob Hope–style comic mayhem. Lots of fun along the way, thanks most of all to Hale. 82 min.

Malcolm X (1992)

40 Acres and a Mule Filmworks/WB. Prod: Marvin Worth, Spike Lee. Dir: Spike Lee. Scr: Arnold Perl,• Spike Lee. Book basis: Malcolm X and Alex Haley, *The Autobiography of Malcolm X* (1965). Cast: Denzel Washington, Angela Bassett, Albert Hall, Al Freeman, Jr., Delroy Lindo, Spike Lee, Theresa Randle, Kate Vernon, Lonette McKee, Tommy Hollis, Giancarlo Esposito, Craig Wasson, John Ottavino, David Patrick Kelly, Shirley Stoler

A major film with a bundle of backstage stories nearly equal to the complications of the real Malcolm's life. The original "property" was Alex Haley's somewhat fictionalized *Autobiography of Malcolm X*. Worth, a jazz producer/manager, comedy writer and former manager for Lenny Bruce, had actually known the young street hustler Malcolm Little back in the forties, acquired the screen rights from Betty Shabazz, Malcolm's widow, and Worth and Haley asked James Baldwin to write the screenplay. When Baldwin worked too slowly for them, Perl was brought in to finish the project. Baldwin's original screenplay (since published as *One Day, When I Was Lost*) had been brilliant (many of the best moments of the final film were his dramatic ideas) but was too difficult to shoot and in many places fatally talky. Perl, an experienced hand at adaptations of all kinds, rewrote the screenplay, but the project languished until the 1980s, when producer-director Norman Jewison dusted it off at WB. Lee, upset that a key African American narrative of resistance would be handled by someone other than a black director, raised his objections in public and managed to gain control of the project. By this time, Perl was gone (he died in 1971). Lee apparently added little more to the screenplay than the ballroom dance scenes at the beginning, and the ending in Mecca, but received co-script credit nonetheless. Perl, a Communist who had turned out first-rate TV work as a director and writer on *East Side/West Side* in the early sixties, also wrote the musical *The World of Sholem Aleichem*, which became FIDDLER ON THE ROOF. Outside of *Malcolm*, however, Perl had virtually no Hollywood credits, not even for *Fiddler*.

The film, at any rate, is epic. Malcolm's tale is narrated carefully and, by the standard of most films, accurately. He is shown as evolving from hipster to dope dealer, prisoner, Muslim, black-power orator and martyr. The final scenes, which accumulate a great deal of power, show his travel to Mecca and his abandonment of racial doctrines for universalism of a sort. His connections with Marxism (his lawyer Conrad Lynn, former Trotskyist of the 1940s, confirmed in his memoirs that toward the end Malcolm read C. L. R. James and established links with the Socialist Workers Party after his break with the Nation of Islam) are, of course, nowhere to be found. 194 min.

The Maltese Falcon (1941)

WB. Assoc. Prod: Henry Blanke. Dir: John Huston. Scr: John Huston. Novel basis: Dashiell Hammett,• *The Maltese Falcon* (1930). Cast: Humphrey Bogart, Mary Astor,

Gladys George, Peter Lorre, Barton MacLane, Lee Patrick, Sydney Greenstreet, Ward Bond, Jerome Cowan, Elisha Cook, Jr., James Burke, Murray Alper, John Hamilton

One of Hollywood's true classics and, along with CASABLANCA, Bogart's best. Also the first directorial effort of Huston (strongly associated with the Popular Front) and the first Hollywood appearance of Greenstreet.

Bogart's predecessors in the role, Ricardo Cortez in the first version and Warren William in the second, were more the lady's men than Bogey's Sam Spade. This detective is almost too haunted for romance, not only with Astor (whom he suspects is a killer even as he's drawn to her), but with his faithful secretary, Effie (Patrick). The killing of his partner shortly after he takes on a case from Astor sets him furiously to solve a rash of murders connected somehow with the pursuit of an invaluable art object, the falcon. The ultimate pointlessness of this search was Hammett's own message about the cupidity that capitalism breeds in everyone. Bogart, like Dick Powell in MURDER, MY SWEET a few years later, faces female treachery that hints at misogyny but is more like a depiction of women scheming on exactly the same terms as men. 100 min.

Mambo (1954)

Para. Prod: Dino de Laurentiis, Carlo Ponti. Dir: Robert Rossen.† Scr: Ennio De Concini, Ivo Perilli, Guido Piovene, Robert Rossen. Cast: Silvana Mangano, Michael Rennie, Vittorio Gassman, Shelly Winters, Katherine Dunham

A fascinating film for many reasons, among them the surrealistic dance sequences choreographed and danced by Katherine Dunham, a West Indian/American associated broadly with left-wing causes from the 1950s to the 1990s. Mysteries abound here. While many U.S. directors, even the friendly witnesses, on occasion tapped into Italian neorealism (the cutting edge of the avant-garde at the time), it is not clear why Rossen chose to follow where mostly blacklistees had likely gone out of sheer necessity (if they wanted to keep working). Writer Perilli also worked on the de Laurentiis production of 5 BRANDED WOMEN with Martin Ritt,• Paul Jarrico• and Michael Wilson,• for example. Also unexplained are the very low production values in this de Laurentiis film, or why the very experienced Rossen, a friendly witness who was in demand in Hollywood, put up with them.

Despite everything, the film holds the interest, most of all in its footage of Venice during its festive moments and daily life, with all its splendor amid impoverishment. The story is told through Mangano, a shopgirl who is spotted by dance-troupe leader Winters as a naïve talent.

To succeed she must leave Venice and her lover Gassman, an out-of-work croupier. She immediately becomes a star, and a gaunt Venice nobleman (Rennie) first cruelly seduces her and then falls in love and proposes marriage. Gassman urges her to accept, knowing the aristocrat, a hemophiliac, is destined for an early grave.

By mid-film the plot subsides into melodrama as Mangano realizes she must choose between art and love. But the Italian sensibility, a mixture of decadent aristocracy, poverty and passion (including a passion for African diaspora culture exceeding the contemporary exoticism of Parisian nightlife), is more effectively captured than in most films of the period. 110 min.

The Man from Colorado (1949)

Col. Prod: Jules Schermer. Dir: Henry Levin. Scr: Robert D. Andrews, Ben Maddow.•† Story basis: Borden Chase. Cast: Glenn Ford, William Holden, Ellen Drew, Ray Collins, Edgar Buchanan

Intense and disturbing western from writers skilled in the genre, the soon-to-be-blacklisted Maddow and the conservative Chase in an unlikely combination. There are no heroes here, merely the mad, the grotesque and those who try to figure out what to do about it.

During the Civil War, a Union captain (Ford) cuts a company of Confederate soldiers to ribbons even though (as we learn) they had tried to surrender. The captain is quickly established as a pyschopath who returns to his home state after the war as the conquering hero to be measured for the robes of a federal judgeship. Just as he is confronting a gang of real-estate thieves bent on keeping land they stole from soldiers while they were off fighting, his own past catches up with him. The conclusion is a hair-raising act of criminal vandalism and cynicism that rivals, at least in spirit, the fate of cities in Germany in World War II—and that might have been the point. 99 min.

The Man from Dakota (1940)

Pleasant action drama about Union soldiers who escape from a Confederate prison and meet a female Russian refugee (Dolores del Rio). Produced by Edward Chodorov• and written by Laurence Stallings from a MacKinlay Kantor novel, *Arouse and Beware* (1936).

The Man from Frisco (1944)

A rare screenplay by radical poet Arnold Manoff• celebrates the achievements of shipbuilder Henry Kaiser, who invented the practice of replacing rivets with welding in ship hulls. A patriotic war drama.

Man from Texas (1948)

An unusual, obscure, low-budget Eagle-Lion western co-written by Jerome Chodorov• with a score by Earl Robinson (whose "Ballad for Americans," sung by Paul Robeson, was a Popular Front anthem) that features the old plot of the outlaw who wants to go straight. The "El Paso Kid," played in good cowboy style by James Craig, is told wife Lynn Bari will leave him if he can't change his ways. He sets up a feed business, but disappointment and a shifty banker drive him back into crime. Remarkable touches here and there, with shock over the march of civilization—decent folks can't carry guns into town anymore without being stopped.

The Man I Married (1940)

20th. Prod: Darryl Zanuck. Dir: Irving Pichel.• Scr: Oliver H. P. Garrett. Novel basis: Oscar Schisgall, *Swastika* (1939). Cast: Joan Bennett, Francis Lederer, Lloyd Nolan, Anna Sten, Otto Kruger, Ludwig Stössel, Johnny Russell, Lionel Royce, Frederick Vogeding, Ernst Deutsch, Egon Brecher

A strong prewar antifascist statement for Hollywood, guided skillfully by Pichel (one of the Hollywood 19) to suggest how Americans off their guard could be lulled, but not if they saw real fascism in action. Pichel sharpened the point by using real Nazi propaganda materials in the set design and Hitler's voice. The film was reportedly pulled shortly after release so as not to offend German distributors.

New York magazine art critic Bennett is newly and happily married to the German citizen Lederer. She pointedly refuses to accept criticisms of his homeland as misguided and bolshevistic. He takes her back to Germany, ostensibly for a visit, and there she discovers (much earlier than he) the suffering imposed by the rulers. In a memorable scene, their train passes another with refugees from Austria, and one prisoner reassures another, with heavy irony, that the Austrians are so ungrateful that they don't want to work on German starvation wages and have to be transported against their will. The movie was pulled from theatres, yet is one of the best films of its kind. 77 min.

The Man in the Trunk (1942)

20th. Prod: Walter Morosco. Dir: Malcolm St. Clair. Scr: John Larkin (uncredited script contribution: Paul Trivers•). Cast: Lynne Roberts, George Holmes, Raymond Walburn, J. Carrol Naish, Dorothy Peterson, Eily Malyon, Arthur Loft, Milton Parsons, Matt McHugh, Charles Cane, Theodore von Eltz, Joan Marsh, Syd Saylor, Douglas Fowley, Tim Ryan, Vivian Oakland

Writer Trivers had few successes in film; his real Hollywood role was as political advisor to John Howard Lawson, a seat close to the throne of the Communist Party. This film offers little evidence of any skilled script or, for that matter, directing touch. In a day when box office hits HERE COMES MR. JORDAN (written by Sidney Buchman•) and *Topper* (its later television version was a favored spot for blacklisted writers) made comical ghosts a subject of commercial interest, the plot of *Man in the Trunk* relies on the discovery of the skeleton of a bookie in Syracuse, New York, ten years after he was murdered. Ghost Walburn is set loose and goes about to solve his own murder. En route he helps Holmes to get his innocent client off the hook and make progress in his romance with Roberts. Meanwhile, THE CANTERVILLE GHOST was the real ghostly property the studios were looking for. 71 min.

A Man to Remember (1938)

Dalton's Trumbo's• screenplay, based on a story by Katherine Haviland-Taylor ("Failure," *American Magazine*, November 1932), concerns a selfless man of science who puts the interests of the community above everything—in this case a small town doctor who battles the medical bureaucrats and profiteers who try to marginalize him but is vindicated when he saves the lives and limbs of local children from the scourge of polio. Garson Kanin's first directing assignment, now apparently lost.

The Man Who Lived Twice (1936)

An Arthur Strawn† co-script with a familiar plot: a criminal has plastic surgery to disguise his identity. But there's a twist: crook Ralph Bellamy eagerly goes under the knife for a change of face *and* brain. The operation is grandly successful and he becomes a top physician—until his past catches up with him. Remade in 1953 as *Man in the Dark*.

The Man Who Reclaimed His Head (1934)

Universal. Prod: Carl Laemmle, Jr. Dir: Edward Ludwig. Scr: Samuel Ornitz,• Jean Bart. Cast: Claude Rains, Lionel Atwill, Joan Bennett, Henry O'Neill, Wallace Ford, Henry Armetta, Lawrence Grant

Produced at the peak of the almost uncontested antiwar sentiment of the 1930s, this strange and remarkable film is also the best by the often-frustrated Ornitz, a Hollywood Left pioneer and the author of the memorable novel *Haunch, Paunch and Jowl*. In the period just before World War I, a pacifist French intellectual and journalist makes a name for himself even as his newspaper dies. He turns to work on a book despite poverty and a wife and child to support. He is offered a top job with a newspaper baron who claims deep sympathy for his ideals. We soon learn that the baron is only playing to the popular sentiment, which changes sharply when war rumors abound (and Rains as Paul Verin, antiwar editor, becomes instantly unpopular). Cynically packed off to war while the baron romances his wife, Rains has lost everything but his pride. Retelling his story to a lawyer in flashback, he comes to a startling conclusion. It is remarkable that the film, an unrecognized peacenik classic, was made at all. 80 min.

The Man Who Turned to Stone (1957)

Clover Films/Col. Prod: Sam Katzman. Dir: László Kardos. Scr: Raymond T. Marcus (pseudonym for Bernard Gordon•). Cast: Victor Jory, Ann Doran, Charlotte Austin, William Hudson, Paul Cavanaugh

An extremely strange low-budget horror film unfairly written off as a drive-in flop. A womens' correctional facility is not an unusual setting for left-wing allegories for social reform, but Gordon added a sci-fi premise: the joint has been seized by a cohort of eternals, eighteenth-century Enlightenment types who had learned the secret of cell rejuvenation in 1780s Paris and freed themselves from aging through animal magnetism. Led by scientist (and head prison administrator) Jory, they have made young women of childbearing age their victims, transferring (in a strange bath apparatus) electrical energy to the old from the young and killing the unfortunates. Unless they get their fix, their skin starts to harden, a prelude to death.

Gordon later commented that he meant the film to treat of memory and guilt. Cavanaugh, going into a last decline, thus reveals the awful weight of class history. Hudson, an energetic prison reformer (and his new squeeze, nurse Doran) uncover the plot and get themselves into another kind of hot water. Too much stock action and too little probing of motivation reduce the larger possibilities of the film, but for the genre it remains rather special. 71 min.

The Man Who Wouldn't Die (1942)

Better than average Mike Shayne mystery written by Arnaud d'Usseau,• one of two in the forties series written by left-wingers (the other was JUST OFF BROADWAY). This one has the private dick on a job in Long Island, where Marjorie Weaver is the dippy daughter of millionaire Henry Wilcoxen, who is under investigation for financial shenanigans. Weaver and Lloyd Nolan (as Shane) pretend to be married while he investigates an apparent murder attempt. Nolan discovers conspiracies oddly involving a financier who thinks he can hire a scientist to invent eternal life and a stage magician who can go into a trance and mimic death. Even the exotic notes are a little pat.

Manhattan Heartbeat (1940)

A two-hankie weeper co-written by Harold Buchman• about a gal, a baby and an airplane—and a husband desperately trying to prove that he deserves them all. Based on the successful novel and play by Viña Delmar, *Bad Girl* (1930).

Margie (1946)

20th. Prod: Walter Morosco. Dir: Henry King. Scr: F. Hugh Herbert. Story basis: Ruth McKenney,• Richard Bransten. Cast: Jeanne Crain, Glenn Langan, Lynn Bari, Esther Dale, Hobart Cavanaugh, Alan Young, Barbara Lawrence, Conrad Janis

Based on short stories by McKenney, a Communist and *New Yorker* writer best known for MY SISTER EILEEN (here helped by husband Bransten), *Margie* was among the films often accused of subversive content, although scriptwriter Herbert himself was in the clear. The accusers may have had a point, despite the apparent innocence of the 1920s adolescence musical, with wholesome family members gathered around the shy if self-doubting protagonist. FBI informers in Hollywood cited the film in reports about innocent-seeming pictures with subversive implications.

Seen in flashback by a grown-up Margie explaining old photographs to a teenager like her old self, *Margie* is an uncorrupted Lolita tale. An underaged high school senior (the youngest in her class), a rabid debater who is also yearning for love, she experiences a series of significant accidents, such as meeting a handsome young French teacher while pinning up her falling knickers. She is rescued by him at a skating party when she loses them entirely and he hides the embarrassing evidence. In the end, in the final up-to-date scene with her 1940s husband home from work, we learn who it was that finally undid the hymeneal knot.

Meanwhile—and this may have attracted the witch-hunters more—Crain stars as a school debater denouncing "dollar diplomacy" and the U.S. occupation of Nicaragua as untrue to the founding fathers' democratic zeal. Her father, a milquetoast undertaker, is so taken by the argument that he becomes ardent against occupation (and, in a bizarre twist, is appointed Minister to Nicaragua by the U.S. Senate!). Meanwhile, loving grandmother Esther Dale, who started the family tradition of radicalism, displays on the family mantle the chains with which she bound herself to the White House for woman suffrage back in the good old 1910s, the same chains in which the cops dragged her away. 94 min., color.

The Mark (1961)
20th. Prod: Raymond Stross. Dir: Guy Green. Scr: Sidney Buchman,• Stanley Mann. Cast: Stuart Whitman, Rod Steiger, Maria Schell, Brenda De Banzie, Maurice Denham, Donald Wolfit

Memorable as Sidney Buchman's return from the blacklist—but only in the United Kingdom, since the prospect of U.S. distribution problems, especially west of the Hudson, still posed difficulties. The film is interesting in its own right as a serious treatment of sex offenders and their rehabilitation, then as now among the touchiest of social issues. *The New York Times* gave it a rave, perhaps in an understated effort to bring the blacklistees home in more ways than one.

Whitman is a paroled sex offender, Steiger his chain-smoking shrink whose dedication (he sometimes sleeps at his desk overnight) and insight help make a new life possible. If group therapy is punishing—others accuse Whitman of being a "mama's boy" afraid of a real woman—a decent job and a loving widow give him the psychic space needed to rebuild his self-confidence. A crisis comes when a tabloid reporter "exposes" Whitman's carnival outing with the widow's daughter (the good child played to the hilt by De Banzie) as proof of a predator's threat to the community. His life falls apart again. Steiger is convincing, Schell remarkably realistic and Whitman more than adequate in this solid if slightly over-long drama, shot in Ireland. 127 min.

Mark of the Vampire (1935)
MGM. Prod: Tod Browing (uncredited: E. J. Mannix). Dir: Tod Browning. Scr: Guy Endore,• Bernard Schubert (script contributions: H. S. Kraft,• Samuel Ornitz,• John Balder-

ston). Cast: Lionel Barrymore, Elizabeth Allan, Lionel Atwill, Bela Lugosi, Jean Hersholt, Henry Wadsworth, Donald Meek, Jessie Ralph, Ivan F. Simpson, Franklyn Ardell, Leila Bennett, June Gittelson, Carroll Borland, Holmes Herbert

Devotees of Lugosi view this as the kiss-off to Bela's grand phase, showing the artifice behind the stock horror features of the early and middle 1930s, but (given the typecasting) leading his career nowhere. Unlike Boris Karloff, who had a stage career and some interesting films ahead, Lugosi was doomed to play in parodies of his early roles, ending up tragically with drugs and Ed Wood, Jr. En route, the thoughtful actor and Hungarian exile was (with Bela Bartok) a symbolic leader of the Hungarian-American Congress, chief Popular Front vehicle of the antifascist movement in that quarter. He somehow escaped being named. Screenwriter Schubert, who mainly did horror films, was never named but believed that he was informally blacklisted, and ended up as a hired man in a Los Angeles synagogue.

This film interestingly poses a Czech legend about a castle in which vampires live (so to speak). Lugosi and daughter Borland appear to be bats who change to human bodies to commit their evil deeds, but whose real identity may be entirely different, as we discover in a gimmick ending devised by Browning at which the actors rebelled. Browning (famous for *Freaks* but also on his way down) rejected the screenplay's hinted-at elements of incest, which had so incited critics of the Lugosi-Karloff vehicle BLACK CAT. Enough remained to make the earlier part of the film a bit of a horror classic. Anything in which the brilliant Marxist novelist and fantasist Endore had a hand (e.g., THE DEVIL DOLL) is worth taking a look at. 64 min.

Marked Woman (1937)
WB. Exec. Prod: Hal B. Wallis. Dir: Lloyd Bacon (uncredited: Michael Curtiz). Scr: Robert Rossen,† Abem Finkel. Cast: Bette Davis, Humphrey Bogart, Lola Lane, Isabel Jewell, Eduardo Ciannelli, Jane Bryan

Based on the trial of Lucky Luciano shortly before he was sent to jail on the testimony of "his" prostitutes, *Marked Woman* comes as close as allowable to describing the struggle of one prostitute (here a "clip joint hostess" who "goes with the customers outside") to crack open the rackets.

Bogart is flat as a flatfoot, the detective who persuades Davis to testify with her friends and see the trial through. Davis here lacks the dose of evil that makes her the great actress, but she is nevertheless incredibly strong as the woman who knows her life is ruined (we are offered her college sister as contrast, and when her sister is kidnapped, she tells crime boss Ciannelli, "I'll get you if I have to crawl back from the grave to do it!").

The weak side of the film is a certain credulity about the honesty of the police force, which Rossen as a former slum resident knew all too well. It is typical of a period with films like RACKET BUSTERS, based on Attorney General Thomas Dewey's anticrime crusades. Still, this is strong Rossen, and the final image of the solidarity of sisterhood as the dames descend the courthouse steps is a classic. 97 min.

Martin Luther (1953)

Louis de Rochemont Associates/Lutheran Church. Prod: Lother Wolff. Dir: Irving Pichel.• Scr: Allan Sloane, Lothar Wolff. Cast: Niall MacGinnis, John Ruddock, Pierre Lefevere, Guy Verney, David Horne, Fred Johnson, Philip Leaver, Egon Strohm, Alexander Gauge, Irving Pichel, Leonard White, Annette Carell

Times critic Bosley Crowther put this film on his top ten list for the year, and it was just as popular with Lutheran audiences around the country (they had helped raise money for the production). There could have been no better choice to direct than Christian Socialist Pichel, who was one of the original Hollywood 19 but died before he could be formally blacklisted (and in any case had already moved his operation out of Hollywood into projects like this).

MacGinnis is particularly effective as the sixteenth-century monk of conscience who confronts the imperial papacy and rallies much of what would become middle-class Germany to his standard (omitted: his late turn against the peasant rebellions). Novice screenwriter Sloane, apparently a Pichel discovery, went on to do some of the sharpest scripts for left-wing TV shows *The Nurses* and *East Side/West Side*. At least one U.S. critic believes the film was the model for the John Osborne bioplay and rivals the late Rossellini for seriousness of purpose. Shot in Germany. 105 min.

MASH (1970)

Ingo Preminger Productions/20th. Prod: Ingo Preminger. Dir: Robert Altman. Scr: Ring Lardner, Jr.• Novel basis: Richard Hooker, *MASH* (1968). Cast: Donald Sutherland, Elliot Gould, Tom Skerritt, Sally Kellerman, Robert Duvall, Jo Ann Pflug, Gary Burghoff

A multiple award-winner and arguably the most shocking political statement ever made in a Hollywood film.

A relatively low-budget production intended for youth audiences, it was heavily (and in its early release days, usefully) patronized by *New Yorker* critic Pauline Kael, who insisted upon the primacy of its artistic merits, the new style of direction by Altman, including much cross-talk and many long takes, as well as near-total irreverence. It was seen by the vast majority of viewers in the United States, but especially abroad, as a fundamental statement against the Vietnam War and the American culture that produced it. Of course, the story of the mobile medical unit was set in Korea, and the novel basis written by a somewhat critical supporter of the military. But in the hands of the vibrant young cast, Altman and, above all, Lardner—who received his vindication here: his first real triumph since previous award-winner WOMAN OF THE YEAR many years earlier—it was filmmaking dynamite. 116 min.

The Master Race (1944)

RKO. Prod: Robert Golden. Dir: Herbert J. Biberman.• Scr: Herbert J. Biberman, Anne Froelich,• Rowland Leigh. Cast: George Coulouris, Stanley Ridges, Osa Massen, Carl Esmond, Nancy Gates, Morris Carnovsky,• Lloyd Bridges†

An overly ambitious film with a strong dose of naiveté about American occupation forces that nevertheless has many strong moments of anti-Nazi melodrama. At the close of the war, German officers are told that the value of Nazi ideologues is at an end but that the true Prussian spirit is destined to continue. Among those advised to scatter, Coulouris is assigned to a small Belgian village engaged in postwar reconstruction. He positions himself among former collaborationists of the middle classes who are too fond of privilege and too weak to resist his blackmail.

The melodrama that follows is one of those possible only in films made during the war. An American officer (Stanley Ridges) encourages the rebuilding of democratic society, while Coularis calls for withdrawal of the U.S. occupiers (as the European Left itself would do a few years later). Meanwhile, the Lloyd Bridges character, back from the war and the prison camps, struggles with others to restore farming through a (suspiciously cooperative) agricultural work brigade; he is slow to discover that the wife he left behind gave herself to the Nazis and that her obviously innocent child is not his. At this fervent moment of Hollywood de-Nazification, no one would guess that soon in real-life Germany prominent Nazi collaborators would be returned to responsible positions in business and government with the help of the U.S. occupiers. 96 min.

Maya (1966)

MGM. Prod: Frank King, Maurice King. Dir: John Berry.•
Scr: John Fante. Cast: Jay North, Clint Walker, Sajid Kahn,
I. S. Johar

A touching children's film with many interesting
sidelights. An Indian version of *Life on the Mississippi*
except that different cultures meet on a basis of near-
equality. After his mother's death, young North (the
boy actor of television's *Lassie*) determines to live with
his father, who happens to be a big-game hunter or at
least a former big-game hunter, in India. No one meets
him at the train, and he finds the grounds in ruins. His
father (a rather wooden Walker) has been clawed and
become gun-shy—although not too shy to shoot a pet
cheetah the boy has found and partially tamed. Feeling
betrayed, North decides to return to the United States.
He leaps from the train at an awkward moment and is
quickly lost in the jungle, where he meets an Indian
boy his age.

The old quest motif sets things in motion: Kahn is
instructed by his dying father to take a sacred, small
white elephant and her mother to a pilgrimage site far
away. The boys go together (with Walker sometimes hot
on their heels) across countryside, through villages,
exotic religious ceremonies and all sorts of adventures.
They learn to love each other as brothers and strive to
learn about each others' lives and cultures. The basis for
a short-lived television series, *Maya* was also director
Berry's triumph in family pictures, unlike his later,
rather painful THE BAD NEWS BEARS GO TO JAPAN. 91 min.,
color.

Mayor of Hell (1933)

WB. Prod: Edward Chodorov,• Lucien Hubbard. Dir:
Archie Mayo (uncredited: Michael Curtiz). Scr: Edward
Chodorov. Story basis: Islin Auster. Cast: James Cagney,
Madge Evans, Arthur Byron, Allen Jenkins, Dudley Dig-
ges, Frankie Darro, Sheila Terry, Robert Barrat, Allen
"Farina" Hoskins, Harold Huber, Dorothy Peterson,
George Pat Collins

A teen's (or for that age, children's) action film of
staggering dramatic action, with scenes of righteous
violence hardly imaginable in movies about adult uprisings against authority. Although adults set the action, boys
carry it out with conviction—probably thanks little to
mediocre director Mayo but much to Chodorov's writing
for Cagney.

The familiar theme of slum boys in trouble with the
law leads to trial and to incarceration as in so many
Depression exposé dramas. The ethnic differentiation of
the youthful criminals is fascinating. The boys are starved
with bad food, beaten and otherwise mistreated until
political boss Cagney investigates the prison and, in the
spirit of New Deal reforms, straightens it out. There, he
falls for nurse Evans, and takes her advice in providing a
healthful, democratic atmosphere.

Lots of action follows, including an insurrection, but
the most instructive moment lies in the self-government
that the kids establish (with Izzy the honest treasurer, who
gives inmates only the candy they earn for labor
expended!), including a court to try their own members
and a handbook for democratic practice. The apocalyptic
uprising makes this a B-movie that compares favorably
with Vigo's *Zero de conduite*. 80 min.

A Medal for Benny (1945)

Para. Prod: Paul Jones. Dir: Irving Pichel.• Scr: Frank
Butler. Story basis: John Steinbeck, Jack Wagner. Cast:
Dorothy Lamour, Arturo de Córdova, J. Carrol Naish,
Mikhail Rasumny, Fernando Alvarado, Charles Dingle,
Frank McHugh

This wonderful Steinbeck story must be the only
anti-establishment political movie Lamour ever made and
is easily one of the most hilarious treatments of the gap
between wartime democratic rhetoric and popular racial
attitudes.

A lead-in explains the presence of "our original
settlers" with "mixed Indian and Spanish blood" (the last
we hear about Indians) as having their own, special lives.
Picaresque treatment has them quaint, poor but musical
and warm-hearted, living as they can in "Sloughtown," a
barrio on Santz Cruz Bay, close to the WASPish village of
Pantera. De Córdova, a lovable no-good, has fallen in love
with Lamour, but she has promised herself to Benny
Martin, a mischievous thief. The plot thickens as we learn
that Martin (whose ignorant but honest and charming
father, played by Naish, is the inadvertent spokesman of
Latino values) was banished from the district for fighting
with police.

The best scene in the film comes when the Pantera
Pepsters (the Chamber of Commerce) are surprised by the
news that the ne'er-do-well Martin has posthumously won
a Congressional Medal of Honor for valor in the Pacific.
Realizing he was Hispanic, they try to salvage the situation
for the sake of national publicity, stumbling into one self-
embarrassment after another. There is too much conde-
scension toward Mexican Americans, but far more ridicule
of petty-bourgeois California racism. 77 min.

Meet Nero Wolfe (1936)

Col. Prod: B. P. Schulberg.† Dir: Herbert J. Biberman.●
Scr: Bruce Manning, Joseph Anthony, Howard J. Green.
Novel basis: Rex Stout, *Fer-de-Lance* (1934). Cast: Edward
Arnold, Lionel Stander,● Joan Perry, Victor Jory, Nana
Bryant, Dennie Moore, Russell Hardie, Walter Kingsford,
Boyd Irwin, Sr., John Qualen, Gene Morgan, Rita Hay-
worth

An effort to put a little anti–ruling class content into
stock Nero Wolfe material (an earlier Stout novel, THE
LEAGUE OF FRIGHTENED MEN, was adapted by Guy Endore●
with less success on this point). Observing a death on the
golf course, Wolfe concludes that a poisoned needle was
triggered when the golfer raised his club; later, his
chauffeur is killed by the bite of a deadly South American
snake, the fer-de-lance. In the Wolfean manner, the
detective gets all the suspects into one room and springs
a surprise on them. 73 min.

Meet the Girls (1938)

20th. Prod: Sol M. Wurtzel. Dir: Eugene Forde. Scr:
Marguerite Roberts.● Cast: June Lang, Lynn Bari, Robert
Allen, Ruth Donnelly, Gene Lockhart, Wally Vernon, Erik
Rhodes, Constantine Romanoff, Jack Norton, Emmett
Vogan, Paul McVey

A Honolulu comedy that was to be the first in a series
created by Roberts exploring "modern girls" who are
working stiffs but adventuresome and resourceful, one
smart and the other pretty but dumb. Only one more in
the series, *Pardon Our Nerve*, was actually produced.

Lots of nice touches, like the opening in which the
girls appear (in an optical illusion) as mermaids in a
fishbowl of a nightclub. They both get fired when they
brush off a wolfish drunk. Looking for excitement, they
board a ship under rather false pretenses, and Lang (the
smart one, which is not saying much) repeatedly enters
crap games and loses their stake. A diamond is stolen
and the girls are offered $5,000 for its return. There are
some good gags (a drink containing the diamond moves
from hand to hand), many perky moments and a happy
ending. Intended for the "neighborhood crowd," it was
probably a few years early: a little later, restyled with
the war effort, it might have been just what Rosie the
Riveter ordered. 66 min.

Meet the Missus (1940)

An entry in the Higgins family series, with a substantial
change in personnel after the same writer's (Val Burton●)

Earl of Puddlestone. In this sitcomic effort, a lost $5,000
in negotiable securities falls into the hands of a neighbor
child, raising the possibility of jail for Dad Higgins and
forcing a reluctant Grandpa to consider raising the money
by marrying a rich widow who had had her eye on him.
68 min.

Meet the People (1944)

MGM. Prod: E. Y. Harburg.● Dir: Charles Reisner. Scr: Sol
Barzman,● Ben Barzman. Cast: Lucille Ball,† Dick Powell,
Virginia O'Brien, Bert Lahr, Rags Ragland, June Allyson

Film version of a left-wing theatrical extravaganza
and the only film actually produced by songster "Yip"
Harburg. It began as a Hollywood revue in 1941 with
producer Henry Blankfort,● lyricist Mortimer Offner●
(assisted by Edward Eliscu●) and choreographer Danny
Dare† and drew raves even from Hedda Hopper. Road
companies were added, mainly to entertain "the boys."
The most class-oriented of the wartime musicals by far, it
was an experiment unrepeated.

A plot constructed mainly by the filmmakers to add
narrative heft to the production has Powell as a machinist in a shipbuilding factory, his lyricist brother off
fighting in the Pacific. Powell successfully persuades
Broadway star Ball to help him produce a patriotic
musical he has written, but the first version is so bad
that he invokes a contract clause, cancels the show and
goes back to his blue-collar job. Ball follows him, taking
a job in the plant. As they prepare for their own show
on a smaller scale, we see lots of working-class musical
dedication to the war effort (also Powell's song and
dance), with Spike Jones the factory musical genius—
invented instruments, satire of classics, physical humor,
and so forth.

Inevitably, the show opens to great success, and at
the climax contains some perfectly amazing numbers. The
best or most representative, the title number, has the hoi
polloi rising over the rich, the day of the common people
finally dawning out of the darkness of war. Popular Front
kitsch to the nth power. 100 min.

The Men (1950)

Stanley Kramer Productions/UA. Prod: Stanley Kramer.
Dir: Fred Zinnemann. Scr: Carl Foreman.● Cast: Marlon
Brando, Teresa Wright, Everett Sloane, Jack Webb

Remembered mainly as Brando's first film, it is
notable as the echo of the progressive hopes attached
to the mobilization of World War II, a sort of tribute film

147

MIDNIGHT COWBOY (1969)

to Veterans Administration services (acknowledged in a printed message before the credits) and to the endurance of the injured veteran. Brando joins others in what will seem to later viewers an anticipation of COMING HOME: the ward of pain, as much psychological as physical, and of men adjusting to more than symbolic emasculation. Victims of serious spinal injuries, these men have lost the use of the lower half of their bodies. And if they do not actually spill their urine (as in *Coming Home*), they talk at length about their feelings, while Sloane as the gruff but kindly doctor provides the medical details to family members. Wright is almost cloying as the loyal fiancée who refuses to give up on Brando, but the moment when he comes home and she realizes what her loyalty has gotten her into as a woman is subtle and devastating. Little is made of fascism, and less of patriotic duty (the Korean War had just begun), but neither is war itself cursed, as it was in the Vietnam epics. 85 min.

The Men in Her Life (1941)
Michael Wilson,• Frederick Kohner and Paul Trivers• adapted Lady Eleanor Smith's novel *Ballerina* (1932), about a young woman determined to become a ballerina whose success leads to romance and tragedy.

Men of America (1932)
RKO. Prod: David O. Selznick. Dir: Ralph Ince. Scr: Samuel Ornitz.• Cast: William Boyd, Charles "Chic" Sale, Dorothy Wilson, Ralph Ince, Henry Armetta, Alphonse Ethier, Theresa Maxwell Conover, Eugene Strong, Gene Layman

Interesting early Depression western starring Boyd in a pre–Hopalong Cassidy role. The cracker-barrel crowd around the general store of a contemporary western village includes purported Indian and Chinese oldtimers who poke fun at former pony express rider Sale's accounts of winning the West. Sale (in real life an oldtime vaudeville comic and literary tale-teller wrapping up his career in films) makes a nuisance of himself by dogging his daughter, who actually keeps the store going and is deeply in love with goat rancher (!) Boyd; he even accuses Boyd of killing an old pal. The real culprits are a gang of jail-breaking bank robbers on the lam and armed with a machine gun. Boyd directs the townsfolk in fighting back against the gang. There are lots of nice small bits. The Old West is deconstructed and the modern West affirmed. 57 min.

Men of the Timberland (1941)
Universal. Prod: Ben Pivar. Dir: John Rawlins. Scr: Maurice Tombragel, Griffin Jay. Story basis: Paul Jarrico.• Cast: Richard Arlen, Andy Devine, Linda Hayes, Francis McDonald

In this unusual eco-western, Hayes inherits some valuable timberland but nearly falls for the schemes of McDonald, who is determined to clear-cut everything. As usual in these plots, honest ranchers and those who treasure the trees (a reflection of the Works Progress Administration reforestation efforts, which ended with the approach of war and the end of New Deal agencies), with Arlen in the lead, intercede to stop the devastation. The film is also memorable for Devine in his irrepressible sidekick role, making him (along with Gabby Hayes) the best of the type. Jarrico later took pride in the theme as "ahead of its time," which it certainly was. 61 min.

Messenger of Death (1988)
Cannon Group. Prod: Pancho Kohner. Dir: J. Lee Thompson. Scr: Paul Jarrico.• Novel basis: Rex Burns, *The Avenging Angel* (1983). Cast: Charles Bronson, Trish Van Devere, Laurence Luckinbill, Daniel Benzali, Marilyn Hassett, Charles Dierkop, Jeff Corey,• John Ireland

Writer Jarrico's last theatrical release and, according to his own account, the only Bronson film in memory in which the protagonist kills no one. This time Bronson is a non-gun-carrying reporter for a Denver newspaper pursuing a story of the murder of an expelled Mormon's three wives and six children. Bronson rapidly finds himself in the middle of a vicious feud (with Corey and Ireland the leaders of respective religious factions). Despite the interesting plot, Bronson fans had to be treated, presumably, to the kind of action (with Bronson mostly on the receiving end this time) they expected, and not to the examination of religious cultism that would have made this a much better film. 92 min., color.

Midnight Cowboy (1969)
Jerome Hellman–Florin Prod./UA. Prod: Jerome Hellman. Dir: John Schlesinger. Scr: Waldo Salt.• Novel basis: James Leo Herlihy, *Midnight Cowboy* (1965). Cast: Dustin Hoffman, Jon Voight, Sylvia Miles, John McGiver, Brenda Vaccaro, Barnard Hughes

This great film marked writer Waldo Salt's return to Oscar glory from the depths of the blacklist and marked the rise of the Hollywood art film. It was a long road back for the writer. Just a year or two earlier Salt was down and out in a New York flophouse, reeling from booze, rotten TV sitcom scripts and very bad screenplays (his last film before *Cowboy* was an animal comedy about a cognac-lapping poodle). Salt shook it all off, and the author of THE SHOPWORN ANGEL (1938) devised a similar but ever-so-much darker tale of an earnest cowpoke adrift in the big city and the women he meets there who've seen it all. At bottom, it's about a little boy in a cowboy suit who never grew up because no one ever taught him how.

Joe Buck, played with extraordinary skill by Jon Voight, believes the popular image of a cowboy is so powerful that he will escape from a lonely life in the Southwest to New York, where well-off women will pay him considerable sums to give them pleasure. There he meets Ratso Rizzo (Dustin Hoffman in his greatest role), a deformed street hustler who first deceives Joe and then finds in his fellow outcast his last connection to humanity. In the end, in the compassion established in the connection between two social castaways, humankind is redeemed, at least for a few hours. And Joe Buck, unlike the bewilderingly cruel society around him, learns how to grow up.

Aside from the power of the storytelling, the film is important for technical and historical reasons. It helped to perfect the flash-forward as a way of establishing urgency in the drive of the narrative toward its crisis, and it lifted the montage out of its ancient clichés (Joe Buck is seen walking down the same bit of New York sidewalk in four identical two-second shots, night alternating with day, to show the passage of 48 hours).

The film is important historically for the way Salt emancipated film from dialogue (in the narrowest sense), turning the stage directions into a systemic visual exposition of the narrative; no longer were directions helpful asides to a director but an integrated and detailed representation of all of the visual elements of the film (Salt was an accomplished artist).

Midnight Cowboy also marked the coming of age of an emerging new film audience that had been to the art house, knew at least something of the European film tradition, and for whom cultural issues were often only slightly less important than the political issues that, in years of a continuing military draft, they often considered a matter of life and death. For that audience, *Cowboy* the represented the right of Hollywood to speak once again of the dark side of U.S. society to clear the way for something more hopeful.

Shocking for 1969, it was the first and last "X-Rated" film to win an Oscar. If the acting and script are first-rate, so are Schlesinger's cinematic inventions in the montages and flash-forwards. Voight and Hoffman both received Academy nominations for best actor. A landmark film of the blacklist. 113 min., color.

Midnight Intruder (1937)
Universal. Assoc. Prod: Trem Carr. Dir: Arthur Lubin. Scr: George Waggner, Lester Cole.• Novel basis: Channing Pollock, *Synthetic Gentleman* (1934). Cast: Louis Hayward, Eric Linden, J. C. Nugent, Barbara Read, Irving Bacon, Robert Greig, Pierre Watkin

Proletarian drama with tragedies and a few laughs. Hayward, an orphan and cotton mill child laborer, had grown up tough and teamed up with ex-newspaperman, ex-hobo Nugent, who spends his time at the track. On the way to the races one day they climb into the window of an apparently empty house, and to their surprise, the service staff mistakes Hayward for the dissolute scion of a fortune. Hayward resolves to live the fantasy as dad and mom are away for some weeks. Complications quickly multiply as Sheila Bromley, wife of the real son, appears to say he has been arrested for murder and to plead for Hayward's help (in return for not revealing his secret). Now definitely a good guy, Hayward sets out to solve the crime, taking a job at dad's newspaper under an assumed name, and, through various maneuvers, even making dad proud of the real son. 66 min.

Millie's Daughter (1947)
Millie is a woman born on the "wrong side," as they say, of the municipal tracks and has lost her daughter to a rich family, which now threatens to disown the girl after she returns to her mother. A rare Edward Huebsch• (best know for *Twilight's Last Gleaming*) adaptation and screenplay of a Depression novel of the same name (1939) by Donald Henderson Clarke.

Million Dollar Legs (1932)
Lively slap-stick comedy co-written by Henry Myers• about an imaginary country ruled by none other than W.C. Fields, who holds off plotters with arm-wrestling, and travels with local superhuman athletes to the Olympics. Great fun: a direct precursor to the Marx Brothers' *Duck Soup*.

The Miracle (1959)
WB. Prod: Henry Blanke. Dir: Irving Rapper. Scr: Frank Butler (front for Jean Rouverol Butler• and Hugo Butler•). Play basis: Karl Vollmöller, *Das Wunder* (1912) Cast:

Carroll Baker, Roger Moore, Walter Slezak, Vittorio Gassman, Katina Paxinou, Dennis King, Isobel Elsom

Ghosted by the Butlers, then living in Mexico, for veteran screenwriter Frank Butler (Hugo's father), this had been a U.S. stage hit (produced by Max Reinhardt on Broadway in 1924) that, on the big screen, was inflated from religious shmaltz to spectacle.

As Napoleon moves into Spain and the English send troops to fend him off, an obviously romance-minded novice (in the stage version it was an actual nun, but this was judged too controversial for the 1950s) falls in love and abandons her calling. When she takes off, a famed statue of the virgin comes to life to take her place (!). Baker's crush on Moore prompts her to pursue him, but he is apparently killed in a battle; she ends up with handsome gypsy King, but he is betrayed by his jealous brother. Slezak, ridiculous in a bandana (but at the least credible as a thief, if not as a gypsy) takes her to Madrid, where she launches a career as a singer (a love-smitten bullfighter is a tiresome sidelight). Though she travels to London and connects with Moore again (he is readying himself for Waterloo), she realizes her virginal duty lies in Spain after all. Everything works out miraculously, with the blessed mother superior (Paxinou, who got an Academy Award in *For Whom the Bell Tolls*) pronouncing the happy solution. All in all, very, very forties, with a budget big enough to distract the audience from the silly plot and acting. 121 min., color.

Miracle of the Bells (1947)
RKO. Prod: Jesse L. Lasky, Walter MacEwen. Dir. Irving Pichel.• Scr: Ben Hecht, Quentin Reynolds. Cast: Fred MacMurray, Alida Valli, Frank Sinatra, Lee J. Cobb†

A self-styled cynical press agent suffering a serious bout of conscience narrates the tale of a working-class diva (Valli) in a great hurry to make her name on Broadway and, if possible, in films. Her coughing suggests she is suffering from TB acquired in her home town, a coal-mining village in Pennsylvania.

She gets her wish when a star quits and as understudy she plays the part she has always wanted—Joan of Arc. In the film within the film, she sings and acts the part with almost inhuman energy, explicable because she is dying and regards her performance as uplifting the common immigrant working class of her home town. The director, convinced that a dead actress will kill the film's box office, decides to reshoot the film without her, just as MacMurray reaches the Pennsylvania town with her remains. In a stunning gambit, he pays to have all the bells in the valley peal without stopping on the day of her funeral; so many people come to visit the impoverished little church, presided over by young priest Sinatra, that the foundation shifts and the plaster saints move to "face" her body. After twists and turns, Sinatra pronounces the sociopolitical homilies of the Popular Front.

Sometimes described as one of the strangest films of the time, both in plot and casting, it is really the Christian crypto-socialism of Pichel, with a St. Joan dying (literally) to play the redeemer of a Slavic working class. Through her selfless death, that working class sees its own nobility, if only as the self-sacrificing creators of value. The cumulative effect of the tolling of the bells is nearly hypnotic. Along with MR. PEABODY AND THE MERMAID and MARTIN LUTHER, this is one of Pichel's most original films, winning Academy Awards for best story and best script; nominated for best picture. 120 min.

Miracle on Main Street (1939)
An odd, dark melodrama about a down-and-out stripper who makes ends meet by rolling drunks and whose life is redeemed when she finds an infant abandoned in the crib of a Christmas crèche. The Frederick Jackson screenplay is based on a story by Samuel Ornitz• and Boris Ingster.

Misadventures of Merlin Jones (1964)
Buena Vista/Disney Studios. Prod: Walt Disney, Ron Miller. Dir: Robert Stevenson. Scr: Tom and Helen August (pseudonyms for Alfred Lewis Levitt• and Helen Levitt•). Story basis: Bill Walsh. Cast: Tommy Kirk, Annette Funicello, Leon Ames, Stuart Erwin, Alan Hewitt, Connie Gilchrist, Dal McKennon, Norman Grabowski

After years of sitcom writing under pseudonyms for shows like *Donna Reed*, blacklisted Al Levitt (best remembered for THE BOY WITH GREEN HAIR) and his wife (a former secretary for John Garfield), teamed up for this followup to "silly" family films like *The Shaggy Dog*. All had in common a strict avoidance of social problems and a gimmick to promote chaos.

College student Kirk is wired up to allow him to read others' thoughts. The film subsequently drifts from one possibility to another as Kirk uses hypnosis to take on assorted subjects, including a chimpanzee and a judge (Ames), who secretly writes crime fiction. Meanwhile, Annette, Kirk's girl, sort of stands around, and Hewitt is the smart aleck prof in the Psych department who gives Kirk a hard time. Not much of a premise, but it held onto the teen audience (who hoped, perhaps, to see bikini-clad Annette take off her clothes) enough to spawn a sequel, THE MONKEY'S UNCLE, also written by the Levitts. 91 min., color.

Miss Susie Slagle's (1945)
Para. Prod: John Houseman. Dir: John Berry.• Scr: Anne
Froelick,• Hugo Butler.• Adaptation: Adrian Scott,• Anne
Froelick. Cast: Lillian Gish, Veronica Lake, Sonny Tufts,
Joan Caulfield, Ray Collins, Billy De Wolfe, Lloyd Bridges†

A superior doctor-and-nurses film, with story basis
by Froelick and Butler, set in a 1910s boarding house for
medical interns and residents. Mothering her tenants,
Gish makes sure the promising young men get past their
crises of confidence (the father of one is an overbearing
physician, another fears the stress of operating, and so
on), and encourages them to find proper mates.

As the tough-but-dedicated administrators bear down
on the students to become good doctors and the romances
burgeon, the story almost loses itself to clichés, but not
quite. Thanks to a good script and good direction, the
humanitarianism of the enterprise pulls together the
wounded egos and near-broken hearts, evoking something
better. One of the 50 top-grossing films of the year. 88 min.

Mission to Moscow (1943)
WB. Prod: Robert Buckner. Dir: Michael Curtiz. Scr:
Howard Koch.• Cast: Walter Huston, Ann Harding, George
Tobias, Oskar Homolka, Eleanor Parker, Richard Travis,
Helmut Dantine, Victor Francen, Henry Daniell, Barbara
Everest, Roman Bohnen, Maria Palmer, Minor Watson

The all-time stinker of apologies-for-Stalinism films,
hailed at the time of its production as a valuable aid to the
war effort and probably commissioned by FDR (at least
by U.S. ambassador to Russia, Joseph Davies, who carried
out orders). It is the story of Davies himself traveling to
the Kremlin. Erskine Caldwell reportedly wrote the first
draft but Koch finished it, which some sources believe led
to his blacklisting even though he never joined the
Communist Party.

The worst parts of the film lionize "Uncle Joe" Stalin
and recall his rugged triumph over the conspirators he
exposed (read: the victims he strung up) in the notorious
Moscow Trials of 1937-1939. Less awful parts show
Huston-as-Davies accurately recognizing that the Russians had carried the burden of the war, at a staggering
human cost (20 million dead), and rightly wanted recognition and financial help from the United States in return.
In a gesture most unusual at any time but wartime, Davies
himself introduces the film. 123 min.

Mississippi Rhythm (1949)
Monogram. Prod: Lindsley Parsons. Dir: Derwin Abra-
hams. Scr: Gretchen Darling. Story basis: Louise Rousseau.• Cast: Jimmie Davis, Lee "Lasses" White, Veda Ann
Borg, Sue England, James Flavin, the Sunshine Boys

A nice western musical including many surprisingly
subtle variations on the shoot-'em-up narrative. The film
begins with the uncharismatic country singer Jimmie
Davis's band singing "Ain't Gonna Study War No More"
("Down By the Riverside"). A thin and familiar (but not
unwelcome) plot shifts from riverboat card sharps to
newly settled territory in East Texas where the leading
citizen (and property owner) aims to keep all economic
activity under his thumb—selling farmers dry land,
overcharging them for water and then foreclosing. Davis,
who has settled in as a singer at dancehall mistress
Borg's saloon, is given a few hours to leave town—
instead, he begins an open campaign for people's
government.

Around this plot, there are many performances of
Grand Ole Opry quality, from a straight-faced (or
straight-lipped) harmonica version of Mozart's "Sonata
in C" to White's sentimental recollection of an oldtime
gambler to Davis' repertoire of hillbilly (and nineteenth-
century popular) favorites. The low point comes when
Jimmie and the Sunshine Boys stage a minstrel show
with a blackface character at each end. But Davis uses
the entertainment to rouse the (white) masses to take
the town away from the corrupters, and a repentant
judge agrees. 68 min.

Mr. District Attorney (1947)
Three of the four films that refer to the title of the long-
running radio show (1939-1951) had Left ties; two of them
with scripters Ian McLellan Hunter• and long-time Samuel
Ornitz• writing partner Robert Tasker, and another had
director Bernard Vorhaus.• This last title is probably the
best, heavily influenced by film noir and with Marguerite
Chapman as the *fatale*. Adolphe Menjou, as he did in real
life (he was a ferocious enemy of the Left), played the
prosecutor.

Mr. Peabody and the Mermaid (1948)
Inter-John, Inc./Universal. Prod: Nunnally Johnson. Dir:
Irving Pichel.• Scr: Nunnally Johnson. Novel basis: Guy
and Constance Jones, *Peabody's Mermaid* (1946). Cast:
William Powell, Ann Blyth, Irene Hervey, Andrea King,
Clinton Sundberg, Lumsden Hare, Hugh French, Fred
Clark, Art Smith, Ivan Browing, Cynthia Corley, Mary Field

Along with Dudley Nichols, writer-producer
Johnson was one of the key Popular Front liberals (he
wrote the screenplay for Ford's THE GRAPES OF WRATH and

for JESSE JAMES). But sometimes that sensibility was gentler, as in *Mr. Peabody*, a wistful comic fantasy about a man delusional over turning 50 (Powell) who accidentally hauls a beautiful young mermaid out of the sea and falls in love with her (she doesn't care about his age). What in less skillful hands might have been another bitter Calvinist melodrama about an older man seduced and exploited is here given an affectionate metaphorical treatment. The mermaid, significantly, is unable to speak and piscine from the waist down. Meanwhile, Hervey has one of her best roles as an attractive wife knowledgeable about what her husband is going through but worried enough, in a fine satirical touch, to drag him off to a shrink (Smith). He, too, is a bit older, and warns Powell not to tell his story to anyone under 50. Good advice, and it might apply to the film audience as well for the fullest appreciation of its wry wisdom. Powell and Hervey are at the top of their form; Pichel never directed a better comedy. 90 min.

Mr. Smith Goes to Washington (1939)

Col. Prod: Frank Capra. Dir: Frank Capra. Scr: Sidney Buchman.• Story basis: Lewis R. Foster, *The Gentleman from Montana* (unpublished). Cast: James Stewart, Jean Arthur, Beulah Bondi, Claude Rains, Edward Arnold, Thomas Mitchell, Harry Carey, Guy Kibbee, Eugene Pallette, Porter Hall, Jack Carson

Reined in by Hollywood censors who insisted that individual senators rather than the Senate at large be condemned, this fictional view of the rebellious Farmer-Labor congressman Charles A. Lindbergh (the flyer's father) is one of the strongest political films of the 1930s. Buchman's script was continually re-adapted by Capra, among others, but the heart of the story survives, no doubt because it suited Capra's own New Dealish mood.

Freshman senator Stewart, newly arrived in Washington and surrounded by lobbyists, learns of a corrupt land deal involving the senior senator of his state and affecting his home district. Attempts to get out the real story are sabotaged with fascist-like brutality back home and political scheming in Washington. His choices narrowed, Stewart enters a memorable filibuster, earning ridicule from politicians and growing support from the honest folks who come to see him as their spokesman and hero. Stewart, who like Capra turned sharply right after the Second World War, is seen at his best here: unsophisticated but sincere, the almost homely face of democracy endangered. It won a combination of more Academy Awards and nominations than any other film scripted from the Left (best story award for writer Lewis Foster and nominations for best actor, best

director, best interior decoration, best picture, best screenplay, best sound, best supporting actor, and best score). 130 min.

Mr. Winkle Goes to War (1944)

Col. Prod: Jack Moss. Dir: Alfred E. Green. Scr: George Corey,• Waldo Salt,• Louis Solomon.• Novel basis: Theodore Pratt, *Mr. Winkle Goes to War* (1943). Cast: Edward G. Robinson, Ruth Warrick, Richard Lane, Robert Armstrong, Ted Donaldson, Bob Haymes, Richard Lane, Richard Gaines, Ann Shoemaker

Strangely touching flag-waver offers Robinson another of his post-gangster roles as a loving family man (in this case, a would-be father) who yearns to be freer but chooses sacrifice. In this case, he gets both. Trapped in a bank desk job he despises, he announces he is quitting and tells his overbearing wife that he wants to open a small repair shop (the newspaper ad begins, "The whole world needs repair") with a boy from the orphanage who would work with him days—like the child he never had. Just as he determines to carry through even if it means divorce from the snobbish Warrick, he is drafted.

In the army, even though he is way too old, he finds comradeship, but once again is stuck in a desk job—until he volunteers for the motor pool. Lots of stock military training and social scenes, like the domestic drama, show Robinson at his best, full of surprises and warmth. His battle glory, perhaps like that of the least citizen-soldier, is unexpected, and the Roman triumphalism greeting him on his return unwanted for the shy, average American. A film that deserves to be much better known. 80 min.

Modesty Blaise (1966)

20th. Prod: Joseph Janni. Dir: Joseph Losey.• Scr: Evan Jones, Stanley Dubens. Comic strip basis: Jim Holdaway, *Modesty Blaise* (1963-1970). Cast: Monica Vitti, Terence Stamp, Dirk Bogarde, Rosella Falk, Harry Andrews, Michael Craig, Scilla Gabel, Clive Revill, Joe Melia

A Pop-Op film, *Modesty* is at once exile director Losey's spoof of the James Bond series and an evocation of Carnaby Street style. Like Pop Art generally, it fails as avant-garde and suffers from a lack of substance, but has some evocative sixties-ish moments. The Cold War has definitely lost its chic here. And if the bourgeoisie is not doomed (as in earlier Left treatments), it is hopelessly out of style. But audiences stayed away in droves, making it Losey's splashiest failure.

Vitti, miscast as the sultry secret agent openly promoting her own agenda, is remarkably unsexy (made just a couple of years later, such a film would look more like *Barbarella*) and equally unlikely to be her own person—although she looks suitably weird in the succession of outlandish costumes. Stamp makes a better Willie Garvin, her cockney assistant and appropriate (but never quite consummated) lover. Taking on a job for British MI5, they fall prey to her old nemesis, played by Losey favorite Bogarde. Here again a delightful psychotic, Bogarde emulates and satirizes Bond antiheroes: he has his own island, his entourage and even his own priest.

Technological games take up too much time, and occasional bursts into song don't amuse much. But when Vitti is thrown into a totally Op-art prison cell looking like an Escher print, and when an Arab army arrives by ship to rescue her on horseback, the wildness of Losey's schemes almost succeed, capped by the image of Bogarde staked out in the desert, his lips cracked, pleading, "Champagne! Champagne!" Still, the essentially humorless Losey never should have tried a comedy. 119 min., color.

The Molly Maguires (1970)

Para. Prod: Walter Bernstein,• Martin Ritt.• Dir: Martin Ritt. Scr: Walter Bernstein. Cast: Sean Connery, Richard Harris, Samantha Eggar, Frank Finlay

An \$11-million financial bust, likely because of the expansive and historically detailed *mise en scène*: no expense was spared for the brilliant cinematographic effort of James Wong Howe (the next to last film of one of Left noir's greatest cameramen) to capture the feel of Irish American working-class life in a Pennsylvania coal town of the 1870s. Made perhaps too early to benefit from popular interest in blue-collar social themes (John Sayles' MATEWAN is a similar but much smaller movie), it is nonetheless a significant contribution to the Hollywood art film. Ritt, blacklisted as an actor, made the film that his generational cohorts had talked of making since the days of radical Depression theater.

The Molly Maguires arise out of the tradition of Irish secret societies, but also the desperate need for a collective response to terrible conditions in the mines. Unable to organize legally and openly, they plan mini-conspiracies against scabs and bosses. Connery, a labor spy for the notorious Pinkerton Agency, is taken to be a dedicated radical, and the story of his dirty work unravels—but too slowly for the film audience, and without the romantic heroism that most film viewers evidently wanted to see. 124 min., color.

The Monkey's Uncle (1965)

Walt Disney Pictures. Prod: Ron Miller. Dir: Robert Stevenson. Scr: Tom and Helen August (pseudonyms for Alfred Lewis Levitt• and Helen Levitt•). Cast: Tommy Kirk, Annette Funicello, Leon Ames, Frank Faylen, Arthur O'Connell, Norman Grabowski

In a sequel to THE MISADVENTURES OF MERLIN JONES, college science whiz Kirk (happily stuck with singing girlfriend Funicello and the annoyingly unforgettable title tune) gets assigned a new set of problems. For instance, there's sleep-learning: first he tries it on his pet chimp, and then on football players who are not much smarter (and manage to bungle anyway). Then college prez Ames learns that in order to get a \$10 million endowment from an alum, someone has to fly without an engine. Kirk devises a turn-of-the-century-style peddle machine and uses it himself, offering the best laughs of the film. Funicello is insensibly jealous now and then, but otherwise plain dull. It was the end of the Levitts' film career, more or less. 87 min.

Monsignor (1982)

20th. Prod: Frank Yablans, David Niven, Jr. Dir: Frank Perry. Scr: Abraham Polonsky,• Wendell Mayes. Novel basis, Jack-Alain Leger, *Monsignore* (1976). Cast: Christopher Reeve, Geneviève Bujold, Fernando Rey, Jason Miller, Joseph Cortese, Adolfo Celi, Leonardo Cimino, Tomas Milían, Robert J. Prosky, Joe Pantoliano, Milena Vukotic

Polonsky's last major film was savaged by the church (and the critics) and very likely would have been repressed altogether a few decades earlier. Father Flaherty (Reeve) is great at maneuvers like seducing nun Bujold (she gives in rather easily), shooting at enemies and scheming to use church funds for a Mafia operation. He's an American priest who joins the staff of the Vatican Secretary in 1944 and does at least some of his scheming in a good cause (if you can call it that), saving the Vatican during the postwar financial crisis at the cost of putting the Mafia into power—something that really happened, though more indirectly, in a deal between the Central Intelligence Agency, officials of the Marshall Plan and the Christian Democratic Party.

The two illicit lovers actually make it on a rooftop with the Vatican dome looming above them. (Admittedly, she doesn't know he's a priest). Next they see each other in a papal audience with pontiff Cimino, who looks remarkably like E.T., and an awfully, awfully surprised Bujold. This is the best and most hilarious moment in a long film. There are lots of other healthily dishonest church types, lovely scenes of Rome and Italian villages, but Reeve is just too innocent-looking to play the rascal of the novel, and poor collaboration evidently got in Polonsky's way of writing the tough and hilarious script that this project demanded. Too bad, and not only for Polonsky: 20 years earlier, director Perry had been the *wunderkind* of *David and Lisa*, a notable American art film (with plenty of left-wing characters); a year before *Monsignor, Mommie Dearest* was also a memorable embarrassment. 122 min.

Monsoon (1952)

Leonardo Bercovici• wrote the screenplay, based on a Jean Anouilh play, depicting sympathetically life and love in modern India. It suffers the handicap of Euro-actors and low production values, but is one of Bercovici's few credited scripts after fleeing Hollywood for Rome (and serving mainly as a script doctor for others). It has a sincerity that Indian film makers themselves will use to greater effect in the era just ahead.

Monsieur Klein (1976)

Adel Productions. Prod: Ralph Baum, Alain Delon. Dir: Joseph Losey.• Scr: Franco Solinas, Fernando Morandi (uncredited: Costa Gavras). Cast: Alain Delon, Francine Bergé, Jeanne Moreau, Michael Lonsdale, Juliet Berto

Losey's account of the famous roundup of French Jews by the police in 1942 and their deportation to Germany is the first and also the most ambitious of his three French-language films. For once, he got a decent budget (18 million francs) and the result was a meticulously well-told story with many superb moments, rich with the director's famous gift for *mise en scène*. It was also one of his most intensely political movies, though its real theme was well hidden through his genius for indirection. *Monsieur Klein* is ostensibly about the madness of the Holocaust, which in a sense makes it uncontroversial. But the deeper theme concerns the resistance of Jewish communists to fascism and how their methods were based on a clear understanding of French society. It is as though that movie were projected on the other side of the screen, invisible to us but driving the action throughout, a story about the techniques a group of resistance fighters use in identity theft, infiltration of German defense plants near Paris and the stealing of munitions for sabotage. This is the movie that we are not permitted to see because we are confined to Monsieur Klein's point of view and must discover for ourselves.

Robert Klein (Delon) is a fastidious little haut bourgeois with manners that are as silken as his dressing gowns. He has a casual predisposition to fascism and makes a living buying paintings from distressed Jews at cut-rate prices. His motto is, "None of this has anything to do with me." But one day he discovers a Jewish newspaper on his doorstep—the first clue that his identity has been appropriated by someone of the same name who wants to disappear into the cover of his identify and who is, as he learns eventually, an enemy of the state.

The rest of the film is a chase to unmask the thief and turn him over to the Gestapo so that the "innocent" Klein can vindicate himself from the fatal charge of being a Jew and a Communist. Along the way, as he gets closer to finding the "other" Robert Klein, he gradually awakens to the social horror around him. Although *Monsieur Klein* has sometimes been called a melodrama with elements of film noir, it is closer in spirit to the thriller genre. It was written by Franco Salinas, who scripted for Rossellini before turning out a half-dozen highly prized Marxist spaghetti westerns and a few of director Gillo Pontocorvo's best films, including those global New Left favorites, *The Battle of Algiers* and *Burn!* and two others for Costa-Gavras, *State of Siege* and *Hanna K.*

Vincent Canby of the *New York Times* almost single-handedly killed distribution of the film in the United States with an uncomprehending (or too comprehending) review, and it never achieved the audience it deserves. One of the most important films of the blacklist. 123 min.

The Moon is Down (1943)

20th. Prod: Nunnally Johnson. Dir: Irving Pichel.• Scr: Nunnally Johnson. Novel and play basis: John Steinbeck, *The Moon is Down* (both 1942). Cast: Cedric Hardwicke, Henry Travers, Lee J. Cobb,† Dorris Bowdon, Margaret Wycherly, Peter van Eyck, William Post, Jr., Henry Rowland, E. J. Ballantine, Irving Pichel

Treachery and resistance in Norway early in World War II with a standout production team and strong cast, probably the high point of director Pichel's prolific career. The Steinbeck novel and play (and eventually the movie) became part of a Hollywood debate over the preferred way to make antifascist films—whether to depict Germans (rarely Italians or Japanese) as three-dimensional characters with an occasional virtue, or as propaganda stick figures. The former method was defended by Dudley Nichols and Johnson, among others, as more effective in the long run than propaganda: they hoped it would lay the foundation for a more sophisticated "low modernism" in the popular arts and create a more sophisticated film art for postwar Hollywood in which the artists would exercise substantially more artistic control than they had in the past. The blacklist resolved this question in the negative.

In the film, both the figure of the Norwegian traitor and the German officer who leads the invasion of the town to acquire its natural resources for the Reich are given a measure of humanity. The King of Norway defended it after a viewing in London, saying it would strengthen the Allied cause by dispelling the myth that the Nazis were supermen. The film has been unaccountably out of print for some time. 90 min.

Moon over Montana (1945)
Monogram cheapie written by Louise Rousseau.• Another Jimmy Wakely oater in which he sings a lot and helps a woman with the little railroad that she owns and manages.

The Moon's Our Home (1936)
Para. Prod: Walter Wanger. Dir: William A. Seiter. Scr: Isabel Dawn, Boyce DeGaw (add. dial: Dorothy Parker,• Alan Campbell•). Novel Basis: Faith Baldwin, The Moon's Our Home (1936). Cast: Margaret Sullavan, Henry Fonda, Charles Butterworth, Beulah Bondi, Henrietta Crosman, Walter Brennan, Dorothy Stickney, Brandon Hurst, Lucien Littlefield, Margaret Hamilton, Spencer Charters, Margaret Fielding

One of the Parker-Campbell team's better efforts at sprucing up someone else's script, this one based on a much-admired novelist of women's lives. In an unlikely premise, movie star Sullavan is compelled to marry a dim-witted cousin (Butterworth) over her protests. Happily, famous writer-adventurer Fonda happens to be in New York autographing copies of his newest book, and after he is overcome by the smell of her perfume and simultaneously races out the door of a department store to escape his fans, he accidentally jumps into Sullavan's horse-drawn carriage (!). They talk amiably without revealing their identities, but later meet in Moonsocket, New Hampshire, at his favorite hotel. There, falling seriously in love, they get married, but on their wedding night, her perfume makes him deathly ill and, misunderstanding the signals, Sullavan heads off for New York. Will they reconcile? 80 min.

Moss Rose (1947)
Leonardo Bercovici• contributed to the screenplay for this costume whodunit set in Victorian England with the key bit of evidence an out-of-season rose.

The Most Dangerous Game (1932)
RKO. Prod: David O. Selznick. Dir: Ernest B. Schoedsack, Irving Pichel. Scr: James Ashmore Creelman (uncredited: John Bright•). Story basis: Richard Connell, The Most Dangerous Game (1925). Cast: Joel McCrea, Fay Wray, Leslie Banks, Robert Armstrong, Noble Johnson, Steve Clemente

A low-budget adventure remade as Game for Death (1945) and Run for the Sun (1956) but never again with a left-wing lineup. Likewise, in Hollywood history, the first film for both Pichel and Bright, and their last together.

Based on a famous short story and shot rapidly on the King Kong location using the two lead stars, it revolves around an insidious "game" of an exile Russian aristocrat who allows prisoners on his hidden island an opportunity to run away, then hunts them down—but spares their lives if they can elude him until dawn. Most memorable to the politically minded viewer is the dialogue between McCrea and fellow passengers on a cruise ship. A big game hunter, McCrea himself expresses contempt for humane attitudes, insisting that animals engage him fairly, as he engages them before killing them. Once on the island, the philosophical tables are turned. 78 min.

Move Over, Darling (1963)
20th. Prod: Aaron Rosenberg, Martin Melcher. Dir: Michael Gordon.•† Scr: Bella and Samuel Spewack. Screenplay basis: Leo McCarey, Bella and Samuel Spewack, My Favorite Wife (1940) Poem basis: Alfred, Lord Tennyson, "Enoch Arden" (1865). Cast: Doris Day, James Garner, Polly Bergen, Thelma Ritter, Fred Clark, Don Knots, Elliott Reid, Edgar Buchanan, John Astin, Pat Harrington, Jr., Eddie Qillan, Max Showalter, Pami Lee, Chuck Connors

The fourth telling of the Tennyson tale on film marked another step in director Gordon's rehabilitation, although it surely would have been bigger and considerably better if Marilyn Monroe had starred in a somewhat different version of the story with Dean Martin, as planned. There is strong acting and direction, but a weak plot, with Day, long thought dead, returning home after surviving a shipwreck on a desert island just as the presumably widowered Garner is about to start his honeymoon with Bergen, wife number 2. In the more innocent 1960s, the reappearance of her companion on the island during the lost years (TV hunk Connors) offers a moral problem. 104 min.

Mrs. Mike (1949)

Alfred Lewis Levitt• adapted a popular novel about the adventures of a proper Boston woman (Evelyn Keyes) who marries a Mountie in the Canadian Northwest with all of the difficulties—and songs!—that go with such a marriage.

Murder in the Big House (1942)

Jerome Chodorov• came up with the plot for this intense B-melodrama. A killer about to die in the electric chair calls a newspaperman and offers to incriminate the respectable people who helped him. What he doesn't know is that the governor has already vacated his execution. Before he learns that, the prison warden announces to the press that "a higher power" has taken the execution into His own hands—by striking the killer down with a bolt of lightning through a window. The corpse shows burn marks on head and feet. Did the warden execute the man to shut him up?

Murder, My Sweet (1944)

RKO. Prod: Adrian Scott.• Dir: Edward Dmytryk.•† Scr: John Paxton. Novel basis: Raymond Chandler, *Farewell, My Lovely* (1940). Cast: Dick Powell, Claire Trevor, Mike Mazurki, Otto Kruger, Anne Shirley, Miles Mander

The film that established the noir detective feature as a potential box office gold mine, it further established Dmytryk (whose HITLER'S CHILDREN a few years earlier had played extremely well) as the leftist with the touch of gold. Part of the success of the film was owed to the casting of Powell, the smooth fellow of so many musicals, against type as the classic out-of-luck private dick whose bruises prove his determination to get to the bottom of a crime. In fact, the actual plotting of the murder becomes decreasingly relevant as Chandler's Philip Marlow enters a world distorted by social disorganization (and brilliant editing, camerawork and special effects). The rich, whose plots lie beneath it all, are reviled for their feigned respectability, although by the time we get to the truth the film seems exhausted by its

episodic stops and starts. It is often described as Chandler's favorite film version of his work, in part because of the effective use of flashbacks, with the subjective contradictions of memory fully exposed. Producer Adrian Scott, a sometime screenwriter, had considerable input into the structuring of the film, including the basic flashback frame. Remade in 1975 with Robert Mitchum as *Farewell, My Lovely*. 95 min.

Murphy's Romance (1985)

Col./Delphi IV/Fogwood Films. Prod: Laura Ziskin. Dir: Martin Ritt.• Scr: Irving Ravetch,† Harriet Frank, Jr. Novel basis: Max Schott, *Murphy's Romance* (1980). Cast: James Garner, Sally Field, Brian Kerwin, Corey Haim, Dennis Burkley, Georgann Johnson, Dortha Duckworth, Anna Levine, Carole King

A good cast is mostly wasted on one of Ritt's lesser films. Garner is just a sweet small-towner here. Field, whose cinematic highpoint was reached in Ritt's union film, NORMA RAE, is a divorcee with a son (Haim) in tow. As they enter into courtship, all the expected complications arise. 107 min, color

Music is Magic (1935)

A silly vehicle for Alice Faye about a fading Hollywood star out to revive her career with song and dance, co-written by Edward Eliscu.• Some music by Oscar Levant.

The Mutineers (1949)

Col. Prod: Sam Katzman. Dir: Jean Yarbrough. Scr: Ben Bengal,• Joseph Carole. Cast: Jon Hall, Adele Jergens, George Reeves, Noel Cravat, Don C. Harvey, Matt Willis, Tom Kennedy, Pat Gleason

A cheapie shipboard action drama before Katzman rose to B-heights with exploitation films, and one of only three credits by the feted left-wing playwright Bengal, who was chewed up by Hollywood.

Seaman Hall finds captain Talbot murdered, his pockets stuffed with counterfeit money. Jaquet takes over the ship for a new run, but passenger Reeves (soon to be known as film and TV Superman) and his sexy moll Jergens assume control with the assistance of the dozen or so new passengers. Hall pretends to go along in a plan to go ashore in Marseilles with the money. The best scenes all involve Jergens, who was (or could have been, with a little more opportunity) a sort of Mae West of the seas. 60 min.

My Favorite Brunette (1947)

Daniel Dare† produced this spoof of death row films, with Bob Hope's flashback of how he got there (through complications with Dorothy Lamour, naturally). One of the 26 best-grossing films of the year.

My Friend Flicka (1943)

Francis Edward Faragoh• adapted the story of a boy and a horse who learn how to grow up together in a dangerous world, with the horse learning from the boy how to trust and the boy learning courage from the horse. One of the more successful in a string of darker children's films turned out by Left writers, with Roddy McDowall taking the kind of role he played so artfully in the Hugo Butler• script for LASSIE COME HOME.

My Girl Tisa (1948)

U.S. Pictures/WB. Prod: Milton Sperling. Dir: Elliott Nugent. Scr: Allen Boretz.• Cast: Lilli Palmer, Sam Wanamaker,• Akim Tamiroff, Alan Hale, Hugo Haas, Gale Robbins, Stella Adler, Benny Baker

Another generic ethnic document in which viewers of the day were likely to see a pointedly Jewish male lead (Wanamaker) playing against an ambiguous female lead (Palmer, better remembered for her role as John Garfield's gal in BODY AND SOUL), both evidently from the same hard-pressed but aspiring immigrant group in the turn of the century Lower East Side. Famed Yiddish actress and dramatic coach Adler has a lesser but nonetheless charming role as landlady of the boarding house where they both live—a middle-aged woman always with a fresh "fiancé" to present.

The not improbable premise has Palmer working nights (after her garment factory job) to bring over papa from the Old Country and Wanamaker trying to make himself into a ward-heeler (as a very unlikely Teddy Roosevelt Republican: in the old Lower East Side, Republicans were not likely to be reformers but out-and-out crooks). He also aspires to become a presidential advisor. There is some slight fun as petty capitalist Hale is tutored in becoming a citizen and Palmer herself faces off against the lecherous Tamiroff to pay for her dad's steerage fee (he tricks her into signing a labor contract with years of back-breaking work as part of the deal). A spectacularly silly ending, featuring Teddy Roosevelt himself, completes a sense of white folks' possibilities in America for those who are willing to fight for them— the classic New Deal message of emancipation and Americanization. Actor Wanamaker left for London and

a life hailing Shakespeare rather than face HUAC, Truman's checkmate of the New Deal. 95 min.

My Kingdom for a Cook (1943)

Harold Goldman• wrote this Charles Coburn comedy about a gourmet Brit with snobbish attitudes about Americans. Then the Englishman runs into a homespun kitchen genius (Almira Sessions), and sets out to lure her away from her employers. After a protracted comic struggle, Coburn admits there's no fool like an old fool and that Yanks are just fine, thus vindicating the common wartime struggle.

My Pal Wolf (1944)

RKO. Prod: Adrian Scott.• Dir: Alfred L. Werker. Scr: Lillian Hayward, John Paxton, Leonard Praskins. Cast: Sharon Moffett, Jill Esmond, Una O'Connor, George Cleveland, "Grey Shadow" as Wolf the dog.

Produced by Adrian Scott and one of his collaborations with progressive writer John Paxton, this "poor little rich girl" film has the daughter of D.C. executives stuck in rural Virginia on their farm, cared for by servants, making friends with the rural folk and pained to learn that the new governess wants to transform her tomboy manner into feminine grace. Luckily, she comes across a raggedy German shepherd who has fallen into an abandoned mine shaft, feeds him secretly, and (through the connivance of the servants) adopts him despite the governess' determined opposition.

All this is sentimental backdrop for the usual wartime message of mobilization. When "Wolf" (as she names the dog) is found to be an army regular (if not an enlistee) and must be returned to Washington, she takes to the road, actually making her way to the apartment of the Secretary of War. This kindly gent explains that the fascists are attacking children all over the world, and that Wolf can save soldiers' lives. 74 min.

My Sister Eileen (1942)

Col. Prod: Max Gordon. Dir: Alexander Hall. Scr: Joseph Fields, Jerome Chodorov.• Story basis: Ruth McKenny, *My Sister Eileen* (1938). Cast: Rosalind Russell, Brian Aherne, Janet Blair, George Tobias, Allyn Joslyn, Elizabeth Patterson, Richard Quine, June Havoc, Arnold Stang, the Three Stooges

The New York apotheosis that made money for years, including a hit play co-authored by Joseph Fields and Jerome Chodorov, two films and the 1953 Broadway musical *Wonderful Town*. It all began with a 1930s series of *New Yorker* short stories by Communist Ruth McKenney, a staffer at the *New Masses* and author of left-wing novels. (The real Eileen married the mordantly comic and radical novelist Nathanael West and died with him in a car crash in 1939.) As a commercial writer with good connections, though, McKenney managed to turn a personal odyssey of Indianians removed to the City (in the play and films, Ohioans) into an archetype that Neil Simon, among others, would ceaselessly exploit in many comedy-dramas to come. Manhattanites, especially those in Greenwich Village, are at once remarkably quaint and cosmopolitan; they show white-bread American girls how to live differently and (more important) think differently about themselves. In this setting anything is possible, but love is inevitable. Who would have thought that such bohemian wackiness, charming as it is, would be the only literary bookmark for the same woman who wrote the novel *Industrial Valley* (1939), an account of the Akron rubber workers' daring sit-down strike to establish a union in the middle 1930s (and the same labor action that inspired the sit-down strike in 1937 in Flint, Michigan). 96 min.

My Sister Eileen (1955)

Col. Prod: Fred Kohlmar. Dir. Richard Quine. Scr: Blake Edwards, Richard Quine. Cast: Janet Leigh, Betty Garrett, Jack Lemmon, Bob Fosse, Kurt Kasznar, Dick York, Lucy Marlow, Barbara Brown

The musical remake of the first film version of MY SISTER EILEEN has considerably less force than the 1942 film, one more reminder of the collapse of the cultural energy of the Popular Front into a disguised version of itself during the Cold War. What remains owes much to the original author's personal angst, scarcely less abundant (but expressed merely as fifties-style kitsch). In this version, Betty Garrett, in real life the wife of friendly witness (and former Communist leader of the Screen Actors Guild) Larry Parks, plays the homely intellectual who finds compensation in her literary talent and verbal wit, while her sister the sparkling beauty and aspiring actress has to fight off the boys with a stick. Jack Lemmon, not quite at his youthful best here, is properly superficial

as a magazine editor. Bob Fosse, who did the choreography, also dances some of it himself. The music by Jules Styne limits the plot to a simple statement of McKenney's themes. One wonders what the author—by this time expelled from the Communist Party and writing a memoir about romantic love in the McCarthy era—thought of the final film production. 108 min., color.

Mysterious Doctor (1943)

Serial decapitations are committed by a headless Nazi ghost in a screenplay by Richard Weil.•

Mysterious Island (1961)

Col. Prod: Charles H. Schneer. Dir: Cyril Endfield.• Scr: John Prebble, Daniel B. Ullman, Crane Wilbur. Story basis: Jules Verne, *L'Ile Mystérieuse* (1874). Cast: Michael Craig, Michael Callan, Gary Merrill, Herbert Lom, Joan Greenwood, Beth Rogan, Percy Herbert, Dan Jackson, Nigel Green

This was the second American version of Verne's fantasy novel (the first was a 1927 silent film), and Endfield's only sci-fi entry, the most traditional among a small group of such films written or directed by blacklistees in the United Kingdom. Union soldiers escape from a Confederate prison during the Civil War in a hot-air balloon, only to find themselves on an island (near New Zealand!) where dwells the brilliant and psychotic Captain Nemo (Lom), who has experimented in the creation of giant creatures. Meanwhile, Cap'n Craig is mighty good at holding off monsters, Merrill and Callan are his hardy crewmen, and Greenwood, the stranded British noblewoman, does her best to keep up standards under these strained and low-budget circumstances. 101 min., color.

Mystery Sea Raider (1940)

Routine B-war actioner directed by Edward Dmytryk•† about Nazi saboteurs working the Atlantic coast of North America; interesting only for striking these notes so early.

N

voice-over at the beginning of *Naked City* (as the camera sweeps over Manhattan), was absorbing the style of the tabloid press for film narration. He repeated the performance on the memorable TV series of the same name (with some graylisted Jewish lefties scripting it), broadcast while Dassin was in full flight from HUAC. The film won Oscars for best black-and-white cinematography and best film editing. 96 min.

Naked City (1948)

Hellinger Prod./U-I. Prod: Mark Hellinger. Dir: Jules Dassin.• Scr: Albert Maltz.• Story basis: Malvin Wald. Cast: Barry Fitzgerald, Howard Duff, Don Taylor, Ted de Corsia, Dorothy Hart

A photographically rich glimpse of Manhattan in its last era as a predominantly white and substantially Jewish working-class city heavily dependent on small manufacturing. Viewed strictly as a political narrative, the film is unmemorable, even retrograde for future blacklistee director and co-writer Maltz. But as an aesthetic adventure in urban noir with a touch of Italian neorealism, especially in the use of black-and-white cinematography, it remains unsurpassed: faces, streets, traffic and bridges are etched as if by a determined act of memory, as if *this* everyday life would soon be destroyed and forgotten (as indeed it was). The score by Miklos Rosza is also memorable as a counterpoint to ostensibly mundane rhythms of the city. The famous title, interestingly, was coined by the newspaper photojournalist Weegee, who sold the right to Hellinger for this film and retitled his own documentary with something less memorable.

A fashion model and playgirl, murdered by unseen hands in the first moments of the film, sets the station house plot in motion around detective Fitzgerald and his assistant Taylor (who unwillingly snatches his overtime from home life as a young husband and father in Queens). The two set out testing one clue after another. Duff, an ex-college boy and middle-class failure, looks good for involvement of some kind, and the uncovered truth about his deception of a rich girl (Hart) provides the only quasi-romantic interest. The film closes with a superb chase through Lower East Side streets and back lots (which look unchanged since the 1890s), onto the Brooklyn Bridge, leaving the cops-and-robbers plot far behind.

The effort to create a mode of documentary fiction, working on the minds of the Hollywood Left since the production of *Native Land* by Leo Hurwitz, Ben Maddow and others, precedes the docudrama by 40 years and offers a promise unfulfilled. Producer Mark Hellinger, offering a

The Naked Dawn (1955)

Universal. Prod: James O. Radford. Dir: Edgar Ulmer. Scr: Herman Schneider, Nin Schneider (pseudonyms for Julian Zimet•). Cast: Arthur Kennedy, Betta St. John, Roy Engel, Eugene Iglesias, Charlita

Hollywood outsider Ulmer's only real western (actually, a Mexican-western) is a real curiosity. Blacklisted writer Zimet really was in Mexico at the time reading Maxim Gorky. He said he adapted the narrative from Gorky's short story "Chelkash," in which the protagonist was described as "a hardened drunkard and a bold and dexterous thief." Zimet turns him into Santiago (Kennedy), a grizzled, whiskey-guzzling Mexican bohemian who joined the revolution after being cheated out of his farmland. The film opens on the moment when the revolution has failed and Santiago and his partner have turned to banditry to survive. When they steal a strongbox from an Anglo railroad station, the partner dies after taking a bullet in the escape. Santiago then finds his way to the home of a peasant and his young wife to hide out. He tries to befriend the peasant, who is envious of his stolen money and the way Santiago throws it around. The peasant's wife, embittered by her virtual domestic slavery, longs for the bandit to take her away. After conjugating greed and eros, Santiago teaches the two of them the art of revolutionary self-sacrifice.

Naked Dawn remains obscure in the United States but was well-regarded in France. François Truffaut claimed to have found in it the dramatic solution to *Jules et Jim*, apparently in the way Zimet depicted the ambivalence of the young peasant wife (played by *Tarzan* series veteran St. John). There is no woman in Gorky's story, however, and a careful viewing reveals that the love triangle is very close to the one in *Shane*. 82 min.

The Naked Jungle (1954)

Paramount. Prod: George Pal. Dir: Byron Haskin. Scr: Philip Yordan, Ranald MacDougall (uncredited: Ben Maddow•†). Cast: Charlton Heston, Eleanor Parker, Abraham Wofer, William Conrad

Exotic adventure mixes sci-fi or creature effects with the subgenre of civilized-lady-and-roughneck-capitalist, the sort of thing normally staged in Africa and shot in Hollywood. Yordan, as so often in this period, had talented blacklistee (and later friendly witness) Maddow doing his work. Cinematography by Ernest Laszlo has its moments in capturing the jungle and the river, but never gets to take flight.

The neurotic Amazon planter Heston (hinted at having no sexual history, or perhaps a conflicted one) can't easily accept mail-order bride Parker from New Orleans because she has been married before. Showing as much cleavage as the times would permit, dishy Parker makes the best of things, hoping for his change of heart but determined to keep her pride. Natives are strictly tribal types (they once had a high civilization, Heston ruminates, but the jungle took them over). Their fondness for shrunken heads reflects the narrative "otherization." By contrast, Heston is almost civilized: though blunt and uncultured, he treats his workers decently (we never quite see them working at anything) and saves them from the cruel planters.

Then the ants advance on the plantation. little red devils by the billions—the real stars of the show. Heston holds on to most of his natives by shaming them in front of Parker—she's not afraid to stay, despite government agent (and later television actor) William Conrad's warnings. This is the revenge of the jungle metaphor, not ecological so much as naturalistic, the test of courage and trust that will make or break the love interest. 95 min., color.

Nazi Agent (1942)

MGM. Prod: Irving Starr. Dir: Jules Dassin.• Scr: Paul Gangelin, John Mehen, Jr., Lothar Mendes. Cast: Conrad Veidt, Anne Ayars, Dorothy Tree,• Frank Reicher, Sidney Blackmer, Martin Koslek, Marc Lawrence†

A tight little drama on the "good German" as an American citizen finds immigrant numismatist Veidt surprised to learn that his twin brother has been appointed German consul—and demands that he spy on his adopted country. The good brother replaces the bad one, intriguing to pass inside information of sabotage plans along to the authorities while running greater and greater risks for himself. Drama reaches its climax when Veidt (a solid antifascist in real life, with a Jewish wife) must decide whether to save himself by going to the authorities with the full truth, or to save loyal assistant Tree and thereby face an angry crowd booing him as he returns to Germany and to certain death. Dassin's first feature. 83 min.

Never on Sunday (1960)

Lopert Pictures/Melinafilm. Prod: Jules Dassin.• Dir: Jules Dassin. Scr: Jules Dassin. Cast: Melina Mercouri, Jules Dassin, George Foundas, Titos Vandis, Mitsos Liguisos, Despo Diamantidou

A film phenomenon that simultaneously put the Greek film industry, Bazouki music, Mercouri, and even Greece on the (tourist) map. Mercouri is the ambivalent but fascinating hooker she had played in *Stella* (1953) against the background of music considered "Turkish" and lower class (or even gangsterish) in Greece. Dassin was a Hollywood exile who had a smashing success in France with RIFIFI and then hit a brick wall. Looking for the mainstream hit, he found it with the theme of an American tourist in search of authenticity who discovers in Mercouri what he believes is the primordial spontaneity of womanhood itself. He tries everything, even a bribe through a mobster, to remove Mercouri from her job as the local prostitute for many shipyard workers. In the process he reveals the character of the uncomprehending American on one side and the possibilities for solidarity between Greek workers and even prostitutes on the other. Stellar from start to finish. 97 min.

Never Say Goodbye (1946)

WB. Prod: William Jacobs. Dir: James V. Kern. Scr: I. A. L. Diamond, James V. Kern Story basis: Ben Barzman,• Norma Barzman,• "Don't Ever Leave Me" (unpublished). Cast: Errol Flynn, Eleanor Parker, Patti Brady, Lucille Watson, S. Z. Sakall, Forrest Tucker, Donald Woods, Peggy Knudsen, Tom D'Andrea, Hattie McDaniel

This feature helped set the guidelines of the standard plot of the cute child who brings the parents back together. Flynn is an artist who is too much of a playboy, Parker his estranged spouse who has wearied of his running around. Their daughter (Brady) has her heart set on their reconciliation, and it would surely work a lot sooner (depriving the film of its thin plot) if only Flynn's model and current girlfriend Watson didn't keep showing up and acting catty.

At turns sexually alluring and motherly, Parker is stymied until she comes up with a scheme about as original as the shy woman taking off her glasses: Parker uses Marine sergeant Tucker to make Flynn jealous. Too predictable and borderline maudlin (Brady was not destined to shine as a child actress), it nonetheless has some clever scenes and hard work by swashbuckler Flynn to become a suave comic lead. Flynn's famous imitation of Bogart was on the money. 97 min.

New Orleans (1947)

Jules Levy/Majestic. Prod: Jules Levy, Herbert J. Biberman.• Dir: Arthur Lubin. Scr: Elliot Paul, Dick Irving Hyland. Story basis: Elliot Paul, Herbert J. Biberman. Cast: Dorothy Patrick, Irene Rich, John Alexander, Arturo de Córdova, Billie Holiday, Richard Hageman, Marjorie Lord (also: Louis Armstrong, Kid Ory, Zutty Singleton, Woody Herman, Meade Lux Lewis)

An important and often overlooked film co-produced and co-written by director Biberman, his last before the blacklist and the famed SALT OF THE EARTH. The narrative about middle-class patriarchal anxiety over debutante daughters slumming in the New Orleans jazz district underlines the social context of the rise of jazz, its repression in New Orleans' Storyville by the U.S. Navy in 1917 and the resulting diaspora of jazz up the Mississippi to Chicago (and the rest of the world).

The film opens amiably by contrasting the world of classical music with the sweaty world of brothel jazz, rather in the mold of the Gershwin biopic RHAPSODY IN BLUE—there is even the kindly German Ph.D. (Richard Hagement) who wants to encourage dialogue and respect between musicians from both worlds. The tale is enlivened considerably by a fine score. This is the only Hollywood feature in which the great Billie Holiday appeared; she plays the girlfriend of bandleader Louis Armstrong in the role of King Oliver (Armstrong's mentor in real life).

Eventually a darker tone takes over the film. After a public controversy erupts over the unchaparoned appearances of the white debs in the jazz bars, a grand jury is convened and the navy clears the eight square blocks of the city named after its alderman (Sidney Story). The crowd scenes of refugees leaving the area during the actual crackdown are reminiscent of newsreels from Germany in the 1930s, effectively driving home the message that the war against jazz was political and racial from the get-go. 89 min.

Night and Day (1946)

Leo Townsend† co-wrote this Cole Porter biopic, considered long and vacuous by critics but loved by audiences. Oscar nominations for musical director Ray Heindorf.

Night and the City (1950)

20th. Prod: Samuel G. Engel. Dir: Jules Dassin.• Scr: Jo Eisinger (uncredited: Austin Dempster). Novel basis: Gerald Kersh, Night and the City (1946). Cast: Richard Widmark, Gene Tierney, Googie Withers, Hugh Marlowe, Francis L. Sullivan, Herbert Lom

Widmark is a tout for a clip joint, offering tourists illicit entertainment while dreaming of becoming a promoter. His girlfriend is the club singer who, off-duty, reminds him continually that he should find an honest job. A barely submerged subplot finds the attractive but older wife of the obese club owner angling for Widmark as her way out of the marriage to manage her own club (for which he must obtain a license). Widmark's chance to become a wrestling manager places him in charge of an aged giant, whose son happens to be the reigning promoter. While he scrambles for cash, manipulating two wrestlers to fight in a staged match, his plans fall apart and the club owner sets him up for a paid killing by the underworld.

Following shortly after Dassin's NAKED CITY and shot at the beginning of his life-long exile, Night can be seen as another vehicle for a psychologically twisted Widmark character. If so, this is better than most because of its sociological features, the antihero who lacks any admirable qualities but is so pathetic as to be almost loveable. Dassin brilliantly manages a nonnaturalistic setting, with shadows everywhere, sweeping wide-angle shots, wharves and broken buildings standing for the broken world that finally overwhelms all the players. 95 min.

Night Club Girl (1945)

Written by Henry Blankfort,• this is the tale of a brother-and-sister team who leave their home town in a blaze of glory on their way to Hollywood (to a nightclub, not the movies). When they arrive they are forced to sleep in parking lots and steal milk from cats to survive. After lots of comic mayhem, all turns right side up. Highlight: Count Basie's band doing "One O'Clock Jump."

A Night in Casablanca (1946)

Roland Kibbee† co-wrote this Marx Brothers send-up of the Warner Brothers classic, which the latter actually tried to halt on the ground of a copyright violation and then wilted under a barrage of Groucho's sarcasm ("What about Brothers? Do you own that, too? Professionally, we were brothers long before you were.") In their last outing together, the boys reveal Nazi spies behind the curtains in an exotic hotel. The fun starts when they suck a spy's toupee into a vacuum cleaner.

Night Plane from Chunking (1943)

Para. Prod: Walter MacEwen. Dir: Ralph Murphy. Story basis: Harry Hervey, "Sky Over China" (unpublished).

Scr: Earl Felton, Theodore Reeves, Lester Cole.• Cast: Robert Preston, Ellen Drew, Otto Kruger, Steven Geray, Victor Sen Yung, Tamara Geva, Soo Yong

A superior antifascist and antiracist update of *Shanghai Express* (1932), which relied on the same Harry Hervey story turning on the familiar plot with odd types trapped in an isolated situation (jungle, desert, island, rescue boat), some proving themselves of noble character and others treacherous. In this case, a Chinese plane is forced down between mountains while the war rages. The survivors are compelled to forage and to make collective life-and-death decisions.

The film opens strongly with an American businessman treating the Chinese as inferiors and planning to make good money from the Japanese invaders. Attempting an escape from a war zone, the businessman and a half-dozen assorted others board a plane flown by Preston, an American archeologist-turned-pilot (he's "making the world safe for archaeologists"). Forced down, they have evidently been betrayed by someone (or some two) among them: the Free French officer, the Dutch diplomat, or someone else? Action (on a small budget) and heated conversation clarify the politics—our protagonist kills one Nazi collaborator "for the millions of people you've starved and mutilated." 69 min.

The Night Riders (1939)
An unusual John Wayne Three Mesquiteers title co-written by Stanley Roberts.† Wayne and the boys turn into night-riding terrorists after they are thrown off their land by a phony baron whose forged Spanish land grant is held up in court, at least until he's exposed. The film is worth a look. The same year, Wayne hit the big time in John Ford's *Stagecoach*.

Nine Girls (1944)
A Karen DeWolf• and Connie Lee• collaboration about a sorority girl who is so detestable that after she is found murdered the suspects multiply quickly. The mystery moves predictably to a remote mountain cabin for a solution preceded by plenty of intrigue. Brightened by Evelyn Keyes and Jinx Falkenburg.

No Down Payment (1957)
20th. Prod: Jerry Wald. Dir: Martin Ritt.• Scr: Ben Maddow.•† Cast: Joanne Woodward, Jeffrey Hunter, Sheree North, Tony Randall, Cameron Mitchell, Patricia Owens, Barbara Rush, Pat Hingle, Robert H. Harris, Aki Aleong,

Jim Hayward, Mimi Gibson, Donald Towers, Charles Herbert

Blacklisted actor Ritt's return, slipping under the blacklist as director, in one of the most important "crack in the picture window" dramas about suburban emotional disorder and one of the key transition pictures to 1960s cinema. Joanne Woodward later recalled in an oral history that this was her first outstanding Hollywood role and one of her best for years to come. The script was clumsy, but with much effort on all sides (and many rewrites on the set), the outstanding cast, with Ritt's guidance, pulled it through.

In a California suburban town safely distanced from the city, commuter and local blue-collar husbands experience a crisis of expectations and values. Unlike *Man in the Grey Flannel Suit*, this comes only in small part because women want more and better material possessions. The thoughtful liberal actor Randall, in one of his early film roles, is especially good as the alcoholic salesman. But each couple has its role in unravelling the narrow-mindedness (emphatically including racial exclusiveness) and insecurity of life on America's new frontier.

Producer Jerry Wald, a non-blacklistee responsible for many of the social films of the 1940s, described it as one of the most courageous and important American films of the McCarthy period. Studio execs vetoed the original ending as too critical of American values and imposed an artificial resolution. 105 min.

No Limit (1931)
Early Viola Brothers Shore• vehicle for Clara Bow, who plays a movie-theater usher whose act of kindness to a stranger propels her into an unknown world of wealth and luxury but that turns out to be a front for gambling interests.

No Minor Vices (1948)
Enterprise/MGM. Prod: Lewis Milestone. Dir: Lewis Milestone. Scr: Arnold Manoff.• Cast: Dana Andrews, Lilli Palmer, Louis Jourdan, Jane Wyatt, Norman Lloyd, Bernard Gorcey, Roy Roberts, Fay Baker, Sharon McManus, Ann Doran, Beau Bridges, Frank Kreig, Kay Williams, Bobby Hyatt

Enterprise was a small and short-lived studio that harbored a large number of leftist writers and directors eager to break out of the established studio system. This was one of its few comedies, a challenge to the regimentation of women within bourgeois marriage, even if the ending was rather conventional.

A cranky artist living next door to a psychiatrist meets the doc's wife and sets her to thinking about how routine her life is. She agrees to model for the artist even as the jealous shrink is tempted by his adoring secretary. Everything is straightened out, but not before the doc learns a thing or two about taking his wife's affection for granted. An early celebration of the postwar bohemianism that would bloom in the 1950s. Beau Bridges' film debut. 96 min.

No More Orchids (1932)

A typical "white telephone" piece, co-written by Gertrude Purcell.† Carole Lombard, a poor little rich girl, is compelled by fate to marry into royalty (how un-American!) to preserve family honor and save her father from financial ruin. But dad (Walter Connolly) turns the tables, sacrificing himself so she can marry someone else. Yawn.

No One Man (1932)

Another Carole Lombard flick from the same period (see NO MORE ORCHIDS), this time from the hand of the usually more interesting Sidney Buchman,• but alas not this time. Lombard, freshly divorced, believes no one man can possess all of the necessary virtues to interest her, so she vows to marry "one virtue at a time." But cynical plans for serial monogamy did not include physician-heartthrob Paul Lukas, who teaches her a thing or two about love and loyalty.

No Sad Songs for Me (1950)

CASABLANCA screenwriter Howard Koch's• last film before the blacklist, one of Dorothy Tree's• final appearances as an actress and also Margaret Sullavan's final film. Self-sacrificing Sullavan, told she is dying of cancer and keeping it a secret, realizes husband Wendell Corey has fallen in love with another woman (Viveca Lindfors), whom she gets to know and, improbably, likes. Adapted from Ruth Southard's novel of the same title (1944).

No Time for Love (1943)

Para. Prod: Mitchell Leisen, Fred Kohlmar. Dir: Mitchell Leisen. Scr: Claude Binyon. Story basis: Robert Lees,• Frederic I. Rinaldo.• Cast: Claudette Colbert, Fred Mac-Murray, June Havoc, Ilka Chase, Richard Haydn, Paul McGrath, Marjorie Gateson, Bill Goodwin, Robert Herrick, Morton Lowry, Rhys Williams, Murray Alper, John Kelly

Fair war-of-the-sexes piece with Colbert cast very much in the image of Margaret Bourke-White, and Mac-Murray the self-educated and dignified proletarian, both set against the real-life backdrop of women's advances in World War II. In Lees' script, Colbert comes off as the sophisticated photographer who, on assignment among the sandhogs (crews digging tunnels for future New York subways) runs into the ruggedly debonair MacMurray. As he becomes her assistant in a classic sex-role reversal, each must adjust values—although the Hollywood drift inevitably finds her doing most of the adjusting toward the last scenes of the film. As Lees reflected, the best moments of role reversal were cut by the studio hacks. Oscar nominations for art-set decoration (Hans Dreier, Robert Usher and Sam Comer). 83 min.

None But the Lonely Heart (1944)

RKO. Prod: David Hampstead. Dir: Clifford Odets.† Scr: Clifford Odets. Cast: Cary Grant, Ethel Barrymore, Jane Wyatt, June Duprez, Barry Fitzgerald, Dan Duryea, George Coulouris

An Odets epic of the slums, no doubt the film in which his creative control was greatest, but paradoxically situated far from the locus of his theatrical triumphs (the Yiddish-tinted New York immigrant life). Still, it's almost entirely successful in transferring the themes of poverty to London's East End and the Yiddish family drama to the worries of a lone drifter played by Grant.

Son of a British veteran killed at Verdun in the First World War, Grant has grown up with a widowed mother (owner of a small junk shop) and a proletarian existentialism. A voice-over explains him as an "unknown warrior" of another kind of conflict, a person who searches "for a free, a beautiful, a noble life in the second quarter of the twentieth century" but finds his world reduced to "victims and executioners." He tells his mother, "Peace, that's what we millions want . . . peace with pride." She answers sadly that it is not to be had in the world, "not in these times."

So the tragedy unfolds. Conscience-stricken to hear that she is dying of cancer, Grant resolves to cease his wandering. But he betrays his long-time girlfriend (Wyatt) for a mobster's ex-wife who says she has "about twenty good kisses left in me" and has no hope for their relationship. Always on the edge of petty illegality, he and his mother go over the edge, with similarly tragic consequences. The Jewish avuncular type ever-present in Odets' ghetto dramas is here a kindly pawnbroker who offers "everything with a kiss." Barrymore won an Oscar for best supporting actress; nominations went to German émigré leftist Hans Eisler for best music, Roland Gross for film editor, and the film captured wide critical praise. It is arguably Odets' one successful transformation of his stage skills to films (by himself), destined to be overshadowed by the blacklist and many related disappointments, with the later THE SWEET SMELL OF SUCCESS his only remaining consolation. 113 min.

None Shall Escape (1944)

Col. Prod: Samuel Bischoff. Dir: Andre De Toth. Scr: Lester Cole.• Cast: Marsha Hunt,• Alexander Knox, Henry Travers, Erik Rolf, Richard Crane, Dorothy Morris, Richard Hale

A forgotten, hard-edged war drama that was one of Cole's best ideological efforts: the making of a Nazi. Former German soldier Knox, psychologically ruined by his experiences in the First World War, cannot readapt to life in his home town. After he rapes a student, he loses Hunt, his girlfriend, and is ripe material for the Nazi party. He returns to his village again as a commandant and terrorizes the inhabitants. As he recalls events at his war crimes trial, he gains the introspection that life denied him. 85 min.

Norma Rae (1979)

20th. Prod: Tamara Asseyev, Alex Rose. Dir: Martin Ritt.• Scr: Harriet Frank, Jr., Irving Ravetch.† Cast: Sally Field, Ron Leibman, Beau Bridges, Pat Hingle, Barbara Baxley, Gail Stickland, Morgan Paull

Every progressive unionist's favorite film (until, for the more literal-minded, John Sayles' Matewan) and Ritt's contribution 30 years late to "Operation Dixie"— the failed organizing drive to transform Southern industrial life. It also turned out to be one of the few nondocumentary films about unionization in an era of badly eroding labor charisma. Reflecting old loyalties (or perhaps repenting old injuries) in Hollywood, the picture was nominated for best of the year. Field, who won for best actress, is at times a bit cute to be the uneducated textile worker who meets and falls somewhat in love (although she is already married) with organizer Leibman, but she smiles at adversity, including the bosses' mean-spiritedness, crosses race lines and brings in a vote for union recognition. Ritt's view of industrial work in the South rings true, even if unionization proved even more difficult to achieve than as pictured. For who knows how many thousands of viewers this is their only positive view of unionism. 114 min.

North of Shanghai (1939)

Maurice Rapf• and Harold Buchman• penned this "premature antifascist" actioner about newspaper reporter

Betty Furness, who goes to the front in China during the Japanese occupation. She joins the resistance, routing spies and creating alliances.

The North Star (1943)

Samuel Goldwyn Company. Prod: Samuel Goldwyn. Dir: Lewis Milestone. Scr: Lillian Hellman.• Cast: Dana Andrews, Walter Huston, Anne Baxter, Farley Granger, Walter Brennan, Erich von Stroheim, Jack Perrin, Dean Jagger

Notorious in the McCarthy era for its happy look at pre-invasion Russian life (and even more for its screenwriter), North Star is best seen as one of the cluster of films (most similar: SONG OF RUSSIA, with script by Paul Jarrico•) that were intended to bolster homefront spirit by romanticizing America's allies. Many Oscar nominations, including best screenplay for Hellman, best cinematographer (James Wong Howe), best art/set decoration (Perry Rerguson and Howard Bristol), best special effects (Clarence Slifer), best music (Aaron Copland•) and best sound recording (Thomas F. Moulton). In 1957, prior to television release, the film was mangled to cut out the Russian element and retitled Armored Attack. Current cable film channels have restored the original.

The film neatly divides in half. During the first portion, greatly aided by the music of Copland and Ira Gershwin, the collective farm is seen as a happy village akin to U.S. prairie life at its best, but less individualistic and more cutely ethnic. Manners and mores are attuned only vaguely to the outside, but the villagers know that their hard work will make a better world, beginning in Russia itself.

The German invasion drastically changes the film, which gains an almost documentary character with stock footage of bombers, civilian casualties, and (the usual character of war films) the courage of the antifascist mobilization. As critics point out, the "Russia" created in both halves has little to do with the actual society. But the war and its effects are dramatized with real feeling. 108 min.

Northern Pursuit (1943)

Hollywood Ten member Alvah Bessie• co-wrote this story about a German-Canadian Mountie (Errol Flynn) who accidentally runs across a pair of German spies who had been dropped off by submarine in Hudson's Bay and who cautiously quiz Flynn about his political loyalties. Much of the rest of the story is a guessing-game on this point.

Northwest Rangers (1942)

Another Mountie tale, this one set in the late nineteenth century by screenwriters Gordon Kahn• and David Lang.† Boys grow up to fighting and fussing over a gambling house in the gold region of the Canadian Northwest, with one going bad and the other good.

Nothing But Trouble (1944)

A credit for additional dialogue went to Margaret Gruen• (Howard Koch's• wife) for this Laurel and Hardy comedy about a kid prince in exile who wants nothing more than to be a Real American Boy.

Not Wanted (1949)

Emerald Productions. Prod: Ida Lupino, Anson Bond. Dir: Elmer Clifton, Ida Lupino. Scr: Paul Jarrico,• Ida Lupino. Story basis: Malvin Wald, Paul Jarrico. Cast: Sally Forrest, Keefe Brasselle, Leo Penn,• Dorothy Adams, Wheaton Chambers, Rita Lupino, Audrey Farr, Carole Donne, Ruth Clifford

Lupino's launch into a short-lived phase of producing and directing her own films started here, with a low-budget effort to portray realistically the condition of the working class in the figure of an unwed mother. Jarrico claimed later that Lupino did not know what she was doing, tampered with his script and produced a melodrama with less realism than feigned pathos. But the theme is interesting, and because it received so little backing at the time, it remains an important, little-examined postwar women's film. It's also interesting as the second film appearance of the blacklisted Leo Penn, father of Sean Penn. 94 min.

The Notorious Lone Wolf (1946)

Col. Prod: Ted Richmond. Dir: D. Ross Lederman. Scr: Martin Berkeley,† Edward Dein. Story basis: William Bowers, based on the character created by Louis Joseph Vance. Cast: Gerald Mohr, Janis Carter, Eric Blore, John Abbott, Peter Whitney, Adele Roberts

Ninth in a series about the adventures of a debonair ex–jewel thief. Series began with Melvyn Douglas in a film oddly titled *The Lone Wolf Returns* (1935), and progressed through several other leads before getting to the dark and handsome Mohr, recognizable for his pencil moustache and lots of Brilliantine. Eric Blore, who was added a few films before Mohr, plays the Jeeves-style gentleman's gentleman, British to a "t" but happy to take a drink now and then, and used mostly as comic relief. Blonde Janis Carter, succeeding such notables as Rita Hayworth, does little acting beyond squeezing Mohr and trying to get her maid (and inadvertent chaperone) Roberts out of the swank Art Deco apartment so she can make love to the Wolf. She wouldn't marry him for a million dollars, she avers—but she wouldn't take a million dollars for him (as a lover), either.

Compared with the sets and apparently sophisticated romance (Blore promises to make breakfast), the plot is fairly incidental. Wolf is back from the war and reluctant to have more adventures. Nevertheless, he is caught up by a stolen sapphire, a couple of visiting East Indian royals, a scheming banker (the only leftish touch of the film), a masquerade by Mohr and Blore in exotic costumes, a couple of murders and the usual false police charges against the ex-thief. Dalton Trumbo• wrote one entry in the series—THE LONE WOLF STRIKES, in 1940. *The Lone Wolf and His Lady* exhausted the series in 1949, with the cast replaced yet again. 64 min.

Nuts (1987)

Universal. Prod: Barbra Streisand. Dir: Martin Ritt.• Scr: Darryl Ponicsan, Alvin Sargent. Play basis: Tom Torpor. Cast: Barbra Streisand, Richard Dreyfuss, Maureen Stapleton, Eli Wallach, James Whitmore, Karl Malden, Leslie Nielsen

A nightmare for Ritt, who could not control Streisand's creative reach (and finances), but a strong movie for its time. Streisand is a prostitute on trial for her life, Dreyfuss her public defender, Stapleton and Wallach her parents who cannot own up to the sexual abuse she suffered as a child. 116 min.

O

Objective, Burma! (1945)

WB. Prod: Jerry Wald. Dir: Raoul Walsh. Scr: Ronald MacDougall, Lester Cole.• Story basis: Alvah Bessie.• Cast: Errol Flynn, James Brown, William Prince, George Tobias, Henry Hull, Warner Anderson, John Alvin, Mark Stevens, Richard Erdman, Anthony Caruso

Documentary-style drama of U.S. paratroopers fighting through the jungles against the Japanese as commander Flynn loses one man after another to a variety of attacks. Proclaimed by critics as one of the best war films ever made, it certainly had the most realistic jungle warfare (though it excluded the barbaric use of flamethrowers and assorted American as well as Japanese atrocities well-known to have occurred on the Pacific Islands campaigns).

The film has little plot except the fatalistic sense of long odds and any but the slimmest air support in the jungles of Burma. After achieving the objective of destroying a radar station and being counterattacked as they wait to be rescued, the group must cross virtually uninhabitable terrain on foot to reach a distant airstrip. The eerie sounds of birds and other animals punctuate the solitude as they move, meeting an occasional attack, more often struggling with the environment. A final vindication comes as the secondary value of their mission is revealed to them at the conclusion, as they meet their rescuers.

The film was banned at first in Britain because of the British Army's absence. Later on it was criticized for occasional racially derogatory references to the Japanese, which Cole swore were put in over his objections. Reviewers complained only that the film was 20 minutes or so too long. Oscar nomination for Bessie. 142 min.

Obsession (1949)

A low-budget film directed by Edward Dmytryk• the same year as GIVE US THIS DAY, likewise on the run in Britain as the curtain closed in the U.S. Originally adapted from novel to an unsuccessful British play, it treats of revenge for infidelity with the familiar "perfect murder" theme, this time a doctor who makes plans for his wife's American lover. Claustrophobic tale of pyschic and physical imprisonment and revealing of the mood of the times. Often titled *The Hidden Room*. 98 min.

Odds Against Tomorrow (1959)

Harbel Productions/UA. Prod: Robert Wise. Dir: Robert Wise. Scr: John O. Killens. (front for Abraham Polonsky•). Novel basis: William P. McGivern, *Odds Against Tomorrow* (1957). Cast: Harry Belafonte, Robert Ryan, Shelley Winters, Ed Begley, Gloria Grahame, Will Kuluva, Richard Bright, Lew Gallo, Fred J. Scollay, Carmen De Lavallade, Mae Barnes, Kim Hamilton, Lois Thorne, Wayne Rogers

Small-budget film with a large secret: Polonsky's sub rosa participation. Killens eventually acknowledged what had been known for decades, that he made only minor contributions to the script. The film had a large impact. *The New York Times*, apparently eager to see a revival of film liberalism on the heels of THE DEFIANT ONES (without ever acknowledging the blacklisted co-scenarist of that film), looked to Belafonte as a torch-bearer of interracial drama. At last, according to Belafonte, who gathered the money for the film, a black actor could play an ambiguous bad guy and still be a star in a film in which artificial "brotherhood" did not prevail.

Behind the innovations, this is a caper film. But in order to carry off a bank robbery, Ryan and Begley need a "colored delivery man." Ryan is the same psychotic racist he played so expertly (as an anti-Semite, that is) in CROSSFIRE, a man utterly dependent on the need to hate. Outside this inner drama is the outer drama of documentary-style location shooting in Manhattan and Hudson, New York, in which the terse criminal drama takes place. Begley (an affable progressive in real life) is a corrupted cop, Belafonte a musician so tied up in gambling debts that he turns to crime. The odds are rightly against success. Polonsky wanted what he called "an ordinary death" of the would-be robbers. Wise, on the verge of launching his own production company and anticipating a possible Oscar, insisted upon an explosion that leaves the robbers racially indistinguishable from each other.

The after-effects of the film could be felt in another important way. Belafonte set out to make a series of films about African American life, researched and written by Polonsky. The first, about a slave revolt in the antebellum South, was finally shelved when Belafonte's more cautious friend Sidney Poitier pulled out his funds, fearful of a backlash that could harm his own career; he was probably right to assume that white American audiences were a long, long way from coming to terms with racism. 96 min.

Of Mice and Men (1939)

Hal Roach Studios/UA. Prod: Lewis Milestone. Dir: Lewis Milestone. Scr: Eugene Solow. Novel basis: John Steinbeck, *Of Mice and Men* (1937). Cast: Burgess Meredith, Lon Chaney, Jr., Betty Field, Bob Steele, Noah Beery, Jr., Charles Bickford

The first and in many ways the most interesting of the two film and one television adaptations of Steinbeck's classic novel, in the manner of the Group Theatre (with an actor or two actually credited as on loan from the Group).

Lon Chaney, Jr. has one of his few serious opportunities (another comes in Renoir's THE SOUTHERNER) to show his talent at drama, playing the retarded Lenny, a mountain of a man who is destined to get into trouble—from which his pal George must extricate him, because he promised his aunt, Lenny's mother. The two of them work the crops and do odd jobs, until they go to work for an agribusiness that is more than usually fascistic. The wife of a brutal and psychosexually damaged foreman longs for attention and mistakenly fixes herself on Lenny. Personal disaster awaits, but in this version, it has the sense of a visitation upon the land; everyone is trapped in the Depression, everyone is struggling to find a way out, and just about everyone is doomed to fail. The musical score by Aaron Copland• is a touch of redemption. 106 min.

Oh Men! Oh Women! (1957)

An intermittently interesting psychosexual musical farce directed by Nunnally Johnson and written by the blacklisted Edward Chodorov,• who was permitted on-screen play credit (at the insistence of Johnson). It was also Tony Randall's major comedy screen debut. The story is a gentle send-up of the psychiatric craze among the upper-middle class of the day.

The Omaha Trail (1942)

A Hugo Butler• screenplay for a B-western about the railroad expansion. Howard da Silva• has a bit part.

On the Waterfront (1954)

Col. Prod: Sam Spiegel. Dir: Elia Kazan.† Scr: Budd Schulberg.† Story basis: Malcolm Johnson (*New York Sun* newspaper articles). Cast: Marlon Brando, Karl Malden, Lee J. Cobb,† Rod Steiger, Pat Henning, Leif Erickson, James Westerfield, Eva Marie Saint

There are other films by friendly witnesses that deal with the blacklist metaphorically, but this is doubtless the most important and most familiar, largely because Brando was at the peak of his art as an actor and Kazan was at the crest of his genius as an actors' director (his cinematic skills were never a match for that talent). A few lines, delivered by Brando as the washed-up boxer Terry Malloy—"I coulda been a contender"—are among the most famous in movie history. As an artistic achievement, the film might be said to be the friendly witnesses' HIGH NOON.

But while the subterranean political basement of an already dark film has received more attention in recent years, many appreciative viewers are still unaware that the filmmakers were essentially creating a narrative alibi for their own roles as informers on their co-workers in Hollywood. The story line of *Waterfront* is Terry's gradual gathering of moral courage to expose the criminality of the gangsters with whom he has associated almost exclusively from the beginning of the film. But it is only after the audience's identification with Terry is complete that it is finally revealed that the "gangsters" are officers of the dockworkers' union and that the union's members almost uniformly regard Terry as an informer ("a pigeon for a pigeon," sobs a youngster who had once looked up to Terry but now throws a dead bird at his feet).

Although organized crime flourished on the docks in the early 1950s (and still does), the Longshoreman's union, the ILA, was not in the hands of gangsters but of their bitter enemies on the Left, who are the real targets of the film. According to one modern source, the decision to change the focus of the story from "mob control" to "Communist control" was made by Columbia studio chief Harry Cohn, a long-time gambling buddy of Hollywood mobsters Johnny Rosselli and Mickey Cohen.

Rarely appreciated is the film's immediate historical context. As John Howard Lawson pointed out in his nearly lost critical appraisal of *Waterfront* in the *Hollywood Review* (Nov-Dec., 1954), when the film was made in late 1953, the Republican governor of New York and the Eisenhower administration were attempting to assert direct political control over the New York waterfront unions as the first step in acquiring control (largely through licensing) of unions nationwide. The target on the docks was the hiring hall, the source of union power, hard-won during the Depression. Dewey and the feds wanted the state to take over the hiring halls, fingerprint and register longshoreman and blacklist "undesirable" workers. It hardly seems a matter of chance that this very issue is at the center of the film.

It is a measure of the time that the two leading films about labor struggle of the day were made and released at virtually the same time, with the one that was unapologetically anti-union (*Waterfront*) opening to declarations of support from Cold War union leaders, while the militantly pro-union, pro-worker SALT OF THE EARTH was barred from theaters nationwide by the mob-controlled projectionists union. 108 min.

One Crowded Night (1940)

Richard Collins† and Arnaud d'Usseau• scripted this tourist camp mixup, memorable (if at all) as Irving Reis' directorial debut.

One Night in the Tropics (1940)

Gertrude Purcell† co-wrote the screenplay (with Charles Grayson) adapted from a 1914 novel by Earl Derr Biggers (creator of Charlie Chan), *Love Insurance*. The film marks the debut of Abbott and Costello on celluloid. Soon they were in better hands with Robert Lees• and Fred Rinaldo.•

One of the Hollywood Ten (2001)

Bloom Street Productions/Canal España. Prod: Karl Francis, Juan Gordon, Stuart Pollack. Dir: Karl Francis. Cast: Jeff Goldblum, Greta Scacchi, Ángela Molina, Christopher Fulford, Antonio Valero, John Pierce Jones, John Sessions, Geraint Wyn Davies

An undeservedly obscure film, ill-treated by distributors and reviewed by only a handful of U.S. publications, *Ten* played only in Jewish film festivals before going to cable. It deserved far better. Authenticity is the touchstone of the film by accomplished Welsh director Francis, from the first moments in 1937, when Gale Sondergaard (played by Scacchi) accepts the first Oscar ever awarded for best supporting actress and seizes the opportunity to plug the Hollywood Anti-Nazi League. Michael Wilson (Wyn Davies) and Sondergaard's husband Herbert Biberman, played most memorably (and for union scale, as a commitment to the project) by Goldblum, are seen taking great satisfaction in this early triumph for the Hollywood Left.

The film passes rather too quickly over Biberman's frustrated but still promising career of the 1940s directly to the 1947 hearings and their consequences, which were the total loss of work for the couple and impending prison for the director. However, at this point the movie gathers its energy, because its real subject is the making of SALT OF THE EARTH, showing the development of the project from informal discussions among left-wing filmmakers to the location shooting in New Mexico, the friendliness of some locals (Chicano strikers and a local priest) and the hateful interference of others, mostly Anglos. There is lots of lovely little stuff, with Paul Jarrico (Sessions) and *Salt* star Rosaura Revueltas (Molina), but the real key to the film is the FBI hotdog played by Fulford, rebuffed back in the 1940s for trying to tackle victims too big for the Bureau but "vindicated" when history goes his way. The role of Harry Truman and the administrative apparatus in suppressing *Salt* even as it was being made is avoided, but the general mood of repression is well established. Not that much has changed: As for FELLOW TRAVELLER, most of the funding for the film had to be raised abroad (in Britain and Spain). 109 min.

One Sunday Afternoon (1948)

Robert L. Richards• made an uncredited contribution to this second filming of the James Hagan play (1933), a soapy musical set in the turn of the century about a dentist's romantic confusion. High point: a mild and semi-satirical bow to suffrage, "The Right to Vote."

Open Secret (1948)

Marathon Pictures. Prod: Frank Satenstein. Dir: John Reinhardt. Scr: Max Wilk, Henry Blankfort.• Story basis: Max Wilk, Ted Murkland. Cast: John Ireland, Jane Randolph, Roman Bohnen, Sheldon Leonard, George Tyne, Morgan Farley, Ellen Lowe

A short, underbudgeted neighborhood thriller that explores postwar anti-Semitism in a vein similar to the prewar (1937) *Black Legion*, but without the Bogart character's divided loyalties about the Klan. The story, by elusive, blacklisted Blankfort, is one of only three readily available titles by this writer (including TALES OF MANHATTAN and THE UNDERWORLD STORY).

The film opens with Ireland and his bride dropping in on war buddy Bohnen on a honeymoon visit, but Bohnen mysteriously disappears. Soon he is found murdered. It turns out he had taken some candid photos of the local Klan-like organization that he had infiltrated, and the leaders desperately want the incriminating evidence back. In the struggle that follows, the opportunity arises for the occasional statement of antiracist, antifascist values.

Sometimes the statements are a little misleading, as when a Klansman defends his pamphleteering by stating, "I can say what I want. It's a free country," and liberal detective Sheldon Leonard responds, "Like shouting 'fire!' in a crowded theater? There's a law against that!" And he snaps on the handcuffs. The ACLU would have had the guy out in minutes. 68 min.

Operation Eichmann (1961)

Bischoff-Diamond. Prod: Samuel Bischoff, David Diamond. Dir: R. G. Springsteen. Scr: Lewis Copley (pseudonym for Lester Cole•). Cast: Werner Klemperer, Ruta Lee, Donald Buka, Barbara Turner, Lester Fletcher, Hanna Landy, John Banner, Steve Gravers, Paul Thierry

Interesting low-cost and forgotten Holocaust drama released two years before Hannah Arendt's book on the subject. The story unfolds as Eichmann carries out extermination plans and escapes Germany with his mistress to Latin America. Israeli agents—in those days still good guys—catch up with him and plot his kidnapping. Footage of death camps and of contemporary Israel add to interest, but Cole was always a rather turgid writer, and it shows. 93 min.

O.S.S. (1946)

Irving Pichel• directed this disappointing docudrama costarring Alan Ladd and Geraldine Fitzgerald about the intelligence service that enrolled so many lefties (including Abraham Polonsky• and Herbert Marcuse), then turned on them and morphed into the Central Intelligence Agency. Purported to be a "composite" of actual events, the film begins with a run-through of department procedures to uncover and halt domestic espionage. Pichel was clearly uninspired by the material.

Our Blushing Brides (1930)

MGM. Prod: Harry Beaumont. Dir: Harry Beaumont. Scr: John Howard Lawson,• Bess Meredyth. Cast: Joan Crawford, Anita Page, Dorothy Sebastian, Robert Montgomery, Raymond Hackett, John Miljan, Hedda Hopper, Edward Brophy, Albert Conti

An early women's film about department store workers Crawford, Page and Sebastian setting out to catch wealthy husbands. Their working and home lives (the latter in an off-the-hall apartment) give good reasons for their mercenary intentions, but only Crawford is levelheaded enough to deal with the difficulty of picking the right fellow and holding onto virtue until the right moment (the wedding night). Page ends up dead after learning that her premarital adventures won't lead to respectability; Sebastian faces the shame of being fooled by (and almost losing "it" to) a fake millionaire. Pursuing Crawford (very much the featured performer) is a young Montgomery, interesting as the bohemian store scion who likes to live in tree houses to "get away from it all." It's far from a great script, but Lawson hints at the chosen method of finding a suitable rich guy for a spirited girl,

especially in screwball features: make him screwball enough to flee the lifestyle of the bourgeoisie. 99 min.

Our Hearts Were Growing Up (1946)

Para. Prod: Daniel Dare.† Dir: William D. Russell. Scr: Norman Panama, Melvin Frank. Cast: Gail Russell, Diana Lynn, Brian Donlevy, James Brown, Bill Edwards, William Demarest

Followup to the film based on Cornelia Otis Skinner's literary memoirs, Our Hearts Were Young and Gay, which had been a solid commercial success two years earlier. This time the two best friends, Cornelia and her intimate pal Emily Kimbrough, come back from traveling through 1920s Europe to resettle in the East, enjoy a social life, make something of themselves if possible and above all find suitable beaux.

The film effectively mixes satire of the young, privileged and silly with the Damon Runyon–style gangster-with-a-heart-of-gold narrative. The girls move to Princeton and promptly run into trouble as they accidentally acquire two cases of bootleg champagne (hauled by Emily's uncle, a sentimental mobster) intended for a major social event. As in a Three Stooges short, the rich become convinced that they have drunk wood alcohol and go into a faint. Socially exiled, the girls take up life in Greenwich Village, replete with hungry artistes and poseurs. Uneven, but with charming moments. 83 min.

Our Vines Have Tender Grapes (1945)

MGM. Prod: Robert Sisk. Dir: Roy Rowland. Scr: Dalton Trumbo.• Novel basis: George Victor Martin, Our Vines Have Tender Grapes (1945). Cast: Edward G. Robinson, Margaret O'Brien, James Craig, Frances Gifford, Agnes Moorehead, Morris Carnovsky,• Jackie Jenkins

An extraordinary film by any standard. Grapes was said to be Trumbo's favorite of his own work, and it's not hard to see why: he showed in this script that he could shape the smallest events of daily life into absorbing drama. The sharpest dramatic conflict in the film derives from the refusal of a girl (O'Brien) to share her skates with a neighbor boy and the lovely, extravagant gesture that her father (Robinson) finds as a way to make up for having to punish her. The moving denouement of the film comes when her parents and the entire community of Fuller Junction, Wisconsin, discover what O'Brien has learned from the lesson of selfishness and sharing that her father taught her.

Quite apart from the craftsman's brilliance of this minimalist narrative, Grapes is in a certain sense the most political film Trumbo ever made. Fuller Junction, while romanticized in the same way American small towns often are in the Hollywood tradition, nonetheless takes on the quality of a society in which kindness, neighborliness and respect for everyone in the community has already been realized—perhaps the closest any of the Left screenwriters ever came to depicting the utopian impulse in concrete terms. The theme of the movie concerns the necessity for educating children and indeed all of the members of the community in the arts of cooperation.

The story is helped immensely by the brightly winning O'Brien, at the time America's most gifted child actor, and her often hilarious sidekick, preschooler Jackie Jenkins as the kid next door. But everyone is kind and open-hearted in this film, including the beautiful young schoolteacher-intern (Gifford), a sophisticated socialist from Milwaukee who can't see what's right in front of her eyes until the committed newspaper editor educates her in the virtues of simplicity. Still, it is Robinson who carries the story as a man who cultivates wisdom from the experience of daily life and turns it into a magnificent harvest. 105 min.

Out of the Blue (1947)
Eagle-Lion. Prod: Isadore Goldsmith, Bryan Foy. Dir: Leigh Jason. Scr: Walter Bullock, Edward Eliscu.• Story basis: Vera Caspary.• Cast: Virginia Mayo, George Brent, Turhan Bey, Ann Dvorak, Carole Landis, Hadda Brooks

An often wildly funny Greenwich Village screwball comedy about a repressed businessman, his bohemian neighbor and a dizzy dame who sets romantic relations in motion. Perhaps the first but definitely the best in a series of left-related comedies about the bohemians and the struggle to overcome the hovering specter of normalcy. Henpecked Brent, whose wife is conveniently out of town, falls for the heavy-drinking and delightfully silly Dvorak, a Village interior designer with a weak heart and propensity for death-like fainting spells. A nice turnabout ending of the sex war punctuates the delightful comedy chase. 84 min.

Out of the Fog (1941)
First National/WB. Assoc. Prod: Henry Blanke. Exec. Prod: Hal B. Wallis. Dir: Anatole Litvak. Scr: Robert Rossen,† Jerry Wald, Richard Macaulay. Play basis: Irwin Shaw, The Gentle People (1939). Cast: John Garfield, Ida Lupino, Thomas Mitchell, Eddie Albert, John Qualen, Aline MacMahon, Jerome Cowan, Leo Gorcey, George Tobias, Robert E. Homans, Bernard Gorcey

An adaptation of Shaw's successful crime tale that combines the Depression social drama, Rossen-style (in Brooklyn, the favorite locale), with a racketeers' portrayal by Garfield that foreshadows FORCE OF EVIL, and a very large dose of O. Henry. Sentimental Irishman Mitchell loves daughter Lupino more than anything in the world but also wants to leave his miserable shop to become a professional fisherman. She can't stand the limits of her life, the empty promise of marriage (even to the proletarian Albert, whom she truly loves) in three rooms with a few babies. He buys a boat with quaint Qualen (who as usual plays a slightly confused and cowardly Swede). But petty mobster Garfield moves in on them, demanding $5 a week in "protection." Then he moves in on Lupino as well, offering her the night-club life, orchids and his own dynamic personality. As he tightens the screws on the men and (it is strongly hinted) gets Lupino to go home with him—kissing him on the docks, she symbolically drops a doll, her innocence, into the murky water—Garfield's fate becomes inevitable. Everything winds up predictably, but Lupino, Mitchell and Thomas are worth watching the whole way through. Even a couple of BOWERY BOYS get into the picture of Brooklyn as it was, before the factories closed and the older immigrant groups started moving to the suburbs. 93 min.

Outside These Walls (1939)
This interesting B-drama written by Harold Buchman• has a con blacklisted from honest work who buys a printing press and goes after political corruption. His warden, a reformer, is elected governor!

Over the Santa Fe Trail (1947)
Cowboy musical written by Louise Rousseau• has star Ken Curtis fall hard for a medicine show entertainer. He joins her in a fight in which a gang of bank robbers try to pin their crimes on the medicine show folks.

Over 21 (1945)
Col. Prod: Sidney Buchman.• Dir: Charles Vidor. Scr: Sidney Buchman. Play basis: Ruth Gordon, Over 21 (1945). Cast: Alexander Knox, Irene Dunne, Charles Coburn, Jeff Donnell, Loren Tindall, Lee Patrick, Cora Witherspoon, Phil Brown

Big-budget Popular Front farce that was a Broadway hit with Gordon managing life in a bungalow court while expressing in a general way the ideals of antifascism. According to critics, Dunne aped Gordon's mannerisms, and Buchman unwisely declined to open up the action cinematically, making for a stagey and talky film, although Coburn as a fat capitalist is amusing. 102 min.

P

Pacific Blackout (1941)

A mildly intriguing B-drama co-scripted by Lester Cole•
(with W. P. Lipscomb) from a Curt Siodmak story about
a blue-collar worker, played by Robert Preston, wrongly
accused of espionage and who escapes custody to find
the real culprit. Some nice action footage.

Palooka (1934)

Reliance Pictures/UA. Prod: Edward Small. Dir: Ben-
jamin Stoloff. Scr: Jack Jevne, Gertrude Purcell,† Arthur
Kober. Cast: Jimmy Durante, Lupe Velez, Suart Erwin,
Marjorie Rambeau, Robert Armstrong, Mary Carlisle,
William Cagney

First of the Joe Palooka pictures, later destined to
become the most consistently left-wing-staffed B-series
of the 1940s (discussed separately as JOE PALOOKA), but
this A-film is the only one with a big-name cast and
includes the story of Joe's origins. Based loosely on Ham
Fisher's comic strip character (and as a term widely
considered a slur on blue-collar Polish-Americans),
Palooka offers a comic journey through a hapless prizefighter's life. The son of a real former champ, Joe
becomes deluded (with much help) into thinking that he
is a contender. As in later pictures, the gang around the
ring adds laughs and gives emotional support to a boy
fighting well out of his league. Here, Durante fixes fights
to arrange for Joe to beat much better boxers, while
Velez (later to have her own series), the gold-digging
Spanish dancer, gets his opponent drunk and takes up
with the new champ. In the end, Joe realizes boxing is
not for him—and Durante gets to sing "Inka Dinka Doo."
Purcell was likely hired to write the Velez dialogue; what
Lillian Hellman's husband Kober was writing can only
be imagined. 86 min.

Pals of the Saddle (1938)

Rep. Assoc. Prod: William A. Berke. Dir: George Sher-
man. Scr: Stanley Roberts,† Betty Burbridge. Cast: John
Wayne, Ray Corrigan, Max Terhune, Doreen McKay,
Joseph Forte, George Douglas, Frank Milan, Ted Adams

A Three Mesquiteers picture with the shifting cast
here including Wayne. It is another in the oddly contemporary western series that contain everything from the
Neutrality Act (passed, 1937) to the U.S. Cavalry. Why
folks with cars and modern weapons would be chasing
each other on horses and using six-shooters is a continuing complication of these seemingly postmodern regional
dramas. Ditto the presence of modern-dressed mobsters
or spies, when our heroes look and act like they stepped
out of 1880.

George Douglas, posing as a guest at a dude ranch,
is smuggling a forbidden war-related mineral. McKay,
who seems to be involved in a conspiracy, is actually a
Secret Service agent. As usual with the Mesquiteers,
Wayne masquerades as an outlaw, in this case posing as
a hillbilly searching for none other than himself! Happily,
just as quantities of the mineral are being sneaked across
the border, the cavalry arrives. Whew. 55 min.

Pancho Villa (1973)

Granada/Scotia International. Prod: Bernard Gordon.•
Dir: Eugenio Martín. Scr: Julian Halevy (pseudonym for
Julian Zimet•). Cast: Telly Savalas, Clint Walker, Anne
Francis, Chuck Connors, Ángel del Pozo, José María Prada

The third treatment after World War II of Mexico's
revolution (there were several other 1930s versions).
Earlier producer-director Torres brought out Pancho Villa
Returns (1950), a Mexican production starring U.S. favor-
ite Leo Carillo; Elia Kazan made a big-budget hit of Viva
Zapata! (1953), whose original screenplay was written by
Lester Cole• but was ripped up and given to John
Steinbeck to rewrite when Kazan changed political sides.

This feature was shot in Spain under the influence
of the Italian Euro-western with heavy American participation all along the line. Not much of a script here,
mainly an action vehicle with a supposed U.S./Mexican
desert border. Still, Savalas is a most sympathetic Villa,
lured across the border and practically compelled to take
over a U.S. Army outpost. Tough Connors is the officer
in charge of the outpost. Walker, as General Pershing, is
a pompous and silly figure who chases Villa back into
Mexico (as in real life). Much of the film's technical
budget went into the final scene, a spectacular train
wreck (staged in miniature) from which Pershing
emerges in a delightfully ludicrous body cast. Silly but
fun, particularly the scene of the northern "invasion."
90 min.

Papillon (1973)

Allied Artists/Solar Corona/General. Prod: Robert Dorf-mann, Franklin J. Schaffner. Dir: Franklin J. Schaffner. Scr: Dalton Trumbo,• Lorenzo Semple, Jr. Book basis: Henri Charrière, *Papillon* (1969). Cast: Steve McQueen, Dustin Hoffman, Victor Jory, Don Gordon, Anthony Zerbe, Robert Deman, Woodrow Parfrey, Bill Mumy, George Coulouris, Gregory Sierra

Trumbo's last screen triumph and one of McQueen's best films. McQueen, a safecracker framed for murder and sentenced to life in 1931, is shipped to a penal colony off French Guyana, the famous Devil's Island. Escape from this hell hole is presumed to be impossible but becomes the singled-minded point of the story. McQueen's newly acquired pal, the desperately near-sighted and very wealthy Hoffman, convicted for counterfeiting government bonds, has the connections to make escape imaginable.

A standard set of characters include a philosophical doctor (Cououris, whose presence recalls 1940s antifas-cist thrillers) and a vicious commandant (in a cameo played by Trumbo himself). There is lots of grim footage of prison life, including cockroach-eating. Happily, McQueen is befriended by Jory, an Indian chief, who runs a sort of primitive socialist colony of his own, with topless native girls to boot. As an instinctive anti-imperialist, McQueen's character makes the best of the situation.

The film accurately reflects the theme of the book, an exploration of the uniquely Catholic French penology of separating wrongdoers from virtually all human contact (and hence from God). Trumbo brilliantly limns the consequences of this dehumanization and the effort to resist it. The result is 1940s-going-on-1970s political cinema cast as a superior entertainment. A landmark. 150 min.

Pardon My Rhythm (1944)

A Universal B-movie co-scripted by Val Burton• and starring teenager Gloria Jean, who is in love with a drummer/impresario played by Mel Tormé in his last attempt at the big screen.

Paris After Dark (1943)

20th. Prod: André Daven. Dir: Léonide Moguy. Scr: Harold Buchman.• Story basis: Georges Kessel. Cast: George Sanders, Philip Dorn, Brenda Marshall, Madeleine LeB-eau, Marcel Dalio, Robert Lewis, Henry Rowland

A B-feature about the French underground. Dorn, a soldier released from a Nazi prison camp after the fall of France, returns to his family in Paris; he is a man broken by the cruelties of imprisonment and convinced the Nazis are bound to triumph. Wife Marshall and friend Sanders convince him that there is hope—but it rests on the courage to fight the Nazis while pretending obedience, not excluding patriotic Frenchwomen's willingness to bed down with the enemy.

Reviewers complained that the film was done in the French style (by exiled, top French film director Mugoy)— that is, deliberate to the point of aching slowness for American tastes. Perhaps they were also offended by the allowance of seeming immorality in favor of a higher morality (something unknown in Hays Office times). Peter Lawford appears briefly as a young partisan. Considering the budget, it is a work of art and arguably B-writer Buchman's most serious as well as most political picture. 85 min.

Paris Blues (1961)

Diane/Jason Films/UA. Prod: Sam Shaw, George Glass, Walter Seltzer. Dir: Martin Ritt.• Scr: Jack Sher, Irene Kamp, Walter Bernstein.• Adaptation: Lulla Rosenfeld. Novel basis: Harold Flender, *Paris Blues* (1957). Cast: Paul Newman, Joanne Woodward, Sidney Poitier, Louis Arm-strong, Diahann Carroll, Serge Reggiani, Barbara Laage, André Luguet, Marie Versini

A film reminiscent of Paul Jarrico's• British-pro-duced ALL NIGHT LONG, released the same year, focusing on another set of U.S. exiles in Europe: jazz musicians. Strangely, Duke Ellington's playing was not acknowledged in the credits. Louis Armstrong, in his largest screen role, almost acts, but mostly he plays—for the first time in a feature film since NEW ORLEANS. Meanwhile, Newman the would-be jazz composer and Poitier the musician hang around Paris, where they pick up a couple of American tourists (Woodward and Carroll), and quickly fall in love.

Naturally, the tourists want to get the boys to go back to the States with them, and so they explain that things are getting better, especially that desegregation is coming soon (if they only knew how exciting life was going to get). Sometimes the film comes close to exploring contro-versial racial themes but always pulls back. In the best moments, Woodward, a widow and single mother drawn to Newman, gets immediately down to erotic cases as an independent woman who wants love but is determined to live her own life, with a man or without. A subplot involves cocaine use by one of the band's musicians: everyone disapproves. 98 min., color.

The Parson of Panamint (1941)

Para. Prod: Harry Sherman. Dir: William C. McGann. Scr: Harold Shumate, Adrian Scott.• Story basis: Peter B. Kyne, "The Parson of Panamint" in *The Saturday Evening Post* (1915). Cast: Charles Ruggles, Ellen Drew, Philip Terry, Joseph Schildkraut, Porter Hall, Henry Kolker, Janet Beecher

Regarded as one of Scott's forgotten gems, this was described by *The New York Times* as "a heartwarming and inspiring film which youngster and adult alike would do well to see in these troubled times." This was the role OUR VINES HAVE TENDER GRAPES would soon play, to a bigger box office.

A western boomtown is soon to be a ghost town when a flood spills into the goldmine that was making Panamint both rich and corrupt. In comes the young parson, played by Terry, and he quickly encounters formidable resistance from all quarters, notably gambling saloon proprietor Schildkraut. Terry also falls for dance hall girl (i.e., prostitute) Drew, a natural Mary Magdalene type, and converts Mexican bandit Puglia to godliness. The story is told in flashback by prospector Ruggles, who surveys the town's economic crash as if it were a sort of metaphor of American experience and looks back to how it all began. A remake of a 1916 film, but done up wonderfully this time for a B-budget and with a B-director. 84 min.

Party Girl (1958)

Euterpa/MGM. Prod: Joe Pasternak. Dir: Nicholas Ray. Scr: George Wells. Cast: Cyd Charisse, Robert Taylor, Lee J. Cobb,† John Ireland, Kent Smith, Claire Kelly, Corey Allen

Ray's first film after *Rebel Without a Cause* and his last before two spectacular clinkers (*King of Kings* and 55 DAYS AT PEKING), is usually regarded as evidence of an uninterrupted downward slide. Certainly, it is not worthy of serious comparison to the artistic quality (or intent) of *They Live by Night, Knock on Any Door,* IN A LONELY PLACE, *On Dangerous Ground* or even the badly confused JOHNNY GUITAR. Still, it has an interesting place in the history of crime drama as Ray's own treatment of the underworld.

Party Girl is best seen as a resumption of the pre-code 1930s gangster film, with the unmistakable sexuality (however mild by later standards) among showgirls and men with money, the equivocal mob mouthpiece and the mistress with the heart of gold. Charisse has limitations as an actress, but her slinky dancing delivers the message (even if it seems to come out of the 1950s, rather than early 1930s Chicago). Taylor is only predictable as the lawyer up from the slums, further damaged by a serious childhood injury (more than a hint that the real damage is psychological). Friendly witness Cobb gives one of his best performances, a mob boss and a former slum hero as a child, who once championed the weak and now believes only in his own strength. This film shows how much Ray needed the Left—and that the return of the noir had to wait until national self-deception eroded and America was noir territory once again. 99 min, color.

Party Wire (1935)

Col. Prod: Roger North. Dir: Erle C. Kenton. Scr: Ethel Hill, John Howard Lawson.• Story basis: Bruce Manning, Vera Caspary.• Novel basis: Bruce Manning, *Party Wire* (1934). Cast: Victor Jory, Jean Arthur, Charley Grapewin, Helen Lowell, Robert Allen, Clara Blandick, Geneva Mitchell

A comedy about gossips who set a small town buzzing when its most eligible bachelor, dairyman Jory, romances Arthur, daughter of the town's most prominent citizen. Arthur's mirthless but lithe portrayal is easily the best thing in the film, although the casting of various character actors as busybodies is effective as well.

Much to-do about family secrets has Arthur declining to be placed in the prestigious flower show competition, and Jory (his all-important business for the town facing bankruptcy in the Depression) essentially using his influence to bludgeon the small-minded citizens to accept Arthur and abandon their gossip. An odd feature for Lawson (and Caspary, too), but much in line with the message that romance will triumph over mean-spiritedness—and an intriguingly unsentimental look at the morals and manners of small town middle America. 75 min.

Passport to Destiny (1944)

RKO. Prod: Herman Schlom. Dir: Ray McCarey. Scr: Val Burton,• Muriel Roy Bolton. Cast: Elsa Lanchester, Gordon Oliver, Lénore Aubert, Lionel Royce, Fritz Feld, Joseph Vitale, Lloyd Corrigan

Lanchester had a fabulous Hollywood avant-garde reputation, shared with husband Charles Laughton, and based less on films than on her decades-long performance of campy blue humor and slightly Left-edged topical quips at the Turnabout Theater, which featured a puppet show by well-known gay puppeteers in its second half.

In this semi-arty, semi-political feature, Lanchester plays a London charwoman, widow of a sergeant major, who decides on her own to kill Hitler. She is guided by a sort of magic that kept her husband out of trouble. Traveling as a stowaway to France, and on to Berlin with her pail and scrub brush (while posing as a deaf mute), she gets the prescribed job in the Reich. She does not actually meet the Führer. But she stirs things up with help from an anti-Nazi officer (Oliver) and his girl (Aubert) before getting away. 65 min.

Peck's Bad Boy (1934)

The fourth film adaptation (but first talkie) of a beloved sentimental literary character from late-nineteenth-century author George W. Peck, this time around co-scripted by Marguerite Roberts• and Bernard Schubert. Independent producer Sol Lessor saw it acutely as a Jackie Cooper vehicle, one of his very best juvenile roles.

The Penalty (1941)

MGM. Prod: Jack Chertok. Dir: Harold S. Bucquet. Scr: Harry Ruskin, John C. Higgins. Play basis: Martin Berkeley,† Roosty (1938). Cast: Edward Arnold, Lionel Barrymore, Marsha Hunt,• Robert Sterling, Gene Reynolds, Emma Dunn, Phil Silvers, Gloria DeHaven

A contrived plot with a good cast and understated class themes has Arnold as mobster and Dunn as his moll, both more or less standard issue, save when he explains to son Reynolds (a child actor who would grow up to become the producer of "M*A*S*H") the solid economics, upsides and downsides, of the armed robbery game. Dunn is especially good as the flashy type vain or foolish enough to display her diamonds in public while the family is supposedly on the run.

The real story, though, starts when the boy is captured and gets sent off to kindly farmer Sterling while his father sits in stir. He resists at first, out of stubborn family loyalty, but the rural life gets to him—especially blind grandpa Barrymore and idealistic schoolteacher Hunt. Just as he happily adjusts, dad returns on the lam, determined to reclaim his boy. Cameo appearance by a young Silvers. 80 min.

People Are Funny (1946)

An unfunny B-movie with story by David Lang† and based on the radio show of the same name. The radio execs and writers compete for rights to buy the small town radio program that will become the next big hit. Includes Rudy Vallee, Ozzie Nelson, Art Linkletter and Frances Langford.

The Perfect Snob (1941)

Partners Lee Loeb and Harold Buchman• wrote this B-film with evident aspirations for something better. The stock plot has Charlotte Greenwood, a socially ambitious mother, throwing daughter Lynn Bari at millionaires. Pop Charles Ruggles, a henpecked veterinarian, is obviously at a loss to deal with it all, but has an ace up his sleeve.

Phaedra (1962)

Joele/Melinafilm/Lopert Pictures. Prod: Jules Dassin.• Dir: Jules Dassin. Play basis: Euripides, Hippolytus. Cast: Melina Mercouri, Anthony Perkins, Raf Vallone, Elizabeth Ercy

Dassin shot this modern-dress version of the Euripides classic on location in Greece, mostly on the island of Hydra, with some work in the amphitheater of Dionysus, where spoken lines (not merely chanted or sung) were first heard "on stage" and where the word "actor" was coined. The original story of the king of Crete who remarries and whose new wife falls in love with his son is here rendered into the tale of a modern king of capital (multimillionaire shipping magnate Vallone), his queen (Mercouri) and prince (Perkins). On Hydra, the summer place of the capitalist's entourage, Mercouri meets Perkins, back from his studies in England, for the first time. Just when the young man grows interested in his father's financial empire and what he might do after inheriting it, the love affair erupts.

The film has many wonderful scenes, like the Greek women seeking news about the probable death of their husbands, all fishermen lost at sea—a tragedy wholly lost on Phaedra, who is interested only in her own romantic affair, and on her husband, for whom it is merely a business problem. The setting is spectacular, and one scene is unforgettable: Perkins driving his Aston-Martin off a cliff with Bach's Toccata and Fugue in F-major cranked on the car speakers while Mercouri prepares herself a lethal drug overdose. This is Euripedes fully realized, and one of Dassin's finest films. 115 min., color.

Phantom Lady (1944)

Universal. Prod: Joan Harrison. Dir: Robert Siodmak. Scr: Bernard C. Schoenfeld.† Novel basis: William Irish (pseudonym for Cornell Woolrich), Phantom Lady (1942). Cast: Franchot Tone, Alan Curtis, Ella Raines, Aurora Miranda, Thomas Gomez, Fay Helm, Elisha Cook, Jr.

A much-discussed noir and a good one. Harrison, a protégé of Hitchcock, teamed up with émigré Siodmak, known for his expressionistic lighting and mise en scène, and hired Schoenfeld, who was not altogether up to the problems of composing an adequate plot for the moodiness of the film but was very good at framing noir suspense drama.

Raines sets out to prove boyfriend Curtis innocent of murdering his wife. Enlisting the suitably overwrought police detective Gomez, she turns late in the film to Curtis' best friend Tone, a neurotic Nietzchean. Cook, a favorite noir supporting actor as a near-psychotic orchestra drummer, has a solo (reputedly by an uncredited Buddy Rich) famous for its leering sexual innuendo. 87 min.

Phantom Ranger (1938)

A Tim McCoy Monogram cheapie in which an undercover government agent pretends to be a cowboy and breaks up a counterfeiting ring. Co-story by Stanley Roberts.†

The Philadelphia Story (1940)

MGM. Prod: Joseph L. Mankiewicz. Dir: George Cukor. Scr: Donald Ogden Stewart• (uncredited: Waldo Salt•). Cast: Katharine Hepburn, Cary Grant, James Stewart, Ruth Hussey, Roland Young, John Howard, John Halliday

Perhaps Stewart's most complex film and Cukor's best feature, its success owing most to the chemistry between Hepburn and playwright Philip Barry, who wrote the Broadway version expressly for her. Four hundred-plus performances later, she bought the rights with, strangely enough, right-wing industrialist Howard Hughes. He insisted, against the wishes of the studios (who blamed her for several flops), that she also play the part in the film.

Hepburn is a star-crossed heiress born to a wealthy Philadelphia Quaker family; she has divorced Grant for his drunkeness and, although it is not spelled out, probably also for his infidelities. Since then she has betrothed herself to a social climbing would-be politician. Grant conspires to get reporter Stewart an inside scoop on the marriage and shows up himself at the family's lavish estate. There, on the eve of the wedding, Hepburn's doubts mushroom, all the more when the men on hand describe her as an unattainable goddess. She falls uncertainly in love with Stewart, who is also an earnest novelist and true-blue democratic American boy, who is, however, practically engaged to photographer Hussey.

Wonderful contributions by bratty Wiedler as a younger sister and lecherous Young as a silly uncle help keep the action going in a farce of gentility with its disguises removed. 112 min.

Pillow Talk (1959)

U-I. Prod: Ross Hunter, Martin Melcher. Dir: Michael Gordon.•† Scr: Russell Rouse, Maurice Richlin. Cast: Rock Hudson, Doris Day, Tony Randall, Thelma Ritter, Nick Adams, Lee Patrick

Gordon's big return from the blacklist earned the studio $8 million and set the pattern for three more Hudson-Day matchups that made her, for at least a few years, the most successful actress in world film. This movie is often cited as evidence of the banality of fifties movies, but the fact that the director was a Communist turned friendly witness is rarely if ever mentioned.

So is it a satire or celebration of the sex war? Actually, it is a return to Ginger Rogers in Moss Hart's *Lady in the Dark*: shunning the unvirile millionaire Randall (already fixed in his role as the fastidious ersatz gay), Day must come to see that her career aspirations (she loves her job, goes out with interesting men) are a form of self-deception allowing her to elude her destiny as wife and mother. Rock (already fixed in his role of virile ersatz heterosexual) must come to a congenial resolution, dropping out of the bachelor's fast lane he has so relished. An annoying telephone party line, a technology now almost forgotten, brings them together and symbolizes the need for the communication modern men and women have obviously lost. The film won an Oscar for best story and screenplay with a handful of nominations, including one for Day and one for Ritter (the nosy maid who always has the keenest perceptions). 103 min., color.

Pinky (1949)

20th. Prod: Darryl F. Zanuck. Dir: Elia Kazan,† John Ford. Scr: Philip Dunne, Dudley Nichols. Novel basis: Cid Ricketts Sumner, *Quality* (1946). Cast: Jeanne Crain, Ethel Barrymore, Ethel Waters, William Lundigan, Basil Ruysdael, Kenny Washington, Nina Mae McKinney

Kazan's race-message film, of a piece with his anti-anti-Semitic GENTLEMAN'S AGREEMENT but with a much weaker script and more a gesture of sentiment than a political statement. The fault lay largely with Zanuck, who had originally commissioned the screenplay from the great Dudley Nichols, who insisted that the ending state explicitly that racism must have a social, not an individual solution. When Nichols refused to back down, Zanuck turned to a more compliant Dunne. Then again, in the years of Disney's *Song of the South,* any statement about regional racism was bound to be softened by Hollywood into a story about some good whites and some bad whites interacting with good (and a few very bad) blacks. There is also a gender angle: "passing" raises questions of intimate (romantic but not actively sexual) social relations for a woman.

Crain is the character of the title, "pink" because her "Negro blood" is not apparent. She returns to Mississippi after being raised in the North and educated as a nurse. When her real identity is found out, she becomes the object of every kind of abuse short of a lynch mob. Her romance with a (white) Northern doctor, depicted in the novel, is carefully avoided, while the kindliness of Old Plantation mistress Barrymore toward her lifelong servant Waters is played to the hilt.

Crain's character is not developed, but some sense of the daily discomforts and abuses of African American life in the South is glimpsed through her eyes. While integration struggles were open in real life in 1949, sentimental solidarity was the only solution Kazan seemed able to summon, perhaps because anything more critical would call into question the "American Way" that he more and more apotheosized in his films. 102 min.

A Place for Lovers (aka Amanti, 1969)

Compagnia Cinematografica/MGM. Prod: Carlo Ponti, Arthur Cohn. Dir: Vittorio De Sica. Scr: Julian Halevy (pseudonym for Julian Zimet•), Peter Baldwin, Ennio De Concini, Tonino Guerra, Cesare Zavatitini. Story basis: Brunello Rondi, "Amanti." Cast: Faye Dunaway, Marcello Mastroianni, Caroline Mortimer, Karin Engh

Arty film that, given the distinguished cast and direction, unexpectedly bombed. Maybe it was an excess of screenwriters that loused up the story of well-heeled American fashion designer and engineer Mastroianni, whom she encountered casually in an airport at some time in the past and whom she immediately makes her lover in a deserted Venetian villa. After they remove to an Alpine village and a continuing idyll, he discovers that she desperately needs medical attention to survive a terrible illness—but they decide to stay and squeeze out all the happiness they can. That the owner of the Venetian villa is returning and plans to stage a fashionable sex orgy is somehow related, though it is not entirely clear how. 88 min., color.

A Place in the Sun (1951)

Para. Prod: George Stevens. Dir: George Stevens. Scr: Michael Wilson,• Harry Brown. Novel basis: Theodore Dreiser, An American Tragedy (1925). Cast: Montgomery Clift, Elizabeth Taylor, Shelley Winters, Anne Revere,• Raymond Burr, Herbert Heyes, Keefe Brasselle

A film adaptation that was recognized immediately as a classic and a timely reminder (with Wilson and Revere) of what cinema was about to lose to the

blacklist—in Revere's case, permanently. This was Wilson's last screenplay before the HUAC curtain fell on Hollywood. Dreiser's famed naturalist novel interpreted the moral erosion of capitalism on the human spirit, as a young man of working-class background begins to make his way and suddenly finds himself bound to a pregnant proletarian girl, whom he drowns in a feigned boating accident. The dramatization softened Clift (in what was the doomed, moody young actor's best film), rendering his guilt ambiguous but without lessening the impact of the story. Taylor is perfect as the spoiled daughter of the factory owner who gives Clift work, but Winters as the spurned working-class girl is simply outstanding, if only a little better than the perfectly cast Revere as Clift's impoverished and self-sacrificing (and to him, deeply embarrassing) mother.

The previous film version, shot with the novel's title in 1931 and directed by Von Sternberg, had Irving Pichel• in a supporting role, but Dreiser proclaimed it had "ruined" his intentions. The author probably would have approved of this version, which updated the setting, but— thanks in no small part to left-wingers who would have held his sympathy—captured the essential meaning, even if communist critics complained that the class message had been lost in the personalization of the tale and particularly in the quality of Clift's courtroom confession. Oscars included best direction, best screenplay, best score (Franz Waxman), best cinematography (William C. Mellor), film editing and costume design. 122 min.

The Plainsman and the Lady (1946)

A "town-tamer" western, with a mixture of family pathos, class and cultural tension, false Indian attacks and Pony Express romanticism. When the St. Joseph, Missouri, saloons are ordered closed at midnight by blue-nosed reformers, owner William Elliott decides to go into the mail delivery business. He also falls in love with a curiously aristocratic eastern transplant, Vera Ralston, who wants him to stay in town and become civilized. Ralston, wife of Republic's mogul, starred in dozens of films as the studio went to the dogs. The story was written by Michael Uris.•

Planet of the Apes (1968)

20th. Prod: Arthur P. Jacobs. Dir: Franklin J. Schaffner. Scr: Michael Wilson,• Rod Serling. Novel basis: Pierre Boule; La planète des singes (1963). Cast: Charlton Heston, Roddy McDowall, Kim Hunter,•† Maurice Evans, Linda Harrison, James Whitmore, James Daly

One of the most popular sci-fi films of all time, *Planet* is also a landmark film of the blacklist because screenwriter Wilson, perhaps the most talented Marxist in the history of screenwriting, recast the action film into a powerful satirical allegory of the blacklist itself.

Three astronauts from the past arrive on earth, are captured by apes and become the center of a political struggle between ruling orangutans, whose government and religion are suspiciously similar to that of U.S. southern conservatives (right down to the coiffed hairdos and investigating committees), while the liberal chimpanzees are scientists who are on the verge of proving that ape creationism is a superstition and that humans might actually have possessed an early civilization. When this dispute erupts into a show trial for the astronaut Heston and the chimpanzees act as his defense attorneys, the deeper theme is revealed. The chief orangutan growls at the chimps: "Let us warn our friends that they are endangering their own careers by defending this animal." The chimps' exchange of shocked glances at this threat of blacklisting had a knowing glint, for the actress in the monkey suit was in reality Kim Hunter, who had been named in the red-baiting publication, *Red Channels,* and blacklisted for four years in the mid-1950s. Later, when Heston and the chimps come across one of the astronauts and discover that the orangs have lobotomized him, Heston shouts, "You cut out his memory, you took his identity, and that's what you want to do to me!" This is Wilson's metaphor for what happened to the "friendly witnesses" who cooperated with HUAC. The famous (and brilliant) final scene in the movie was written by Serling before Wilson made his contribution and contains an additional political warning, this one against nuclear war.

There may have been no more devastating revenge in the fight against the blacklist than the image when Heston, stripped naked before his accusers, watches the orangutans of HUAC cover their eyes, ears and mouth in the ancient image of determined ignorance. Critics and the public did not get the joke in 1968, and so the film became Wilson's literary time capsule, buried deep in the imagery of popular culture, to be excavated in the twenty-first century. All of this was anticipated, eerily enough, by Bertold Brecht• in 1947, when he emerged from his HUAC testimony and remarked to Joseph Losey• that his experience was like "a zoologist being cross-examined by apes." 112 min., color.

Port of New York (1949)

A poor cousin to THE NAKED CITY and likewise shot on the streets of New York, but despite some good direction, it lacks Dassin's• verve and suffers from weak characterizations and plot. It is a dope-peddling drama, co-written by Leo Townsend† in which Scott Brady and Richard Rober are determined to track down smugglers and murderers. Yul Brynner, who is more interesting than anyone else, has a role.

Portrait of Jennie (1948)

Vanguard Films. Prod: David O. Selznick. Dir: William Dieterle. Scr: Leonardo Bercovici,• Peter Berneis, Ben Hecht (uncredited: David O. Selznick). Cast: Joseph Cotten, Jennifer Jones, Cecil Kellaway, Ethel Barrymore, David Wayne, Lillian Gish

One of the handful of films influenced by surrealism made in Hollywood's studio days, adapted and written in part by the Communist writer deeply involved in questions of psychoanalysis, *Jennie* won several nominations and an award for special effects.

Cotten is a frustrated artist (in real life a frequent figure in Group Theatre and WPA Federal Theater) drawn to a woman whom he increasingly suspects is a ghost. To make her real, partly against her own better judgment, he must bring her to light on the canvas. Tinted green, the last reel climaxes in Technicolor. Always a fantasy, it expresses the determination of an all-consuming love to conquer reality. 86 minutes, partly in color.

Possessed (1947)

WB. Prod: Jerry Wald. Dir: Curtis Bernhardt. Scr: Silvia Richards,† Randall MacDougall. Novella basis: Rita Weiman, "One Man's Secret," *Hearst's International-Cosmopolitan* (1943). Cast: Joan Crawford, Van Heflin, Raymond Massey, Geraldine Brooks.

Police find an elegantly dressed woman wandering in Philadelphia at dawn, apparently in a trance and repeatedly asking to see "David." Through narcosynthesis or dream analysis, doctors learn her story. She was the personal nurse to the invalid wife of an industrialist but obsessively in love with a young engineer who is cold to the suggestion of their continued involvement and eager to move onward with his career. Left behind at a lake property with the invalid, she is tortured by the woman's charges of having an affair with the absent husband.

Arguably Joan Crawford's best film and the one for which she claimed to have worked the hardest as an actress, it fails only because the motivation for her obsession with the narcissistic engineer (Heflin) is assumed rather than explained. Nevertheless, it achieves high marks for its highlighting of gender themes within the noir modes of dream-like states. Distorting camera angles give the viewpoint of a neurotic driven mad, perhaps to show the constraints in the lives of ordinary women of the time. 108 min.

The President's Mystery (1936)

Rep. Prod: Nat Levine. Dir: Phil Rosen. Scr: Lester Cole,• Nathanael West. Story basis: Rupert Hughes, "The President's Mystery Story," *Liberty* (1935), based on an idea by Franklin D. Roosevelt. Cast: Henry Wilcoxon, Betty Furness, Sidney Blackmer, Evelyn Brent, Barnett Parker, Mel Ruick, Wade Boteler, John Wray

The first of the Popular Front films and an effort to use the popularity of the New Deal in reaching voters for the 1936 re-election campaign. According to legend, FDR (but more likely certain writers for *Liberty* magazine) supplied the plot based on the notion that a Wall Streeter might disappear from public life and reappear unnoticed in public service. On that unlikely premise, Cole and West devised a plot that had Wilcoxon, a lobbyist who has just blocked a (historically fictitious) bill in Congress that would have helped turn bankrupt companies into cooperatives, go on a fishing trip, meet and fall in love with a small town maiden and see the error of his ways. She is Furness, the bankrupt capitalist's daughter who wants to reopen under cooperative management and bring the economic life's blood back to the little town. Efforts to frustrate this effort fail, and something better than capitalism is presented as possible. The story was also published in book form in 1935, with seven mystery writers, including the noted S. S. Van Dine of the Philo Vance series, contributing a chapter each. 81 min.

Pride of the Marines (1945)

WB. Prod: Jerry Wald. Dir: Delmer Daves. Scr: Albert Maltz• (uncredited: Delmar Daves). Adaptation: Martin Borowsky. Book basis: Roger Butterfield, *Al Schmid, Marine* (1944). Cast: John Garfield, Eleanor Parker, Dane Clark, John Ridgely, Rosemary DeCamp, Ann Doran, Ann Todd, Warren Douglas

Powerful film used for Marine Corps Guadalcanal Day ceremonies in many cities until writer Maltz was attacked as a Communist. Based on the real-life story of Marine John Schmid, this is one of those Garfield working-class epics whose heartbreaking sincerity overwhelms its occasional maudlin elements and stock plot points and nearly wipes away Hollywood's built-in cynicism. The ethnic angle is fascinating: Garfield's best buddy Clark explains that the "handicap" of being a Jew is not so different from being a blind person, and both of them want a postwar America where no one gets kicked around anymore.

In rowhouse Philly where the film opens, factory operative Garfield seems happy-go-lucky with a vague sense of not yet finding himself. Sister Todd and brother-in-law Ridgely urge him to settle down to the modest but satisfying family life they enjoy. Meeting Parker makes him uneasy: he doesn't want to get tied down, or does he? Then comes Pearl Harbor, and he manfully enlists. The romance becomes stronger at a distance, an expression of their mutual need for a "normal" life.

Pride suddenly accelerates into a war film, creating in less than 30 minutes one of the most powerful battle scenes in the vast contemporary genre. This owes something to Daves' direction of buddies staring down hundreds of Japanese from a machine-gun nest on the Solomon Islands near Guadalcanal. But it owes more to Garfield's performance as the possessed machine-gunner holding on somehow as his friends die around him.

The remainder of the film, for which it is best remembered, constitutes the compulsory return of the blinded and embittered Garfield into the "community" of love and extended family. Nurse DeCamp is splendid in rehab, and Clark gets to deliver the "message" dialogue. Against a tear-jerking background of "America, America," he tells the recovering vets, "I know why I fought—for the right to live in the United States," insisting that things will be different for ordinary Americans, not just those en route to upward mobility through the GI Bill. Some critics have attacked the parade ground scenes as an example of Hollywood Communists unthinkingly supporting the kind of jingoism that did in the whole of the U.S. Left after the war. Academy Award nomination for screenplay went to Maltz. 119 min.

Prince of the Plains (1949)

Louise Rousseau• co-wrote the screenplay for this fictionalized account of the life of Bat Masterson, starring Monte Hale.

The Princess and the Pirate (1944)

Samuel Goldwyn/Goldwyn Pictures. Prod: Samuel Goldwyn. Dir: David Butler, Sidney Lanfield. Scr: Everett Freeman, Don Hartman, Melville Shavelson. Story basis: Sy Bartlett. Adaptation: Curtis Kenyon, Allen Boretz.• Cast: Bob Hope, Virginia Mayo, Walter Slezak, Walter Brennan, Victor McLaglen, Bing Crosby

An exotic historical romp into the generic quasi-Italian, quasi–Middle Eastern world of kings, caliphs and pirates. Hope is a no-talent vaudevillian who gets caught up—accidentally, of course—in an adventure protecting a secret princess, who has run away to escape an arranged marriage. The more mature Mayo slowly falls in love with the seemingly virginal Hope, releasing the tension built up by constant flight and disguise. One of the genuinely antifascist but future right-wing comedian's finest moments.

Best are the scenes of life on a pirates' island, where everyone is a crook and the authorities (Slezak as chief) are only more powerful, not more crooked, than anyone else. This could be capitalism writ large, but no morals are offered. Worst moments: painfully silly musical and pseudo-exotic dance numbers. Yes, that's the same Sy Bartlett who, a quarter of a century later, ruined Michael Wilson's script for CHE! Academy Award nominations for art-set decoration (Ernst Fegté, Howard Bristol) and music (David Rose). 94 min., color.

Prison Ship (1945)
A wrongly neglected antifascist war film co-written by Josef Mischel.• POWs find out that the prison ship transporting them to Tokyo is only a decoy to draw out an American submarine. They revolt, at great loss of life, but will it be in time to warn the sub?

Promise at Dawn (1970)
Nathalie Prod. Prod: Jules Dassin.• Dir: Jules Dassin. Scr: Jules Dassin. Novel basis: Romain Gary, *Promise at Dawn* (1963), and play by Samuel A. Taylor, *First Love* (1961). Cast: Melina Mercouri, Assi Dayan, Didier Haudepin, François Raffoul, Despo, Jean Martin, Fernand Gravey, Jacqueline Porel, Elspeth March, Maria Machado, Perlo Vita (pseudonym for Jules Dassin), René Clermont

A virtual all-Dassin production for his wife, Mercouri, about a woman who sacrifices everything for her son (played at different stages of life by Dayan, Haudepin and Raffoul). Filmed in the USSR, Paris and Nice, it posits Mercouri as a beloved actress of the early Soviet silent film with an illegitimate son conceived with a contemporary screen idol. After a theatrical tour closes in Kharkov, she pretends to be a famous Paris designer, is exposed and moves to Nice, where she works to support her son. As he grows up, he enlists in the Free French Air Force and the RAF for World War II and is awarded the Cross of Liberation, which he presents to her as reward for her sacrifices. When he arrives in Nice, he learns something that astonishes him. Dassin played the Russian silent actor and heartthrob of the Czarist era. 99 min.

The Prowler (1951)
Eagle/Horizon. Prod: S. P. Eagle (Sam Spiegel). Dir: Joseph Losey.• Scr: Hugo Butler• (uncredited: Dalton Trumbo•). Story basis: Robert Thoeren, Hans Wilhelm. Cast: Van Heflin, Evelyn Keyes, John Maxwell, Katherine Warren, Emerson Treacy, Wheaton Chambers, Robert Osterloh, Sherry Hall, Louise Lorimer

Rightly considered a classic of Hollywood in the last, lingering moments of genius before the blacklist, this is an allegorical treatment of greed and moral corruption infecting U.S. society in the postwar period. According to recent testimony, Trumbo was the principal writer, but under the pressure of being named as one of the Hollywood Ten, he withdrew, and Butler (who had not yet been named) substituted for him. Producer Eagle/Spiegel would later guide various projects for blacklistees in Europe.

Van Heflin is an L.A. cop who is called in by Keyes after she spots a prowler peeping into her bathroom window. Keyes' hubby, an unsympathetic and rather creepy all-night DJ played by Maxwell, has no time for her, and she soon falls hard for the designing Heflin. Some months after arranging for an "accidental" murder of Maxwell, Heflin takes Keyes to a desert ghost town to have their child—which brings up the point of the late Maxwell's impotence, and was considered very dicey for mixed audiences by theater-booking agents of the time. As Keyes begins to realize that his death was no accident, Heflin makes a run for it and the cops give chase. Edgy, tough and intelligent. In short, great stuff. 72 min.

Psyche '59 (1964)
Col./Troy-Schenk/Royal Films International. Prod: Philip Hazelton. Dir: Alexander Singer. Scr: Julian Halevy (pseudonym for Julian Zimet•). Novel basis: Françoise des Ligneris, *Psyche 59* (1959). Cast: Curt Jurgens, Patricia Neal, Samantha Eggar, Ian Bannen, Beatrix Lehmann, Elspeth March, Sandra Leo, Shelley Crowhurst

The film that, along with *Young Lovers* and *Circus World* the same year, marked Julian Zimet's successful return from the blacklist (albeit under a pseudonym, "Julian Halevy"). Sadly, he did not get much further, save a notable co-script for the classic HORROR EXPRESS and his single best film, written for Edgar Ulmer, the western NAKED DAWN.

Here, a solid cast (including Neal, who had recently won an Oscar) struggles through the difficulties inherent in adapting an existentialist novel to the screen. Neal is the mysteriously (psychosomatically) blind wife of industrialist Jurgens. The cause of her blindness is apparently his affair with Eggar, which Neal primordially witnessed. But is she faking it? Meanwhile, avant-garde film sexiness of the day dictates that Eggar will stand in a flimsy gown before a mirror, rubbing herself suggestively while Bannen sulks and moons for her. Lehman is the screwy grandmother of Neal consulting her astrological chart. Even the title is a bit of a mystery. 94 min.

The Public Enemy (1931)

WB. Prod: Darryl F. Zanuck. Dir: William A. Wellman, Harvey F. Thew. Scr: John Bright,• Kubec Glasmon. Cast: James Cagney, Edward Woods, Leslie Fenton, Joan Blondell, Mae Clarke, Jean Harlow

One of the most important films ever written from the Left and one of the earliest. As he tells the story, former bootlegger Bright left Chicago for Hollywood working on a crime novel. The film, a descendent of the novel (sold to MGM and itself never produced or published), was an experiment in sound with "street talk," as Bright put it. The gangster film had been around since the later 1910s, and actor Cagney (along with writer John Wexley, his later favorite) had been part of Brooklyn theater in which street toughness casually fit the various entertainment formulae. But the stock market crash prompted a thirst for a kind of social revenge against the system, and *Public Enemy* offered a new realism—before censorship tamed both violence and the sexual references.

In order to justify and explain itself, *Public Enemy* uses the criminal type as a social lesson. Cagney emerges from urban working-class experience, the disappointments of lower-class life and the temptations of the street. Although his mother is sentimentally kind and his brother is noble, Cagney is drawn to the fast life. There he finds money and action, along with danger aplenty, and he becomes ruthless in the chief racket of the age: selling illegal hooch. As we follow him through a repertoire of social relationships, he demonstrates his callousness and his odd innocence (Jean Harlow, with a past of "dozens" of men, is quick to grasp his sincerity). He will risk his life to avenge a pal as surely and unflinchingly as he will take a life, and that makes him something more than a psychotic. As the written prologue and afterword (looking more like silent film trailers) stress, this is a phenomenon that society must cope with somehow.

In many ways, this is a silent film with sound, often using 1920s music rather than dialogue to make its point, as if the film were accompanied by the organist in the theater. Perhaps in that sense (among others), it remains an art work unique in the Left canon. 83 min.

Q

Quality Street (1937)

RKO. Prod: Pandro S. Berman. Dir: George Stevens. Scr: Mortimer Offner,• Allan Scott (uncredited: Jack Townley). Cast: Katharine Hepburn, Franchot Tone, Fay Bainter, Cora Witherspoon, Estelle Winwood, Florence Lake, Bonita Granville, Eric Blore

This adaptation of a London play by James Barrie (of *Peter Pan* fame) poses interesting questions of women's culture and aging despite an awkward premise that pops up mid-picture. Apparently intended to be one of Hepburn's winsome roles, it fails as historical drama but succeeds as a gender picture.

In 1805 England, most of the men have gone off to war and the women left behind must reconcile themselves to spinsterhood. They decide to reject the (adult) male presence entirely, from the dirty boots to smelly tobacco pipes. Old prunes for the most part, seen unsympathetically (except for the plump, plain but affable Bainter), they offer a contrast to the 20-year-old Hepburn. Her heart is set on the kindly local physician, Franchot Tone, but the gentility is too thick for her even to hint that he propose marriage, and he misunderstands her intentions as urging him to enlist in the Napoleonic wars. With him gone, Hepburn and household set up a school for local children, including a vicious set of boys puberty-bound to another warring generation.

Ten years later, Tone returns, fearful that she now must have aged, only to find Hepburn posing as her 20-year-old niece. Does Tone suspect or not? The drama cannot possibly be strong enough to overcome the absurdity of the dual role, but Hepburn's anguish at her loss and her moments of happiness at potentially achieving love are worth clambering through the theatrical plot apparatus. 84 min.

Queen of Burlesque (1946)

A true curiosity from director Sam Neufeld, distributed by Producers Releasing Corp., humblest of the Poverty Row operations, which occasionally hired left-wing B-writers like Louise Rousseau.• Here, David Lang† delivered a convoluted plot about a pair of dames competing on the burlesque stage for star billing, complete with a murder subplot. An exploitation flick, it actually featured Rose La Rose, described by *Variety* as "a runway peeler with considerable experience." A collector's item.

Quicksand (1950)

UA. Prod: Mort Briskin. Dir: Irving Pichel.• Scr: Robert Smith. Cast: Mickey Rooney, Peter Lorre, Jeanne Cagney, Barbara Bates, Peter Lorre, Taylor Holmes

One of the best of the generally forgotten noir features, and arguably Pichel's best noir. It may also be Rooney's most interesting dramatic performance until his later television work and his sharpest portrayal of the blue-collar "little man" who urgently wants a bigger life.

Set memorably in a sleazy California seaside amusement park, *Quicksand* has Rooney as a car mechanic unwilling to accept Cagney's love. Instead, he pursues a new girlfriend whom he badly wants to show a good time. Short on cash, he borrows $20 from his garage's cash register. Caught short the next day and desperate, he buys a $100 watch on time and pawns it for $30, only to learn that in doing so he has violated a fine-print contract and committed a jailable offense. Then he steals several hundred dollars and, trapped by arcade-operator Lorre, has to steal an automobile: finally he is convinced that he has committed a murder. As his personal crisis deepens, the amusement park provides noir moments of crowds, rides, nickelodeon music and a perfect sense of the glittering materialism that will destroy him. A Hollywood ending of sorts is all wrong, but does not detract from the quality of the images. 79 min.

R

Racket Busters (1938)

WB. Prod: Samuel Bischoff (uncredited). Dir: Lloyd Bacon. Scr: Leonardo Bercovici,• Robert Rossen.† Cast: George Brent, Humphrey Bogart, Gloria Dickson, Allen Jenkins, Walter Abel, Penny Singleton

"If he could think as straight as he hits, he'd be terrific," says the truck-driver oldtimer, Walter Abel, about young Brent, his natural successor. But Brent has a typically American independent streak and a pregnant wife (Dickson). When the mob, led by Bogart, moves in on their cooperative (only the word "association" is ever used) of truck drivers and Pop is murdered, he is finally forced into action by his wife's moral admonitions.

Hollywood studios' slant on organized labor gave this film many unpleasant angles. D. A. Jenkins is a stand-in for Tom Dewey, the crusading politician of New York state and future Republican presidential nominee, the subject of a half-dozen other contemporary films. A teamster "strike" is staged by the mob—perhaps a slap at the heroic Minneapolis teamster strike that was a labor high point of the earlier 1930s—and resisted by working-class women. Such historical distortions weaken (or pervert) the film, yet something survives: portrayals of working-class life and its leaders. Brent is allowed to give the moral: "We've got to stick together." 71 min.

Rachel and the Stranger (1948)

RKO. Prod: Richard Berger ("presented by Dore Schary"). Dir: Norman Foster. Scr: Waldo Salt.• Story basis: Howard Fast.• Cast: Loretta Young, William Holden, Robert Mitchum, Gary Gray, Tom Tully, Sara Haden, Frank Ferguson, Walter Baldwin, Regina Wallace

With this film and THE BOY WITH GREEN HAIR, Schary held out the promise of a sustained relationship with top Left writers—until the blacklist intervened. Rachel is memorable as the first work of novelist Howard Fast to reach the screen—to be followed by Spartacus and others after Fast got out of prison. The film suffers from the passing of decades because the themes of nineteenth-century frontier heroism (especially the fending off of

Indian attacks) do not translate into the 1940s. But it does capture the extreme loneliness of the post-Revolutionary frontier life. Widower Holden realizes that his son (Gray) needs a mother and acquires a bonded servant (Young) whom he then takes as help-meet and wife. Along comes the wanderer, Mitchum, an old friend, to settle in for awhile. Strumming the guitar, playing with the boy and generally looking virile as only Mitchum can, he charms Young—but not quite to the point of active romance. Fate intervenes with a Shawnee attack, and Holden finally realizes that he must woo the wife he took for granted. The most important element in the film, however, is the subjectivity of Young, who often played the strong (but "traditional") woman over the decades—sometimes on the Left, more often on the Right. 93 min. (later cut to 79 min.)

Rage in Heaven (1941)

MGM. Prod: Gottfried Reinhardt. Dir: W. S. Van Dyke (uncredited: Robert B. Sinclair). Scr: Robert Theoren, Christopher Isherwood (uncredited: Edward Chodorov•). Novel basis: James Hilton, Dawn of Reckoning (1925). Cast: Ingrid Bergman, Robert Montgomery, George Sanders, Lucile Watson, Oskar Homolka, Philip Merivale, Matthew Boulton

A psychological thriller with Homolka the Freud-goateed shrink on hand at the last moment to explain everything (in a heavy Viennese accent) and save the day. Before that, a "veddy, veddy English" Montgomery, a troubled scion of capital who has been confined to a mental institution, escapes and makes his way back to his palatial home, joined by his college chum, Sanders. There they greet Montgomery's mother, dowager Watson, and her nurse-companion, Bergman. Both fall in love with Ingrid but the gallant Sanders realizes that Montgomery's happiness depends wholly upon marriage, while he can roam as an engineer and make his own life. The two marry happily, despite the occasional outburst that reveals Montgomery's mental instability. At his mother's insistence, he also takes over the family mill, and proves himself almost immediately both incompetent and tyrannical.

When workers learn that their pay has been cut and they will not be provided with the new mill housing they had been promised, they riot, and only the quick thinking of Sanders (conveniently on hand) saves his skin. But Montgomery has been plunged into the darkness of his own fears and hatreds, and events spin out of control.

Montgomery was one of Hollywood's most conservative actors (and gutsy: he stood up to real-life mobsters), and he is particularly good here in his role as a troubled capitalist. Bergman plays the familiar dewy ingénue. Although the ending is too pat, the film comes out well even if Van Dyke had to substitute for the ailing Sinclair. Montgomery won two acting awards from the National Board of Review—for this and for HERE COMES MR JORDAN). 82 min.

Rampage (1963)

Seven Arts/Talbot. Prod. William Fadiman. Dir: Phil Karlson. Scr: Robert I. Holt, Marguerite Roberts.• Novel basis: Alan Caillou, *Rampage* (1961). Cast: Robert Mitchum, Elsa Martinelli, Jack Hawkins, Sabu, Cely Carillo, Émile Genest, Stefan Schnabel

Roberts' second credited film after her rehabilitation from the blacklist was a return to working with Karlson, a favorite Left director of the later 1940s who would happily have gone on making "their" films if only conditions had been different. Unfortunately, this is not much of a picture. Like so many other Third World big-game hunting films of the time (still more popular in the 1950s), it leads to a romantic triangle, this time in the Malay bush in pursuit of an elusive feline predator (Karlson also directed THE BIG CAT) for a German zoo. How is it different from *Mogambo* et al.? Well, there's lots of talk about trapping versus hunting (a version of sheepherding vs. cattle ranching), and the aged hunter mentor (Hawkins) loses his mind in the manner of Conrad's *Heart of Darkness*. Hawkins' mistress Martinelli is centrally involved, not to mention guide Sabu, who repeatedly suggests that Mitchum sleep with Sabu's wife (Carrillo). Elmer Bernstein's score and footage from the San Diego Zoo (!) are probably the most memorable features. 99 min., color.

The Raven (1935)

Universal. Prod: Carl Laemmle, Jr. Dir: Louis Friedlander (pseudonym for Lew Landers). Scr: Ernest Boehm (uncredited contributions: Guy Endore,• Dore Schary, Clarence Marks, et al.). Title: Edgar Allan Poe. Cast: Bela Lugosi, Irene Ware, Boris Karloff, Lester Matthews, Inez Courtney

A horror classic with some extraordinary expressionistic moments, great makeup work for Karloff, prime Lugosi and a dreadful cast of supporting players. The title is little more than a rip-off of Poe's famed poem. Physician Lugosi keeps a stuffed raven as a totem of death, and the poem's best-remembered verses are recited several times with some effect. Ward, a modern dancer, has suffered a brain injury and only the famed, reclusive doctor can operate successfully. Lugosi agrees, but quickly falls in love with the girl and plots to take her from her betrothed (and her financier father). One of the most extraordinary moments of the film has Ward, in homage to his effort, dancing a "Raven" number in a black mask against a Caligari-style background. The plot would dissolve into melodrama at this point if not for Lugosi's cruel trick on the criminal-on-the-run Karloff. Rather than giving him the new face he needs as a disguise, Lugosi makes him a twisted monster (who sees his new face for the first time in a shot with six surrounding mirrors). Together, they carry out fiendish plots that must be foiled so that the real lovers can be reunited and propriety restored. Too bad. 62 min.

Raw Deal (1948)

Reliance/E-L. Prod: Edward Small (uncredited). Dir: Anthony Mann. Scr: Leopold Atlas,† John C. Higgens. Story basis: Arnold B. Armstrong, Audrey Ashley. Cast: Dennis O'Keefe, Claire Trevor, Marsha Hunt,• Raymond Burr, John Ireland

A low-budget but well cast and tightly plotted noir that is memorable as Hunt's major starring role before the blacklist. It begins as a classic jailbreak film, with O'Keefe managing to evade pursuers, thanks to sentimental moll Trevor driving a getaway car. O'Keefe kidnaps his lawyer, Hunt, who has seen something in him that she hoped to rescue. The film unpredictably becomes a combination road movie and romantic triangle. The odyssey seems destined for doom, and not only because crime boss Burr intends to "pay off" O'Keefe for taking an earlier rap for him by having him killed. O'Keefe is beyond redemption, and for that reason, the emotional core of the drama belongs to Trevor and Hunt. Born and raised in the slums of San Francisco, Trevor craves love and increasingly suspects that her man is drawn to her rival. Hunt, who pulled herself up from a more typical Depression home of economically defeated middle-class parents, sees in O'Keefe's violent nature his deserved end, but also feels drawn to him as doom approaches, perhaps (although this is never explicated) because he so clearly represents the lower-class society whose suffering and fatalism she has come to understand. Violence and gunplay disguise or perhaps amplify the strong class interpretation of the ending. Shot on a small budget and probably in a few weeks, *Raw Deal* goes as far as it can. 79 min.

Reckless Age (1944)

Gertrude Purcell† and Henry Blankfort• teamed up for this rarely seen B-film with an almost casually delivered Popular Front message. Issues of class and worker morale were quietly insinuated into this harmless tale about the heiress of a department store fortune who runs away from home when her grandfather informs her that the demands of ownership require that her entire life be planned out to the minute. After skipping town, she winds up working for her grandfather's chain under a pseudonym, and her hands-on experience make her an expert observer of working conditions and her suggestions lead to improvement in employee morale. These rather harmless themes are interspersed with occasional misunderstandings and mayhem (animals loose in the store), but the gender issues are resolved when grandpa agrees she has the right to live her own life—and she signs up to fight fascism!

Red Dust (1932)

MGM. Prod: Victor Fleming, Hunt Stromberg (uncredited). Dir: Victor Fleming (uncredited). Scr: John Lee Mahin (uncredited script contribution: Donald Ogden Stewart•). Play basis: Wilson Collison, *Red Dust* (1928). Cast: Clark Gable, Jean Harlow, Gene Raymond, Mary Astor, Tully Marshall, Forrester Harvey, Willie Fung

One of the original exotic location talkies (as much exoticism as a Hollywood backlot and lots of fake rain could convey), the film provided the model for many hot-climate romances to come. Gable manages a rubber plantation somewhere in what was called French Indo-China (could be Vietnam, Thailand or Cambodia), and seems to have little passion beyond beating the natives to get out his production quota. Harlow comes over from Saigon, an émigré floozy (i.e., hooker) for the European crowd, with a platinum hairdo (where would Harlow be without it?) and acid wit—thanks, perhaps, to Stewart's contributions.

After much repartee, and as she begins to soften Gable, she leaves for distant parts and young engineer Raymond comes into the scene. As he falls victim to fever, his wife Astor hangs out and becomes enamored with Gable: a kiss tells audiences in pre-Code days that they are sleeping together. Harlow returns (her ship never made it out of the harbor) and sets things right all around, sending the married couple off and settling in for a long, happy stretch in primitive conditions with the big hunk of a man with the flappy ears. Remade as *Mogambo*, with an African subtheme and little of the thirties' sauciness. 83 min.

Red River Range (1938)

Rep. Assoc. Prod: William A. Berke. Dir: George Sherman. Scr: Stanley Roberts,† Betty Burbridge, William Colt MacDonald, Luci Ward. Story Basis: Luci Ward (characters created by William Colt MacDonald). Cast: John Wayne, Ray Corrigan, Max Terhune, Polly Moran, Lorna Gray, Kirby Grant, Sammy McKim

Another of the Three Mesquiteers series, memorable mainly for Wayne's appearance and the modern setting. This time the Mesquiteers respond to the Red River Cattlemen's Association, which has obtained the help of the state attorney to investigate rustling. Wayne takes on the identity of outlaw "Killer Madigan," who works at a dude ranch and feigns being a greenhorn as he is "taught" to ride. Encroachments on the myth of the West are everywhere, from the proliferation of dude ranches to the sight of cows being towed off to market by truck. The political angle, never strong, is emphasized slightly by the determination of the town hotel manager to get rid of the Mesquiteers, a point reinforced near the end of the film when a naïve member of the Cattlemen's Association reveals a secret plan to the town banker, who has been working with the rustlers all along. 55 min.

The Remarkable Andrew (1942)

Para. Prod: Richard Blumenthal. Dir: Stuart Heisler. Scr: Dalton Trumbo.• Cast: William Holden, Brian Donlevy, Ellen Drew, Rod Cameron, Porter Hall, Nydia Westman, Montagu Love, Jimmy Conlin

A fairly silly wartime evocation of patriotically liberal values with sometimes good acting, making the script seem better than it is. Holden is an unassuming auditor who has the yearly job of going over his small town's financial records. He knows that city officials line their pockets in land deals, but keeps quiet because no outright illegality has taken place. This time, however, sums of money have disappeared, and attempted persuasion by various officials can't compel him to overlook the gaps. This also puts a dent in his romance, but only as a distraction to the central theme.

The crisis calls back the ghost of President Andrew Jackson (Donlevy), whose picture stands on the bookkeeper's wall and for whom he was named. The real slave-owner and Indian killer Jackson is nowhere to be found. But the crusty moralist and whiskey drinker, seen only by Holden, offers large chunks of folksy philosophy and some intelligent advice. When Holden is himself imprisoned on trumped-up charges, a barrage of other Founding Fathers appears (Jefferson, Washington, Franklin and a Revolutionary War soldier who complains that the ordinary people are always forgotten), remarkably reaffirming New Deal programs. Could have been better, considering it's Trumbo. 80 min.

The Return of October (1948)

Col. Prod: Rudolph Maté. Dir: Joseph H. Lewis. Scr: Norman Panama, Melvin Frank. Story basis: Karen DeWolf,• Connie Lee.• Cast: Glenn Ford, Terry Moore, Albert Sharpe, James Gleason, Stephen Dunne, Dame May Whitty, Henry O'Neill, Frederic Tozere, Samuel S. Hinds

The Runyonesque world of the racetrack is contrasted with the respectable but ultimately unsatisfying worlds of riches and book learning. Moore is horse-crazy, bonded to her uncle and to his buddies at the track, but he dies just as she wins enough cash on craps to buy the horsefeed for the promising October. She is packed off to grandmother's mansion, where she grows into a fashionable but restless young lady.

Meanwhile Ford, a psychology professor at a nearby university interested in emotional bonding of people and animals, is quickly drawn into the picture, and decides to write a monograph on Moore's delusion that her uncle's spirit continues in the horse. The film closes with a bizarre trial concerning her sanity (with a few bows to human/animal lore), and the inevitable Derby running. Pleasant and original. 98 min., color.

Reunion in France (1942)

Enterprise/MGM. Prod: Joseph L. Mankiewicz. Dir: Jules Dassin.• Scr: Marvin Borowsky, Leslie Bush-Fekete. Story: Jan Lustig, Marc Connelly (uncredited: Charles Hoffman). Cast: Joan Crawford, John Wayne, Philip Dorn, Reginald Owen, Albert Bassermann, John Carradine, Howard da Silva,• Anne Ayars, J. Edward Bromberg

Despite big-name casting, this is a run-of-the mill antifascist feature backed by equally big-name producer Mankiewicz, and of interest primarily as the first major directorial assignment for Dassin.

Crawford is the center of attention as the frivolous Parisian bourgeoise who sees her world disintegrate around her as the Nazis take over, seizing control of the city's social life as well as its political and economic institutions. Collaboration and resistance are the chief themes, and the Americans never looked so comfortable in sophisticated surroundings. Dassin resists the temptation to demonize the Germans. Instead, he draws them with a fine satirical edge, as tourists wandering past the shops and boulevards, as when a troop of Wehrmacht

soldiers, Baedekers in hand, snap their gazes from guidebooks to monuments in unison, as in close-order drill.

After a strong opening in which the character of the still-luminous Crawford is explored and tested, the story gives up and turns into an actioner, with John Wayne playing John Wayne but not without an occasional well-turned moment. As the plot grows heavier with reversals and the more familiar artifacts of martial suspense, one looks for vignettes like da Silva's wonderfully comic turn as a low-level Nazi collaborator. 100 min.

Revenge of the Creature (1955)

U-I. Prod: William Alland.† Dir: Jack Arnold. Scr: Martin Berkeley,† William Alland. Cast: John Agar, Lori Nelson, John Bromfield, Robert Williams, Nestor Paiva, Clint Eastwood (uncredited)

The second creature epic of producer Alland (best remembered as the back-of-head narrator in CITIZEN KANE) and, like Creature from the Black Lagoon, an ecological warning with a beauty-and-the-beast subtheme. This time, sci-fi pic regular Agar is the scientist who oversees the capture of the creature from its South American lair and its removal to a kind of Seaworld amusement part in Florida. It is pitilessly chained to the bottom of a tank, swimming around enough for tourists to gape through portals. It espies Agar's fiancée and fellow scientist Nelson (who stops action long enough to mull the unfairness of women needing to choose between family and career), and eventually escapes to capture her.

The hunt for the creature through coastal Florida offers especially bizarre moments of sunbelt suburbanites facing the survivor of a lost world. The gloom of the monster's inevitable demise marks the pervasive sense of loss—or so claims the film's real creator Alland, who hired his directors as virtual walk-ons. Cameo by young and unknown Eastwood is a plus only for the hard-core fan. 82 min.

Rhapsody in Blue (1945)

WB. Prod: Jesse L. Lasky. Dir: Irving Rapper. Scr: Howard Koch,• Sonya Levien. Story: Elliot Paul (uncredited: Clifford Odets†). Cast: Robert Alda, Joan Leslie, Alexis Smith, Charles Coburn, Oscar Levant, Paul Whiteman, Al Jolson, George White, Hazel Scott, Anne Brown

A composer's version of The Jazz Singer, with Alda as the young George Gershwin, who yearns to deliver a uniquely American musical message and in the process creates an assimilated Jewish Americanism, thanks to the apparent adoption of the African American idiom. Unlike

Jolson (who plays a cameo as the star who lifts young Gershwin to commercial success), a vaudevillian drawing on the minstrel tradition, Gershwin has a more serious purpose: he wants to incorporate these traditions into contemporary art music (tending, like the late French romantics, toward the popular). And so he leaves Broadway behind for the concert hall and Europe.

In real life as in the film, the adoption of Gershwin's work by Paul Whiteman is critical to "making a lady" (as Whiteman puts it) out of jazz. But while the orchestration in "Rhapsody in Blue" captured a certain urban ambience, it all but abandoned the black idiom. Gershwin's similar rhapsodies about Paris and Cuba have broadly similar touches—the folkish idiom lovingly combined with the metropolitan, which was to remain his contribution to music.

The surrounding plot is mostly gratuitous. Gershwin leaves singer Joan Leslie in New York, discovers artist Smith in Paris and spends a long time coming back to his true love. Ira Gershwin, in real life a solid left-winger (and life-long friend of Yip Harburg•), is seen as part of the larger Jewish family life that binds the composer to his ideals. 139 min.

Rhythm Parade (1942)

Monogram. Prod: Sydney M. Williams. Dir: Howard Bretherton. Scr: Carl Foreman,• Charles R. Marian. Cast: Gale Storm, Nils T. Granlund, Robert Lowrey, Margaret Dumont, Chick Chandler, Candy Candido, Yvonne DeCarlo

An extremely light musical piece, which apart from being Foreman's second writing credit, is notable mainly for its gendered politics. Singer Storm's sister has gone to Hawaii, leaving her infant son in Storm's hands. This poses, in the terms of the era, the supposed problem of "explaining" why a would-be celebrity, though unmarried, has a child. Dumont (better remembered as delivering the straight lines for the Marx Brothers) is the tough-as-nails sister of an agent, determined to secure for Storm the booking she deserves. En route to a Hollywood ending, Dumont gives a short and improbably eloquent lecture on what should be a performer's and presumably every woman's own private business.

Apart from a brief "Russian Dance" (and a rare film appearance by the Mills Brothers), the most compelling moment of the film is a transsexual musical number sung by the freakishly multi-octaved Candy Candido—later known as a voice of cartoon characters—acting both parts as boyfriend (with deep voice) and girlfriend (high voice, many campy gestures). 68 min.

Rhythm Round-Up (1945)

Charming comedy oater in the high style of the forties, with a Louise Rousseau• story showing an early example of Arizona land fraud. A pair of cattle rustlers have set up shop on the top floor of a hotel in the desert from which they are (a) sending out hundreds of letters to unsuspecting marks informing them that they have inherited the hotel and can claim it for a $146 fee, and (b) spreading tales that the hotel is haunted so the prospective heirs will leave town as quickly as they arrive. The plan works fine until the day Cheryl Walker and the failing band, the Hoosier Hot Shots, arrive in town, determined not only to move in but to use the hotel for nationwide radio broadcasts. Merry mayhem, as they say, ensues. Musical highlight: "That's What I Learned in College," by Bob Wills.

Rich Man, Poor Girl (1938)

MGM. Prod: Edward Chodorov.• Dir: Reinhold Schünzel. Scr: Edward Chodorov, Joseph Fields. Cast: Ruth Hussey, Robert Young, Lew Ayres, Lana Turner, Guy Kibbee, Rita Johnson, Don Castle

Strong performances and some good dialogue almost save this weak story from sinking into romantic shmaltz. Hussey is the executive secretary to hands-on construction magnate Young, who proposes to take her out of the New York slums. Ambivalent about the leap across social classes, Hussey insists that Young meet her family. With that premise, we enter the lower-middle-class life of the Depression years among generic gentiles who have no bad habits and mostly work hard but still cannot advance themselves. Brother Ayres is a gabby anticapitalist, perennially quitting work because he can't stand to be bossed. Teen-aged Turner, in one of her earliest roles, is the little sister who wants a glamorous life. Guy Kibbee is the lovable dad and, like mom Johnson, only wants the family to be happy. Repartee foreshadows the Chodorov-Fields stage-and-film successes like Junior Miss. As in The Philadelphia Story, Hussey is wonderfully cast as the perky career girl. 65 min.

Riding The Wind (1941)

RKO. Prod: Bert Gilroy. Dir: Edward Killy. Scr: Morton Grant,• Earle Snell. Story basis: Bernard McConville. Cast: Tim Holt, Ray Whitley, Lee "Lasses" White, Mary Douglas (Joan Barclay), Eddie Dew

For once, the love interest (Douglas) of a western has no crooked uncle and no mistaken involvement with the bad guys to confuse our hero and move the plot. Instead, we have windmills (hence the title), brought west unassembled by an aged engineer and his daughter. This seems to be just the thing for the water-starved ranchers, beset by a capitalist water hog who has dammed the river. But of course, sabotage of various kinds ensues, until Holt gets to the bottom of things.

Sidekick White is an embarrassing show in himself. A popular cowboy second lead, his middle name came from the diminutive for "Molasses," a stage name from the country black-face act in which he got his start (which also included signature eye-rolling, fear of ghosts, and other clichés of the genre). Poignant moments of the film include a hoedown that reveals a community threatened by the power-hungry and their bought-off officials. Will the masses rise up violently? Not while Holt can appeal to higher authorities to bring back a just decision on water use: yet more echoes of conservation issues in the New Deal. 60 min.

Rififi (aka Du Rififi chez les hommes, 1955)

Indus Films/Prima Films. Prod: René Gaston Vuattoux. Dir: Jules Dassin.• Scr: Ben Barzman• (uncredited), Jules Dassin, René Wheeler, Gabriel Arout, Jose Giovanni. Cast: Jean Servais, Carl Mohner, Robert Manuel, Jules Dassin

The granddaddy of modern heist films, *Du Rififi chez les hommes* is Dassin's masterpiece, combining American film noir with French poetic realism to evoke the streets of Paris and the cheap hoods who hustle goods and women while dreaming of bigger scores to come. The modern techno-thriller can be traced directly to this film, which Dassin himself ransacked years later for his own *Topkapi*. It was also the first film to appear in the United States with the credit of a blacklisted filmmaker intact (it ran briefly in New York).

The jewel theft at the heart of the tale is executed in a 20-minute tour de force of absolute silence interrupted only by a footfall or the clanking of tools. With extraordinary technical skill, four lower-class thieves avoid all of the traps and security measures; if they fail, it will be because of the flawed social relations among them. They have no central organizing principle that would permit them to conclude their business effectively. Rather like *On the Waterfront* by friendly witness Elia Kazan (but without the stool pigeon message), this film is best understood as Socialist Realism without the socialism. In French with English subtitles. 120 min.

Road Gang (1936)

WB. Prod: Bryan Foy. Dir: Louis King. Scr: Dalton Trumbo.• Story basis: Abem Finkel, Harold Buckley. Cast:

Donald Woods, Kay Linaker, Carlyle Moore, Jr., Joe King, Marc Lawrence†

Trumbo's first credited film is a social shocker of the prison exposé variety. A probing journalist (Woods) is sent to a Southern prison, thanks to the conniving stepfather of his new girlfriend. There, he comes across a road gang working under monstrous conditions: denial of water in the hot sun, beatings with whips for the exhausted or ill and—in a prison film cliché that was all too true-to-life— denial of medical treatment for emergency cases.

If that were not bad enough, Woods is sent to "Blackford," the prison coal mine, where death is almost preferable to the slavery of the work. But the hardest cons prove surprisingly generous with each other, rebelling against outrages (and for their efforts almost murdered in a gas counterattack). Meanwhile, legal forces and a Chicago newspaper begin the challenge that will bring down the corruption and brutality of state prison officials. Often gripping, with remarkable crowd action scenes. 59 min.

Road House (1948)

Fox. Prod: Edward Chodorov.• Dir: Jean Negulesco. Scr: Edward Chodorov. Story basis: Margaret Gruen, Oscar Saul. Cast: Ida Lupino, Cornell Wilde, Celeste Holm, Richard Widmark, O. Z. Whitehead, Ozzie Carnes, Robert Karnes

This crisp noir becomes a vehicle for Lupino at her best, playing the tough-talking (and gravel-voiced) lounge singer whose appearance in a bowling alley/tavern of a blue-collar town near the Canadian border sets its owner (Widmark at his psychotic best) and Cornel Wilde (almost acting here, and terribly manly in a bowling shirt) at each other's throats.

Noir had broken down some boundaries by this time, and there's no doubt that Widmark has brought in the new girl as a prospective bed partner (he has hired similar songbirds on earlier road trips). But Lupino is no pushover. She wows the customers, practices bowling in her off hours and pushes Widmark away by snuggling up to Wilde. This sets off a psychological storm of the kind that is so frequent in films of this period and brings out the petty criminal record that is being held over the head of the loyal (but resentful) Wilde. The film ends with a memorable chase in and around a hunting lodge, where the dame has to go all the way with the available gun. Seemingly destined for better things in a dozen ways, real-life Lupino had to settle for a brief directing career and a successful run at Golden Age television. 95 min.

Roads to the South (1978)

France 3/Profilmes S.A. Prod: Yves Rousset-Rouard. Dir: Joseph Losey.• Scr: Jorge Semprún. Cast: Yves Montand, Miou-Miou, Laurent Malet, Roger Planchon

Les routes du sud is one of Losey's least-known films and one of his most personal, even though he was not the author. The screenplay was written by the highly regarded Jorge Semprún. He worked extensively with left-wing directors Alain Resnais and Costa-Gavras and served for a time as the minister of culture for the social democratic government of Spain after the events portrayed in the film, which deal with the last days of the Franco government as the old dictator lies dying in his bed of Parkinson's disease.

The film responds to the very specific question, "Who was the last person to die in Spain in the 40-year resistance to fascism?" The answer is a middle-aged, happily married woman, a Spanish exile in France who is killed on the highway to Barcelona while acting as a courier for the Communist Party. Left behind in France to mourn her are her husband, a novelist and filmmaker (Montand), and his son (Malet), who has brought his girlfriend (Miou-Miou) to his father's home to help in communicating with the grieving husband. The lovely young girlfriend remains behind after Malet suddenly leaves the house in frustration. She seduces the much older man, then accompanies him to Barcelona to witness the end of fascism.

As the film opens, Montand is obsessed with a screenplay in which a German soldier in World War II who is also a Communist risks his life to cross the battle lines and warn his comrades in the Red Army that they are about to be attacked. The Russians listen to his story and then kill him without another thought. This allegory for what his son later calls "the cult of Stalinism" hangs over the rest of the film. Montand (himself, as actor-activist, but like his famous wife, Simon Signoret, by this time disillusioned) plays an intellectual contemplating the fact that he devoted his life to a cause that ended badly, notwithstanding its supporters' courageous roles in class struggles large and small, its (sometimes grudging) support for anticolonialism and, most memorably in France, its resistance to fascism. Sometimes slow but often riveting—a small masterpiece. 100 min.

The Roaring Twenties (1939)

WB. Prod: Hal B. Wallis, Jack L. Warner. Dir: Raoul Walsh. Scr: Jerry Wald, Richard Macaulay, Robert Rossen† (uncredited: John Wexley•). Cast: James Cagney, Priscilla Lane, Humphrey Bogart, Gladys George, Jeffrey Lynn, Frank McHugh, Paul Kelly

Another of Cagney's classic (and best) films as the tough guy and tender romantic, which is narrated with stock footage to reveal three eras in U.S. history: wartime, the dizzy twenties, and the post-prohibition thirties.

Cagney, Bogart and McHugh are blue-collar Doughboys in the First World War who stumble into each other and swear that if they get out alive, they will help each other make it in civilian life. Bootlegging is the obvious way up, and Cagney eventually brings in Bogart, who is working for another gang. However, Cagney has fallen in love with would-be singer Lane (who is, in turn, in love with Cagney's lawyer) and promotes her into modest stardom. After Prohibition is repealed and he loses the girl, Cagney slips into a bottle; he is cared for by his erstwhile cabaret partner-singer, Gladys George.

The last scenes, with Cagney set to protect his true love and her husband (now a prosecutor) from mob boss Bogart, are some of the best in 1930s melodrama, and will unfailingly touch the heart of the viewer who can look beyond the all-too-familiar stylization for a glimpse of as much real humanity as Hollywood could allow. 106 min.

The Robe (1953)

20th. Prod: Frank Ross. Dir: Henry Koster. Scr: Philip Dunne (uncredited: Albert Maltz•). Adaptation: Gina Kaus. Novel basis: Lloyd C. Douglas, *The Robe* (1942). Cast: Richard Burton, Jean Simmons, Victor Mature, Michael Rennie, Richard Boone, Jay Robinson, Dawn Addams, Dean Jagger, Jeff Morrow, Ernest Thesiger

The first film shot in CinemaScope (at vast expense), *The Robe* opened amid huzzahs for technical improvements in the wrap-around effect, leading briefly to a picket line from musicians at the Roxy in New York who feared the new movie technology would make the stage spectacular obsolete (the move's tagline, playing on the tinted spectacles of 3-D, was, "The modern miracle you see without glasses!"). The premiere featured Hollywood's brightest celebrities—surrounded by a rubbernecking crowd of 6,000 Fox execs, who sank $4,600,000 into the picture and struck special gold medallions to the four big stars. Who knew that its original screenwriter was the notorious Albert Maltz? Probably Zanuck, but if so, he kept mum.

The Robe offered a narrative breakthrough as well. It was the first of many biblical films to follow in which a Hollywood Communist, in this case also a secular Jew, wrote dialogue for Christian revolutionaries who were forced into hiding and suffering for their ideology—or, as in *The Robe*, suffering from remorse that they had done the wrong thing. Who could blame Maltz for seizing with such relish the opportunity presented by Douglas' reverential novel to explore the guilt of a man who betrayed the cause of creating a better world?

Burton is Marcellus Giallo, the centurion in the Gospels who is put in charge of crucifying Christ and, drunk on imperial cynicism, gambles for Jesus' simple garment after the crucifixion. Confused by his remorse, Marcellus tries to find out why his conscience tortures him, and once he figures it out (as a few friendly witnesses in Hollywood actually did), he rallies to the cause, finding Judas, who begs him not to lose the faith. The failed revolutionary then goes into exile to gain the courage necessary to return in support of the slaves' ideology. While the biblical soap opera will continue to evolve through the 1950s, the first is still the best. 135 min., color.

Robin Hood of El Dorado (1936)
MGM. Prod: John W. Considine, Jr. Dir: William A. Wellman. Scr: Melvyn Levy.† Cast: Warner Baxter, Ann Loring, Margo, Bruce Cabot, J. Carrol Naish.

An extraordinary exercise in popular antiracism and anti-imperialism, all the more extraordinary for the early date of its production. A highly fictionalized biography of Joaquin Murrieta, it explains the actions of the nineteenth-century California social bandit by pointing to the rape and murder of the simple farmer's wife by gold-crazed and ruthless "Americans" expropriating everything in sight. Taking to the hills but refusing the company of Mexican American bandit gangs, Murrieta (Baxter) changes his mind after a key defeat. He soon heads a quasi-revolutionary army whose hidden encampment is the site of lots of merriment and folk-dancing, along with military training—the old Robin Hood scenes reborn.

At the political turning point in the film, Baxter plans to rob the rich Mexican landowners only to find that they, too, have been expropriated. Their proudest señorita (Margo) joins his gang, and they plan a collective getaway to a peaceful life in Mexico. At this moment the Yankees attack the camp, surrounding the Mexicans with devastating gunfire. The film has a maudlin conclusion, and an often weak story, but many wonderful moments turn the standard western stereotypes upside-down. Melvyn Levy's best work. 86 min.

Rocketship X-M (1950)
Lippert Pictures. Prod: Kurt Neumann. Dir: Kurt Neumann. Scr: Kurt Neumann, Orville H. Hampton (uncredited: Dalton Trumbo•). Cast: Lloyd Bridges,† Osa Massen, Hugh O'Brian, John Emergy, Noah Beery, Jr.

One of the most left-wing of the kids' films, this low-budget, small-cast production has a spaceship that loses direction and whose crew discovers that a planet not so different from Earth has been destroyed by something very much like atomic war. The shipboard romance between Bridges and Massen (a favorite of antifascist films) is unconsummated but grows intense when they discover they are doomed. Interesting for the day, and just one more of the Lippert/Neumann collaborations, it nonetheless foreshadowed the work of other producers who also scrounged for blue-light specials on first-rate talent reduced to hack work by the blacklist—but often the work was far less progressive than this. 77 min.

Rockin' in the Rockies (1945)
The Three Stooges were a part of Popular Front culture, performing at a benefit for a maritime workers union and at a Communist Party–sponsored writers conference (along with Henry Fonda) in 1941, but this film is their only creative tie to the Left. In a story basis by the prolific Louise Rousseau,• the boys head out West, pick up a coin dropped by a drunk in a saloon and use it to hit the roulette jackpot. The winnings are turned into the stake for a gold-prospecting trip—and then the true madness begins.

Roman Holiday (1953)
Para. Prod: William Wyler. Dir: William Wyler. Scr: Ian McLellan Hunter• (front for Dalton Trumbo,• uncredited), John Dighton. Story: Dalton Trumbo. Cast: Audrey Hepburn, Gregory Peck, Eddie Albert,• Tullio Carminati

A much-honored film with Hunter, soon to go on the blacklist, still able to front for the already notorious Trumbo (who received a posthumous Oscar for this film four decades later). Like Edgar G. Ulmer's B-version exploration of Paris in *Bluebeard* (1944), this is a work of love about a city, no doubt in contrast to suburbanized Cold War life at home. The Romans' zest for living is brilliantly juxtaposed to the ancient urban environment of endless carved façades and fountains. They sit in cafés, they dance joyously to American music, they drive madly—and they believe in love.

That atmosphere prompts a bored and restless visiting princess (Hepburn) to escape her palatial surroundings, now "drunk" with a drug given earlier to sedate her. She accidentally meets American expatriate journalist Peck, who wants more than anything to get back to New York. With the help of photographer Albert,

Peck plots to write a sensationalist exposé of the city and the princess—but falls in love as he and the princess spend the day together. Hepburn is brilliant and real-life progressive Hollywoodite Albert is more than adequate, but Peck lacks the temperament to get far with the comic element. Never mind. The film won Oscars: best actress, best costume design, best story basis. Nominations: art direction, black-and-white cinematography and film editing. 118 min.

Romance of a Horsethief (1971)

Allied Artists. Prod: Gene Gutowski. Dir: Abraham Polonsky.• Scr: David Opatoshu, Abraham Polonsky. Cast: Yul Brynner, Eli Wallach, Jane Birkin, Oliver Tobias, Lainie Kazan, David Opatoshu

An underbudgeted but intensely political version of Eastern European ghetto life—something like FIDDLER ON THE ROOF, but considerably tougher. It was also the only opportunity for director Polonsky (who took over the project mid-film) to deal with Jewish themes after his classic BODY AND SOUL, FORCE OF EVIL and I CAN GET IT FOR YOU WHOLESALE.

Old and young horse thieves Opatoshu, Wallach and Tobias are concerned only with making (or stealing) a living among those for whom horse-trading is an art as well as a business. The little Polish *shtetl* feels the effect of the Russo-Japanese war when Cossack commander Yul Brynner arrives to requisition all the available livestock. The village responds with a sense of political awareness, and the horse thieves–turned-partisans hide the horses in the village whorehouse (run by Kazan).

Adding to the fun, Paris-educated Birkin comes back to the village with revolutionary ideas, and meets and falls for the crude but vigorous Tobias. Even Brynner, devoted to duty and his own aristocratic sensibility, is charmed by the cleverness of this crew.

Taking liberties with history—but no more so than the usual popular versions of the classless *shtetl* society—*Romance* made some cinematic history with Jewish-identified figures as rascals and revolutionaries. Too bad the production ran out of money for editing and a decent score, and that many other details suffered. Polonsky and the capable actors deserved better, but it still has some superb moments. 101 min., color.

The Romance of Rosy Ridge (1947)

MGM. Prod: Jack Cummings. Dir: Roy Rowland. Scr: Lester Cole.• Novel basis: MacKinlay Kantor, *The Romance of Rosy Ridge* (1937). Cast: Van Johnson, Tho-mas Mitchell, Janet Leigh, Marshall Thompson, Selena Royle, Charles Dingle

One of Hollywood Ten figure Cole's few big-budget films, a serviceable adaptation of a Kantor allegory about the difficulty the United States had in overcoming the social divisions left by the Civil War and the compelling reasons for doing so. A young Northern veteran with a secret (Johnson) lands in a rural community in Missouri that is still divided by the war. Both sides are tormented by unexplained barn-burnings, but a budding romance between Johnson and the daughter of a Southern loyalist starts to knit the community together after they organize a community dance. Difficult obstacles punctuated with sentimental moments drive toward the necessary conclusion. 105 min.

Romance of the Rio Grande (1941)

An adventure of the Cisco Kid, with Hollywood's biggest gay star, Cesar Romero, as the handsome outlaw. This time he must save the ranch of heroine Patricia Morison from scheming relatives (who always seem to scheme next to open windows where they can be overheard). Reviewers commented that at the end of such sagas, Cisco would ordinarily hand over the marriageable women to some other hero. They didn't know the half of it. Co-written by Harold Buchman.•

The Romantic Englishwoman (1975)

Dial Films/Les Productions Meric-Matalon. Prod: Daniel M. Angel. Dir: Joseph Losey.• Scr: Thomas Wiseman, Tom Stoppard. Novel basis: Thomas Wiseman, *The Romantic Englishwoman* (1971). Cast: Glenda Jackson, Michael Caine, Helmut Berger, Beatrice Romand, Kate Nelligan, Nathalie Delon, Michael Lonsdale

A showcase for Losey's dim estimation of human nature, at least of the suburban variety, and one of his weaker films, with a sometimes compelling but ultimately disappointing story. Jackson, wife of successful pulp novelist Caine, makes a faint protest against her husband's small domestic brutalities by leaving home for the German baths and the gambling of Baden Baden. There she comes across Berger, a poet making a living smuggling heroin. After carelessly losing the drugs, Berger flees the resort and his angry supplier and surreptitiously follows Jackson home to suburban England. When Berger shows up on their doorstep, Caine jealously reconstructs the meeting of poet and wife as a plot for his next story. More fascinated by the poet than his wife, Caine invites the poet-playboy-crook (played with understated skill by

Berger) to stay with them. Just as Caine hoped, a romance springs up between his two suspects, and the prize is Jackson's obvious guilt, suitable for novelization.

Gifted actor Caine, here evidently of lower-class origins as in real life, is given too little to do; he seems too typical of yesterday's Angry Young Men who have made it in British literary circles and now find themselves fascinated with the materialistic, swinging lifestyle. But maybe that was part of the point. In any event, Losey clearly despises all of this but is caught up in it every bit as much as the Caine character. The residue is an often confused portrait of the characters, their uncertainties and their ennui. In lesser hands, the film would not have been an interesting failure but an outright disaster. 115 min.

Roughshod (1949)

RKO. Prod: Richard H. Berger. Dir: Mark Robson. Scr: Hugo Butler• Geoffrey Homes (pseudonym for Daniel Mainwaring). Story: Peter Viertel. Cast: Robert Sterling, Gloria Grahame, Claude Jarman, Jr., John Ireland, Jeff Donnell, Myrna Dell, Martha Hyer, Jeff Corey•

A gender study in the form of an action drama, one of progressive director Robson's first features and Butler's only real western. Sterling and kid brother Jarman are riding westward to start a ranch when they find themselves waylaid, first by four unemployed dance hall girls (with their sexual pasts none too disguised) and then by an outlaw gang. Most of the non-action treats the ways in which the men must come to understand that "purity" is not a matter of virginity, that these proletarian women are full of character and, if given the chance, ripe with the human potential for love (and motherhood). Corey is one of the rascals. 88 min.

Rubber Racketeers (1942)

Monogram. Prod: Maurice King. Dir: Harold Young. Scr: Henry Blankfort.• Cast: Ricardo Cortez, Rochelle Hudson, William Henry, Barbara Read, Milburn Stone, Dewey Robinson, John Abbott

An antifascist B-movie, with Henry as a defense factory prole who organizes his fellow workers to find the rubber racketeers after a pal dies when a bad used tire blows on his truck. Cortez is the former bootlegger just out of jail on an income tax evasion sentence who goes big into rubber racketeering. The climax of the film features rubber workers confronting criminals at mob headquarters until the cops arrive. The wartime propaganda message to the public: don't buy unofficial recap tires. 65 min.

Ruby Gentry (1952)

20th. Prod: King Vidor, Joseph Bernhard. Dir: King Vidor. Scr: Sylvia Richards.† Story basis: Arthur Fitz-Richard. Cast: Jennifer Jones, Charlton Heston, Karl Malden, Tom Tully, Bernard Phillips, James Anderson, Josephine Hutchinson, Phyllis Avery, Herbert Heyes, Myra Marsh, Charles Cane, Sam Flint, Frank Wilcox

A film about a strong woman confused by class issues, a 1950s motif that fails to make a credible Southern melodrama out of a soap opera plot.

Jones is Ruby, born on the other side of the tracks in a narrow-minded little town. Beautiful, obviously talented and tough, she makes an error in agreeing to marry the town's richest citizen (Malden) to spite Heston, scion of a decaying Southern aristocratic family and a man with whom she is none-too-secretly in love. A few steamy sex scenes would have helped, but in contemporary antirealist fashion, even a symbolic suggestion of her easy virtue is barely allowed.

When Malden accidentally dies, tongues wag: she is so wanton, she must be guilty somehow. Emotionally dispossessed like one of Ibsen's heroines, she takes out her revenge against everything and everyone, not excluding Heston. The film is a big disappointment after Richards' riveting script for *Possessed* and is one of her last. She gave testimony against her ex, Robert Richards, then faded out of the Hollywood scene. 82 min.

Rusty Leads the Way (1948)

Col. Prod: Robert Cohn. Dir: Will Jason. Scr: Arthur Ross. Story basis: Nedrick Young• from characters created by Al Martin. Cast: Ted Donaldson, Sharyn Moffett, John Litel, Ann Doran, Paul Raymond, Peggy Converse, Harry Hayden

Another forgotten animal story of the Left, this one based on a *Saturday Evening Post* writer's tale about a guide dog, published at the very moment when the *Post* began to lead the way for the crucifixion of tainted writer/actors like Young.

An almost documentary feel is given to the narrative of training seeing-eye dogs for the job. Donaldson, a lad himself, tries to solve the problems of blind girl Moffett through love, understanding and one mighty good dog. Step by step, dog and "master" (it's a little hard to say which is which) teach each other about the roles they will play together; Moffett regains confidence and the will to live, while Flame (the actor-dog) gets his biggest starring part. 58 min.

Ruthless (1947)

E-L. Prod: Arthur S. Lyons. Dir: Edgar G. Ulmer. Scr: Alvah Bessie,• S. K. Lauren, Gordon Kahn.• Novel basis: Dayton Stoddardt, *Prelude to Night* (1945). Cast: Zachary Scott, Louis Hayward, Diana Lynn, Sydney Greenstreet, Lucille Bremer, Martha Vickers, Raymond Burr

One of the neglected gems of the Hollywood Left, this psychological study of the finance capitalist surrenders to Ulmer's always low-budget methods (mainly in a certain lack of cinematic continuity), but features fine acting and a script full of Abraham Polonsky–style bon mots.

A poor boy (Scott) raised in a single-family home with an embittered mother manages to save a rich girl from drowning, earning himself the opportunity for the upward path he needs. Warned by the experiences and advice of his father (a gambler who lives across town) to make a killing or be crushed, he charms his way into an adopted family, then gets financial assistance to Harvard and eventually leaves school for a banking position, thanks to a new fiancée, whom he will soon discard. Learning that he cannot defeat utilities king Greenstreet outright, he seduces the rich man's wife and, with her help, continues his climb. A crucial moment is reached late in the film when his childhood friend, Hayward, brings a lookalike of his first girlfriend (she played both parts) to a party and Scott proposes that they run off together. In the vivid climax, Greenstreet, Hayward and Scott put the pieces together politically. "It wasn't a man, it was a system," Lynn memorably remarks, in Scott's only epitaph. 104 min.

S

amid more serious work in theater before being black-listed—in this exotic drama-romance with Alan Ladd, Veronica Lake and Morris Carnovsky.• A mediocre U.S. flyboy story, but ironically enough about Vietnam. Careful viewing shows few anticipatory insights.

Saboteur (1942)

Dorothy Parker• contributed to the screenplay for one of Alfred Hitchcock's best films, the most effective of the wartime domestic-spy dramas. Robert Cummings plays it straight as the protagonist who must vindicate himself outside the law after he is falsely accused of sabotage in a war-production factory. Cummings escapes with the help of a blue-collar pal and replays a FRANKENSTEIN theme delightfully when he comes across the blind hermit who can "see" innocence. The dame, Priscilla Lane, at first convinced that Cummings is guilty, finally joins forces with him in the adventure to find the real saboteur.

Trademark Hitchcock action scenes (at the Boulder Dam and the Statue of Liberty) are practiced here first, with better political valence. The shocker ending, another big part of Hitchcock's charm, is on display. The film is weak only in its political premises (practically none at all, except the danger of subversion).

Sahara (1943)

Columbia. Prod: Harry Joe Brown. Dir: Zoltan Korda. Scr: Zoltan Korda, John Howard Lawson.• Cast: Humphrey Bogart, Bruce Bennett, J. Carrol Naish, Lloyd Bridges,† Rex Ingram, Richard Nugent, Dan Duryea

One of the great war dramas of film history and one of the very first to feature a black hero (albeit described as African) and one of Bogey's best films. Based more or less directly on the 1937 Russian film *The Thirteen*, it has a British-American tank unit isolated and stranded in the path of a Nazi regiment's line of march in North Africa, with the water running low and a sneaky captured German officer trying to demoralize the crew. Bogey holds them together. Naish as the Italian, always eager to defect, shows the Germans to be the real villains, and Ingram is the courageous black. Only a Hollywood ending could save them, and did. But who could complain? 97 min.

Saigon (1948)

Julian Zimet• briefly lifted his career above B-westerns—

Salt of the Earth (1954)

Independent Productions/International Union of Mine, Mill & Smelter Workers. Prod: Paul Jarrico,• Adolfo Barela, Sonja Dahl Biberman. Dir: Herbert J. Biberman.• Scr: Michael Wilson,• Herbert J. Biberman. Cast: Rosaura Revueltas,• Will Geer, David Wolfe, Mervin Williams, David Sarvis, Juan Chacón, Henrietta Williams, Ernesto Valazquez

This was the grand film project of the blacklist, and it was made almost literally under fire. As late as 1954, the filmmakers of *Salt of the Earth* still believed they could break through the cultural iron curtain of the Cold War and find an audience for the kinds of films that they had been forbidden to make in Hollywood. While Pauline Kael jeered, Bosley Crowther cheered them on in the pages of the *New York Times* as they made a picture on a verboten theme—a strike, this one in Silver City, New Mexico, by largely Latino families against the Empire Zinc Mine. The filmmakers faced problems larger than hostile critics—local armed vigilantes, busybodies in Hollywood ratting them out (led by actor Walter Pidgeon) and mob-dominated film unions. Roy Brewer refused to permit his IATSE members even to show the film, and the theater chains joined the boycott. A last-gasp alternative of union screening collapsed when the ostensibly liberal United Auto Workers leader Walter Reuther banned auto locals from becoming, in effect, blue-collar film societies. The film got raves from European critics—and not only from Communists. But without the domestic market, the film never had a chance.

Salt is the tale of Mexican Americans striking for improved safety conditions and wage parity with Anglo miners after speed-ups and job cutbacks cause a series of accidents. The miners' wives complain that their concerns are being ignored in the strike demands—a lack of the same sanitation and running water provided to the white miners' homes. As the women say, "Maybe we need to have equality in plumbing, too." The women's demands are largely ignored by the men until the union's picket line is slapped with a federal injunction and the women courageously step forward to take their places. The result, naturally, is that the women's concerns are integrated into the strike demands as they join the leadership. (When the men are forced to take up domestic chores at home while their wives picket, one miner says, "I'll never go back to that job unless they install running water for us." Then he makes his son help wash the dishes!)

The high point of *Salt of the Earth* is the community-based resistance, most memorably the struggles of Latinas against their miner husbands as well as against the employers, for dignity and a change of social status. The luminous photography of the women, with Mexican actress Revueltas at their head, remains a vivid image for many viewers long after the details of the film have been forgotten. American film had simply never seen anything like her or it. *Salt of the Earth* did indeed achieve cult status on college campuses, and an entire conference was devoted to it by the College of Santa Fe, New Mexico, in 2003. Interest has been sustained in no small part by feminists and younger labor historians. *Salt* may not be great filmmaking, but it is remarkable that it exists at all. No study of the blacklist is complete without an understanding of how it was made and the people who made it. Biberman wrote a memoir about the making of the film that was published in 1965. 94 min.

San Quentin (1937)

Forgotten Big House drama from a story basis by writing partners John Bright• and Robert Tasker. The latter actually had been incarcerated there only a few years earlier, and escaped the blacklist only by being killed under mysterious circumstances in Mexico in the mid-1940s. Here, convicts ultimately learn to cooperate with a prison reformer; some sequences were actually shot at the prison.

The Sandpiper (1965)

Among the bigger latter-day flops of Dalton Trumbo• and Michael Wilson,• thanks in part to overacting by Elizabeth Taylor (as a bohemian artist in Monterey) and Richard Burton (as a lusting if proper schoolmaster).

Sands of the Kalahari (1965)

Pendennis Productions/Paramount. Prod: Stanley Baker, Cyril Endfield.• Dir: Cyril Endfield. Scr: Cyril Endfield. Novel basis: William Mulvihill, *The Sands of the Kalahari* (1960). Cast: Stuart Whitman, Susannah York, Stanley Baker, Theodore Bikel, Harry Andrews, Nigel Davenport

Endfield's "other" African film stands in the shadow of the far better known ZULU, which, oddly, had been made just one year earlier on a much larger budget with some of the same themes and a similar ending. It even has Stanley Baker as an actor and co-producer. So is *Kalahari*

Endfield's comment on *Zulu,* the way MCKENNA'S GOLD was Carl Foreman's• comment on HIGH NOON? If so, the heroics of the British colonial army have been replaced and analogized to the ferocious society of desert baboons, highly intelligent and totally dominated by individual strength and the will to conquer.

After a commercial airliner cancels a flight out of an African capital, six passengers decide to charter a small plane together. All goes well until it hits a giant swarm of locusts, plunging the plane into virtually uninhabited desert hundreds of miles from any settlements. Quickly, the survivors set out to husband their resources, and locate scarce fruit and equally scarce game until help can be located. The survivor situation features odd personalities, such as the UN relief worker (Bikel), the German humanitarian (Baker), the erstwhile hunter (Whitman) and the beautiful woman (York), among others.

Whitman, who owns the gun (too much symbolism) wins York through his virility. But he aims to survive by cutting down the competition for food, driving out or killing off most of the men. York must decide how she feels about a lover who is also a monster. But the antifascist speech of the film goes to the German who lived through World War II by obeying the murderous orders of Nazi officers: he has learned to recognize the type, and sees it again in survivalist Whitman. An interesting scene has one of the group actually managing to get to the ocean—only to find himself in a diamond mining district where the company makes the laws and considers any stranger a thief whom they may beat or murder without compunction. Endfield, who grew increasingly disillusioned with his early days as a Communist, aimed his later shafts at the transhistoric wounds of the human spirit. 119 min., color.

Satan Met a Lady (1936)

WB. Prod: Henry Blanke. Dir: William Dieterele. Scr: Brown Holmes. Novel basis: Dashiell Hammett,• *The Maltese Falcon* (1930). Cast: Bette Davis, Warren William, Alison Skipworth, Arthur Treacher, Marie Wilson, Porter Hall

A strange adaptation of Hammett's story, so strange that it barely appears to be the same film as the cult favorite Bogey version of 1941. This time around, *femme fatale* Bette Davis yields the screen to William, a B-style detective quick with the quips and suave as all get-out. Unfortunately, William is not up to Gerald Mohr of the Saint series and lacks the Irish copper credentials of Lloyd Nolan's Mike Shane: he isn't all that witty or sexy. Davis also seems wooden in a role that should have been "bad" enough for her to sparkle in, and the surprises that (in the novel and later version) reveal the commodity fetishism of capitalism through the object so ardently pursued come through here as mere upper-class villainy. A bomb. 66 min.

Saturday's Hero (1951)

Col. Prod: Buddy Adler. Dir: David Miller. Scr: Millard Lampell,• Sidney Buchman.• Novel basis: Millard Lampell, *The Hero* (1950). Cast: John Derek, Donna Reed, Sidney Blackmer, Alexander Knox•

An extraordinary film about the corruption and hypocrisy of college athletics in the age of growing crowds and media enthusiasm. Buchman obviously had this in mind as the kind of social film he intended to make before the blacklist ended his career as a studio exec. *Saturday's Hero* is about social mobility and its costs, as well as the reality behind the spectacle of democratic (or merito-cratic) claims to the glory of American youth.

Derek is a mill town boy with a kindly Italian immigrant father and brother on disability from wounds suffered in the Pacific. A high school gridiron hero, he is offered athletic scholarships everywhere but chooses to get a good education at "Jackson State." There, he quickly learns from his buddies of equally modest origins that part-time jobs involve no work, that grades can be fixed and that big bonuses can be arranged for athletic stand-outs. He also gains a mentor in an English prof who helps him grapple with Balzac, Dostoyevsky and Whitman.

Romance with Reed, whose guardian is (not so ironically) a bullying mill owner, dilutes the impact of the sports scenes but allows a sort of analogy to the wounded spirits of the American century ("That's rare these days, someone all in one piece.") Derek's days as a college hero end with a gridiron injury—treated between halves with drugs. But like so many working-class boys, he's unde-feated in spirit. Available only in film archives, this film needs to be reissued. 111 min.

Savage Mutiny (1953)

Col. Prod: Sam Katzman. Dir: Spencer Gordon Bennet. Scr: Sol Shor.† Story basis: Characters created by Alex Raymond. Cast: Johnny Weissmuller, Angela Stevens, Lester Matthews, Nelson Leigh, Charles Stevens, Paul Marion, Gregory Gaye, Leonard Penn, Ted Thorpe, George Robotham, Tamba the Chimp

Shor's last film before his testimony was another in the "Jungle Jim" series written by lefties for the beefy, middle-aged Weissmuller, the former Tarzan with the huge chest and the soft voice. As so often, Columbia used stock footage from earlier days, this time including Frank Buck travel documentaries, to fill in a thin plot. There's also a soft humanistic or animal message, this time bent toward Cold War themes.

Responding to appeals from the U.S. and British governments, Jungle Jim urgently wants to get natives off an island that is to be used for an atom bomb test. Those sneaky Russian agents try to get the indigenous peoples to remain, expecting to use photos of the tests as anticap-italist propaganda. Seen through older eyes many years later, the struggle of indigenous peoples protecting their land is heroic—and, of course, ignored. As Weissmuller got on in years, Katzman and other producers filled in absent action scenes more and more with animals, and this assortment of domesticated wild creatures is the best thing in the film. Shor's only solo credit—perhaps a reward for his testimony. 73 min.

School for Scoundrels (1960)

Guardsman Films. Prod: Hal E. Chester. Dir: Robert Hamer. Scr: Patricia Moyes, Hal E. Chester, Frank Tarloff• (denied credit). Novel basis: Stephen Potter, *One-Upman-ship* series. Cast: Ian Carmichael, Terry-Thomas, Alastair Sim, Janette Scott, Dennis Price, Peter Jones, Edward Chapman

Tarloff's debut in British films, thanks to his old connection with Chester, a former BOWERY BOYS actor who was trying to work upward from B-pictures. Taken from Stephen Potter's then-popular satirical book series on "One-Upmanship"—corporate logic as modern life—and especially *How to Win Without Actually Cheating*. This film established the career of the gap-toothed antic, Thomas, who so ably twitted the British upper class.

Carmichael is a loser who wants to be a winner and Sim runs the school that teaches him unethical ethics. Thomas is Carmichael's rival for the heart of Scott and the undoing of his acquired guile. Typically broad British humor, a bit tasteless for contemporary Hollywood stan-dards—but the masses loved it. 94 min.

The Sea Hawk (1940)

WB. Exec. Prod: Hal B. Wallis. Dir: Michael Curtiz. Scr: Howard Koch,• Seton I. Miller. Cast: Errol Flynn, Claude Rains, Donald Crisp, Alan Hale, Flora Robson, Brenda Marshall, Henry Daniell, Gilbert Roland

In the days of the Spanish Inquisition and shortly before the Spanish Armada, England is a center for freedom of work and expression and Spain's autocracy a threat to the advance of proto-democracy. In other words, this is the Second World War projected backward several centuries. Much of the film is pure swashbuckling, with Flynn the jolly privateer. But the antifascist subtext is unmistakable: Flynn must flatter and bribe his queen into spending the necessary government funds to match the military buildup of the powers of darkness and, as Roosevelt discovered, persuading stingy and isolationist legislators is no easy task. The queen, deceived by her ties to European royalty and by some treacherous figures around her, foolishly believes negotiations will palliate the evil ones. Acting on his own when necessary and with the help of his democracy-loving shipmates (remarkably and unlike real-life British captains, he operates more like a democrat than a commandant), Flynn will steal the gold Spain looted from the new world and help prepare the nation for the life-and-death struggle ahead. 128 min.

Sea of Grass (1947)

MGM. Prod: Pandro S. Berman. Dir: Elia Kazan.† Scr: Marguerite Roberts,• Vincent Lawrence. Novel basis: Conrad Richter, *The Sea of Grass* (1936). Cast: Katharine Hepburn, Spencer Tracy, Melvyn Douglas, Phyllis Thaxter, Robert Walker, Edgar Buchanan, Harry Carey

Late in life, screenwriter Marguerite Roberts observed in an interview that one of her most heated struggles with a director had been on this film. She insisted that Hepburn's character stand up to Tracy's character, but Kazan was a "chauvinist" who would hear none of it. Roberts' view would surely be supported by the other work of preeminent Pennsylvania Dutch novelist Richter, who all but specialized in depicting strong women on the frontier, and it may also have been retrospective personal criticism of Kazan, who as a friendly witness ruined many careers while nurturing his own. But it also cuts to the seemingly contradictory nature of the film.

Tracy is a hugely successful cattle rancher in the post–Civil War southwest and Hepburn his St. Louis bride. In the philosophy he seeks to impart to her, he is God's caretaker over the grasslands that once knew the Indians and buffalo and are now populated by his cattle. To allow "nesters" (farmers) to settle would be to upset the delicate balance, drain the water table and subject the land to unacceptable stress. How a cattle rancher would not see his own activity as overwhelmingly harmful to the natural environment is surely a mystery; Roberts interpreted the narrative as an untenable attempt to render a typical American agri-businessman into an idealist.

Interestingly, Hepburn's character suspects the same. But the plot loses direction when she commits

adultery with a pro-settler lawyer (Douglas) and becomes part of the settlement narrative (the advance of demographic democracy against the lords of the West) so typical of Popular Front cinema. 131 min.

The Sea Wolf (1941)

WB. Prod: Hal B. Wallis, Jack L. Warner (both uncredited). Dir: Michael Curtiz. Scr: Robert Rossen.† Novel basis: Jack London, *The Sea-Wolf* (1904). Cast: Edward G. Robinson, Ida Lupino, Alexander Knox, Gene Lockhart, John Garfield, Barry Fitzgerald

More or less faithfully adapted from London's famous novel, the film recasts the black-hearted Captain Wolf Larson (Robinson) as a variation on the actor's gangster film archetypes, philosophical enough to comprehend himself as a totalitarian and to seek vindication in the brutish behavior of others. Around him range the novelist and the escaped woman convict (Knox and Lupino), both accidentally on board, the alcoholic ship's doctor (Lockhart) who was once a famous physician, the stool pigeon (Fitzgerald) who doubles as ship's cook and the tough youngster (Garfield), along with the rest of the degraded crew.

This is a journey on The Ghost, in London's time a veritable hell, but now with unmistakable asides about fascism and democracy. Garfield, not seen much of the time, plays himself, the proletarian pug who has fled from shore but is trying to figure out a philosophy of life. Lupino is a working-class existentialist trying to give herself a reason to survive. As others disintegrate amid the cruelty, the increasing blindness of the captain, attempted mutiny and approaching disaster on the seas, the doomed writer explores the scene and Garfield and Lupino seek hope in each other. A film with an accumulating and ultimately terrifying power. 90 min

The Search (1947)

MGM. Prod: Lazar Wechsler, Oscar Düby. Dir: Fred Zinnemann. Scr: Richard Schweizer, David Wechsler, Paul Jarrico.• Cast: Montgomery Clift, Aline MacMahon, Wendell Corey, Ivan Jondl, Jarmila Novotna, Karel Malik, Mary Patton, Leopold Borkowski

An important early response to the huge success of Italian neorealism, filmed in the U.S. zone of occupied Germany under difficult conditions. As the Holocaust-surviving (and apparently orphaned) children receive care from U.N. agencies, they learn not to sneak food, not to fear beatings and almost learn to trust adults again. Of the children, the most pathetic is a Czech boy, Malik (played by Jandl) who refuses to identify his nationality. His mother (Novotna), who has somehow survived and has gone from camp to camp looking for her son, is first told that he has been found—and is led to a choir boy (Borkowski) who as a Jew has been pretending to be a Christian and has adopted her son's name. Slowly, through flashbacks, the story of the real son comes out: he wandered through bombed-out Germany until GI Clift took him under a friendly wing. Borkowski, released from false identity, can regain his real Jewishness and leave for Israel. 105 min.

The Searching Wind (1946)

Para. Prod: Hal B. Wallis. Dir: William Dieterle. Scr: Lillian Hellman.• Play basis: Lillian Hellman, *The Searching Wind* (1944). Cast: Robert Young, Sylvia Sidney, Ann Richards, Dudley Digges, Albert Bassermann, Douglas Dick

The ultimate Popular Front gossip film, not because its protagonists are the "beautiful people" but because they are diplomats and journalists among the brightest and best, bluebloods turning to the Left in defense of the American tradition that is now in their charge. Young is perfectly cast as a weak-willed American aristocrat, son and grandson of diplomats stationed in Italy during the 1920s. He urgently wants to marry Sidney, and in more peaceful times she would probably set aside her reservations. But he doesn't know what to feel about fascism, and she is becoming a committed antifascist. The plot thickens slightly with the appearance of various family members who outline how the older America (personified in the newspaper publisher) responds to the bad news in Europe, and how others who are young begin to understand what is really at stake.

Like other Hellman dramas, this possesses the dramatic virtue of confining the discussion to the elite that she knew so well—and the limitation of never reaching beyond them. 108 min.

The Second Woman (1951)

Cardinal Pictures/UA. Prod: Mort Briskin, Robert Smith. Dir: James V. Kern. Scr: Mort Briskin, Robert Smith (uncredited: John Howard Lawson•). Cast: Robert Young, Betsy Drake, John Sutton, Florence Bates, Morris Carnovsky, Henry O'Neill, Jason Robards, Sr.

Typical psychodrama of the period has Young (a depressive in real life) as an architect in a semi-rural California village who is suspected of having intentionally killed his fiancée in an automobile accident. As he is

wooed by new resident Drake, who eventually solves the mystery, the film explores the potential role of mental illness in memory (Young suffers from blackouts) and in public perceptions.

Despite some real acting talent, this is a distinctly second-rate noir and one of the weakest of the low-budget Briskin-Smith catalogue (QUICKSAND, THE MAGIC FACE). Unlike better versions of psychic stress, it lacks any social dimension. The psychological terms are reduced to pure family drama, and the "dark" forces do not seem especially dark. 91 min.

Secret Ceremony (1968)

World Film Services/Universal. Prod: John Heyman, Norman Priggen. Dir: Joseph Losey.• Scr: George Tabori. Novella basis: Marco Denevi, *Ceremonia secreta* (1960). Cast: Elizabeth Taylor, Mia Farrow, Robert Mitchum, Peggy Ashcroft, Pamela Brown, Michael Strong, Robert Douglas

A bit of a big-budget mess, re-edited and reshot continually in a vain attempt to fill holes in the plot and render it more avant-garde (a bathtub scene of Mitchum and Farrow was replaced by one of Farrow and Taylor!) or less avant-garde (for television release).

Taylor, an aging London prostitute, is visiting the grave of her daughter when she is followed by Farrow, who urgently misses her own late mother and is convinced Taylor is a lookalike. They develop a mother-daughter relationship, and Taylor comes to live with Farrow's aunts, Brown and Ashcroft. Stepfather Mitchum earlier has been booted out for trying to seduce Farrow, and she soon claims that he has returned and raped her. Taylor learns from him, however, what she might have guessed all along: that Farrow is mentally unbalanced and prone to imaginative flights. Losey pursued similar themes more successfully in other films, particularly in THE SERVANT. 109 min.

Secrets of the Lone Wolf (1941)

Needlessly fussy caper film directed by Edward Dmytryk•† has the recovering jewel thief guarding gems on loan to the United States that once belonged to Napoleon, the object of thievish desire by scheming Frenchmen.

Semi-Tough (1977)

Walter Bernstein• co-scripted this lively sports-and-sex comedy from a novel of the same name by Dan Jenkins

(1972), adapted by Ring Lardner, Jr.• (who had his name taken off the credits). One of Burt Reynolds' best roles, he plays a pro football star who, like teammate Kris Kristofferson, is in love with Jill Clayburgh. Worthy satire of big-money sports, but mostly just fun. Adapted to a short-lived television series.

Señorita from the West (1945)

Early version of the enduring *Three Men and a Baby* plot has a trio of grubby western prospectors secretly striking gold but unable to persuade their real treasure, the young Bonita Granville, to leave New York and the bright lights to join them. She thinks she has hit paydirt of her own by landing a job as an elevator operator in a radio station. So Cap, Rosebud and Dusty mosey off to the cold canyons of the East Coast and hover protectively over her until she ties the knot and all secrets of the heart are disclosed. Formulaic fun written by Howard Dimsdale,• but not without charm.

Sergeant York (1941)

Howard Koch• was the last of four scriptwriters, and apparently an influential one, who penned this stirring interventionist piece about a backwoods WWI soldier (played with much hick emphasis by Gary Cooper) who first refuses to betray his antiwar sentiment, then becomes a hero sharpshooter and later declines, out of modesty, even a home town parade in his honor. Drawn from life, if obviously heroized, and made to justify impending U.S. entry into war. Some painful jingoistic moments.

Serpico (1973)

Para./Produzion De Laurentiis. Prod: Martin Bregman. Dir: Sidney Lumet. Scr: Norman Wexler, Waldo Salt.• Novel basis: Peter Mass, *Serpico* (1973). Cast: Al Pacino, John Randolph,• Jack Kehoe, Biff McGuire, Barbara Eda-Young, Cornelia Sharpe, Tony Roberts, John Medici, Allan Rich, Norman Ornellas, Edward Grover

Serpico was made in a time when stories about serious and deep-rooted police corruption were rare—then as now the preferred narrative dealt with the occasional rogue cop. The film was all the more shocking because it depicted an honest cop hated by his fellow officers, a story line hardly known since 1940s and film noir. Veteran cop Frank Serpico was shot and nearly killed for giving testimony to the Knapp Commission; he returned long enough to sit in on story conferences with Salt, Lumet and Pacino.

Filmed largely in and around Manhattan station houses, the film was gritty and tough, a muted version of the style of filmmaking being done abroad at the time (for example, *Z* and *State of Siege)*. All of the considerable talent on the project remained true to the radical thrust of the book, which explored a corrupt system through the eyes of a blue-collar but somewhat bohemian cop who learns about himself and gains extraordinary courage in the process. Pacino was nominated for an Oscar, as were Salt and cinematographer Haskell Wexler. 129 min.

The Servant (1963)

Elstree/Springbok. Prod: Joseph Losey,• Norman Priggen. Dir: Joseph Losey. Scr: Harold Pinter. Novella basis: Robin Maugham, *The Servant* (1946). Cast: Dirk Bogarde, Sarah Miles, James Fox, Wendy Craig, Catherine Lacey, Richard Vernon, Patrick Magee, Harold Pinter

Along with ACCIDENT, this is Losey's most important film. It was based on a novella written by a nephew of Somerset Maugham, a rather misogynistic 90-page tract that Pinter radically rewrote. In the novella, Tony is an officer who served as a tank commander in World War II in North Africa along with Maugham's narrator (also an officer, and a bore, whom Pinter immediately removed from the screenplay). The two officers celebrate their reunion by inviting Tony's girlfriend to a drunken spree that seems intended to cement their postwar friendship. On the advice of his friend, the spectacularly idle Tony takes on a "manservant" to look after him while he devotes his little energy to studying for the bar. Barrett, the servant, is carefully identified by Pinter's biographer as a servile sort with pretensions to an advanced taste in everything from food to flowers. He understands how to manipulate everyone around him by giving them exactly what they secretly desire and by becoming the indispensible supplier of that pleasure. In Tony's case, it's creature comfort. Barrett even changes the socks on his feet. After Tony has become utterly dependant on Barrett, the servant introduces his 16-year-old "niece" to Tony, and she moves in. As Tony is an incautious drinker, it is not long before he and the girl excite each other's passions—considerably helped in her case by the fact, asserted with no trace of irony by Maugham, that she is a "nymphomaniac." Now Tony is twice dependent. By the end, Barrett has tossed the girl into the streets and begun to supply a steady stream of other 16-year-olds for his own and Tony's mutual pleasure. The once merely indolent officer has become a serial child molester.

It is surprising to note that the Pinter and Losey film, which has such a reputation for darkness, is actually less sordid than Maugham's tale—but it is narratively far more effective. The filmmakers started by throwing out the ending. After removing the temptations represented by 16-year-old girls, Pinter set Tony and Barrett at each others' throats in a squalid mutual psychosis culminating in the famous "orgy scene," implied more than depicted, with one of the most shocking kisses in cinematic history. Barrett the drunken and insolent servant kisses his master's girlfriend—and the squeamishness of the audience is moved nearly to nausea when it becomes obvious that his daring has actually aroused her. Nothing of this sort occurs in the book.

Maugham's novella also provides an answer to the lingering speculation about homosexual content in The Servant. In the novel, homosexuality makes an appearance only in silhouette, as a suggestion in the friendship between the narrator and Tony, and never in connection with the servant himself. Maugham did write at least two novels with frankly gay themes, but in his 1946 novella the matter was handled with the kind of casual tact that gentlemen with public school backgrounds hardly needed to articulate. What Pinter preserved was a sense of revulsion at Tony's degradation—but it was not entirely or even necessarily sexual. Much more terrifying in Maugham's work was the utter incapacity of either the gentleman or the manservant to maintain their class distinctions, which turns them into monsters. By comparison with this fundamental "corruption," sexuality of any sort is merely symptomatic and incidental. What the conservative Maugham presented as horrifying, Pinter depicts as grandly ridiculous.

The Servant is always listed as among the top two or three films of 1963, and its effect on filmmaking and on the culture at large was enormous. Writing in the New York Times in 2001, film historian David Thomson called Losey's film "a movie that altered England's sense of itself." The seamless collaboration between writer and director raised for the first time the prospect of an art cinema at once intelligent and uncompromising and as political as it needed to be. The Servant would be among the most memorable Marxist films ever made. 112 min.

Shadow in the Sky (1951)
MGM. Prod: W. H. Wright. Dir: Fred M. Wilcox. Scr: Ben Maddow.•† Story basis: Edward Newhouse. Cast: James Whitmore, Ralph Meeker, Nancy Davis, Jean Hagen

A tense and realistic Maddow drama about the consequences of war for civilian life, close in temperament to THE MEN but focused on the mental rather than the physical price soldiers pay. In any case, it's a far cry from the upbeat heroism of wartime Popular Front cinema.

Whitmore and Meeker, buddies in the Pacific theater's rough action, are drawn together again through Whitmore's marriage to Davis. But Meeker is a victim of shell shock, driven over the edge every time it rains because it reminds him of near-death experiences. Confined to a vets' hospital, he desperately wants out, but Davis, fearing for the consequences on the family and her two children, overrules Whitmore's sense of obligation to offer Meeker a room in their home.

Eventually, with the help of hospital nurse Hagen, Meeker makes his return to civilian life. But he is pulled first in one direction and then another: does he want marriage, perhaps joining Whitmore in his small gas station, or should he build a boat to sail away to a peaceful life? Through extended discussion hinging on his mental condition—punctuated by the fears of neighbors about men with "mental troubles"—various issues of the vets are explored. That the recollection of individual survival during battle now weighs heavier in memory than the pride of personal sacrifice hints at the difference between attitudes about World War II and the unmentioned (but for the audience unavoidable) Korean War then raging; it also anticipates the later Hollywood attitudes toward war in the Vietnam era. A scene in which a bird is trapped in an attic room, an image representing madness, was a typically adept Maddow touch. 78 min.

Shall We Dance (1937)
RKO. Prod not given. Dir: Mark Sandrich. Scr: Allan Scott and Ernest Pagano. Story: Lee Loeb and Harold Buchman.• Adaptation: P.J. Wolfson. Cast: Fred Astaire, Ginger Rogers, Edward Everett Horton, Eric Blore, Jerome Cowan, Ketti Gallian, William Brisbane

Second pairing (with eight more to follow) of Astaire and Rogers that transformed the screen musical also marked a comeback of sorts for George Gershwin, who with progressive brother Ira (later a central figure in the Committee for a First Amendment) composed the music and lyrics that shaped the plot (Vincente Minnelli reportedly supplied the title). Most famous scene has Astaire and Rogers on roller skates accompanying "Let's Call the Whole Thing Off." (Happily, "They Can't Take That Away from Me" received an Oscar nomination, but the film proved a minor disappointment.)

Thin plot has American ballet dancer in Paris wooing a musical revue star. Romance takes place on boat, accompanied by cute dog. 101 min.

She (1935)

RKO. Prod: Merian C. Cooper. Dir: Irving Pichel,• Lansing C. Holden. Scr: Ruth Rose. Novel basis: H. Rider Haggard, *She: A History of Adventure* (1887). Cast: Helen Gahagan, Randolph Scott, Helen Mack, Nigel Bruce

Pichel's second directorial assignment and the second of four screen versions of Rider Haggard's exotic classic locates the mysterious kingdom somewhere in icy Asia rather than (as in most other versions) tropical Africa. Scott's distant ancestor discovered the kingdom but fled with a mortal woman and died before returning to England. Nigel Bruce (best remembered for playing Watson to Sherlock Holmes) is his descendant's faithful companion on the trip, and Mack is picked up en route, an orphan suffering at the hands of a stern stepfather but remarkably perky and modern-American nevertheless.

"She who must be obeyed," played by Gahagan, the future congresswoman who was red-baited and defeated for re-election by Richard Nixon (amid many accusations of Hollywood disloyalty), is apparently eternal yet still longing for the return of a Scott-like figure. Around her is an absurd but beautifully eclectic set in Flash Gordon decor, including a high priest, a castle with cliffs, and generic "natives" whose heavily choreographed and high-angle ritual dance is orientalism run amuck. Unlike the later Ursula Andress version, Gahagan does not seem to be a white goddess ruling dark peoples but simply an exotic regent of some unbelievable land.

After the usual adventures, the visitors prepare to flee, Mack gives a soliloquy about the virtues of merely mortal romance and She faces an unprecedented crisis. The secret of eternal life is evidently something that He (i.e., most of the rest of the audience) was not meant to know. 95 min.

Sherlock Holmes and the Voice of Terror (1942)

John Bright• co-scripted this most class-conscious story of a present-day Holmes, discovering the Nazi spy is a ruling class imposter, brought down with the help of the subterranean masses of London.

Shoot Out (1971)

Universal. Prod: Hal B. Wallis. Dir: Henry Hathaway. Scr: Marguerite Roberts.• Cast: Gregory Peck, Patricia Quinn, Robert F. Lyons, Susan Tyrrell, Jeff Corey,• James Gregory, Rita Gam, Dawn Lyn

The studio's effort to replicate the extraordinary success of TRUE GRIT, with the same producer, director and

screenwriter, but sans John Wayne. Not even Peck can match Wayne's charisma as a broken-down gunfighter playing against his own reputation. Now back from prison and wired for revenge, he proves a sentimental softie when his young daughter (Tyrrell) is put into his care. He is heading into town to kill Quinn, who wronged him, and how can he focus on the task when he's becoming, unwittingly and unwillingly, a family man? Too cute, too talky. 95 min., color.

The Shopworn Angel (1938)

MGM. Prod: Joseph L. Mankiewicz. Dir: H. C. Potter. Scr: Waldo Salt.• Story basis: Dana Burnet, "Pettigrew's Girl," The Saturday Evening Post (1918). Cast: Margaret Sullavan, James Stewart, Walter Pidgeon, Nat Pendleton, Alan Curtis, Sam Levene, Hattie McDaniel

Along with MR. WINKLE GOES TO WAR, this is Salt's most memorable film until he returned from the blacklist with a bang with the 1967 hit MIDNIGHT COWBOY. A sentimental drama, made earlier as a silent film and later remade as *That Kind of Woman* (1959), it offers an ambivalent reflection on the social effects and meaning of World War I at a time when World War II was looming on the horizon.

Beautiful showgirl Sullavan, filled with the longueurs of a Broadway star's life and impatient with the decadence of wealthy suitor Pidgeon, accidentally meets democratic everyguy Stewart as he is training on Long Island for combat overseas. He is fresh from a Texas cattle ranch (although he sounds more like an Indiana farmer) and filled with the great Romantic virtue of sincerity, a quality in him that eludes her as much as her *ennui* escapes him. The writing that contrasts these attitudes is High Hollywood. Sharing a cab with Sullavan on their accidental first meeting, Stewart is informed that New York, too, has its share of cattle drives. "But where do they pasture?" Stewart asks wonderingly. "In Central Park," she replies. "But what do they live on?" Sullavan: "They beg from *door* to *doo-oo-oor!*" But Stewart's native honesty gradually wears down her cynicism, and she begins to take a broader view of the society she lives in.

In one effective scene after Sullavan has sung "Pack Up Your Troubles" to the troops at an evening performance on the Long Island base, Stewart shows her around the camp, including what appears to be a row of life-size dolls. "Oh, aren't they cute," Sullavan sing-songs girlishly before the close-up shows that the dolls are straw dummies, minus the stuffing in places, used by the soldiers in bayonet practice. The embarrassing silence that follows is filled with the beginning of her change in character as she realizes that the dummies are the ghosts of men, perhaps including Stewart, who have not yet died on the battlefield. The antiwar message has rarely been expressed so effectively. 85 min.

Short Cut to Hell (1957)

Albert Maltz• rewrote his early screenplay for one of the all-time great films noir, THIS GUN FOR HIRE, for this new Paramount version, made in the depths of the blacklist on a negligible budget and directed and introduced by none other than Jimmy Cagney (his only directorial effort). The ground-breaking style of cinematography of the original is virtually dispensed with, so what remains of interest is the way Maltz re-adapted the themes of the Popular Front developed in GUN FOR HIRE (and in Graham Greene's source novel) to the Cold War and the McCarthy era. By working anonymously, he actually had more freedom to attack his enemies. The film is scarce, if not rare, and rewards patient study.

The Sign of the Cross (1932)

Scripted by (Jewish) Sidney Buchman,• the first sandals-and-salvation film epic of the sound era helped set formula for the Roman noble who falls for Christian dame and, if unable to save her, joins her martyrdom. Hanky-panky is what the Romans do when they're not cheering on the slaughter, and the lions are hungry.

Singin' in the Corn (1946)

Richard Weil• wrote this Judy Canova vehicle, one of several with a script or story by lefties. In this outing, Judy is a carnival mindreader (with some good sight gags) who inherits an estate from her uncle. The only provision: that a ghost town be given "back to the Indians." Jay Silverheels must have been a bit embarrassed by appearing in this aptly titled film, but at least the Indians are a far cry from the thievin', murderin' savages of western lore. They even sing!

Sinners in Paradise (1938)

Universal. Prod: James Whale. Dir: James Whale. Scr: Harold Buckley (also story), Louis Stevens, Lester Cole.• Cast: John Boles, Madge Evans, Bruce Cabot, Marion Martin, Nana Bryant, Milburn Stone, Don "Red" Barry

A low-budget film with a cross-section of individualist Americans who are stranded and compelled to live cooperatively (thus many similarities to FIVE CAME BACK, co-scripted by Dalton Trumbo•). This time, it's an uninhabited Pacific isle—uninhabited, that is, except for Boles, a doctor on the run, and his Chinese servant. A plane bound for China goes down and eight stragglers make their way ashore.

We learn on the doomed plane that the passengers include a few gangsters and a moll, a millionairess avoiding a sitdown strike at one of her properties (!), a self-sacrificing nurse, two munitions salesmen and an extremely pompous U.S. senator. Stone, the politician, offers the perfect caricature of the bourgeois, indignant at the manual labor forced on him but too unskilled to do anything else. Evans is the nurse who falls for Boles and convinces him that paradise is no real escape: they must seek to help a troubled world. There are lots of laconic asides on class, war and human nature, including some saucy working-girl repartee by blondie Martin. Curiously, this crypto-political B-picture was directed by Whale, famous for FRANKENSTEIN. 65 min.

Sins of the Children (1930)

MGM. Prod: Unknown. Dir: Sam Wood. Scr: Clara Lipman, Samuel Ornitz.• Story basis: J. C. Nugent, Eliott Nugent. Cast: Louis Mann, Robert Montgomery, Elliott Nugent, Leila Hyams

Among the early experiments with social themes in sound film, this obscure feature is remarkable in several ways, particularly in its opening scenes.

Mann is a widower with four children, a loving father with a handlebar mustache and a job (barbering) that gives him away as an Italian immigrant. In a small commercial town, he has saved several hundred dollars to invest in a new savings and loan company, his exit from daily toil. But fate intervenes: a son has come down with tuberculosis, needing sustained treatment in a far-off climate. As the children naively offer Mann a celebratory wreath for what would have been his last day at the shop, he concludes that success was not for him: a child counts more.

His simple, loving kindness faces a new test 20 years later. The town has grown into a city and the other partner (who had urged him to invest in the bank, not the boy's health) of his unconsummated partnership is the rich man. Montgomery, his gay blade son, is bound to fall in love with Mann's daughter, diluting the class themes or perhaps realizing (and reconciling) them in the only way Hollywood knew. At its best, the film has a humanity that contrasts with its commercial ambitions—an interesting if thoroughly sentimental message for Depression-era America. 86 min.

Sis Hopkins (1941)

Rep. Assoc. Prod: Robert North. Dir: Joseph Santley. Scr: Jack Townley, Milt Gross, Edward Eliscu.• Cast: Judy Canova, Bob Crosby, Charles Butterworth, Jerry Colonna, Susan Hayward, Katharine Alexander, Elvia Allman

Co-scripter Eliscu later reflected that every Judy Canova comedy is more or less the same vehicle for the unglamorous but spunky girl to show that she can amount to something (if not always get her man). This time around, she is remarkably restrained—for Canova. Perhaps it's the formula: the popular stage hayseed comedy in which an out-of-town cousin learns city ways and, amid pratfalls and music, teaches the city folks a thing or two.

With what the *Times* called "the sawmill voice and the hayrick legs," Canova heads for college, where she runs into wacky prof Colonna and band leader Crosby. Happily, she has a Daddy Warbucks uncle (Butterworth) to fall back on, and that helps account for her getting the opportunity to sing not only a few country numbers but also an operatic aria. 98 min.

Sister, Sister (1982)

A TV production directed by John Berry• but held back from release several times, perhaps with a sense that the cachet of the script and the story original (both by Maya Angelou) had not found their moment. Two sisters deal with assorted domestic problems of middle-class black women as they look, even after his death, back to their father, a unionist who seems strangely like A. Philip Randolph, the great hero who became in old age a labor hack.

Slaves (1969)

The sad end to the directing career of Herbert Biberman,• his only feature after SALT OF THE EARTH. Dionne Warwick, Ossie Davis and others in the Old South look to prospects for rebellion after a slave who was promised freedom by a kind master is instead sold to a greedy merchant. A large-scale rebellion breaks out. The few critics who saw it panned it, and it dropped out of sight. Biberman's wife Gale Sondergaard,• once an Oscar winner, has a nameless, almost bit part, which was also her last.

633 Squadron (1964)

Howard Koch• of CASABLANCA fame wrote this World War II film with great action scenes, but he forgot the plot. Cliff Robertson is the American airman given command of a

British squadron, this time to enter Norway's airspace and bomb a German missile factory. Some critics insisted that only mediocre dialogue and a limp romance deprived the film of epic status, but that surely depends upon a critical soft spot for air warfare. A sluggish late film for the usually superb Koch.

Smart Woman (1948)

Allied Artists. Prod: Hal E. Chester. Dir: Edward A. Blatt. Scr: Alvah Bessie,• Louis Morheim, Herbert H. Margolis. Story basis: Leon Gutterman (adaptation: Adela Rogers St. Johns). Cast: Brian Aherne, Constance Bennett, Barry Sullivan, Michael O'Shea James Gleason, Otto Kruger, Isobel Elsom, Richard Lyon, Selena Royle, Taylor Holmes, John Litel, Nita Hunter, Iris Adrian

This was child actor–turned-director Chester's biggest film before going abroad in the 1950s-1960s, where he once again employed (or exploited) blacklistees in the Philip Yordan manner. It was also Bessie's last credit under his own name before he became one of the Hollywood Ten. The tale is the familiar gender clash of crusading D.A. Aherne locking horns with defense attorney Bennett. Naturally, the two also fall in love, and as the plot proceeds, she realizes that she has to make a crucial admission as a defense lawyer: to reveal that her client (gangster Sullivan) is also her former husband. This revelation may damage her relationship with her son (Lyon) and with Aherne. Will she put work ahead of love? Whaddya think? 93 min.

Smartest Girl in Town (1936)

RKO. Prod: Edward Kaufman. Dir: Joseph Santley. Scr: Viola Brothers Shore.• Story basis: Muriel Scheck, H. S. Kraft.• Cast: Gene Raymond, Ann Sothern, Helen Broderick, Eric Blore, Erik Rhodes, Harry Jans

A mildly amusing gender comedy on the all-too-familiar mistaken identity theme with some sharp edges. Fashion model Sothern has determined that she and her sister will marry rich. But when she rebuffs the attentions of the wealthy Raymond after mistakenly sizing him up as a penniless male model, she creates the misunderstanding that drives the plot. In the meantime, Sothern dates a wacky Italian baron who is an inept lover, giving Raymond a chance to out-romance him. Raymond, taking advantage of Sothern's ignorance of his wealth, pretends to be the very male model Sothern had taken him for and arranges for fashion shoots that force the two together. The most vivid moment: an erotic hair-washing scene in which

Sothern recoils in horror at the idea that she is "mothering" Raymond. 58 min.

Smash-Up, the Story of a Woman (1947)

U-I. Prod: Walter Wanger. Dir: Stuart Heisler. Scr: John Howard Lawson.• Story basis: Dorothy Parker, Frank Cavett. Cast: Susan Hayward, Lee Bowman, Marsha Hunt,• Eddie Albert, Carl Esmond, Charles E. Brown

Hayward's first starring role and Lawson's last major screenplay in a story that offered an opportunity to depict a tortured soul drinking herself into oblivion—as many contemporary Hollywoodites did as the hand of McCarthyism fell on the film capital.

In the formal plot, Hayward the nightclub singer gives up her career for marriage and family but finds herself almost inexplicably sinking when her increasingly famous husband, an emcee, is gone all the time. True to the time, a German-accented doctor (Esmond) explains to her husband about the unmet needs of modern women, and the emcee's sympathetic best friend (Albert, himself destined to be associated with many progressive causes, particularly for agricultural workers) gives good advice to the confused husband. But the best moments in the film belong to the booziness of Hayward, shot sometimes in the noir style. Clearly a "non-political" opportunity for Lawson, but one to which he lent his very real dramatic skills. 103 min.

Snafu (1945)

Louis Solomon• and Harold Buchman• wrote Robert Benchley's only feature film and the closest Hollywood would come to spelling out the 1940s title from GI slang about military bureaucracy ("Situation Normal: All Fucked Up"). Benchley and Vera Vague have their 15-year-old son honorably discharged and sent home from the army. Innocent comedy.

Society Lawyer (1938)

MGM. Prod: John W. Considine, Jr. Dir: Edwin L. Marin. Scr: Frances Goodrich, Albert Hackett, Leon Gordon, Hugo Butler.• Cast: Walter Pidgeon, Virginia Bruce, Leo Carrillo, Eduardo Cianelli, Lee Bowman

A slight film about hard-working criminal lawyer Pidgeon and the mess he gets into with showgirls and the underworld. Inheriting his father's law firm, he breaks with its corporate practice to defend the demimonde and wins a dramatic case for Runyonesque gangster Carrillo

(here with an Italian accent that sounds remarkably like his later Spanish accent as the Cisco Kid's sidekick, Pancho).

After Pidgeon breaks with a social climbing girl-friend, she is murdered and a college friend is charged with the crime. Pidgeon enlists the aid of Virginia Bruce, who, full of vim (though not much of an actress), takes on a mob competing with Carrillo's operations and inevitably cracks the case. Bruce sings the almost memorable "In Love with the Honorable Mr. So and So" about the backstreet affair of the stage beauty with the gentleman who cannot afford to be seen with her in polite society. Best scene: Carrillo on the floor of his private suite, playing with an elaborate toy train set. 78 min.

So Dark the Night (1946)

Thanks more to good direction (by Joseph H. Lewis) and camera work than to the plot, this is probably screenwriter Martin Berkeley's† best picture, a moody little number about a murder in France. The middle-aged Parisian detective (Steven Geray) falls for a young country girl (Micheline Cheirel) already betrothed to another (Theodore Gottlieb), a farm boy who stalks out of a social event in a rage. Later, he and the girl are found strangled, and Geray must make sense of a case that potentially points toward him. Not much else happens, but his drift into psychopathology is fascinating.

So Dear to My Heart (1949)

Disney. Prod: Walt Disney. Dir: Harold D. Schuster. Scr: John Tucker Battle, Hamilton Luske. Adaptation: Maurice Rapf,• Ted Sears. Cast: Bobby Driscoll, Burl Ives, Beulah Bondi, Harry Carey, Luana Patten

This may be the best of the postwar Disney mixtures of live and animated action, unburdened by the sentimentalization of African American subservience in Song of the South (for which Rapf wrote the original script, to his later considerable embarrassment). This is a 1902 rural South with folks so poor and isolated that not even the county fair boasts an African American porter or vendor. And yet, it is an undeniably beautiful and touching film about a boy's life in a hamlet that revolves around a general store. Raised by his hard-pressed grandmother (Bondi) and a family friend (Ives), and lacking any friends but neighbor girl Patten, Driscoll adopts a black baby lamb that quickly wreaks havoc with the farm. The worse the mischief becomes and the more Bondi threatens to sell it, the more the boy becomes fixated on winning a prize at an upcoming county fair.

At another level, the moral lessons are dispensed freely. No one wants black wool, and so the animal (like the orphan boy) begins with a disadvantage. This is explained repeatedly by an animated owl to an animated lamb, with background singing by Burl Ives who also sings a half-dozen other tunes. Through various adventures and the final triumph, "Stick-to-it-ivity" is the final Protestant message: reject fatalism. 82 min., color.

Sodom and Gemorrah (1962)

With screenwriter Hugo Butler• falling apart physically— he would soon have a fatal stroke—this Robert Aldrich/ Sergio Leone biblical melodrama reveled in sins of the flesh, particularly betrayal and torture (rather than the sins, more shocking at the time, that were promised by the title). Nor was there much of the semi-nudity associated with sandal epics. Stewart Granger, Pier Angeli and Anouk Aimée share the hammy opportunities. (The opening line is famous among gay film fans: "Beware of Sodomite patrols!") The film's only importance is historical: Leone learned the art of the "dark western," which he later refashioned as the "spaghetti western," at Aldrich's knee.

Soldiers Three (1951)

MGM. Prod: Pandro S. Berman. Dir: Tay Garnett. Scr: Marguerite Roberts,• Tom Reed, Malcolm Stuart Boylan. Novel basis, Rudyard Kipling, *Soldiers Three* (1899). Cast: Stewart Granger, Cyril Cusack, Robert Newton, David Niven, Walter Pidgeon, Greta Gynt

Billed as *"Rudyard Kipling's Soldiers Three,"* this is a remake of *Gunga Din* (1938) without a star like Cary Grant or the romantic interest of a Joan Fontaine. The addition of Robert Newton—the rubber-faced actor best remembered for his role in the fifties remake of *Treasure Island* (mumbling "ahr, ahr" between dialogue)—is the big plus. Newton, Cusack and Granger have been privates for 18 years in India of nineteenth-century colonial days, drinking, wenching and fighting. All this is told in a flashback, as their colonel (Pidgeon) recalls their antics and heroics, under Niven's formal command, to a group of fellow officers.

Screenwriters (no doubt Marguerite Roberts in particular) attempted to tone down the inherent racism of the comical colonials and the treacherous natives. They succeed, to a degree, through a Wild West–style narrative of the rebel leader rising to arms to "protect our land" against unwanted intruders. However, the old native

chiefs who grasp the necessity for *gradual* change are seen as kindly and open to dialogue; the young hotheads have to be stopped and the heroics of the Soldiers Three ("Her Majesty's Hard Bargain") will accomplish it against all odds, laughing their way into the presumed postcolonial but actually neocolonial future. 92 min.

Solid Gold Cadillac (1956)

Col. Prod: Fred Kohlmar. Dir: Richard Quine. Scr: Abe Burrows.† Play basis: George S. Kaufman, *The Solid Gold Cadillac* (1953). Cast: Judy Holliday,† Paul Douglas, Fred Clark, John Williams, Arthur O'Connell

This was Holliday's next-to-last film, shot while she was being harassed by HUAC. Because of her renunciation of communism she was not blacklisted, though it did her little good. It was an exceedingly early comeback for friendly witness Burrows as well, who was too hot as a writer to be confined by mere political considerations.

As in BORN YESTERDAY, Holliday is the apparently dumb beauty who is actually smarter than she seems. Here she is a small stockholder who realizes that the corporate execs are a bunch of crooks and organizes a campaign to outsmart them.

The casting and corporate setting have more of the feeling of one of the crypto-Left television plays of the era rather than a product of contemporary Hollywood, then in the political deep-freeze. 99 min., partly in color.

Something to Shout About (1943)

Col. Prod: Gregory Ratoff. Dir: Gregory Ratoff. Scr: Lou Breslow, Edward Eliscu.• Story basis: Fred Schiller. Cast: Don Ameche, Janet Blair, Jack Oakie, William Gaxton, Cobina Wright, Veda Ann Borg, Jaye Martin, Cyd Charisse

An absolutely charming musical comedy, perhaps Eliscu's best screenplay, brightened by the flashbulb smile of Ameche, luminous songs by Cole Porter and the film debut of the glowing Charisse (as Lily).

A cynical young golddigger (Wright) with little talent arranges for a down-and-out Broadway producer to create a show for her that she will finance after marrying a millionaire, with an eye on a divorce settlement. Contrasted with Wright and her bunch is a bright young songwriter (Blair) from Altoona and her Manhattan theatrical boardinghouse full of unrecognized but talented singers and dancers who, after a plotful of complications and misunderstandings, are destined to carry the day. Caught in the middle is publicist Ameche, who is (of course) teetering between the demands of love and money. In embryo here is the old show business sense of a tight-knit group of artists who must rely on each other's talent to survive while facing powerful outside forces bent on exploiting them. Soon these sentiments would take on a direct political expression.

Porter's "You'd Be So Nice to Come Home To" was nominated for best song at the Oscars the following year, and Morris Stoloff was nominated for best score. 90 min.

Somewhere I'll Find You (1942)
MGM. Prod: Pandro S. Berman. Dir: Wesley Ruggles. Scr: Marguerite Roberts.• Cast: Clark Gable, Lana Turner, Robert Sterling, Patricia Dane, Reginald Owen, Lee Patrick, Charles Dingle

A romantic vehicle for Gable and (to a lesser degree) Turner, this film uses a war setting to throw the potential lovers together (she chasing him rather than vice-versa), separate and reunite them. Thanks to Roberts, this is a better-than-standard patriotic message film, but the politics still barely transcend the plot about the taming of the wild wolf.

Returning from the Pacific with his brother, Gable hears about a mysterious girlfriend who will presumably become his sister-and-law soon. But wait: she is not only alluring but also has been in love with Clark since he broke a date with her years earlier. Between that date and the later complications comes the war. Through it all, his brother knows the real score. Antifascist values are remote through all of this, but not altogether absent. Toward the end, an extended battle sequence on Bataan improbably brings the protagonists together in a common sacrifice in the service of democracy. 108 min.

Song of Russia (1943)
MGM. Prod: Pandro S. Berman, Joe Pasternak. Dir: Gregory Ratoff. Scr: Richard Collins,† Paul Jarrico.• Story basis: Guy Endore,• Leo Mittler, Victor Trivas (uncredited: Edgar G. Ulmer). Cast: Robert Taylor, Susan Peters, John Hodiak, Robert Benchley, Felix Bressart, Joan Lorring, Darryl Hickman

Hollywood screenwriter John Wexley• once recalled in an oral history that he was brought onto the set of Song of Russia not to write but to reassure star Robert Taylor (a staunch anti-Communist who, however, respected Wexley) to act in one of the most pro-Russian films ever made in Hollywood and to speak his lines as written. There were even more unlikely connections. In an interview late in life, cult director Ulmer claimed to have written the original script. Guy Endore was a

Communist, but a writer whose specialty was the fantasy-horror genre. Although the film earned respectable notices when it was released, after World War II it was one of three films (along with NORTH STAR and MISSION TO MOSCOW) that were most often cited by conservatives as evidence of Communist propaganda and that Hollywood leftists tended to dismiss as wartime kitsch. What the conservatives overlooked was that the small and short-lived "Russia is our Ally" subgenre was created in part at the request of the Roosevelt administration around the time Russians were making a heroic stand against the Nazis at Stalingrad and elsewhere, and what the Left rarely mentioned was how much the subgenre really did owe to the sensibilities of writers like Anna Louise Strong, an erstwhile American labor poet who had lived off and on in Russia over the years and had spent some time glamorizing it for U.S. audiences. But none of this seemed to concern the critics when the film was released; it was only after the war that these films came to be treated as post hoc evidence of subversion.

The story seems harmless enough. American orchestra conductor Taylor, flattered into accepting a Russian engagement in Moscow, immediately finds himself pursued by Peters, who hails from a village on the Western front named for the composer Tchaikovsky. Although they fall in love, she is drawn back to her village, and when he follows her, he learns about Russian life and spirit, which is surprisingly like American life and spirit out on the vast plains—but with some differences, such as the fact that talented violinist Peters proudly runs a tractor on a collective farm when she is not giving music lessons or learning to shoot a machine gun. But everyone loves classical music (naturally), giving ample opportunity for dance numbers and lending the film a NORTH STAR quality. With the Nazi invasion, however, the mise en scène is transformed into a battleground filled with desperately heroic people, driving home the lessons that Taylor must take back with him to the American people. 107 min.

Song of the Thin Man (1947)
MGM. Prod: Nat Perrin. Dir: Edward Buzzell. Scr: Steve Fisher, Nat Perrin. Story basis: Stanley Roberts.† Based on characters created by Dashiell Hammett.• Cast: William Powell, Myrna Loy, Keenan Wynn, Dean Stockwell, Philip Reed, Patricia Morrison, Leon Ames, Gloria Grahame, Jayne Meadows

The sixth and last film of the Thin Man series, this time co-written and produced by a comedy writer who suffered blacklisting for a few days due (he claimed later in an interview) to a misunderstanding, but more likely to his friendship of many years with a circle of fellow comedy writers like Allen Boretz,• themselves future for-real blacklistees.

Child actor Stockwell (who was also in THE BOY WITH GREEN HAIR) steps in as Nick, Jr.; borderline avant-gardist Meadows makes a youthful appearance; and the suave Wynn is a piccolo player. But, mainly, it's the same old stuff. As usual, the plot is a bit too complex to be the heart of the film. The clues come fast and furious as Powell wanders through nightclubs trying to find out who shot a bottle of scotch out of his hand after the killing of a bandleader. He also tries to figure out the meaning of musicians' jive talk, a reference to the postwar bebop phenomenon (also notable is that Powell and Loy lose their black maid, by this time evidently considered a bit embarrassing). Although they are still funny and Wynn in particular is very good, perhaps the emerging Cold War culture was too much for the crew. The crime is solved but they have all had enough of the detecting business. 86 min.

A Song to Remember (1944)

Sidney Buchman's• fanciful biopic of young composer Frederic Chopin (Cornel Wilde) in Paris as he gains control of his talent. He is faced with a serious struggle with teacher Paul Muni; rivalry with Franz Liszt (Stephen Bekassy); and love in the form of his affair with Georges Sand, played by Merle Oberon. The film is mainly a vehicle for the music. For the modern feminist reading of the same material, Judy Davis as Sand in *Impromptu* is the must-see.

Sorority House (1939)

Dalton Trumbo's• fine little drama of disillusionment in the campus Greek system is a rarely seen gem. The daughter of a small town grocer goes to college on money that dad has borrowed, learns quickly to covet the sorority system and later comes to see how morally corrupt it is. Able direction by minor auteur John Farrow and good acting.

The Sound and the Fury (1959)

20th. Prod: Jerry Wald. Dir: Martin Ritt.• Scr: Irving Ravetch,† Harriet Frank, Jr. Novel basis: William Faulkner, *The Sound and the Fury* (1929). Cast: Yul Brynner, Joanne Woodward, Margaret Leighton, Stuart Whitman, Ethel Waters, Jack Warden, Albert Dekker†

A failed follow-up to Ritt's adaptation (with the same screenwriters) of Faulkner material in THE LONG, HOT

SUMMER, weakened by the absence of actors Paul Newman and Orson Welles from the earlier film. It was weakened further because Ritt was forced to shoot indoors to lower costs, rather than using the abundant Southern setting that offered him an artist's palette. The melodrama of a decaying South gave Woodward in particular too little to work with, and CinemaScope didn't help at all. 115 min., color.

Sounder (1972)

Radnitz/Mattel Productions. Prod: Robert B. Radnitz. Dir: Martin Ritt.• Scr: Lonne Elder III, William H. Armstrong. Cast: Cicely Tyson, Paul Winfield, Kevin Hooks, Carmen Mathews, James Best, Janet MacLachlan, Sylvia Kuumba Williams

Former blacklistee Ritt's effort to create the perfect film about African American historical and personal life, *Sounder* often falls into sentimentalism, but the lushness of the scene and the seriousness of the effort overcomes the limitations. It is a rural Louisiana Depression story of a child's awakening. The father-sharecropper is imprisoned, and the son simultaneously learns that he can attend school, acquire knowledge about his people's long saga and escape the life of his parents. With their emotional support (and that of his dog, whose name gives the film its title) he will move on toward life in a different and better South—or so the hopeful film attempts to show through moving scenes of what is mostly a family drama. 105 min., color.

So Well Remembered (1947)

Rank Film Organization/RKO. Prod: Adrian Scott.• Dir: Edward Dmytryk.•† Scr: John Paxton. Novel basis: James Hilton, *So Well Remembered* (1945). Cast: John Mills, Marsha Scott, Patrician Roc, Trevor Howard, Richard Carlson, Reginald Tate, Hayley Mills (uncredited, as infant), James Hilton

The fourth and final collaboration of the fabled team of Scott, Dmytryk and Paxton before the blacklist broke it up (it was preceded by MURDER, MY SWEET, CROSSFIRE and CORNERED) and sometimes overlooked because it was shot in England and departs from the film noir mold. It remains a Popular Front film with themes more familiar to U.S. movies of the period but sharpened by the English ability to be more honest about issues of class.

Yorkshire newspaper editor and town councilman John Mills falls in love with the daughter of a much-despised mill owner who has refused to clean up worker housing or the sewers that run through it. An outbreak of diphtheria accelerates the issue of responsibility, costing the Labor Party activist Mills his marriage as well as a seat in Parliament when he takes the principled position. The ruling interests and their politicians are seen as ravenous exploiters willing to sacrifice "500 children, if necessary" to maintain their class position; greed gnaws away at the gothic hearts of three generations of mill owners. As usual in U.S. films, the Marxist is played by the doctor (Howard), his postwar disillusionment about the possibilities for change underlined by his heavy drinking, which does not slow his activism. When V-Day comes, the doc hauls out his most expensive cognac and pours Mills a shot: "We'll drink to victory, no matter how sad it tastes." Mills responds, referring to the latest incarnation of the mill-owning family: "We've not seen the last of her yet. We've a long way to go." After 1947, these warnings against domestic fascism (whether in England or the United States) would rarely if ever be heard again. Which, after all, was the point of the blacklist. 114 min.

The Southerner (1945)

UA. Prod: Robert Hakim, David L. Loew. Dir. Jean Renoir. Scr: Jean Renoir (uncredited: William Faulkner, Hugo Butler,• Nunnally Johnson). Novel basis: George Sessions Perry, *Hold Autumn in Your Hand* (1941). Cast: Zachary Scott, Betty Field, Beulah Bondi, Norman Lloyd, Bunny Sunshine, Estelle Taylor, Percy Kilbride, J. Carroll Naish

A moving tale from the director of *Rules of the Game*, *Grand Illusion* and other classics of the European cinema, and from left-wing screenwriter Butler, who skillfully minimized any indulgence in pastoral sentimentality. Oddly, uncredited contributor Faulkner counted this as one of his favorite Hollywood projects, probably because it handled poor Southern white characters with a sensitivity virtually unknown in other American productions. Renoir worked hard for that effect, according to assistant director Robert Aldrich, who later said of the production, "Renoir truly believed that a transfusion takes place from the physical surroundings to the performances and the picture itself. . . . He would bring the actors there a week early, get them into costumes, and have them walk around barefoot" (Edwin T. Arnold and Eugene L. Miller, Jr., *The Films and Career of Robert Aldrich*).

Scott plays a field hand who makes up his mind to become a tenant farmer. He sets up his family on bottomland that has not been worked for three years and puts his life into it as his loyal wife (Field) struggles by his side. The poverty that dogs their hopes reduces them to helplessness when their son comes down with "spring sickness" (pellegra) for lack of milk and vegetables. Much

of the story turns on the viciousness of a neighbor who had his own plans for the bottom land and who at times threatens to take over the picture with his astonishing displays of inhumanity (as when he slops his pigs with the milk that would save Scott's son from the disease).

There are remarkable moments of celebration as well, however. The Popular Front effort at blue-collar folksiness is transcended with a natural presentation of country manners, as at a wedding dance. The same note is struck more self-consciously in a conversation between Scott and his city friend, a factory worker, in which both come to an understanding about why they prefer their own way of life while declaring that society would collapse without the efforts of people like them.

Scott, more often associated with B-films, is wonderfully vernacular and subtle in this picture, and the supporting cast is fine throughout, including the always incandescent Field in a confining role. 92 min.

Spartacus (1960)

Bryna/U-I. Prod: Edward Lewis. Dir: Stanley Kubrick. Scr: Dalton Trumbo• (uncredited: Calder Willingham, Peter Ustinov). Story basis: Howard Fast,• *Spartacus* (1951). Cast: Kirk Douglas, Laurence Olivier, Jean Simmons, Charles Laughton, Peter Ustinov, John Gavin, Tony Curtis, Woody Strode

Remembered in film circles as the movie that broke the blacklist (not least because John and Jacqueline Kennedy attended the Washington premiere), effectively breaking the campaign by the Catholic Legion of Decency to destroy the film's box office and reinstate Hollywood blacklisting. It should be remembered politically as the novel that Howard Fast wrote while in jail for refusing to testify and that Trumbo and Kubrick adapted, only to have Douglas decide where self-censorship should draw the line. As impossible as it was to make the film without Douglas (as Fast put it), *Spartacus* was also impossible to make with him, at least in the political form Fast intended.

The tale of the great slave revolt was a natural for CinemaScope's big screen and for the civil rights epoch. Ustinov (known in real life as a noncommunist opponent of the Cold War) saves Douglas from a death sentence by placing him in the gladiatorial academy. A great fighter, Spartacus captures the moment, rousing slaves against the decadent Roman empire. Tony Curtis, who owed his rise partly to left-wing screenwriters who lifted him out of "sand and sandals" features in hopes of making him another John Garfield, memorably treats the role of a bisexual slave with a dignity unusual for the day. (A noted bath scene was cut from the film but restored in 1991.)

Ultimately, the battle scenes (Willingham's contribution) create narrative interest, at least for most viewers, before the film subsides into the anticlimax that has the *Viva Zapata!* sensibility of romantic but inevitable defeat. As history, it is Hollywood; but for the time, it is very good indeed. 187 min., color.

The Spy Who Came in from the Cold (1965)

Salem. Prod: Martin Ritt.• Dir: Martin Ritt. Scr: Paul Dehn, Guy Trosper. Novel basis: John Le Carré, *The Spy Who Came in from the Cold* (1963). Cast: Richard Burton, Oskar Werner, Claire Bloom, Sam Wanamaker, Peter Van Eyck, Cyril Cusack, Rupert Davies, Michael Hordern

This heavily nominated but not heavily awarded British production of the Le Carré novel emphasizes the immorality of both sides in the Cold War. Burton, who must infiltrate the East German secret service, is an alcoholic and psychologically wearied if still tactically alert and extraordinarily skilled veteran of MI5. He finds his CIA counterparts both untrustworthy and hypocritical but comes to see his own boss, Smiley, as equally unscrupulous in the purported defense of the West (i.e., the advancement of British interests).

The many fine moments include Burton seeking to explain to his lover (Bloom), an idealistic British communist, that individuals have no chance between the Cold War combatants—and yet he doesn't dare crush her hopes for a better world. Or Burton in an East German secret court of security agents who explain their own high-handed behavior as defense of their "democratic state"; or Burton on the grim streets of East Berlin, where the price has been paid for Cold War fury. Ironically, the film's attempts at near-documentary realism, including its black-and-white photography, damaged it badly at the box office. More a critic's (or filmmaker's) than a popular movie, *Spy* nonetheless established Ritt as an important artist. It was also the last hurrah for liberal Popular Front screenwriter Guy Trosper. 110 min.

Square of Violence (1961)

A neglected World War II drama and the best Italian feature of Leonardo Bercovici• in his decade of exile, this film was based on a real incident. After partisans killed 33 Germans in 1944, the Nazis rounded up 335 men and boys and massacred them in the caves along the Appian Way. Highly regarded in Italy, the film was buried in the United States, thanks to Bercovici's status as a blacklistee. Co-scripted by son Eric Bercovici.

Stanley and Iris (1990)

Lantana. Prod: Arlene Sellers, Alex Winitsky. Dir: Martin Ritt.• Scr: Irving Ravetch,† Harriet Frank, Jr. Novel basis: Pat Barker, *Union Street* (1983). Cast: Jane Fonda, Robert De Niro, Swoosie Kurtz, Martha Plimpton, Harley Cross, Feodor Chaliapin, Jr., Julie Garfield.

A distinctly disappointing final note to the ailing Ritt's directorial career, but full of earnest effort as modern blue-collar uplift. Perhaps Fonda could not be credible as a factory worker living with her sister and an abusive husband, or De Niro as an illiterate fellow worker who finds in her the means to gain control over his destiny; but the two give it the old college try. The location filming was chased out of Cleveland (and moved to Toronto) because of continuing local red-baiting over Fonda's antiwar past, and in gutting the novel of its more violently depressing elements, the screenwriters may have given the tumble-down New England factory town too little realism. Oddly, First Lady Barbara Bush adopted the film for a public literacy campaign; still more oddly, it didn't do any good. Perhaps the next generation of working-class cinema belonged to the new working class of non-white immigrants and to independent filmmakers? Notable for a supporting role by John Garfield's daughter, Julie. 104 min., color.

A Star is Born (1937)

Dorothy Parker• and Alan Campbell• co-scripted (with Robert Carson) this weepy melodrama based loosely on the plot from George Cukor's *What Price Hollywood?* It won an Oscar for the story basis (and another for cinematography) by Carson and director William A. Wellman. Parker discounted it as art, but audiences loved the tragic energy between leads Fredric March (a rising star destined for an early eclipse) and Janet Gaynor (a promising actress who must accept the consequences of her continued rise as part of hubby's breakdown). The eternal Lionel Stander• appears in a supporting role. Cukor remade it in 1954 with a bravura musical cast, and Barbra Streisand appeared in a particularly drippy version in 1976, with a co-script by Joan Didion.

Steaming (1985)

World Film. Prod: Paul Mills. Dir: Joseph Losey.• Scr: Patricia Losey. Play basis: Nell Dunn, *Steaming* (1983). Cast: Vanessa Redgrave, Diana Dors, Patti Love, Brenda Bruce, Felicity Dean, Sally Sagoe

Attacked at the time as a dull and talky feminist tract, this film looks better in retrospect as the dour Marxist

Joseph Losey's final outing, an attempt at the political uplift he had for most of his career studiously avoided. What began as a sort of consciousness-raising theatrical piece (briefly on Broadway) with an admixture of *Hair*—the topless and sometimes total frontal nudity of the protagonists an unmistakeable major feature—was toned down to a discreet nudism for the film. Screenwriter Patricia Losey, the director's last wife, had earlier been secretary to Hugo Butler,• after Butler and Losey worked together on EVE.

A rundown London public bathhouse becomes the ideal locale for a cross-section of British women to strip off their symbolic class dignity and "steam" about their status in a patriarchal world. Diana Dors, the 1950s British sex symbol, played her last role (dying a few weeks before Losey, just before the film was released) as the bathhouse manager. Suburban matron Redgrave, the real star of the film, vents along with erstwhile jet-setter turned lawyer Miles, and Love, a free-spirited working-class woman.

These characters find common purpose in keeping the bathhouse open, frustrating the plan of developers to tear it down. And they find a certain cinematic clarity, thanks to Losey's famed fluid visual narrative, tested here by the confining set. There's something odd, alluring and unique about the mixture of stripping and feminism, with the gruff Losey hitting a bright note at the very end of his career. 102 min.

Stella Dallas (1937)

The all-time champion weepie with "dramatization" by Gertrude Purcell† has Barbara Stanwyck unwilling to stand in the way of her daughter's success but perfectly capable of martyring herself for it. What happens when a woman marries "above" her station? *Stella* fed on the doubts that can weaken the strongest women. Jaw-droppingly maudlin in places.

Stormy Weather (1943)

20th. Prod: William LeBaron. Dir: Andrew L. Stone. Scr: Frederick J. Jackson, Ted Koehler. Adaptation: H. S. Kraft.• Story basis: Jerry Horwin, Seymour B. Robinson. Cast: Lena Horne, Bill Robinson, Cab Calloway, Katherine Dunham and Her Troupe, Fats Waller, Nicholas Brothers, Dooley Wilson

A thin story line of Robinson recalling to black children his career and his on-and-off romance with a famous singer (Horne) offers the opportunity for perhaps the most condensed and best collection of music and dance numbers ever offered in a single short film. Fats

Waller, who rightly complained that he was never offered a serious opportunity in Hollywood in the 1940s, makes an appearance here (unfortunately, still limited to clowning). Robinson and Calloway, backed up by plenty of others, dance up a storm, reminding the viewer of what Spike Lee sought to capture in the early scenes of MALCOLM X. Dunham's rendition of the title song is (along with some of her numbers in Robert Rossen's† MAMBO) the best glimpse of her astonishing work during these years. 77 min.

The Story of GI Joe (1945)

Lester Cowan Productions: Prod: Lester Cowan. Dir: William A. Wellman. Scr: Leopold Atlas,† Guy Endore,• Philip Stevenson.• Cast: Burgess Meredith, Robert Mitchum, Freddie Steele, Wally Cassell, Jimmy Lloyd, John R. Reilly, William Murphy

A neglected film that successfully transfers battle journalist Ernie Pyle's columns into a film script about the ordinary dog-face soldier of World War II. Loaded with documentary material, including lots of Signal Corps footage of the North African and Italian campaigns, it traces the opening of the long-awaited second front (a favorite demand of communists in wartime, eager to relieve the Eastern Front) through Meredith's eyes and his effort just to survive while telling the story. The film shows the bitterness of the conflict, with slow—and for months, no—progress moving northward into Italy. Meanwhile, German troops were aiding collaborators who would in only a few years be regarded as U.S. allies against former Italian partisans.

There is little if any of the glory usually associated with war films. Like A WALK IN THE SUN, this film captures the antifascist determination of the soldiers along with the senselessness of war. Mitchum's first of many soldier roles. 109 min.

The Story of Louis Pasteur (1936)

Cosmopolitan/WB. Prod: Henry Blonke. Dir: William Dieterle. Scr: Sheridan Gibney, Pierre Collings (uncredited script contribution: Edward Chodorov•). Cast: Paul Muni, Josephine Hutchinson, Anita Louise, Donald Woods, Fritz Leiber, Porter Hall, Akim Tamiroff

An Oscar winner for Muni and writers Gibney and Collings, a film much admired (even beloved) during its time. Muni, who so often played the outcast, got one of his most idealistic roles as the outcast humanitarian. Chemist Pasteur in mid-nineteenth-century France must win over a medical profession skeptical about his discovery of germs. He is repeatedly scorned and ridiculed (Tamiroff, a noted physician, is his nemesis), but true-blue wife Hutchinson supports him emotionally through it all, and daughter Louise likewise (as she slides into love and marriage with Muni's assistant, played by Woods).

Medical-scientific highlights: decades after discovering the most common cause of maternal death during childbirth, Muni (much aged) swears to find a cure for rabies and even has himself inoculated to prove his solution. Nice scenes of the heretic against the elite and of his deserved triumph. This is a very 1930s idealistic view of science, untainted by the realities of what comes after. 87 min.

Strange Love of Martha Ivers (1946)

Hal Wallis Productions/Paramount. Prod: Hal B. Wallis. Dir: Lewis Milestone. Scr: Robert Rossen† (uncredited: Robert Riskin). Story basis: John Patrick, "Love Lies Bleeding" (unpublished). Cast: Barbara Stanwyck, Van Heflin, Lizabeth Scott, Kirk Douglas

An almost accidental death of a tyrannical aunt at the hands of a child causes the child to grow up to be a classic "strong woman" of the period, taking over a small family-owned factory and turning it into a war-production plant employing almost everyone in the little Midwestern industrial town. Her husband, played by Kirk Douglas in his first starring role, is the weak, psychologically tortured plant manager who witnessed her crime and shares her guilt. Into this scene returns the cynical former GI and current drifter Sam (Heflin), who happens to be romantically involved with a nearly broken (or perhaps "fallen") ex-jailbird local woman he has just met. Sam knows all about the aunt. Seeing the danger of their exposure but also drawn to Sam since their childhood, Stanwyck suggests he kill her husband and gives him a pistol.

One of Rossen's most effective films, Martha Ivers combines emerging class themes with gender themes, here the strong woman who makes her way in a man's world and is proud of it but perhaps inevitably surrounds herself with weak men. The class issues turn on the fruit of wealth and war profits. Heflin succeeds in bringing down the little town's leading citizens but declines to stick around for the consequences. Committed to being uncommitted (except, perhaps, to his new lover), he is the noir antihero of the age. 116 min.

A Stranger in Town (1943)

MGM. Prod: Robert Sisk. Dir: Roy Rowland. Scr: William Kozlenko, Isobel Lennart.† Cast: Frank Morgan, Richard Carlson, Jean Rogers, Porter Hall, Robert Barrat, Donald MacBride, Walter Baldwin, Andrew Tombes, Olin Howlin, Chill Wills, Irving Bacon, Eddie Dun, Gladys Blake, John Hodiak

Dumbed-down or politically diluted version of TALK OF THE TOWN, which celebrated the morals of a small town anarchist who, amid screwball antics, dragged a respectable judge into defending him. This film lacks Cary Grant and Jean Arthur, too, but has a few good points.

A Supreme Court justice (Morgan) goes on a duck-hunting vacation. By accident, he lands in the middle of a town rife with crooked politics where a mayoral election pits boss Barrat against young lawyer-idealist Carlson. Involved against his will, Morgan helps to break the power of the machine and in so doing makes it possible for romantic interest Rogers to become Carlson's true love. 67 min.

Stranger on the Prowl (1953)

Tirrenia-Riviera. Prod: Noël Calef (front for John Weber•). Dir: Andrea Forzano (front for Joseph Losey•). Scr: Ben Barzman.• Story basis: Noël Calef. Cast: Paul Muni, Joan Lorring, Vittorio Manunta, Luisa Rossi, Aldo Silvani, Franco Balducci, Enrico Glori

A picture with one of the strangest backstories in blacklist history. Weber, a former Hollywood Communist functionary, screen-analysts' guild founder and agent, anticipating the blacklist ahead and looking for solutions in exile, put together a team in Paris (later Italy) for a Losey film starring Muni. The scenario, he recalled, was borrowed from Crime and Punishment and The Bicycle Thief. A miniscule budget, State Department–directed harassment (via the Italian government), location and technical problems were all capped off by the refusal of U.S. distributors to carry the film unless the blacklistees' names were stripped from the title. Despite conceding to these demands, the film received little play, and the vision of a series of productions (with Bernard Vorhaus making B-films along the way as part of the team) that would allow artists to sit out the blacklist and await better times was doomed. Only Luxury Girls, directed by Vorhaus, came out of the same group, and it was his last film.

But at least Stranger was made. Muni, a former Yiddish actor with left-wing sympathies, came back from retirement (with a heart condition) to play a loser who sells his sole possession, a gun, to raise money to get out of Italy illegally. No one wants to purchase the weapon, however, and, increasingly hungry, he snatches some cheese in a store, then accidentally strangles the storekeeper (Manson) while trying to keep her from screaming for the cops.

Now really on the run, he is shot and wounded by police, then adopted by the waif Manunta. Both of them are given shelter by Lorring, maid in a ruling-class home. After a romantic episode, Muni and Lorring realize the hopelessness of the situation. Muni flees again—his temporary escape including a dramatic scene running through an Italian circus—and eventually he meets his fate. Originally made at three hours and cut twice. Along with LAWLESS and THE PROWLER, this is early Losey at his best. 82 min.

Strawberry Roan (1948)

Julian Zimet• provided the story for a Gene Autry Production/Columbia remake of a 1933 film of the same title, wholly rewritten as an Autry vehicle, a singing cowboy film. The horse of the title is free, one of a herd of wild horses perhaps never meant to be tamed. Autry, the foreman at a small ranch, captures him and reluctantly turns him over to the owner's son to be broken, but with tragic results: the roan throws the boy, apparently crippling him for life. Gene saves horse and cures boy. Autry's first color pic, it was also the debut of Pat Buttram, a sort of B-version Gabby Hayes, who rose to semi-stardom in Autry's shadow.

Studs Lonigan (1960)

Philip Yordan/United Artists. Prod: Philip Yordan. Dir: Irving Lerner. Scr: Philip Yordan (uncredited contribution: Bernard Gordon•). Cast: Christopher Knight, Frank Gorshin, Venetia Stevenson, Carolyn Craig, Jack Nicholson, Dick Foran

A highly curious example of Yordan's production factory, first because it was a cut far above his usual fare, and second because an erstwhile Communist writer (Gordon) recreated the structure of a film based on a trilogy by James T. Farrell, the Trotskyist writer whose work served to precipitate the 1946 "Maltz Controversy" in Hollywood. More than a decade later, the rather conservative Yordan brought in the radical Gordon to make something out of a film project that was over budget and near collapse. The highly detailed novels surrendered no easy narrative, and director Lerner (a former film writer for the *New Masses* who somehow escaped the blacklist) was no match for the problems. Ultimately, this was an arty film that looked too commercial and a commercial film that lacked the narrative strength to deliver.

Knight, in his film debut, is Studs, the Chicago Irish working-class boy who works his way through the slum life on the old South Side, never becoming a hero in anything but neighborhood pranks but now and then expressing aspirations to his boyhood friend Gorshin (i.e., novelist Farrell). The racism of his parents is softened in the film, and father Foran in particular comes off as a quietly decent proletarian. Studs' girlfriend Stevenson tries futilely to steer him onto a better path, but to no use. The film preceded a television mini-series, which, even with more time to develop the plot and characters, still failed to overcome the difficulties of adaptation. 95 min.

Summertime (1955)

Donald Ogden Stewart• made an uncredited script contribution to this David Lean idyll. Katharine Hepburn plays a spinster falling for married man Rossano Brazzi in Paris. It was adapted from graylistee Arthur Laurents' play. Location shooting was the film's prime accomplishment.

Sunday Dinner for a Soldier (1944)

Low-key wartime unity story co-scripted by Melvin Levy† about a Florida family saving their money to provide you-know-what for John Hodiak, with Anne Baxter as the widow, Charles Winniger as the grandpop and Anne Revere• as a neighbor. Interesting pacing and tone.

Suspense (1946)

Directed by Frank Tuttle† with a script contribution by David Lang,† this was billed by poverty-row studio Monogram as its first "million dollar release," boasting big production skating scenes and a minor melodrama.

The Sweet Smell of Success (1957)

Hecht, Hill & Lancaster/Norma-Curtleigh Prod. Prod: James Hill. Dir: Alexander Mackendrick. Scr: Ernest Lehman, Clifford Odets† (uncredited: Alexander Mackendrick). Cast: Burt Lancaster, Tony Curtis, Martin Milner, Barbara Nichols, Sam Levene

The only satisfactory Odets screenplay after DEADLINE AT DAWN, SUCCESS offered him the opportunity to repent his sins of testifying against his friends and strike a blow at old enemies on the Right. Indeed, it was for many years Hollywood's only comment on the effect of the blacklist.

Lancaster and Curtis, whose informal links with the Left had also been tenuous at best for career reasons, are brilliant as the gossip columnist J. J. Hunsecker (i.e., Walter

Winchell) and his pimpish press agent. Together, they cover Broadway with their sleaze, extracting favors of all kinds in return for kind treatment or forbearance from bad treatment, saving the worst for the uncooperative (metaphorically, the reds). When a jazz musician falls for J. J.'s sister and she returns his ardor, Lancaster goes on a tear, from charges of dope use to communist sympathies. Like the real world, in which the red-baiting Winchell lost face after attempting to ruin Josephine Baker's career, it seems inevitable he will fall, but even so the world is not likely to be a better place. 96 min., color.

Swing Hostess (1944)

Bottom-drawer PRC effort co-scripted by Louise Rousseau• in the wartime genre of young women seeking to break into show business but thwarted in one way or another until romantic interest provides a solution. Here, a telephone operator struggles to get a record contract with a good band. Strong on women's friendship.

Swing in the Saddle (1944)

Morton Grant• co-scripted this B-western musical about two gals working on a dude ranch. Amazingly, the film found a way to include an interracial music scene with Nat King Cole (not yet a solo act and well known in left-wing entertainment circles).

Swing It, Professor (1937)

Conn Pictures. Prod: Maurice Conn. Dir: Marshall Neilan. Scr: Nicholas Barrows, Robert St. Claire, Connie Lee.• Cast: Pinky Tomlin, Paula Stone, Mary Kornman, Milburn Stone, Pat Gleason, Gordon Elliott, the Gentle Maniacs, the Four Singing Tramps, the Four Squires.

A low-budget, high fantasy comedy that represents a paradigm shift in U.S. popular culture. It is one of the first movies to deal with the political context of swing music, a theme that would be explored at great length into the late 1940s in dozens of films, often by lefties.

Bandleader Tomlin is a music professor at a small university down on its luck. He refuses to go along with the silly demands of students and administration to get with the jive. Fired for his troubled dignity, he hits the road, and there he meets some hobos who have amazingly recherché tastes in classical music (the sextette from *Lucia di Lammermoor*) as well as a deep interest in jazz. Through their mentoring, he gets into a nightclub act,

becomes a jazz star and gets the girl he left behind on campus (Stone). Jack Greenhalgh's camera work, for the period, is very inventive, especially on the hand-held angles, and several of the songs (and lyrics) are by Connie Lee. Charming. 62 min.

Swing Out, Sister (1945)

The able Henry Blankfort• wrote this literate story about a young vocalist, Jessica Mariman (played by Billie Burke), who can perform with equal facility in swing and opera and is torn between the two worlds, each represented by a separate suitor and the social standing of their families. Anything written by Henry (younger brother of the famous friendly witness, Michael Blankfort†) is worth watching.

Swiss Tour (1949)

Praesens-Film. Prod: Lazar Wechsler, Lou Wechsler, Oscar Dilby. Dir: Leopold Lindtberg. Scr: Curt Siodmak (English dialogue: Ring Lardner, Jr.•). Novella basis: Richard Schweizer, *Swiss-Tour* (1947). Cast: Cornel Wilde, Josette Day, Simone Signoret, Richard Erdman, John Baragry, Alan Hale, Jr., George Petrie.

A Swiss production that took advantage of the blacklist to match Lardner's talents with some left-wing actors, notably French Popular Front favorite Signoret. Director Lindtberg's earlier work included the low-budget antifascist drama *Last Chance*, about an escape from Italy with the assistance of Spanish Civil War vets.

This time, more obviously in the commercial vein, Wilde (a liberal actor who often expressed the desire to break the blacklist) is a U.S. sailor on a Swiss leave who falls in love with Day, a watchmaker's daughter. The film makes the most of a ski holiday, with virtual documentary footage of what was then an exotic sport for most Americans. Signoret is the romantic competition, and, in her prime, an arresting if not classic beauty. GI pals hang around for the action. 79 min.

Sylvia Scarlett (1935)

Mortimer Offner• was one of three scriptwriters for this Katharine Hepburn set piece about the daughter of a French merchant who, fleeing to Britain with her father, disguises herself as a young man until she falls for a bohemian artist. After assorted adventures, they discover each other. Directed by George Cukor.

T

Take It or Leave It (1944)

A spin-off by Harold Buchman,• Snag Werris, and Mac Benofft† from real-life radio celebrity Phil Baker's program, with a handful of personalities, including former top banana Phil Silvers. Some fun as satire on commercial broadcasting, providing a sense of the sponsors' control and misdirection—but not much of a picture.

Tales of Manhattan (1942)

20th. Prod: Boris Morros, S. P. Eagle (Sam Spiegel). Dir: Julien Duvivier. Scr: Ben Hecht, Ferenc Molnár, Donald Ogden Stewart,• Samuel Hoffenstein, Alan Campbell,• Ladislas Fodor, László Görög, Lamar Trotti, Henry Blankfort.• Film basis: Un carnet de bail (1937). Cast: Charles Boyer, Rita Hayworth, Thomas Mitchell, Eugene Pallette, Ginger Rogers, Henry Fonda, Cesar Romero, Gail Patrick, Roland Young, Charles Laughton, Elsa Lanchester, Marion Martin, James Rennie, Victor Francen, Edward G. Robinson, Christian Rub, George Sanders, James Gleason, Harry Davenport, Paul Robeson,• Ethel Waters, Eddie Anderson, Clarence Muse

American version of a French film directed by Duvivier, himself by this time in exile, like many French artists during the German occupation. Best remembered as Robeson's final film, which came at the end of a disappointing series of efforts on his behalf in Hollywood and only five years before he was blacklisted from public concerts and indeed all other possible public appearances, as well as travel abroad. The film was also destined to be controversial within the Left itself.

In spite of its problems, *Manhattan* is a rare anthology film that actually works. Known at the time as an experiment in form, it is what newspapers call a "journey story," following the fortunes of a full-dress, swallow-tail tuxedo as it passes from one hand to the next. In the first story, matinee idol Boyer discovers that his lover Hayworth, someone else's wife, is herself fickle, with disastrous consequences; the suit passes on successively to a pianist (Laughton), a bum (Robinson) attending a college reunion in style and to a crook (Mitchell) on the run.

Finally it falls (with a wallet full of money) out of an airplane and into the hands of a deeply religious and grateful African American community in the South.

The film has many intriguing moments, as when Laughton's suit jacket rips out as he conducts a symphony, the audience at first laughing uproariously and then being won over to him (the men taking off their own jackets in solidarity) as he resumes. It is notable, too, for having more visual time for African American actors concentrated in non-servile roles than any other major film of its time save the musicals STORMY WEATHER and CABIN IN THE SKY. Some critics nevertheless objected at the time to the "praise de Lawd" framing of black rural culture, and some Communists (that is, cultural functionary V. J. Jerome) retrospectively complained that the picture typified the treatment of race by "Hollywood." Nonetheless, Henry Blankfort's dialogue for Robeson was often eloquent, as in these lines : "We're gonna buy tools with edges so sharp the earth will rise up to meet 'em. And we're gonna work that ground side by side, raisin' corn and cotton, and what we gets, we shares. There won't be no rich, and no more poor. Yes, folks, a new day is dawnin'!" 118 min.

Talk About a Lady (1946)

A Jinx Falkenburg musical, this time backed up by Stan Kenton's band and the antics of a future substitute Stooge, Joe Besser. Tunes are included by noted antifascist Oscar Hammerstein II among others as jazzed-up wholesomeness wins over the shabby aristocracy of mere cash. Scripted by Richard Weil• and Ted Thomas.

Talk of the Town (1942)

Columbia. Prod and Dir: George Stevens. Scr: Irwin Shaw, Sidney Buchman.• Story basis: Sidney Harmon. Cast: Cary Grant, Jean Arthur, Ronald Coleman, Edgar Buchanan, Glenda Farrell, Charles Dingle, Rex Ingram, Lloyd Bridges,† Lee "Lasses" White

A fine example of left-wing dramatists depicting an imagined Yankee life, with a near-perfect mixture of screwball comedy and cross-examination of justice in contemporary law. Grant has one of his best roles as the small town New England radical—even if he only gives speeches on streetcorners because he is too anarchistic to be part of anything outside his small world. He is on the run from the phony charge of setting the factory on fire and burning a man to death. Coleman is the prominent law professor and, we learn, probable next appointee to the U.S. Supreme Court, intent on enjoying himself during a working vacation. Pert Jean Arthur, whose house is rented by Coleman but also used for a hideout by Grant, is the creature who entrances both.

Some of the best moments have Grant and Coleman, who thinks his new conversationalist friend is the gardener, debating legal issues, with the usual contrast of the letter and the meaning of the law. Meanwhile, the town capitalist, judge, sheriff and cops would like nothing better than to throw a lynching party. Arthur spins in confusion as she realizes that she is in love with both of them.

This is one of those great 1930s-1940s films with a rock 'em, sock 'em windup including everything from car chases to a philosophical recognition that something in society has gone wrong. Screenwriter Shaw, close to several future blacklistees since their mutual Brooklyn boyhoods, later chose personal exile over work in Hollywood. 118 min.

Tamango (1957)

Le Films du Cyclope (France). Prod: Sig Shore, Gaston Vuattaux. Dir: John Berry.• Scr: Lee Gold,• Tamara Hovey,• John Berry.• Novel basis: Prosper Merimee, *Tamango* (1829). Cast: Dorothy Dandridge, Curt Jurgens, Jean Servais, Roger Hanin, Guy Mairesse, Alex Cressan

A slave revolt drama considered overwrought at the time, but now thought to be far ahead of its time— *Amistad*, for example, suffers by comparison. Dandridge, in her most "serious" role (save in all-black films) and en route to an early death from depression and drugs, returned to work with the left-wingers who "discovered" her during the 1940s by taking the role of the slave who is also mistress to slave-ship captain Jurgens. Critics rightly complained about the low-budget crudeness of the production, giving shipboard scenes a "studio" feel, but the blame properly falls on the problems of producing, at that time, an ardently antiracist film *about a slave uprising.* Performances were solid and heartfelt, especially those of Dandridge and Jurgens.

Gold, his wife Hovey, and Berry set out to make a picture that was not likely to be distributed at all in the United States. But somehow it managed to find its way to U.S. theaters in 1959 and, in partly dubbed form, was such a hit that Shore went on to make a fortune producing blaxploitation "Superfly" films. American audiences enjoyed it as black drama—one of the first times, filmed or live, when that genre had a wide popular reception. French critics, however, considered it "American" and badly wounded its reputation as well as that of director Berry, who after a career in exile with some real triumphs was finding it difficult to get good work in France. 98 min., color.

Taras Bulba (1962)

Avala Film/Harold Hecht Productions. Prod: Harold Hecht.† Dir: J. Lee Thompson. Scr: Waldo Salt,• Karl Tunberg. Novel basis: Nicolai Gogol, *Taras Bulba* (1842). Cast: Yul Brynner, Tony Curtis, Sam Wanamaker, Brad Dexter, Guy Rolfe, Perry Lopez, George Macready, Ilka Windish

Produced by friendly witness Hecht, who also produced several other films with blacklistees, this is an adventure in semi-Asiatic otherness (and semi-European familiarity), with Cossacks as a captive people. The proud Cossacks of sixteenth-century Ukraine have joined with Poles in a successful fight to ward off invading Turks but are betrayed by the Polish rulers; they want to continue their occupation of the steppes, then move to break up the Cossacks once and for all. Resisting assimilation, horseman/warrior Brynner leads his people back to the hills, burning their villages before departing (much like Polish villagers did against the Nazi invasion). But then a generation passes, and the sequestered Taras Bulba decides that he must send his sons, above all his favorite (Curtis), into Kiev for education. There the brothers encounter racist and religious persecution, including an intolerant and nationalistic Polish Catholicism (quietly suggesting real-life Jewish memories of the Holocaust). But they persevere as long as allowed, and, to no surprise for Curtis fans, he wins the heart of a Polish beauty (Windish). Politics merges back into a family struggle as the brothers escape mob violence and set off a struggle for national liberation. Often turgid, and not one of Salt's proudest moments. 122 min., color.

Tarnished Lady (1931)

Para. Prod: Unknown. Dir: George Cukor. Scr: Donald Ogden Stewart.• Cast: Tallulah Bankhead, Clive Brook, Alexander Kirkland, Phoebe Foster, Osgood Perkins, Elizabeth Patterson

This was Cukor's first sound film and Bankhead's film debut. *New York Times* critics complained, "only in a few spots is the author's fine hand discernable." The script did not lend enough strength to a film with poor photography, bad editing (usual for 1931) and a weak plot. Still, the film has its moments.

Financial plunger Brook has made his fortune in the stock market, then realizes suddenly that he's wiped out. Wife Bankhead raises the question of divorce and lives it up in cabarets while hubby mopes in his town house. She is in love with younger man Kirkland, if unwilling to abandon the prospect of Brook's financial recovery. Foster, who had always wanted Brook to herself, now sees her chance and pounces. But a classic Hollywood ending cancels all bets. 83 min.

Tarzan's New York Adventure (1942)

MGM. Prod: Frederick Stephani. Dir: Richard Thorpe. Scr: William R. Lipman, Myles Connolly (uncredited: Gordon Kahn•). Based on characters created by Edgar Rice Burroughs. Cast: Johnny Weissmuller, Maureen O'Sullivan, Johnny Sheffield, Virginia Grey, Charles Bickford, Paul Kelly, Chill Wills

This is by far the most political of the Tarzan features and the last in which O'Sullivan adds the erotic touch of the well-bred Englishwoman who chooses the life of the ape-man over what Western civilization can offer her.

Big game hunters invade Tarzan's domain to kidnap animals for their own commercial ventures. In the only sign of real Africans in the film, painted tribesmen unsuccessfully attempt to drive the hunters out. Tarzan's first impulse is to do the same. But the invaders stay long enough to kidnap Boy after Tarzan and Jane have been knocked cold from swinging on a loose vine. The two follow Boy to Manhattan amid much explaining by Jane to Tarzan of modern technology and civilization's rules, making him seem at once ignorant and sage. In a court battle, Tarzan exposes the fraud and corruption of life in the jungle of buildings, but in seeming to lose the case, must counter Jane's advice with direct action. Swinging through the city, diving from the Brooklyn Bridge in a beautiful Olympic-quality swoop (a stunt Weissmuller performed himself) and making his way to the circus, where he rouses the captured animals to come to his aid, he frees Boy and they all return to their proper home, with the elephants leading the revolution against cage slavery. The fine comic scenes with the chimp busting up corporate decorum in an office will have four-year-olds and all sympathetic parents rolling on the floor. 71 min.

Tarzan's Savage Fury (1952)

A failed effort by Cyril Endfield• to get hack directorial work to tide him over through blacklist period. Interesting only because he turned to Africa for his best subject matter once he was in Britain.

Taxi! (1932)

WB. Prod: Darryl Zanuck. Dir: Roy Del Ruth Scr: John Bright,• Kubec Glasmon. Story basis: Kenyon Nicholson, "Blind Spot." (N.d.) Cast: James Cagney, Loretta Young, George E. Stone, Dorothy Burgess, Ray Cooke, Matt McHugh, David Landau

In its first half, at least, this is the most political of the half-dozen films written by Bright and Glasmon for Warners in 1931 (the others: PUBLIC ENEMY, SMART MONEY, BLOND CRAZY, THE CROWD ROARS, UNION DEPOT). Because of conflicts with the studio, it also marked the end of Bright's early, phenomenal success. Looking for more money (he was paid $250 per week) and enraged at Zanuck's abuse, he punched the boss and tried throwing him out of a window—according to Hollywood legend.

The screenwriters turned the early part of the film into a cabbies' struggle for unionization. In the second half, it turns to action, with the disappointed Cagney pursuing vendettas, using his fists too often and even planning to murder Landau, who killed his brother. Happily, his girl (Young) stops him from shooting through a door at the trapped Landau, who obliges by jumping out of a window to his doom. Bright later recalled that *The Nation* praised the film's social significance and Zanuck (who never heard of the magazine) reflected, "I'll be a son of a bitch. I thought it was all cops and robbers." Highpoint: Cagney speaking several lines in Yiddish! 70 min.

Tell Me a Riddle (1980)

Godmother Productions. Prod: Mindy Affrime, Rachel Lyon, Susan O'Connell. Dir: Lee Grant.• Scr: Joyce Eliason, Alev Lytle. Story basis: Tillie Olsen, *Tell Me A Riddle* (1961). Cast: Melvyn Douglas, Lila Kedrova, Brooke Adams, Dolores Dorn, Bob Elross, Zalman King

A low-budget epic based on the famous work of Olsen, a "proletarian novelist" of the 1930s and the favorite of left-leaning 1970s feminists. It is also Douglas' next-to-last performance. He plays the husband of a dying Kedrova, and the recollection of their lives together is stretched a bit thinly over the circumstances of their granddaughter, played by Brooke Adams, as an artist with man trouble. Still, between Douglas and Kedrova, through memories of Depression blue-collar life and the anxieties of aging, there's an awful lot here to see and admire. It was actress Lee Grant's directorial debut. 90 min.

Tell No Tales (1939)

Loew's/MGM. Prod: Edward Chodorov.• Dir: Leslie Fenton. Scr: Lionel Houser (uncredited: Edward Chodorov). Story basis: Pauline London, Alfred Taylor. Cast: Melvyn Douglas, Louise Platt, Gene Lockhart, Douglas Dumbrille, Florence George, Halliwell Hobbe

An unusual murder mystery involving a newspaper baron's manipulation of the press for his own ends. At the seventy-fifth anniversary of the *Evening Guardian*, crusading editor Douglas finds out that the paper is being closed to eliminate competition with another paper owned by the same man (Dumbrille). He sees the worst in the yellow competitor's treatment of Platt, a schoolteacher who bravely came to the police as an eyewitness of a kidnapping and is now kept virtual prisoner by a police guard. Striking up a relationship with her, Douglas follows the trail as it winds from one suspect to another and finally to the mob. Winning a gunfight, he publishes the full story in the final issue—and the owner retracts his decision as the public marvels at the revelations. 69 min.

Tell Them Willie Boy Is Here (1969)

Universal. Prod: Jennings Lang, Philip A. Waxman. Dir.: Abraham Polonsky.• Scr: Abraham Polonsky. Book basis: Harry Lawton, *Willie Boy: A Desert Manhunt* (1960). Cast: Robert Redford, Katherine Ross, Robert Blake, Susan Clark, Barry Sullivan, Charles McGraw, John Vernon

Blacklistee Polonsky returned to the screen as a director after 20 years to make his most popular picture, which was condemned by Pauline Kael and other Cold War liberal critics, and for good reason—Polonsky called *Willie Boy* his testimony to the antiwar movement. His first two films, made in the 1940s (BODY AND SOUL and FORCE OF EVIL) used the boxing business and the numbers racket, respectively, to frame his leftist critique of American business culture, but *Willie Boy* dealt with the war of business interests on the Third World and traditional cultures.

The story of Willie is one of an Anglo-led posse in pursuit of a Chemeuevi laborer (Blake) who has run off with Lola (Ross), a young woman of the same tribe, after he has killed her father in a "marriage by capture." It is based on a real incident of 1909, widely accepted as the last armed resistance in California of a Native American. The pursuit is told in the context of two love stories, the one between Willie and Lola and another between Sheriff Coop (Redford) and the Indian agent (Clark) who has befriended Lola. The movie shows what American empire, then in its first throes of consolidation, extracted from the ordinary humanity of the four protagonists, whose love story Polonsky intercuts with great skill. Coop, by the way, is Polonsky's jibe at Gary Cooper, the westerner with the star on his chest who testified so disingenuously against the Left before HUAC.

This is one of the most important westerns ever made, not only for the subtlety of the storytelling at many

different levels but also for the performances (it's one of Blake's best films), the cinematography of the desert in elegant desaturated whites and silvers, and the music—which changed forever the way U.S. westerns would sound. 96 min.

The Tempest (aka *La Tempesta*, 1958)

DeLaurentiis-Bosna Film. Prod: Dino DeLaurentiis. Dir: Alberto Lattuada. Scr: Alberto Lattuada, Louis Peterson, Ivo Perilli (uncredited: Michael Wilson•). Story basis: Alexander Pushkin short stories. Cast: Silvana Mangano, Van Heflin, Viveca Lindfors, Geoffrey Horne, Oskar Homolka, Robert Keith, Agnes Moorehead, Finlay Currie, Vittorio Gassman, Helmut Dantine

A Yugoslavian-French-Italian collaboration from the years when Yugoslavia was (along with Hungary) the East Bloc country where blacklisted filmmakers could work with some freedom. De Laurentiis' 5 BRANDED WOMEN, directed by Martin Ritt,• also featuring Mangano and Heflin, was made there the same year. With a $2 million budget bankrolled in part by Paramount, the film was shot primarily in English with an emphasis on spectacle. Intended to follow up De Laurentiis' *War and Peace*, it had considerably less box office appeal.

Horne, an officer of the Russian empress's guard in the nineteenth century, is punished by being assigned to the distant hinterlands. En route, he saves a Cossack from freezing to death and learns to his surprise that he has saved and released the famed rebel Pugacev (Heflin), who roused a revolt against Catherine II. Once he arrives at the fort to which he has been assigned, Horne falls for Magnano, the daughter of the fort's commandant (Keith). When Pugacev attacks the fort, Horne is captured but given his freedom when the rebel recognizes him. Back in Moscow, he is suspected of being a spy and flees to rebel territory, where he convinces Pugacev that he should be permitted to marry Magnano.

Reviewers praised the battle scenes, including the execution of the fort commander by the rebels and the final capture of Pugacev by the Czar's forces. Heflin, in one of his best roles, got to be a revolutionary of sorts—decades after working as a young actor surrounded by radicals (at the Group Theatre) in real life. Later commentators on the film were not so charitable, treating it as just one more none-too-deep spectacular. 120 min.

Temptation (1946)

U-I. Prod: Prod: Edward Small. Dir. Irving Pichel.• Scr: Robert Thoeren. Play basis: James B. Fagan, *Bella Donna*

(1911). Adapted from the novel by Robert Smythe Hichens, *Bella Donna* (1909). Cast: Merle Oberon, George Brent, Paul Lukas, Charles Korvin, Lenore Ulric, Arnold Moss, Aubrey Mather

In this historical drama, Oberon plays the woman with a past who sheds her identity, marries archaeologist Brent but begins seeing the exotic Korvin (an Oxford-trained Egyptian intellectual) on the side. Like other strong-women protagonists of the time, Oberon offers scathing monologues on the exploitation and domination of women by men and how she intends to avoid this fate through her own scheming. If not admirable, she is at any rate erotic, slipping out into the Cairo night to satisfy her desires.

In an interesting plot sidelight, Lukas as the exile German doctor and friend of her husband reprises, in a sense, his role in WATCH ON THE RHINE and those of so many other German intellectuals in this time: as the most immediate witnesses to human criminality, they record its meaning. 98 min.

Tender Comrade (1943)

RKO. Prod: David Hempstead. Dir: Edward Dmytryk.•† Scr: Dalton Trumbo.• Cast: Ginger Rogers, Robert Ryan, Ruth Hussey, Patricia Collinge, Mady Christians,• Kim Hunter,† Jane Darwell, Mary Forbes, Richard Martin

One of the films most often attacked during the McCarthy Era and one of the most soapish of the Left's Hollywood work. Ryan and Rogers (she playing the simpering innocent, as always) are childhood sweethearts who marry not long before he is drafted and sent overseas. She moves into a collective household of women in a similar situation. Many emotional tokens of cooperative life are in evidence, notably the famous line, "Share and share alike—that's the American way." It was a line much regretted by Rogers and cited as communistic by McCarthyites seeking proof of subversion. One of the women is a "good German" (a refugee), another is vaguely alienated from U.S. participation in the war because it has driven up prices and taken her husband.

Incredibly, the most subversive message in the film was overlooked by nearly everyone. In a closing monologue, Rogers addresses the audience (by way of confiding to her infant) that the social gains in American society secured by the sacrifices of her husband and others in the war against fascism would have to be protected after the war by continuing the struggle against domestic reactionaries. Trumbo phrased it more ambiguously, but there was no mistaking his meaning. Nearly 60 years later, THE MAJESTIC would pick up precisely this theme. 102 min.

Tension (1949)

MGM. Prod: Robert Sisk. Dir: John Berry.• Scr: Allen Rivkin (uncredited: John Berry). Story basis: John Klorer (unpublished). Cast: Richard Basehart, Audrey Totter, Cyd Charisse, Barry Sullivan, Lloyd Gough,• Tom D'Andrea, William Conrad

Police lieutenant Sullivan faces the camera at the beginning of this film and tells the audience that success in his racket depends on putting enough stress on the suspect: "when they're stressed so tight, they can't take it any more." And so it proves in a better-than-average noir.

Basehart is crushed when wife Totter takes off with another man, the shady Gough. He develops a second identity in a scheme to murder both of them—and then falls for Charisse, which gives him second thoughts about murder. Drawn to a beach house of Gough's, he discovers that the man has already been killed, and he is the inevitable suspect. The cheating wife/*femme fatale* is the real culprit, but the outcome is less important than the appearance of shadowy characters, nearly all of them cynical, and above all the obsessions (mostly revenge) that drive people over the edge.

This was an early showcase for Berry's directing talents, and not only that: he rewrote the script (according to his recollections) without taking any credit, and shot a scene with Basehart behind bars (neither approved nor funded by the studio), on an improvised set. 95 min.

Tenth Avenue Kid (1937)

Directed by Bernard Vorhaus• and scripted by Gordon Kahn• with a story basis by Kahn and Adele Buffington, this was the low-budget debut of child actor Tommy Ryan, won over from a neighborhood gang to law and order.

10:30 P.M. Summer (1966)

Argos/Jarilie. Prod: Jules Dassin,• Anatole Litvak. Dir: Jules Dassin. Scr: Jules Dassin, Marguerite Duras. Novel basis: Marguerite Duras, *Dix heures et demie du soir en été* (1960). Cast: Melina Mercouri, Romy Schneider, Peter Finch, Julián Mateos, Isabel María Pérez, Beatriz Savón

A little film aimed at the arthouse crowd and featuring Schneider (best remembered for *Last Tango in Paris*) as a bisexual youngster. Finch and his alcoholic wife Mercouri are tourists traveling in Spain with Schneider, both under stress for reasons that are never altogether clear. They are plunged into tragedy by an incident with a fugitive (supposed wife-killer Mateos) in a village. Mercouri's character may or may not have imagined that her husband is sleeping with Schneider; Schneider certainly is taking showers with

Mercouri. The novel by famed French writer Duras was too subjective for adequate film plotting, although Dassin and his cameramen almost make up the deficit with lovely night scenes. 85 min.

Terror in a Texas Town (1958)

Seltzer Films. Prod: Frank N. Seltzer. Dir: Joseph H. Lewis. Scr: Ben L. Perry (front for Dalton Trumbo,• uncredited). Cast: Sterling Hayden,† Sebastian Cabot, Nedrick Young,• Carol Kelly, Gene Martin, Victor Millan

A mind-bogglingly improbable movie and a vital, if obscure, document in the history of the blacklist. Young, who won an Oscar the same year under a pseudonym for co-writing THE DEFIANT ONES and wrote INHERIT THE WIND two years later, co-starred as a cheap gunman in this ultra-low budget western. Young's grim, unshaven face (he had been hired to replace Bogart at Warner Brothers when Bogey left that studio) menaces the town as the two-gun enforcer for local boss Cabot, who has hired him to get rid of all the local ranchers around Prairie City after he has secretly discovered oil.

The fly in the ointment is Hayden, in real life the penitent friendly witness who afterward toured the country to confess his error. Whaler Hayden returns from the high seas to avenge the death of his sod-busting father, dead at the hands of Cabot and Young. The picture features a western walkdown on Main Street that tops the shootout in JOHNNY GUITAR for campiness: a man bent on revenge and armed with nothing more than a whaler's harpoon and with a bad Swedish accent "draws" on gunslinger Young.

Luckily, the unlikely duel was directed by Lewis. Unluckily, this would prove to be the able Lewis' last film (he did some TV afterward), which he shot in ten days on a budget of $80,000, a daunting task for anyone save perhaps Ed Wood. There is one school of thought (although the number of critics who have actually seen the film is so small that opinion can hardly be said to be divided) that views the project as in part a comment on the stylistic excesses of Nicholas Ray and, more largely, the social conservatism that the genre had come to embody by 1958. It was in any case an odd departure for Trumbo and Young and a strange final note for Lewis, whose GUN CRAZY, also written by Trumbo, is a B-classic. 80 min.

That Midnight Kiss (1949)

MGM. Prod: Joe Pasternak. Dir: Norman Taurog. Scr: Tamara Hovey,• Bruce Manning. Cast: Kathryn Grayson, Mario Lanza, José Iturbi, Ethel Barrymore, Keenan Wynn, J. Carrol Naish, Jules Munshin

Lanza's debut, in a film that vaguely resembles his own personal climb from Philadelphia obscurity to operatic renown, with a love affair with upper-crust Grayson and plenty of music. Thin plot has Main Line dowager Barrymore, long ago a frustrated singer herself, bankrolling the campaign to launch a new opera company—in no small part so that her niece Grayson can become a star. After she finds her available male leads fat and middle-aged (what did she expect?), she discovers a truck driver (after giving up on a stage career, he used a GI loan to buy his vehicle) with a voice of gold and a handsome face. For non-operatic viewers, some of the best scenes feature Wynn as Lanza's blue-collar pal and manager, with fellow truck drivers as his kidding enthusiasts. As the Garfield films with the violin signal "Jewish," opera here signals "Italian," and the same basic quest of the ethnic masses to rise above their disadvantages through high culture. 96 min., color.

That Uncertain Feeling (1941)

Ernst Lubitsch/Sol Lesser Productions. Prod: Ernst Lubitsch. Dir: Ernst Lubitsch (uncredited: Sol Lesser). Scr: Donald Ogden Stewart• Adaptation: Walter Reisch. Play basis: Victorien Sardou, Emile de Najac, Divorçons (1883) Cast: Merle Oberon, Melvyn Douglas, Burgess Meredith, Alan Mowbray, Olive Blakeney, Harry Davenport, Eve Arden

An oversophisticated comedy about a neurotic wife (Oberon) who becomes convinced her "ideal" marriage to an insurance executive (Douglas) is the cause of her hiccups and insomnia. She consults a psychiatrist, and at the shrink's office she meets a wacky pianist (Meredith) who sweeps her off her feet.

Very much in the tradition of Stewart's early 1930s film comedies (and earlier Broadway hits) about adultery as an overrated concern of the American middle class. This adultery can be allowed to happen only at the emotional level, but Oberon clearly wants to shake up the marriage by any means possible, and Meredith is it. The film has lots of witty Stewart dialogue, not much action, and a disappointingly inevitable resolution. Still, it was the last of this kind of Stewart (and Lubitsch) film and with the highest production values (thanks to changing technology): a final look at a cinematic era. 84 min.

That Way with Women (1947)

Written by Leo Townsend,† this was a vehicle for Dane Clark, then a bobby-sox favorite, who falls for the daughter of a retired magnate, who plays cupid.

Theodora Goes Wild (1938)

Col. Prod: Harry Cohn. Dir: Richard Boleslawski. Scr: Sidney Buchman.• Story basis: Mary McCarthy. Cast: Irene Dunne, Melvyn Douglas, Thomas Mitchell, Thurston Hall, Elisabeth Risdon, Margaret McWade, Spring Byington

The first comedy role for a mesmerizing and very funny Dunne is a critical addition to the screwball genre and one of Buchman's best screenplays. It is also arguably the best of McCarthy, who was better remembered as an ex-Catholic who despised Communists and wrote THE GROUP; that, too, was directed by Buchman after he returned from the blacklist and was her last story to be filmed. Oddly—if only because *Theodora* was such a success—the rest of McCarthy's Hollywood career was undistinguished and she gave no hint of interest in her time there in her memoirs.

Although she is a church organist and Sunday school teacher, Dunne has written scandalous bestsellers from her small town in Connecticut. When the local paper serializes her latest story, the editor receives outraged complaints from none other than her respectable aunts (Risdon and McWade). After the serial is suppressed locally, she goes to Manhattan to see her publisher (Hall), who urges her to participate in a publicity campaign for the book. At first she demurs, but then begins to behave as she thinks her *nom de plume* would, having too much to drink and going to the apartment of her handsome illustrator (Douglas).

Although Dunne resists his advances, Douglas follows her to Connecticut and insists that she hire him as a gardener. They fall in love, she misses her church performance and follows him back to Manhattan, but fate intervenes. He cannot divorce his wife, notwithstanding their years-long separation, until his father, lieutenant governor of New York, retires from office. Defiant of bourgeois convention, Theodora moves into his apartment and holds a press conference there. The rest is erotic history. One of the scripts that the Breen office rejected on first sight because of its ridicule of small town and middle-class morality, but accepted in revised form. We'll never know what it lost. 94 min.

There Was a Crooked Man (1960)

Knightsbridge Films/Lopert. Prod: Albert Fennell, James Bridie. Dir: Stuart Burge. Scr: Reuben Ship.• Cast: Norman Wisdom, Alfred Marks, Andrew Cruickshank, Reginald Beckwith, Susannah York, Jean Clark, Timothy Bateson, P. Whitsun-Jones

Before the blacklist, which led to his deportation to Canada as an "enemy alien," Reuben Ship wrote radio scripts for *The Life of Riley*. After he was escorted to the border—on crutches and in handcuffs despite his osteomylitis—Ship wrote a celebrated radio play for the CBC called *The Investigator* (audio files are accessible online) in which a U.S. senator with a wheedling voice dies in a plane crash, goes to heaven on a "temporary visa" and finds it is his turn to be investigated (by Torquemada and Cotton Mather!). Ship had no film credits before the blacklist, and this caper film was his first.

A down-on-his-luck but honest demolitions expert is duped by a gang of crooks (headed by Marks) who intend to crack a bank vault. After the crime, the expert (Wisdom) becomes the fall guy and is caught and jailed. When he is released he goes straight and then notices a leading citizen in his Northern working-class village controlled by a swindler and vows to clean it up by any means at hand. The film is notable as York's screen debut—the honey Wisdom falls for in the factory town. 90 min.

These Are the Damned (1962)

Hammer Films/Col. Prod: Anthony Hinds. Dir: Joseph Losey.• Cast: Macdonald Carey, Shirley Anne Field, Viveca Lindfors, Alexander Knox, Oliver Reed, James Villiers

One of Losey's better-known films because of the haunting imagery of radioactive children locked in an underground vault by a national security madman of the familiar type. Their radioactivity, expressed as an extreme coldness of the hands, is thought to give them some kind of immunity to the effects of an imminent nuclear war. The children come to understand their fate, thanks to the intervention of a courageous figure from the Old Left (Carey), a middle-aged American exile in Britain—rather like Losey himself. The film has both an outer and an inner story. The inside story is about the radioactive kids (whose situation is not so different from that of THE BOY WITH GREEN HAIR in Losey's first film), and the outer story concerns a bunch of motorcycle teddy boys led by none other than Reed, who is insanely jealous of his attractive sister, whom he dangles as pickup bait for tourists like Carey before rolling them for their money. In a twist, the sister (Field) finds herself drawn to Carey, probably as a ticket out of the confinement of an English port city.

Not only the children "scientifically" prepared for all-out war, but those who are left to drift in the streets of a postindustrial city are, collectively, *The Damned*. 87 min.

They Gave Him a Gun (1937)

An antiwar picture with Spencer Tracy and Franchot Tone as World War I buddies. Tracy's character hates war but is a master marksman, and, in the postwar disillusionment, he becomes a mobster. A sentimental subplot in this movie written by Maurice Rapf• spoils the pacificist sentiment somewhat, but never entirely. There are several great speeches.

They Live in Fear (1944)

Interesting World War II propaganda film (written by Samuel Ornitz•) about an anti-Nazi teenager in Germany who helps a concentration camp victim and afterward flees to the United States, where fear for his family's fate makes adjustment difficult. In the spirit of Edward Dmytryk's•† HITLER'S CHILDREN.

They Shall Have Music (1939)

Samuel Goldwyn, Inc/UA. Prod: Samuel Goldwyn, Robert Riskin. Dir: Archie Mayo. Scr: John Howard Lawson.• Story basis: Imogen von Cube. Cast: Gene Reynolds, Jascha Heifetz, Joel McCrea, Walter Brennan, Marjorie Main, Porter Hall, Dolly Loehr (Diana Lynn), Terry Kilburn

One of the most entertaining of the proletarian uplift films. Poor kids yearning to listen to and play classical music look for an opportunity, which is almost stolen away but then restored, thanks to Heifetz (who plays six violin solos—the performance feature of the film, along with some remarkable kid piano playing and singing).

Child star Reynolds (decades later the producer of TV's M*A*S*H and still surrounded by left-wingers) is a bit of a delinquent with an abusive stepfather and a kindly mother (Main). His real father was a fiddler and left behind an instrument, which Reynolds finds and hocks, then buys back after he accidentally gets a ticket to hear Heifetz play. Though his stepfather smashes the violin, Reynolds happens upon a settlement house music school, with Loehr and McCrea in charge of administration, while kindly old Brennan is the real teacher. The school is about to go under, its instruments and furniture to be seized for nonpayment, but after various adventures (including the schoolchildren's mothers blockading the entrance against the cops—a very funny standoff) Heifetz is persuaded to come to a performance and saves the day. 109 min.

They Were So Young (1955)

Corona Cinematografica. Prod: Kurt Neumann. Dir: Kurt Neumann. Scr: Felix Lützkendorf, Kurt Neumann (uncredited: Dalton Trumbo,• Michael Wilson•). Cast: Scott Brady, Raymond Burr, Johanna Matz, Ingrid Stenn, Gert Fröbe

A German production on the imperial (and gender) theme of the American tycoon capitalist, played by Burr, who practically owns large sections of Brazil and is planning a government takeover. As the lead-in explains, an anonymous dead woman washed up on the beach at Rio unravels his plan.

Brady is an oil engineer who discovers that the young "models" trained and brought in from various parts of Europe are coerced into becoming call girls for Burr's clients. Matz, a lively German orphan, at first has difficulty convincing Brady of the existence of the white slavery racket, but he comes to believe her after Burr discovers her treachery and has her kidnapped hundreds of miles into the interior to shut her up. Brady manages to pick up her trail and free her. After they fall in love, he enlists in the struggle against empire. In and around the adventure and romance there is a lively description of the practices once known as colonialism and now called globalization. Very low production values belie an interesting and fast-moving story by two of the best writers of the blacklist, Trumbo and Wilson. In different hands and with a larger budget, it might have been a forties-style tropical noir. Alternatively entitled *Violated* and *Party Girls for Sale*. 80 min.

They Won't Believe Me (1947)

RKO. Prod: Joan Harrison. Dir: Irving Pichel.• Scr: Jonathan Latimer. Story basis: Gordon McDonell. Cast: Robert Young, Susan Hayward, Jane Greer, Rita Johnson, Tom Powers, George Tyne, Don Beddoe, Frank Ferguson, Harry Harvey

A neat noir with Young a vapid middle-class character on trial for the murder of his lover, pleading that he is a louse but not a killer. He married Johnson for money and position, while having an affair with Greer on the side and planning to run away with her. Appealing to his greed and still loving him, Johnson gets him to move to L.A., where she owns part of a stock brokerage. There he begins an affair with secretary Hayward, running off to Reno with her when Johnson finds out. From there, the tale spirals into a very noir conclusion.

Hardly a normal venue for Pichel, whose humanism dominated most of his large repertoire, the film is nonetheless one of the little-remembered gems of the genre, with bankrupt values of the California middle class posited as the heart of the modern malaise. 95 min.

They Won't Forget (1937)

WB. Prod: Mervyn LeRoy. Dir: Mervyn LeRoy. Scr: Robert Rossen,† Aben Kandel. Novel basis: Ward Greene, *Death in the Deep South* (1936). Cast: Lana Turner, Claude Rains, Otto Kruger, Allyn Joslyn, Elisha Cook, Jr., Edward Norris

Rossen's first successful script is one of the important social classics of the 1930s. A Southern factory girl is murdered and a Northern supervisor blamed. Shades of the notorious Leo Frank case, in which a Jewish factory owner was lynched by a Georgia mob for just such an alleged crime; in Rossen's home neighborhood, intellectual giant of the Jewish ghetto, Abe Cahan, devoted almost an entire volume of his personal memoirs to the Frank case.

The accused man's wife, played by Turner, joins his attorney, Kruger, in a hopeless defense against the prejudice of the town. This prejudice has been neatly redirected away from race (virtually impossible to treat in contemporary film) to decadent regionalism; the crowd lusts for vengeance and the news media exploit the story. Prosecuting attorney Rains, eager for a political career, performs brilliantly as the chief conspirator, concocting evidence and playing on the prejudices of the locals.

But it is the New Dealish ambience that seems most remarkable just a year or so after the Communist Party turned toward the Popular Front. Left filmmakers were evidently eager to make the turn, and the film offers a most revealing scene with the patrician governor seeking to save the defendant's life (he is soon dragged off a train and lynched anyway), perhaps reflecting more hope for enlightened leadership than the power of an enraged proletariat. All this works to the benefit of the drama, with Turner as the voice of justice, delivering the kind of moral address that would become more accepted as entertainment when the nation turned to war. 95 min.

Thieves' Highway (1949)

20th. Prod: Robert Bassler. Dir: Jules Dassin.• Scr: A. I. Bezzerides. Novel basis: A. I. Bezzerides, *Thieves' Market* (1949). Cast: Richard Conte, Valentina Cortesa, Lee J. Cobb,† Barbara Lawrence, Jack Oakie, Millard Mitchell, Joseph Pevney , Morris Carnovsky,• David Opatoshu

One of the late 1940s Dassin classics (along with BRUTE FORCE and NIGHT AND THE CITY) in which he displayed his talent for depicting the urban nightmare—before leaving for Europe to elude the blacklist. It also compares closely with Nicholas Ray's *They Live by Night* as an early road film with mythic qualities and tragedy tattooed all over the hopeless mission.

Ex-GI Conte arrives home in rural California to find his father crippled in a truck accident. Just as the world (and the screen, in sunny, wide shots) seems open and he plans to marry his old girlfriend Lawrence, he puts his savings into a surplus troop truck to sell apples in the produce market of San Francisco. Then he is injured when the truck slips off the jack as he fixes a flat. He is not seriously hurt physically, but emotionally he faces a constricting world. While he is distracted, his apples are sold on consignment by crooked wholesaler Cobb, who has two confederates steal the money from Conte. Lawrence arrives, finds him broke, and dumps him. Things do not turn out badly, but the corruption runs too deep for an entirely happy ending. There is an additional sense that the generation that stared death in the face during World War II would no longer accept the contrived happiness of traditional endings, though a qualified optimism could still survive. 94 min.

The Thin Man (1934)

MGM/Cosmopolitan Films. Prod: Hunt Stromberg. Dir: W. S. Van Dyke. Scr: Albert Hackett, Frances Goodrich. Novel basis: Dashiell Hammett,• *The Thin Man* (1932). Cast: William Powell, Myrna Loy, Maureen O'Sullivan, Nat Pendleton, Minna Gombell, Porter Hall, Henry Wadsworth, William Henry, Natalie Moorhead

The first of the Hammett-based films and a grand success, foreshadowing five more adventures in the Thin Man series and other, darker Hammett mysteries. It was one of the top ten box office hits of the year, and the greatest of lasting triumphs for the famous team of stars.

This success owed far less to plot than to the combination of antibourgeois ironies (with its parallel in the violence of the mobster films) and the chemistry of Powell and Loy. In this first episode, the respectable O'Sullivan's inventor father (Henry) leaves on a mysterious business trip shortly before her wedding, then goes missing. Her mother, remarried but broke, goes to see the father's current mistress (Moorhead) and finds her dead. Ex-police detective Powell becomes involved in the case with his wealthy mate Loy after she encourages him, and when their famously cute terrier, Asta, finds a skeleton in Henry's laboratory. Powell demonstrates that it belongs to Henry himself, and sets up a dinner party in which all the suspects are on hand. Powell solves the case neatly, but what fans liked so much, the Breen office hated: risqué remarks (Loy about her dresser: "What's that man doing in my drawers?"), heavy drinking and big city sophistication *in extremis.* 91 min.

The Thin Man Goes Home (1944)

MGM. Prod: Everett Riskin. Dir: Richard Thorpe. Scr: Robert Riskin, Dwight Taylor. Story basis: characters created by Dashiell Hammett,• *The Thin Man* (1932). Cast: William Powell, Myrna Loy, Lucile Watson, Gloria DeHaven, Anne Revere,• Donald Meek

The first of an intended new series of Thin Man adventures for the 1940s (the last was SONG OF THE THIN MAN). This one is remembered mainly because detective Powell goes back home and introduces to the audience his parents (Davenport and Watson), who had wanted him to be anything but a detective. Probably the weakest of the series in dramatic terms, but marginally antifascist in treating intrigues of an Axis espionage ring to steal paintings, resulting in two murders actually touched off by Powell's appearance in his home town. Old social-sexual chemistry of Powell and Loy is paramount, not far from Hammett's own life (with Lillian Hellman), like the heavy drinking all around and the novelist's enduring charm. 100 min.

The Thin Red Line (1965)

Security Pictures/AA. Prod: Sidney Harmon, Philip Yordan. Dir: Andrew Marton. Scr: Bernard Gordon.• Novel basis: James Jones, *The Thin Red Line* (1962). Cast: Keir Dullea, Jack Warden, Kieron Moore, James Philbrook, Robert Kanter, Ray Daley, Merlyn Yordan

Gordon wrote or directed no fewer than seven socially conscious films for deal-maker Yordan, who only gradually allowed the blacklisted writer to use his own name or take any credit. The best, by Gordon's own account, were based on novels he adapted himself, and this may have been the best of those. At any rate, it supposedly pleased the best-selling author of the original. The film offers a contrasting study of the patriotic and antifascist films that were produced during World War II or shortly afterward. In this unromanticized battle story, survival is the one thing on the mind of the soldiers and the key figures reach a sometimes creative desperation in tactics because they come to see survival as impossible.

Ordered to take a mountain fortress in the Pacific, C Company is positioned for disaster. Warden, the tough sergeant, warns against field officers thinking for themselves or wanting to save their men; it is too much of a luxury. The "Japs," meanwhile, are seen as sinister, but not for racial reasons; rather, they are the foes who adopt various tactics that the Americans might just as easily have chosen themselves.

A rare moment of ease between battles finds one soldier cross-dressing in a small group, then forced by Warden into the larger circle, where he faces psychological if not physical gang rape. At that moment, the Japanese attack. The handful of survivors decide to take the mountain fortress anyway. There Warden reaches his moment of truth. Alienation, fear and fanatical loyalty to the immediate group become the new lingua franca of the war film. 99 min.

Thirteen Women (1932)

RKO. Exec. Prod: David O. Selznick. Dir: George Archainbaud. Scr: Bartlett Cormack, Samuel Ornitz.• Novel basis: Tiffany Thayer, *Thirteen Women* (1932). Cast: Ricardo Cortez, Irene Dunne, Myrna Loy, Jill Esmond, Florence Eldridge, Kay Johnson, Julie Haydon, Harriet Hagman, Mary Duncan, Peg Entwistle

A perverse women's film and one of the rarities: a red script that can be seen as dabbling, if slightly, in the "Yellow Peril" theme. Loy is a half-Hindu, half-Javanese former college girl who managed to get into an exclusive academy, which she left because of ill treatment from her sorority sisters. Time has passed and the 12 sisters have gone on to husbands and families. The film traces her maddened revenge: teamed with a phoney swami (Gordon in heavy makeup), Loy writes letters to each of them, predicting personal tragedies and attempting to bring them all about. The power of suggestion is enough to cause some of the sisters to go over the edge—as British actress Entwhistle did in real life, committing suicide soon after production wrapped by jumping to her death off the cliff in the Hollywood Hills that bore the "Hollywoodland" sign.

Much of the film concerns Dunne, whose determination to save her son (Albright) from falling under the same curse opens the road to detective Cortez solving the evidently incomprehensible series of deaths. The reality of racist treatment of Loy at the sorority, which ruined her life as a "half-caste," only comes out at the end and too late to make much sense of the action. She is charming when she makes the "evil eye," though—a power that seems to provoke sleep. 73 min.

The 13th Letter (1951)

20th. Prod: Otto Preminger. Dir: Otto Preminger. Scr: Howard Koch.• Film basis: Georges Clouzot, *Le corbeau* (1943). Adapted from the novel by Louis Chavance, *Le corbeau* (1937). Cast: Linda Darnell, Charles Boyer, Michael Rennie, Constance Smith, Judith Evelyn, Guy Sorel, June Hedin, Camille Ducharme

A remake of Clouzot's notoriously cynical film *Le corbeau*, lightened up a tad for American audiences.

Someone is trying to destroy the reputation of a new doctor in a Quebec town with poison pen letters, but unlike the original, it's the whole town that is made rotten by these actions, not just a few unscrupulous busybodies. Koch turned the story on the discovery of who wrote the notes. Was it Boyer the old doctor, driven by jealousy; or Smith, his wife, obviously being ignored by Rennie; or could it be her sister Evelyn, an embittered old maid? Or someone else—Darnell, a troubled nurse with one leg shorter than another, or even Rennie, the young doctor himself, in some odd psychological gesture? The suicide of a World War II veteran casts new doubt upon the mentality of the inhabitants.

The atmosphere of fanatically Catholic small town Quebec is in itself interesting, a change from the usual treatment of American small towns traditionally depicted as too virtuous for what Chavance had in mind. But finally, in the atmosphere of psychosexual repression and potential revelation, it is the metaphor for McCarthyism that becomes the driving impulse of the film. 85 min.

Thirty Seconds Over Tokyo (1944)

MGM. Prod: Sam Zimbalist. Dir: Mervyn LeRoy. Scr: Dalton Trumbo.• Book basis: Ted W. Lawson and Robert Considine, *Thirty Seconds Over Tokyo* (1943). Cast: Spencer Tracy, Van Johnson, Robert Walker, Phyllis Thaxter, Tim Murdock, Scott McKay, Robert Mitchum

A film treatment adapted from the actual diary of one of the participants in the first bombing of the Japanese homeland by the United States in World War II. Air Force volunteers, under the supervision of famed Lt. Col. James Doolittle, set out to bomb Japan on a 1942 raid—with serious consequences for both sides. The planes carried out their mission, then crash-landed in China, with some surviving. The film traces the background life of flyer Johnson and his wife, Thaxter, the training received, transfer to a Navy aircraft carrier and the aftermath. With large sections done in virtual documentary form, it was, along with BACK TO BATAAN, the closest thing to a nonfictional film ever done by the reds working in the Office of War Information.

Seen in other terms, however, it has much the same feel as TENDER COMRADE, in the crescendo of emotions between warrior husband and pregnant wife, with the future of the nation at one with the child's future. Thaxter is invariably perky when not overwrought, and Johnson lacks the tiniest doubt about his role in combat, even when warned by avuncular Tracy that all those with family obligations should back out, with no hard feelings. Trumbo's internationalism is realized in the kindly Chi-

nese, who lavish the downed flyers with ancient jewelry and modern medical skill (feeding them, however, healthy vegetarian meals rather than the steak and french fries that they crave). Air combat scenes provide the most spine-tingling moments.

An instantly beloved piece of patriotism, the film was one of the top grossing of the winter season. It won an Academy Award for special effects (A. Arnold Gillespie, Donald Jahraus, Warren Newcombe) and a nomination for cinematography (Harold Rosson, Robert Surtees) and placed in several prestigious top ten "best" lists. 138 min.

This Gun for Hire (1942)

Paramount. Prod: Richard Blumenthal. Dir: Frank Tuttle.† Screenplay: Albert Maltz,• W. R. Burnett. Novel basis: Graham Greene, *A Gun for Sale* (1936). Cast: Alan Ladd, Veronica Lake, Robert Preston, Laird Cregar, Tully Marshall, Yvonne DeCarlo.

Linking noir moods to patriotic antifascism, this is by far the most dramatic of Maltz's scripts and one of Ladd's best films. Its good-bad criminal and its psychological complexity have appealed to French audiences and critics eager to pinpoint early and influential noir films

A professional gunman is hired by an obese and evil nightclub owner to kill a potential informant who might reveal the secret of a Los Angeles chemical magnate: he's selling chemical secrets to the Nazis. The gunman (Ladd) does the job but is given marked bills from an earlier robbery, attracting a police lieutenant to his trail. The cop is engaged to a dancer in a nightclub filled with government intrigue, and by chance it is the dancer whom Ladd kidnaps to cover his tracks. She comes to understand him as the product of an abusive home, a driven animal who urgently needs understanding. Will he get it? Does it matter?

Devotees of left-wing novelist Greene will find little here resembling his work; in the novel, the assassinated figure is a socialist minister, the last man in Europe who could prevent World War WII, but Hollywood could hardly mention that. Regardless, the film is a classic. 80 min.

This Island Earth (1955)

U-I. Prod: William Alland.† Dir: Joseph M. Newman. Scr: Franklin Coen, Edward G. O'Callaghan. Novel basis: Raymond F. Jones, *This Island Earth* (1952). Cast: Jeff Morrow, Faith Domergue, Rex Reason, Lance Fuller, Russell Johnson

A sci-fi film produced by William Alland finds jet pilot Morrow suddenly frozen in a green haze that strips him of control of his plane and then sets him down safely. He discovers that aliens have set up secret laboratories around the world to recruit earth scientists—purportedly to help bring world peace but, as our hero learns when he meets up with scientist Domergue, actually for some other, hidden purpose. As they reveal more and more of their authoritarian tendencies, guys with enormous prosthetic foreheads forbid the scientists to talk with each other, and finally spirit away Morrow and Domergue to a distant galaxy.

The two earthlings learn that the aliens are on the losing side in an interplanetary war that has depleted their uranium supplies; now they must find a new fissile material for fresh weapons to protect themselves against their own alien invaders. In a set that is too cheap to approach anything resembling good production values but so evocative even in its kitsch that it mimics surrealist paintings, the end of their planet and way of life becomes all too visible. Several of disillusioned Communist Alland's concerns are repeated here: fear of the secret totalitarianism of "intellectuals from the future" to save humanity from war, and an almost Trotskyist sense of mourning for a social revolution that could not survive the attacks of its internal enemies. 80 min., color.

Those Endearing Young Charms (1945)

RKO. Prod: Bert Granet. Dir: Lewis Allen. Scr: Jerome Chodorov.• Play basis: Edward Chodorov,• *Those Endearing Young Charms* (1943). Cast: Robert Young, Laraine Day, Ann Harding, Marc Cramer, Anne Jeffreys, Lawrence Tierney

A moody drama that, like *The Enchanted Cottage*, locates Robert Young perceptively in his real-life depressive character. This time he is an Air Force officer on leave in New York who steals the girlfriend of well-intentioned sap Tierney (repeating his wide-eyed role in Odets' DEADLINE AT DAWN). Perfume-counter clerk Day doesn't take too much effort to get stolen, but her innocence overwhelms the conscience of Young. Son of a department store owner, who has gone through life uncertain of what he wants except to use his power over people, he admits his manipulation, and more romantic angst occurs. Day's mother (Jeffreys), as so often in melodramas, had given up her chance at true happiness long before. Against a setting of men who anticipate possible death in battle, the struggle for a normal life is a trial. 81 min.

Thousands Cheer (1943)

MGM. Prod: Joe Pasternak. Dir: George Sidney. Scr: Paul Jarrico,• Richard Collins.† Story basis: Paul Jarrico. Cast:

Kathryn Grayson, Gene Kelly, Mary Astor, John Boles, Ben Blue, Frances Rafferty, Mary Elliott, Frank Jenks, Frank Sully, Dick Simmons, Ben Lessy, Mickey Rooney, Judy Garland, Red Skelton, Eleanor Powell, Ann Sothern, Lucille Ball, Lena Horne, Marsha Hunt•

There is lots of singing and dancing, not much dialogue and even less dramatic action in this MGM star parade. The film ends on a Popular Frontish choral anthem to the United Nations and the bright future ahead (with Grayson soloing against a spectacular background). It has little other social content but is a famous example of Hollywood Communist kitsch. The familiar progressive Gene Kelly is an aerialist who resents being drafted and taking military orders, all the more so when he falls for the colonel's daughter, Grayson. Returning for a special show with his family high-wire troupe, he must be reminded that only discipline turns a fool-crazy routine into a death-defying but perfectly executed stunt—just as soldiers like him will have to do in service abroad. Minor plots barely materialize or are lost in the livelier of numbers, like "Honeysuckle Rose," sung by Lena Horne. 126 min., color.

Three Faces West (1940)

Rep. Assoc. Prod: Sol C. Siegel. Dir: Bernard Vorhaus.• Scr: F. Hugh Herbert, Joseph Moncure March, Samuel Ornitz• (uncredited: Doris Anderson). Cast: Charles Coburn, John Wayne, Sigrid Gurie, Sonny Bupp, Russell Simpson

A curiously antifascist John Wayne western, notable for its evocation of rural values (rather than gunplay) and anti-Nazism that extends even to a critique of regressive nativism and praise for the "good German." Of all Wayne films (and despite his personal ties with a handful of individual lefties, such as Marguerite Roberts•), this doubtless comes closest to critical cinema.

The film opens with an appeal for American communities to accept refugee physicians from Europe. Coburn is splendidly typecast as the portly Austrian who had fled with his daughter to the new land. He accepts a position as community doctor in the Dust Bowl during a bitter winter, although his daughter (Gurie, anything but the average Wayne woman) at first despises the bleakness of the scene. Saving lives and mending the ill, Coburn quickly fits in, and Gurie falls for local farm leader Wayne. Romantic and other complications result when a former boyfriend (an antifascist who risked his life to save father and daughter) reappears as if from the dead. After a community decision to move to untilled land in Oregon, Wayne is put in charge of a kind of rural army. Lots of underlying themes of New Deal land programs, a sort of cooperative "people's development" entirely at odds with the subsidized individualism of the postwar era. 79 min.

Three Husbands (1950)
Gloria Productions. Prod: Isadore Goldsmith. Dir: Irving Reis. Scr: Edward Eliscu,• Gertrude Purcell,† Vera Caspary.• Story basis: Vera Caspary Cast: Eve Arden, Howard da Silva,• Ruth Warrick, Vanessa Brown, Sheppard Strudwick, Jane Darwell, Emlyn Williams, Billie Burke

A mildly interesting sex comedy, especially for the match-up of da Silva (soon to be blacklisted) and Arden (known to have non-left politics, but personally the strong female in radio and television's *Our Miss Brooks*). Here they present the bickering husband and wife risen from the working class to wealth in San Francisco but not made happy by it. The larger frame is a letter from a playboy, Strudwick, after his death to the husbands of three women, two of whom he squired around town and the other his nurse. Multiple triangles allow for many jabs at marriage in the postwar years of financial prosperity and emotional insecurity. The film was a sequel to *A Letter to Three Wives*. 78 min.

Three Kids and a Queen (1935)
Samuel Ornitz• and Mortimer Offner• wrote this class-based Depression comedy focusing on a ditzy rich lady who is indifferent to the ordinary materialist cravings of her class. May Robson's character is so eccentric that she buys a prime plot of urban land for her dog to run on and stops the construction of a skyscraper. As her relatives move to declare her incompetent, she has an accident during a carriage ride in the park and is taken in by the slum teens who were driving the car that hit the carriage. Once there, in modest surroundings, she learns to love the youngsters and to become more tolerant of humanity's foibles.

Three Married Men (1936)
A slight comedy from the talented if in Hollywood often under-utilized Dorothy Parker• (and husband Alan Campbell•) based on an unremarkable story by Owen Davis, Sr. Like Romeo and Juliet, the offspring of two commercial families fall in love and vow to marry despite an old feud between their families. Comic complications follow the efforts of her brothers to persuade the prospective groom (Roscoe Carns) of the pitiless drudgery of married life. He bucks up his courage by listening to recordings of advice

to young marrieds and dressing up in an outfit he imagines is seductive but that inspires in her (Mary Brian) nothing but humiliating laughter. Will the relationship survive the family feud and his feckless wooing?

Three Men in White (1944)
MGM. Prod: Carey Wilson. Dir: Willis Goldbeck. Scr: Martin Berkeley,† Harry Ruskin. Based on characters created by Max Brand. Cast: Lionel Barrymore, Van Johnson, Marilyn Maxwell, Keye Luke, Ava Gardner, Alma Kruger, Rags Ragland

The only one of the dozen popular Dr. Kildare series with notable Left connections, although the co-star of most of the series, Lew Ayers, was famed as a pacifist. The series was inspired in part by MEN IN WHITE, which owed its origins to the Group Theatre's early 1930s box-office triumph.

In the film version of novelist Brand's treatment of the hospital drama, romance and healing (with a heavy dose of tragedy) go hand in hand. Gruff but lovable Dr. Gillespie, played by Barrymore in a wheelchair, usually occupies the most footage, ordering subordinates around, instilling the doctorly (almost military) values of self-sacrifice with wisecracks on the side. Meanwhile, nurses and patients crave the co-star Ayers and, in later films, Van Johnson. A host of greater or lesser stars show up in minor parts, including Gene Lockhart, Lana Turner, Robert Young and even Red Skelton. No film lacked two or three subplots and none had the hospital gore later considered *de rigeur* for 1990s television successors like *Chicago Hope* and *ER*.

Three Men in White finds Marilyn Maxwell hot on Van Johnson, offering invitations to come up to her place as lascivious as the censors allowed (even with marriage implied later). He gets waylaid by Ava Gardner, who is taken in for drunken driving but turns out to be a seriously confused girl who relies on sedatives for her nerves. Meanwhile, Johnson and Keye Luke (in a notably sympathetic Asian-American role) compete for their appointment as Kildare's chief assistant—Luke wants a springboard to work in the New China, the only Popular Front reference. The film winds on pleasantly for those who like this kind of drama with a dash of comedy. 85 min.

Three on a Match (1932)
First National/WB. Prod: Darryl Zanuck (uncredited: Samuel Bischoff). Dir: Mervyn Le Roy. Scr: Lucien Hubbard, Kubec Glasmon, John Bright.• Cast: Joan Blondell,

Warren William, Ann Dvorak, Bette Davis, Grant Mitchell, Lyle Talbot, Glenda Farrell, Humphrey Bogart

Critics at the time considered this the least of Glasmon and Bright's half-dozen earliest for First National/Warners, despite a distinguished cast. It was subsequently viewed as one of those pre-Code gems of sin and near-realism—at least by the standards of what was to follow.

The title refers to the famous World War I warning against the supposed bad luck for three people to light their cigarettes on one match (because it would give time for a sniper to draw a bead). Here it's a metaphor for the lives of three women at risk. Former school mates Blondell, Dvorak and Davis set themselves up in various ways after meeting accidentally ten years after graduation. Blondell, a working-class girl, earlier let a man get her involved in unspecified criminal activity and did a term in jail. Upper-class Dvorak (especially good) is terribly bored with her stockbroker husband (William) and hangs out in cabarets drinking and dancing with good-for-nothing Talbot. Davis looks on as Dvorak (either an alcoholic or drug addict) leaves her husband and young son and falls into poverty, while Blondell marries the guy and takes over the home. Tragedy strikes as William tries to recoup his gambling debts by helping crooks Talbot, Phelps and (bit actor) Bogart kidnap the kid.

The best part of the film is the experimental use of newsreels (the stock market crash, and repeated predictions by Wall Street that things will turn around soon), and laconic comments by people about the crisis of the society at large. 64 min.

Three Russian Girls (1944)

UA. Prod: Gregor Rabinovitch. Dir: Fyodor Otsep, Henry S. Kessler. Scr: Aben Kandel, Dan James.• Adaptation: Maurice Clark, Victor Trivas. Film basis: Serge Mikhailov, Mikhail Rosenberg, *The Girl from Leningrad* (1941). Cast: Anna Sten, Kent Smith, Mimi Forsythe, Alexander Granach, Kathy Frye, Paul Guilfoyle, Dorothy Gray, Feodor Chalipin, Jr.

An American remake of a Russian film with a famed Russian director and actor on hand. Didactic, like the original, it tells the heroic story of Russia's volunteer nurses at the front in 1941. Smith, an American technical engineer, is injured in a plane crash and brought into a Red Cross unit headed by the tough Sten. They develop a mild romance as he pulls back from death's door. The whole operation has to be moved as the Germans force evacuation of Leningrad, then moved again as the Soviets counterattack. Footage from the Soviet production details

military and medical operations in subzero weather, and it's better dramatic material than most of television's *World at War*. Too earnest, but an unforgettable period piece by James; he was a close friend of Leonardo Bercovici• but never successful in films, with the brief exception of two British horror features toward the end of his life (written under assumed names), *Behemoth* and *Gorgo*. This film won an Academy Award for cinematography. 80 min.

Three Strangers (1946)

WB. Prod: Wolfgang Reinhardt. Dir: Jean Negulesco. Scr: John Huston, Howard Koch.• Cast: Sydney Greenstreet, Geraldine Fitzgerald, Peter Lorre, Joan Lorring, Robert Shayne, Marjorie Riordan

An unusual film that marks the first notable script collaboration of Huston and the Left, en route to several more before his allies were cut down by the blacklist. Rather than a social theme per se, this offbeat and sometimes disjointed film fatefully brings together three unhappy people.

Lorre, who gets the best part, is a drunk and small-time crook who hangs out in lower-class London's mean streets, while sweet Joan Lorring attempts somehow to save him from his inevitable end. Fitzgerald is a distraught woman separated from her husband, who returns from London to announce that he wants a divorce. Greenstreet is a mediocre businessman. They share a lottery ticket and are destined to win (because, most improbably, a statue of a goddess in Fitzgerald's apartment grants such a favor), but turn out to be utterly ill-suited to enjoy their good fortune. Something is definitely off here, and it just may be the sublimated recognition of the unpleasant society emerging from the great war against fascism. 92 min.

Thunder Below (1932)

Para. Prod: Unknown. Dir: Richard Wallace. Scr: Sidney Buchman,• Josephine Lovett. Novel basis: Thomas Rourke, *Thunder Below* (1931). Cast: Tallulah Bankhead, Charles Bickford, Paul Lukas, Eugene Pallette, Ralph Forbes, Leslie Fenton, James Finlayson, Edward Van Sloan

In this melodramatic love triangle Bickford never suspects that his best friend (Lukas) is secretly in love with his wife (Bankhead), and that she loves the rival in return. Together in a bungalow in the imaginary Central America republic of San Mateo, oil geologist Bickford learns that he is going blind. Yet another love possibility, oil man Forbes, appears on the scene and woos Bankhead, arousing Bickford's rage. After being ordered from the camp, he leaves with Bankhead, followed closely by Lukas. Bankhead resolves the confusion in a rather indelicate manner. The undirected and then love-directed anxiety of the modern woman also has a certain charm. Briefly allied with the Left and then swinging violently rightward, sometime coke-head Bankhead could be quite an actress. 67 min.

Till the End of Time (1946)

RKO/Vanguard. Prod: Dore Schary. Dir: Edward Dmytryk.•† Scr: Allen Rivkin, Novel basis: Niven Busch, *They Dream of Home* (1944). Cast: Dorothy McGuire, Guy Madison, Robert Mitchum, Bill Williams, Tom Tully, William Gargan, Jean Porter, Ruth Nelson

Dmytryk's version of the themes of the more distinguished *Best Years of Our Lives* (released a few months before): servicemen returning to civilian and especially to family life. It's also far and away the most serious film by Madison, known for his B-work and destined to make television's *Wild Bill Hickock* his real occupation.

Ex-Marine Madison, who was hardly out of high school before leaving for war, is back at home in small town California and can't convince his parents, Tully and Nelson, that he must work out his own life off the beaten track. Meanwhile, he falls for war widow McGuire in a troubled relationship that has each misinterpreting the other, then breaking off, only to yearn for reconciliation. His two pals, Mitchum and Williams, are in worse shape: the former has a silver plate in his head (a metaphor for ex-servicemen's psychological instability), and the latter is a prizefighter who has lost his legs and his occupation.

Dmytryk's (and Rivkin's) special pleading for Left causes is just a bit contrived, such as a barroom scene during which the trio confront anti-Semitism and right-wing veterans organizations. If not for *Best Years*, this movie likely would have survived with more credibility. At least the title song, based on Chopin, was a big hit. 105 min.

Timber Stampede (1940)

RKO. Prod: Bert Gilroy. Dir: David Howard. Scr: Morton Grant.• Cast: George O'Brien, Marjorie Reynolds, Chill Wills, Morgan Wallace, Guy Usher, Earl Dwire, Frank Hagney, Robert Fiske, Robert Burns

A politically interesting shoot-'em-up. Dunlap is the virile cowboy whose dad (Dwire) owns the town newspaper of Wagon Wheel. Into this relative paradise come the timber barons and swindlers—Wallace, Fiske, and their stooge-sheriff Burns—promising to bring needed "development" to the territory.

Female angle: Reynolds is a newspaperwoman covering what she thinks is railroad progress (the train line has only been created to haul out lumber). She takes over the paper from her father, whose mortgage has been seized. She is the mouthpiece of the new bosses, hardly noticing such outrages as taverns re-signed to prohibit cowboys, as actually happened in a few Calvinist Kansas towns. The swindlers arrange faked homesteading papers for dozens of drifters and scalawags, planning to steal the lumber—until O'Brien gets into action. Wills, en route to big parts as a sidekick of the greats, is notable as the tall tale–telling pardner who has not quite perfected his act of being permanently silly. 59 min.

Time Without Pity (1957)

Harlequin Productions Ltd. Prod: John Arnold, Anthony Simmons. Dir: Joseph Losey.• Scr: Ben Barzman.• Play basis: Emlyn Williams, *Someone Waiting* (1956). Cast: Michael Redgrave, Leo McKern, Ann Todd, Paul Daneman, Peter Cushing, Alec McCowen, Renee Houston

An all but forgotten melodrama from Joseph Losey's early British period with more than a few riveting moments, thanks largely to a superb performance by Redgrave and Losey's mastery of the noir narrative.

A young man is sentenced to death for the murder of his girlfriend, and his father (Redgrave) a fumbling journalist and alcoholic who has not been much of a father, arrives in England from Canada to see what he can do about his son. His son rejects his help, but, convinced of his innocence, Redgrave undertakes his own investigative reporting to find the real murderer in the few hours left until the scheduled execution. How he copes with the tycoon (McKern, later Rumpole of the Bailey), whom he comes to believe did the deed, not to mention his own desire to take a drink, is expertly handled, if not much more than the kind of B-film Losey handled so expertly in Hollywood. 88 min.

To the Ends of the Earth (1948)

Kennedy-Buchman Pictures/Col. Prod: Sidney Buchman.• Dir: Robert Stevenson (uncredited: Sidney Buchman). Scr: Jay Richard Kennedy. Cast: Dick Powell, Signe Hasso, Ludwig Donath, Vladimir Sokoloff, Edgar Barrier, John Hoyt, Luis Van Rooten, Fritz Leiber, Vernon Steele, Peter Virgo

A big production, reputedly costing $2 million, arranged by Buchman in praise of the very government that was poised to ruin him. Ironically, the Motion Picture Association had a difficult time persuading assorted church and civic groups of its virtue, and even the Production Code regulations had to be modified just to handle the subject of drug smuggling. Introductory sequences were shot inside the narcotics division of the Treasury Department.

This is clearly the extension of the wartime Popular Front as Powell, in the service of the real-life (and plenty ominous) national drug czar of the day, Harry J. Anslinger—who appears briefly on camera as himself—tracks down the source of opium-making poppies. Beginning in Shanghai, where he meets and flirts with the suspicious Hasso, he traces the source of the drug back to the Middle East. A bit of "Yellow Peril"—and Persian Peril, for that matter—are thrown in, but not overdone as badly as the politics of drug interdiction. Too bad Powell didn't uncover the CIA connection, which by this time was sending the horse through reliably anticommunist French mobsters. Nevertheless, the drama is well-staged, with good performances all around, a certain moral ambiguity and a fine surprise ending. Even the Asians are not so otherized as a decade earlier. 109 min.

Together Again (1944)

Col. Prod: Virginia Van Upp. Dir: Charles Vidor. Story basis: Stanley Russell, Herbert Biberman.• Cast: Irene Dunne, Charles Boyer, Charles Coburn, Mona Freeman, Jerome Courtland, Elizabeth Patterson, Charles Dingle, Shelley Winters

Boyer chases Dunne, the widow of a mayor of a small Vermont town who has carried on in his office out of a sense of obligation. Coming to New York to hire a sculptor for a statue of her late husband for the town square, she hires Boyer and is mistaken for a striptease dancer in a nightclub while at dinner. She fires him, but he shows up in town anyway to do the work and woo the mayoress. A bit of woman-who-doesn't-want-a-career sentiment, but mostly romantic nonsense of the usual kind and of interest only to see what SALT OF THE EArth director Biberman was up to a decade earlier. 96 min.

Tom, Dick and Harry (1941)

RKO. Prod: Robert Sisk. Dir: Garson Kanin. Scr: Paul Jarrico.• Story basis: Paul Jarrico. Cast: Ginger Rogers, George Murphy, Burgess Meredith, Alan Marshal, Phil Silvers

On its face, a Rogers vehicle in which an apparently empty-headed bride confronts the problems of marriage and class in the modern age. But dream sequences are used effectively as political satire (a rarity), and the consequences of marriage for women are explored. Comparing one potential suitor to another, Rogers slowly realizes that neither the capitalist nor the salesman (played with special vigor by future right-wing senator Murphy) would be a good partner.

According to Jarrico, the lead had been written for Jean Arthur. The casting of Rogers meant loads of simpering, which took the edge off the satire and reduced the protagonist to silliness. *Tom, Dick and Harry* could rightly be compared to KITTY FOYLE, in which Rogers' limited talent for portraying a woman's subjectivity was much stronger.

The film nevertheless was considered one of the year's ten best, and scriptwriter Jarrico and his partners received an Academy Award nomination—one of the first for left-wing writers after the prestigious Donald Ogden Stewart• and a promise of better assignments to come. Today it may be best remembered as the film that introduced longtime burlesque top banana Phil Silvers, this time playing an annoying ice cream salesmen. 86 min.

Tomahawk (1951)

U-I. Prod: Leonard Goldstein. Dir: George Sherman. Scr: Silvia Richards,† Maurice Geraghty. Story basis: Daniel Jarrett. Cast: Van Heflin, Yvonne De Carlo, Alex Nicol, Preston Foster, Jack Oakie, Tom Tully, John War Eagle, Rock Hudson

An A-western, thanks more to its big stars than its script or direction. But its hints of pro-Indian sentiment were still rare in 1951, and particularly interesting in a biopic of Jim Bridger (Heflin), a distinctly lesser Daniel Boone. It turns out that Colonel Bridger actually likes Indians for all the reasons he has fled civilization (while willingly leading it westward into Indian territory), but his lieutenant (Nicol) is more bloodthirsty than any Indian around.

Into this duel of nerves and continual battles in Technicolor comes *chanteuse* De Carlo and her wagon-train show, looking remarkably out of place—but, by endangering herself, commanding the interest of the good Heflin. Reviewers pointed out that at this real historical juncture, Bridger was in his middle sixties. 82 min., color.

Tomorrow is Another Day (1951)

First National/WB. Prod: Henry Blanke. Dir: Felix E. Feist. Scr: Art Cohn, Guy Endore.• Story basis: Guy Endore. Cast: Ruth Roman, Steve Cochran, Lurene Tuttle, Ray Teal, Morris Ankrum

An interesting, low budget near-noir about an unhardened con, a couple on the run and the potentially redemptive power of blue-collar community. Cochran is just out of the can after a considerable stretch, hardly knows where to turn and is almost ensnared in more crime when he leaves L.A. for New York. There, he meets bottle-blonde taxi dancer Roman, who inadvertently tangles him up in worse trouble by implicating him in the killing of her mobbed-up former boyfriend.

The pair go on the lam together in a journey that includes riding the rails and lots of hoofing. Finally they get to central California, where kindly Teal tells them about the open-air joys of lettuce picking. Amazingly, we see no Latinos here, just the remnant of Okies and Arkies from another era living in extreme modesty but treating each other with great decency. Cochran and Roman (now a brunette), play husband and wife but fall in love for real—until exposure threatens and a final adventure intervenes.

If the film feels a bit outdated, it's only because the genre went in a different direction. But it remains an important bridge between the noir genre of the 1940s and the youth-rebel road films of the 1950s, showing the continuity more directly than perhaps any other movie of the period. Much of the accomplishment must be attributed to the great Endore and his unique sensibility. 90 min.

Tomorrow Is Forever (1946)
International Pictures/RKO. Prod: David Lewis. Dir: Irving Pichel.• Scr: Gwen Bristow, Lenore J. Coffee. Story basis: Gwen Bristow. Cast: Claudette Colbert, Orson Welles, George Brent, Lucile Watson, Richard Long, Natalie Wood

This wartime melodrama appeared too late for the war issues to have maximum impact and begins slowly, but, with Pichel's acute direction of an above-average vehicle for Colbert and Welles, it still has vivid moments toward the climax. Welles goes off to World War I after a few years of marriage to Colbert and is announced dead on virtually the last day of the war in a government telegram to Colbert, who is crushed by the news. Pregnant, she is taken in during her grief and then married by kindly businessman Brent.

Twenty years later, on the verge of another world conflict, Welles returns, so terribly disfigured that she does not recognize him at first (the odds of this, or of Welles going to work for her second husband, as the plot calls for, require a great suspension of disbelief). Meanwhile, their son contemplates joining the RAF to fight the Nazis. His adopted daughter (a charming

Watson), orphan of parents murdered by the Nazis, adds emotional weight to the call to antifascist combat. Moments of Welles reading Tom Paine with son Richard Long must stand among the best examples of patriotic kitsch of left-wing filmmaking. 105 min.

Tomorrow, the World! (1944)
Lester Cowan Productions. Prod: Lester Cowan, David Hall. Dir: Leslie Fenton. Scr: Ring Lardner, Jr.,• Leopold Atlas.† Play basis: James Gow, Arnaud d'Usseau,• *Tomorrow the World* (1943). Cast: Frederic March, Betty Field, Agnes Moorehead, Joan Carroll, Edit Angold, Skippy Homeier

Adapation of the successful stage play that was the apex of d'Usseau's career and in the mold of the red-written propaganda plays in the forties that focused on children as the hope for a German future without fascism. Again, an indoctrinated German boy (Homeier, reprising his stage role) is taken in by a welcoming liberal U.S. family; he is suspicious and aloof until he is softened by the generosity of the community he has joined.

The wartime collaborations of Gow and d'Usseau attracted the attention of Sen. Joseph McCarthy's investigating committee in 1953, which (according to documents released in 2003) summoned d'Usseau to face secret questioning from McCarthy aide Roy Cohn. "COHN: How about James Gow, the co-author, was he a member of the Communist party? D'USSEAU: He is dead. COHN: Was he a member of the Communist party? D'USSEAU: Do you want me to dig him up and ask him?" Apparently considered too hot to handle, D'Usseau was spared further questioning. 86 min.

Tomorrow We Live (1942)
A project of cult director Edgar G. Ulmer and producer Seymour Nebenzal, who financed both the German (Lang) and the U.S. (Losey) productions of the classic M. Financing and distribution came from the rock-bottom Producers Releasing Corp., known for its microbudgets. The film is further interesting for being one of the rare solo original screenplays by later friendly witness Bart Lytton.† Sadly, the movie itself is a mess, though the early treatment of urban gangsters exiled in the desert is prophetic. Coed Jean Parker goes back home to her "Pop's" café in the middle of the Arizona desert to be propositioned by "the Ghost" (Ricardo Cortez), the tough guy who owns everything in sight, including a nightclub called The Dunes—13 years before the Vegas casino-hotel of the same name was built. One critic said it was "a little

picture that confuses itself beyond the point of bearing any analysis," a most portable phrase. 64 min.

Tonight We Raid Calais (1943)

20th. Prod: Andre Daven. Dir: John Brahm. Scr: Waldo Salt.• Story basis: L. Willinger, Rohama Lee. Cast: Annabella, John Sutton, Lee J. Cobb,† Beulah Bondi, Blanche Yurka, Howard da Silva,• Marcel Dalio

One of those war action films later ridiculed for its melodrama, inadequate sets and thin plotting—nor was it the talented Salt's finest hour by a long stretch. But the film earnestly seeks to portray occupied France of 1942, with British pilot Sutton landing behind enemy lines. He must elude the Nazis and negotiate with a French peasant family that includes mom (Bondi), dad (Cobb) and the difficult daughter (Annabella) enraged at the British for sinking French ships and inadvertently killing her brother. Annabella changes her mind when Nazis execute Cobb (with a Stalin-style mustache) and Bondi. Da Silva is a Nazi villain as in other films (memorably REUNION IN FRANCE), Yurka the widow who leads French peasants in field-burning to aid the British. Too many close escapes in the film rival cowboy B-flicks, but the conclusion is genuinely moving. 70 min.

Too Late for Tears (1949)

UA/Streamline Pictures. Prod: Hunt Stromberg. Dir: Byron Haskin. Scr: Roy Huggins.† Novel basis: Roy Huggins, Too Late for Tears (1947). Cast: Lizabeth Scott, Don DeFore, Arthur Kennedy, Kristine Miller, Barry Kelley, Denver Pyle

A noir of minor importance puts the greedy and murderous Scott at center stage when she and her second husband (the first was a suicide) suddenly get $60,000 in stolen cash mysteriously tossed into their moving car and must decide what to do with it. Duryea, an erstwhile petty criminal who blackmailed an executive into swindling the cash from insurance premiums, appears when Scott's husband is at work and demands the money. Realizing her husband is too "weak" to hang onto the prize, Scott sets out on a murderous plan that is chilling even by noir standards.

Here and there the film, based on a Huggins novel serialized in the Saturday Evening Post, moves beyond crime drama to look at seedy Los Angeles and the desperation of the lower-middle class (as Scott describes her background) to escape the ranks of those near the working class into luxury and excitement. Huggins, who went on to produce The Rockford Files, television's all-time most popular detective show in residuals (his

sometime writer, Meta Rosenberg, was also a friendly witness) had often tried out the noir theme in his early days on the Left. 99 min.

Top Banana (1954)

Roadshow Productions/UA. Prod: Ben Peskay, Albert Zugsmith. Dir: Alfred E. Green. Scr: Paula Stone, Mike Sloane. Play basis: Hy Kraft,• Johnny Mercer, Top Banana (1951). Cast: Phil Silvers, Danny Scholl, Rose Marie, Judy Lynn, Jack Albertson, Herbie Faye

A movie version of Phil Silvers' nostalgic look at burlesque, with the name of Kraft, the writer for the Broadway hit's book, suppressed from the Hollywood version. A vehicle for Silvers (then at the height of his fame as television's Sergeant Bilko), it's an anthology of his routines filmed in the Winter Garden Theater, with a weak love story and lots of music.

Silvers is Jerry Biffle, a Milton Berle–like television star who has risen to fame in the burlesque circuit and manages to maintain much the same persona on the small screen. The bumps-and-grinds and the double-entendre jokes are perhaps the least offensive ever heard anywhere; somehow, the absolute sexualization of burlesque women has been rewritten as mere showbiz pizzazz and the legendary horniness of the top banana is reduced to mere girl watching.

As the plot stumbles along, Biffle manipulates those around him to move his intended sweetie (Rose Marie) up the success ladder—and, unintentionally, into the arms of his romantic rival (Scholl). This new romance helps introduce endless love songs but is only incidental to Silvers' rapid patter, his censored recuperation of burlesque routines and above all his dialogue with gofers Albertson and Faye. For decades afterward, Faye remained a favorite of burlesque revivals as well as a beloved television commercial actor. 100 min., color.

Topkapi (1964)

Filmways Pictures/UA. Prod: Jules Dassin.• Dir: Jules Dassin. Scr: Monja Danischewsky. Novel basis: Eric Ambler, The Light of the Day (1964). Cast: Peter Ustinov, Melina Mercouri, Maximillian Schell, Robert Morley, Akim Tamiroff

Comic version of the caper film with two layers of added crypto-political interest: daily life in Istanbul, as seen in colorful footage of the exotic as workaday; and the operations of a police state revealed and ridiculed.

Mercouri, Schell, Morley and Tamiroff are practiced thieves planning the heist of their careers, the Topkapi

Palace Museum. They hire the engaging petty hustler and small-time smuggler Ustinov to bring in a car from Greece, but he is picked up by Turkish security forces, convinced that an assassination plot is underway to discredit the Turkish state. Working as a double-agent (but a bumbling one), Ustinov goes along with the caper, for which the troupe spends much time and energy in various technical preparations. Mercouri, recast from earlier Dassin films, seems out of place; the rest have unusual charm, especially the perennially fey Morley.

Ultimately, things fall apart, but not because security forces have any idea what is going on. Confusion after confusion reveals a world befuddled both by materialism and the craving for control, a world at which one can only laugh. Dassin's satire on himself in RIFIFI. 122 min., color.

Toys in the Attic (1963)
Claude Prod./Mirisch Corp./UA. Prod: Walter Mirisch. Dir: George Roy Hill. Scr: James Poe. Play basis: Lillian Hellman, *Toys in the Attic* (1960). Cast: Dean Martin, Geraldine Page, Yevette Mimeux, Wendy Hiller, Gene Tierney, Nan Martin, Larry Gates, Frank Silvera, Charles Lampkin

A savage play, a psychically violent counterpart to Hellman's forties Southern films—and undoubtedly a measure of revenge against American blacklisting of the avant-garde in Hollywood. Incest, imbecility and adultery abound in decadent New Orleans as Martin returns home with child bride Mimieux, bringing calamity to the household. Martin's role is one of the few serious ones in his career, and he succeeds better than might be imagined.

Page, as the spinster sister whose lust for Martin is the closeted secret of the family, gives a good performance even though the ending is changed to suit movie audiences. Mother Tierney is having an affair with the African American Silvera, and so on. Perhaps the transition from play to film was simply too difficult, or perhaps the real edge had been worn off Hellman's vision of Confederate cupidity as a key to the dark side of the American character. The interracial romance theme, even at this late date, was controversial, however, and her use of it remains historically interesting. 90 min., color.

Traffic in Crime (1946)
A typical gang-buster show, written by David Lang.† Police spy Kane Richmond is out to bust up gambling syndicates in small town America, here conveniently in the California fruit district. He meets hoods, a gun moll with an eye for him and the sweet girl who is destined for

him. He comes up with a successful plan to get the two mobs to shoot each other, Hammett-style, sparing police the trouble.

The Train (1964)
UA. Prod: Jules Bricken. Dir: John Frankenheimer, Arthur Penn. Scr: Franklin Coen, Frank Davis (uncredited script contribution: Walter Bernstein●). Book basis: Rose Valland, *Le Font de l'Art.* (N.d.) Cast: Burt Lancaster, Paul Scofield, Jeanne Moreau, Michel Simon, Suzanne Flon, Wolfgang Preiss, Richard Münch

One of the most impressive World War II films of its era: glossy, really long and documentary in style. In this case, the Nazis (one in particular, a colonel played by Scofield) are smuggling the contents of France's great art museums to Germany near the end of the war. Antifascist Lancaster is on the job to foil the heist until the Allies arrive, and no matter the cost in human lives to prevent the looting of priceless objects, it's demanded for the French nation's élan. Hardly anything else happens. Shot beautifully in black and white. 133 min.

Trapped By Television (1936)
Col. Prod: Allen G. Siegler. Dir: Del Lord. Scr: Lee Loeb, Harold Buchman.● Story basis: Sherman Lowe, Al Martin. Cast: Mary Astor, Lyle Talbot, Nat Pendleton, Thurston Hall, Henry Mollison, Wyrley Birch, Robert Strange, Marc Lawrence†

The film is interesting mainly as an anticipation of the then-experimental medium. Television inventor Talbot gets a job as bill collector to see him though while he invents TV. Seeking a collection from Astor, he runs into a maze of plots within the Paragon Broadcasting Company. When Astor helps Talbot get a demonstration of his machine, manager Strange sabotages the effort. Astor even pawns her fur coat for working capital, and when Strange sends thugs to beat up the couple, she turns on the transmitting mechanism, broadcasting the fracas and bringing the cops. 64 min.

The Traveling Saleswoman (1950)
Col./Joan Davis Productions. Prod: Tony Owen. Dir: Charles Riesner. Scr: Howard Dimsdale.● Cast: Joan Davis, Andy Devine, Adele Jergens, Chief Thundercloud

Remake of *Traveling Saleslady* (1935) with Joan Davis replacing Joan Blondell, selling her father's soap, instead of the toothpaste made by her father's competitor in the earlier version. Usually considered inferior to the original's higher production values, it is full of charming moments with Davis, who made it a "Joan Davis Production" and shortly after launched a syndicated television comedy—the only show ever to negotiate a contract with the blacklisted Television Writers of America.

Faced with her father's imminent financial collapse, Joan goes on the road, replacing her incompetent fiancée, Devine. Heading west from Pennsylvania, she finds herself somehow in a cow town near Indian Territory. She becomes hilariously drunk, precipitates the first of several slapstick brawls (she does some mock Errol Flynn chandelier-swinging), and heads out, but is captured by the reputedly ferocious Indians. She helps the chief with his dandruff and promptly wins his friendship, later saving the town and finding the needed workforce for the soap factory she has inherited. Rather than the standard racist treatments of the time, Davis offers a woman's hand, healing all misunderstanding. She also explains the function of a girdle to Devine: "You know where it says in the Constitution that all men are equal? This does the same thing for women." 75 min.

Treasure Island (1934)

MGM. Prod: Hunt Stromberg. Dir: Victor Fleming. Scr: John Lee Mahin (contribution to treatment: John Howard Lawson,• Leonard Praskins). Novel basis: Robert Louis Stevenson, *Treasure Island* (1883). Cast: Jackie Cooper, Wallace Beery, Lionel Barrymore, Otto Kruger, Lewis Stone, Nigel Bruce, Charles "Chic" Sale, Douglass Dumbrille

Of the four film versions, this is the best or second-best (lacking the "ahr ahr" Long John Silver played by Robert Newton in the 1950 Disney version), though the 1972 British film with Orson Welles and Lionel Stander also has its moments. This one is played over the top by just about all concerned. Cooper is too sweet and innocent to be believed, but Barrymore as the alcoholic seaman dying in the eighteenth-century English roadhouse owned by Cooper's widowed mother comes off splendidly. Stone and Kruger are fine as the bourgeois investors in the plan to find the treasure depicted on the dead captain's map, and Beery is the best as Long John Silver, leading the rebellious crew in an attempt to beat the gentry to the prize.

Vaudeville comic "Chic" Sale marvelously plays Ben Gunn, the fabled refugee of the novel left behind by the pirates years earlier, living Robinson Crusoe–like but becoming daffy. Rapport between one-legged rascal Beery and the boy idealist takes up much of second half of the film. The ending is splendid, with Beery lying like a

trouper to the last second of the film, but delivering the sentimental lines that keep little Jackie tearful. Lots of adventure and very high quality production values for the period almost make the seafaring realistic; but what part of the plundered Third World was that treasure island in, anyway? 105 min.

A Tree Grows in Brooklyn (1945)

20th. Prod: Louis D. Lighton. Dir: Elia Kazan.† Scr: Tess Slesinger, Frank Davis (uncredited: Anita Loos). Novel basis: Betty Smith, *A Tree Grows in Brooklyn* (1943). Cast: Dorothy McGuire, Joan Blondell, James Dunn, Lloyd Nolan, Peggy Ann Garner, James Gleason, Ted Donaldson

A theatrical, triumphant transfer of a novel to film—overlong, slow and overwhelmingly sentimental in parts but never quiet maudlin. Along with PINKY and GENTLEMAN'S AGREEMENT, as uncompromisingly humanistic (without the standard celebration of American materialism) as Kazan got before his friendly testimony—or after. This owes much to Slesinger (a disillusioned left-winger from the 1930s) and Davis, and even more to Smith's novel, but Kazan's direction effectively captured a public perception of New York tenement life.

The Williamsburg Irish family of the tale is always on the verge of total impoverishment. Dorothy McGuire, who plays mom, washes tenement steps to help cover the mounting family bills; Blondell, an aunt and constant presence, seems perpetually switching husbands; Ted Donaldson, the beloved youngest, wants food variety the family can't afford. But the real key players are dad (Dunn), who means well but is melancholy and given to boozing, and a teenager (Garner, obviously the author's stand-in), who wants to grow up and be a writer. A new baby on the way means that Dunn's hope to be a great singing waiter goes down the drain (he comes home late, his tips blown on drinks), but he is determined to find work somehow so that Garner can continue in school. Eventually he dies trying, of pneumonia. The tree grows in spite of everything, bent and twisted but a survivor. 128 min.

Triple Justice (1940)

A George O'Brien western written by Morton Grant.• Riding from Wyoming to Arizona and stopping to attend the wedding of a friend, O'Brien runs into three men and accompanies them to Star City. The three rob the bank, shoot his pal and ride away. As so often, the stranger is taken for an outlaw and arrested—by the deputy sheriff who is the real brains of the mob. After a shootout, the action moves to a border village in Mexico, and this is easily the unique feature of the film; gracious officials, happy citizens, brave cowboys and singing maidens all around. Most charmingly, three Mexican sisters get triple justice: three bridegrooms.

Triumph of the Spirit (1989)

Nova International Films. Prod: Shimon Arama, Arnold Kopelson. Dir: Robert M. Young. Scr: Andrzej Krakowski, Laurence Heath (script contribution: Millard Lampell•). Story basis: Shimon Arama, Zion Haed. Cast: Willem Dafoe, Edward James Olmos, Robert Loggia, Wendy Gazelle, Kelly Wolf, Costas Mandylor, Kario Salem

A miscarried Holocaust tale that, according to Lampell's recollections, was a project that director Young could not finish with the existing script. He asked Lampell to restructure it, and finished it himself—unsuccessfully, because of the difficulty of the material.

Based on the story of a Greek-Jewish boxer who is sent to Auschwitz and survives temporarily by entertaining his Nazi captors, it contrasts the sweetness of his former life with the present overwhelming sense of doom. Olmos, whose significant supporting role was added by Lampell, contributes a *Cabaret*-style element as a magician who performs for the Nazis and subtly satirizes their beastliness.

The story dwindles in the face of tragedy, which (as Lampell noted) Stephen Spielberg handled more successfully, perhaps because more obliquely, in *Schindler's List*. Still, although it is almost impossible to watch (prisoners are marched to the showers on screen, the poison gas is released and the bodies go to the crematorium) and therefore a box office bomb, it is a tribute to Young's determination and to the moral convictions of Dafoe and Olmos. 120 min., color.

The Trout (1982)

Gaumont/Triumph Releasing. Prod: Yves Rousset-Rouard. Dir: Joseph Losey.• Scr: Monique Lang, Joseph Losey. Novel basis: Roger Vailland, *La truite* (1964). Cast: Isabelle Huppert, Jacques Spiesser, Jeanne Moreau, Jean-Pierre Cassel, Daniel Olbrychski, Alexis Smith, Craig Stevens

One of Losey's blandest films, with Moreau the older wife and Huppert in a rather more naïve version of the kinds of roles Moreau once played. The crowd of rich Europeans suffers from boredom; naturally, girl-chasing fits in with a life of discos, bars and (amazingly enough) bowling. At the alley, rich guy Casell spots Huppert, who is married to the bisexual Spiesser.

Wooing Huppert with financial treats and mundane bourgeois excitements (and disgusting his wife), Cassell will inevitably bag her, or is it the other way around? Along the way, Huppert—or is it perhaps everyone in this materialistic society?—comes to resemble more and more the cold-blooded trout who run in icy mountain streams. Both elusive and predictable, the story is millions of miles from Losey's tougher films. 104 min.

True Grit (1969)

Para. Prod: Hal B. Wallis. Dir: Henry Hathaway. Scr: Marguerite Roberts.• Novel basis: Charles Portis, *True Grit* (1968). Cast: John Wayne, Glen Campbell, Kim Darby, Jeremy Slate, Robert Duvall, Dennis Hopper, Alfred Ryder, Strother Martin, Jeff Corey•

It is an enduring irony of the blacklist that John Wayne, the sheriff of Hollywood in more ways than one (for a time, he and Ward Bond had the power to grant amnesty to blacklistees who begged for forgiveness) won his only Oscar with the help of a former Communist. Roberts refused to name names and eventually returned to work with her dignity intact. It was an odd reminder of how closely Left and Right once had to work together in the studio system, and at least sometimes still needed each other as artists in their latter days.

In any case, Roberts, the native westerner and experienced ranch hand, was the perfect writer for the story of Matty Ross, the bull-headed teenage girl who sets off to find the varmint who robbed and murdered her father. She enlists the aid of an aging and drunken wreck of a lawman (Wayne) to help her track down the man and bring him to justice. Roberts wisely hewed closely to the book, a western classic, and brought it brilliantly to life. Wayne had the spirit to parody himself in the early scenes, but of course (like a similarly positioned Clint Eastwood in *The Unforgiven*), regathers all of his frontier "virtues" for the final shootout. The Writers Guild nominated Roberts that year for best adaptation. 128 min.

True to Life (1943)

Para. Prod: Paul Jones. Dir: George Marshall. Scr: Don Hartman, Harry Tugend. Story basis: Ben Barzman,• Bess Taffel,• Sol Barzman.• Cast: Mary Martin, Franchot Tone, Dick Powell, Victor Moore, Mabel Paige, William Demarest, Clarence Kolb, Beverly Hudson

This comedy about a soap-opera writer who moves in with a family to get fresh ideas began with Taffel listening to radio soaps. Her friends, the brothers Barzman, filled out the story and it sold, more or less intact, with the happy addition of comic effects specialist and the film's associate producer, Paul Jones (late of Preston Sturges pics). Powell appropriates one idea after another from the family until he and Martin announce their budding love for each other. (He also sings a couple of Hoagy Carmichael tunes.) Moore is a Gyro Gearloose–style Pop, crazy about inventions, and Paige is a loving but deeply sarcastic mom. Tone, as Powell's erstwhile collaborator, also shows up to inflict himself as a romantic rival for Martin. Pretty funny satire of the radio game through the life of a participant. 94 min.

Try and Get Me (1950)

UA. Prod: Robert Stillman. Dir: Cyril Endfield.• Scr: Jo Pagano (uncredited: Cyril Endfield). Novel basis: Joe Pagano, *The Condemned* (1947). Cast: Frank Lovejoy, Lloyd Bridges,† Kathleen Ryan, Richard Carlson, Katherine Locke, Adele Jergens, Art Smith

Blacklistee Endfield went into exile in England after making six films in the United States, including two important noir titles—this and THE UNDERWORLD STORY one year earlier. The picture's reissue title, *The Sound of Fury*, is more apt, evoking the sound of a lynch mob that has been inflamed by a reactionary press in a manner not unfamiliar to Hollywood artists of the period.

The story opens on California newcomer Lovejoy, who has been searching for a job without success. In a scene close in feeling to the opening of THE ASPHALT JUNGLE, Lovejoy is offered a job as a getaway driver by a leering, flashy Bridges. After a series of small holdups, Bridges grows more ambitious and forces Lovejoy against his will to join first in a kidnapping, and then in the murder of a young man from one of the town's wealthiest families. (This is one of the few American films to dwell exclusively on issues of class from beginning to end.)

The final mob scenes are shot (in late-forties Phoenix) so effectively that Endfield returned to the same device many times in his career, most notably in ZULU and in SANDS OF THE KALAHARI. Endfield remains one of the most underappreciated of the blacklisted directors. Many of his films are hard to find, but the results are always worthwhile. 85 min.

Tugboat Princess (1936)

A tugboat captain (Walter C. Kelly) borrows money from a rival skipper to pay for an operation for his tiny daughter, then must race against time to keep ownership of his vessel. Based on a lesser story by Dalton Trumbo.• Maudlin.

Two Bright Boys (1939)

A western melodrama co-written by Val Burton• about a hard-pressed family fighting off an oil baron. Jackie Cooper, by this time more teenager than child, helps widowed mom (Dorothy Peterson) try to bring in their own wildcat well on their Texas farm as the baron plots against them. Ho-hum.

Two Girls on Broadway (1940)

Remake of THE BROADWAY MELODY about two singing sisters (Lana Turner and Joan Blondell) and the boy they both fall for (future right-wing senator George Murphy). The studio was building up Turner as a star. The Jerome Chodorov• co-script turns on the difficult transition of show biz people from vaudeville to night clubs. Comedy weakens after the first half as the romance soars. Basically a low-cost vehicle for Turner, then the most glamorous box office draw on the lot.

Two Guys from Texas (1948)

Color re-make of *The Cowboy from Brooklyn* (a Dick Powell and Pat O'Brien vehicle) and intended to be a laugh-or-a-song-a-minute extravaganza. Curly haired Dennis Morgan and wisecracking (but neurotic) Jack Carson, Manhattanites driving to California by way of Texas, have a breakdown and somehow land in a dude ranch whose entertainment is managed by their own friend (Denny Edwards). Everything is played for gags and romance, with Morgan turning on the charm for the ranch owner (Dorothy Malone). Even Allen Boretz• couldn't save this story.

Two Mules for Sister Sara (1969)

Malpaso/Universal. Prod: Carroll Case, Martin Rackin. Dir: Don Siegel. Scr: Albert Maltz.• Story basis: Budd Boetticher. Music: Ennio Morricone. Cast: Shirley MacLaine, Clint Eastwood, Manuel Fábregas, Alberto Morin, Armando Silvestre

A superb western, made by a still modest Eastwood under his newly formed production company and under the guidance of some of the best hands in Hollywood. (Boetticher was a fabled director of westerns in the 1950s.) This was one of the new wave of U.S. political westerns made under the influence of Italian Euro-westerns, many of which (though not Sergio Leone's) were explicitly antiwar. Morricone's score emphasizes this connection, as does the appropriation in the very first scene of an incident in Leone's *For a Few Dollars More*.

Like almost all Euro-westerns, *Two Mules* is absorbed with the question of personal motives and suspicions of betrayal during the Mexican revolution. Who is working for gold and who is working for revolution (against the French occupation)? The film answers all of these questions in the sauciest manner, with MacLaine at her most charming, carrying the film almost single-handedly as Eastwood perfects his Clint Stare. 116 min.

Two O'Clock Courage (1945)

Remake of *Two in the Dark* and a slow-moving mystery involving amnesia, murder and romance. Tom Conway, found wandering in the streets by cutie cabdriver Ann Rutherford, is implicated in the murder of a theatrical producer. Conway and Rutherford get to know each other as they follow assorted leads, pose as newspaper reporters to elude police and put themselves in line to be bumped off as well. Naturally, they fall in love as the fickle world of the theater is revealed (surprise) to be full of snooty celebs and conniving characters. There are some funny newspaper gags along the way. Conway was taking a break from the Falcon series, and director Anthony Mann was still a fledgling.

Two Señoritas from Chicago (1943)

Hotel garbage collector Joan Davis gets herself into trouble by pretending that an original play she produces is her own. Two actresses (Jinx Falkenburg and Ann Savage, with terrible accents) are presented as Portuguese sisters of the playwright and the show's stars. Closely follows *Two Latins from Manhattan*. Written by Stanley Rubin.†

Two Smart People (1946)

MGM. Prod: Ralph Wheelwright. Dir: Jules Dassin.• Scr: Ethel Hill, Leslie Charteris. Story basis: Ralph Wheelwright, Allan Kenward. Cast: Lucille Ball, John Hodiak, Lloyd Nolan, Hugo Haas, Lenore Ulric, Elisha Cook, Jr., Lloyd Corrigan, Shelley Winters

An early work of Dassin's, shot on a low budget and hamstrung with a familiar sentimental division of financial crookedness and love, but with a spectacular scene in Mardi Gras New Orleans and some other interesting moments. Ball and Hodiak (here, rarely enough, a romantic figure) are locked up in a mixture of swindling and romance, with Nolan the faithful New York cop. Hodiak is the swindler with a fortune in bonds, but Nolan has caught up with him just as Ball, a small time scam artist, meets him and falls in love.

Most of the film takes place on a transcontinental train from California for Hodiak's return to Sing Sing, with stop-offs to Mexico and New Orleans. Dassin later commented about these years, "I didn't know what I was doing, and God forgive me, I didn't care," a rather harsh judgment for uneven but occasionally quite interesting B-work that was better than he remembered. 93 min.

Two Wise Maids (1937)

Rep. Prod: Nat Levine. Dir: Phil Rosen. Scr: Samuel Ornitz.• Story basis: Endre Bohem. Cast: Alison Skipworth, Polly Moran, Hope Manning, Donald Cook, Jackie Searl, Lila Lee, Luis Alberni, Max "Slapsie Maxsie" Rosenblum, Marcia Mae Jones

A sentimental schoolhouse drama by Ornitz, which, like several scenes from the more notable BACK DOOR TO HEAVEN, recalls the fond relations of women teachers and their troubled students.

Teacher Skipworth is known affectionately as "Old Lady Ironsides" by her students and, approaching the end of her career, is up for promotion at the elementary school she has taught at for years. But when she and her roommate, a fellow teacher, set out to get a troubled girl (Jones) out of jail for stealing a pair of roller skates, she finds she has lost the promotion and is even urged to retire as "too old" by the new principal. Heartbroken, she refuses, and sticks to her desk.

Enough subsequent complications, lies, jealousies and misunderstandings large and small follow to build a picture of a small town no different from thousands of others across America—towns in which a few honorable teachers with a clear eye on the welfare of their pupils redeem the gossip and small-mindedness they must put up with to do their jobs.

Two Wise Maids is hardly great cinema—there is even a traditional "courtroom" drama to tie up loose ends—but in its compassion and decency it represents what Popular Front filmmaking aspired to when given the chance. 79 min.

Two Years Before the Mast (1946)

Para. Prod: Seton I. Miller. Dir: John Farrow. Scr: Seton I. Miller (uncredited: Val Burton•). Book basis: Richard Henry Dana, *Two Years Before the Mast: A Narrative of Life at Sea* (1840). Cast: Alan Ladd, Brian Donlevy, William Bendix, Esther Fernandez, Howard da Silva,• Barry Fitzgerald, Albert Dekker

A rather muddled version of Dana's famous book but marked with some occasionally astonishing examples of seamen's semi-feudal working conditions, attempts by the contemporary ruling class to suppress information and the metaphorical references to the real-life Seaman's Bill of Rights (which passed Congress in 1944 but was ignored during wartime and often afterward).

Dragooned from a seaside tavern onto ship, ship-owner's son Ladd finds himself experiencing the fate of the working man. Donlevy, who plays the historical Dana, keeps a log to record the cruelties. Ship's captain da Silva, in one of his man-you-love-to-hate roles, deprives the crew of adequate food, throws dissenters into chains and justifies himself morally by leading prayers over the corpses before they are thrown overboard. Bendix, as ship's mate, carries out the orders but begins to perceive the moral calamity. Ladd warns da Silva, "When people back home learn about butchers like you . . ."

Though the stockholders conspire against publication, Dana's book is published, putting the case before the public. Controversy is stirred, rich against poor. In the final courtroom scene Dana and Ladd get to plead the case of the sailors and of themselves, and it is almost worth watching all the movie to get to that ending. Easily the best effort of Burton, who labored in B-genres the rest of his career. 98 min.

The Two-Headed Spy (1958)

Alfred Lewis Levitt and Michael Wilson• contributed to this Brit film, which lacks the humor of Levitt's other work but recuperates the World War II anti-Nazi thriller. Jack Hawkins, a British agent who rises to the rank of Nazi general, feeds the Allies information through an antique clock dealer (Felix Aylmer) while eluding suspicion. Soon he must turn to Gia Scala, a beautiful singer, feigning an affair (but actually falling in love) while she acts as his agent. Cut-rate production used considerable stock footage, although the portrayal of the German elite was regarded as more than adequate. Michael Caine is a Gestapo agent.

U

Under Age (1941)

Columbia. Prod: Ralph Cohn. Dir: Edward Dmytryk.•†
Scr: Robert Hardy Andrews. Story basis: Stanley Roberts.† Cast: Nan Grey, Alan Baxter, Mary Anderson, Tom Neal, Leona Maricle, Don Beddoe, Yolande Mollot (Yolande Donlan)

Deepest B-film, aimed at a youth audience, with a sometimes strong message about the exploitation of young women—but an equally strong exploitation angle. The film is best remembered in the trade for having been shot shortly before the Hays Office decreed against "sweater girls" showing overly sharp profiles. Here these sweaters are prolific.

Homeless girls just out of detention camps are forced to work for gangsters as come-ons to tourists to spend big and be swindled. Grey and her sister Anderson find themselves working for the tough Maricle, boss of the camp, and caught up in a theft of gems. Neal is the jewelry salesman who comes to their rescue and helps bring down the mob. Best part of the film is the interaction of the blue-collar/slum girls trying to create a community among themselves under the worst conditions. In this period in history, the real-life equivalent of these characters were waiting for war work. 59 min.

Under Colorado Skies (1947)

The voice-over narration for this Louise Rousseau• screenplay of a Monte Hale shoot-'em-up states that the Panic of 1873 knocked the bottom out of the regional economy, and as "our country was swept by marauding groups of desperadoes," the "leaders of these groups found willing followers in men taught to kill by the Civil War." All of this is layered over a sibling betrayal plot and a scene in which Hale sings a charming version of Bob Wills' "San Antonio Rose."

Under Ten Flags (1960)

Dino de Laurentiis/Para. Prod: Dino de Laurentiis. Dir: Duilio Coletti. Scr: Vittoriano Petrilli, Duilio Coletti, Ulrich Mohr (uncredited contribution: Leonardo Bercovici•). Story basis: Bernhard Rogge, *Schiff 16: die Kaperfahrt des schweren Hilfskreuzers Atlantis* (1955). Cast: Van Heflin, Charles Laughton, Mylène Demongeot, John Ericson, Cecil Parker, Liam Redmond, Alex Nicol

An Italian American production of war action in Italian cinematic style, too herky-jerky to achieve its aims. A Nazi raider plays cat and mouse with the British admiralty (headed by Laughton) by posing as a friendly freighter and adopting a variety of flags and disguises. Eventually, it is caught by Americans breaking the Nazi codes. But along the way, captain Heflin is the sympathetic figure, almost a Nazi Robin Hood of the seas to Laughton's Sheriff of Nottingham. Bad editing and poor coordination across the Atlantic evidently overrode Bercovici's efforts to make the thing coherent for American audiences (and for his friend, de Laurentiis), but it does successfully point up the bully boys that top British officers remained even when fighting the worst of enemies. This was Heflin's third de Laurentiis film in a two-year period. 92 min.

The Undercover Man (1949)

Robert Rossen,† now acting as a producer (the film was directed by Joseph H. Lewis) and aiming at the same subgenre as Jules Dassin's• NAKED CITY, with a newsreel-like quality recording the street life of the city but bound by the conventions of law-and-order themes. An IRS agent (Glenn Ford) sets out to nab a mob boss on tax evasion.

Undercurrent (1946)

MGM. Prod: Pandro S. Berman. Dir: Vincente Minnelli. Scr: Edward Chodorov,• Marguerite Roberts,• George Oppenheimer. Story basis: Thelma Strabel, "You Were There," in *Women's Home Companion* (1944-1945). Cast: Katharine Hepburn, Robert Taylor, Edmund Gwenn, Robert Mitchum, Marjorie Main, Jayne Meadows

An unlikely Hepburn role has her sprightliness turn to morbid curiosity and fear as she discovers more and more about the sinister Taylor (in real life, a Hollywood conservative and eager friendly witness). The unmarried daughter of a kindly scientist (Gwenn) and facing spinsterhood, she is swept off her feet by Taylor—an entrepreneur, playboy and famed industrial inventor. But he has a problem and a secret. He is given to irrational moods and outbursts, and he has a brother (Mitchum) who believes he is guilty of a heinous crime with the most venal motive. Is he? That's the question Hepburn becomes obsessed with in a gothic romance that works hard but fails to sustain interest all the way through. 126 min.

Underground Agent (1942)

Anti-Nazi drama in which government agent Bruce Bennett invents a word scrambler that stops Nazi saboteurs from eavesdropping at a defense plant. Directed by Michael Gordon.•†

The Underworld Story (1950)

Filmcraft Productions. Prod: Hal E. Chester. Dir: Cyril Endfield.• Scr: Henry Blankfort.• Story basis: Craig Rice, "The Big Story" (apparently unpublished). Cast: Dan Duryea, Herbert Marshall, Gale Storm, Howard da Silva, Michael O'Shea, Mary Anderson, Frieda Inescort

An accurate and chilling view of the newspaper business at its most venal. When an unscrupulous reporter who specializes in shaking down businessmen is fired from a big-city paper in New England, he borrows money from a mob boss to buy a half-interest in the sleepy little *Lakeville Sentinel* (circulation 2,200) in an upscale suburb. The reporter (Duryea) unwittingly walks into a big story when the daughter-in-law of the state's newspaper magnate is found murdered moments after Duryea has bought the *Sentinel*. The new owner ruthlessly cashes in on the story by selling it to competing news services when the murder suspect walks into the *Sentinel* office seeking help from her old friend, the former editor—Storm in her best dramatic role.

The Underworld Story, also called *The Whipped*, is blacklistee Endfield's second stand-out noir film, along with TRY AND GET ME. Devotees of the newspaper picture will prize it because of the tough, knowing script by blacklistee Blankfort. His newspaper patter is genuine, and the description of the social and political forces at work in framing the innocent woman never strikes a false note. Duryea's character gradually develops a social conscience only because that's where the story leads him. Meanwhile, the leftists and liberals who organize to defend the black maid, in a group very much like the real-life Civil Rights Congress (1946-1956), launch a mass protest and then scatter (in the familiar manner of Cold War liberals) when members of the small circle that actually runs the town start putting on the pressure.

One of the prolific but obscure Blankfort's most telling lines comes in this picture, just three years after the first HUAC hearings. Mrs. Eldritch (the Lovecraftian reference must be intentional), a member of the defense committee, says of Lakeville and one of its inner circle: "If your ancestors weren't present at the original witch burnings in this town, the Major thinks you are an interloper." 91 min.

Union Depot (1932)

First National. Prod: Unknown. Dir: Alfred E. Green. Scr: Kenyon Nicholson, Walter De Leon (uncredited script contribution: John Bright,• Kubec Glasmon). Play basis: Gene Fowler, Douglas Durkin, Joe Laurie, Jr., *Union Depot* (unpublished). Cast: Douglas Fairbanks, Jr., Joan Blondell, Guy Kibbee, Alan Hale, George Rosener, Dickie Moore, Ruth Hall

A sort of "Grand Hotel" or *Street Scenes* of a busy metropolitan railroad station, with Blondell at the center of the action (as usual in Bright's early efforts). A chorus girl encountered by a shell-game operator (Fairbanks, acting remarkably like James Cagney), she wants a train ticket to Salt Lake City and a free dinner. This simple desire leads to a violin case full of money, which turns out to be counterfeit, which brings down the G-men on the assorted hustlers and hangers-on at the train station. The set, said to be one of the most expensive in Hollywood to date, accommodates the real subject of interest: "types," including new immigrant Europeans, social swells, tired clerks, Chinese (played by Occidentals) awaiting their relatives, and many others. 67 min.

Unseen Enemy (1942)

Universal. Prod: Marshall Grant. Dir: John Rawlins. Scr: Roy Chanslor, Stanley Rubin.† Story basis: George Wallace Sayre. Cast: Leo Carrillo, Andy Devine, Irene Hervey, Don Terry, Lionel Royce, Turhan Bey, Frederick Giermann

A fine B-cast wrestles with a mediocre plot and low production values in this melodrama about enemy agents on the Frisco waterfront (where, in real life, communists were pretty much in charge, usually with the cooperation of shipowners).

Waterfront café owner Carillo, who collaborates with "the Japs" to assist his stepdaughter's rise in social position (!), tries to help get a crew together for a daring raid on ships along the coast, and runs up against government agent Devine. Stepdaughter and café singer Hervey becomes the patriot as she begins to suspect the too-frequent requests to sing "Lydia" (a signal) as German sailors gather. She also gets romantic with Terry, a Canadian government agent who assists Devine. Not much else happens except what *Variety* called a "rousing chase." 61 min.

Up Front with Mauldin (1951)

Stanley Roberts† wrote the screenplay dramatizing the adventures of cartoon figures Willie and Joe, World War II dogfaces on the Italian front invented by Bill Mauldin and based on one of his books. The pair of lowbrow GIs are good soldiers when the bullets fly but notoriously disrespectful to the officers and eager to celebrate the arts of peace with wine, women and more wine.

V

Valley of Hunted Men (1942)

Rep. Assoc. Prod: Louis Gray. Dir: John English. Scr: Morton Grant,• Albert DeMond. Story basis: Charles Tedford. Cast: Bob Steele, Tom Tyler, Jimmie Dodd, Anna Marie Stewart

Unintentionally hilarious bottom-budget wartime western (and the forty-seventh Mesquiteers film) in which escaped Nazis, distinguishable by their black hats, cause mayhem—until white-hatted cowboys track them down.

As a soon-to-be martyred storekeeper says, "fightin' Nazis is like fightin' Comanches." And Hitler is "just a galoot with a toothbrush mustache." (For that remark, the storekeeper is gunned down.) Mean-spirited or just ignorant ranchers at first turn their hatred toward the German immigrant scientist who is trying to teach them to spray their crops (presumably with insecticides) for larger yields. A German agent, posing as the scientist's nephew, arrives to steal the "secret" of this agri-development for the homeland and dumps harsh chemicals into the trial batch, with predictable results. Lots of shoot-'em-up action until the Three Mesquiteers sort things out. 60 min.

Vanity Street (1932)

Col. Prod: Unknown. Dir: Nick Grinde. Scr: Gertrude Purcell.† Story basis: Frank Cavett, Edward Roberts. Cast: Charles Bickford, Helen Chandler, Mayo Methot, George Meeker, Arthur Hoyt, Raymond Hatton, Ruth Channing

A light women's film, Purcell's métier. The forgotten Chandler turns in a fine performance as a showgirl who reaches a dead end after fruitless job-hunting during the depths of the Depression. After she tosses a brick through a drugstore window, planning to spend a few days warm and fed in jail, cop Bickford saves her, and she in turn falls in love with him. But she misunderstands his silences and moodiness, and takes up with young rogues, including Meeker, finding herself in the middle of a murder investigation that Bickford must resolve. In this far-gone age of low-key technical wonders, even a radio patrol car seemed marvelous. 67 min.

Variety Girl (1947)

Para. Prod: Daniel Dare.† Dir: George Marshall. Scr: Edmund L. Hartmann, Frank Tashlin, Robert Welch, Monte Brice Cast: Mary Hatcher, Olga San Juan, DeForest Kelley, Glenn Tryon, Nella Walker, Torben Meyer, Jack Norton, William Demarest, Frank Faylen, Frank Furguson, Sonny Tufts, Sterling Hayden,† Howard da Silva,• Alan Ladd, Dorothy Lamour, Veronica Lake, Bob Hope, Barbara Stanwyck, Gary Cooper, Ray Milland

A boffo all-star musical of Paramount contract players that celebrates the decency of show people, with Pearl Bailey (her film debut: one song), Spike Jones and a horde of others popping up in a thinly plotted tale (Hatcher and San Juan seeking their fortunes in Hollywood). The true story behind the story is about these entertainers' philanthropic movement, called the Variety Club, that started in 1929 when traveling vaudeville artists discovered a homeless child in the Sheridan Theater in Pittsburgh. The Variety Club was organized to raise money for orphans and to find sponsors for them. In the film, Hatcher, supposedly a grown-up orphan, shows up and is "adopted" again, this time by the studios.

There are close-ups of Paramount Studio, Hollywood pool parties, lunches at the Brown Derby, a bit of self-satire and in-jokes about current and past films and a lot of collective self-congratulation. It is all topped off by the Variety Club benefit show, hosted by Bob Hope. All in all, an insider's close-up of Hollywood, or of how Hollywood regarded itself at its best, which audiences loved even while critics attacked the film as vacuous. A George Pal puppetoon sequence in color revealing how sound is dubbed on film is one of the high points. 93 min., part color.

Varsity (1929)

Para. Famous Lasky Corp. Prod: Unknown. Dir: Frank Tuttle.† Scr: Wells Root, Howard Estabrook. Cast: Chester Conklin, Charles Rogers, Mary Brian, Phillips R. Holmes, Robert Ellis, John Westwood

One of the part-dialogue experiments at the end of the silent era "exposing" the high life at Princeton. Conklin, a gin guzzler, has fallen to the lowly status of janitor at the college after he spent the cash needed to buy medicine for his late wife. Rogers, an undergraduate, is his unknowing son. Dad, now dry, keeps an eye on junior without the kid knowing it. How does Rogers make the college scene? Not boozing like his classmates (at one point they force whiskey down his innocent throat), but by being honest and studious. He also improbably falls in love with Brian, the star of a Wild West show(!). Conklin's heart is breaking (everyone calls him "Pop" but his own son) until he accosts some speakeasy gangsters who attempt to rob sonny of the money collected for the college fund. In a fadeout, the two young lovers walk into the sylvan campus, a sort of American Dream come true. 67 min.

The Very Thought of You (1944)

WB. Prod: Jerry Wald. Dir: Delmer Daves. Scr: Alvah Bessie,• Delmer Daves. Story: Lionel Wiggam. Cast: Eleanor Parker, Dennis Morgan, Dane Clark, Faye Emerson, Beulah Bondi, Henry Travers, Margaret O'Brien

A neglected wartime romance and family drama that has many of the usual clichés but some charming and occasionally powerful bits on psychological dislocation in wartime. Parker is a Pasadena girl in a parachute plant (some shots of parachute production are quite detailed), Morgan a former medical student who has enlisted in the navy and is awaiting overseas duty. He and pal Clark blow into town. They meet Parker and Emerson on a trolley and romance blooms all around in a whirlwind courtship of factory girls.

The best of the film takes place in Parker's family home, sometimes described as the single most dysfunctional family in all of Popular Front homefront drama. Indeed, slackers and isolationists appear on all sides. The disappointed mother (Bondi) takes out her own frustrated urge for upward mobility on everyone around her, but especially dad; she also fears the war will end and ruin the economy. Parker's sister, faithless to her overseas husband, gets to be the unpatriotic villainness, while a 4F brother-in-law complains about U.S. involvement.

The best lines of the film go to dad, a loveable failure at money-making, a former relief recipient who now works as a lowly clerk. He advises Parker to take chances and find her own way in the world. More complications and patriotic gestures follow as Parker gets pregnant and the film winds down, despite the interestingly unfriendly welcome home for erstwhile heroes. Described as a "distasteful and irritating picture" by the *New York Times*. 99 min.

The Vicious Circle (1948)

UA. Prod: W. Lee. Wilder. Dir: W. Lee Wilder. Scr: Heinz Herald, Guy Endore,• Noel Langley. Play basis: Geza Herczeg, *The Burning Bush* (1947). Cast: Conrad Nagel, Lyle Talbot, Reinhold Schünzel, Edwin Maxwell, Philip Van Zandt, Eddie LeRoy, Frank Ferguson, Fritz Kortner

A historical treatment of anti-Semitism that recounts a factual courtroom drama from 1880s Hungary, where five Jews are accused of murder. Unfortunately, this low-budget effort lacked the means to get beyond a staged drama on film. Economies in production are evident on all sides. Nagel is the courageous lawyer, Kortner the main defendant and Schünzel the aristocratic enemy of the Jews. Evidently intended to appeal to Jewish audiences, it went nowhere. Not to be confused with a 1959 British film, released both as *The Circle* and *The Vicious Circle*. 77 min.

Violence (1947)

B&B Pictures Corp. Prod: Jack Bernhard, Bernard Brandt. Dir: Jack Bernhard. Scr: Louis Lantz, Stanley Rubin.† Cast: Nancy Coleman, Michael O'Shea, Emory Parnell, Sheldon Leonard, Peter Whitney, Pierre Watkin, Frank Reicher

One of those FBI dramas about subversive organizations that a little later usually turned out to be the very Communist Party that Rubin, among many others, had joined himself. Rubin became an early friendly witness to save his career, but not without regrets or later efforts to make up for his sins to some blacklistees. Here, the "United Defenders," a secret organization bent on rousing discontent, is ideologically vague but at this date probably most likely fascists of some stripe. Coleman, an undercover operator for a photo mag, is out to bust these nasties, but she suffers memory loss after an automobile accident and FBI man O'Shea has to step in, besting the sneaky efforts of Leonard and others to rope in confused veterans. 72 min.

Virgin Island (1959)

Countryman Films. Prod: Pat Jackson. Dir: Pat Jackson. Scr: Philip Rush (pseudonym for Ring Lardner, Jr.•) and Pat Jackson. Novel basis: Robb White, *Our Virgin Island* (1953). Cast: John Cassavetes, Virginia Maskell, Sidney Poitier, Colin Gordon, Isabel Dean, Howard Marion Crawford, Ruby Dee, Julian Mayfield

An update with color, location shooting and racial themes of the old white-visitors-in-the-Caribbean film. Maskell, on a luxury cruise with her mother (Dean), meets a handsome young bohemian writer (Cassavetes) on the beach. They marry, and he convinces her to buy a deserted island for $85 and they set up as castaways. Assisted by Poitier as the comic islander, they meet assorted problems: a birth, in-law troubles and hassles with the territorial governor (Gordon). Reviewers complained that the screenplay shifted to satire—no doubt Lardner's touch—

too late to be effective. But the rich tones of the Caribbean setting photographed by Freddie Francis make this unserious film pleasantly good-natured. Lardner himself considered it routine work, with all possibilities ruined by the director's plot changes and bad editing. 84 min., color.

The Virgin Soldiers (1969)

Col./Highroad/Open Road. Prod: Carl Foreman,• Lester Gilliat. Dir: John Dexter. Scr: John Hopkins (uncredited: Carl Foreman). Novel basis: Leslie Thomas, *Virgin Soldiers* (1966). Cast: Lynn Redgrave, Hywel Bennett, Nigel Davenport, Nigel Patrick, Rachel Kempson, Tsai Chin, Jack Shepherd, Michael Gwynn

Oscar winner as best foreign film, another major vindication (like MASH, the same year) of the blacklistees in a moment when most of them who were lucky enough to make a comeback in films inched into the mainstream. It shares with *MASH* its theme and several extended antiwar metaphors. This time it's the "innocents abroad" model, with British recruits in Singapore during World War II. Virginal in the arts of war and love alike, they deal with the prospect of death in the surrounding jungles by trying to make it with babes in the brawling, boozing capitol.

Bennett hooks up with hooker Chin (despite her cameo role, the only smart woman in the picture), while aspiring to Redgrave, schoolmistress daughter of Sergeant Patrick, the ludicrous martinet. Redgrave's role is mainly sulky, and Kempson plays dumb as the wife of Patrick. The best moments are extended versions of *Carry On Nurse*–style Brit comedy: lads demanding circumcision to get sick leave, Bennett losing his shorts in a cat house and so on. The film climaxes in a jungle scene with an ambushed troop train, where the courageous and the merely boastful are given their respective deserts. 96 min.

Virginia City (1940)

WB. Prod: Jack Warner. Exec Prod: Hal B. Wallis. Dir: Michael Curtiz. Scr: Robert Buckner (uncredited script contribution: Howard Koch•). Cast: Errol Flynn, Miriam Hopkins, Randolph Scott, Humphrey Bogart, Victor Kilian, Frank McHugh, Alan Hale, Guinn "Big Boy" Williams

A big-budget western made on the heels of *Dodge City*, also starring Flynn (and best remembered for providing Mel Brooks an object for his satire, *Blazing Saddles*). But like several Cold War westerns, the film is loaded down with the dark impulse to reunite Yanks and Rebs in a common Americanism.

As the Civil War moves to a close and the South grows desperate for funds, Virginia City saloon showgirl Hopkins volunteers to bring $5 million in gold back from the west. The commander of the notorious Libby prison (Scott) agrees to her plan and sets out to direct the project himself, but is overheard making plans by Flynn, a Union intelligence officer who escapes from the prison and goes west to intercept the shipment. By coincidence sharing a stage, the unknowing Hopkins and Flynn fall in love. She avoids him once in Virginia City and focuses on the gold, but eventually is asked by Scott to lure Flynn into a trap. She submits and the gold train heads across the desert with Flynn as prisoner. After he escapes, the wagon train is attacked by Mexican bandit Bogart (sporting a pencil mustache). Scott, mortally wounded, pleads with Flynn (who has come to the rescue) to save the gold for rebuilding the South after the war. Loyally, Flynn hides it from the bandit, is rescued by the cavalry, but refuses to divulge the location and almost goes to his death at an army court martial. But wouldn't you guess? Hopkins appeals to Abe Lincoln (Kilian), who permits the lovers, like the country, to be reunited. Somehow, this narrative leaves out the fate of free Southern blacks and the Northern bankers who squeeze the postwar South strictly for their own benefit. 121 min.

The Visit (1964)

Deutsche Fox/20th/Cinecittà. Prod: Julien Derode, Anthony Quinn. Dir: Bernhard Wicki. Scr: Ben Barzman.• Play basis: Frederich Dürrenmatt, *Der Besuch der Alten Dame* (1956). Cast: Ingrid Bergman, Anthony Quinn, Irina Demick, Claude Dauphin, Paolo Stoppa, Romolo Valli, Valentina Cortese, Eduardo Ciannelli

German-French-Italian production of Swiss Dürrenmatt (with a Swiss director to boot) is uneven and melodramatic but fascinating in parts. Critics complained that the stage drama was about old people, but Bergman and Quinn added erotic possibilities, squeezing out the symbolism for more familiar cinematic stargazing.

The heiress Bergman returns to the broken-down middle European town where she was wronged decades earlier. A prostitute who married a millionaire, she buys up the industries of the town to shut them down, in preparation for her revenge. She demands the assassination of Quinn, the man who impregnated her and then had her driven from town, and she offers up a $2 million bounty. Ultimately—a change from the play—she decides to let him live among the people who were perfectly willing to kill him for her. Best scene: Bergman looking at the town from a balcony with a leopard by her side. 100 min.

W

A Walk in the Sun (1946)

Lewis Milestone Productions/20th. Prod: Lewis Milestone. Dir. Lewis Milestone. Scr: Robert Rossen.† Novel basis: Harry Brown, *A Walk in the Sun* (1944). Music: Millard Lampell.• Cast: Dana Andrews, Richard Conte, John Ireland, Lloyd Bridges,† Sterling Holloway

The often gripping story of the Italian campaign waged by GIs and presented almost entirely from the GI point of view. From their landing through their bloody advance, they act like ordinary, mostly working-class Americans (like the author himself, from blue-collar neighborhoods in greater New York), feuding, passing time and preparing themselves for the likelihood of death. They use up their heavy ammunition on an enemy tank, exposing themselves to later assault and making heavy casualties certain. In the final frames, seen from behind the Axis soldiers in the farmhouse, GIs die until the last of them break through. In the tradition of soldierly multiculturalism, urban argot and the courage of the ordinary dogface, this film is one of the better ones. 117 min.

Watch on the Rhine (1943)

WB. Prod: Hal B. Wallis. Dir: Herman Shumlin. Scr: Lillian Hellman,• Dashiel Hammett.• Play basis: Lillian Hellman, *Watch on the Rhine* (1941). Cast: Bette Davis, Paul Lukas, Donald Woods, Beulah Bondi, Geraldine Fitzgerald, George Couloulis, Henry Daniell, Helmut Dantine

An adaptation of a Broadway play (also directed by Shumlin) and the only complete (or perhaps, as Ring Lardner, Jr., has suggested, the only acknowledged) full collaboration between the famed detective writer and Hellman. It was also the first play—embarrassingly for some, appearing at the time of the Nazi-Soviet Pact—to portray the evil of Nazi ideology. It is unique in one other important respect: it is Hellman's respite from the South, as in the blistering histories of THE LITTLE FOXES and ANOTHER PART OF THE FOREST, to deal with the present. It is consequently rather sentimental about "American" values. Somehow, in the face of fascism, race relations

seem better and the perennially wicked persona of Bette Davis has morphed into a self-sacrificing progressive wife.

Davis and Lukas (who won an Academy Award as best actor, among many nominations for the film) have fled Nazi Germany with their child, but as a leader of the resistance, he is morally compelled to return. Landing in Virginia (near Washington) with family, she is received warmly but by Americans typically unable to make sense of international issues. Davis must explain (everybody is against fascism, but people like Lukas do something about it), and does so at some length. Her sister's husband, the delightfully amoral Woods, meanwhile conspires with Nazi consular officials, hoping to return to Europe in a position of power. The ending had to be changed to satisfy censors. 114 min.

Way for a Sailor (1930)

Novelist W. L. River,• one of the older generation of Hollywood radicals, wrote this curious and borderline silent/talkie, which combines explanatory intertitles with occasional music and stage-like dialogue (some of it contributed by Charles MacArthur). It's also rather salty, with sex and bathroom jokes impermissible after the Code. Sailor Wallace Beery is every bit the protean proletarian in the maritime style of Popeye and the real center of the film, while John Gilbert romances clerk Leila Hyams between sea voyages. Interesting faux-realistic footage of waterfront life at home and the whorehouses of Singapore.

The Way We Were (1973)

Col./Rastar Production. Prod: Ray Stark. Dir: Sydney Pollack. Scr: Arthur Laurents (uncredited: David Rayfiel). Novel basis: Arthur Laurents, *The Way We Were* (1972). Cast: Barbra Streisand, Robert Redford, Bradford Dillman, Viveca Lindfors, Herb Edelman, Murray Hamilton, Patrick O'Neal, James Woods, Sally Kirkland

This multiple award-winning film, made in the wake of the restless 1960s, was the postponed recollection of the blacklist and the historical experience of Hollywood's Old Left. Unlike THE FRONT, with which it is often compared, this film has a love story par excellence and a narrative that ties together Jewish experience in every decade from the 1930s to the 1960s. It also offered Streisand (who co-produced) an opportunity to become the cinematic political activist that she has often been in life (and often at considerable risk, as in her determined opposition to Israel's invasion of neighboring Lebanon).

Streisand is the left-wing and very Jewish campus activist Katie, whom pretty-boy gentile Redford meets in the tumultuous 1930s. Unlike earlier depictions (in which Streisand was seen as unattractive, even "homely"), here she seems extremely fetching, not least for her raw political and personal energy and idealism. Opposites attract, and they begin a passionate, stormy relationship that develops into marriage in postwar Hollywood, with him as a screenwriter and her as an L.A. political activist. When the crunch came, he would support the blacklistees—if it didn't threaten to harm his career. She is seen, quite realistically, as burying her personal problems in political mobilizations, but also carrying the burden of the liberal Left during the Cold War, when others opted for private life.

Old-fashioned doomed romance earns new resonance, as in politics, with time and distance. (For one thing, as it often was in real-life Hollywood, the friendly witnesses were also gentiles). Reviewers pointed out that the film dropped the broad references in Arthur Laurents' novel to the informers, to Richard Nixon, Jews and the Holocaust, and treated Katie's politics with considerably less seriousness. One of the key moments of the novel, in which she might have saved the marriage by becoming an informer herself, was dropped, according to director Pollack, after a "sneak preview" (more likely, it was a studio decision). All that said, no film Communist (even if the word is hardly used) had received such sympathetic treatment since the mid-forties. And Hollywood stood up to applaud, with Oscars for best song, best original score and nominations for best actress, best art direction, best direction, and best costume design. 118 min., color.

The Way West (1967)

Harold Hecht Productions/MGM. Prod: Harold Hecht.† Dir: Andrew V. McLaglen. Scr: Ben Maddow,•† Mitch Lindemann.• Novel basis: A. B. Guthrie, Jr., *The Way West* (1949). Cast: Kirk Douglas, Robert Mitchum, Richard Widmark, Lola Albright, Michael Witney, Stubby Kaye, Sally Field

A transition western from 1940s heroism and 1950s angst to post-1960s multiculturalism, but with the old-time "winning of the West" ideology somehow (uncomfortably) intact. There would have been little reason for the sixties movie buff to detect the hand of the Old Left here save in a few characteristic flourishes, like the turning of a key plot element on the issue of sexual repression. Or maybe Maddow was invoking the weirdness of JOHNNY GUITAR at a more commercial and self-conscious level. In

any case, the fact that it appeared in the same year that produced HOMBRE and the first two Eastwood/Leone spaghetti western collaborations already gave it an antique flavor. It was produced by Hecht, a friendly witness who would later make a habit of hiring former blacklistees.

Douglas is a former senior U.S. senator from Illinois (his party affiliation is not given) who has lost his wife to suicide and given up his political ambitions to become a Moses—or an immigrant-smuggling coyote, depending on your vantage point—by leading a wagon train to the promised land of Oregon. The eternally dour Mitchum is the veteran scout who has also lost his wife, a Blackfoot woman. (Asked if they are the same as whites, he cracks that he hasn't been with a white woman in so long, he "disremembers," using a bit of African American dialogue for punctuation.)

The wagon train encounters all of the usual problems and many more than most. Chubby-faced Sally Field in her movie debut is impregnated by a married man but goes on to make a match with an affable teenager. The son of an Indian chief (portrayed as a noble savage) is murdered, and the murderer is actually punished. Rivers, canyons, lust for gold must all be surmounted. In one important scene by Maddow, a guilt-ridden Douglas commands a former slave to flog him; whereupon the ex-slave explains, "You can't get nothin' from a whip." The fate of the Indians displaced from the Willamette Valley is not revealed. 122 min., color.

We Go Fast (1941)

20th. Prod: Lou Ostrow. Dir: William McGann. Scr: Thomas Lennon, Adrian Scott.• Story basis: Doug Welch, "We Go Fast," *The Saturday Evening Post* (1939). Cast: Lynn Barie, Alan Curtis, Sheila Ryan, Don Deforest, Ernest Truex, Gerald Mohr, Tom Dugan

A forties-style didactic comedy about a couple of motorcycle cops, rivals for the affection of a coffee-shop waitress (Barie). The cops' authority is undermined when an heiress flouts a traffic ticket after driving 90 mph in a 45-mph zone. When a judge upholds her argument that the ticket is invalid because the traffic signs have only numbers on them (and no "mph"), the town is taken over by speeders (and the city attorney points out that speeders caused 100,000 accidents the year before). A subtheme involves the extortion of city officials by a "businessman" who wants a bribe in exchange for a big order to a local factory, but the speeding metaphor for the lawlessness of class privilege is the heart of the story. 64 min.

We Who Are Young (1940)

Dalton Trumbo• scripted this Depression drama about a couple of newlyweds deeply in love but struggling to overcome crisis after crisis, including a delightfully mean capitalist played by Gene Lockhart. Seymour Nebenzal produced for Loew's/MGM.

The Web (1947)

U-I. Prod: Jerry Bresler. Dir: Michael Gordon.•† Scr: William Bowers, Bertram Millhauser. Story basis: Harry Kurnitz. Cast: Edmond O'Brien, Ella Raines, William Bendix, Vincent Price, Maria Palmer

Minor crime-drama with vaguely noirish tinges has people's lawyer O'Brien demanding payments to a client from big shot corporate exec Price, who is drawn steadily into intrigue and romance with Price's secretary, bombshell Raines. Impressed with O'Brien's pugnacity, Price hires the lawyer to protect him for a few weeks. O'Brien then shoots a former business partner and finds himself suspected of murder. Bendix, in one of his better dramatic roles, weighs in as the police detective who aims his investigation at O'Brien but also struggles to learn the real story. Between the rising romantic ardor and the manipulative evil of Price, the story finds an unsurprising resolution. The interesting premise that O'Brien seeks clues that can only lead to more suspicion of himself is never psychologically explored. 87 min.

Web of Danger (1947)

Screenwriter David Lang's† talky action film, about rival bridge-builders (Bill Kennedy and Damian O'Flynn), squeezed into its corset-tight budget by using a lot of stock footage for floods and construction. Kennedy and O'Flynn both lust for Adele Mara, but come together to complete a bridge to get flood refugees out of an endangered valley. There is something vaguely New Dealish about all this, one supposes, but nothing definite.

Weekend for Three (1941)

RKO. Prod: Tay Garnett. Dir: Irving Reis. Scr: Dorothy Parker,• Alan Campbell.• Story basis: Budd Schulberg.† Cast: Dennis O'Keefe, Jane Wyatt, Philip Reed, Edward Everett Horton, Zasu Pitts, Franklin Pangborn, Marion Martin, Hans Conried

Described as "chucklesome"—but probably not nearly as much as if Parker and screenwriter husband Campbell had creative control—the film falls considerably short on plot. Cleveland housewife Wyatt wants to make hubby O'Keefe jealous by flirting with Broadway playboy Reed. She tires of the game, however, as a weekend with him proceeds, and commences to strategize with O'Keefe on methods of getting rid of an increasingly unbearable pest. Not much else happens. The dialogue is far and away the best part of the film. 65 min.

West of Rainbow's End (1938)

A Stanley Roberts† screenplay about railroad dick Tim McCoy coming out of retirement to find and convict the land thieves who are conspiring against the railroad.

What's Cookin'? (1942)

Universal. Prod: Ken Goldsmith Dir: Edward F. Cline. Scr: Jerry Cady, Stanley Roberts.† Story: Edgar Allan Woolf. Cast: Jane Frazee, Robert Paige, Gloria Jean, Leo Carrillo, Charles Butterworth, Billie Burke, Donald O'Connor, Franklin Pangborn

Universal produced a string of profitable musicals mainly featuring younger performers, all intended for youthful, swing-minded audiences. Most were so heavily performance-oriented (like this one, with no fewer than 14 tunes) that the plot virtually disappeared into a sort of cinematic MTV format.

In this typically backstage setting, a group of youngsters seeks to hit the big time. Luckily, they find themselves booked on a radio show with big shots like Woody Herman's band and the Andrews Sisters. Plugging products (with the help of Gloria Jean, a kindly capitalist's niece), they score. O'Connor, in one of his first screen appearances, sings and dances up a storm while being pursued by the romance-minded Jean. Happy endings all around, except for the moviegoer looking either for a plot or a few black musicians. 69 min.

Where the Hot Wind Blows (1958)

Cité Films/GESI Cinematografica. Prod: Jacques Bar, Malena Menotti. Dir: Jules Dassin.• Scr: Jules Dassin (uncredited: Diego Fabbri). Novel basis: Roger Vailland, La loi (1957). Cast: Gina Lollobrigida, Pierre Brasseur, Marcello Mastroianni, Melina Mercouri, Yves Montand, Paolo Stoppa, Raf Mattioli

In the days when Mastroianni, Mercouri and Montand were all left-wingers, this was a French-Italian sex farce (dubbed for English-speaking audiences) with some social pretensions. Lollobrigida is the virginal village temptress who gets local kids to steal for her so she can collect a dowry for a proper marriage. Montand is a hood who, for the sake of son Mattioli, wants respectability. Her hopes set on engineer Mastroianni, Gina spurns the gangster, marries an aristocrat for his money, and successfully manipulates Mastroianni. Mercouri, Montand's mistress, comes to grief, bringing down his house and hopes. The film is shot largely to show off Lollobrigida's allure, which is considerable, but Dassin's skill at observation is ever-present and probably more socially significant than the plot. 126 min.

Where the West Begins (1938)
Another Stanley Roberts† script in which ranch foreman Jack Randall tries to protect employer Luana Walters against swindlers when, unbeknownst to her, valuable mineral deposits are discovered.

Where There's Life (1947)
Para. Prod: Paul Jones. Dir: Sidney Lanfield. Scr: Allen Boretz,• Melville Shavelson. Cast: Bob Hope, Signe Hasso, William Bendix, George Coulouris, Vera Marshe, George Zucco, Dennis Hoey

Typical Hope vehicle from his best era. The king of Baravia is assassinated by a Bolshevik but Hope, the heir-apparent to the throne, wants to stay home and marry girlfriend Marshe instead—until he lays eyes on Hasso. A figure (in more ways than one) among the plotters who kidnap him, Hasso is the strong character to match Hope's weak one. He is, as usual, suddenly up to his eyebrows in trouble, and the movie becomes an endless series of mostly enjoyable chase scenes as kidnappers seek to elude both the cops (including Marshe's brother Bendix, who wants Hope at his sister's alter) and those frisky Bolsheviks, headed by real-life progressive Coulouris. If anything else is funny about this film, it's hardliner Boretz, who yielded not an inch to revisionists and Mensheviks like his pal Groucho Marx. 75 min.

Wherever She Goes (1953)
Allied Australian Films/Ealing Studios, Australia. Prod: Arthur Mayer, Edward Kingsley. Dir: Michael Gordon.•† Scr: Michael Gordon, Barbara Woodward. Cast: Eileen Joyce, Suzanne Parrett, Muriel Steinbeck, Nigel Lovell, John Wiltshire, George Wallace, Tim Drysdale, Syd Chambers

Gordon's exit from Hollywood led him to Australia (the only blacklistee to take refuge there), where a small film industry grew up after the war. This biopic romantically chronicles the early life of the nation's first noted concert pianist, Eileen Joyce, played by herself in a cameo as a mature woman and by Parrett as a young girl. A precocious child who overcame great personal difficulties as the daughter of a miner, she faces poverty (including a lack of music lessons), lack of sympathy (as she plays a harmonica outside a miners' bar), and eventually enters the music competition that gains her a scholarship.

Miners are won over by her talent and sincerity and raise the money among themselves to send her on to represent their community. Joyce provides the soundtrack, and even if it is slow-moving, it is a genuine working-class document of the British type as well as an important film in Australian cinema. 80 min.

Whirlpool (1949)
20th. Prod: Otto Preminger. Dir: Otto Preminger. Scr: Lester Barstow (pseudonym for Ben Hecht), Andrew Solt. Novel basis: Guy Endore,• *Methinks the Lady* (1945). Cast: Gene Tierney, Richard Conte, Jose Ferrer, Charles Bickford, Barbara O'Neil, Eduard Franz, Constance Collier

Based on Endore's most highly regarded novel, about a hypnotist (Ferrer) who convinces Tierney that she has committed a murder. Actually, she's a kleptomaniac so devious that not even her husband, psychologist Conte, is aware of her illness. The unlikelihood of Tierney driving around L.A. and breaking into houses while under a hypnotic spell failed to convince critics, and the actual murder committed by Conte while he has hypnotized himself to cover the pain of a gall bladder operation is a bit much. It's a slick production, but vastly unequal to the complexity of the novel, and pronounced "bleakly artificial" by the *New York Times*. 98 min.

Whistling in Brooklyn (1943)
MGM. Prod: George Haight. Dir: S. Sylvan Simon. Scr: Nat Perrin (script contribution: Stanley Rubin†). Cast: Red Skelton, Ann Rutherford, Jean Rogers, Rags Ragland, Ray Collins, Henry O'Neill, William Frawley, Sam Levene

Third and last in a series of Skelton comedies that began with *Whistling in the Dark*. As in the others, Red is a radio detective who finds himself taking on cases in real life. A mysterious criminal called the "constant reader" particularly enjoys killing cops and manages to get Skelton implicated. Rogers, a cub reporter, tries to advance her story, while Rutherford is Red's heartthrob. High point: an appearance by the Brooklyn Dodgers, one of whom Skelton impersonates in Ebbets Field (with a beard, yet).

Interestingly, Perrin (according to his own recollections) briefly faced the prospect of blacklisting. He had so many comedy-writing pals on the Left—and later on the list—that the connection was inevitable. He managed to get off, however, without testifying, thanks to his "clean" record and his connections in the industry. 77 min.

The White Tower (1950)

RKO. Prod: Sid Rogell. Dir: Ted Tetzlaff. Scr: Paul Jarrico.• Novel basis: James Ramsey Ullman, *The White Tower* (1946). Cast: Glenn Ford, Allida Valli, Lloyd Bridges,† Cedric Hardwicke, Oskar Homolka

The last pre-blacklist credit for Jarrico had possibilities—if the scenes explaining motivation had not been almost fatally cut. An adventure film about mountain climbing in the post–World War II era has ex-Nazi Bridges cooperating with a former American flyer (shot down in the same Alps they set their sights on) in a party led by Valli, with Hardwicke and Homolka the oldtimers of the group. The "White Tower" peak, which has never been scaled, awaits them, and in some measure reveals something about each climber—Hardwicke the failed writer, Ford the existential American and Valli the love-seeking romantic.

Most of the action is strictly nonpolitical: Technicolor shots of grimacing climbers grabbing cliff edges, moving along with ropes and picks, and so on. Bridges gets in an occasional observation about his success because of a superior ideology (unlike the Allied victors, the West's "softer" champions), but it ain't much. Jarrico has expressed disappointment, in interviews, that even such an ostensibly straight commercial job might have been considerably better. Ford, by this time rather familiar to blacklist-related films, was beginning his turn to safer fare. 98 min., color.

Who Done It? (1941)

Universal. Prod: Alex Gottlieb. Dir: Erle C. Kenton. Scr: Stanley Roberts,† Edmund Joseph, John Grant. Story basis: Stanley Roberts. Cast: Bud Abbott, Lou Costello, Patric Knowles, William Gargan, Louise Allbritton, Mary Wickes, Thomas Gomez, Willliam Bendix

One of the weaker early Abbott and Costello films, full of energy and some strong acting but without much of a plot or the gag lines that Robert Lees• and Fred Rinaldo• supplied in so many other of the comedy team's films. Most of the time, the two stars look like vaudeville actors in front of a camera.

The boys are would-be radio writers who pretend to be detectives, convincing even the perpetrators of a studio murder that they are on the job. Bendix, as a half-wit cop, is pretty funny at times. So is Wickes as a caustic secretary. But it's Lou who carries the burden of laughs, teetering on window ledges and confusedly making change, among many routines. It's funnier yet to think of straight man Gomez becoming, in a few years, one of the remarkable noir actors of the era. 75 min.

Who Is Hope Schuyler? (1942)

Average B-mystery of a special prosecutor (Joseph Allen, Jr.) who gets help from a girl (Mary Howard) to expose a corrupt D.A. Written by Arnaud d'Usseau.•

Wild and Wonderful (1964)

Harold Hecht† produced this dreadful Waldo Salt• film, which was his first on returning from the blacklist. Tony Curtis waltzes through a role as a bridegroom who has a poodle (the real star of the film) that laps cognac and is infatuated with a bride-to-be. Based on a Dorothy Crider story, "I Married a Dog."

The Wild Man of Borneo (1941)

MGM. Prod: Joseph L. Mankiewicz. Dir: Robert B. Sinclair. Scr: Waldo Salt,• John McClain. Play basis: Marc Connelly, Herman Mankiewicz, *The Wild Man of Borneo* (1927). Cast: Frank Morgan, Mary Howard, Billie Burke, Donald Meek, Marjorie Main, Connie Gilchrist, Bonita Granville, Phil Silvers, Dan Dailey

Medicine-show grifter Morgan in the early years of the century seeks to retire and reform because he is convinced that his daughter has inherited a fortune. Later he learns that his daughter (Howard), whom he rejoins for the first time in years, is broke. He offers her blarney instead of a loan, and they go to live in a theatrical boardinghouse where the limited action and humorous byplay take place—more often than not with Morgan speaking into the camera. Too little use is made of the always entertaining Burke as housekeeper, the great comic actor Meek as Professor Birdo (a vaudeville whistling specialist), and comedy virtuosi Main and Silvers. Dailey comes in tardily as the romantic lead. 78 min.

Winchester '73 (1950)

U-I. Prod: Aaron Rosenberg. Dir: Anthony Mann. Scr: Borden Chase, Stuart N. Lake, Robert L. Richards.• Cast: James Stewart, Shelley Winters, Stephen McNally, Dan Duryea, Millard Mitchell, Will Geer, Rock Hudson, Tony Curtis

Historical epic of sorts shows a stolen high-tech rifle passing through various hands with cowboy Stewart, a Confederate veteran and the son of a murdered farmer, in pursuit. This is a western made in a torrent of political and artistic transition, with some parts leftish, such as kindly sheriff Geer's no-guns-in-town ethic, while other parts are traditional, such as the Indian shootout with white settlers. A great deal lies somewhere in-between. References abound to Custer's last stand and Indians' attempt to learn from the rare strategic victory, but the affect remains vague—both sides are heroic fighters, but with savages resisting civilization.

The first teaming of Stewart and Mann, the film was said to have played a powerful role in setting off the western craze of the 1950s. Marked by good acting and fine photography, it hits a high or low point when Young Bull (Hudson), gun in hand, leads warriors in the raid of a U.S. Cavalry camp. 82 min., color.

The Wistful Widow of Wagon Gap (1947)

Universal. Prod: Robert Arthur. Dir: Charles T. Barton. Scr: Robert Lees,• Fred Rinaldo,• John Grant.• Cast: Bud Abbott, Lou Costello, Marjorie Main, George Cleveland, William Ching

Arguably the best of the many Abbott and Costello films (along with THE LITTLE GIANT, written by Paul Jarrico•) because of the tight script, fine direction and comically exaggerated setting, all of which make for a mixture of slapstick and a kind of social comedy.

Traveling salesman Lou, in one of those notoriously lawless western towns, shoots his gun in the air and mysteriously brings down a troublesome local. By a mythical law of the West, he must now take care of the widow and her family. Marjorie Main, who plays the traditional battleaxe with breathtaking zest, is so fierce that Lou needs only to show her photo to intimidate the rough characters around town. He therefore makes a perfect sheriff, and in some magnificently choreographed scenes (such as the boys at the bar forced en masse to follow Costello's example in drinking milk, a quote from DESTRY RIDES AGAIN) demonstrates the little man's power of will. In another satire on the satire Destry, the women of the town (led by Lou, in drag) take clubs in hand, attack the rowdy saloon crowd and triumph after an intergender skirmish. That there are lots of other, more standard comic asides (like Lou confronting a frog in his soup) should not distract from the originality of the humor or Main's contributions. 78 min.

Without Honor (1949)

Merit Productions. Prod: Robert and Raymond Hakim. Dir: Irving Pichel.• Scr: James Poe. Cast: Laraine Day, Dane Clark, Franchot Tone, Agnes Moorehead, Bruce Bennett, Frank Marlowe, Harry Lauter

That this was intended to be a film noir is revealed in the first choices for a title—*Twilight* and *Deep End*—and in the fact that the notorious Hakim brothers produced it (they were famous for backing strong left-wing noir projects on a shoestring and then interfering). It is still noir, but the moment for the genre had passed. What remains is a very dark crime melodrama of the suburbs, in its overwrought and soapish way anticipating films of suburban angst to come, such as Ritt's NO DOWN PAYMENT a few years later.

It's also Pichel's turn away from studios to independent production, which continued during the rest of his (brief) remaining career.

Poe's story has a classic shape. One day a married man (Tone) arrives at the home of his married lover (Day) to inform her that her husband has discovered their affair and is on his way over with Tone's wife (the scary Moorehead) to confront the vixen in her own den. Tone wants to break off the affair, but Day, caught in a loveless marriage to a slob (Bennett), thought she had seen a way out of her prison and now, despairing, threatens to kill herself with that metaphor of the suburbs, a shish-kebob skewer. Tone tries to prevent her from plunging it into her chest, but in the struggle finds himself fatally kebobbed instead.

Now with a corpse hidden away in a back room, Day is deluged with visitors. First up is her loutish brother-in-law (Clark), who arrives ostensibly to warn her that Tone, Moorehead and Bennett are all on their way over in various stages of indignation. During this conversation we learn that the discovery of the affair was all Bennett's doing; he had hired a private detective as an act of revenge because Day, before she married his brother, had cuttingly rebuffed Bennett's own sexual advances.

And so the visitors pile up as Day comes apart at the emotional seams and her lover's body molders invisibly nearby—or does it? Poe and Pichel raise and reverse expectations in fine melodramatic style in a series of twists that resemble the shape of the murder weapon. 69 min.

Without Love (1945)

MGM. Lawrence Weingarten. Dir: Harold S. Bucquet. Scr: Donald Ogden Stewart.• Play basis: Philip Barry, *Without Love* (1942). Cast: Spencer Tracy, Katharine Hepburn, Keenan Wynn, Carl Esmond, Lucille Ball, Patricia Morison, Felix Bressart

Superior match-up of Tracy and Hepburn, one of the best after WOMAN OF THE YEAR and KEEPER OF THE FLAME. Stewart used to say modestly that his greatest talent lay in keeping out of the way of good theater, and this adaptation of Barry's Broadway production deploys the stage drama to its best advantage.

Seeking a place to live in overcrowded wartime Washington, D.C., scientist Tracy happens across an inebriated Wynn and talks himself into an overnight stay in a big house that turns out to be owned by the usually absent Hepburn. The daughter of a scientist who had revered Tracy's father and a bereaved widow of some years standing, she is prepared to fall in love again but does not know it (nor does Tracy, a confirmed bachelor). The taste of comedy is in the bite of the dialogue between these two, enhanced by the incisive character bits of Wynn (forever tipsy, as a privileged parasite and henpeckee), and ex-red Ball (her biggest comedy role so far) as Wynn's ex-girlfriend. As in WOMAN OF THE YEAR, the politics are mostly sexual. 113 min.

The Wizard of Oz (1939)

MGM. Prod: Mervyn LeRoy. Dir: Victor Fleming (uncredited: King Vidor, Richard Thorpe). Scr: Noel Langley, Florence Ryerson, Edgar Allan Wolfe. Novel basis: L. Frank Baum, *The Wonderful Wizard of Oz* (1900). Cast: Judy Garland, Margaret Hamilton, Ray Bolger, Bert Lahr, Jack Haley, Frank Morgan, Charley Grapewin, Clara Blandick, Billie Burke

Undoubtedly the most popular musical of all time, with lyrics by left-wing E. Y. "Yip" Harburg,• which not only set the tone and push the action but insert important themes like the "rainbow," absent from the literary original. The score won an Academy Award.

L. Frank Baum, literary pulp writer and attentive son-in-law of one of the most radical of the suffrage pioneers, Matilda Joselyn Gage, wrote a series of children's fantasies that grew more egalitarian and feminist as the volumes progressed. This second (and first sound) film version of *Wizard* combined several of these volumes and added Kansas to the mis en scène for a certain Depression-style authenticity. Garland, who won a special Academy Award for her performance, brilliantly acts out the part of a child who desperately fears the death of a close relative and craves exotic adventure. The Oz setting, with all sorts of magical features and some of the best dancers on the planet, allows her to deal with her fears. And it allows the film audience to realize a key element of Baum's political dimension, revealing the Wizard (stand-in for politicians and above all, bankers with their gold standard) as a fake.

Meanwhile, the Tin Man, Scarecrow and Cowardly Lion were, respectively, allegorical representations of workers, farmers and William Jennings Bryan (famed enemy of the gold standard) who, in Baum's Populism, were too feckless to unite against the bankers. Of course, at another level it remained just a superb children's story. With fine casting and extraordinarily innovative use of color, the film survived repeated changes in directors and other over-budget near-disasters. Gay viewers of the 1950s-1980s added a new and special fondness for the androgynous Garland, asking if a potential friend or lover "knows Dorothy." 101 min., part color.

Woman in Hiding (1949)

U-I. Prod: Michael Kraike. Dir: Michael Gordon.•† Scr: Oscar Saul, Roy Huggins.† Story basis: James Webb, "Fugitive from Terror," in *The Saturday Evening Post* (1949). Cast: Ida Lupino, Howard Duff, Stephen McNally, Peggy Dow, John Litel, Joe Besser

A slight but surprisingly radical story of a Southern woman who finds that her new husband (McNally) has probably murdered her father to get possession (through their marriage) of a profitable mill. Former mistress Dow confronts wife Lupino with the truth, and Lupino tries to flee and seek an annulment, but her car's brakes have been cut. Believed dead, she turns up in another town, where she is spotted by former GI and current newspaper vendor Duff, who is dreaming of a life as a boat builder but unable to afford it. Pursued by McNally, unable to decide whether Duff is sincere or just seeking a reward, Lupino reveals the desperation of the title (but with a script that didn't allow her to do much). Taut, with good action, but lacking substance. 92 min.

A Woman of Distinction (1950)

Col. Prod: Buddy Adler. Dir: Edward Buzzell. Scr: Charles Hoffman, Frank Tashlin. Story basis: Hugo Butler,• Ian McLellan Hunter.• Cast: Rosalind Russell, Ray Milland, Edmund Gwenn, Janis Carter, Mary Jane Saunders, Francis Lederer, Lucille Ball

A gender comedy described by Butler's widow as a desperate attempt by two men on the run to make some money. In the writing of Hoffman and Tashlin, the twists become hackneyed, but some of the edge remains, thanks to Russell's spirited performance.

A dean at a Connecticut women's college has been an achiever all her life—and man-free all the while, from her student days to distinguished war service (as we see in a flashback when she shuns a French military award-cum-kiss) to her current educational renown. Then comes a British astronomer (Milland), on a lecture tour, who brings her back a watch she'd lost during the war. They are thrown together by a conniving newspaper journalist (Carter), and go through many ups and downs (with Russell encouraged by her adoptee daughter Saunders, and her kindly father Gwenn) with love hanging in the balance. 85 min.

Woman of the Year (1942)

MGM. Prod: Joseph L. Mankiewicz. Dir: George Stevens. Scr: Michael Kanin, Ring Lardner, Jr.• (uncredited: John Lee Mahin). Cast: Spencer Tracy, Katharine Hepburn, Fay Bainter, Reginald Owen, Minor Watson, William Bendix, Gladys Blake, Dan Tobin

Coming after Hepburn's box office comeback with THE PHILADELPHIA STORY (scripted by Donald Ogden Stewart•), this is the film that made her a permanent superstar and won her the first of a string of Academy Award nominations. She requested and got Lardner as a writer. Apart from the Hitler-Stalin Pact, which like most liberals she detested, Hepburn had a perfect sympathy with his politics (while never getting closer to the party than a ringing endorsement of Henry Wallace).

Critics have complained in recent years that the proto-feminist journalist-diplomat Hepburn plays ridicules and emasculates Tracy, a more stodgy journalist type. More properly, it is a gender turnabout, as she has the language skills for international assignments, the wit and the attraction that Tracy lacks. As opposites, they feud and then clinch, after the usual problems are straightened out. She softens (as Hepburn had to), and wins him over despite his gruffness, finally settling down to be a good wife. Academy Awards went to Kanin and Lardner, with a nomination for Hepburn. It was one of the top-grossing films of the year, guaranteeing the Hepburn-Tracy match in future films. 112 min.

A Woman's Face (1941)

MGM Prod: Victor Saville. Dir: George Cukor. Scr: Donald Ogden Stewart,• Elliot Paul. Play basis: Francis de Croisset, Il était une fois: Pièce en trois actes et six tableaux (1932). Cast: Joan Crawford, Conrad Veidt, Melvyn Douglas, Osa Massen, Reginald Owen, Albert Bassermann, Marjorie Main, Donald Meek, Charles Quigley, Henry Daniell

Remake of original 1938 Swedish version with Ingrid Bergman fails to show Crawford to best advantage, but she has many fine moments in a courtroom drama. She plays a woman horribly scarred since childhood (her father drunkenly set her room on fire and died saving her—a lot of grist for the Freudian mills). She has become a blackmailer to take revenge on a Swedish society repelled by her looks. She is also an intellectual and plays the piano beautifully. Pioneering surgeon Douglas, whose unfaithful wife Crawford had been blackmailing, volunteers to perform the necessary restorative surgery, and thus begins her rehabilitation as a human being and a woman.

She has meanwhile fallen in love, however, with aristocratic scoundrel Veidt, who plans to seize his own extended family's fortune through the murder of the competing heir, a child. Playing nursemaid to the child in a charmingly unsophisticated northern province of Sweden, Crawford must choose. The political moment arrives when Veidt announces that evil is taking over the world and he wants the power to join the evil side. A surprise ending follows the testimony of witnesses. 106 min.

The World Changes (1933)

Occasionally fascinating tale of a farm boy's rise to meatpacking multi-millionaire in Gilded Age Chicago, scripted by Edward Chodorov.* Best scene: stock market crash of 1893, obviously drawing upon panic spirit of recent 1929 catastrophe.

World for Ransom (1954)

Plaza Productions. Prod: Robert Aldrich, Bernard Tabakin. Dir: Robert Aldrich. Scr: Lindsay Hardy (uncredited: Hugo Butler•). Cast: Dan Duryea, Gene Lockhart, Patric Knowles, Reginald Denny, Nigel Bruce, Marian Carr

An exotic little film, an appendage to Duryea's syndicated television vehicle, China Smith (1952-1955). Our lad is an aging American privateer in Singapore (shot, like the television show, in Mexico, where Aldrich's friend Butler was in exile) who still carries the torch for his former girlfriend (nightclub singer Carr), now married to the debonair Knowles, whose life has been saved on an earlier occasion by Duryea.

The law is uncertain at best here, with gangsters operating openly along with the drug trade (Carr sings at The Golden Poppy), and the British colonial office is well-meaning but not especially competent. The plot winds around the kidnapping of an A-bomb scientist and the betrayal of Duryea by Knowles, ending up in a one-man invasion of the kidnappers' retreat. The best scene could not have been shown on television: Carr admits, without quite using the words, that she had become a prostitute before she met Knowles, and that when Duryea puts her on a pedestal she can't get aroused. 82 min.

Wreck of the Hesperus (1948)
An Edward Huebsch• adaptation of the Longfellow poem and an attempt to flesh it out. The poem is about an 1830s sea captain who realizes that his boss, a supposed ship salvager, is actually destroying viable ships for profit. Like much of Longfellow, it is touched both with strangeness and an all-too-obvious search for "American" qualities.

Wyoming (1940)
MGM. Prod: Milton H. Bren. Dir: Richard Thorpe. Scr: Jack Jevne, Hugo Butler.• Story basis: Jack Jevne. Cast: Wallace Beery, Marjorie Main, Ann Rutherford, Lee Bowman, Leo Carrillo, Paul Kelly, Bobs Watson, Henry Travers

First pairing of Beery and Main in an otherwise rather abysmal film. Reviewers found solace for the thin plot in the mannerisms of Beery, beloved for his cowboy imitations, tobacco-spitting and all. Rustlers and cattle-men (led by Beery) shoot it out against a background of picturesque mountains, with infernally troublesome Indians on the side. His courtship of Main offers a light touch (she is the lady blacksmith with malapropisms for every occasion). All done tongue in cheek; occasionally delightful. 89 min.

Y

Yank on the Burma Road (1942)

MGM. Prod: Samuel Marx. Dir: George B. Seitz. Scr: Gordon Kahn,• Hugo Butler,• David Lang.† Cast: Laraine Day, Barry Nelson, Keye Luke, Stuart Crawford, Victor Sen Yung, Philip Ahn, Knox Manning, Turhan Bay

A strong Popular Front action adventure covering the period from the "premature antifascist" struggle to just before World War II. Nelson, a New York cabdriver who heroically captures a bank robber while the police stand around confused, is asked by the Chinese anti-imperialists (reds) to help get a shipment of medical supplies past the Japanese invaders on the Burma Road. With the help of Asians (a few of them played by Asian actors) and Day, a reporter, and in the middle of attacks (some shown with stock footage), he succeeds, at last turning toward the camera and pleading with the audience to grasp the importance of Chinese national liberation for Americans. 66 min.

Yanks (1979)

CIP Filmproduktion/UA. Prod: Joseph Janni, Lester Persky. Dir: John Schlesinger. Scr: Colin Welland, Walter Bernstein.• Story basis: Colin Welland. Cast: Richard Gere, Vanessa Redgrave, William Devane, Lisa Eichhorn, Rachel Roberts, Chick Vennera, Arlen Dean Snyder, Annie Ross

A big-budget feature on Americans in England during World War II, the film moves slowly but with picturesque background and affecting characterization. In the main plot, Gere falls in love with Eichhorn, daughter of a proper middle-class family in a middling industrial/commercial village. Redgrave, a minor aristocrat but avid war worker, becomes involved with American officer Devane.

The most telling element of the film is the impact of the soldiers on British popular culture and, especially, on women's sexuality. In contrast to IF WINTER COMES, in which the stiff-upper-lippers rule patriotic Britons, here, and more realistically, the omnipresence of romantic American films, music and boys with money (and the absence of British men) makes sexual contact almost inevitable. The struggle against upper-lipism is, then, the struggle for love against the tragic fate of war. It is also the cultural conquest of a people almost conquered, but who cling tenaciously to their dignity. 139 min.

Yellow Jack (1938)

MGM. Prod: Jack Cummings. Dir: George Seitz. Scr: Edward Chodorov,• Paul De Kruif, Sidney Howard. Play basis: Sidney Howard, Yellow Jack (1941). Cast: Robert Montgomery, Virginia Bruce, Lewis Stone, Stanley Ridges, Charles Coburn, Buddy Ebsen, Andy Devine, Sam Levene

An adaptation of the Broadway play about Dr. Walter Reed's experiments at the close of the Spanish-American War in occupied Cuba to cure yellow fever. Clichés abound, including the portrayal of the disease as "this insidious thing that comes out of the dark jungles of Africa" and threatens all civilization. Heroically (if predictably), Reed refuses to close his project after months without progress, accepting at last the hypothesis reached twenty years earlier by a British physician (here, Coburn) that mosquitoes alone carry the germs.

Within this historical drama, scripter Chodorov made the most of the political opportunity. The working-class guys (the ignorant southern farmer, the regular aspiring American and the ethnic type), taking orders from Irish American Montgomery and laughable sergeant Devine, work out their own reasons for taking part in the experiment. Levene, the avowed Marxist who semi-jokingly describes his group as "pawns of imperialism" and who wishes he "could be in Chicago right now, helping the movement," at first hopes to gather enough cash to launch a left-wing newspaper. Purified by Montgomery's praise of Reed, he joins mates in a prison-like hut, volunteering to accept the mosquito bites that will likely kill—suffering for an ungrateful humanity. 83 min.

You Belong to Me (1941)

Millionaire playboy Henry Fonda marries a lady doctor and is so jealous of her male patients that he buys a bankrupt hospital and reorganizes it to keep an eye on her. Barely funny. Remade as Emergency Wedding in 1950. Based on a story by Dalton Trumbo.•

You Can't Ration Love (1944)

Paramount. Prod: Walter MacEwen. Dir: Lester Fuller.• Scr: Val Burton,• Hal Fimberg. Story basis: Muriel Roy

Bolton. Cast: Betty Rhodes, Johnnie Johnston, Bill Edwards, Marjorie Weaver, Marie Wilson, Johnnie "Scat" Davis, Jean Wallace

One last (alphabetically speaking) World War II youth musical, like so many others based on college life. The unique premise is that dates with boys are being rationed for the duration, like sugar or gas, and, better, on the basis of the more desirable girls to the less desirable guys. Moved by jealousy, one of the coeds pygmalions Johnston into being the crooner adored by all. Led by Rhodes, they now swoon as if he were Sinatra. Her vocalization of "Nothing Can Replace a Man" captures the mood of wartime longing for romance. 78 min.

You Gotta Stay Happy (1944)

U-I/Rampart Productions. Prod: Karl Tunberg. Dir: H. C. Potter. Scr: Karl Tunberg (script contribution: Allen Boretz•). Story basis: Robert Carson, "You Gotta Stay Happy," *The Saturday Evening Post* (1948). Cast: Joan Fontaine, James Stewart, Eddie Albert, Roland Young, Willard Parker, Halliwell Hobbes, Stanley Prager,• Mary Forbes

You'd think heiress Fontaine, now working on her sixth fiancé, would be used to the idea of getting married. But she's still terrified of the wedding night, so she makes a run for it and winds up in the hotel room of airline pilot Stewart in an early example of meeting cute. All Stewart wants is some shut-eye, but she persuades him to take her along to California along with a planeload of funny animals, a casket, a corporate crook and so forth. Zany, not brainy. 100 min.

Young Ideas (1943)

MGM. Prod: Robert Sisk. Dir: Jules Dassin.• Scr: Ian McLellan Hunter.• Story basis: William Noble. Cast: Susan Peters, Herbert Marshall, Mary Astor, Elliott Reid, Richard Carlson, Allyn Joslyn, Ava Gardner

Sophisticated comedy, more or less, about a sophisticated distaff novelist on a book tour who disappears after unaccountably falling for and marrying a stuffy, conservative professor in a small Pennsylvania college. Her own college-age kids are horrified and set the comic complications in motion by getting the prof to read his new wife's last novel, saucily titled *As I Knew Paris*, believing he will be scandalized by it. Will it work? Overtones of THEODORA GOES WILD but without the sparkle. 77 min.

Young Man with a Horn (1950)

WB. Prod: Jerry Wald. Dir: Michael Curtiz. Scr: Carl Foreman,• Edmund H. North. Novel basis: Dorothy Baker, *Young Man with a Horn* (1938). Cast: Kirk Douglas, Doris Day, Lauren Bacall, Hoagy Carmichael, Juano Hernandez

Based on a *roman à clef* by Baker about the life of Bix Beiderbecke and produced by frequent left-collaborator Wald, the film drifts far from the famous real-life trumpeter's tragic story into a vehicle for actor Kirk Douglas' emerging angst. And yet the film does not desert entirely the central contradiction of the white musician playing black music. Hernandez, African American trumpeter and Douglas mentor, seeks to guide him toward reconciling his musical aspirations with a family and private life. Day, not yet reduced to her virginal role in fifties cinema, is the sugary sweetheart who mistakenly introduces him to the intellectual Bacall, a psychoanalyst-in-training who marries Douglas although she can't stand his music. There are moments, especially in the sex war between Bacall and Douglas, when the film transcends its artifice and provides a deeper glimpse of humanity than the particular trumpeter's fate. 112 min.

The Young One (1951)

Olmeca. Prod: George P. Werker. Dir: Luis Buñuel. Scr: H. B. Addis (pseudonym for Hugo Butler•) Luis Buñuel. Story basis: Peter Matthessen, "Travellin' Man." Cast: Zachary Scott, Bernie Hamilton, Key Meersman, Graham Denton, Claudio Brook

A remarkable little story, the final cooperation of paired exiles Buñuel and Butler and not as successful as ADVENTURES OF ROBINSON CRUSOE—but with a similar atmosphere and low budget. Also memorable as one of the outstanding Mexican art films of the day.

The laconic loner Scott, a handyman living hermit-like on a southern coastal island, is drawn to the Lolita-like Meersman. The death of her guardian, a beloved grandfather, forces the two together alone on the island until the improbable arrival of Hamilton, an African American fleeing a mob that thinks he committed a rape. She supplies Hamilton with food and a gun, but Scott accuses him of molesting the girl, at least for the moment. Complications arise with outsiders, who realize that Hamilton is the fugitive—now protected by the erstwhile racist Scott. For its time, a militantly antiracist film. 96 min.

Young Tom Edison (1940)
The better of the two Edison biopics, by far. Hugo Butler•
also collaborated on *Edison the Man*.

Young Winston (1972)
Col./Open Road. Prod: Carl Foreman,• Richard Attenbor-
ough.• Dir: Richard Attenborough. Scr: Carl Foreman.
Book basis: Winston Churchill, *My Early Life: A Roving
Commission* (1930). Cast: Simon Ward, Peter Cellier,
Ronald Hines, John Mills, Anne Bancroft, Russell Lewis,
Robert Shaw, Jack Hawkins, Jane Seymour, Anthony
Hopkins

An unlikely project for Foreman's last major film is
a strangely sympathetic biopic of the determinedly conservative and deeply racist Tory politician. The fate of the
young man has been pressed upon him by his family, and
he struggles for his identity while advancing from junior
officer in India to journalist in the Boer War and his initial
election to parliament. Duty to family means duty to
empire. 145 min.

The Younger Brothers (1949)
The story basis was written by Morton Grant•—yet
another Jesse James variation about innocent criminals.
Gunplay, an outlaw brother and a female (Janis Paige)
with notably low-cut blouses add up to very little.

You're a Lucky Fellow, Mr. Smith (1943)
Ben Barzman• co-scripted this service musical version of
the girl-must-marry-to-secure-an-inheritance vintage.
More songs than plot.

Youthful Cheaters (1929)
Frank Tuttle† in his pre-political days directed this "White
Telephone" silent film (the analogy is to the Victorian
"Silver Fork" novel) about the good life on Long Island
and the efforts of a few to escape the sinful ways of the
leisured classes.

Z

Z (1969)

Office National pour le Commerce et l'Industrie Cinematographique/Reggane Films. Assoc. Prod: Eric Schlumberger, Phillipe d'Argila. Dir: Costa-Gavras. Scr: Jorge Semprún, Costa-Gavras (uncredited: Ben Barzman•). Novel basis: Vassilis Vassilikos, *Zeta*. Cast: Yves Montand, Irene Papas, Jean-Louis Trintigant, Jaques Perrin, Charles Denner, François Périer, Pierre Dux

Barzman made an uncredited but essential structural contribution to this Costa-Gavras classic. He advised the director to throw out the first screenplay that Costa-Gavras had sent him and rewrite it, staying true to the Vassilikos novel and adopting a documentary style with a telegraphic delivery. Costa-Gavras took the advice. Barzman was engaged to write a new adaptation of the book, and the director called in the gifted Semprún to write the screenplay, and between them they very effectively got out the "message" about the Greek "colonels" who seized power with the assistance of the U.S. State Department. The terse style would be imitated many times.

Montand stars as an idealistic professor opposed to nuclear weapons who comes to Athens to give a talk on the subject. After he is attacked by right-wing thugs, he throws himself into the peace movement. Perrier is the reporter who digs out the truth about the assassination of a prominent antifascist.

Semprún went on to become the minister of culture for the post-Franco Socialist government in Spain, wrote a unique cycle of four Marxist "spaghetti westerns" and wrote one of Joseph Losey's• best films, MONSIEUR KLEIN. 127 min.

Ziegfeld Girl (1941)

Loew's/MGM. Prod: Pandro S. Berman. Dir: Robert Z. Leonard. Scr: Marguerite Roberts,• Sonya Levien. Cast: James Stewart, Judy Garland, Hedy Lamarr, Lana Turner, Tony Martin, Jackie Cooper, Edward Everett Horton, Philip Dorn, Paul Kelly, Eve Arden, Dan Dailey, Fay Holden

Heavy on the production numbers and light on plot, this backstage musical follows the lives of three girls chosen for the Ziegfeld follies. All have serious man trouble, but Judy's problem is her kind, old vaudevillian pop, while Hedy's and Lana's boyfriends don't want them subordinating personal relationships to their careers. Here and there class themes lurk (especially for Turner, whose boyfriend is the proletarian Stewart, considering crime as a means of upward mobility). The film repeatedly suggests the familiar assumption that rich men usually pick up the chorus girls they want.

But mostly, these are clichéd roles to situate the music and dancing. In this regard, too, the film is a disappointment: the most lavish scenes feature women in choreographed strolling, with spectacular costumes but few of the visual gymnastics that mark Busby Berkeley's (and MGM's) best films. Now and then Garland turns on the charm, looking like nothing so much as an overgrown Dorothy in a new and far less attractive Oz. 132 min.

Zis Boom Bah (1942)

Monogram. Prod: Sam Katzman. Dir: William Nigh. Scr: Connie Lee,• Jack Henley. Story basis: Connie Lee. Adaptation: Harvey Gates, Jack Henley. Cast: Peter Lind Hayes, Mary Healy, Grace Hayes, Huntz Hall, Benny Rubin

A better than average "Hey, kids, let's get together and put on a musical!" feature, with underlying themes of backstage sentimentalism and campus life during wartime. Hayes is the middle-aged star of the "cheap musical show" (as she calls it), belting them out for decent pay but losing interest and concerned about the son she sent off to be raised by others. Packing it in, she heads for the college town where a financially failing school has been kept alive with her quiet contributions, but where her (real-life) son Peter has become a free-spending, skirt-chasing egoist.

Mother Hayes is the real star here as she buys up a restaurant and turns it into a club, then backs a show that will put the college back in the black. Looking thoroughly unglamorous for the part and full of gendered *bon mots*, she strikes up a quasi-romance with a professor—while first punishing her son and then backing him as impresario. The film slides into the song-and-dance phase almost casually, with an air of oldtimers appreciating the music of the younger generation. It ends with a sentimental, predictable but charming conclusion. 61 min.

Zulu (1964)

Diamond Films Prod: Stanley Baker, Cyril Endfield.• Dir: Cyril Endfield. Scr: John Prebble, Cyril Endfield. Cast: Stanley Baker, Jack Hawkins, Ulla Jacobsson, James

Booth, Michael Caine, Nigel Greene, Patrick Magee, Chief Mangosuthu Buthelezi

Endfield's most famous film, an action spectacular based on real events in 1879, when Zulu warriors handed the British empire one of its bloodiest defeats in a battle that cost it 1,500 soldiers. This film concentrates on a second and much smaller battle a few hours later, when 4,000 warriors surrounded a British supply camp guarded by just 139 Welsh infantrymen. Critics have attacked its accuracy and objectification of the Zulu people, but in the early 1960s it could have been perceived as nothing other than a critique of colonialism by virtue of the choice of a famous defeat (as Australian Peter Weir did in *Gallipoli*) rather than a victory as its subject. The brutality of war is examined with no disrespect for the individual soldier on either side. Socialist Stanley Baker was also celebrating his working-class Welsh heritage (he lost a brother in the coal mines), notably in the soldierly set pieces of choral singing. The ending, practically trade-marked by Endfield, must be experienced in a theater to fully grasp its meaning, and the movie should be seen in tandem with the Baker/Endfield production of SANDS OF THE KALAHARI (released a year later) for a complete reading. This was Michael Caine's debut, and of course he is an absolute standout. 138 min.

Zulu Dawn (1979)
The "prequel" to ZULU, written but not directed by Cyril Endfield• and lacking the extraordinary sweep of the earlier film. This time it's about the actual Battle of Isandlwana in 1879, with the unexplained presence of American officer Burt Lancaster. A disappointment.